A Catalogue of the South

A Catalogue of the South

Oxmoor House, Inc. · Birmingham, Alabama

Book Division of The Progressive Farmer Company
Publisher of *Southern Living*®, *Progressive Farmer*®, and *Decorating & Craft Ideas*® magazines.
P.O. Box 2463, Birmingham, Alabama 35201.

Eugene Butler — Chairman of the Board
Emory Cunningham — President and Publisher
Vernon Owens, Jr. — Senior Executive Vice President

Conceived, edited and published by Oxmoor House, Inc., under the direction of:

Don Logan — Vice President and General Manager
Gary McCalla — Editor, *Southern Living*®
John Logue — Editor-in-Chief
Jerry Higdon — Production Manager
Mary Jean Haddin — Copy Chief

A CATALOGUE OF THE SOUTH

Editors: Karen Phillips Irons, Mary Jean Haddin, Jo Voce

Editorial Assistant: Annette Thompson

Book Design: James R. Weldon

Special Photography: Mike Clemmer, John O'Hagan, Judy Nemeth

Book Reviews: Susanna Van Hoose

Library of Congress Catalog Number: 79-87641
ISBN: 0-8487-0502-5

Manufactured in the United States of America
First Printing

Cover Art: Donny Finley

Special thanks to Mary Elizabeth Johnson and Mary Jo Sherrill and the staff of *Decorating & Craft Ideas*® for their assistance with the Handwork section.

Contents

A FEW WORDS ABOUT THE USE OF THIS CATALOGUE:

Any orders or requests for additional information for merchandise must be directed to the supplier whose address is given, not to the *Catalogue*.

All prices are subject to change, although we have endeavored to give the most up-to-date information possible.

The editors have made every effort to verify the quality of all items mentioned in the *Catalogue*; however, we cannot be responsible for any lapse in quality on the part of the manufacturer.

Introduction

Books have been written on the old South, the new South, the enduring South, and the changing South. But however it is labelled, the South is still considered a distinct region. In *A Catalogue of the South* we have gathered together the abundance of good things the South has to offer. There are things to buy, places to go and things to do, and definitely things to eat. You will find reviews of useful and interesting books from Southern presses, as well as prints, line drawings, paintings, and photographs.

No catalogue of the South would be complete without its history and its people's love of history. In the Heritage section you will find an article on how several enterprising families have restored old houses—followed by entries of hard-to-find hinges and elegant moldings, plus such items as hot pepper jelly, antique maps, and goose quill pens.

The sense of history involves attachment to place—to the climate and landscape that Southerners call home. The Earth section is devoted to the many, often year-round, activities (and accessories to those activities) that can be enjoyed in the South: a wild flower trek and balloon ride, snake boots and pea shellers, nuts and fishing lures, and a "garden monster" to scare the pests away.

In the highlands, on the coast, on the farms of the South, though handwork is no longer a necessity, the pleasure and pride remain. In our Handwork section you will find pottery, stained and blown glass, leather work, wood carving, weaving and basket weaving, stuffed and wooden toys, wrought iron and copper, batik, glass and lead sculpture, guitars and dulcimers.

Pleasures and Places, our last section, is a potpourri of some of the delights of the South: a mint julep, flea markets, tales of Southern ghosts, a steamboat ride on the Mississippi, hang gliding, homes of famous people, zoos, and wildlife refuges.

We hope our *Catalogue of the South* will reflect the South in all its moods and idiosyncrasies—the real, old, new, and unique South.

Jack Jeffers

HERITAGE

No one remembers the songs
originally played on its keys
and for the serious organist
it is just mediocre—or less—
but the patina increases still
from the touches of strangers
who, through the tips of their fingers,
give it the tunes of their own memories
and save the good in the time that was.

JV

Heritage Index

THE PHOTOGRAPHY OF
JACK JEFFERS

Jack Jeffers believes that the camera can be a tool for producing fine art and that a good photographic print can hold its own in competition with oils and watercolors. We think you will agree when you see his work. Jeffers' subject matter is most often the scenes of rural America. He produces original limited editions and one-of-a-kind prints for the connoisseur of fine art photography. He has exhibited his work in more than 200 all-media art shows and has taken many awards in those shows. To date, close to three thousand prints have been acquired by private collectors, museums, and fellow artists. Jeffers' prints occupy a place in the collections of such notables as Earl Hamner, Jr., Irving Desfor, John D. Rockefeller IV, Dr. Norman Vincent Peale, Chrysler Museum, Shenandoah National Park, and many others.

We think that the best way to present his work is simply to let you see some of it. Shown here are "Old Store," photographed near Appomattox, Virginia, "Steam Locomotive" at Cass, West Virginia, and "A True Mountain Dweller." We thought so much of the photographs that we used them to open three sections of our book; these appear on pages 1, 63, and 185.

For catalogues and pricing information, send $1.25 (U.S.), $1.50 (foreign) to defray shipping and handling costs to:

Jack Jeffers
RD. 1, Box 148
Lyndhurst, Virginia 22952

Restoring period houses to live in has been gaining momentum all across the South, a vital way of saving the region's rich heritage of domestic design. Here are some shared experiences from the plaster-dust crowd.

Home, Sweet Restoration

by PHILIP MORRIS

The people that are written about in this article are among a special breed—the growing ranks of Southerners who have restored houses to live in. Most of them have done part or all of the work themselves, covered with plaster dust for weeks and months, living in one room while the next stands bare to the studs, expecting one problem and uncovering a dozen. None will say it was easy, but all are proud and pleased with the results.

On the pages that follow, we present a collection of houses and the owners who have restored them, briefly touching the experiences that any one of them could elaborate on for hours. We found a great diversity of both houses and owners. The architecture of the houses featured here ranges from late 18th century through the 19th, from elaborate townhouse to simple country cottage. Some of the restorers have done it as their first house, while others have come to it later with a family grown.

The grand restored museum houses of the South are wonderful to see, but what a nice surprise now to come across, unexpectedly, a long-neglected house in the country reclaimed for living or a whole street of a town brought back to the best of its era.

Restored houses make wonderful places to live, and many young families find even more modest ones a value in space and quality. For anyone, there is the pleasure of seeing something old cared for and the region's cultural record of building vitally maintained. There are also lessons to be learned from much early architecture, and—not incidentally—about living with style.

There are degrees of restoration, of course, and while these houses are authentic and true to style, most have been adapted somewhat for today with such conveniences as indoor bathrooms or kitchens in the house rather than in another building. The important fact is that the houses have been restored in the spirit of their original condition, not compromised.

While each experience is different, most owner/restorationists agree on three basic suggestions to others who might be contemplating such a project: 1) Go slow, they say, and don't expect an overnight transformation. (This also helps avoid mistakes.) 2) Do exhaustive research on architectural and decorative periods of the house to fully understand and appreciate it. 3) Supervise any work done, especially if carpenters and other tradesmen are not accustomed to working with old houses.

Dwight Young, Southern regional director for the National Trust for Historic Preservation, recommends state and local historical commissions as the best place to start research. He also acclaims *The Old-House Journal* (199 Berkeley Place, Brooklyn, New York 11217) as a helpful guide, both for technical information and ways to live with a vintage structure. Another place to seek assistance is the Historic House Association of America (740 Jackson Place N.W., Washington, D.C. 20006).

We know there are hundreds of other fine restorations; we're delighted there are so many engaged in this movement, frustrated not to be able to include more. But we don't mean to imply, either, that the South should live in the past architecturally, and we continue our encouragement of good contemporary design. An appreciation of early structures might be a good foundation for care in building today. The region would surely miss their grace and presence and the stories they tell.

They bought the house in 1972 for $100, had it moved, and have been working on it ever since.

It's called the Deanes House and was built in the early 1800's on Murfreesboro, North Carolina's, Main Street. Ed and Bobbi Wooten learned it was to be destroyed in order to make way for a commercial development, so they purchased it for a song—a song with a very long refrain.

After moving the two-story house with weatherboard exterior to a 1-acre plot near town, the Wootens began the slow process of restoration. They found out very soon that someone needed to be on site constantly to supervise work and receive materials, so they moved into a small trailer (a little larger than a camper) with their young children and lived there for three months until the house could be occupied. "We are a very close family," they now say with a smile.

Although the seven-room house is being adapted for living requirements, the Wootens are keeping it as authentic as possible. The major change is the use of a former kitchen wing as a den, with the kitchen taking space at the rear of the main house.

"We were fortunate in that the floor plan was very practical," observes Bobbi Wooten. "We had the house livable after about a year and a half, but we are still working on the living room, dining room, and foyer and expect to finish this year."

The Wootens did their own research and have repaired and refinished much of the interior themselves. "We were lucky in that Ed (a teacher) had an opportunity to spend one summer in Williamsburg doing graduate work, so we packed up the children and went. We used the library there and, of course, the houses for our study," explains Bobbi. "It was essentially the right period and style for this house."

The most important thing the Wootens learned early about restorations was that they could not rely solely on the professional help available.

Local carpenters and brickmasons did not have experience in working on old

houses, and most of the repairs had to be done by hand on an hourly basis. But the Wootens were prepared for the task, mentally.

"We set up a five-year plan when we started, and feel that's the only way to do it. Sure you get tired of it, but if you are prepared from the beginning not to expect it all to be done overnight, that helps."

Would they ever do it again? "Yes, it's still what we want, and we couldn't find anything like this. We would do it again."

"This is a Low Country simple house, and the best advice we had from a restoration architect was to keep it simple and not pretend it was a grand Charleston house."

So comments Jane Hazzard about the house she and husband Hap restored at 405 Front Street in Georgetown, South Carolina. Not only did they take the simple architecture of the 1737-vintage house as a virtue, they removed certain Victorian columns and railings that had been added during the 19th century.

The design direction came from Architect Russell Wright, AIA, of Annapolis, Maryland, who is in Georgetown consulting on a waterfront redevelopment plan. The town made him available to homeowners doing restoration.

The young couple's house was in terrible condition, and the restoration included complete rewiring, replumbing, insulation, new baths, plus refinishing all floors, walls, and woodwork. They worked on the house for six months before moving in, doing much of the tearing out themselves.

The Hazzards are delighted with what they feel is both a livable and notable dwelling. They have 2,700 square feet of living space, including three bedrooms and three baths, heart-pine floors with a practical polyurethane finish, a living room and dining room each measuring 20 x 22 feet and each with a fireplace.

In adapting for living, one small upstairs bedroom was converted to a bath and dressing area for the master bedroom. But the interiors have been kept true to period with much research done on colors, paper, and furnishings.

Bill and Frances Gay have gone slowly with restoration of their Victorian house—a room a year—working on a budget, but doing it right.

And going slow has turned out to be of benefit, they find. "By taking our time and doing one room at a time, we've uncovered a lot of things we might have missed if we'd had it all redone at once," observes Bill Gay.

"By living in the house, we came to understand it better. For example, we first thought about turning a small room into a closet, but instead we picked up old wardrobes to use for storage, just like they would have done then, keeping the room intact."

Victoria, as it's named, was one of two identical houses built in 1895 in downtown Charlotte as wedding gifts for two sons. The house was moved in 1913 to the edge of town as business took over the location—quite a feat in those days. Older residents of Charlotte have told the Gays the house was rolled on logs, with horses and mules pulling it slowly out to the new site.

The Gays bought the house in 1970. Though rundown, it was habitable and they moved right in. Step by step, room by room, they began restoration, he doing the heavy work and she, an artist, applying final touches, such as the stenciled borders seen everywhere.

To date they have completed 7 rooms out of the total of 15 (which includes room-size baths). They have done extensive research and now have their own library on Victorian architecture and decorative arts. Restoration is authentic, even to replacement of stained glass lost during the original move.

One major change in the appearance of the interiors has come from getting back to the original wood tones. Shellac used in those days darkened with time to the point that it looked like black paint. Bill Gay painstakingly removes wood trim, strips it, refinishes and reinstalls it as work in each room is completed.

Warm weather, as in seasons past, will find the couple back on the outside of the house, painting and patching—slowly, like things used to be done.

Selden's Point, a historic place in Norfolk, is being restored by one of the city's oldest families. It's restoration at a grand scale.

Built in 1807 out in the country, the Selden-Grandy house is now virtually in downtown Norfolk, but on quiet Freemason Street where other houses are being restored for living. The grounds occupy 1 square block, with a countrylike rear garden overlooking the harbor. Dr. and Mrs. Albert Roper II are engaged in its restoration—for the love of it.

The frame house is 2½ stories on a raised-brick English basement, making it tower over the street. Built in Federal style, with a five-bay front and a Georgian Revival porch, the house was later embellished with two large dormers.

Along with general abuse received over the past years, the house had a fire recently with damage limited to its left interior. One measure of the durability of the structure: during the fire, heavy timbers charred to the point that they sealed themselves and helped in preventing collapse.

For just a glimpse into the intricacies of restoration, read the first two steps for repair of the central stair prepared by Architects Spigel, Carter, Zinkl & Herman: "1. Handrail, balusters, and newel shall be dismantled for refurbishing. Treads, flooring, and aprons, not to be replaced, may be reworked in place. 2. Where required, replacement materials shall match existing (walnut) and shall be solid (not veneered) wood. The following shall be an approximate guide to replacement materials: 16 linear feet of railing, 36 balusters, 135 linear feet of nosing, 14 linear feet of stringer apron, 13 linear feet of landing apron, 16 linear feet of baseboard."

The eight-room raised cottage in Galveston, Texas, looked grim, but underneath asbestos siding the clapboard was in good condition and inside, there was much of the original furniture.

Charles and Barbara Lawrence had to be optimistic when they purchased the 1895-vintage house for $20,000 in 1975. Neglected for years and classed as uninhabitable by the city building department, the structure turned out to be essentially sound, unmarred by interior or exterior remodelings and with no thick layers of paint or wallpaper to be removed from walls and woodwork.

Victorian drawing-room furniture, wardrobes, beds, and dressers that came with the house were a boon to furnishing, all believed to have been purchased by the original owners.

The house exterior is cypress, explaining its durability, as are the original shutters which the Lawrences found piled in the backyard where they had been for 25 years.

The structure is 3,000 square feet, including a basement apartment that has helped finance the restoration. The Lawrences occupy the upper story and a half, where there is a central hall measuring 7 x 30 feet with a den, bath, and bedroom on the left and a parlor, dining room, and kitchen on the right. Upstairs

there are two large bedrooms with dormers.

Chuck Lawrence, who is executive director of the Galveston Chamber of Commerce, refinished the heart-pine floors himself, but most of the work was contracted, much of it to young craftsmen from Woodmasters, a refinishing shop on The Strand in Galveston.

"The house has been appraised at much more than we've got in it," notes Barbara. "But anyone trying restoration should not expect instant change. You never know what you are going to get into, so you take it as it comes."

The 1892 House, as it's known, was built for coolness in summer, and it still works.

Works so well, in fact, that Marcus and Elsie Fields, who have lived in the house for 10 years bringing it back to mint condition, seldom use air conditioning even in the middle of South Carolina summers.

"There are wide halls through the center of the house both upstairs and down; the downstairs hall is a full 75 feet long," explains Elsie Fields. "So air is continually drawn through the house when doors and windows are open. And there are porches all around the ground floor where we virtually live during nice weather." The 11-foot-high ceilings also help keep the house cool.

Located in the tiny community of Pomaria, some 30 miles from Columbia, the 1892 House is half town, half country. It faces the town, but the 36-acre site is open country to the sides and rear.

The house was in poor repair when the Fields bought it from the original family heirs. But since it had been entirely built of heart pine cut from the estate, the house was in good structural condition. There are 5,500 square feet of living space and a fireplace in every room. It is a little hard to heat, since walls cannot be insulated, but the Fields live with that, using the fireplaces as needed in the winter.

"We have no complaints about the house at all. We did much of the work ourselves on-and-off over the years," says Elsie. "All our friends love the house, too, and in the summer it's almost like a hotel."

The gambrel-roofed house had never been wired or fitted with plumbing and it had been given only one coat of paint since it was built in the 1760's.

When John Parker bought it about two years ago, the house had stood vacant for some 20 years. Built by an ancestor, Francis Parker, the property had been in his family for six generations, only to be sold in 1943.

To get the house back, John bought it, moved it 7 miles to 400 acres he owns in Northampton County, North Carolina, and set about authentic restoration on a three-year timetable.

With its barnlike roof, the house sits high on a brick English daylight basement. He's adapting the structure but going to great lengths to keep it in the restoration class. The brick is a special handmade type from Webster Brick in Maryland; roof shingles are the same as those used in Williamsburg restoration; nails come from Massachusetts.

Upper floors will be kept intact and will even have special low-voltage lighting using candle fixtures. The basement will have a kitchen, a small bath, small bedroom, and a 20 x 20 foot all-purpose room.

Parker, like many other restorationists doing their own work, believes in going slowly and carefully. He is getting advice from experts in Winston-Salem, and Master Restorer Ned Hipt is repairing his doors.

Parker teaches school, as does his wife, and they have a young son. Going slowly and doing much of the work himself permits him to get quality usually found only with a large budget.

"The quicker you do it, the more money it's going to take," he cautions. "If you can't do a good portion of the work yourself, a good restoration will ruin your pocketbook."

"Helena occupies one of the prettiest situations on the Mississippi. Her perch is the last, the southern-most group of hills which one sees on that side of the river . . .

"Helena is the second town in Arkansas, in point of population—which is placed at five thousand. The country about it is exceptionally productive. Helena has a good cotton trade; handles from forty to sixty thousand bales annually; she has a large lumber and grain commerce; has a foundry, oilmills, machine shops, and wagon factories—in brief, has one million dollars invested in manufacturing industries. She has two railways, and is the commercial center of a broad and prosperous region. Her gross receipts of money, annually, from all sources, are placed by the New Orleans Times-Democrat *at four million dollars."*
Mark Twain, LIFE ON THE MISSISSIPPI

A Waltz With Jeb Stuart

My grandmother's thin bracelets jingled like faraway chimes. "Yes, back in '62 near Baltimore when I wasn't even as old as you, I danced with Jeb Stuart. I remember . . . they played a waltz."
Diary of Patsy Lane Lanier
April 19, 1907

The moon was mazed in gold that night
with tatters of cloud streaming from her
like ribbons from a gypsy tamborine.
The academy blazed with candles
and jewels sputtered on the dresses of my sisters
and all the ladies swirled through the great hall
with soldiers,
faces wild and shadowed,
fantastic in wavering, flowing light.
Dizzy from the ice fizz I had sneaked,
I watched the quadrille from the galleries.
I went down to the gardens
cool and sweet there
the academy hurled out in hot brilliance,
its glare mingling with shades
of roses and goldenrod
that gusted on the tender wind
—summer memories of Maryland—
and I was glad to be a girl then
and not to know men yet.
I remember thinking of the music
. . . a flick of reins over the post
a soldier's step
firm between the moving shadows
and he stopped   His cloak
lashed back scarlet
like the plume in his hat
crimsoning the winds.
His eyes flashed like the glints
of light on his French saber
and gilt sash.
Gold spurs thrusted
from tall calvalry boots that came
almost to the hip and I could tell
he did not want to surrender the night yet.
. . . he started toward the hall
seeing me   he stopped
the band began a waltz
and he brought down his hat
in careless challenge
and offered me his arm—
almost one motion— and suddenly
we were back inside the mad laughter
and smoke and

whirling   his eyes the blue of Virginia rivers
scooped-up snow glove holding mine
not even as old as my brother

my sisters stopped,
their glitter—still

whirling   my left glove on grey buttoned to the chin
brushed his beard, a rich brown
the burnished floor clearing for us

everyone fixed
murmuring, watching

whirling   his hand on the curve of my waist
and I glad for my turning grace
swirling in strange sovereignty

whispering "beautiful"
and it was me

whirling   and he smiled, eyes full of dance
and his hand urged the curve of my waist
faster, now everything blurring

the hall hushed

whirling   each round a wash of colours
and faces, the music fevered
a sorcery of sound   snapped

shocked, violins shuddered to
silence
and the hall tightened like a gunlock

a soldier next to us, I don't know how
"the enemy, sir, they've driven our pickets
and are comin' on" . . . he was gone, new motion
spurs jarring the gleaming floors
saddles groaning from forced weight, pounding
pounding   and gone too

and the air full of perfume, burnt . . . gone

my sisters threw a shawl over the muslin
my mother had made me wear, and they
pressed against me, shrill, saying things
and some soldier stepped towards us especially,
no danger   our men always   my apologies   I couldn't hear
only music still

fast goodbyes, worried gossip, whose carriage was that
and ours to come soon repeated my oldest sister
I'll wait in the garden, I said, and they were confused
and talking to neighbors and I slipped out
trembling

once again   calm
carriage dust settling over asters
into shadows and the moon was smothered
in cloud but still holding through,
and the crisp dark broke into rifle cracks
as the lathered horse galloped to the gate
and he swung his hat down
the wild plume against the night
"Thank you for the waltz."

Susanna Van Hoose

The lower section of this window opens into small doors, which become an exit to the gallery when the lower window sash is raised. (This is called a jib door.) The jib door and window facing and trim are of heart pine.

The floor of this entrance hall is reclaimed 8-inch wide Southern Yellow Heart Pine, face nailed with square head nails. The stair treads are also pine.

A REDISCOVERED LEGACY

The virgin longleaf yellow pine, discovered and used by the colonists of Georgia, Alabama, Mississippi, Louisiana, and North Florida, is now almost extinct. The giant trees were timbered out in the early 1900s.

It was a slow-growing tree, taking from 150 to 450 years to mature. At maturity, the tree consisted mainly of heartwood, with little of the sapwood of most other species. Because of the predominance of heartwood, virgin longleaf yellow pine had great strength and hardness and was widely used in heavy construction, shipbuilding, railroad bridge construction, and as pilings. (The keel of the U.S.S. Constitution is made from a single heart-of-pine timber from Darien, Georgia.) The wood was also used in home building because of its strength and beauty, and the fact that it was virtually bug- and rotproof.

Period Pine, Ltd., a firm specializing in locating, salvaging, and recycling the rare wood, is trying to rectify the situation. Period Pine seeks out old mills, warehouses, factories, and other structures built with virgin longleaf yellow pine. When the buildings are razed, the massive structural beams and other sources of the wood are carefully removed, cleaned, denailed, and shipped to the firm's mill in Duluth, Georgia, for resawing. The lumber is salvaged and recycled under the watchful eye of Wilmer Stanley, a 60-year veteran of sawmill operations and timbering in the South. Stanley, one of the few Master Sawyers left in the United States, began the business by locating Southern Yellow Heart Pine for European furniture makers. His talent and experience assure only fine quality wood—carefully graded, priced and resawed for today's purposes. Period Pine's current inventory comes from a mill built near Lawrenceville, Georgia, in 1885.

Heart of Pine is not pine as most of us know it today. It is the finest pine lumber ever grown; therefore, its modern uses are mostly decorative. Flooring, paneling, millwork, furniture, exposed beams, and mouldings are a few of the areas where heart pine adds to the beauty and elegance of a structure. It can be used to grace both contemporary and traditional settings.

For information write to:

Period Pine, Ltd.
P.O. Box 77052
Atlanta, Georgia 30309
(404) 876-4740

THE STREETCARS OF NEW ORLEANS

by Louis C. Hennick and E. Harper Charlton

Pelican Publishing Company, Inc.
630 Burmaster Street
Gretna, Louisiana 700531

For over 100 years, the life of historic New Orleans has been enlivened by the colorful streetcar. In 1831, the first railway line was established and provided a very effective means of transportation throughout the sprawling city. The development of New Orleans' streetcar and urban railway system served as a model for innovations and transportation refinements elsewhere.

Illustrated with some 200 old and rare photographs and dozens of early maps, *The Streetcars Of New Orleans* is appealing to the historian, the student of traction, and the plain old New Orleans-lover. One chapter is devoted entirely to Canal Street, so named in 1804 because of the large drainage ditch running down its center. This street is the main artery of traffic in New Orleans, serving also as the traditional line of demarcation between the French and American sections. At one time, five streetcar tracks traversed this historic street.

Today, with the establishment of huge shopping complexes in the suburbs, the flow of traffic toward downtown in New Orleans, as in most American cities, has been altered. New Orleans, like the rest, has succumbed to the passion for private transportation and although rapid transport systems are now being instituted, the street railway is a thing of the past. A small group of citizens (self-styled Streetcars Desired) attempted to save the Canal Line for the sake of its charm and character. However, New Orleans soon went the way of other cities, and the colorful streetcars no longer sound on her streets as they once did. (There are only 3 streetcars still in operation there.)

The authors of this book have managed to preserve in photographs and words something of this way of life. Also, there are detailed descriptions of the two basic passenger lines and the many historic routes and operating companies. Altogether, this book offers an intriguing and thorough examination of life in a slower, and (some claim) a richer, more fulfilling world.

—S.V.H.

ARCHITECTURAL ARTIFACTS

Whether you are restoring an older home and need to replace a missing door or just want a beautiful old brass door knocker to decorate your otherwise modern home, Artifacts, Inc., of Alexandria, Virginia, may be able to help you. They sell (or buy) architectural salvage.

There are generally over 1000 items in stock, including old hardware, mantels, columns, doors, newel posts, stair spindles, wood brackets, and pedestal sinks. Since the items are those which are saved from old buildings, the stock changes constantly. From a partial list of inventory which was sent to us, we noted that Double Victorian mantels sell for $150–$550; newel posts in various woods, sizes, and styles cost $25–$250; and pedestal sinks run $75–$100.

If you are interested in purchasing an item which they might have in stock, write and tell them what you are looking for. They will furnish you with photographs, dimensions, and shipping information. With a little luck, that something you are wanting may be the something they have just brought back from a buying expedition.

Write to:

Artifacts, Inc.
702 Mt. Vernon Avenue
Alexandria, Virginia 22301

HABERSHAM PLANTATION

Habersham Plantation handcrafts replicas of 17th and 18th century furniture modeled after designs of the early American settlers. In the days when the people of the Blue Ridge Mountains lived in isolation from the rest of the world, it was common for them to build most of the things that were needed in the home. These items were fashioned in unpretentious beauty with truly functional qualities. This is the tradition that the craftsmen at Habersham Plantation work to uphold.

There are over 200 pieces in the Habersham Plantation furniture collection. Each piece is handcrafted, handcarved, finished, and waxed. Recent additions to the collection are even handpainted with delicate designs copied from furniture, fabric, and wallpaper of the 17th and 18th centuries.

The two catalogs that we have seen, *The Habersham Plantation Collection* and the *Connecticut River Valley Collection* offer an infinite variety of beautiful pieces. One of the most exquisite items we have seen (in any catalog) is the 18th century Wedding Chest with its intricate painted design. This chest was a traditional part of every maiden's world in the 1700s. It was filled with linens and laces from the moment a young lady learned to sew. Great care went into the construction and decoration of this first hope chest.

Ask your local dealer to show you these beautiful catalogs.

Habersham Plantation
P.O. Box 1209
Toccoa, Georgia 30577

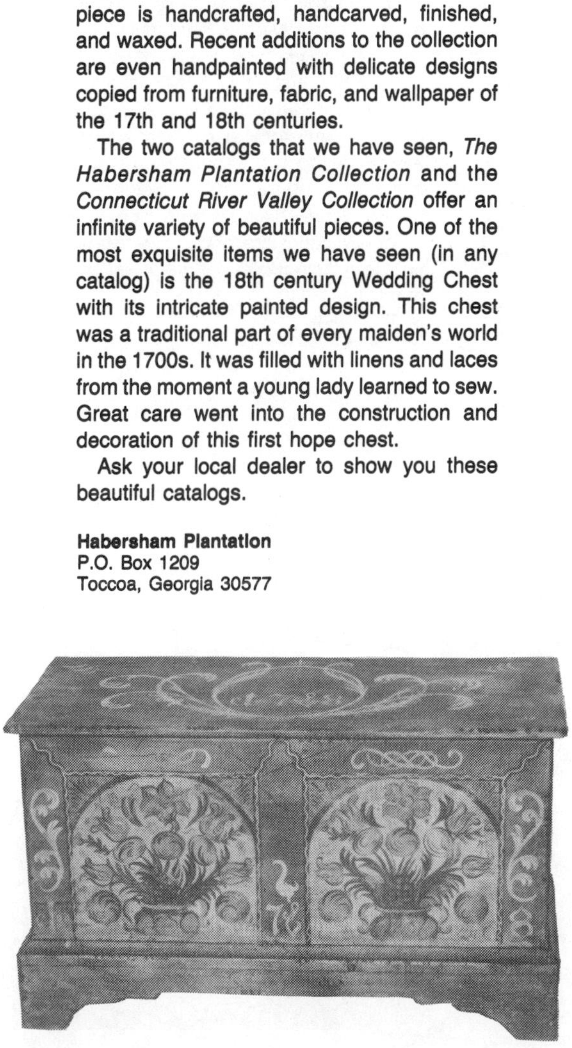

A SWEET STORY

The praline was invented by the cook of Count Plessis-Praslin, a 17th-century French soldier, hence the name, pronounced "praw-leen" by some, "pray-leen" by others, and "proh-leen" by a very few. This cook took some almonds and, after crushing them, boiled them in sugar until they were brown and crisp. The recipe swept through French kitchens and was brought to Louisiana by the French colonists.

The Louisiana version of the praline was made with more accessible pecans, with brown sugar being substituted for refined sugar. This version as quickly became a part of the Creole culinary tradition as the original version had of the French.

New Orleans is perhaps more closely associated with the praline than is any other place. In days gone by, *pralinieres* in starched white apron and tignon (a madras handkerchief worn as a headdress) went around the streets of the town vending *Pralines aux Pacanes*. In the cookbook *Recipes and Reminiscences of New Orleans*, published for the Old Ursuline Convent there, there is a good recipe for Pecan Pralines as made by the Ursuline Nuns:

Pecan Pralines

1 cup brown sugar
1 cup white sugar
1 cup pecan meats
½ cup cream
2 tablespoons butter

Dissolve sugar in cream and bring to a boil, stirring occasionally. Add the butter or margarine and pecans and cook until the syrup reaches the soft ball stage (238°). Cool without disturbing, beat until somewhat thickened but not until it loses its gloss, and drop by tablespoons onto a well-greased flat surface or a waxed-paper-lined surface. The candy will flatten out into large cakes. Yield: 20 pralines.

Recipes and Reminiscences of New Orleans is available for $4.95, plus $.75 postage and handling, from Old Ursuline Convent Cookbook, Box 7491, Metairie, Louisiana 70010. It is an excellent cookbook, full of interesting sidelights on New Orleans lore.)

There may be many of you who would rather have the experts make your pralines for you. If so, there are several good confectioners in the South who specialize in perpetuating the tradition of the *Creole sucreries*, as well as making a few improvements of their own.

Evans Creole Candy Factory, located in New Orleans on Decatur Street in the historic French Market, makes pralines of great taste and texture, in the old tradition, with some additions such as chocolate creamy pralines, maple creamy pralines, and rum creamy pralines. If you write, they'll send you a brochure that will put your sweet tooth in gear.

Evans Creole Candy Factory
848 Decatur Street
New Orleans, Louisiana 70116

Lamme's Candy, of Austin, Texas, makes a special "Texas Chewie Pecan Praline" which is just that: the flavor of a pecan praline with a caramel texture. The "Texas Chewie" was invented by the grandfather of Lamme's present president in 1885. Lamme's also ships candy assortments and boxes of divinity, chocolates, caramel-covered pecans, almond toffee, flint stick candy, and mint kisses.

Lamme's Candies Since 1885, Inc.
P.O. Box 1885
Austin, Texas 78767

NOSTALGIA—FOR THE EIGHTEENTH CENTURY

There is nothing new under the sun—especially in this time of reverence for the near and distant past: nostalgia for lost generations is at an all-time high and the hallmarks of the particular generations longed for are an integral part of the contemporary scene. Not to be forgotten in this race for remembrance is the eighteenth century. Salem House, in Williamsburg, Virginia, that city whose very existence is a monument to nostalgia, has made available several items that will indeed "take you back." Among these are an 18th Century Herb Garden, an 18th Century Flower Garden, and handmade 18th Century work and dress shirts. The garden packets each contain 10 packages of seeds of plants that were prevalent in Colonial gardens. Instructions for planting—and for drying the flowers—are included. Each packet sells for around $4.00.

The Colonial work shirt (available in white, red check, chambrey blue and unbleached muslin) can be worn by men as a sport shirt, and by women as either a sport shirt, bathing suit cover-up, or even maternity smock. The dress shirt (in white only), with its ruffles at the neck and cuffs, can be worn with formal evening wear. Sizes (with corresponding women's sizes in parentheses) are neck size 13—13½ (6—8); 14—14½ (10—12); 15—15½ (14—16); and 16—16½ (18—20). Work shirts retail for around $22.50; dress shirts, around $24.50—plus $2.75 postage and handling.

Salem House also features dollhouse miniatures. If you need Williamsburg wallpapers with matching fabrics or a working barometer for your dollhouse, this is the place to inquire. Other miniatures include English Staffordshire replicas; Early American, Victorian, and Eighteenth-Century furniture; petit point firescreens (# 40 gauze), trinket boxes, footstools, pillows, bellpulls, and candle screens.

For additional information, please write and include a self-addressed stamped envelope:

Salem House
209 North Boundary Street
Williamsburg, Virginia 23185

SHIRLEY PEWTER

Pewter is an integral part of the colonial tradition and perhaps that is why the Shirley Pewter Shop of Williamsburg, Virginia, excels so completely in its pewter craftsmanship: the craftsmen in the shop can feed on the atmosphere engendered by Colonial Williamsburg and the result is a product almost unequalled in quality.

Shirley's catalogue displays such items, made in its workshop on Jamestown Road in Williamsburg, as whale-oil lamps with shades or chimneys; sconces; a time light (burns for 8 hours—the time can be read by the oil level); keys; candlesnuffers; inkwells; fruit bowls; plates; trays; small dishes; candlesticks; sugars and creamers; chambersticks (used by our forefathers when retiring to their bed chambers); wine and water goblets; punch bowls; highball and old-fashioned beakers; jiggers; seven-arm candelabra; spoons of various types and sizes; Jefferson cups and miniature cups of the same style for use as cordials; porringers; baby cups—and many other items selected by Shirley from other outstanding foreign and domestic pewterers.

For your catalogue, send $2.00 to:

Shirley Pewter Shops
P.O. Box 553
Williamsburg, Virginia 23185

8 CUP COFFEE & TEA POT, SUGAR & CREAMER, ON A 16" TRAY.
A fine service for a large group. Insulated handles. Tray is hammered so scuff marks do not show up. Elegant!
$445.00 complete.

COFFEE SERVER.
Made in limited editions for taverns in Colonial Williamsburg. Each is numbered and dated. This server holds 3 quarts of liquid and stands 12" tall.
$175.00

INK WELL.
This 18th Century designed ink well is just the right touch on a desk. 2" tall, 3½" wide.
$30.00

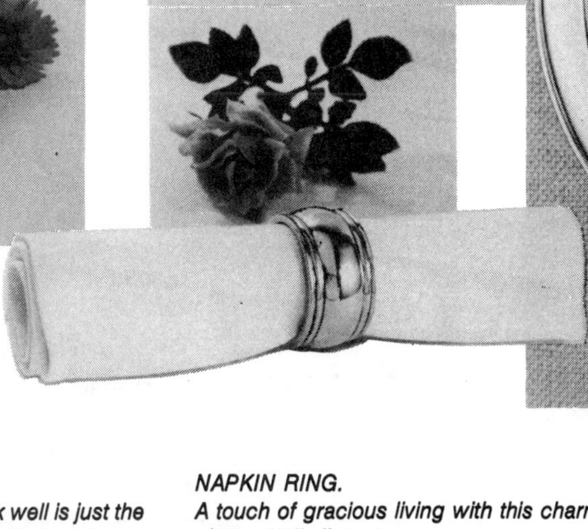

NAPKIN RING.
A touch of gracious living with this charming piece. 1½" diameter.
$9.00

WHALE OIL SCONCE.
A decorative piece of simple lines and charm. Beautiful for hanging in foyers or dens. 10" high, 8¾" wide.
$70.00

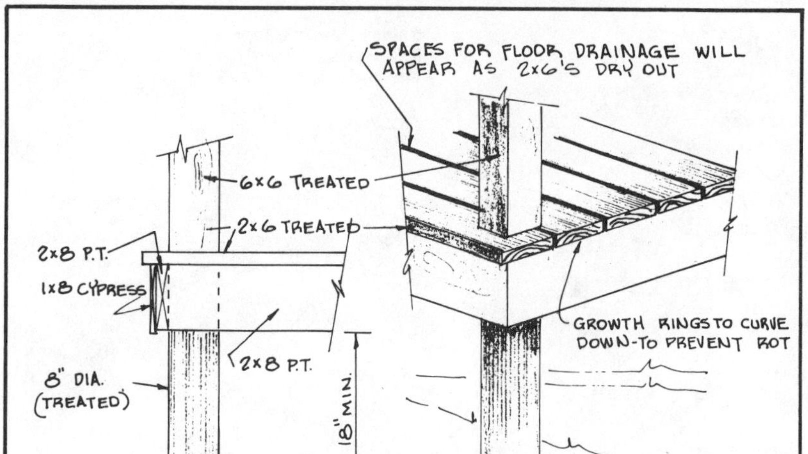

CUSTOM HOME PLANS

Just reading through a copy of *Country Plans* by Natalie Howard gives one a pastoral feeling. Many of her homes reflect a leisurely, carefree pace through designs using keeping rooms and parlors, rail fences, and much stone and wood.

Should your taste run to a rambling country home, there are plans available for one with 2,675 square feet; or if a country cottage is appealing, why not a tiny two-story one with 795 square feet?

These homes can be first homes, vacation homes, cabins, or ski lodges—the variety is endlessly fascinating.

A book of 65 country plans is available for $4.80, and we suggest you order this first. Afterward, when you are ready to build, complete sets of house plans can also be ordered. Reversed plans are for sale with mirror images and dimensions backward; therefore, Natalie suggests that you order an additional regular set to accompany the reversed sets.

Prices for plans are:

5 sets.. $50.00
3 sets.. $40.00
2 sets.. $35.00
1 set.. $25.00

Natalie has two other books for sale—*Country Features* and *Log Home Plans*. *Country Features* contains 20 ideas and directions on how to build country porches, homemade doors and shelters, window seats, wide plank floors, and more. It sells for $5.80. *Log Home Plans* contains the plans for 18 log homes and sells for $3.80.

To order the books or plans, the address is:

Custom Home Plans, Inc.
Route 1, Lake Burton
Tiger, Georgia 30576

NORMAN'S NATCHEZ
An Early Photographer and His Town

by Joan W. Gandy and Thomas H. Gandy

The University Press of Mississippi
3825 Ridgewood Road
Jackson, Mississippi 39211

It is seldom that a town is fortunate enough to have its buildings, its beauty, and its citizens recorded for posterity by a great photographer. Natchez is indeed a favored city. Not only is the photographic skill of Henry Norman employed in this remarkable book, but also the work of his son is featured. Same subjects, same talent. In addition to the Normans' photographs, the work of the Gurney brothers for whom Henry Norman first worked is included. Their studio began in 1851, and thus the book records Natchez during its decade of greatest wealth. Following this comes the Civil War, and the pictures immediately take on a more somber tone. Dirty Confederate soldiers, Federal gunboats, and deserted streets all exemplify the appalling effects of the conflict.

However, the majority of the pictures belong to Henry Norman and mirror a world of manners, gaiety, and historic solemnity during important events like a visit from President Taft. There is an astonishing collection of river photographs. Both Henry and his son Earl Norman loved the majestic, lonely beauty of the Mississippi. The river was the reason for the town and perhaps that accounts for their fascination. Also, it was the waterway for the proud steamboats—the grandest being the *J. M. White.* Norman photographed the sumptuous salons and rooms within. The richly ornate main cabin and giant silver water cooler surrounded by glistening parquet floors reflect a luxury unequaled on the river. Tragically, the *J. M. White* burned in 1886, but in a sense, Norman saved its contents and its grandeur in his pictures.

The people of Natchez are not neglected by the camera by any means. Memorable "little things" are preserved on film. A child muses among scattered cards, four young ladies peer coyly from beneath floppy bonnets, men's baseball teams share equal billing with women's tennis. Mardi Gras whirled the elite of Natchez from the 19th to 20th century, and the romantic photographs of the revelers are among the book's best.

It is difficult to describe in words a book of visual delights. The town, the river, the countryside, and the people all helped create the unique attractiveness of *Norman's Natchez: An Early Photographer and His Town.* But interestingly enough the lure of this book does not confine itself to any particular region. Like all great photography, its appeal is universal. A bygone era, old-fashioned pastimes, historic houses, and celebrations are here, but the people enjoying them are those we all have seen and known many times, many places.

—S.V.H.

NATCHEZ SCENES

Carolyn Harper has drawn up a set of prints depicting some of Natchez, Mississippi's famous antebellum homes and has also sketched some of the steamboats that once plied the waters of the mighty Mississippi. A set of the four house prints sells for $5.00; a set of four steamboat prints sells for $10.00. A box of notepaper bearing a print of a house on each of 12 prints is $2.50.

To order write:

Natchez In Pen & Ink
Carolyn Harper
130 John Glenn Drive
Natchez, Mississippi 39120

Stanton Hall

BELLE OF MEMPHIS
OF THE ANCHOR LINE FLEET
1880

Longwood

NATCHEZ VIII
BUILT AT JEFFERSONVILLE, INDIANA
1891

SOMETHING OLD—SOMETHING NEW

Now you can make your own pie safe from a kit, which (if you're queasy about making furniture) looks like a good thing to begin on. The wood panels are tongue-and-groove construction, assembled with screws and dowels. The authentic punched-tin designs are available in several patterns. The safe is 54 inches high, 32 inches wide, and 14 inches deep, and costs $149.95. Or if you would prefer to start small, you might want to try a colonial doll cradle kit for $19.95 or a primitive doll cradle kit for $15.95. Also available in kits are a regular-sized colonial cradle, a dough box, a spice cabinet, and a bench table.

Heritage Shoppe makes custom furniture and wood-carved signs as well. For information write to:

Heritage Shoppe
P.O. Box 418
Sullivan's Island, South Carolina 29482

The South's Great Gardens

by KAREN LINGO

Some of the most powerfully beautiful spots in the South are in the public gardens. Most are open all year, with seasonal masses of color. But probably the most popular time of year to visit is from February through April, when the camellias, azaleas, and spring bulbs bloom. This is when color is piled upon vibrant color in beds, banks, and along the wandering paths.

People like Walter Bellingrath, Cason Callaway, A. J. Hodges, and Henry Middleton helped make it this way. Their efforts to create a monument to nature and a sanctuary for man resulted in the gardens that bear their names.

These, then, are the Great Gardens of the South.

Bellingrath Gardens

About 20 miles south of Mobile, Bellingrath Gardens stretch quietly along the banks of the Isle-aux-Oies River, and winding paths make their way through carefully groomed plantings. This is a garden for walking, and throughout you'll find benches where you can sit and relax.

Just inside the entrance is a rose garden and beside it a conservatory that houses delicate and exotic plants.

One area is devoted to camellias, which are in full bloom in January and February. And just when they're beginning to fade, elsewhere you'll find the hyacinth, narcissus, and pansy warming up for their debut. But it's the azaleas that steal the show. They usually begin opening in February and are in full bloom in March and April. In the meantime, tulips, dogwood, pyracantha, amaryllis, Japanese flowering cherry, and many other plants add their beauty to the gardens.

Midway through the gardens is the elegant Bellingrath home. Tours, lasting 45 minutes, are conducted daily from 8:30 a.m. to 4:15 p.m. Admission is $3. Located next door to the home is the Gallery of Boehm Porcelains, the largest public display of these works in existence.

An area where visitors probably spend the most time is the Oriental-American Garden. Here, surrounded by bridges, stepping stones, and floral displays on the water's edge, long-legged pink flamingos and fat swans provide a continuous show.

Bellingrath Gardens is south of Mobile in Theodore, Alabama, off U.S. 90 and State 59. It is open daily year-round, from 7 a.m. to dusk. Admission is $2.40 for adults and $1.20 for children 6 through 11. Breakfast, lunch, and snacks are served in the entrance building from 7:30 a.m. to 4 p.m., and a free pet motel is provided for animals.

Callaway Gardens

Spring comes gently to Callaway Gardens in the Piedmont area of Georgia. It breathes life into the waiting acres of native plants and wildflowers. And the legions of azaleas that reach their peak from mid-March to April give reality to the dream of Cason J. Callaway, who wanted to build "the most beautiful garden since Adam was a boy, built to last until Gabriel blows his horn."

Along the way, Callaway Gardens became known not only as a horticultural area, but as a resort as well. It has overnight accommodations and facilities for golf, tennis, fishing, horseback riding, swimming, and hunting. And of course, it has the gardens.

Within the resort are 13 miles of scenic drives and a number of woodland trails. The larger plants are easily seen from the roads, but the exquisite, tiny wildflowers are best seen on foot and sometimes on bended knee. Along the Wild Flower Trail, you can see native plants all year.

A visit should begin at the Information Center, where you can see a brief multiscreen presentation about the gardens. Then you can either drive your own car through, or take a 2½-hour guided bus tour with a naturalist. At scheduled times, a naturalist conducts nature walks, which usually last about an hour and 45 minutes. Another way to see the gardens is by bicycle, and rentals are available at $2 for two hours.

Callaway Gardens is on U.S. 27 near Pine Mountain, which is about 80 miles southwest of Atlanta. The Information Center is open from 9 a.m. to 5 p.m. daily, and the gates to the gardens are open from 7:30 a.m. to 6 p.m. Admission is $2 for adults and $1 for children 6 through 11. The only cost for a bus tour is gate admission; the tour departs the Callaway Gardens Holiday Inn. Inside the gardens is a restaurant that serves lunch between 11:30 a.m. and 2:30 p.m., and dinner between 5:30 and 9 p.m.

Hodges Gardens

In the early part of this century, the land where Hodges Gardens now grows was a sorry sight. Lumbermen had come to the longleaf pine forests of Louisiana and stripped the land, leaving it barren and virtually useless. But A. J. Hodges, a lumberman himself, was interested in reforestation. He chose as his experimental arboretum an area near Many. Today it bears his name.

Much of the gardens is left in a natural state, forested in the pine seedlings that A. J. Hodges planted. You can drive through it on 10 miles of paved roads. The cultivated gardens with masses of flowers are in and around an old quarry and are designed for leisurely walking. Atop a knoll is an observation tower, from which you can survey the display of colors below.

The cool weather of winter brings out the camellias, some blooming as early as November. Peak times are January and February, and azaleas bloom from mid-March through April. Also with the advent of spring comes the flowering of wisteria, dogwood, tulips, and many others. The flower with the longest blooming season here, though, is the rose. It can be seen from March to November in the three rose gardens.

The greenhouses are open to the public, and sometimes there are extra plants for sale. No restaurant facilities are inside the gardens, but picnic areas are provided.

Hodges Gardens is 15 miles south of Many on U.S. 171. It is open from January 15 through December 24, from 8 a.m. to sunset daily. Admission is $3 for adults and free for children under 12 with an adult.

The Gardens of Charleston

If there is one distinct garden city of the South, it has to be Charleston. For within a few miles of the city are three major public gardens: Cypress, Magnolia, and Middleton Place.

Camellias and azaleas are the springtime mainstay of this area, with drapes of wisteria and vignettes of flowering bulbs filling in. The peak season for camellias is from February until mid-March, followed by the azaleas, which reach their peak and fade by the last of April.

Cypress Gardens is the smallest of the three gardens. It grows around a lagoon of black water punctuated with cypress knees. You can walk the paths that lead over the banks, but a luxury here is a 40-minute boat trip that covers virtually the same territory in a more relaxed manner.

Located 24 miles north of Charleston off U.S. 52, Cypress Gardens is open daily, February 15 through May 1. Hours are 8 a.m. to sundown, and admission is $3 for adults, $2 for children 12 through 16. The boat ride is an extra 50 cents. No restaurant facilities are available, but picnicking is permitted.

Magnolia Gardens is one of the oldest in the country and is listed in the National Register of Historic Places. Its oldest camellias were brought from France and England more than a century ago, and some of the azaleas were imported from Asia.

The pathways are designed for walking and cycling alike, and for those who want to explore the gardens by water, canoes rent for $1 an hour. The plantation home is open to visitors; an art gallery is upstairs. Admission is 50 cents to the downstairs displays. A children's petting zoo is on the grounds.

Located 12 miles northwest of Charleston off State 61, Magnolia Gardens is open daily from 8 a.m. until dark. Admission is $3 for adults, $2 for students, and $1.50 for children 7 through 12. Lunch is served from the plantation's 170-year-old kitchen every day from noon to 4 p.m.

Middleton Place, boasting the oldest landscaped gardens in America, is basically of a formal design. It also has the country's oldest camellias, brought to the area in 1783 from France.

Aside from its gardens, Middleton Place offers tours through its house museum and stableyards. Admission to all three is $4 for adults and $2 for children 4 through 12. Admission to only the gardens and stableyards is $3 and $1.50.

Located 15 miles northwest of Charleston on State 61, Middleton Place is open daily from 9 a.m. to 5 p.m. The house is open from 10 a.m. Monday through Saturday and 2 p.m. on Sunday. Lunch is served from a kitchen on the grounds from noon to 3 p.m. (except December and January).

More of the South's Beautiful Garden Spots

ALABAMA

Birmingham Botanical Gardens, Birmingham; daily, dawn to dusk; free.

Jasmine Hill Garden, 8 miles north of Montgomery on U.S. 231; weekends only December-February, Tuesday through Saturday March-November, 9 a.m. to 5 p.m.; $1.50 for adults, 50 cents for children 6 through 12.

ARKANSAS

The Arkansas Territorial Restoration, Little Rock; daily, 9 a.m. to 5 p.m., and from 1 p.m. on Sunday; $1 for adults, 25 cents for children.

FLORIDA

Alfred B. Maclay Gardens State Park, 5 miles north of Tallahassee; daily, 8 a.m. to sunset; $1 for adults, 50 cents for children.

Busch Gardens, Tampa; daily, except Sundays and holidays, 9 a.m. to 4 p.m.; free to gardens area.

Cypress Gardens, Winter Haven; daily, 8 a.m. to 5:15 p.m.; $4 for adults, $3 for students 12 through 16, $2 for children 6 through 11.

Leu Gardens, Orlando; daily, 9 a.m to 5 p.m.; free.

Ponce De Leon Springs, 6 miles north of DeLand on U.S. 17; daily, 9 a.m. to sunset; $1.25 for adults, $1 for students 12 through 18, 75 cents for children 4 through 12.

Ravine Gardens State Park, Palatka; daily, 8 a.m. to sundown; free.

GEORGIA

American Camellia Society Headquarters Garden, Fort Valley; daily, dawn to dusk; free.

Forsyth Park, Savannah; daily, dawn to dusk; free.

Founder's Memorial Garden, Athens; daily, 7 a.m. to 5:30 p.m.; free.

KENTUCKY

Bernheim Forest, Arboretum, and Nature Center, Clermont; daily, 9 a.m. to sundown, March 15-November 15; free.

LOUISIANA

Jungle Gardens, 7 miles southwest of New Iberia at Avery Island; daily, 9 a.m. to 5 p.m.; $1.75 for adults, 75 cents for children 6 through 12.

Live Oak Gardens, 7 miles southwest of New Iberia at Jefferson Island; daily, 9 a.m. to 5 p.m.; $2.25 for adults, $1 for children 4 through 16.

MARYLAND

Brookside Gardens, Wheaton; daily, 9 a.m. to 5 p.m.; free.

Sherwood Gardens, Baltimore; open three weeks each May; free.

MISSISSIPPI

Mynelle Gardens, Jackson; daily, dawn to dusk; $1 for adults.

NORTH CAROLINA

Airlie Gardens, Wilmington; daily, March 1-September 30; $1 for adults, 50 cents for children.

Biltmore House and Gardens, Asheville; daily, 9 a.m. to 5 p.m.; $5 for adults, $4 for children 6 through 16.

Orton Plantation Gardens, 19 miles south of Wilmington on State 133; daily, 8 a.m to 5 p.m.; $2 for adults, $1 for children 6 through 12.

Reynolda Gardens, Winston-Salem; daily, sunrise to sunset; greenhouses, Monday through Friday, 7:30 a.m. to 4 p.m.; free.

OKLAHOMA

Honor Heights Park, Muskogee; daily, dawn to dusk; free.

Will Rogers Park Horticulture Gardens, Oklahoma City; daily, 8 a.m. to dark; free.

SOUTH CAROLINA

Clemson Horticulture Gardens, Clemson; daily, sunrise to sunset; free.

Edisto Gardens, Orangeburg; daily, dawn to dusk; free.

Glencairn Gardens, Rock Hill; daily, dawn to dusk; free.

Hopeland Gardens, Aiken; daily, 10 a.m. to sunset; free.

Swan Lake Iris Gardens, Sumter; daily, 8 a.m. to 5 p.m.; free.

TENNESSEE

Memphis Botanic Garden, Memphis; daily, sunrise to sunset; free.

Tennessee Botanical Gardens (Cheekwood), Nashville; daily except Mondays and major holidays, 10 a.m. to 5 p.m., from 1 p.m. on Sundays; $1 for adults, 50 cents for students 12 through 18.

TEXAS

Botanic Gardens, Fort Worth; daily, sunrise to sundown; free.

McAshan Arboretum and Botanical Garden, Houston; daily, arboretum open from 8:30 a.m. to sunset, botanical hall from 9 a.m. to 5:30 p.m.; free.

Sunken Gardens, San Antonio; daily, dawn to dusk; free.

Tyler Rose Park, Tyler; daily, 8 a.m. to 5 p.m.; free.

VIRGINIA

Bryan Park, Richmond; daily, dawn to dusk; free.

Gardens-by-the-Sea, Norfolk; daily, 8:30 a.m. to sunset; 50 cents for adults, children under 5 free.

WEST VIRGINIA

Oglebay Park, Wheeling; daily, dawn to dusk; free.

SOUTHERN COUNTRY COOKBOOK is a volume of 1,400 recipes fresh from the countryside—all kitchen-tested. There are 16 pages of color photographs and original artwork and 20 chapters including "Foods with a Southwestern Flavor," "Crowd Cooking," "Favorite Oldtime Southern Foods," "Wild Game," and "Food Preservation." OXMOOR HOUSE has published this book and sells it, hardcover, for $12.95.

FOR NEWS OF THE PAST AND PRESENT

THE *VIRGINIA* GAZETTE.
Containing the freshest Advices, Foreign and Domestick.
Founded By William Parks August 6, 1736
Post Office Box 419 Williamsburg, Virginia 23185

Williamsburg's own newspaper "containing the freshest advices, foreign and domestick" since 1736.

In addition to all the news of local government, breaking events, and in-depth reports, *The Virginia Gazette* offers these special features:

PEOPLE AROUND TOWN — notes on newsmakers

SOCIAL — scheduled events, personalities, features

EDITORIALS — emphasizing local topics

PUBLIC FORUM — opinion by local leaders

SPECTATOR — 2 pages on the arts

SPORTS — exclusive Youth League coverage and perceptive features

HIGH PRIEST — a tough columnist evaluates our town's events

BUSINESS — no other paper covers the local economy so completely

JUSTICE — courts and crime news in one complete page

52 ISSUES FOR ONLY $10.00 IN-STATE, $12.00 OUT-OF-STATE.

The Virginia Gazette
P.O. Box 419
Williamsburg, Virginia 23185

TRY A TRUNK

If you've spent so much money renovating your old house that you can't afford furniture, dig grandma's old trunk out of the attic to sit on or store things in. You can cover unsightly holes or spots with some of these carved or embossed wood ornaments, available from Charolette Ford Trunks. If you are just missing a hinge or lock or corner, you can also get them from Charolette Ford. A free 24-page catalogue will show you a variety of the above plus handles, clamps, doll trunk hardware, drawbolts, fancy nails, and decorative rings. You can also order tools, such as nippers, tack claws, and brushes. For $3.50 prepaid, Charolette will send you *Heirloom Treasures from Antique Trunks:* a how-to book for restoring, refinishing, and decorating antique trunks. Or you can get a *History of Antique Trunks* for $1.50 prepaid. (Texas residents add 5% sales tax.) Write to:

Charolette Ford Trunks
Dept. HC, Box 536
Spearman, Texas 79081

Lewis Glaser

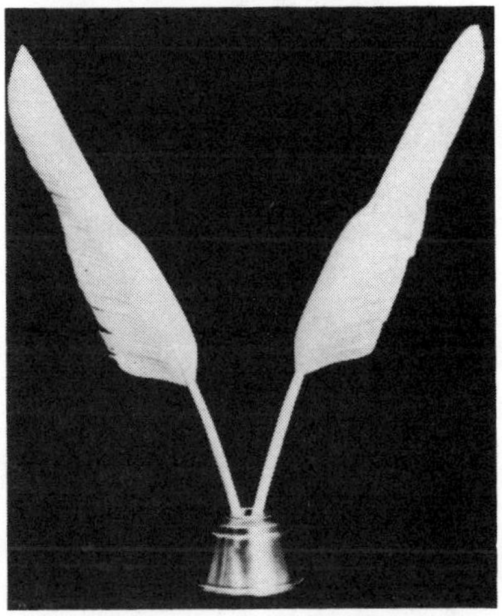

GOOSE QUILL PENS

Each day the Supreme Court of the United States is in session, reminders of its historic dignity lie on the counsel tables.

Each lawyer who appears to argue his case finds before him a pair (right and left) of crossed goose quill pens on a ruled sheet of white paper. He is permitted to carry them away as a memento of his appearance.

The quill pens for many years have been handcut by Lewis Glaser of Charlottesville, Virginia. They are required to be exactly 10 inches long, one side smoothed, and pure white. Mr. Glaser's only tool is a penknife, a gift from the late President Eisenhower. The wing feathers of Embden geese—shipped from Europe—are used to fashion the quill pens because Embden provide the most nearly perfect white feathers.

Goose quill pens—a bit longer than the court pens—are available in Charlottesville and by mail as a handsome set paired with a colonial pewter inkstand, 3 inches in diameter and 2 inches high.

The colonial inkwell and quill pen sets gift-boxed sell for $15.00 each, postpaid.

On the box in which Mr. Glaser packages his quill pens and the inkwell appears this pointmaking quotation from a letter Thomas Jefferson wrote on Dec. 26, 1808, to his granddaughter, Cornelia Jefferson Randolph: "I rejoice that you have learned to write for another reason: for as that is done with a goose quill, you now know the value of a goose. . . . "

Because Mr. Glaser is a one-man industry, working only with a penknife, you may have a waiting period until he can process your order. Be patient! Address orders to:

Lewis Glaser
Handcut Colonial Style Goose Quill Pens
P.O. Box 123
Charlottesville, Virginia 22902

HISTORY.

At the dawn of her history, Alabama contained four tribes of aborigines, the civilized and hospital Cherokees, in the northeast, in a region that they always called Chiaha; the warlike and heroic Chickasaws, in the northwest, along the Tennessee, the Tombigbee and the Upper Yazoo; the friendly Choctaws, in the west and southwest; and the Muscogees (or Creeks), called by Bancroft "the most powerful nation north of the Gulf of Mexico," west of the Ocmulgee.

STATISTICS.

Settled at	Mobile Bay
Settled in	1702
Founded by	Frenchmen.
Admitted to the U. S.,	1819
Population in 1860,	964,201
In 1870,	996,992
In 1880,	1,262,505
In 1890 (U. S. Census),	1,513,017
White,	662,185
Colored,	681,431
Voting Population,	259,884
Vote for Harrison (1888),	57,197
Vote for Cleveland (1888),	117,320
Net Public Debt,	$11,992,619
Area (square miles),	52,250
U. S. Representatives,	8
Militia (Disciplined),	2,587
Counties,	67
Post-offices	1,933

THE "KEARSARGE" AND "ALABAMA."

On Sunday, June 19th, 1864, the *Kearsarge* and *Alabama* were engaged in mortal combat off the port of Cherbourg, France. The *Alabama* was a powerful steamer, a swift sailer, and, carrying guns of the heaviest calibres. She had been the terror of our commerce as far as the Indian Ocean, from which she had just returned and entered the port of Cherbourg for repairs. Captain Winslow, commanding the *Kearsarge*, had long been in search of her, and the moment he heard of her arrival, set sail and lay off the mouth of the harbor for the purpose of following her to sea, when she again left port. On the 14th Captain Semmes sent Captain Winslow a challenge to fight, which was entirely unnecessary. He had come to Cherbourg for no other purpose and intended, by no means, to leave until he could follow the bold corsair out on the deep, and then sink him or be sunk himself. The bells of the churches of Cherbourg had not yet done pealing when the pirate steamer cast off her fastenings and began to steam slowly out of port. Captain Winslow, as soon as he descried his adversary approaching, turned his ship's head seaward to avoid the question of jurisdiction. The *Alabama* followed after till the former was about seven miles from shore, when Winslow turned short about and steered straight for the privateer, intending to run her down. The latter immediately sheered off and slowed her engines, presenting her starboard battery to her enemy. The battle now commenced in earnest; the firing was rapid and incessant, and the two guns of the *Kearsarge*, carrying eleven-inch shells, sent their ponderous missiles with terrible accuracy into the hull of the *Alabama*, and, bursting within, opened huge gaps, through which the water poured in torrents. Semmes, finding his ship was sinking, hauled down his colors and dispatched a boat to the *Kearsarge* to state that he had surrendered. In the meantime he lowered the boats that had not been shot away, to receive the sick and wounded; but, before all could be got off, the stern of the steamer sank deep in the sea, lifting her bow in the air, and then with one heavy lurch she went to the bottom. The English yacht *Deerhound*, that had hovered about the scene, now approached and picked up Semmes, with others of the crew who were struggling in the water.

RAPHAEL SEMMES.

REPRINTS OF HISTORY

If you enjoy browsing through the pages of the old "Harper's Weekly" and other publications of the Civil War era, Donald Brundage of Atlanta, Georgia, has a service that should appeal to you: he reproduces historical prints, making them look like originals, sometimes even better. Mr. Brundage began this business as a hobby which combined his interest in graphic arts with his collecting old history books and from a start reproducing maps, he moved on to making prints of the major battle scenes of the Civil War. After finding a print he wants to reproduce, Mr. Brundage uses a special camera to make an enlarged negative of the print which, after retouching, is made into a printing plate. The crucial step in his process is the "antiquing" of the finished print, a step accomplished with the help of a secret formula Mr. Brundage has devised. The result of the use of the secret formula is an authentic-looking, aged print.

Mr. Brundage lists prints from Alabama, Georgia, Florida, Kentucky, Louisiana, Pennsylvania, South Carolina, Tennessee, Maryland, Colorado, Michigan, North Carolina, California, Rhode Island, Texas, Illinois, West Virginia, Massachusetts, Ohio, Virginia, Washington, Missouri, Montana, New Jersey, Idaho, and England. He also stocks portraits of various Civil War generals, maps, and train prints. Also available is a box of notepaper imprinted with a drawing, in color, of the "General," famous for its Civil War great locomotive chase.

A box of the "General" notepaper is $1.50 (for 10 notes and envelopes). Prints, through the size of 10" x 14", are $2.95 each prepaid.

Order from:

Donald J. Brundage
P.O. Box 9966
Atlanta, Georgia 30319

Foxfire

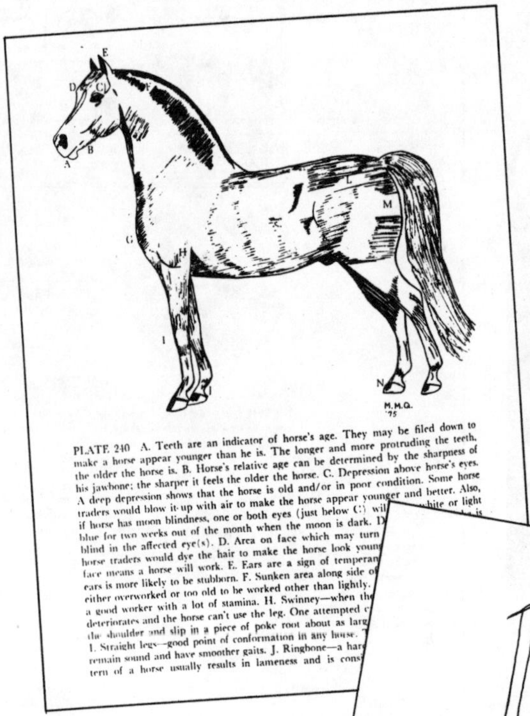

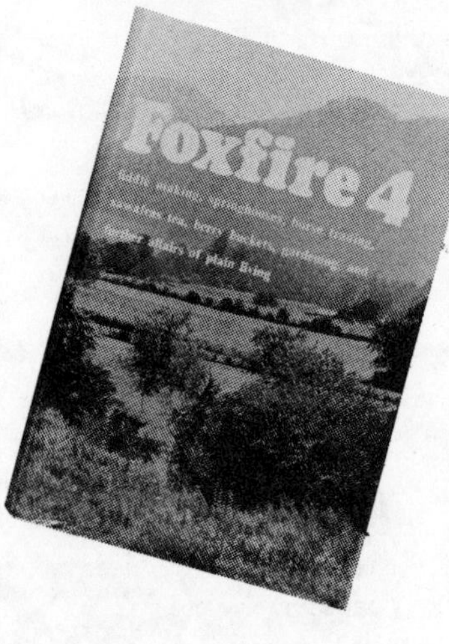

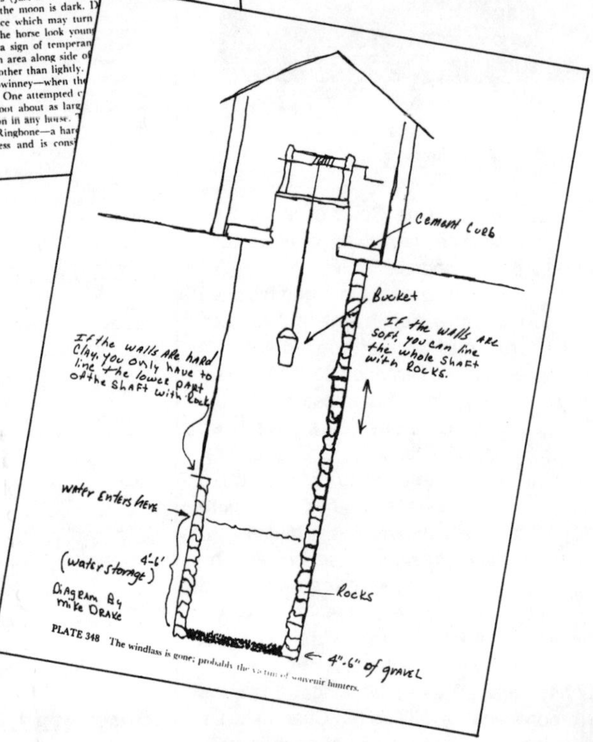

Foxfire is a plant that glows in the dark. It is also a quarterly magazine published by students in a small Appalachian high school. Many have called it the most extraordinary magazine by high school students in this country. One indication that this may be true is the fact that it received two $10,000 research grants from the National Endowment for the Humanities in Washington, D.C. Another is the fact that it has been written about by virtually every other magazine of note around. And still another is the fact that it has over 10,000 subscribers representing every single state and several dozen foreign countries.

The primary concern of the students who put *Foxfire* together is a distinctive culture that is uniquely theirs. The concern of the adult advisors is the quality of the educational experience the students have as they run what has become, since its founding in 1967, a staggeringly complex operation.

Battery-powered tape recorders and cameras in hand, the editors sometimes disappear for days at a time into the Appalachian highlands in search of families who still live in log cabins—families who remember vividly how it was that they survived in a pre-supermarket, pre-flight, pre-television age. The students return with exact, step-by-step instructions for self-sufficiency; and they write, lay-out and publish these detailed instructions as articles which are fully illustrated with photographs and diagrams.

Whole issues have already been printed that deal comprehensively with such topics as how to build a log cabin, how to plant by the signs of the zodiac, how to slaughter a hog and cure and smoke the meat, how to build a stone chimney, how to spin and weave, how to heal the sick and bury the dead—all told in the exact words of those who remember best: those who had to know how in order to survive.

In the process, these twelve- to sixteen-year-olds learn not only how to write and edit and proofread full, rich articles; but also how to lay them out, design the issues, run the entire circulation and distribution system, handle all the funds, answer most of the correspondence—in short, run a very real business in a very real world.

In 1972, a selection of articles from the magazine was published in book form by Doubleday. *The Foxfire Book* is now well on its way to passing two million copies in print. Additional volumes are also available in what has become an open-ended, continuing series.

THE FOXFIRE BOOK

Contents: Hog dressing, log cabin building, mountain crafts and foods, planting by the signs, snake lore, hunting tales, faith healing, moonshining, chimney building, working with white oak splits, quilt making, soap making, weather signs, home remedies, and more.

FOXFIRE 2

Contents: Ghost stories, spring wild plant foods, spinning and weaving, midwifing, burial customs, corn shuckin's, wagon making, bee keeping, washing clothes in an iron pot, more personality interviews, and more affairs of plain living.

FOXFIRE 3

Contents: Animal care, banjos and dulcimers, hide tanning, summer and fall wild plant foods, butterchurns, and other affairs of plain mountain living.

FOXFIRE 4

Contents: Fiddle making, spring houses, horse trading, sassafras tea, berry buckets, gardening, and further affairs of plain living.

FOXFIRE 5

Contents: Blacksmithing, gun making, and iron making.

The Foxfire program has been extended into video through shows which are broadcast each week over the Rabun County CATV system, through a series of records devoted to traditional music and contemporary songwriters, through a press which has published an oral history of the Tallulah Falls Railroad, and through Foxfire Furniture, which produces exact copies of traditional mountain hardwood furniture made under the supervision of genuine mountain craftsmen.

To subscribe to the *Foxfire* magazine:
One year: $8.00
Two years, $13.00

The Foxfire Fund, Inc.
Rabun Gap, Georgia 30568

SMITHFIELD PACKING COMPANY HAMS

The Smithfield Packing Company has three product lines: Luter Genuine Smithfield Hams; Jamestown Country Hams; and Jordan's Genuine Virginia Hams. Each is similar to the other, with all being dry-cured (the curing process indicative of all "Smithfield" hams), and with the Jamestown hams being slightly milder than the other two varieties.

The Luter Genuine Smithfield Hams are the premiums of the company. These are available both cooked, ready to serve, and uncooked. You can also obtain a boneless Luter ham—boned after cooking then either reformed into its natural shape or pressed into a "boxcar" loaf shape, and then browned. The Luter line also includes a picnic ham, from the front leg of the hog, and a half slab of bacon.

The milder Jamestown ham is available both cooked and uncooked.

Perhaps the most historic of all the Smithfield Packing Company hams is the Jordan ham. To quote from *Gourmet* magazine:

"It was 131 years ago that Jordan's Old Virginia Smokehouse began curing and smoking hams at Smithfield. In 1890 the firm expanded and moved to Richmond. Truly great are these hams. To start with, not just any ham can wear the Jordan label. Seldom more than 15 out of 100 hogs purchased on the hoof are graded high enough to earn the honor.

"The hams are first salt-packed in cool cellars for 50 days, being turned frequently during this period. After the salt is removed the ham is allowed to mature for two weeks, then is thickly coated with pepper and hung over hickory fires. For weeks the hams are left in the pungent smoke to come to a deep mahogany tone. Next they go to the aging room to rest for long months protected from light.

"When it's cooking time the ham is taken into the Jordan kitchen to be soaked 18 hours, then to simmer slowly for 3½ hours. After cooling in the stock, the heavy skin in removed, the fat trimmed, and a brown sugar glaze is added. Then the ham is baked, well-sauced with wine. The meat has a savory nut-like sweetness that only care in curing and time in aging can give."

Also, from a Confederate diary comes this mention of a Jordan ham, the name of which evidently was used during that era as almost the generic term for country ham: " . . . Christmas Day dawned bright and cold over Richmond. There was an air of gaiety, of anticipation, as the lovely belles in their crinolines and the handsome officers in the Confederate gray left church services and stepped into carriages for the drive home. Soon they would be feasting on Jordan's ham—mahogany-hued, wine-flavored, and sliced paper-thin. Though Lee's gallant men are in bivouac north of Manassas, the War seems very far away . . . "

It is evident that you will be getting a ham with the weight of tradition and experience behind it if you buy any of the Smithfield Packing Company hams.

For more information about the Luter or Jamestown hams, write:

The Smithfield Packing Company, Inc.
Mail Order Department
P.O. Box 447
Smithfield, Virginia 23430

For more information about the Jordan Ham products, write:

Jordan's Virginia Ham Company
Mail Order Department
P.O. Box 447
Smithfield, Virginia 23430

How to Carve

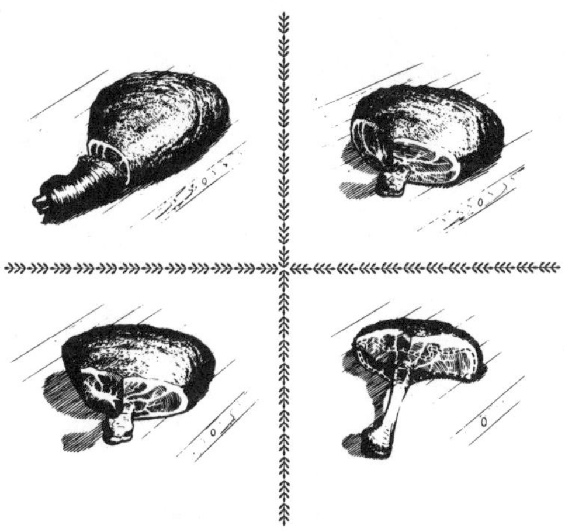

Use long, thin, very sharp knife. Slice as THIN as possible; thin slices are tastier, go farther.

1. Fat side up, start about six inches from bone end, cutting straight down to and around the bone. Take out small wedges down to bone. Slice at right angle to bone, and clean from bone all around as you go. Small slivers are best you can do until past hock joint. Then remove hock and save to flavor soups or vegetables.

2. Grip bone, turn ham and slice from one side, then the other.

3. Soon slices become larger, and therefore difficult to keep thin; so cut back at sides and take smaller slices from three faces as shown.

4. When you hit the "cross" bone about three-fourths of way back, slice on other side from back to front . . . until you hit bone at bottom. Now bone underlies much of remaining ham. Slope the cut back at top, until all possible slices are taken from top of bone. Finish cleaning bone by cutting away all meat in small THIN slivers . . . good for sandwiches.

Remember, shape or size of slice is secondary. Keep slices thin, however small.

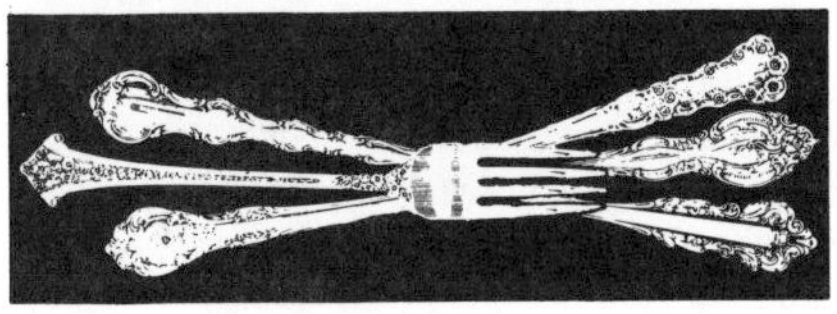

HARD-TO-FIND SILVER

Julius Goodman & Son has been in the jewelry business in Memphis since 1862. For the past 30 years the Goodmans have assembled from purchases of estates, individuals, and other jewelers a unique storehouse of active, inactive, and obsolete patterns of sterling silver flatware not readily obtainable elsewhere. Today they have over 1,000 patterns to offer.

Goodman and Son also sells antique and unusual holloware, antique and fine jewelry; but sterling flat silver remains the firm's specialty.

Because the stock consists of many one-of-a-kind items, changing frequently, Goodman's has found it impractical to issue a catalogue. However, the jewelers do offer price lists, free. They accept any sterling flat silver or jewelry items in trade as part-payment against the purchase of all other merchandise they supply and do a volume of their business by mail-order.

Write to them:

Julius Goodman & Son
P.O. Box 3195
Memphis, Tennessee 38103

"I found the half-forgotten Southern intonations and elisions as pleasing to my ear as they had formerly been. A Southerner talks music. At least it is music to me, but then I was born in the South. The educated Southerner has no use for an r except at the beginning of a word. He says 'honah,' and 'dinnah,' and 'Gove'nuh,' and 'befo' the waw,' and so on. The words may lack charm to the eye, in print, but they have it to the ear."
Mark Twain, LIFE ON THE MISSISSIPPI

Benne cheese straws and wafers and ginger chutney are specialties of the city of Savannah and are also specialties of the house at the Cottage Shop there. The shop's brochure gives a little history of the cottage. The benne products and chutney may be ordered, as may hot pepper jelly and *The Savannah Cook Book*. For more information write:

The Cottage Shop
2422 Abercorn Street
Savannah, Georgia 31401

CENTER FOR SOUTHERN FOLKLORE

The Center for Southern Folklore is located in a large brick house at 1216 Peabody in Memphis, Tennessee. Founded in 1972, it is a non-profit corporation with the purpose of collecting and preserving the folklore of the South. The directors are William Ferris, Yale history professor, and Judy Peiser, a documentary filmmaker. Through films, records, and books, the folk traditions of the South are preserved.

An archive houses 30,000 photographs and color slides, 1000 hours of taped recordings, 200,000 feet of film, and many pieces of folk art and craft—all indexed. Diverse photographs make up the collection of the Center for Southern Folklore. L. O. Taylor (1922-1967), a black minister, recorded life in the Memphis black community: Baptist conventions, baptisms, high school football games, the Cotton Maker's Jubilee Parade, portraits of celebrities such as Joe Lewis and W. C. Handy, and thousands of private individuals. Charles Faulk, photographer and writer for the *Vicksburg Evening Post,* recorded forty years of Vicksburg life in approximately 2600 photographs, including photographs of the 1953 Vicksburg tornado, the 1935 and 1937 Mississippi River floods, the burning of the sternwheeler *Sprague* in 1974, and the 1940-41 mobilization for World War II. Sixteen-millimeter films cover such subjects as "Gravel Springs Fife and Drum" and "Black Delta Religion."

Another endeavor, a traveling exhibition called "Folk Art and Crafts: The Deep South," has been created for the Smithsonian Institution and will be seen there and at other museums around the country. Eighteen panels and twenty-five objects tell the story of southern folk art and crafts.

"Sacred Harp Singing" Stitchery by Ethel Mohamed.

Painting "Cotton to the Gin" by Theora Hamblett.

Center for Southern Folklore Archives/photographer:Jane Moseley

The Center is also serving as a clearinghouse for information about work being done. It published, in 1976, a comprehensive listing of over 1800 films and videotapes; this index, *American Folklore Films and Videotapes: An Index,* fills a 350-page book.

The Center for Southern Folklore Newsletter is a semi-annual publication with a summer supplement. Sent to us was an issue of 16 pages, which contains an 8-page section devoted to recorded folklore and features articles about the people who make recordings and the people who make the music. Types of music are varied: blues, country, Afro-American, psalm-singing, ballads, Acadian, and gospel. The paper guides the reader to these recordings. It also provides news of how various groups proceed with their projects. Books and films are the subjects of articles in this issue. Each edition contains a calendar of meetings which are of interest to folklorists. Reports of in-progress field work and information on new publications appear in each edition. Subscriptions to the *Newsletter* (published semi-annually) are $5.00 for one year or $7.50 for two years.

A set of twelve, full-color 4" x 6" postcards—reproductions of artifacts in the exhibit prepared with the Smithsonian Traveling Exhibition Service—are available by mail. We are showing two of the designs: "Sacred Harp Singing" which is from needlework by Ethel Wright Mohamed and "Cotton to the Gin" by Theora Hamblett. Other card designs include white oak baskets, clay sculpture, a bottle tree, tire art, and a folk sign. A set of twelve cards sells for $1.80 or individual cards are $.15 each.

To order cards or subscribe to the *Newsletter,* write:

Center for Southern Folklore
1216 Peabody Avenue
P.O. Box 4081
Memphis, Tennessee 38104

FOLKLORE
for the time of your life
by Elaine S. Katz

Oxmoor House, Inc.
Birmingham, Alabama

With the renewed interest in ancestry and roots, this book should be welcomed. But it is significantly different from most others of its type. The emphasis is not so much on the "who's in your past" as on the "what's in your past and present." It is an adventurous do-it-yourself guide to the colorful lives around you, the expressions you always thought were so hilarious and quaint, and the stories your grandmother told you that you always wished you could remember.

There are all kinds of stories in everyone; you just have to discover them. Like a quilt, stories often piece together to make up a life. Or as Marie Webster would say, "How much piecin' a quilt is like livin' a life! Many a time I've set and listened to Parson Page preachin' about predestination and free will, and I've said to myself, 'If I could just git up in the pulpit with one of my quilts I could make it a heap plainer to folks than parson's makin' it with his big words.' " There are many Marie Websters in your life, full of patches of tragedy, comedy, and plain old good sense. But like everything else, culture is becoming faster, quicker, and more and more the same. People take less time listening and being with each other, and too late, they realize what they miss (if they're lucky).

Folklore promotes a good hobby for these confusing modern times. It tells how to start collecting the verbal expressions and rhymes of those around you. And slowly you branch out to gathering tales, beliefs, and songs others will be more than happy to share with you. What tools do you need? Photographs, slides, index cards, tape recorders, and notebooks are recommended. Using a tape recorder to collect folklore in the form of an oral biography is especially helpful. This book offers useful interviewing techniques for the beginner. And for the experienced collector, it tells of the rich veins to be mined in the form of craftspersons, social folk groups, and folk artists. Even the process of tracking down a legend can be fascinating; as you discover reading the story of the murderous Hazel Farris, whose body has not decayed since her death in 1906.

So, no matter where you come from, how old you are, or how much money you have, you can achieve satisfaction for yourself and preserve valuable grass-roots experiences for others. You will meet all kinds of interesting people and can learn more about your own heritage. And the best part is that it's so much fun!

—S.V.H.

THE CANE-ERY

2747 MURPHREESBORO ROAD
ANTIOCH, TENNESSEE 37013
PHONE 615/367-2019

This company services caners and seat weavers nationwide, and has been doing so for several years.

They will ship your order in 24 hours—check or money order is required.

LONG SELECT CHAIR CANE
(For Seats With Holes)

		App. 1000' Hank
Carriage	1½MM	$5.15
Superfine	2MM	5.25
Fine-Fine	2¼MM	5.35
Fine	2½MM	5.65
Narrow Medium	2¾MM	5.85
Medium	3MM	6.05
Common	3½MM	6.25

(1 Hank Does 3-4 Average Size Seats)

BINDING CANE

Narrow 3/16"	– 4MM	$4.10	App. 500'
Wide 7/32"	– 5MM	4.20	App. 500'
X-Wide 1/4"	– 6MM	4.40	App. 500'

PER FOOT .01

OPEN WOVEN CHAIR CANE
(For Seats With Groove)

FINE OPEN 1/2 INCH MESH

12"	Per Running Foot	$1.20
14"	Per Running Foot	1.40
16"	Per Running Foot	1.60
18"	Per Running Foot	1.80
20"	Per Running Foot	2.00
22'	Per Running Foot	2.20
24"	Per Running Foot	2.40
36"	Per Running Foot	3.60

50' Rolls – $1.00 square foot
10 or more Running Feet .... 10% Discount

RATTAN SPLINE
(For Installing Woven Cane)

Heavy	$ .05 per foot
Medium	.05 per foot
Light	.05 per foot
100'	4.50

A Guide to use to determine the size of Cane required

SIZE OF HOLE IN SEAT FRAME	DISTANCE BETWEEN HOLES - CENTER TO CENTER	SIZE OF CANE
1/8	3/8	Super Fine
3/16	1/2	Fine Fine
3/16	5/8	Fine
1/4	3/4	Narrow Medium
1/4	3/4	Medium
5/16	7/8	Common

TERMS: Check or Money Order – No Cash or C.O.D.
No Open Accounts
QUALITY – SERVICE

POSTAGE

On orders up to	$10.00 – $1.00
On orders up to	15.00 – 1.45
On orders up to	20.00 – 1.70
On orders up to	30.00 – 2.25
On orders up to	40.00 – 3.25
On orders up to	50.00 – 4.25

Orders over $50.00 – $5.00

FIBRE-RUSH
5/32" Brown

1 Coil (2 lbs)*	$ 3.10
Reel (app. 14 lbs)	12.50

(*will do average size seat)

ORIENTAL SEAGRASS
(Hong Kong Grass)

1 Coil (app. 3 lbs) *	$ 3.10
(*Will do Large Size Seat)	
10 or more coils	10% discount

RATTAN
SPLINTS OR REEDS
(For Weaving Over the Rail)

3/8" Flat Split	$3.10 bundle
1/2" " "	3.20 bundle
5/8" " "	3.30 bundle
3/16" Flat Oval Reed	4.10 bundle
1/4" " " "	4.40 bundle

(1 bundle will do average seat)

INSTRUCTION BOOKS

Seat Weaving, L. Day Perry	$3.00
Basketry, Christopher	2.50
Stool Seating (Booklet)	.55
How to Re-Cane (Booklet)	.55
How to Re-Rush (Booklet)	.55
How to Re-Splint (Booklet)	.55

TOOLS

Pegs	$ .75 Doz.
Awls	.60 Each
Wedges	.75 for (5)

BASKET REEDS

No. 1 (App. 1 lb. Reels)	$3.20
No. 2 (App. 1 lb. Reels)	3.20
No. 3 (App. 1 lb. Reels)	3.20
No. 4 (App. 1 lb. Reels)	3.20
No. 5 (App. 1 lb. Reels)	3.20
No. 6 (App. 1 lb. Reels)	3.20

FINE PINE FURNITURE

The craftsmen at Hux-Craft, Inc., are local men who make each piece of white pine furniture individually. They work in a small shop in Pickens County, Georgia, handcrafting reproductions of early American furniture. Hand sanding, staining, and rubbing produce the quality finish that you see here on a sample of their work, the Buffet Table. Hux-Craft will custom-make a table to fit any area in your home. For information write to:

Hux-Craft, Inc.
279 East Paces Ferry Road
Atlanta, Georgia 30305
(404) 237-1161

"We picked up one excellent word—a word worth traveling to New Orleans to get; a nice limber, expressive, handy word—'Lagniappe.' They pronounce it lanny-yap. It is Spanish—so they said. We discovered it at the head of a column of odds and ends in the Picayune the first day; heard twenty people use it the second; inquired what it meant the third; adopted it and got facility in swinging it the fourth. It has a restricted meaning, but I think the people spread it out a little when they choose. It is the equivalent of the thirteenth roll in a 'baker's dozen.' It is something thrown in, gratis, for good measure. The custom originated in the Spanish quarter of the city. When a child or a servant buys something in a shop—or even the mayor or the governor, for aught I know—he finishes the operation by saying:

"Give me something for lagniappe."

Mark Twain, LIFE ON THE MISSISSIPPI

Charleston is a unique city in America—one that is outstanding for its cultural heritage as evidenced in its architecture, cuisine, festivals, and citizenry.

CHARLESTON

In the old peninsula city of Charleston, South Carolina, three centuries of architectural beauty combine with an elegant cultural legacy and important historical Americana to portray the city-state that played major roles in the creation, the dividing, and the reforming of the American Republic.

Here, within a half-mile radius, the visitor may see and touch and experience events that helped make America. A short stroll, or a carriage ride, or a bicycle, or an automobile carries one to the spot where South Carolina's decision to secede made the Civil War certain; to the place where the hanging of Stede Bonnett and 37 other pirates meant the end of piracy on the Atlantic Coast; to the oldest theater in America; to a former slave market or to an ancient church where Sabbath services once were timed to coincide with the tides.

While taking a look into the past, the visitor can count on being taken care of in the present. There are fine motels, elegant hotels, convention facilities, excellent restaurants, art galleries, museums, and antique shops in addition to the usual facilities found in an American city today.

In the old city, built on a peninsula that juts into the great harbor between two bold rivers, many of the houses and public buildings are maintained today in the same fine condition as when they were built, some more than two-and-a-half centuries ago.

Charleston's architectural heritage is unique in America, for she was the first American city to protect and preserve the fine old buildings that had witnessed so much history. Today, the houses are still lived in and some are still owned by the families that built them. The public buildings still function for government, for cultural organizations, and for learned societies. Lawyers and bankers still function in buildings that predate the American Revolution.

It was from these buildings that came the men and women who helped shape the Revolution, who pioneered in the first American railroad of any consequence and who stood with their state in the crisis that generated the Civil War.

From the point of the peninsula–White Point Gardens–the visitor may stand and see the spreading panorama of the firing of the first shot of the Civil War. Immediately before him, in the harbor center, looms old Fort Sumter, while on all sides are the forts and sites from which the Confederate artillery poured a withering fire on April 12, 1861, initiating 4 years of fighting that saw the Confederate States defeated and the United States reunited as one nation.

It was on this strategic peninsula, nearly an island, that the early settlers decided to build their city just a few years after their first landing in 1670, several miles away. It was here that they erected a fortress wall along the Cooper River and inland to completely surround the new town named in honor of King Charles of England, the patron king who generously rewarded eight noble friends by giving them a strip of land that encompassed what is now North and South Carolina and Georgia and that stretched westward to the Pacific Ocean.

GEORGE EVERLEIGH HOUSE on Church Street is a fine example of the Charleston House with its wrought iron gate and walled-off garden.

Charleston was to become the city-state that dominated the infant colonies through an era of rule by the eight Lords Proprietors into a return to the status of a Royal Colony under the king himself and then into the holocaust of rebellion against the might of Great Britian.

In September of 1776, Charleston's Sons of Liberty forced the last royal governor, Lord William Campbell, to flee the city and 9 months later defeated a British fleet and army that attacked the harbor while delegates to the Continental Congress at Philadelphia were still debating the issue of separation from the mother country.

On June 28, an ill-equipped and badly outnumbered colonial garrison repelled the British fleet, neutralized its accompanying army and sent a courier galloping toward Philadelphia with the news of victory. It was that news, reaching the Congress in mid-July, that persuaded faltering delegates that the British could be beaten and a nation could be birthed.

South Carolina was to be the scene of 172 battles and skirmishes before the American victory at Yorktown, and Charleston was captured, occupied and sacked by the British just before the war's end.

Nearly 2 decades later, a Charlestonian, Charles Cotesworth Pinckney, told the great powers of Europe: "Millions for defense but not one damned cent for tribute," very nearly precipitating a war with France. Charlestonians, rising to the threat, met in old St. Michael's Episcopal Church and raised funds to assist the United States with completion of harbor defenses. Then they went out and personally built the harbor-side fort themselves, named Fort Mechanic in honor of the men who did most of the work.

The War of 1812 found the city outfitting ships for defense and supporting artillery and infantry units. In 1830, the nation's first operating railway train made its first run out of Charleston on Christmas Day.

Today's visitor may visit the Railway Historical Society's museum and see an exact reproduction of that first railway engine and the building in which it was planned.

That building, and more than 1,000 others, are protected under a zoning and protective code that is a half-century old, the first such historical protective law in the United States. The treasury of architectural gems that is unique to Charleston is the result of an ongoing program that has helped preserve the old city as a lived-in museum.

The city and its buildings are a composite of the varied ethnic backgrounds of the people who built Charleston. The first were mainly English and Scotch, Irish and Welsh. Then came the French Huguenots fleeing the persecutions in France. Later waves of German Lutherans were welcomed as refugees from the religious wars in that nation, and the Dutch came also, along with Jews, seeking religious freedoms guaranteed under the first Carolina Constitution.

The second oldest Jewish synagogue in America is in the old city along with one of the nation's oldest Roman Catholic churches, and the old Quaker Burying Ground contains the remains of such stalwart Quakers as Mary Fisher Bayley Cross, whose lone voyage to confront the Sultan of Turkey in 1660, when she was only 21, was one of the great feats of womankind.

The old city, and the once agricultural empire it ruled, are today offering a new look at an antique way of life . . . one that encompasses the warp and woof of the entire history of America.

From the comfortable and enjoyable Charleston of today it is only a few steps into the easy pace, the elegant culture and the beautiful settings of the Charleston of yesteryear.

HISTORIC CHARLESTON REPRODUCTIONS

Those of you who visit Charleston, or even have just read about Charleston, may want to bring a little of the flavor of the city into your own home. You may do this by sending for a copy of the *Historic Charleston Reproductions* catalogue and then ordering an item or items. This 1979 Catalogue contains photographs of over 250 beautiful, heirloom pieces that have been reproduced or adapted from the originals. These pieces are copies of the originals that were in Charleston homes starting in the 17th century and on up to the early 19th century; they range in price from $5 to $5000 and more.

We have reproduced one of the opening pages in the catalogue and several of the exquisite pieces of furniture. You may order a catalogue for $3.50, which will be credited against any future purchase of $25.00 or more.

Historic Charleston Reproductions
51 Meeting Street
Charleston, South Carolina 29401

HISTORIC CHARLESTON · CHARLESTON, S.C. · REPRODUCTIONS

THE STORY OF HISTORIC CHARLESTON REPRODUCTIONS

Fine furnishings imported from abroad, or made by master craftsmen in Charleston, are part of Charleston's unique heritage. Important furniture, silver, porcelains, crystal, luxurious fabrics and decorative accessories, comprise this store of treasures cherished still in private houses or loaned for exhibition in museum buildings which are open to the public daily.

Generous Charlestonians, because of their love for their city and their determination to save her historic buildings, have permitted their heirlooms to be reproduced by Historic Charleston Reproductions. These reproductions, available in fine stores across the country, or by mail order, generate royalties used for preservation and restoration.

Each heirloom chosen for reproduction has a relevance to today's living, multipurpose usage and Charleston style. Each is small-scaled enough for modern rooms, although Charleston houses boast high ceilings and generous space.

Each original is meticulously copied by the finest craftsmen working today, some in the United States and some abroad. New pieces are added to the expanding Collection each year, as Charleston shares its treasures to bring history to life again.

HISTORIC CHARLESTON REPRODUCTIONS AND THE HALLMARKS

ARE TRADEMARKS OF HISTORIC CHARLESTON FOUNDATION

Reprinted by permission of Historic Charleston Reproductions, Charleston, South Carolina.

Baker's Historic Charleston Reproductions are grouped around a typical Charleston fireplace. To complete the Charleston "look," the furniture is shown with accessories and fabrics which create the inimitable ambience of the historic Southern port city.

Porcelains from Mottahedeh; lamps from Norman Perry; and fabrics from P. Kaufman are all participants in the Historic Charleston Reproductions program, along with many other leading reproduction manufacturers.

A unique mahogany Pembroke Breakfast Table, with butterfly drop leaves and fretwork apron. The prototype, made in the mid-18th century, perhaps by Charleston master cabinet maker, Thomas Elfe, may be seen in the Heyward-Washington House Drawing Room.

An unusual Chippendale-style mahogany bookstand with four shelves and fretwork panel ends. The 18th century English-made original is in an historic private house.

THE APPALACHIAN PHOTOGRAPHS OF DORIS ULMANN

Preface by Jonathan Williams
Remembrance by John Jacob Niles

The Jargon Society

Doris Ulmann was born in New York City in 1884. She was educated in public school, later at the School of Ethical Culture and Columbia University. She studied photography with Clarence H. White for 2 years, but as John Jacob Niles says in his remembrance, ". . . basically she was self-taught, for she was a genuine artist and as such, had to find her own way. She was a completely remarkable woman and one who gave her life, and as much of her estate as was necessary, to the idea of photographing simple Americans."

The "simple Americans" Doris Ulmann devoted her life to photographing were the residents of the Southern Appalachian Mountains, mostly in North Carolina, Kentucky, Georgia, and Tennessee. Miss Ulmann found that "I have been more deeply moved by some of my mountaineers than by any literary person. (Editor's note: Miss Ulmann had published a book entitled *A Portrait Gallery of American Editors* in 1925.) A face that has the marks of having lived intensely, that expresses some phase of life, some dominant quality or intellectual power, constitutes for me an interesting face." In *The Appalachian Photographs of Doris Ulmann,* 63 of these interesting faces, out of the thousands she captured on film during her many trips through the South, were reproduced for the first time since the late 1930s. The story of their reissuing is a saga in itself.

Jonathan Williams *is* The Jargon Society. He also spends much time on the road within the United States, traveling to various colleges for readings of his poetry or for symposiums on literary subjects. It was on one of the "poetry-reading, snake-oil-dispensing sessions," as Williams terms them, at Berea College in 1967, that he took time to go through the thousands of Doris Ulmann prints in the archives there. From these thousands he picked 81; he then had Ralph Eugene Meatyard drive down to Berea from Lexington to go over the whole lot independently and make his selection. Meatyard chose 251, some of which duplicated Williams's. The total 300 were then taken to New York City where they "were scrutinized by non-blue-grass-eyes." From these, the final 63 were chosen.

John Jacob Niles, a friend of Williams and a fellow traveller with Doris Ulmann on many of her trips through the Southern Appalachians, wrote the moving remembrance which provides the only commentary necessary for the book. Mr. Niles entitles his remembrance, "Doris Ulmann: As I Remember Her," and his memories are fond and far-ranging. Mr. Niles and Miss Ulmann met when the now-famous folk song collector-composer was struggling as an actor in an "Off-Off-Broadway" revue. As Mr. Niles puts it, "Doris Ulmann saw exactly what she had been waiting for a long while—an active, youngish man with a strong back and what she hoped were strong arms, a man with an accent that sounded faintly like the Southern mountaineers she had met, but best of all, a vagabond type who was ready and willing for any kind of novel experience and a ballad singer, to boot." What followed this discovery was several years of a mutually beneficial relationship, one that ended only with Miss Ulmann's death. Mr. Niles would "do his thing," ferreting out new songs and singers, all the while assisting Miss Ulmann in her photography—carrying her heavy equipment, driving her car at times, even, during one memorable outing, ferrying her piggyback across a wide and shallow stream in Kentucky called Cutshine Creek. Mr. Niles also attempted to get Miss Ulmann to follow a proper diet, since she had suffered from a stomach ulcer since her childhood and, even with several operations, had never really recovered. On this front, Mr. Niles was unsuccessful, since strong, black coffee—gallons of it—was Miss Ulmann's favorite "food," and cigarettes her constant companions. Ultimately Miss Ulmann fell prey to her ulcer and these excesses and, during a working trip with Mr. Niles in the mountains of North Carolina, became so ill that he had to drive all night to get her back to her New York doctors. She died, at age 50, in New York City on August 28, 1934.

Now, 40 years later, Jonathan Williams has had the inspired good sense to rejoin Jacob Niles and Doris Ulmann. For Mr. Niles, the task was undoubtedly difficult: as he wrote to Mr. Williams, "You young men who enjoy the health of youth cannot imagine what this has done to me." We can only hope that Mr. Niles also realizes, as he surely must, that the pain of his labor has resulted in deserved new life for the art of Doris Ulmann. We are indebted to him for his present portrait of her, and for his past assistance to her.

To Jonathan Williams should go our thanks for yet another example of what one critic has termed "Jargon's cultural husbandry." The strength and character revealed in the faces of the mountain people captured by Miss Ulmann's camera are qualities to be revered and re-possessed. Jonathan Williams and The Jargon Society have reminded us of what modern-day life has tempted us to forget: the dignity and the enduring worth of simplicity.

—C. H.

The book is now available in paperback for $8.50 from Gnomon Distribution, P.O. Box 106, Frankfort, Kentucky 40602.

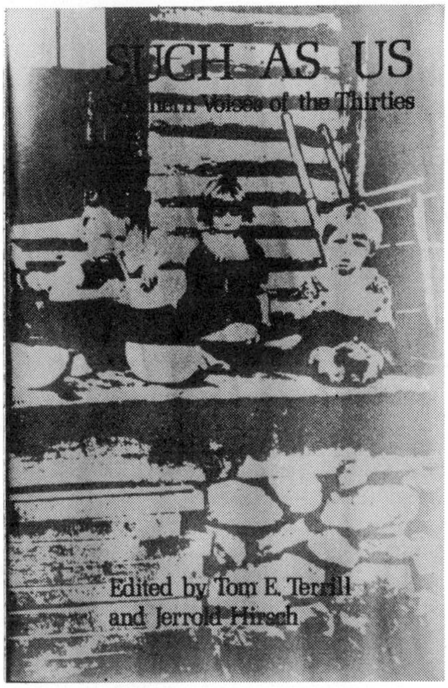

SUCH AS US
Southern Voices of The Thirties

Edited by Tom E. Terrill and Jerrold Hirsch

The University of North Carolina Press
Box 2288
Chapel Hill, North Carolina 27514

For all the many books claiming to illuminate that detached, illusory, magical, bizarre section of the country known as the South, few deliver. *Such As Us* is a noteworthy exception. It is a book that primarily works because it lets the South speak for itself. And it also lets a time (the 30s) speak for itself. So together, the land and the time produced the true authors of this amazing book.

Some of the voices have a unique poignancy as that of Lettice Boyer: "I don't look a hundred and ten year old? I's beginning to feel it. I got no blood pressure as I knows of: it ain't never been tuk."

And some are wrenching in that terrible agony of the little people like Emaline: "I knowed Abel daid. I tuck de baby way from him an' started to de house to tell Mr. Carrington. De teahs wuz er-streamin so I could hardly see. I wuz about 16 I reckon, an wid mah fust baby an' I loved my man. Hit mos' broke mah heart . . . I doan't specks a gal ever gits over her fust man. I sho didn't."

From an anonymous factory worker from Landgrove, North Carolina, comes a statement of his individual (yet sadly universal) experience: "You'd like to know what a day in my life is like. Well, t'aint no trouble at all fer me to tell you because every one is so much like the other I've learned the pattern by heart long ago."

James Edmonds' decision to support a local weavers' union against the exploitation of the owners reflects the courage of the individual in the country, towns, mills, and factories of the South. It describes a bravery echoed many times throughout this remarkable book: "To me the saddest part of it all was that the people because of their lot in life was too ignorant to protect themselves from what was being forced on them. It was like taking advantage of a child. I knew what a man was up against if he tried to point out some sort of way. I felt awful ignorant and not big enough for the job. But I had seen all I could stand."

Not all of the voices are heroic. Many are selfish and shrill and some reflect the division of wealth or race. But most are reminiscences that are compelling portraits of humanity in adversity and in prosperity. The life histories extend as far back as slavery times and reach forward as far as World War II. The experiences go beyond the South, embracing the problems of Everyman: death, religion, sex roles, poverty, and old age. Yet they are peculiarly Southern, from individual Southern people about their private feelings. And one is once again reminded that in everyone's life there is something that will break your heart.

—S.V.H.

MARYLAND'S WAY

One gets the distinct impression while leafing through *Maryland's Way—The Hammond-Harwood House Cook Book* that Maryland's way may be the *best* way, if the delicious-sounding recipes are any indication of other pleasures to be found there.

Seafood and game recipes are highlighted, since Maryland has long been noted for the bounty from both the waters of and skies above the Chesapeake Bay. For these alone the cookbook would be worth $8.95, but for that price you also get excellent photographs and drawings depicting Maryland vistas, as well as fascinating glimpses into its history via excerpts from the notebooks of notable Maryland personalities.

One of the more interesting recipes in the cookbook is this one for Diamond Back Terrapin, taken from Commodore Rodger's Sion Hill Papers:

Diamond Back Terrapins A. Aubrey Bodine

Diamond Back Terrapin

TO PREPARE AND COOK DIAMOND BACK TERRAPIN It is a question of choice whether the terrapin's head should be cut off, some claiming that it should be, that it may bleed, others that it should be put in the pot alive. If the head is cut off, place the terrapin with the neck down for a few minutes so the blood can run from it.

Have two vessels of boiling water, put them in one and let them remain for five or six minutes, then take them out, and a flaky skin can be easily removed from all the exposed meat by rubbing with the fingers. This cannot be done after the terrapin has been cooked and the meat has become soft.

Put them now in the other pot of boiling water and boil until you can, with the forefinger and thumb, easily press through the foot. For a five inch terrapin this takes about one hour, for larger ones of course

90

longer. But, by taking it out of the pot and testing in this way, a mistake cannot be made. The great success of the dish is this cooking, for unless this is properly done they are apt to be stringy or tough.

After the terrapins are done, take them from the pot and put in a vessel that will hold the liquor that runs from them. Remove the top shell; if it is inclined to stick, use a thin knife to run up between the shell and the meat. Some little tidbits are apt to adhere to the shell. Save them. Sometimes the sand bags adhere too; these are one of the few things about the terrapin you must throw away. After removing the upper shell you will find the sand bags or lungs, unless they have remained on the top shell, on top of the meat. Remove these with a fork; they are thin and leathery looking.

Carefully open the meat, find the liver, open it and remove the gall with as little of the liver attached as possible. Some epicures break one gall to six terrapins. All the rest of the meat is good except some of the intestines at the extremity. Do not pick the meat too fine. Save the liquor that has come from the terrapin in the vessel in which they were placed, and add to this enough liquor taken from the pot in which they were last boiled to use when they are put in the chafing dish. A great many people never think of this and use plain water to make the necessary liquor; this is not nearly so rich.

When ready to serve, put the meat in the chafing dish, and add the liquor that has been saved as above, as you prefer, in good quantity or enough to keep from burning. A good quantity is recommended for it is delicious. Before this, butter should have been used; indeed when first the terrapin is put in the chafing dish lumps of butter should be placed all over; then light the chafing dish, give a stir so the butter will melt, stir again, add more butter, add a little more butter; just before serving season with red pepper and salt, add a little more butter, and then just a little more butter.

The chafing dish is not to cook it, simply to make it piping hot, and as soon as it reaches that stage, serve on hot plates. Should any be present who wishes wine, let him add it after it is served. Never put wine in when cooking.

Maryland biscuit should be served with terrapin.

Commodore Rodger's way
Sion Hill Papers *Harford*

91

The Hammond-Harwood House, whose association published the cookbook, is a National Historic Landmark in Annapolis. The house was designed by William Buckland for Matthias Hammond and was built in 1774. It is now open as a museum every day except Mondays and Christmas Day.

For your copy of *Maryland's Way,* send check or money order for $8.95 plus $1.25 postage to:

The Hammond-Harwood House
19 Maryland Avenue
Annapolis, Maryland 21401

NEW OLD-TIME KITCHENS

Have you thought about the kitchen? When re-doing your old house, you may not want to break the authenticity of the period by installing a sterile-appearing modern kitchen. Yet you probably can't quite see yourself building a wood fire in the range every morning before your first cup of coffee. In that case, the Country Charm Range may be your answer.

The Country Charm Range, made by the House of Webster, looks just like your great-grandmother's wood range and will fit beautifully with your nineteenth century decor, but will still give you coffee at the flip of an electric switch. (The coffee mill on top is the electric timer.) You can get the Country Charm Deluxe Electric Range—with exhaust fan and automatic receptacles for small appliances—for $715.00. If you prefer a wall oven, you can get one with a cast iron front with old-time scrolling finished in black enamel for $395.00.

House of Webster also makes an electric cast iron skillet for $59.95 and an electric cast iron 5-quart bean pot for the same price. (Prices do not include postage or freight charges.) And for real purists there is even an electric cast iron patio cooker with tripod.

For information write to:

The House of Webster
Box 488, U.S. 62, North
Rogers, Arkansas 72756

CHARLESTON RICE STEAMER

As almost any cook will tell you, there is a definite art to preparing good—but not dry—rice. This is an art that has been known and practiced in Charleston for 300 years, more recently with the aid of what is known in many parts as the "Charleston Rice Steamer." The steamer is actually manufactured by many companies, in all parts of the country, but for the purist, who must cook rice the Charleston way with a Charleston product, we have found that James F. Condon & Sons, Inc., a Charleston department store, handles a couple of varieties of steamers for your selection. We tried the Wear-Ever Aluminum one and found it improved our own rice perceptibly. (That once glue-y mass became a collection of actually distinct grains!)

To improve your own chances of luck with rice, or just to get a good 6-quart pot with 2-quart steam inset pan for $13.99 plus $1.00 postage, write:

James F. Condon & Sons
425 - 37 King Street
Charleston, South Carolina 29403

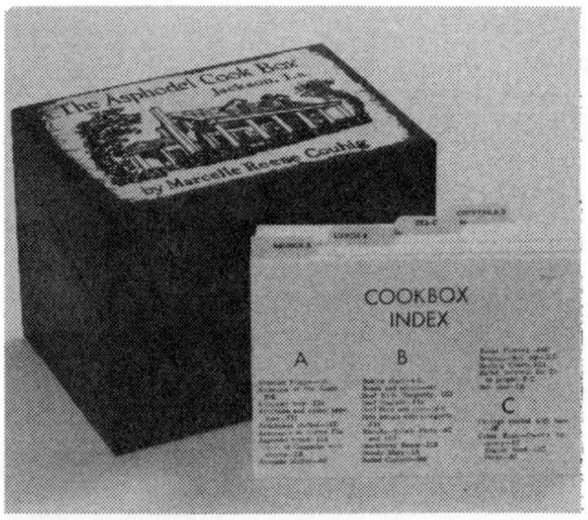

WHY DIDN'T WE THINK OF IT? A COOK BOX!

Mrs. Marcelle Reese Couhig has "invented a better mousetrap." She has taken the housewife and cook's file box and converted it into a readymade cook box, almost filled with recipes and clever hints accumulated through the years at Asphodel Plantation, an historic resort in Louisiana's Feliciana country. We say "almost filled" because there is plenty of room for personal recipe additions. With 256 cards, the Cook Box is available in blue, red, mustard, and green boxes, and sells for $19.95.

The Asphodel Cook Box
Pelican Publishing Company
630 Burmaster Street
Gretna, Louisiana 70053

The Valley Forge

If you find yourself without the proper fireplace accessories in your renovating, you may want to contact The Valley Forge. They handforge every item, using the same methods passed down from craftsman to craftsman for generations. Therefore, it may take awhile before you get your order, but the wait will have been worth it.

You can order many different types of fireplace screens (with brass trim and/or glass doors), log hoops, candleholders, andirons, baskets, and tool sets (with extra long handles, if you desire).

Write to:

The Valley Forge
1010 3rd Avenue, N.W.
Hickory, North Carolina 28601
(704) 327-2943

Grate

G-601

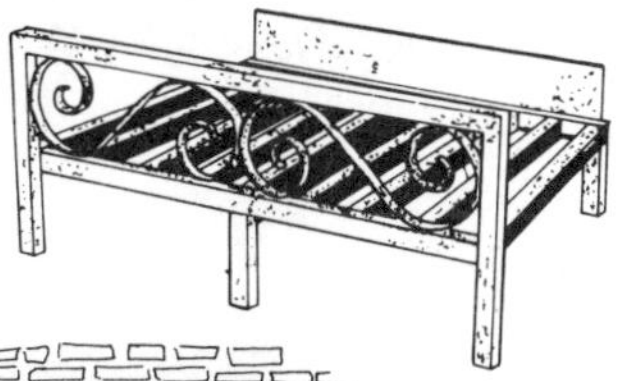

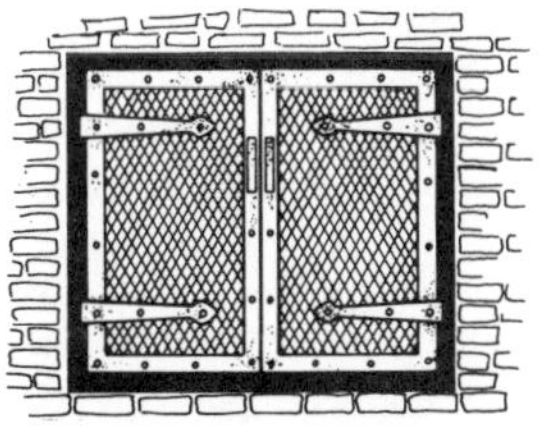

Screen
S-101

All screens may be ordered
with brass trim and/or glass doors

Candleholder

C-111

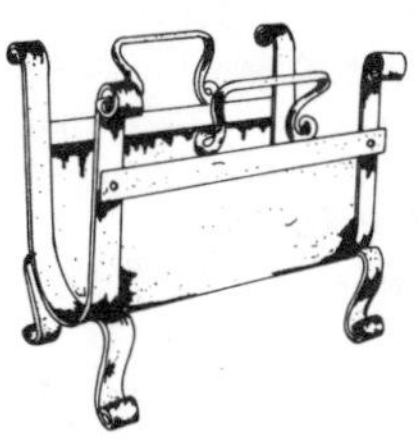

501

Basket

LYNCHBURG HARDWARE & GENERAL STORE

The Lynchburg Hardware & General Store was established back in the early 1900s by Mr. Lem Motlow. That esteemed gentleman was, in case you are not up on your Lynchburg, Tennessee genealogy, the favorite nephew of the famous stiller of Old No. 7 Black Label, Mr. Jack Daniel. (Yes, Virginia, there was indeed a real Jack Daniel!) The familial ties between the distillery and the Hardware & General Store were maintained until Mr. Conner Motlow, Lem's younger son, sold the proprietorship to Mr. Herb Fanning some years back.

Herb, who for years was the purchasing agent at Jack Daniel's, runs his store with the same frugal eye for a bargain and quality as he did the country's oldest registered distillery. One can still supply his farm with all the needed nails and nuts and bolts and buckets as before, but Herb's big interest these days is his mail order operation. He has loaded his down-home, highly readable little catalogue with all manner of exclusive goodies—authentic reproductions of actual turn-of-the-century Jack Daniel Advertising items—as well as folk craft collectibles for all ages. A must for the Daniel buff, a gold mine for the insatiable explorer, the Lynchburg Hardware & General Store catalog is only $1.00.

Lynchburg Hardware & General Store
Herb Fanning, Proprietor
P.O. Box 359
Lynchburg, Tennessee 37352

A MATCHING SERVICE

Buschemeyer & Company has an active silver matching service. They match pieces of sterling silver and silverplate dating from the turn of the century. In their stock, they carry over 50,000 pieces of flatware, in more than 500 different patterns. If they do not have the particular piece that is needed in stock, they search the market for it at no charge.

Buschemeyer & Company, established in 1865, is one of the oldest jewelry companies in Kentucky. They also do fine silver repair and replating.

For information, write to:

Buschemeyer & Company
515 River City Mall
Louisville, Kentucky 40202
Toll free number: 1-800-626-4555

A LITTLE HONEY, AND A LOT ELSE BESIDES

Remember Erskine Early and his Honey Stand? He writes fabulous letters when he is not packing hickory smoked sausage, bacon, and hams into mail order packages.

For those of you who missed his letter about his mail order "authentic Tennessee Hill Country foods":

". . . In 1925 my Dad was a beekeeper. Mom got the idea of putting a little 'stand' out beside the road (now U.S. 31) with various sizes of honey in jars, cans, etc.; nailed a tin can to a post with a little sign saying to select the items and then put the money in the can through a small slot in the top. Believe it or not, this 'system' worked for a time . . . never did have a thing stolen! That summer we added apples and peaches, etc., to the 'stand.' That fall and winter when we butchered hogs, a 'tourist' stopped and asked could he get, maybe, some sausage. Dad made up his sausage and one thing led to another; pretty soon we were selling sausage and all the extra meat we had plus all we could buy from the neighbors. The name 'Early's Honey Stand' stuck and we are still using it. Today, we still sell honey of course but 90% of my total business is in smoked meats (pork) . . . country hams, sliced country ham, smoked bacon, smoked sausage.

"Getting back to the early days of the 'stand' . . . we got into the mail order business of pure necessity. Folks would write back and want another ham or something shipped to them . . . all over the country. We really at that time didn't care anything about mail order . . . it was just an evil necessity we thought. We would save the orders till about Friday night and Dad and I would get in the kitchen and wrap and tie and sack and box and get them ready to ship. Mom kept fussing about us messing up her kitchen so much that we finally built a little lean-to onto the Stand and we were in the mail order business whether we wanted it or not. In spite of more or less erratic attention to the M.O. business, it kept growing steadily. Then along in the late forties and early fifties, we kept hearing talk about the 'interstate highway' program. We discovered that one through here (I-65) would miss us by several country miles . . . I took another good, long look at the mail order part of the business. The more I looked at it and the closer the Interstate came to being finished, the better the M.O. looked. It was sort of like the fellow who was raised up with this local girl and never gave her a second look or thought . . . then, suddenly, one day she started looking good."

Now, here is what has recently happened to Erskine and his Honey Stand:

"There has been some changes in the business itself. First, we have had a rather dramatic growth in the past 4 years . . . to about double what my volume was formerly. This always presents some problems . . . but 'problems' of a nice kind I must say. Mainly we had run out of space in my former shipping building. I had already enlarged the rather ample building I put up in 1967. But last season and in this one particularly, we are 'stumbling over our feet' so to speak for space. We are solving this by constructing a new and about twice as big a shipping building. This new one will be (initially) 70 by 125 feet. Construction is now under way and we expect completion some time in the spring. It is being built in such a manner that additional space can be obtained as needed rather easily. The new building will incorporate our offices and also a retail store of ample size. Our 'stand' that we have had for so many years had become extremely too small to take care of our retail trade. Our present shipping building (30 by 140) will be used for storage of boxes and supplies.

"Edie and I are not spring chickens anymore . . . I'm 61 and she is close behind. Not wanting to end up at 65 or 70 years old with far more work and responsibilities on our shoulders than we had when we were 45, I have sold a 49% interest in my business to a fine young man named Benton Jones. Benton or 'Benny' is 31, married to a fine little lady with two cute little girls. Benny and Diane (his wife) are highly qualified for this work. They are both local folks, as plain and simple country folks as you can imagine, honest, decent, God fearing and hard working. The main thing Benny brings to the business is youth, vigor, intelligence and a love of the mail order business. He has at least 30 years of 'sweat equity' to put into it. To me this is more important than anything else. Benny was formerly in a managerial position with Dairymen, Inc. . . . one of the South's largest dairy operations as you well know.

"Of course Edie and I will still be here same as ever. But ever so gradually I am going to turn more and more things over to Benny. I'll be watching him . . . guiding . . . counseling and in general seeing to it that he don't make too many mistakes or get off on the wrong track. I really don't think that will be too much of a job however. He is a fine boy.

"Then as Benny comes along, I will have more time to play the part of the senior, all-wise 'old man' . . . more time to fish, hunt, camp, girl watch, to engage in tobacco chewing contests, whittling, tall story telling (sometimes rudely referred to as 'lieing'), etc . . . the really important things of life.

"Incidentally . . . and this ain't got a thing to do with the subject at hand . . . I won the Tennessee state wide champion liars contest at the spring convention of the National Campers and Hikers Association at Carthage, Tenn. this past spring. There was about 2000 people there and expert liars from all sections of the state (11 contestants to be exact). The competition was something fierce but I walked away with the blue ribbon. I am plum proud of that ribbon and keep it on my office wall. If you should insist . . . in fact even hint . . . that you want to know what my story was that won first place, I will be glad to send it to you."

For all who might wish to get a catalogue from Early's Honey Stand, and, if you're lucky, a letter from Erskine Early, write:

Early's Honey Stand
Route 2, Box 100
Spring Hill, Tennessee 37174

EARLY'S TENNESSEE COUNTRY HAM

RECIPE SHEET

There are almost as many ways to cook an old time Tennessee country ham as there are cooks. Cooking an EARLY'S TENNESSEE COUNTRY HAM can be a tradition whether you bake, boil or fry it. The following are some of the time tested methods that Williamson Countians in Tennessee use in cooking their hams.

THE EARLY'S BOILING & BAKING METHOD

Scrub ham thoroughly & soak in cold water 24 hours. Place in boiler with a handfull of brown sugar and cover with water. Let come to a boil and then simmer 20 minutes per pound keeping ham covered with water while cooking. The ham is done when the meat seperates from the bone at the hock end. . . .and when these bones can be pulled out without too much trouble. Allow ham to cool in its own liquor. Remove skin from ham while still warm. Score the fat, dot with cloves and sprinkle with brown sugar. Bake in a shallow pan in a 400 degree oven til brown. Cool well before slicing. If meat crumbles when sliced it indicates that the meat is over done.

NOTE: A 15 lb. ham will yield enough for 150 to 200 average biscuits, even more of the smaller, party size.

NOTE: We recommend only the boiling and then baking method. Baking a country ham without first boiling it can result in the meat being overly dry and hard. This is especially apt to occur with the inexperienced.

THE EARLY'S RED-EYE GRAVY METHOD FOR FRYING

Slice ham about ¼ inch thick being sure to include the fat. Lay slices in a cold skillet. . . . an electric skillet is fine. Cook on medium heat till it is lightly browned on both sides and fat is clear. Do not over cook as this toughens the ham.

TO MAKE RED-EYE GRAVY: Remove ham slices from skillet. Heat the remaining grease and "fryings" in skillet very hot. Add ¼ cup warm water, stir, allow to boil a bit and then pour over ham slices. The gravy is delicious over biscuits, grits, ripe tomatoes, corn, etc. We recommend serving a sweet and a sour with ham.

FOR MILDER TASTING HAM: Fry as above. Then pour ¼ cup of water over ham slices, cover and simmer for 20 minutes. This method automatically makes red-eye gravy, takes out some salt and makes ham softer. Sprinkle sugar over the ham slices if it is too salty for your taste.

HOW TO STORE A HAM

Our guarantee as to soundness and freedom from taint is good for 30 days only after receipt. Properly cured and stored in our smokehouses, a ham will keep almost indefinitely. However, since you probably do not have comparable facilities, there is SOME danger of spoilage or insect contamination if you keep the ham for 30 to 60 days after receipt. It you do keep the ham for some time, unwrap completely, place a paper (NOT PLASTIC!) bag loosely around the ham, tie securely at the top and hang in a ventilated place. Be sure there are no holes in the sack. If you slice the ham for frying, the ideal way to store is to wrap the slices and freeze them. This is excellent for up to 90 days. After a ham is once cut, always refrigerate the unused portion.

HOW TO ORDER A HAM

Additional hams may be ordered at any time. Obviously, a 15-pound ham will cost more than a 12-pound ham. Also, it costs more to send a ham to the 8th zone than to the 2nd. Then too, we may not always be able to ship you a ham of the EXACT weight requested. For these reasons you can see how it is IMPOSSIBLE for us to tell you the EXACT amount of money to send for a ham. Therefore, we suggest that you send a "rule of thumb" amount of from 35 to 40 dollars. We will ship you a ham to match the money (less shipping costs) figured at______ per lb. West of Denver add 10%. PLEASE SEND REMITTANCE WITH ORDER. NO C.O.D.'s. We will ship you a ham as near the size you ordered as possible. In any event, we refund to you every penny not used. NOTE: About 75% of my regular accounts solve the problem of how much to remit by sending a "LIMITED CHECK". This is simply your check, across the face of which you have written these words: "This check is not valid for more than $40.00." We fill in the correct amount and advise you.

WRITE FOR FREE CATALOG OF FINE FOOD & GIFTS

HOT PEPPER JELLY

Mrs. H. A. Bailey of Natchez, Mississippi, is the "Hot Pepper Jelly Lady" in those parts and she'll send you some of her "Aunt Freddie's Sweet Hot Stuff" to enjoy with your meats or as an hors d'oeuvre with cream cheese.

Each minimum order contains four 5-ounce jars of Mrs. Bailey's hot pepper jelly (2 red and 2 green) and is just $3.00 plus postage. There are also cartons available with 6, 8, 12 or 24 5-ounce jars (red and green) at $.75 a jar plus postage. A cookbook is also available and fits in the top of the 4 jar or 6 jar box at $2.50 plus postage. Gift packaging (at Christmastime, glossy gift paper with red and green bows and a cutout Santa Claus with cotton beard; year-round, hand-printed paper of Natchez scenes) is $1.00 extra. Mrs. Bailey asks that you let her bill you, since postage costs vary according to mailing zones.

Bailey's Jelly Kitchen
c/o Mrs. H.A. Bailey
400 South Commerce Street
Natchez, Mississippi 39120

THE DAVIS ROUND TABLE *in Orlando, Florida, offers custom-built, handcrafted, round oak tables. Due to the varied wood grains and the individual workmanship, each piece will have a uniqueness of its own. Consequently, a round oak table is often handed down from generation to generation. The tables are available in standard sizes: 42", 48", 54", 60", 66", and 72". Davis also makes an attractive lazy susan that is available in sizes: 18", 24", 30", 36" and 42". Write to 1726 Austell Road, Marietta, Georgia 32803 for prices.*

Mission Concepción is the oldest church in Texas that has remained intact and in use.

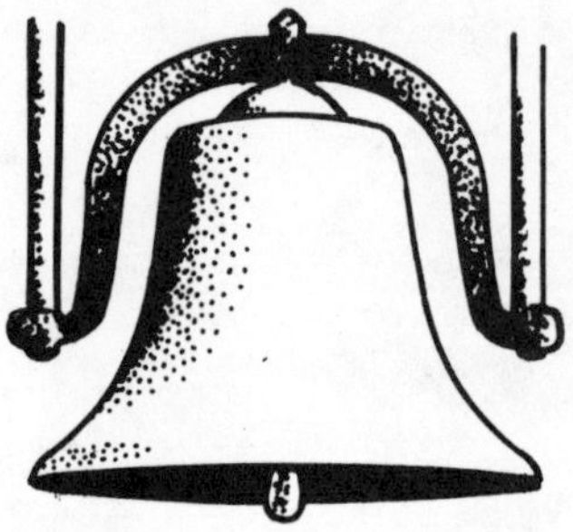

San Antonio's Mission Trail

Four magnificent 18th-century missions are now connected by a road into the past.

A special roadway has been developed in San Antonio that leads you quickly and easily to four historic missions that played such vital roles in the founding and growth of the city.

It's best to pick up Mission Trail at the intersection of Lone Star Boulevard and Roosevelt Avenue, just south of the downtown area. Less than a mile away on Mission Road is Mission Concepción, established in 1731. It is the oldest church in Texas that has remained intact and in use for religious services.

Drive another 2 miles down the road and you arrive at Mission San José, a state park that has been called the "Queen of the Missions." Surrounding the church, with its famed "Rosa's Window"—described as one of the finest pieces of Spanish Colonial ornamentation in the country—are the 84 compartments of an Indian pueblo, a granary, mill, and five cloisters. It was established in 1720.

Mission San Francisco de la Espada, also still active as a church, is 6.8 miles from the starting point. It was established in 1731, but the present chapel dates back only to 1868.

Mission San Juan Capistrano, also founded in 1731, is noted for its open bell tower. Inside the chapel are rare and ancient figures of Christ and the Virgin Mary made of cornstalk pith, a process perfected by the Indians of Mexico, then lost as an art form shortly after the Spanish Conquest. San Juan is about 2.1 miles from Espada.

The Mission Trail, for all practical purposes, guides you down narrow roads that are off the beaten path in San Antonio. It gives you a feeling of traveling in a countryside that has changed very little since the padres first trekked into the mesquite-brush hills.

The road is easy to follow if you pay attention to the large blue and white signs that direct you.

All of the missions, except San José, are open from 10 a.m. to 6 p.m. The hours at San José are 9 a.m. to 6 p.m. A $1 ticket allows you admission to all four missions, or you can see them separately for 50 cents each.

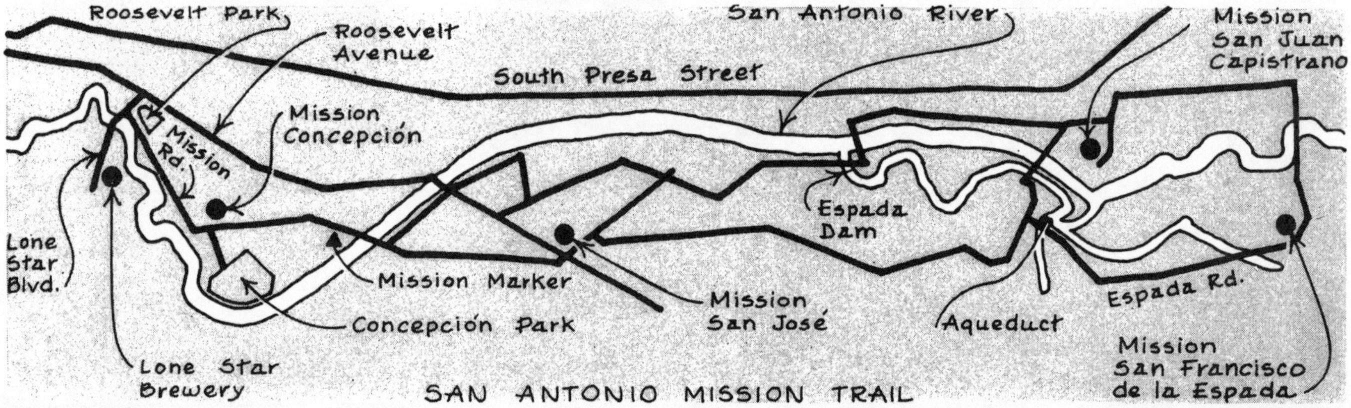

ROCKING CHAIR OF HISTORY

The first Brumby Rocker, a man-sized chair handmade from solid oak and woven by hand, was built around 1875 in Marietta, Georgia. During World War II, production of the rocker was suspended when Oriental cane, needed for the weaving, became impossible to obtain.

In the ensuing years, the Brumby Rockers became valuable collector's items. A whole new generation of Americans was introduced to this symbol of the past when in 1977 the Brumby found its way to the White House during Jimmy Carter's presidency.

In 1966, the late Frank H. Melson of Marietta obtained the rocker's manufacturing rights from the Brumby family. Because some of the machines necessary to the manufacture of the rockers had been specially designed for the original Brumby Chair Company, 5 years were needed to locate the machines, bring them back "home" to Marietta from spots all around the country, and recondition and modernize them. Some of the craftsmen who had built the rockers prior to World War II were called back into service. By 1971 all was in readiness to produce the new generation of Brumby Rockers, but Frank Melson's untimely death delayed the start of production for a year until his widow, Carole, could acquire the knowledge she felt necessary to running the business as it should be run. In 1972 the first four rockers were given to the State of Georgia and were put on the Governor's Mansion porches for its visitors to enjoy.

Along with the news that the Brumby Rockers are being manufactured again has come a wealth of correspondence from owners of the original rockers, most requesting possible manufacturing dates of their rockers and many detailing the parts that the Brumby Rockers have played in their lives. Mrs. Melson is interested in compiling a book of these stories because of the wonderful thread of American life that is reflected in them.

The Brumby Rocker can be ordered and shipped directly from the manufacturer:

The Rocker Shop of Marietta, Georgia
P.O. Box 12
1421 White Circle N.W.
Marietta, Georgia 30061

THE BRUMBY ROCKER
SPECIFICATIONS

- The posts are turned out of 2½" solid prime oak.
- The back posts are steam-bent for comfort.
- The portions of the back of the chair which cradle your back are steam-bent for comfort.
- The alternation of kiln-dried and air-dried wood was designed to accommodate the contraction and expansion of the component parts so that the chair would give maximum performance under varying climatic changes as occurs under outside conditions and interior conditions of central heating and air-conditioning in the home.

- The rocker runners are off-set and bolted so that they can be adjusted when climatic conditions dictate.
- The arms are wedged by hand to allow for expansion and contraction. Wood is a living material that adjusts itself to changes in the atmosphere. The wedge of wood in the arm keeps the arm tight under all conditions.
- The seats and backs, which are very large, are caned by hand in the "old manner," which is patterned on both sides in a very tight weave. The cane is of the best "Blue Tie" quality, and is woven wet so that when it dries it tightens like a drum.
- The rockers will have a hand-rubbed finish in a soft warm antique oak.
- The weight of the rocker makes it a good selection for use in areas that have high winds.

SAVING THE BEST OF THE PAST

The huge wrecking ball has become an accepted—almost a constant—part of any urban scene. Large crowds gather at the implosion of an old building—some, no doubt, in the spirit of a funeral and some for the spectacle.

Luckily, The Wrecking Bar of Atlanta often arrives just before the spectacle—to cart away and preserve what may be irreplaceable. Before the fine buildings of the world's major cities are destroyed in the path of change, the Wrecking Bar saves some of the unique and unreproducible architectural features. That is why they may have "the world's largest collection of interesting or valuable architectural antiques," running "the gamut from marble fireplaces from a French chateau to a silver chandelier from an American mansion."

They have wood, marble, and even cast iron mantles; ornamental wood doors (some as tall as 12 feet); glass-windowed doors, etched, beveled, or stained; stained glass, and beveled and leaded glass windows; wood

and marble balusters; crystal, brass, iron, and silver chandeliers and sconces; columns and pilasters; wrought iron railings and gates; and a "wondrous" assortment of door hardware, old pub signs, carousel horses, and such.

The stock at the Wrecking Bar varies continually, of course, and most of the items are one of a kind. Therefore, they do not try to put out a catalog, but suggest that you write and tell them of your needs. Please specify dimensions, style, period, material, and general price range. Some idea of the setting would be helpful, too. They will let you know what they have that might suit you and will send photographs. Since they have items ranging from a few dollars to thousands, they can probably help you out.

The Wrecking Bar is in an old mansion in Atlanta, about a mile off one of the main expressways, I-20 East. They are open from 10 until 5 every day, except Sunday. (However, if you are coming in from out of town they suggest you call in advance.) Or write:

The Wrecking Bar
292 Moreland Avenue, N.E.
Atlanta, Georgia 30307
(404) 525-0468

"I had myself called with the four-o'clock watch, mornings, for one cannot see too many summer sunrises on the Mississippi. They are enchanting. First, there is the eloquence of silence; for a deep hush broods everywhere. Next, there is the haunting sense of loneliness, isolation, remoteness from the worry and bustle of the world. The dawn creeps in stealthily; the solid walls of black forest soften to gray, and vast stretches of the river open up and reveal themselves; the water is glass-smooth, gives off spectral little wreaths of white mist, there is not the faintest breath of wind, nor stir of leaf; the tranquillity is profound and infinitely satisfying."
Mark Twain, LIFE ON THE MISSISSIPPI

Regimentals is a business specializing in items of, or connected with, the British Forces: Royal Navy, British Army, Royal Marines, and Royal Air Force. The business began about 9 years ago when Earl Levitt of Williamsburg, Virginia, carried in his menswear shop a large selection of regimental neckwear and a handful of cuff links, badges, and blazer buttons. The traffic in these items became so brisk that Mr. Levitt began expanding his stock to include British military antiques, works of art, books, and a much larger selection of the ties, blazer badges, cuff links, and blazer button sets from many regiments and corps in the British Armed Forces.

Today, Regimentals is a British militaria outlet. The term "militaria" covers such items as uniforms (with the accoutrements mentioned above), service gear, weapons, tools of the military trade, books, artwork—anything that has a military connotation. Regimentals specializes in British militaria because of the tremendous variety of items and large amount of history produced as a result of the British regimental system whereby each regiment had its own uniform details as well as its own unique customs and traditions. While most other armies were founded upon a centralized system of command, the British Armed Forces regimental system, begun over 300 years ago, required that the members of each regiment look only to their own command and colors for inspiration.

Regimentals features items that are useful, historical, and decorative. It does not carry swords, guns, medals, or miniature soldiers since these items are themselves highly specialized. In stock are crest-pattern ties from most of the services. The blazer badges of the regiments are resplendent with gold bullion, silver wire, and red velvet—they are suitable for wearing on a blazer as well as for collecting and framing. Many blazer buttons are carried in stock.

Also in stock are old-style, regimental gold-gilt brass button cuff links, particularly interesting since most of these buttons were replaced by anodized aluminum ones and the original ones are now very hard to find.

Regimentals sends out a catalogue each year covering the expanding stock of militaria.

Included are such items as uniforms; belts; epaulets; helmet plates; walking out sticks; trench art; campaign beds; books on the histories of the Scottish Highlands, clans, and regiments; biographies; personal campaign accounts; war weeklies; cartoons; old periodicals; 18th, 19th, and 20th century engravings; mezzotints; aquatints; color lithographs; photogravures; and many, many more fascinating items.

The "Militaria Catalogue" is available for $1.00. Also shown here is a photograph of one of the many blazer button sets which Regimentals offers. These sets sell for around $17.25.

Regimentals
P.O. Box 2348, 303 Indian Spring Road
Williamsburg, Virginia 23185
(804) 229-5742

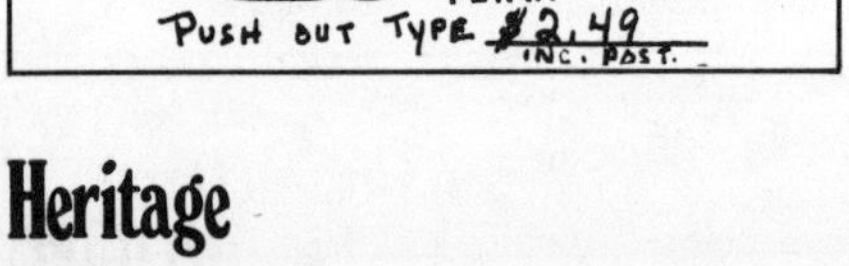

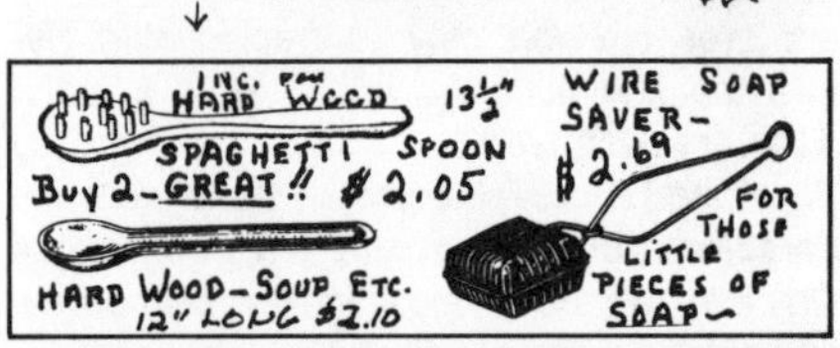

The Yancey County Country Store has a catalog which lists numerous items available for mail order. If you wish a copy of the latest "Blue Ridge Bugle," send $.25 to the address below.

Yancey County Country Store
Box 8B
Burnsville, North Carolina 28714

RARUS LIBER

A "rarus liber"—rare book—is, as the name implies, hard to find. Sometimes even harder to find is a good dealer in such books. F.M. Hill—Books of Kingsport, Tennessee, is a rare book dealer, and a good one. By their own description, Hill's specialty is "anything: books, periodicals, maps, prints, documents, autographs, old letters related to the Southern States in any way, including Southern Appalachians and the Southern Indians. We buy in any quantity from single copies to large collections. We sell by, and issue regularly, catalogues and will be glad to send catalogues to anyone requesting them. We also sell by appointment."

For the current catalogue write:

F.M. Hill—Books
P.O. Box 1037
Kingsport, Tennessee 37662

THE ATLANTA CENTURY

When Norman Shavin was Sunday Editor of the *Atlanta* (Georgia) *Journal-Constitution,* he conceived *The Atlanta Century,* a prize winning national history series which recorded events of the years 1860-1865 in newspaper format. The series—the longest in world journalism—was published each Sunday for almost five and a half years, as a page in the *Journal-Constitution.* Mr. Shavin explained, "The *Century* was not a reprint of any existing paper; it was a new product, written in the 1960s and based on the author's research." In fact, "the *Century* told of each week's events (exactly a century later) for the period between March, 1860, and mid-May, 1965." After the last of the series, which occupied 272 pages, Mr. Shavin's series was published as a huge, "coffee-table" book.

Shavin's original *Atlanta Century* series won the National Civil War Centennial Commission's first and highest award for excellence. The late Carl Sandburg wrote of the volume: "I catch myself reading one news story after another and getting the feel of the days a century ago when history every day was portentous and ran hot and wild. . . . " Said Bruce Catton, noted Civil War historian: "This is a very graphic way and an appealing way to provide an understanding of the background and the general course of events in America's greatest war. There is a sense of immediacy about the daily newspaper that one gets no other way. I don't believe there is a better method to show, in genuinely readable style, how the nation moved into and through its most tragic experience. . . . "

In the preface to the bound volume of the weekly pages Mr. Shavin tells the story behind the *Century:* "This book contains the 272 complete pages of a weekly newspaper which, in fact, wasn't a newspaper, but a unique method of chronicling this nation's years of most poignant agony. For more than five years, *The Atlanta Century* ran as a page of the *Atlanta* (Ga.) *Journal-Constitution* each Sunday. The *Century* appeared as the front page of a newspaper as it might have looked if its editors enjoyed immediate and accurate accounts of events more than a century ago."

The Atlanta Century is available for $24.95 (postage included) from Capricorn Corporation of Atlanta. Excerpts from the *Century* are also available in a 52-page booklet (8½ x 11), titled *Illustrated Tales of the Civil War,* at $2.50 each (delivery cost included). Capricorn Corporation also has available other interesting items in an 8½ x 11 booklet format: *The Million Dollar Legends: Margaret Mitchell and Gone With the Wind* (52 pages, including rare photos of Ms. Mitchell), $2.50 by mail; and *Atlanta Then, Atlanta Now* (52 pages), filled with old and new photos and anecdotes about Atlanta ($2.50 by mail).

Mr. Shavin later served as editor and publisher of *Atlanta* magazine, and in 1978 became the Director of the Special Products Division—the newly-formed publishing arm of Perry Communications, Inc., of Atlanta. In 1978 that Division published a hardcover, 128-page picture book entitled *Atlanta: A Celebration,* which Shavin co-authored with Bruce Galphin; and a 68-page picture-and-text paperback (8½ x 11) entitled *The Wonderful World of Coca-Cola,* conceived by Shavin and co-authored by him and Martin Shartar.

For a fascinating look at the past or the present of Atlanta (including *Atlanta: A Celebration,* $21.95 by mail, and *The Wonderful World of Coca-Cola,* $3.75 by mail), write:

Capricorn Corporation
4961 Rebel Trail, N.W.
Atlanta, Georgia 30327

FROM THE LIBRARY OF CONGRESS

Established in 1800 as a reference library for the United States Congress, the Library of Congress has become world-renowned as a source of knowledge and national repository of our country's treasures of books, manuscripts, musical scores and recordings, prints and photographs, maps, rare books, and motion pictures.

Visitors to Washington can use the vast collections of over 74 million items housed in several buildings on Capitol Hill, across the plaza from the U.S. Capitol. The Library of Congress Building, a landmark since 1897, is worth a visit in itself. Designed in Italian Renaissance style, its murals, mosaics and sculpture are symbolic of the learning housed within its walls.

The Library of Congress offers a number of collectibles to the public—gifts, books, posters, and recordings. Each fall the Library publishes a catalogue of greeting cards, note paper, and facsimiles of some of the Library's more notable works. The greeting cards, including Christmas cards, sell for between $.15 and $.25 individually and are available in packages of 10 and 20 cards.

The historical facsimiles available include the first page of Genesis from the Library's copy of the Gutenberg Bible ($1.75); the Paul Revere engraving of the Boston Massacre ($1.00); *Long Remembered: The Gettysburg Address in Facsimile,* which includes reproductions of the five known drafts of the Gettysburg Address in Lincoln's own handwriting ($2.00); two rebuses of the American Revolution ($1.00); Captain John Smith's Map of Virginia ($1.75); and the *Declaration of Independence* ($2.00).

A number of posters are for sale: Arabic Calligraphy, which denotes the beauty of this ancient art ($4.95); A Wonderful Invention, a colorful poster using the historical photograph of Thomas A. Edison at work in his laboratory ($4.95); Folk Art and Folklife, a five-color poster featuring Georgia folk art, commemorating a major exhibition held at the Library ($10.95); China: 19th-Century Drawings by Unknown Artists, displaying the image of the Imperial Dragon of China ($4.95); Printed on Vellum, a handsome poster depicting an ancient craftsman cutting animal skins that were used to make vellum ($4.95); and Building a Better Mouse, a poster commemorating the 50th anniversary of animation ($3.00).

Other gifts include the Calendar for Children ($3.00); Calendar of Panoramic Maps, of American cities ($6.95); the New Game of Steeplechase, a 19th Century children's game ($3.00); the Reward of Merit Scarf, brown on tan or navy on red ($5.95); Library of Congress tote bags, red or blue, ($5.95); and a "Meet me on the Plaza" LC lunch tote ($3.95).

Books on sale via mail order include *A Guide to the Study of the United States of America* ($12.00); the *Lessing J. Rosenwald Collection,* a catalogue and explanation of his gifts to the Library, 1943-1975 ($17.25 clothbound, $13.25 paperbound); *Television, The Book, and The Classroom* ($4.95); *The Development of a Revolutionary Mentality,* consisting of papers and commentaries presented by 10 distinguished historians at the first Library of Congress symposium on the American Revolution ($3.50); and *Papermaking, Art and Craft,* named by the American Institute of Graphic Arts as one of the Fifty Books of the Year ($6.95).

Captain John Smith's Map of Virginia, reproduced from an engraving in the Library of Congress.

Library of Congress Facsimile No. 1a

The complete list of publications in print currently and a catalogue of greeting cards and other gift items may be obtained by writing: Library of Congress, Central Services, Washington, D.C. 20540. In addition, copies of prints, photographs, xerox copies, or microfilm copies of rare items in the collection may be obtained by ordering specific items in detail from the Library's Photoduplication Service.

Of further interest to the public and available from the Library's Recording Laboratory is *Folk Music in America,* an anthology of 15 long-playing records issued by the Library, with music selected from a diversity of ethnic and regional backgrounds, recorded between 1890 and the present. Individual records, ranging from religious music to songs of humor and hilarity, may be ordered at $6.50. Please note that an additional $.50 for postage must be added with the price of every record ordered. The public may also order *Our Musical Past,* a set of two long-playing recordings in stereo, containing music popular during the 1850's and 1860's ($10.00).

Many more recordings are for sale including those of folk music and tales: *Animal Tales Told in the Gullah Dialect* ($15.00); *Music of the American Indian* ($6.50); *American Sea Songs and Shanties* ($6.50); *Negro Blues and Hollers* ($6.50); *Cowboy Songs and Ballads* ($6.50); and *Songs from Morocco* ($10.00). A particularly interesting set of recordings is *The Ballad Hunter,* five records made by John Lomax from a lecture on American folk music with musical illustrations ($26.00).

Available from the Archive of Recorded Poetry and Literature are many spoken recordings of poets reading their own poems. The listening public may enjoy hearing T.S. Eliot read "The Waste Land," plus other famous poems, ($6.50); Robert Frost reading "A Soldier," and others ($6.50); an interview with H.L. Mencken ($10.00); readings by Julio Cortezar ($6.50); and an *Album of Modern Poetry—An Anthology Read by the Poets* ($18.00). The most recent recording issued by the Library is *Robert Lowell Reading His Own Poems,* available at $14.00 for the two-record set. Note again the additional $.50 required for postage on all of these orders.

For a copy of the catalogues for either the folk music recordings or poetry, write to:

The Library of Congress
Recording Laboratory
Washington, D.C. 20540

"Bear Creek—so called, perhaps, because it was always so particularly bare of bears—is hidden out of sight now, under islands and continents of piled lumber, and nobody but an expert can find it. I used to get drowned in it every summer regularly, and be drained out, and inflated and set going again by some chance enemy; but not enough of it is unoccupied now to drown a person in."
Mark Twain, LIFE ON THE MISSISSIPPI

SHILOH—IN HELL BEFORE NIGHT

by James Lee McDonough

The University of Tennessee Press
Knoxville, Tennessee

April has always been the cruelest month for wars. Shiloh happened in April of 1862. A year before, the opening guns of the war had sounded at Fort Sumter in April. Three years after Shiloh, the war would end on an April Palm Sunday at Appomattox Courthouse.

Shiloh was a unique battle in many ways. Up until that time, it was the biggest battle in American history—involving 100,000 men. According to many participants, it was the bloodiest battle they had ever fought in, or ever would fight in. Sherman, according to Mr. McDonough, was for the first time caught by surprise at the outset of the battle. Furthermore, the general concluded during the fight that, because of the "horrid nature of this war," he probably would not survive it.

This book does a very creditable job of explaining why Shiloh was such a critical battle. The loss at Shiloh was the beginning of the end for the Confederacy. Unfortunately, it was not the swift, clean end that the Federals hoped for but a finish that would drag on unmercifully for three more tortuous years, impoverishing the South and wasting her sons on innumerable battlefields. For with Shiloh, the Confederates lost their opportunity to smash a vulnerable Blue line situated in an undeveloped defensive position with their top commanders not expecting an attack.

Instead, the Rebels surrendered their chance to stop the decisive Union drive and their chance to reclaim much of Tennessee and the West. Also, had the South won, Grant and Sherman—the two men who emerged to lead the North to victory—would probably have been ruined in their careers. Mr. McDonough comes up with some thought-provoking answers to some very strategic puzzlements offered by Shiloh. Why was the Union army situated with a river to its back? Why was Grant absent when his army was attacked? Could the Rebels have won the battle or were they fated from the start to have it slip through their fingers? Did Beauregard with his swagger and out-dated Napoleonic concepts of war throw away the victory?

Most intriguing in this book are the accounts and vignettes of the soldiers themselves. Their courage, their suffering, their remembrances, and their loneliness make for very moving reading. Especially shattering is the story of one Union general's wife who ignored the warnings of her family and friends and journeyed South to be with her husband only to arrive to witness his dying. In contrast to the beautiful spring-blue skies and budding trees, the corpses among the peach blossoms served as a shocking reminder that war transcends all seasons and that Shiloh, a Biblical word meaning "place of peace," was one of the ugliest battles of one of our ugliest wars. —S.V.H.

DOROTHY'S RUFFLED ELEGANCE

For long, ruffled elegance, Dorothy's Ruffled Originals may have what you want to frame your windows. Most of the curtains are floor length and fall in the long, luscious folds that only yards and yards of good material can produce. Dorothy uses "26 yds. of fabric per 96-inch-long window." According to the brochure, "We offer a unique service in that all of our curtains are custom-made for each person." Therefore you must "measure carefully and make the correct choice in fabric." Dorothy's ruffled originals include ruffled wreaths, ruffled pillows, ruffled placemats, ruffled chair pads and ruffled lampshades. For information, write to:

Dorothy's Ruffled Originals, Inc.
6721 Market Street
Wilmington, North Carolina 28405
(919) 791-1296

SHILOH MILITARY TRAIL, INC.
Historical Hiking Trails, Inc.

Boy Scout Troop 343, headquartered at Kingsway Christian Church in Memphis, Tennessee, has an extremely unusual, but truly enterprising troop project. It has formed a non-profit corporation to sponsor hiking trails on several battlefields where General Nathan Bedford Forrest rode and also at Shiloh National Military Park. To help finance the trails, as well as to furnish supplementary material useful to trail-users and other history buffs, the troop has published trail maps and informative booklets about each of the 17 different educational historical hiking trails that it sponsors. The 17 trails are located in the following places:

11 at Shiloh National Military Park (near Savannah, Tennessee);

2 at Fort Pillow State Park (near Henning, Tennessee);

2 at Nathan Bedford Forrest State Park (near Camden, Tennessee);

1 at Brice's Crossroads National Battlefield (near Baldwyn, Mississippi);

1 in historic part (river front) of Memphis, Tennessee.

Another popular publication available from Boy Scout Troop 343 is *Hiking Trails of America*—a booklet listing over 600 different hiking trails throughout the United States. Edition No. 15 (for 1979) is now available for $1.00 per copy postpaid. Write to:

Historical Hiking Trails, Inc.
P.O. Box 17507
Memphis, Tennessee 38117

Colonial Model M-143/18—of solid brass, lacquered for long-lasting finish. There are 12 arms on the bottom row and 6 on the top row on this excellent Williamsburg-style design. $600.

CHANDELIERS FIT FOR A KING

Some of the most beautiful chandeliers we have seen were made by a family-owned and operated company in North Carolina: King's Chandelier Company in Eden (Leaksville), North Carolina. Durward F. King and his nephew, Franklin King Ricks, are continuing the tradition of fine quality workmanship at moderate prices which D. F. King, the company's founder, began in 1935.

Each fixture is designed especially for the customer. Durward King explains: "I design all of the chandeliers, and I design the parts that go to make up the chandeliers; the parts are made to my specifications in Czechoslovakia, Austria, Italy, Germany, etc. I import large quantities of these parts and each chandelier is made up as we get the order. I sometimes copy antique chandeliers and sometimes I will design things of my own—but perhaps as though I were designing in the 18th century. You will find many 18th century designs among the chandeliers, and you will find a number of 19th century ones that are particularly good now because so many people are re-doing houses of that era. I am happy that we do have (in the U.S.) a number of good 19th-century houses that can be restored, because of course we were just sort of getting started in the 18th century and not many that were built then are still standing. You will find a section in the catalogue that is devoted to my designs in which I have used the hanging crystal of Swarovsky Strass, which is certainly the most brilliant crystal made. These do not show up in the photos, but if one is familiar with this type of crystal, then he can get an idea of the design and imagine it with the brilliance of the Strass."

In addition to chandeliers, you can also buy sconces and candelabra from King's. Designs in both the sconces and candelabra and the chandeliers vary from extremely ornate crystal ones to the more simple lines of Colonial brass and crystal ones. Any of the chandeliers may be made with hurricane shades or with candelabra tapers. All fixtures are furnished with matching ceiling plates and standard ⅜" F. connection. You may choose between a chain or close ceiling connection—one foot of chain comes with each chandelier; if more is needed, there is a slight extra charge per additional foot. Satisfaction is guaranteed and, after seeing the catalogue, we are sure that that guarantee is a proper one.

For your catalogue, send $1.00 to:

King's Chandeliers
Highway 14
Eden (Leaksville), North Carolina 27288

HOME-COOKED SALTED PEANUTS

You must try these peanuts prepared in small batches by a special and difficult water blanching process unique to traditional Tidewater Virginia. The time has been well spent because we think they're delicious!

The selected Virginia Jumbos are completely free of additives and preservatives. In fact, they are perishable and you must refrigerate them to preserve their freshness. Grown in the sandy loam soil of Southampton, Virginia's largest peanut producing county, the peanuts are painstakingly graded, water-blanched, cooked in coconut oil, salted and packed in tins.

Since making its way to the pre-Civil War American South from the Old World tropics and South America, the peanut has established a solid nutritional reputation. You might not know that peanuts contain more protein per pound than steak, more vitamins and minerals than beef liver, and more food energy than sugar.

The Packing Shed will be pleased to send you a current price list.

The Packing Shed
Route 1
P.O. Box 11
Weyers Cave, Virginia 24486

THE ARCHITECTURAL LEGACY OF THE LOWER CHATTAHOOCHEE VALLEY IN ALABAMA AND GEORGIA

Edited by D. Gregory Jeane
Associate Editor Douglas Clare Purcell

The University of Alabama Press
University, Alabama

This book should be of great interest to the architectural student or to the lover of "old things." It provides a thorough record of the Chattahoochee Valley from its earliest days to the turn of the century. The authors point out the structures that are in good condition, those that are endangered, and the construction details, size, and history of those that are beyond repair.

This book defines many of the types of houses that we have seen, heard of, or read about all our lives. The first-generation, second-generation, and third-generation dogtrot houses are defined according to their similarities and differences as well as is the single-pen log house. Not so numerous or as easily recognizable as the single-pen or dogtrot house, as far as their developmental stages were concerned, were the double-pen and the saddlebag house. The saddlebag house was distinctive as being the only folk house with a central chimney.

Around 1820 and extending to 1860 was the Greek Revival architecture reminiscent of that used to build houses in the Tidewater Virginia area. The most common of these early types was the hall-and-parlor house. Later, this characteristic broadened into the two story central-hall house so widespread throughout the South. Greek Revival architecture reached its zenith in mid-19th century America. It became synonymous with wealth and huge plantations. More than any other style, Greek Revival retained a visual dominance over the Southern scene. It has become the essence of "antebellum" and includes some of the most impressive simplicity and symmetry to be seen in the buildings of that time.

Not only homes but also businesses such as mills, banks, jails, and courthouses had a certain style. Examples of each type of structure are given in this book, with a detailed analysis and fascinating photographs of exterior and interior details. There are 61 sets of drawings which serve as a reference for architects, an aid to historians, and an informative guide for the general reader. —S.V.H.

A SILVER LINING

Your Victorian tilting ice water pitcher may not be in such a decrepit state as this one before restoration. (A fire had melted away almost half of this family heirloom. The silversmiths at Simmons Silver Plating Company took over, filled in the missing metal sides and made handles and feet so nearly like the originals that they defy detection.) But whatever state your old silver is in, it is probably precious to you at least for the memories and perhaps for the monetary value as well.

Simmons Silver Plating Company does plating, repairs, and refinishing on gold, silver, copper, and brass. They are specialists in sterling and pewter. The skilled hands and the practiced eyes of the silversmiths in their workrooms are their chief assets, as it has been with metalworkers since Paul Revere's day.

Simmons' first step in restoring an antique metal piece is expert inspection. Then the necessary repair is carefully planned. Next, painstaking repair of damaged areas and replacement of missing parts is begun. Missing parts of precious antiques are duplicated with such skill that they blend perfectly. When this delicate assignment is completed, the heavy, rich coating of pure silver is applied. Then follow many steps of hand-buffing and polishing, until the restored piece gleams with renewed beauty.

Simmons offers a choice of finishes: Butler, a dull or satin finish; Colonial, a soft, medium-bright finish; and Polished, a bright, polished finish. They also do oxidizing and lacquering.

You can protect your fine silver with Simmons Polish. With Simmons Miracle Silver Polish and Tarnish Preventive you can polish your fine silver easily and quickly but won't need to do it often. And with Simmons Silver Kotton Polish you can give a quick last-minute polish.

For the polish or information on restoring, write to:

Simmons Silver Plating Company, Inc.
409 Whitehall Street, S.W.
Atlanta, Georgia 30303
(404) 523-2852

DOWN COMFORTS

Even way down South, we have a few cold winter nights. What better way could there be to relax than with a down comfort—and one comfort will provide all the warmth you need.

For years, Alden Comfort Mills has been marketing extra fine quality comforts made from the finest quality of down—their business is strictly a mail-order business which affords a buyer the best possible price. These comforts are beautifully covered in satins and non-skid cottons; they are just like the ones your grandmothers used to have.

Their stock includes colors to complement any bedroom decor; they are available in twin, standard, queen, and king sizes. The standard size prices start at $107.95.

For further information:

Alden Comfort Mills
P.O. Box 55
Plano, Texas 75074

History For Sale

Colonial Williamsburg's craft shop program is the activity under which the trades and crafts of colonial times are carried on in authentic, working shops at 20 locations scattered throughout the historic area. Some of them have been in operation for a quarter of a century. In recent years many additional crafts have been added as the program increased in scope and effectiveness.

Admission to the craft shops is included under the general admission ticket which enables visitors to see more than 30 colonial homes, shops, public buildings, and 90 acres of gardens; attend evening films and lectures; and use the continuous bus service circling the historic area of the city. The general admission ticket good for three days during the regular season is priced at $15.00 for adults and $7.50 for children aged 6-12.

The craft shops are a key facet of a broad endeavor to reveal 18th-century Williamsburg in the light of human personalities—to make present-day visitors truly feel the companionship and presence of the patriots who proclaimed the rights of man in words and deeds no American should ever forget.

Here, the colonial society is portrayed not only as the gifted, the articulate, the famous, but as men and women who lived useful lives, who scolded their children, who knew illness, fun, toil, ambition, and sorrow. Authentically furnished and equipped after extensive research, the shops are staffed by artisans who wear workmen's clothing of the colonial period and perform their chores by hand.

The tools in the silversmith's shop came from a London shop in use since 1726. They were the property of a silversmith named Wickes, and they are still in use today.

The shops and their activities are organized into three subdivisions—crafts, professions, and domestic crafts. Under the basic crafts are the cabinetmaker, wigmaker, silversmith, wheelwright, engraver, jeweler, printer, cooper, musical instrument maker, brass founder, pewterer, bookbinder, papermaker, bootmaker, blacksmith, gunsmith, miller, carpenter, and milliner. There are three professions: apothecary, music teacher, and postmaster. Classed as domestic crafts are the textile dyer, harnessmaker, weaver, candlemaker, baker, shinglemaker, flaxbreaker, and basketmaker.

The primary function of the craft shops is interpretation and demonstration rather than manufacture, and this type of mission makes it necessary for Colonial Williamsburg to subsidize the various shops. Part of the operating cost, however, is covered by the sale of handmade products, which are limited due to the conditions of manufacture. Products from the various craft shops are sold in the Prentis Store and Tarpley's Store, both located on Duke of Gloucester Street.

For example, andirons, toasting forks, hinges, and other wrought iron items are made by the blacksmith; leather drinking mugs, belts, and hornbooks are made by the bootmaker; the silversmith makes numerous items of silver including coffee pots, bowls, bracelets, and trays. The baker kneads, bakes, and sells bread, cookies, and gingerbread men; the printer and bookbinder combine their forces to reproduce a storybook of children's tales; the sails of Robertson's Windmill turn majestically as the miller grinds Indian corn into meal.

The printer and bookbinder demonstrate their operations in two shops on the site of William Parks' *Virginia Gazette,* first newspaper published in the Virginia Colony. A feature of this facility is a postal headquarters, reminiscent of the day when the colonial Printing Office was an important way station for postal riders from the North and South. Today, letters and cards may be mailed here, receiving a handstamped postmark patterned after one used in Williamsburg in 1771.

More than 100 full-time craftsmen and interpreters, at least two in each shop, are employed in the program. The shops are open, variously, 6 and 7 days a week on an overlapping schedule. Tours by "Great Lanthorn" are held several nights each week except during the summer months when extended hours make evening visitation possible on a regular basis. When scheduled, the "Lanthorn" tours consist of a craftsman leader and a group of approximately 20 lantern-carrying visitors who inspect a selection of four shops during an hour-long tour.

Williamsburg's master craftsmen, above all, must be well-qualified artisans. They come from many corners of this country and abroad. One cabinetmaker was apprenticed for 6 years in Europe; two craftsmen are natives of England; another is from Austria. The remainder of the craftsmen come from more than a dozen states in this country.

Many times the craftsmen are called upon to work on a product that becomes well-known. Five different craftsmen worked on the silver tea service and cribbage board presented to Elizabeth, the Queen Mother of Great Britain, as gifts for her grandchildren when she visited here in 1954. Two craftsmen created the silver Town Crier's bell and leather-covered case presented to the late Sir Winston Churchill on December 7, 1955, as the symbol of the Williamsburg Award.

In 1961 the master silversmith fashioned reproductions of Paul Revere lanterns for the late President Kennedy as a gift from the White House Correspondents Association. Since then the W.H.C.A. has commissioned the silversmith to make other silver articles for

The Galt Apothecary Shop on historic Duke of Gloucester Street in Williamsburg exhibits for modern travelers an imposing array of elixirs and ointments of colonial medicine, as well as "compleat Setts of amputating Instruments."

President Johnson, Vice-President Humphrey, and President Nixon.

To learn more about the Williamsburg Craft Shops and their wares, write:

Craft Shops
Colonial Williamsburg
Williamsburg, Virginia 23185

The master gunsmith and his apprentices in Williamsburg make muskets, pistols, and long rifles entirely by hand, carving the stocks, casting the brass, and executing fine inlays and reliefs.

The bootmaker and other craftsmen in Williamsburg demonstrate more than 30 trades and handcrafts of 200 years ago. Bootmakers, gunsmiths, silversmiths, blacksmiths, and many others use hand tools and age-old methods to fashion the wares of the 18th century.

At the Raleigh Tavern Bakery in Williamsburg costumed bakers mix their dough by hand and bake bread, cookies, and gingerbread men daily in brick ovens.

The bookbinder in Colonial Williamsburg gives careful attention to old books in his tiny shop. Using the tools and methods of 200 years ago he produces handsome leather covers, colorful endpapers, and sturdy, lasting bindings.

CRAFT HOUSE CATALOGUE

Reproduced here are a few pages from *Williamsburg Reproductions: Interior Designs for Today's Living,* the official catalogue of Colonial Williamsburg's Craft House reproduction program. For $4.95 you can receive this 286-page, paperbound book and its wealth of historical information interwoven among the display of over 1,500 items licensed for manufacture by Colonial Williamsburg.

The catalogue contains such chapters as *Williamsburg* furniture reproductions and adaptations; *Williamsburg* fabrics and wall coverings; *Williamsburg* important accessories (mirrors, lamps, lighting fixtures, fireplace accessories, and brass hinges and locks); *Williamsburg* decorative pieces (brass pieces, wooden items, Delftware, china objects, maps, and prints); *Williamsburg* decor for dining (sterling silver reproductions, flatware, plated silverware, pewter, glassware, dinnerware, and pottery); and a potpourri of gifts (from trivets and pins to games, needlepoint, and books).

One of the latest books available from Colonial Williamsburg is *"Fashionable, Neat, and Good . . . "—The Williamsburg Collection of Antique Furnishings.* This is a fantastically well-produced book with beautiful pictures of over 2,000 objects from the Colonial Williamsburg collection, selected by the curator of the historic area, Graham Hood, and his staff. Each photograph is carefully identified, with the result that, when one even casually glances through the book, a few new insights into history are gleaned. For information about this book and the many other items available from Colonial Williamsburg, including the catalogue from the Craft House, write:

Colonial Williamsburg Foundation
Williamsburg, Virginia 23185

CRAFT HOUSE CATALOGUE

WILLIAMSBURG REPRODUCTIONS:
Interior Designs for Today's Living

Now, a new, revised and enlarged edition of the Craft House catalogue with hundreds of beautiful color photographs of room scenes and vignettes. A presentation of furniture and accessories from the Colonial Williamsburg collection which have been reproduced for today's homes. Included are many decorating ideas plus special sections on such subjects as furniture design, fabrics, and wall coverings. 286 pages, 8½ x 11⅛. Paperbound..... $4.95 postpaid.

At right—Reprinted from *Williamsburg Reproductions: Interior Designs for Today's Living.*

The Reproductions Program

THE EIGHTEENTH CENTURY IN EUROPE was a brilliant period in the history of domestic furnishing, a time when skilled craftsmen designed and produced objects in styles admired to this day—furniture and silver, brass and pewter, fabrics and wall coverings, looking glasses, chandeliers, glassware, porcelain, and earthenware. Colonial commerce and communication with England brought to Virginia many fine products from this flourishing era of design and craftsmanship, and stimulated their production in this country. When examples of these furnishings were installed in the exhibition buildings in the mid-1930s, the response of visitors was immediate: how can we obtain accurate reproductions of such pieces?

Facsimile of Certificate of Authenticity that accompanies each hallmarked reproduction

Obviously, original pieces, both rare and fragile, could not meet the demand. Colonial Williamsburg then carefully considered its rapidly expanding collections of period furnishings and selected a number of them based on the criteria of beauty, soundness of design, and appropriateness for daily use in modern American homes. Subsequently, Colonial Williamsburg turned to a few manufacturers, with both the resources and the desire to produce fine replicas, and licensed them to turn out reproductions bearing the Colonial Williamsburg hallmark. In 1937 Craft House was opened to serve as the public display and sales area for the Reproductions Program.

But it was not merely to enter the merchandising field that Colonial Williamsburg inaugurated this effort. From the start, the handsome, durable, and useful items have been regarded as interpretive objects, part and parcel of the Colonial Williamsburg Foundation's educational activity. A sturdy wing chair purchased in 1937, for example, has not only served its household in a utilitarian sense; its beauty of design also has been a constant reminder of eighteenth-century craftsmanship. In fact, the program has been credited with elevating public taste. Thus, these items fulfill an educational purpose and, as they have been produced largely by handcraftsmen and as the older pieces will soon be forty years old, it may be said that they are in truth becoming heirlooms in their own right.

The building program was cautious and slow. Manufacturers realized that their artisans had to meet the rigid standards of quality and design mutually developed with Colonial Williamsburg. The painstaking proccess of selection and the specifications controlling acceptable reproduction have been continued since the outset of the program.

The Director of Merchandising selects an article to be reproduced or adapted (with changes in design for modern use). The original is temporarily removed from exhibition and the manufacturer copies it in detail—though small variations in handcrafted work are inevitable now, as they were characteristic of their period.

The reproduced article then goes before the Craft Advisory Committee, a team of experts from many divisions of the foundation, including the director of research, the curator, master silversmith, interior design consultant, director of archaeology, and architectural historian. After thorough critical analysis, the item is approved, suggestions made for resubmission, or disapproved. Following approval the manufacturer is then consulted, and if there is agreement production begins.

The reproductions are strikingly similar to the originals. For years, in fact, one of Colonial Williamsburg's most popular displays has consisted of two pieces of furniture, the antique and the copy—so nearly identical that the layman's eye can hardly detect a difference.

This program has been so successful that at least a dozen of the original manufacturers still participate in the program some thirty-five years later. Today, twenty-five manufacturers produce a total of 1,500 items.

There are exceptions to this process of selection. The department of archaeology, for example, unearths fragments of earthenware of porcelain, from which reproductions or adaptations are made. This provides the program with unique items and strengthens its ties with the eighteenth century.

In recent years the Adaptations Program has grown rapidly in importance and influence. In this phase of furniture manufacture, the foundation and its licensed manufacturers have followed a process commonplace in every period of design: originals have been modified to meet changed use requirements. This frequently means that the adaptations, though handcrafted with the same care given to reproductions, are redesigned to smaller scale so that they fit the smaller rooms in homes and apartments of modern America.

Of course no one can say with assurance precisely how every room in eighteenth-century Williamsburg was furnished—but the collections, the basis of our Reproductions Program, have become more complete and authoritative each year. Behind thousands of items is a mass of data, documentary and archaeological, to lend the authority of authenticity to the original pieces and thus to the reproductions.

Fortunately for this endeavor, men of many stations in life who died in early Williamsburg left inventories of their estates—governors, blacksmiths, tavern-keepers, and merchants alike. Armed with these, and with an array of wills, deeds, letters, diaries, shipping invoices, contemporary newspaper advertisements, and other evidence, Colonial Williamsburg's curators have assembled one of the largest and most distinguished collections of seventeenth-, eighteenth-, and nineteenth-century English and American furnishings.

Though these collections are constantly expanding, the purpose of the growth is to reflect faithfully the life of tidewater Virginia and Williamsburg in colonial days. The most important guideposts in the acquisitions program are those set by the foundation's specialists in documentary history, colonial social life, architecture, and archaeology. They now work from an enormous body of cumulative data and insure the continuing validity of the Reproductions Program, which has become an important by-product of Colonial Williamsburg's efforts in this field.

Williamsburg AND THE HALLMARK

WILLIAMSBURG · C W · RESTORATION

"Williamsburg" and the hallmark, both registered trademarks owned by the foundation, may be used only on reproductions and adaptations made by licensed manufacturers. The Williamsburg hallmark, shown at right was designed from old and new symbols. The letters "C.W.," for Colonial Williamsburg, have been joined to the central symbol, an elongated "4" ending in what appears to be a double "X." This symbol was used by English shippers of the 17th and 18th centuries and was sometimes combined with the initials of merchant and consignee.

Origins of the merchants' and makers' mark are obscure and possibly ancient. One legend has it that the mark traces back to the Greek god Hermes, patron of commerce and trade, in whose honor the symbol "4" was worshipped. The double "X", according to one theory, symbolized man looking up to a benevolent god. Yet another theory is that the symbol "4" is of runic origin—that its past is buried in the unwritten and little-known history of early European alphabets. Some scholars suggest that it might have been intended as a sign of the cross. Whatever its origin, this central symbol has appeared on merchandise of quality for centuries and continues today in the Colonial Williamsburg hallmark.

Many products in the Colonial Williamsburg program are displayed and sold in fine stores throughout the United States, as well as at Craft House.

Selections may be purchased at Craft House or ordered from this catalogue for prompt delivery. Careful attention is given to mail orders, instructions for which may be found on page 286.

Reprinted here is the list of products available from the Prentis-Tarpley's Stores, the retail outlet of Colonial Williamsburg's Craft Shops. This list includes only items reproduced by Colonial Williamsburg's outside manufacturers, since the resident craftsmen could not possibly keep up with a mail-order business. Leather goods, printed items, silver, and pewter items made in the Shops by the craftsmen are available on a limited basis. Craftsmen in all the shops will take custom orders from visitors coming to town. Direct all orders and inquiries to Colonial Williamsburg Gifts, 201 Fifth Avenue, Williamsburg, Virginia 23185. Make all checks payable to Colonial Williamsburg Foundation.

THE PRENTIS STORE AND TARPLEY AND COMPANY ARE THE SALES OUTLETS FOR THE CRAFT SHOPS OF COLONIAL WILLIAMSBURG.

The stores stock items made by the Williamsburg craftsmen, as well as reproductions of products of the type sold in Williamsburg in the eighteenth century. The stores are located on the Duke of Gloucester Street in the restored area of Colonial Williamsburg.

Delft A selection of delft reproductions from the Colonial Williamsburg collection of antique furnishings. Reproduced by Messrs. Oud Delft of Nijmegen, Holland.

E.e Scord—Blue-and-white delft dry apothecary jar. Height, 7⅛".
20.00 each
2.00 mailing costs

C: Malvae—Blue-and-white delft dry apothecary jar. Height 6¾".
20.00 each
2.00 mailing costs

P. Rudy—Blue-and-white delft ointment pot. Height, 3½".
15.00 each
1.00 mailing costs

Inkwell—Blue-and-white delft inkwell with landscape design. Signed Edward Herbat, 1755. Height, 1⅝".
10.00 each 1.00 mailing costs

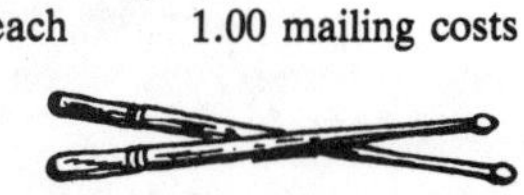

Sturdy Rosewood Snare Drumsticks
15.00 the pair .75 mailing costs

Fine Maple Fife 5.95 1.00 mailing costs

Bilbo Catcher or Bilboquet A popular stick and ball toy of the eighteenth century neatly turned in wood. The Bilboquet is reproduced from one in the Colonial Williamsburg collection of antique furnishings. Bilbo Catcher (Boxed) 3.00 .50 mailing costs

Playing Cards The cards, the package, and the duty stamp are reproduced from a Mogul deck made in England for importation to the colonies in the eighteenth century and now in the Colonial Williamsburg collection of antique furnishings.
Playing Cards 2.75
.50 mailing costs

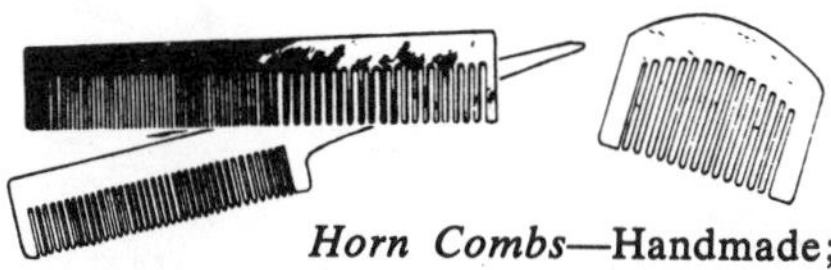

Horn Combs—Handmade; from England. Subtle colorations of black, brown, and beige horn.

Straight—length 6"	3.40 each,	.25 mailing costs
Rattail—length 7½"	2.95 each,	.25 mailing costs
Curved—length 2½"	2.95 each,	.25 mailing costs

Strong Brass *Pipe Tamps* made from eighteenth-century designs.
Harlequin— Height, 2½" 4.50 each
.85 mailing costs
Slipper— Length, 2½" 4.50 each
.85 mailing costs

Fine Tricorn Hats of heavy black felt
Small, medium, large, extra large. Please list size.
3.50 each
.75 mailing costs

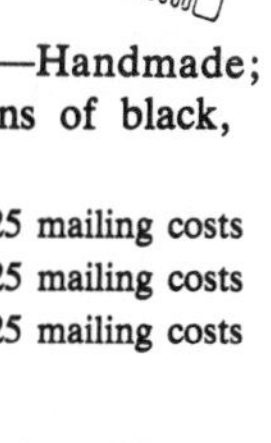

Fine Coffee especially blended by James G. Gill Co. Inc.
Columbian Supremo A mild breakfast coffee typical of coffee grown in Central and South America in the eighteenth century. It is similar to Dutch West Indian coffee that would have been served in the coffee houses of Williamsburg at that time. Packaged in attractive muslin sack.
Columbian Supremo—Bean or Ground Form— 6.50 the pound
.75 mailing costs

Mocha Java An after-dinner coffee with a strong definite taste. It resembles most closely, among modern blends, the coffee that would have been served in Williamsburg in the eighteenth century. Packaged in attractive muslin sack.
Mocha Java—Ground Form only—6.50
.75 mailing costs

Fine Tea imported by James G. Gill Co. Inc., from Jackson's of Piccadilly.

Oolong—A rich, mellow tea that is black and silky in appearance.
Lapsang Souchong—A fine and rich traditional Chinese tea. Black, long-leafed, and only lightly fired.
Darjeeling—This large-leaf variety is the finest and most distinctive of the Indian teas.
Pinhead Gunpowder—Well-known in the eighteenth century, this green Chinese tea is of a pale straw color when brewed.
Young Hyson—A green Chinese tea prepared from the youngest and tenderest of leaves.
Earl Grey—A delightfully pungent tea that is a mixture of Indian and Ceylon teas.
2.35 each package
.50 mailing costs

Pomander A spicy, clove-studded lemon covered in a cotton print and tied with satin ribbon to ward off the plague or merely to scent closets and bureaus.
3.75 each
.50 mailing costs

Bayberry Soap Bars Each carefully packaged in beige printed paper.

4 soap bars—	2.40	.50 mailing costs
6 soap bars—	3.60	.60 mailing costs
the dozen—	7.20	1.00 mailing costs

Best Virginia Tobacco
A large-flake cut tobacco containing some Virginia bright and latakia in a primarily Burley mixture. It is naturally cured and lightly aromatic.

½-pound tin—2.75
.75 mailing costs
One-pound tin—4.75
.75 mailing costs

Please send all orders and inquiries to:
Colonial Williamsburg Gifts
201 Fifth Avenue
Williamsburg, Virginia 23185
Please make check or money order payable to the Colonial Williamsburg Foundation
Residents of Virginia please add 4% sales tax.

FRUITCAKES

A tradition at Christmastime, and a treat generally throughout the year, is the fruitcake: either dark or white (depending upon whether the cake is made with jam or without). The South seems to be the principal purveying point for these delicacies, and three bakeries which have themselves become traditions in their association with fruitcake-baking are mentioned here. Each bakery stakes a "unique" claim to fruitcake excellence; we thought all were great, with the Claxton and Collin Street fruitcakes bearing a close resemblance to one another, and the Gordon Smith one having a distinctly different flavor.

Old Fashion Claxton Fruit Cake

BAKED IN THE DEEP SOUTH, ACCORDING TO A FAMOUS OLD SOUTHERN RECIPE.

WORLD FAMOUS!

CLAXTON "OLD FASHION" FRUIT CAKE

The Claxton Bakery was established in 1910 by Mr. Savino Tos, an Italian immigrant, who operated the business until 1945. It was taken over at that time by Albert Parker who continues as its president. Claxton Fruit Cakes are found in many neighborhood stores and are often sold by civic clubs or church groups as a Christmastime fund-raising effort. Year-round baking produces over six million pounds of fruitcake. Visitors and chartered bus tours are welcome to take a guided tour through the bakery, daily from 7 a.m. to 7 p.m.

Claxton Fruit Cakes are sold in boxes, but for $1.00 extra a five-pound cake will be sent in a tin.

Costs:

3 lb. light or dark (packed either solid or in three 1-lb. cakes)—$6.50

5 lb. light or dark (packed either solid or in five 1-lb. cakes)—$9.50

Add $.75 to a 3 lb. or $1.00 to a 5 lb. shipped west of the Mississippi River. Add $1.00 or $1.50 outside the U.S.

Claxton Bakery, Inc.
P.O. Box 367
Claxton, Georgia 30417

Gordon Smith
MANUFACTURER OF
Smith's White Fruit Cake
A DELICACY FROM DIXIE
MOBILE, ALA.

A DELICACY FROM DIXIE

Gordon Smith Bakery bakes the fruitcake you wish your mother used to make: rich but light; fine-textured and full of fruit. This fruitcake gives an old-timey sense of great care having been taken, a hint of fragrant pantries and parties and mistletoe.

The Bakery began in 1906 when a friend of Mr. Smith's allowed him to use her family's white fruitcake recipe to bake cakes upon request. He continues to operate a relatively small mail-order business with cakes baked on order only.

Gordon Smith White Fruit Cakes are shipped in metal tins that you can use again and again.

Costs prepaid anywhere in the United States: 3 lb. cake, $11.50; 5 lb. cake, $16.75. A 4% discount is given on orders of 10 to 24 cakes from one customer; special discounts are given for larger orders.

Gordon Smith Bakery
1100 Dauphin Street
Box 109
Mobile, Alabama 36601

ORIGINAL
DeLuxe
"That Famous 'Corsicana Fruit Cake'"
CORSICANA, TEXAS SINCE 1896

COLLIN STREET BAKERY

"THAT FAMOUS CORSICANA FRUITCAKE"

The origins of the Collin Street Bakery and its white fruitcake were in the business partnership of a young German baker, August Weidmann, and a wealthy promoter, Thomas McElwee. In 1896, McElwee christened the fruitcake "the Original Deluxe" and 10 prosperous years later, at the opening of a new location for the bakery, he engineered a brilliant promotional ploy: the new bakery's entire second floor was made into an elite private hotel, where the celebrities of the day were invited to stay. Such guests as Enrico Caruso, Will Rogers, John J. McGraw, and "Gentlemen Jim" Corbett rested at the "hotel" and took away good impressions of the Collin Street Bakery and fruitcake. The first great Christmas order brought to the bakery was by John Ringling and his circus troupers: several hundred Original Deluxe Fruit Cakes destined for foreign lands—implanting the cake's reputation of international favor. Today Collin Street claims orders from 158 countries and all states and possessions of the United States. Since Collin Street concentrates on the Christmas season, only a portion of its 750-man work force remains on the job during the entire year, but for two mad months the conveyor belts roll out over two million pounds of fruitcake. You can get the fruitcake at any time, however.

Collin Street Fruit Cakes are sold in a "keepsake" tin at no additional charge. Costs:

Prices Include Delivery*

1 thru 24 Cakes	
2 lb.	@ $ 7.65
3 lb.	@ $10.90
5 lb.	@ $17.70
25 thru 99 Cakes	
2 lb.	@ $ 7.45
3 lb.	@ $10.60
5 lb.	@ $17.20
100 or More Cakes	
2 lb.	@ $ 7.25
3 lb.	@ $10.30
5 lb.	@ $16.70

*PRICES INCLUDE delivery to the 50 states, all U.S. possessions, Puerto Rico, and APO-FPO addresses.

For surface mail delivery from Texas to foreign countries, allow 6 to 9 weeks. Add $2.25 per cake for foreign postage. For Canada allow 3 weeks and add $2.00 per cake.

Collin Street Bakery
Corsicana, Texas 75110

FAVORITES FROM·THE·PAST

2951 HARRIS STREET
KENNESAW, GEORGIA 30144

(404) 427-3921

THE MINIATURE SHOP

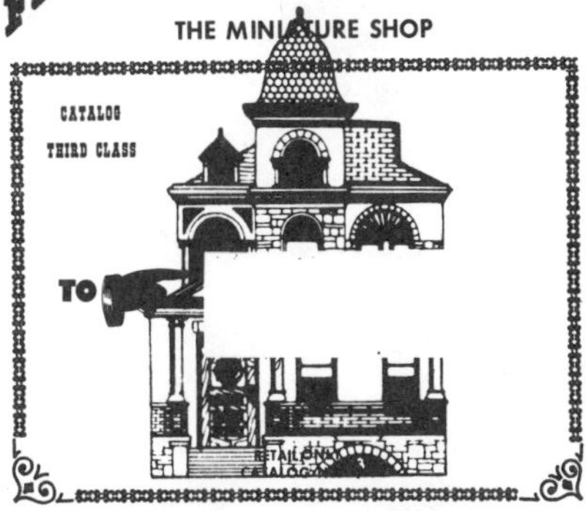

The wonderful catalog of The Miniature Shop includes *everything* you could possibly want for a dollhouse—rugs, lamps, wallpaper, shelves, hardware, staircases, and many other fascinating items. To order the catalog, write: Favorites From The Past, 2951 Harris Street, Kennesaw, Georgia 30144.

COLLECTOR'S MEDIA

Kermit, Texas, may be the center of the current vogue of nostalgia: no less than five publications celebrating antiques and their collection have their base there, all under the wing of Collector's Media, Inc. They include "The Collector" (formerly "Collector's Weekly"), a monthly newspaper-format journal of collectables of the last 100 years; "The Plate Collector," a monthly magazine featuring limited edition plates, prints, figurines, bells, etc., and averaging over 300 pages; "Bottle News," a monthly magazine of old bottles, fruit jars, insulators, and related collectables; "Antique Price Report," a monthly magazine of fine antiques featuring current price information, research and historical information and current news; and "Plate Newsletter," an eight-page weekly newsletter, sent via first class mail, with latest information on limited edition plates.

Each publication has its own separate post office box—more than likely providing the bulk of Kermit's postal business. Here is a list of the Collector's Media, Inc., publications, their addresses, and their current subscription rates:

	Annual Subscription
The Collector Drawer C Kermit, Texas 79745	**$8.00**
The Plate Collector Box 1041 Kermit, Texas 79745	**$15.00**
Bottle News Box 1000 Kermit, Texas 79745	**$8.00**
Antique Price Report Box 974 Kermit, Texas 79745	**$10.00**
Plate Newsletter Box 981 Kermit, Texas 79745	**$100.00**

Collectors No. 40021
QUEEN ANNE FIRE SCREEN
Circa 1725-1760
Measures 3¾" tall when finished
Kit $2.95

Collectors No. 40019
CHIPPENDALE DRY SINK
Circa 1750-1790
Measures 3" high x 3⅛" wide when finished
Kit $5.95

Collectors No. 40012
CHIPPENDALE NIGHT STAND
Circa 1750-1790
Measures 2½" high x 1¾" wide when finished
Kit $3.95

Collectors No. 40022
CHIPPENDALE STRAIGHT-TOP HIGHBOY
Circa 1725
When finished, measures 6-1/2" high x 3-1/2" wide x 2" deep
Kit $14.95

Collectors No. 40023
CHIPPENDALE BROKEN-BONNET HIGHBOY
Circa 1725
When finished, measures 7-1/6" high x 3-1/2" wide x 2" deep
Kit $17.95

Collectors No. 40024
CHIPPENDALE LOWBOY
Circa 1725
When finished, measures 2-7/8" high x 3-1/2" wide x 2" deep
Kit $8.95

Collectors No. 40025
CHIPPENDALE SIDEBOARD
Circa 1725-1750
When finished, measures 2-7/8" high x 4-1/2" wide x 2" deep
Kit $9.95

Collectors No. 40034
DOWER CHEST
Circa 1790
When finished, measures 1-3/4" high x 3" wide x 1-3/4" deep
Kit $5.95

Collectors No. 40031
CHIPPENDALE BENCH
Circa 1760
When finished, measures 1-1/2" high x 2-3/16" wide 1-9/16" deep
Kit $4.95

Collectors No. 40015
CHIPPENDALE SOFA
Circa 1750-1790
Measures 6¼" long when finished
Kit $7.95

Collectors No. 40016
CHIPPENDALE WING CHAIR
Circa 1750-1790
Measures 3¾" tall when finished
Kit $5.95

Collectors No. 40014
CHIPPENDALE CANOPY BED
Circa 1750-1790
Measures 7" tall x 6⅛" long x 5¾" wide when finished
Kit $8.95

CUMBERLAND GENERAL STORE

Cumberland General Store in Crossville, Tennessee, invites you to "come by and visit a spell"—but until you can, we suggest shopping through their catalog, *The Wish and Want Book.* All the "old-fashioned" items are new goods. Do you need a Conestoga wagon, a cast iron souse pan shaped like a hog's head, or a brass cuspidor? Or, on a somewhat more practical day, how about a harness, a mechanical pea and bean sheller, a fireplace grate, or a milk can?

For your 250-page catalogue from the store which bills itself as the "outfitters for your journey back to basics," send $3.00 to:

Cumberland General Store
Route 3
Crossville, Tennessee 38555

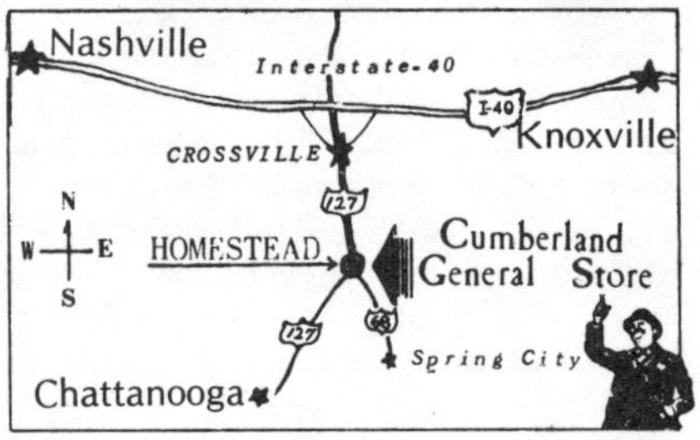

THE OUTDOOR PORTABLE PIT

When the W.C. Bradley Company of Columbus, Georgia, went into business, making cast iron skillets and stoves, it was 1853, in the "Good Old Days" before charcoal. It weathered the storm of the War Between the States as a gun boat producer for the Confederate Navy. The Bradley Company is now perhaps best known as the maker of Char-Broil products for the patio and fireplace.

One of the Char-Broil products harks back to the "Good Old Days," but makes use of "modern" charcoal: the Outdoor Portable Pit (part of the Bradley Company's registered trademark). A whole steer might not quite fit on this pit, but who could afford that much beef anyway? The "Outdoor Portable Pit" sells, depending upon the particular style, for anywhere from $130.00 to $350.00.

Request information from:

Char-Broil Outdoor Portable Pit
W.C. Bradley Enterprises, Inc.
Box 1240
Columbus, Georgia 31902

". . . We were in the absolute South now—no modifications, no compromises, no half-way measures. The magnolia trees were lovely and fragrant, with their dense rich foliage and huge snowball blossoms. The scent of the flower is very sweet, but you want distance on it, because it is so powerful—we were certainly in the South at last; for here the sugar region begins, and the plantations—vast green levels with sugar-mills clustered together in the middle distance—were in view. And there was a tropical sun overhead and a tropical swelter in the air. And at this point, also, begins the pilot's paradise: a wide river hence to New Orleans."
Mark Twain, LIFE ON THE MISSISSIPPI

THE HATFIELDS AND THE McCOYS

by Otis K. Rice

The University Press of Kentucky
Lexington, Kentucky 40506

Their feud covered two states. Often, the governors of both West Virginia and Kentucky had to intervene to enforce the law. Just as often, it really didn't make much difference—the families had their own notions about settling disputes. But even as strange as the truth of this most famous vendetta of the Southern Appalachians really was, there still exist distortions and fictionalized accounts of what happened. In this book, Mr. Rice uses court records, public documents, official correspondences, newspaper accounts, and other evidence to rub the legend and the lies off the facts. He succeeds, and the resulting book is a captivating account of two families whose stubbornness and loyalty were exceeded only by their capacity for a terrible revenge.

The beginning of the feud is shrouded somewhere in the Civil War when the conflicting allegiances in those crucial border states divided many a neighbor against a neighbor. The critical years of the feud in the 1870s were ushered in after the Hatfields accused the McCoys of stealing a hog. After this seemingly minor incident came some of the bloodiest ambushes and killings. No one was safe—not even women or friends—who allied himself with one of the two warring factions. Even though there was one notable intermarriage—when the chips were down, the husband went to his family (the Hatfields) and the wife and children to hers (the McCoys). One McCoy daughter, spurned by her Hatfield lover, grieved herself to death.

In his rendering of all the events and factors which went into this remarkable feud, Mr. Rice maintains an objectivity that is as unusual as it is professional. He faithfully records the origins and progress of the conflict, rejecting the temptation to embellish or sensationalize any of the facts. He tells of the exemplary citizens that the Hatfield and McCoy families produced as well as the feudists. The participants in this unique drama are unforgettable. Without a doubt, the Hatfield-McCoy feud will reign supreme as the most fascinating vendetta on the American scene.

—S.V.H.

NO. 709 SUNBURST. *The traditional sunburst design shown here looks well in almost any setting, taking on the formality of a drawing room or the informality of a wicker-filled porch.*

FOCAL POINT, INC.

"Originals reborn" and "architectural artwork from the past engineered for today" are at least two ways of describing the beautiful moulding produced by Atlanta's Focal Point, Inc.

When we first saw pictures of the moulding, it was impossible to tell it from the "real thing," that is, the conventional driwood moulding. However, because Focal Point reproduces artwork in modern polymers, it is of a considerably lighter weight.

Focal Point moulding can be nailed, drilled, or screwed. It can be sawed by hand or by machine. The moulding can be made to conform to any severe wall irregularities by paring down the backside with a knife. Normal wall irregularities are taken care of by the natural resilience of the material. Fitting of corners can be handled with a pocket knife. Ordinarily there would be no reason for sanding, but the material does sand easily. It is factory primed so only a final coat of paint is necessary. Because the product is pre-engineered, considerable savings on labor can be realized.

Focal Point also produces ceiling medallions with the soft texture of plaster but composed of especially compounded urethane and shipped easily and inexpensively in a cardboard box.

A recent addition to the Focal Point product line is a series of overdoor pieces.

About 70% of Focal Point's business is in new construction; however, the company also works in the field of restoration.

To inquire about products or local dealers:

Focal Point, Inc.
4870 South Atlanta Road
Smyrna, Georgia 30080
Phone: 404-351-0820

CORNICE MOULDINGS. Installed as a single member. The material is approximately the density of white pine. Factory priming should receive any paint. A stain effect can be achieved.

THE HERMANN RUSCH GREENBRIER COOKBOOK

What better way to learn to prepare the delicious dishes that have made The Greenbrier world famous for its cuisine than from the man who has made it so? *The Hermann Rusch Greenbrier Cookbook* is a complete guide to Continental cooking and offers recipes for everything from hors d'oeuvres to desserts, including many traditional Greenbrier favorites. Mr. Rusch includes numerous cooking hints and basic information on stocks, sauces, glazes and pastries as well.

You can order the Cookbook (at $9.75 plus $1.00 postage and handling) by writing The Greenbrier, White Sulphur Springs, West Virginia 24986. If you plan a visit there, pick up a copy at The Greenbrier Newsstand.

Another beautiful idea from The Greenbrier is the elegant initial "G" cast in solid brass. The trivet can be used to hold casseroles or a wine bottle, or hang it on the wall as a shining graphic memento of a visit or promise of a trip to come. Five inches in diameter, it is available for $9.50 (plus $1.00 postage and handling) from The Greenbrier.

ENERGY ALTERNATIVE

All of us experience the feeling from time to time that we would like to find a viable way to cut down our energy consumption in the home. Summerwood Stove Company has an alternative for us—a wood-burning stove. They offer a complete selection of forty stoves and furnaces in many shapes and sizes so that you can choose one to fit in with your existing decor.

Summerwood has a package available by mail for $1.00—it's called "Beautiful Heat." Each package includes a price list and a wealth of information about the airtight, fuel-efficient wood stoves. Summerwood also has a line of accessories for your stove and for your home. Some of the items you may order include insulated stovepipe, glass fireplace doors, chimney brushes, fire-tile hearths, and kerosene lamps.

Summerwood Stove Company
111 Jefferson Street North
Huntsville, Alabama 35804

ANTIQUE MAPS: GOING, GOING, GONE

If you want to own a *real* old map and grandma's attic doesn't have one, try bidding for one through Tim Coss's Antique Map Mail Auction. Maps dating back as far as 1550 have been sold through the auction. The mail auctions include low-, medium-, and high-priced items. Whether you are a collector or dealer, you may find something in this catalog.

The catalog—free—is published quarterly. Bids may be entered by mail or phone up to a closing deadline. There is no floor bidding. Consignments are accepted, with a 20% commission on sales of consigned items payable by the consignor. The catalog includes descriptions of the maps, a bid sheet, and full instructions.

An Old Newspaper Mail Auction operates along the same lines. For information about either auction or to request a catalog, write:

Antique Map Mail Auction
5614 Northfield Road
Bethesda, Maryland 20034

EPHRAIM MARSH COMPANY

Ephraim Marsh Company has two catalogues of furniture, one they call Heirloom and the other Distinctive Furniture.

The Heirloom group consists of reproductions and offers a fine selection of bedroom, dining room, and living room pieces. The entire group is made of solid Honduras mahogany with solid brasses like those on the originals and, in further imitation, the pieces are hand-fitted, sanded, and rubbed.

The Distinctive Furniture is just that. There is heavy emphasis on the traditional style, with upholstered items offered in your choice of fabric, including leather, and you have the option of sending your own fabric. The line also includes an array of executive furniture—chairs, tables, desks, and lamps. This furniture catalogue is one of the most helpful we have seen in assisting you in making an intelligent choice without actually having the furniture in your presence. Finish chips are available for wood furniture as well as fabric swatches for upholstered pieces.

The catalogue gives detailed descriptions and pictures of every piece offered. There is a running first person commentary throughout, setting the mood of a fine old house with its memories and furnishings.

The catalogues are $1.00 each, and all price, ordering, and shipping information is clearly indicated. Be sure to indicate which catalogue you are requesting, the Distinctive Furniture or the Heirloom. Write to:

Ephraim Marsh Company
Box 266
Concord, North Carolina 28025

Console Card Table is of African mahogany and with the top closed is 33¾" x 16⅞"; with the top open, 33¾" x 33¾" and 30" tall.

PLEASURE AND PAIN REMINISCENCES OF GEORGIA

Emily Burke

The Beehive Press
321 Barnard Street
Savannah, Georgia 31401

This description of people and places, adventures and discoveries was written by a New England schoolmarm who spent the 1840's in Georgia. With charm, sentiment, affection and detail, she tells about life in Savannah, tours to several plantations, various aspects of slavery, poor whites in the countryside and a camp-meeting in the woods. She loves the South and its people, but she is surprised to find Georgia still a frontier and she is troubled by slavery. Thus, she leaves Georgia at last with "mingled emotions of pleasure and pain."

A BIT OF OLD CHARLESTON

Birlant's of Charleston, exclusively, sells an authentic reproduction of the famous Charleston Battery bench. These graceful seats are a compliment to any garden, patio, or lawn.

The Charleston Battery bench has sides made in original molds of hand-cast iron and the slats are from Low-country cypress trees. The bench measures 48" long by 29" high and is available in Charleston dark green.

Each bench comes unassembled and sells for $119.50—shipping is freight collect. South Carolina residents add 4% sales tax.

Order from:

Birlant's
191 King Street
Charleston, South Carolina 29401

Time Washes Maryland's Eastern Shore

Change has crossed Chesapeake Bay, yet watermen hold to their solitary lives, and townships keep their identity.

by IRENE PRESTON

Not 40 miles from Washington, D.C., as the crow flies, is the Eastern Shore of Maryland, a sawtooth peninsula full of quaint towns and peaceful ports.

Three centuries of geographic isolation have kept the Eastern Shore somewhat remote, a place where change has not happened fast. The oysterman still harvests under sail, and crab women continue to pick and clean the catch by hand. With its wide bay and tiny towns, the Eastern Shore provides a vast inheritance of an earlier way of life, and we are its beneficiaries.

The Chesapeake Bay Bridge was completed in 1952. The newer 17.6-mile-long Chesapeake Bay Bridge-Tunnel to Norfolk, longest bridge-tunnel in America, opened in 1964. Between them, they have finally begun to alter the provincialism of the Eastern Shore. Land along the major roads has been developed, and tourism and immigration from the urban mainland have increased.

Running through the deep stands of loblolly pine, U.S. 50 cuts through a sizable portion of the Eastern Shore. Hundreds of acres of flat, sprawling farms spread out from the highway, kept from being monotonous by the lush vegetation and the haunted, weathered look of the buildings. The Eastern Shore was once the chief producer of truck crops and chickens for markets on the East Coast, but modern transportation and the network of interstate highways changed all that, leaving abandoned farms and ghost towns spread throughout the countryside.

A century before Baltimore was founded, bay towns like Easton and Oxford were prosperous places, thriving on European trade which brought in slaves and manufactured goods and shipped out cargoes of tobacco, the Eastern Shore's first—and most profitable—crop.

Although the enormous profits of the plantation system are now gone, agriculture remains an important part of bay life. Proximity to the ocean promotes a long growing season. Land is fertile, and rainfall plentiful. In fact, areas around Easton in Talbot County still advertise themselves as the tomato and strawberry capitals of the United States.

Back in the 1920's tomatoes were a prime cash crop on the Eastern Shore, second only to wheat. At one time 30 tomato canneries operated in Talbot County, running eight months of the year. Today there are two.

Easton, the county seat of Talbot County, is known as the Colonial Capital of the Eastern Shore. Settled as an agricultural center by the Quakers in 1682, the broad tree-lined streets and brick Federalist buildings give Easton something of the flavor of a New England village.

Easton grew up around the Third Haven Friends' Meeting House on South Washington Street. Founded in 1682 and believed to be the oldest frame church in America, it was built on the Tred Avon River. The congregation came by boat to attend services, several of which were led by William Penn.

Washington Street was founded as a major commercial thoroughfare, a place for produce and livestock sales and public meetings. Many of the old Federalist buildings survive. A good example is the Talbot County Courthouse. First built in 1711, the present courthouse, constructed in 1795, now stands on the original site. Here in 1774 the "Talbot Resolves" were adopted, later to become one of the foundations for the Declaration of Independence.

Down the Tred Avon River from Easton is tiny Oxford. Today corn grows right up to the edge of town, but Oxford's layout and architecture—especially the row of merchant houses on Morris Street—indicate the thriving port it once was.

In the center of town a small brick museum details the life story of Oxford and its famed ferry. Built in 1682, the Tred Avon ferry is the oldest operating cable-free ferry in the United States. Shuttling carriages back and forth all day, the ferry made 17th-century Oxford a major port of entry to the Eastern Shore.

Just down the street from the ferry is the Robert Morris Inn, a rambling frame structure which dates back to 1710. It was once the home of financier Robert Morris, at the time the wealthiest man in America, who used much of his private fortune to underwrite the American Revolution. Ironically, he later lost all his money, partially because he was never repaid the loan he made to the Continental Army, and spent three years in a debtor's prison in Philadelphia.

Much of the credit for the growing recognition of the Eastern Shore's irreplaceable beauty goes to people like Karl de Rochefort-Reynolds and to both local preservation organizations and to the Maryland Historic Trust, which has provided guidelines and some tax relief for private restoration. In St. Michaels on the Miles River, for instance, through the aid of the St. Michaels Historic District, pastel houses along the harbor have been restored by their owners to newborn freshness, each with its own individual detail—gable, door knocker, or window box.

The waterfront homes of St. Michaels look out upon an unusual museum—the Chesapeake Bay Maritime Museum, which commemorates the early days of St. Michaels. Like a reflection in a giant glass, the museum illuminates the workaday world of the St. Michaels shipyards and, indeed, of the entire Eastern Shore. Major exhibits range from a hexagonal frame lighthouse, brought about 60 miles upshore from Hooper's Strait, to the *Rosie Parks,* the finest example of a working skipjack in America. The museum, at Navy Point, is in the former heart of the once prosperous shipbuilding industry.

TIMES DOWN HOME
75 Years with Progressive Farmer
Edited by Mary Elizabeth Johnson
Research and Narrative by Mary Jean Haddin

Oxmoor House, Inc.
Birmingham, Alabama

In the early 1900s, reading matter in most farm homes was sparse and might include only the Bible and perhaps the *Progressive Farmer* magazine. It is not too surprising, under those circumstances, that the *Progressive Farmer* had a women's section which included requests and all sorts of advice, from how to make lye hominy to how to cure a broken heart. The richness of this material, from 1902 to the present, has thankfully been preserved in the pages of *Times Down Home.* As one reads through the book noticing the old-fashioned dress, cars, and look of the people, he cannot help but be aware of the startling similarities in the basic way of thinking between that time and ours. There are many superficial contrasts, but the spirit of these people—who rushed out to buy government bonds for World War I, survived the devastating depression, and planted victory gardens during World War II—that spirit is still alive and well today.

The liberation of women was as much on the early twentieth century mind as it is today. In an article entitled "Thank Heaven For Tennessee" (Tennessee was the last state to ratify the 19th amendment—giving women the right to vote), there is the following: "And thus did we women cease to be classed with idiots, imbeciles, and criminals, as dependents of the state and become citizens entitled to vote on the same basis as men."

Grooming aids and home improvement suggestions abound. "Don't have a parlor—it is always inane, characterless. . . . " "Drink hot water with lemon or with salt in it for a fine complexion." The modern term "workaholic" is not used directly but the problem existed even then: "It would be far better for many families if their conditions were not so easy and their family life richer . . . there must be the giving of the self." And the importance of good cooking is brought home with this chilling observation: "Many wrecked homes, many divorces, many crimes have been traced directly to a bad digestion, the result of wrong methods of cooking."

Times Down Home is liberally sprinkled with illustrations of every imaginable kind of advertisement. "Dandruff Is Inexcusable!" "Too Late! Too Late! Stammerer you will soon be too late to be cured!" (This one goes on to inform the public that a noted voice specialist who cures this specific affliction can now be found in a certain North Carolina hotel.) "She fought radio for three years—now see what she says!" Those are just a few of the things that caught our forbears' eye.

For the nostalgia buff, the history fan, or the collector of curiosity pieces, this book contains an unbeatable record of Americana. Anyone over fifty will enjoy again those times, "down home," and anyone under fifty will chortle at the differences and marvel at the samenesses. Brimming with humor, advice, ads, war reminders, and fashions, *Times Down Home* makes good reading and, for many, will bring back great memories of the "little" things.

—S.V.H.

DO-IT-YOURSELF

No need to tell you that old-house renovation is expensive. Here is one way to save money and have fun at the same time. The Emperor Clock company is still making Grandfather, Mantel, and School Clock Kits, but they have broadened out into other furniture kits as well. Can you imagine making your own Queen Anne secretary or coffee table, writing desk or lowboy and saving from $100 to $250 by "doing-it-yourself"?

According to the catalogue, there is no guesswork involved. All kit pieces are pre-cut and sanded smooth on both sides for ease of assembly. Complete hardware and step-by-step assembly instructions are furnished. (To avoid breakage, glass is not included in most kits.) To ease your mind, each kit piece may be reordered separately. The customer service department is staffed by experts who can handle any problem you might have. And for the faint-hearted, you can also buy most of this furniture assembled and finished.

Write to:

Emperor Clock Company
Emperor Industrial Park
Fairhope, Alabama 36532
(205) 928-2316

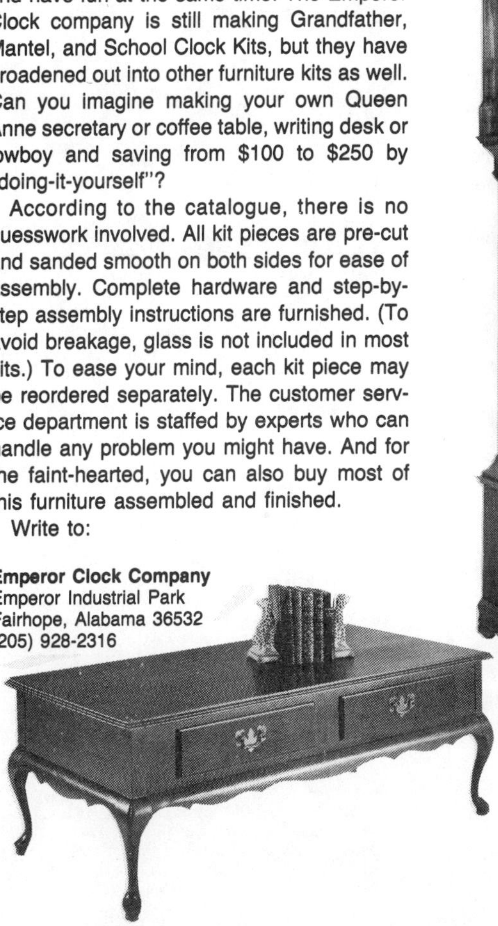

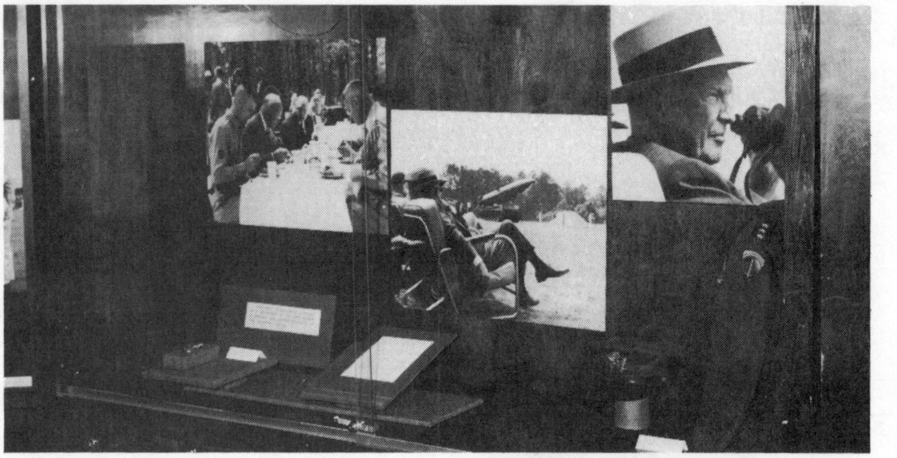

NATIONAL INFANTRY MUSEUM

The National Infantry Museum at Fort Benning, Georgia, houses thousands of interesting and unique items and reflects the role played by the Infantryman in the defense of the nation. Two hundred years of proud history are on display.

The museum collection is continually growing. There are some 2,300 firearms ranging from a 16th century Spanish cannon to an early Japanese matchlock musket; also the Gatling gun which helped win the West; the nation's smallest atomic weapon (the Davy Crockett); and an experimental grenade launcher developed for use in Southeast Asia.

Of special interest to young and old alike is the Sutler's General Store located in the museum. This store is an authentic re-creation of a turn-of-the-century general store and its merchandise. You will see tobacco cutters, a potbelly stove, a barber shop, spitoons, oil lights, advertisements, coffee grinders, straw hats, and bear traps as part of the well-stocked store.

Colorful antique Oriental screens grace the display of centuries-old Japanese armor. Temporary displays of contemporary art works, military badges and equipment, as well as mementos and gifts from around the world create a never ending kaleidoscope of interesting exhibits.

The museum has memorabilia of several distinguished officers. A partial list includes: General of the Armies John J. Pershing, General of the Army Dwight D. Eisenhower, General of the Army George C. Marshall, General of the Army Omar Bradley, General George Patton, General Manton Eddy, General Courtney Hodges, Secretary of the Army Gordon Gray, and First Commander of Camp Benning, General Farmsworth.

Dick D. Grube, curator of the National Infantry Museum, made a special point when writing to us: "We hope that you will point out to your readers that more important than the mementos of these famous men are the mementos of the dog-faced Infantryman, the GI, whose deeds in general we commemorate and honor. . . ."

Admission to the museum is free, and it is open Tuesday-Friday, 10 a.m. to 4:30 p.m., and Saturday and Sunday, 12:30 to 4:30 p.m. The museum, which is located in Building 396, Baltzell Avenue, is closed on Thanksgiving, Christmas, and New Year's Day.

PUT SOME DELFT ON YOUR SHELF

"Delftware" is a kind of pottery that is made of soft earthenware covered with a lead glaze. It is sometimes made opaque with ashes or oxide of tin. Before it is glazed, a painter paints a scene or a pattern, as if working with watercolor, on this white absorbent surface. Since it is very difficult to erase any mistakes, painting on this white surface requires great skill. Today, Delft Blue Ltd. applies much the same techniques as those used in earlier times.

This work is not to be confused with printed, decaled, or silk-screened items that are brush-washed for a handpainted appearance. Delft Blue, Ltd., work is completely handpainted and signed by the artist. The formula used to make these exquisite pieces is made up of the finest-quality clay bisque.

Delft Blue, Ltd., tiles are available in 74 traditional handpainted designs. These tiles can be used around fireplaces and in bathrooms and kitchens. Special orders for table tops, tableaus, and wall hangings are also available. Send one dollar for catalogue and price list to:

T. T. I.
P.O. Box 103
Ellicott City, Maryland 21043

Bring Back The Drugstore Fan

The paddle-blade ceiling fan was introduced (in resemblance to its present form) for 19th-century tropical climates. The fan was then used to circulate the air, keeping insects away and moving, if only slightly, the heavy humid air. This function stayed with the fan when in the late 19th century a motor was added. The ceiling fan's full potential was realized and began to be used in meat markets, drugstores, hotels, and other establishments. When applied to the home (particularly the dining room), the fans became elaborate and ornate and included elegant light fixtures, sometimes of leaded glass in the Tiffany style.

The paddle-blade ceiling fan was almost forgotten with the advent of central air conditioning. But a few years ago people (particularly in the South where porch living has been an evolutionary part of the culture) began to rediscover the air-moving function of the fan (even one of the smaller size fans will circulate air in a 20- x 20-foot room with 10-foot ceilings) and appreciate the beauty in the old machine. The fans are now being used on screened and open porches, in summer houses, and in breezeways for not only their function and pleasure, but also for the soothing hum of the blades, which has an almost tranquilizing effect.

Designer Bill McGregor suggests that with the addition of enamel paint to the metal motor housing and stem, the fans can work as an accenting interior design element in such places as breakfast rooms, kitchens, dens, and bathrooms, or even above a workbench.

The once-plentiful fans from drugstores and department stores are becoming scarce. But the original paddle-type blade fans are still being produced and sold. Most are made in 36-inch and 52-inch sizes (distance from blade tip to opposite blade tip) and have a two-speed motor, high and low. The 36-inch model takes approximately a 1½-foot clearance below the ceiling, while the 52-inch model needs a 2-foot clearance. On some larger models there is an air adjustor which adjusts the angle of the blades to either direct the air flow to the ceiling or floor. Also, an option on some larger models is an adaptor which can be installed at the base of the fan for a light fixture.

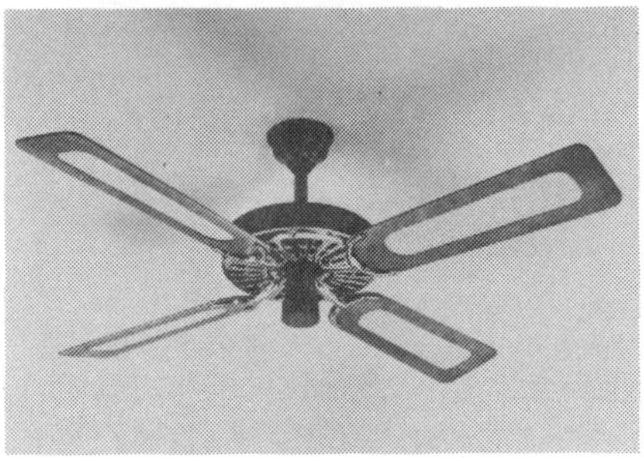

CEILING FAN MANUFACTURER

Hunter Olde Tyme Ceiling Fans are noted for their graceful looks, but their real beauty is in their performance and energy efficiency. In summer, the ceiling fan supplements and enhances air conditioning by keeping the air circulated. This added air movement allows homeowners to set their thermostats six, eight, even ten degrees higher and still maintain the same level of cooling comfort. During winter, the same fan, at slow speed, can recycle heat. Rising warm air from the heating system is pushed down by the ceiling fan to colder areas, preventing heat stratification. The savings can be astounding, because a ceiling fan operates on as little power as a light bulb.

Available in 36" or 52" diameters, the Hunter fan collection features seven motor colors—black, chestnut brown, antique white, brass, as well as black/brass, brown/brass, and white/brass combinations—with matching irons and canopies. Wooden blades, in antique white or pecan finish, are available with or without woven-cane inserts. Fans operate at two speeds with traditional pull-chain switch unless the buyer wants the optional solid-state control.

A full-color, eight-page catalogue with a companion energy bulletin is available for $1.00. Write to:

Hunter Division of Robbins and Myers, Inc.
P.O. Box 14775
Memphis, Tennessee 38114

Old Carolina Brick Co.

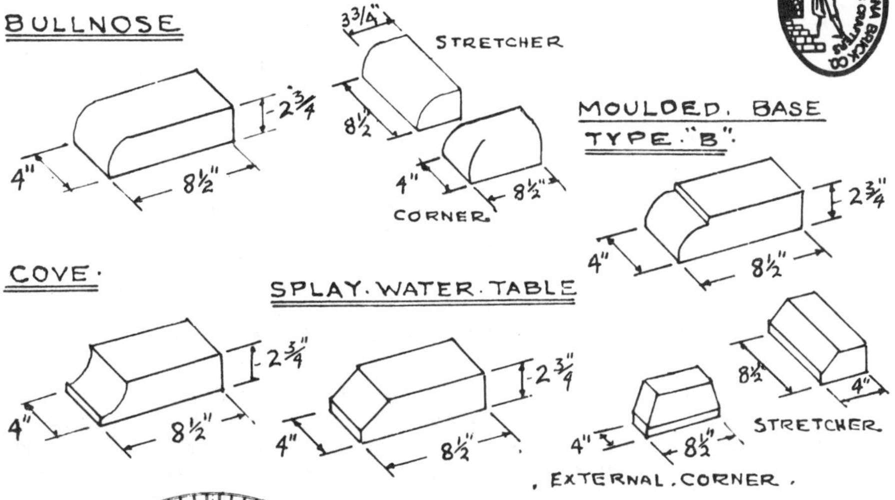

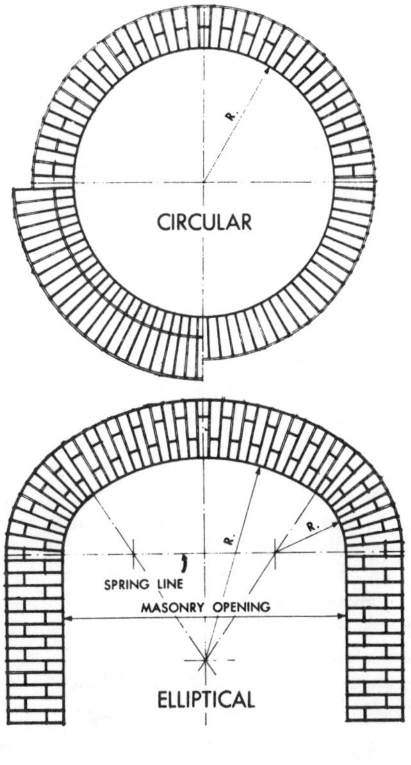

NEW-OLD BRICKS

If you want to build a truly authentic new-old house from the ground up, you may want to contact the Old Carolina Brick Company, ceramic crafters. They actually handmold each brick in a wood mold and individually characterize each to make it unique. To complement the old bricks, they also offer 8" x 8" Dutch pavers, split pavers, jack arches, and a variety of special shapes.

If you have an old brick house with a few holes or tumbled down areas that need matching brick, you are in luck. Old Carolina offers its expertise in matching its handmade brick to existing old brick. Send a representative sample of the brick to be matched, along with the approximate quantity desired, and Old Carolina Brick Company will return a sample of its brick with a price quotation.

Write to:

Old Carolina Brick Company
Route 9, Box 77
Majolica Road
Salisbury, North Carolina 28144
(704) 636-8850

COUNTY DIRECTORY.

The name following the name and occupation of citizens refer to their postoffice, the two numbers indicate the township and range of their residence.

The Directory proper, though not so accurate as could be wished, is as nearly so as the nature of the work permitted. There are so many citizens of a transient character, that it was impossible to avoid some little inaccuracy.

A.

Abernathy, Thos S, methodist preacher and planter, Spring Hill; 16, 3 e
Adams, Benjamin, planter, Linden
Adams, Thos J, clerk, Linden
Adams, Charles J, Jefferson; 17, 2 e
Adams, Spencer, planter, Shiloh; 14, 3 e
Adams, Homer, planter, Shiloh; 14, 3 e
Adams, Felix G, planter, Linden; 15, 4 e
Adams, Jno H, planter, Linden; 15, 4 e
Adams, Josephus A, shoemaker, M'Kinley
Adams, Rich H, planter, Uniontown; 17, 5 e
Alexander, J W, physician, Nanafalia; 13, 1 e
Alexander, Jno W, planter, Nanafalia; 13, 1 e
Alexander, J M, planter, M'Kinley; 16, 5 e
Alexander, D C, planter, M'Kinley; 16, 5 e
Alexander, J D, planter, M'Kinley; 16, 5 e
Allen, Robt E, hotel-keeper, Linden
Allen, Jno G, planter, Spring Hill
Allen, Wm C, planter, Spring Hill
Allen R H, planter, Nanafalia; 13, 1 e
Allen, H G, planter, Dixon's Mills; 13, 3 e
Allen, W B, teacher, Dixon's Mills; 13, 3 e
Agee, Isham A, planter, Shiloh
Agee, Z D, planter, Shiloh; 13, 4 e
Agee, J P, merchant, Hampden
Anderson, Jesse M, planter, Hampden; 13, 4 e
Anderson, Lewis, planter, M'Kinley; 16, 5 e
Anderson, J E, planter, M'Kinley; 16, 5 e
Anderson, W L, physician, M'Kinley
Anderson, Isaac, planter, M'Kinley; 16, 5 e
Anderson, Thos, laborer, Hampden; 13, 4 e
Anderson, T C, overseer, Spring Hill; 17, 2 e
Andrews, A S, methodist preacher, Dayton
Andrews, Jonathan, laborer, Shiloh; 13, 3 e
Armstrong, J H, overseer, Demopolis; 18, 2 e
Armstrong, Alex, planter, Newburn; 18, 5 e
Abrahams, E W, lawyer, M'Kinley
Abrahams, W T, physician, M'Kinley
Ayres, Saml H, planter, M'Kinley
Alston, Jas Y, tanner, M'Kinley
Alston, Nathl Y, planter, M'Kinley; 15, 5 e
Archa, P B, steward female academy, Dayton
Ash, W C, physician, Demopolis
Alvis, E S, overseer, Demopolis; 17, 3 e
Axom, Soloman, overseer, Spring Hill; 17, 8 e
Askew, M G, merchant, Dayton
Askew, H J, planter, Dayton
Autrey, R, planter, Dixon's Mills; 13, 3 e
Autrey, Noah, planter, Hampden; 12, 4 e
Autrey, Absolom, planter, Shiloh; 13, 3 e

ROBERT D. HART,

ATTORNEY AT LAW,

Linden, Marengo County, Alabama,

Will practice in this and the adjoining Counties, and in the Supreme Court at Montgomery.

J. P. JONES,

ATTORNEY AT LAW

AND

SOLICITOR IN CHANCERY,

Will practice in the Courts of Marengo and adjoining Counties.

OFFICE AT McKINLEY, ALA.

R. A. SAUNDERS,

ATTORNEY AT LAW,

LINDEN, ALABAMA,

Will practice in all the Courts of Marengo and the adjoining Counties, Ala.; and also in the Circuit and Probate Courts of Lauderdale and Kemper Counties, and the High Court of Errors and Appeals, Miss.

Z. O. RIDDLE. JAMES WOOLF.

RIDDLE & WOOLF,

COMMISSION MERCHANTS,

45 North Front & 46 North Commerce Streets,

MOBILE, ALA.

REGULAR SATURDAY EVENING PACKET.

The Fine Passenger Steamer

ALICE VIVIAN,

S. W. ABELS, CAPTAIN,

Will leave Mobile every SATURDAY EVENING, at FOUR o'clock P. M., for DEMOPOLIS and MERRIWETHER'S LANDING. Returning, will leave DEMOPOLIS at NINE o'clock A. M., the following TUESDAY, BICKLEY'S LANDING at TEN o'clock A. M., and all other Landings in proportion.

J. F. STANTON'S

AMBROTYPE GALLERY,

47 & 49 DAUPHIN STREET, MOBILE.

The subscriber takes much pleasure in informing his numerous friends and the public generally, that he still continues the

AMBROTYPING,

AT HIS OLD AND WELL KNOWN STAND,

47 and 49 DAUPHIN STREET,

And hopes that by giving his personal attention to all his patrons, and producing pleasing and perfect *Likenesses*, to merit a continuance of that patronage so liberally conferred upon him for the past eight years.

PERFECT LIKENESSES

Taken in all kinds of weather, and at prices within the reach of all.

DAGUERREOTYPES & AMBROTYPES

Carefully copied and enlarged.

J. F. STANTON.

LIFE IN THE PRE-CIVIL WAR ALABAMA

Even if you do not claim forebears in Marengo County, Alabama, you will enjoy browsing through the pages of *Tharin's Marengo County Directory for 1860-61.* This directory, reproduced photographically from the original copy by the Marengo County Historical Society, includes many interesting facts in addition to a complete list "embracing the names of the voters in the county, alphabetically arranged, their occupation, post office and residence . . . ." Such things as the statistics of mortality for the year ending June, 1860, showing many unusual causes of death, ranging from "eating dirt" and "putrid sore throat" to pneumonia; a nativity list of all voters of Marengo County, showing that citizens came from 12 foreign countries and 21 states; a recapitulation of the taxes for 1860 (playing cards were taxed at $.10, Bowie knives and revolvers at $2.00, silver watches at $.25); and a capsule history of the county and its principal "cities" are given. Also, there are numerous advertisements for goods throughout the book, making it a good source of information as to what items were important to people in those days. Each copy costs $3.00 (add $.50 postage).

Another interesting book offered by the Historical Society is *Days of Exile* by Winston Smith. It is the first detailed history, fully documented and footnoted, of the French settlers who came to Marengo, Greene, and Hale counties in 1817. The principal villages established in the nearly 100,000 acre French grant were Demopolis, Aigleville, and Arcola. The narrative includes the stories of the exile of the Bonapartists from France, their reunion in Philadelphia, their appeal to Henry Clay and Thomas Jefferson and James Monroe, their dangerous voyage to Mobile, the building of their settlements, their social life in the wilderness, and the ultimate failure of their experiment. Each copy costs $11.00 postpaid.

Order these books from:

Marengo County Historical Society
P.O. Box 159
Demopolis, Alabama 36732

Clifty Farm Real Tennessee Country Ham

Clifty Farm Country Meats is a family business—Truman Murphy, J. D. Murphree, and their sons. They tell us that the narrow little strip right around Paris has always been the most perfect place in the world to cure hams. They started offering their first hams for sale in the spring of 1955 and haven't caught up with production since that time.

We learned about the process of curing country hams from their detailed brochure: "They'd prepare a salt rub (a mixture of salt, molasses, and other "secret" ingredients that suited each family's taste) and smear it on the ham by hand. Then the meat was set on shelves in the smokehouse and left to "take the salt"—usually six to eight weeks but you had to add a day for every day the weather was below freezing. Another rule of thumb was to allow seven days per inch of thickness.

"The second stage of the curing process was smoking the meat. That usually took place in the early spring when the peach trees began to bloom. The hams were washed and hung from the rafters of the smokehouse. The fire was built right there on the dirt floor and a fellow had his choice of using hickory wood or oak or apple or peach bark or corncobs or sassafras or whatever he wanted. Whatever you chose, you had to keep that smoke going continuously for six to seven days or until the meat took on a thick, delicious, brown crust. If you did it too long, your meat was dry and tough. But, done just right, that crust served to seal in all the wonderful natural juices."

We think that the Murphrees and the Murpheys do it just right. Write to them for their interesting brochure, complete with recipes, and a pricelist.

Tennessee Valley Ham Company, Inc.
Clifty Farm Country Meats
P.O. Box 1146
Paris, Tennessee 38242

A CURTAIN CHARM

Now that you're "into" old houses, or old-*style* houses, you'll need to be thinking about curtains authentic to the period. Mather's has a wide selection of early-American-style curtains to add a touch of country charm. In some cases there are also matching bedspreads, shams, and canopies. And you can often get "old country" charm with "new country" convenience. A self-fringed textured-homespun tablecloth is "stain resistant, machine washable and permanent press." Most of the curtains are ruffled and/or valanced and look as if they would require only a sunny breeze to take you home.

Armchair decorators will delight in the gay prints, checks or stripes of actual fabric samples included in the "Old Manor House" catalog, which you can receive for $1.00. There is also a free brochure. Write to:

Mather's
31 East Main Street
Westminster, Maryland 21157

NOT YOUR RUN-OF-THE-MILL HARDWARE

It is plain from looking at the catalogue from Blaine Window Hardware, specialists in replacement hardware, that they have replacement parts for any kind of hardware you could imagine: for windows; lockers; toilet partitions; closets; patio or garage doors; plus screen splines, weatherstripping, and more. They stock over 15,000 different hardware parts. We had no idea that there *were* so many variations of casement locking handles, tube and tape balances, awning operators, screen clips, spring catches, etc., etc., etc.—let alone that one place might carry them all. No wonder they ask you to send a sample so that they can match it. You can get a catalogue for $1.00 by writing to:

Blaine Window Hardware Inc.
1919 Blaine Drive, R.D. 4
Hagerstown, Maryland 21740
(301) 797-6500

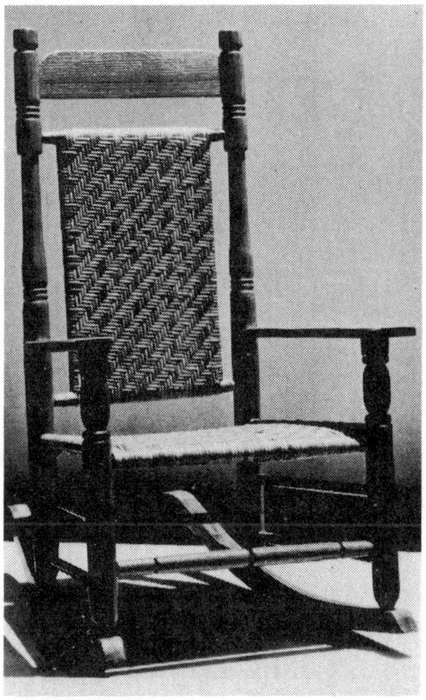

JUMBO ROCKERS

The Thomastown Chair Works, run by Sam Swearenger III in Thomastown, Mississippi, has been in business for almost 6 years now, manufacturing the large, comfortable rocking chairs everyone is so fond of remembering. The chairs are solid oak, with handwoven cane back and bottom, and can be used either indoors or out. They are available in either a natural or walnut finish. Currently, the chairs are available for $105.00 each—subject to change. Payment may be made by check or by Visa or Master Charge (give number and expiration date).

For more information, write:

Thomastown Chair Works
Box 93
Thomastown, Mississippi 39171

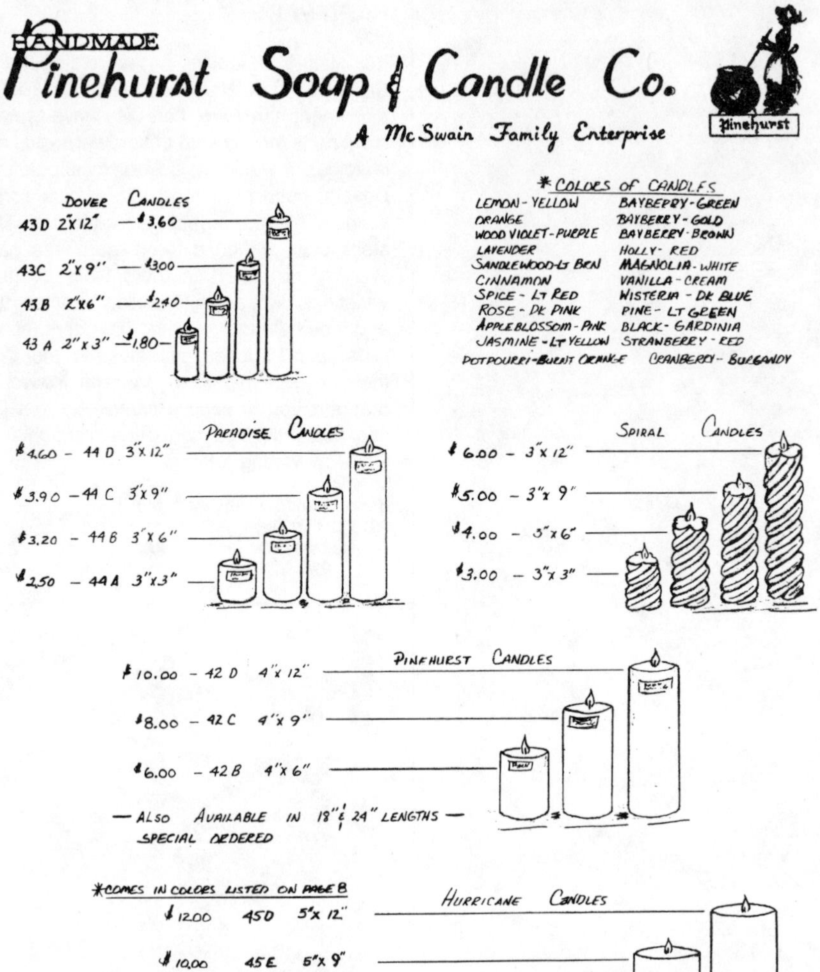

The Pinehurst Handmade Soap and Candle Company has a free catalog full of all kinds of candles. Reproduced is a spread from the catalog with price information. Add $1.25 for shipping, insurance, and handling; add $2.25 if you live on the West Coast.

Pinehurst Soap and Candle Company
Box 1148
Pinehurst, North Carolina 28354

OPELOUSAS' ANSWER TO THE FRENCH CHEF

Opelousas, Louisiana, bills itself as the "Gateway to Acadiana" and one of the premises upon which it bases this claim is the excellence of its "Cajun" cooking as epitomized by that practiced by Tony Chachere. Tony, described as a "noted sportsman, gourmet, businessman, raconteur, master salesman, chef and bon vivant of the area," has published a cookbook incorporating recipes that he has tried out during over 40 years of cooking. His watchwords, as he enters a kitchen to whip up some of his famous "All-Purpose Creole Seasoning" or "Tony's Oyster Chowder," are "Tonight, I'm gonna make 'em cry!" Maybe, if you buy Tony Chachere's *Cajun Country Cookbook,* you can make someone you love cry tonight! Send $5.50 plus $.75 tax and postage.

Order from:

Cajun Country Cookbook, Inc.
P.O. Box 1687
Opelousas, Louisiana 70570

"In the old times, whenever two fast boats started out on a race, with a big crowd of people looking on, it was inspiring to hear the crews sing, especially if the time were nightfall, and the forecastle lit up with the red glare of the torch-baskets. Racing was royal fun . . .

"In the 'flush times' of steamboating, a race between two notoriously fleet steamers was an event of vast importance. The date was set for it several weeks in advance, and from that time forward the whole Mississippi valley was in a state of consuming excitement. Politics and the weather were dropped, and people talked only of the coming race."
Mark Twain, LIFE ON THE MISSISSIPPI

HE MAKES FURNITURE "LIKE THEY USED TO"

Peter Kramer makes "reincarnated 18th century furniture." Though he uses power tools, he employs methods similar to those colonial cabinetmakers used. To increase the authenticity, Mr. Kramer has in mind, as he makes each piece, a fictional community named Cloven Mill. Thus, the "distressing" on each piece is done creatively, keeping in mind the actual marks that this piece of furniture would have acquired through use. Marks on colonial furniture, says Mr. Kramer, are "a clue that something happened." Each mark tells a story about the way the furniture would have been used. Each mark, along with the simple design, denotes character.

"Since I was quite young," explains Mr. Kramer, "I have gone to restorations and museums and studied pieces of furniture I would love to have owned. However, I could neither find them in antique shops nor afford them if I did. That's what got me started designing and making [this furniture]."

These pieces "look old but are my designs just as I would have made them had I lived 200 years ago . . . If you desire to order you may find that we have an interesting piece in our inventory that will meet your needs. I will be glad to send you pictures of a specific item if you cannot come to the showroom. If there is nothing suitable on hand I will design something special."

As you will see from these pictures, all Mr. Kramer's furniture is "something special."

Peter Kramer
Washington, Virginia 22747
(703) 675-3625

HISTORICAL DOCUMENTS

Henry Maslansky runs the Historical Documents N.O. company, a concern in New Orleans that publishes antiqued reproductions on parchment that "look old and actually feel old." Mr. Maslansky has selected several items which should be of interest to history buffs and has packaged them according to their subject matter. The packages, whose contents are listed here, sell for $2.00 each, plus a $.50 handling charge.

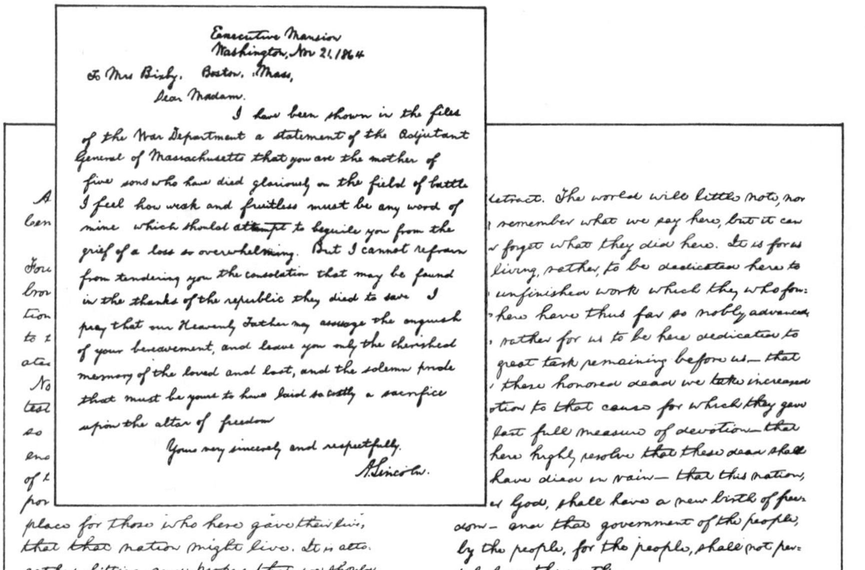

Executive Mansion
Washington, Nov 21, 1864

To Mrs Bixby, Boston, Mass,

Dear Madam.

I have been shown in the files of the War Department a statement of the Adjutant General of Massachusetts that you are the mother of five sons who have died gloriously on the field of battle. I feel how weak and fruitless must be any word of mine which should attempt to beguile you from the grief of a loss so overwhelming. But I cannot refrain from tendering you the consolation that may be found in the thanks of the republic they died to save. I pray that our Heavenly Father may assuage the anguish of your bereavement, and leave you only the cherished memory of the loved and lost, and the solemn pride that must be yours to have laid so costly a sacrifice upon the altar of freedom.

Yours very sincerely and respectfully.

A. Lincoln.

place for those who here gave their lives, that that nation might live. It is altogether fitting and proper that we should do this.

But, in a larger sense, we can not dedicate— we can not consecrate— we can not hallow— this ground. The brave men, living and dead, who struggled here, have consecrated it, far above our poor power to add

detract. The world will little note, nor remember what we say here, but it can forget what they did here. It is for us living, rather, to be dedicated here to unfinished work which they who fought here have thus far so nobly advanced. rather for us to be here dedicated to great task remaining before us— that these honored dead we take increased devotion to that cause for which they gave last full measure of devotion— that here highly resolve that these dead shall have died in vain— that this nation, God, shall have a new birth of freedom— and that government of the people, by the people, for the people, shall not perish from the earth.

Abraham Lincoln.

November 19. 1863.

Package #1: *Abraham Lincoln—Selected writings bearing his own signature.*
Contents: The Emancipation Proclamation 1863; Gettysburg Address 1863; letter to Mrs. Bixby (mother who lost five sons in Civil War) 1864; and Second Inaugural Address 1865.

Package #2: *General Robert E. Lee—Selected writings bearing his own signature.*
Contents: 1858 letter to Major McDowell; 1858 letter to President Buchanan; 1861 letter to his sister; 1861 letter to U.S. Army Commander, resigning his commission; 1863 letter to Jefferson Davis; 1865 Farewell Address; and Lee's last will and testament.

Package #3: *Civil War Battlefield Map and Recruiting Posters.*
Contents: Battlefield Map showing 78 locations; "The Union is dissolved" message; "Men of Virginia, to the Rescue" poster; and "Southern men avenge their wrongs" poster.

Package #4: *Louisiana Purchase and New Orleans—Selected letters and documents of Louisiana freedom, bearing signatures.*
Contents: Treaty of 1803 between the U.S. and the French Republic; Louisiana Purchase 1803; Letter by the first governor of Louisiana; and the report by Andrew Jackson of the Battle of New Orleans.

To order any or all of the above packages, write:

Historical Documents N.O.
333 St. Charles Avenue
New Orleans, Louisiana 70130

CHARLESTON RECEIPTS

The Charleston Receipts cookbook is a charming collection of recipes, Gullah sayings, line drawings of Charleston landmarks, and introductory verses, such as this one:

Throughout this book, as you will see,
We never mention *recipe*,—
The reason being that we felt,
(Though well aware how it is spelt!)
That it is modern and not meet
To use in place of old *receipt*
To designate time-honored dishes
According to ancestral wishes.

Indeed, many of the receipts (if you will) do trace themselves back to an earlier era, but most have been translated from the original "pinch of this, size of an egg of that" to more accurate measurements. We get the flavor of that bygone time, however, in such Gullah exchanges as this:

"No, Ma'am, I ain' fuh measure. I jes' jedge by my own repinion. I teck muh flour en' muh brown sugah, en' two-t'ree glub un muhlassis."

"What do you mean by glub?"

"You know de soun' muhlassis meck w'en 'e come fum de jug? Glub! Glub!"

Cookbooks are $5.00, postage and handling $.75.

Order from:

Charleston Receipts
Junior League of Charleston
P. O. Box 177
Charleston, South Carolina 29402

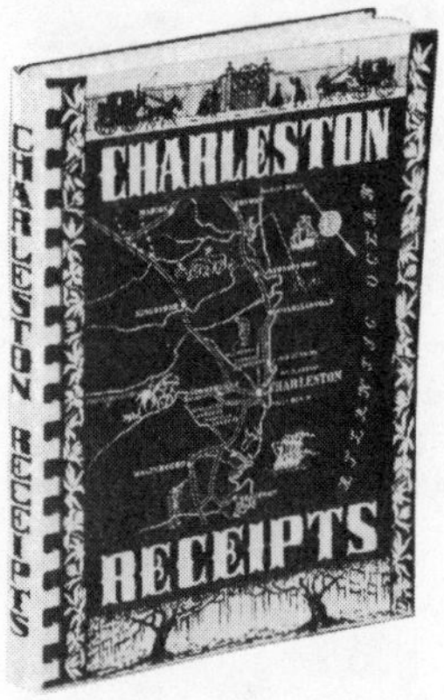

CHARLESTON RECEIPTS

Baked Hominy

2 cups cooked hominy, preferably hot
⅔ cup milk
⅓ stick butter
2 eggs

Beat butter into hot hominy (if using cold hominy, melt butter before adding). Beat eggs until light, add milk to eggs, then stir this mixture into hominy. Put in oven dish and set in pan of water. Bake in moderate oven (375°) for about an hour. (A little more butter and another egg may be added for extra richness.) Serves 6.

MRS. LOUIS T. PARKER (Josephine Walker)

Fried Hominy

HOMINY & RICE CHEESE & EGGS

Man, w'en 'e hongry, 'e teck sum egg or cheese an' ting an' eat till e' full. But 'ooman boun' fuh meck wuck an' trouble. 'E duh cook!

Never call it "Hominy Grits"
Or you will give Charlestonians fits!
When it comes from the mill, it's "grist";
After you cook it well, I wist,
You serve "*hominy*"! Do not skimp;
Serve butter with it and lots of shrimp.

Hominy

Hominy has long been a favorite in the Carolina Lo... This corn preparation, boiled with water and salt, was ... most every household for breakfast—not as a cereal ... and cream, but mixed with butter and eaten with a ... bacon, eggs or fish cakes. It was not frequently used f... was often on the supper table, either cooked in the ... or, more often, in the form of fried hominy, bal... "Awendaw." These concoctions...

CHARLESTON RECEIPTS

Boiled Hominy

1 cup grist
4½ cups water
1 rounded teaspoon salt

Formerly, the grist which could be procured in fine, medium, or coarse grind, according to preference, had to be washed in several waters. It was often soaked overnight or for several hours in a pot and then boiled in that utensil with the same water. When it began to cook, it was allowed to boil hard, uncovered, being stirred constantly to keep from scorching. It was then covered and cooked on a slower heat, stirred from time to time for the last ½ hour. The hominy was sometimes beaten up with butter before being served. Today, the packaged "grits" may be added directly to boiling water and cooked for a shorter time, but should still be stirred frequently until done. (Hot water may be added if it becomes thicker than desired.) Serves 4.

MRS. LOUIS T. PARKER (Josephine Walker)

Pressure Cooked Hominy

A modern way of cooking an old favorite.

1 cup grist
3½ cups water
1 teaspoon salt

CHARLESTON RECEIPTS

Hasenpfeffer

1 rabbit
Vinegar and water
1 sliced onion
Butter
3 cloves
1 bay leaf
1 cup thick sour cream
Salt and pepper

Disjoint rabbit, wash and place in crock or jar with enough vinegar and water in equal parts to cover. Add onion, a few cloves, bay leaf, salt and pepper to taste. Let the meat soak for 2 days. Then wipe dry and brown in hot butter, turning frequently. Slowly add some of the solution used for soaking the meat to the depth of ¼ of an an inch. Cover tightly and simmer until done (about 30 minutes). Do not boil. Just before serving stir sour cream into sauce.

MRS. R. O. DION (Eleanor Walker)

Squirrel

Squirrel is one of the finest and tenderest of all wild meats. Its flavor is mild, rarely gamey. There is no need for soaking, and seldom any need for parboiling. They should be cleaned as soon as possible after shooting, but skinning may wait until they are to be cooked.

MISS MARGARET WALKER

Broiled Squirrel

Clean squirrels and rub with salt and pepper. Brush with fat and place on hot broiling rack. Broil 40 minutes, turning frequently and basting with drippings every 10 minutes. Serve with gravy from drippings and season with 1 to 2 tablespoons of lemon juice.

MRS. W. W. HUMPHREYS (Martha Lynch)

137

HARVESTING RICE

138

CHARLESTON RECEIPTS

Mrs. Ralph Izard's "Awendaw"

1½ cups hominy, cooked
1 heaping tablespoon butter
3 eggs
1½ cups milk
¾ cup corn meal
½ teaspoon salt

While hominy is still hot, add butter and eggs beaten very light. Then gradually add milk and when well mixed, add corn meal and salt. The batter should be like thick custard. Pour in deep greased pan, bake in moderate oven. (375°). Serves 6-8.

MISS EMMA GAILLARD WITSELL

Grainy Hominy

2 cups raw grist
Salt to taste

Wash grist and drain carefully; place in double-boiler, cook for 2 hours, stirring frequently with a fork. Add salt after 1½ hours of cooking time. When done, hominy should be white and flaky with every grain apart. This is an old plantation dish and is served with gravy. It is delicious. Serves 4-6.

MRS. STUART DAWSON (May Hutson)

Hominy Surprise

2 cups grist
1 tablespoon salt
8 cups water

...ok grist until thick (about 30 or 40 minutes). Pour into ...ixing bowl and add:

...w eggs
...p grated sharp cheese
...lespoon black pepper
1 tablespoon Worcestershire
1 cup milk
1 tablespoon butter

...horoughly and pour into baking dish, reserving enough ...ver top. Sprinkle with paprika. Bake 1 hour, or longer, ... oven. This is good with cold sliced ham. Serves 8.

MRS. JACK W. SIMMONS (Irene Robinson)

142

HANDMADE TILE FOR STYLE

Something about handmade tile makes you think of the warmth of your grandmother's kitchen or the sunny breeze as you sat on her tiled porch. The tile shown here (Elon's "Saltillo") is unglazed terra cotta with the variations in color and surface that bespeak individual construction. You can get several styles from Elon Tile, including two-inch round, ten-inch octagonal with four-inch insert, hexagon (4", 6", 8", 10", 12", 15"), square (2", 4", 6", 8", 10", 12", 15"), and lattice (4" x 8" or 6" x 12"). (Since these tiles are handmade, all the sizes are approximate.) There are other styles with fanciful names like "Venice," "Dijon," and "Espana." They are also available in unglazed "chocolate."

For your fireplace or to adorn your kitchen or bathroom, there are handmade decorative tiles in soft, glowing colors. Especially interesting for the kitchen are the designs of flowers, fruits, and vegetables. A choice of colors is offered on most of the designs. Four-inch tiles of this type are regularly in stock, with some two inch and six inch. Eight-inch tile must be special-ordered. Custom designs can be accommodated.

You can even get handmade sinks, decorated with colorful birds and flowers (that remind you of your grandmother's pitcher and wash bowl) and accessories: towel racks, recessed soap holders, tooth brush and tumbler holders, hooks and toilet roll holders.

For information write to:

Elon Tile of Florida, Inc.
1320 Stirling Road
Dania, Florida 33004
(305) 923-8103

SOLID COMFORT

Often upon entering an old house, one gets a feeling of solidity, of things that matter, of attention to detail—all of which contribute to a sense of peace, a sense of being taken care of. One feels that someone—someone of taste and judgement—cared. The smooth utilitarian lines of today have their place, but for comfort, solidity, and charm, nothing can beat the cornices and paneling of some of the more ornate 18th century houses.

To have such mouldings and cornices and wall panels hand carved today, however, would be so expensive as to be out of the question. If you are looking for the elegant solidity in your new house that these old-time touches can provide, the Driwood Moulding Company may be your answer.

Driwood Period Mouldings are not composition. They are not plaster. They are machine-processed mouldings embossed out of hardwoods, in some instances in combination with wood fibers to give economy in price, durability, and adaptability. And they are authentic in design—architecturally correct. Driwood Mouldings will not chip or crack. They are stocked in poplar suitable for use in white or color work. They can also be obtained to order in genuine maple, walnut, oak, or mahogany. They are easy and economical to erect due to the fact that they are supplied in lengths from 6 to 16 feet. You can get ceiling cornices, plate rails, ceiling panels, chair rails, wall panel mouldings, bases, door and window casings, and pilasters.

You may also be interested in Driwood custom millwork, produced by skilled craftsmen working to classical details and standards of the Architectural Woodwork Institute. Custom woodwork items include entrances, special doors, raised panel work, case and cabinet work, overdoor and mantel treatments, straight and curved stair work and handrails.

A catalogue is available for $1.00. For it or information write to:

Driwood Moulding Company
P.O. Box 1729
Florence, South Carolina 29503
(803) 662-0541

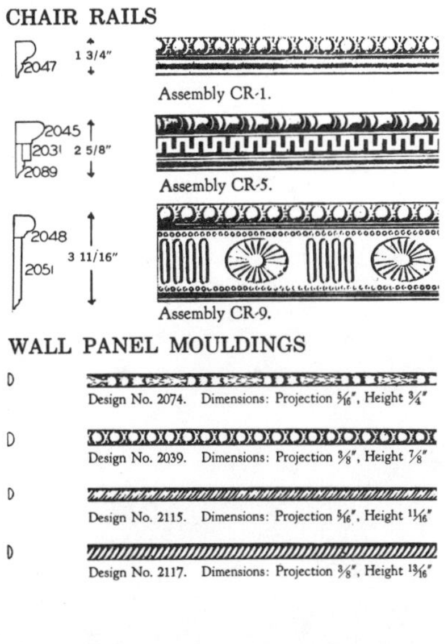

This elegant ceiling piece is made of styrene stock and molded under pressure. W. T. Weaver's catalogue suggests: "Only the pocketbook knows the difference."

NO MORE SMOKE-FILLED ROOMS

Established in 1889 by W. T. Weaver and his brother, W. T. Weaver and Sons specializes in hard-to-get hardware items. From them you can get colonial-style rim locks, front door hardware and knockers, foot scrapers, and shutter dogs. You can get handcrafted light fixtures. You can get brass towel rings, robe hooks, and switch plates. You can get polished brass and polished or brushed chrome bathroom fixtures and decorated washbowls.

These are just a few of the many items. One of the more unusual is a fireplace damper reminder. (It is a sign on a chain that says "Damper is closed." No more smoke-filled rooms!) Another is The Philadelphia Busybody ("Ben Franklin's Burglar Alarm"): a unique arrangement of mirrors which, when installed outside a second story window, allows you to see who is at your door or coming up the street without being seen yourself.

For information write:

W. T. Weaver and Sons, Inc.
1208 Wisconsin Avenue, N.W.
Washington, D.C. 20007
(202) 333-4200

"When we presently got under way and went poking down the broad river, I became a new being, and the subject of my own admiration. I was a traveler! A word never had tasted so good in my mouth before. I had an exultant sense of being bound for mysterious lands and distant climes which I never have felt in so uplifting a degree since."
Mark Twain, LIFE ON THE MISSISSIPPI

Jack Jeffers

EARTH

Water in large amounts,
earthbound and cumbersome,
laces itself into the gravity of its boundaries,
but a single sun-drenched droplet
resting on the fragile symmetry of a lilypad
somehow whispers infinity.

JV

Earth Index

The Earth is Full of Thy Riches

"In speaking of a natural thing most men assume a natural law. All things in nature are governed by this law. Man begins by saying, 'of course,' before any of his senses have a chance to come to his aid with wonder and surprise. The result is that he dies, and his neighbors and his friends murmur with the wind, 'of course.'"

Nobody would say "of course" about Walter Inglis Anderson, who wrote the above in his notebook. The two books that concern his work, *The Horn Island Logs* and *A Painter's Psalm: The Mural in Walter Anderson's Cottage* (Memphis State University Press), both testify to the "wonder and surprise" of which his senses were capable.

The most recently published, *A Painter's Psalm:* is a beautiful little book, each page of which is exquisitely bordered by screened running motifs from Anderson's paintings. The first color plate is of a modest cottage amid lush southern greenery. The second is a photograph of what might be paradise, or at least

fairyland. It is, however, a room: every inch of the walls and ceiling of this room is covered with warm loving colors and uncontainable light—light bursting from the walls, light carrying the natural sunlight streaming through the windows into the very heart of the reader. A wonderful foldout of the room's four walls surrounds us with a fairyland of nature: deer, birds, a possum, cats, an alligator, fish, frogs—all melting out of their natural setting. The colors and strokes of the figures are so like the background that they literally seem to form or "materialize" out of it—a veritable frenzy of creation. (I have never encountered such a happy marriage of Post-Impressionist strokes and colors to the natural world.) The ceiling is a giant zinnia of which Anderson wrote:

Oh, Zinnias,
Most explosive and illuminating
Of flowers,
Summation of all flowers,
Essence of excentric form,
Essence of concentric form!

Perhaps most extraordinary of all the feelings of "wonder and surprise" induced by this incredible room is the viewer's impression of its being filled with light and yet, for all the light in the room and despite the superb artistry plainly at work, the simultaneous impression that his eye is drawn through the window to the outside. Intrigued, one reads the sympathetic commentary by Redding Sugg and absorbs the paintings (photographed with consummate skill by Gil Michael). One discovers that Walter Anderson painted the room's east wall so that its glowing, crowing cock would top the rising sun itself. He painted the south wall to embellish, with thunderheads and rainbows and birds and animals, the noonday sun. And he painted the west wall as a frame for the sunset. After viewing such a tribute to the cycles and laws of nature, one is not surprised to learn that Walter Anderson's survivors discovered, copied in his own hand, one of the great human tributes to the divine plan of the world. It was Psalm CIV from the King James Bible, which includes the verse:

> *Oh Lord, how manifold are thy works! In wisdom has thou made them all: the earth is full of thy riches.*

It was his copying of this psalm that gave the book, *A Painter's Psalm,* its title.

But where is this room that has brought the outside inside and yet directs the richly satisfied eye outside again? And who is or was this man, who was able to create such an ecstasy of nature? Why have we not heard of him or seen his work before? Why are the great museums of this country not clamoring for his paintings? Why have we been deprived hitherto of the delight of his work? All these questions arise as one eagerly devours this enchanting little book.

The answers are fascinating. Walter Anderson lived as a recluse in this modest house for the last eighteen years of his life. Apparently no one knew of this great work of his life until after his death in 1965 when his family entered the locked room for the first time. Redding Sugg suggests: "It burst upon the Anderson family, bereaved and thinking they had to do only with the liquidation of the remains of a tragically aborted talent, as a note of affirmation, as exhilarating as it was unexpected."

Anderson's artistic talent had already been recognized at the Pennsylvania Academy of the Fine Arts, where he was formally trained and was influenced by a teacher who had been a "familiar of the Impressionists." After his graduation from the Academy, he received an award for travel and study and went to France in 1928. Then at the age of 26 he returned to his family in Ocean Springs, on the Gulf Coast of Mississippi. Here his family had bought a large tract of wooded land and his older brother Peter had built the now-famous Shearwater Pottery. When Walter married in 1933, he and his bride were given a cottage (the cottage which was to become the site of his great work) on the property. He and his younger brother James built an annex to the Shearwater Pottery "where they designed and produced the amusing and inexpensive figurines which they called 'widgets.' " He supplemented his income with commissions from the Works Progress Administration (this being the heart of the Depression) for murals in public buildings. But, according to Sugg, "Anderson was extremely ambivalent about selling or exhibiting his work—drawings, watercolors, and surely the cottage mural—that most directly expressed his painterly commitment. He was likely to state his occupation when he had to . . . not as artist or painter but as 'decorator.' In that capacity and with an eye to the market, he designed pottery, now much sought by collectors, for production in his brother Peter's nearby Shearwater Pottery, and linoleum block prints. His paintings . . . were private affairs conducted on principles very different from those of artists who aim for reputation." This is one reason, no doubt, why we have been deprived of Anderson's work for the last fifty years.

However, another reason may be that in 1937, the year of his first child's birth, Walter Anderson had what was later "tentatively diagnosed" as a schizophrenic episode and asked to be hospitalized. At that time one of his doctors at a clinic at Johns Hopkins "ventured the opinion that if he [Anderson] could return to Ocean Springs in circumstances relieving him altogether of pressure he had the personal resources to work out an adjustment." Over the next several years he was in and out of hospitals and finally returned home. According to Redding Sugg, "From this point began, if not anything which can intelligibly be called a cure, the adjustment which culminated in the romance with Horn Island."

Horn Island is "one of a series which comprises the barrier separating the Mississippi Sound from the Gulf of Mexico." To it Walter Anderson, after his return, would often row, and camp on it in a rude hut or even under his careened boat. He would make a fire and cook and eat the contents of cans that had been washed up by the waves. He would often trail a particular bird or animal for days, recording its actions and appearance in his logs, describing how he felt about it and how he thought it felt about him. He recorded an almost social relationship between them, much as an 18th century diarist might have described the various characters he met at tea parties:

> *. . . in clear water between two pools, a very ancient and barnacled horseshoe crab, very still with the clear water moving over him, and the ripple marks beneath.—He moved, put his nose into the sand, rose up and turned a complete somersault—on his back, all his legs kicking—he rolled over on his side and was his still self again. It was as if Mr. Chesterton while promenading the deck of the Queen Mary had done the same thing.*

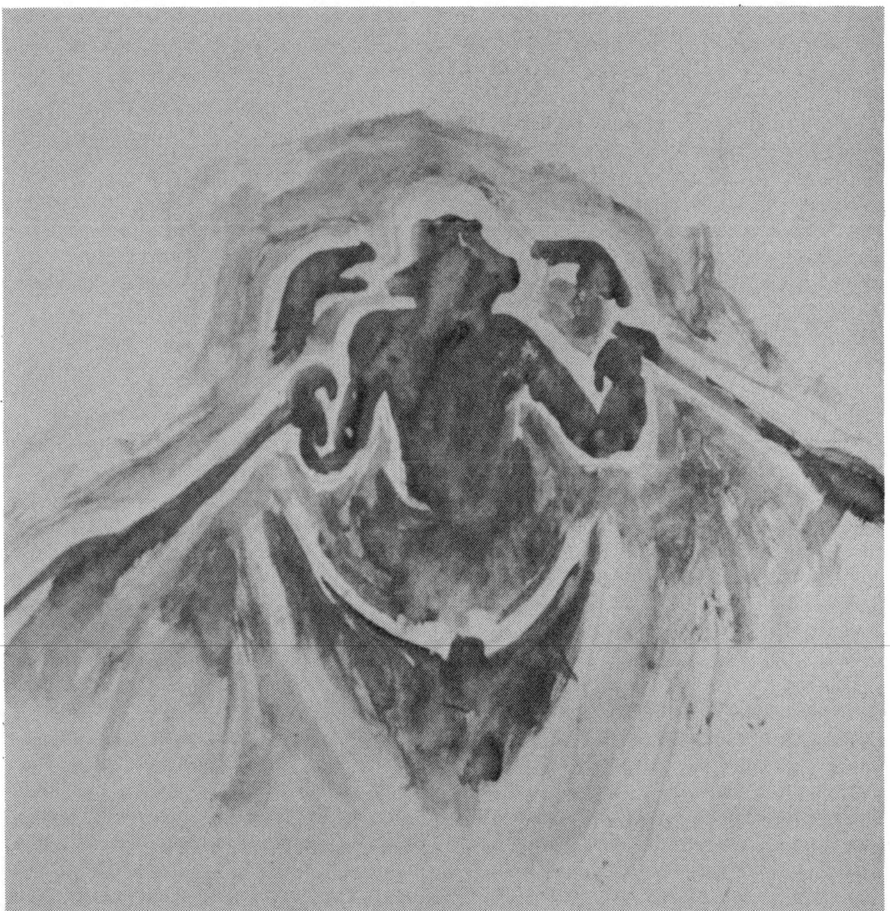

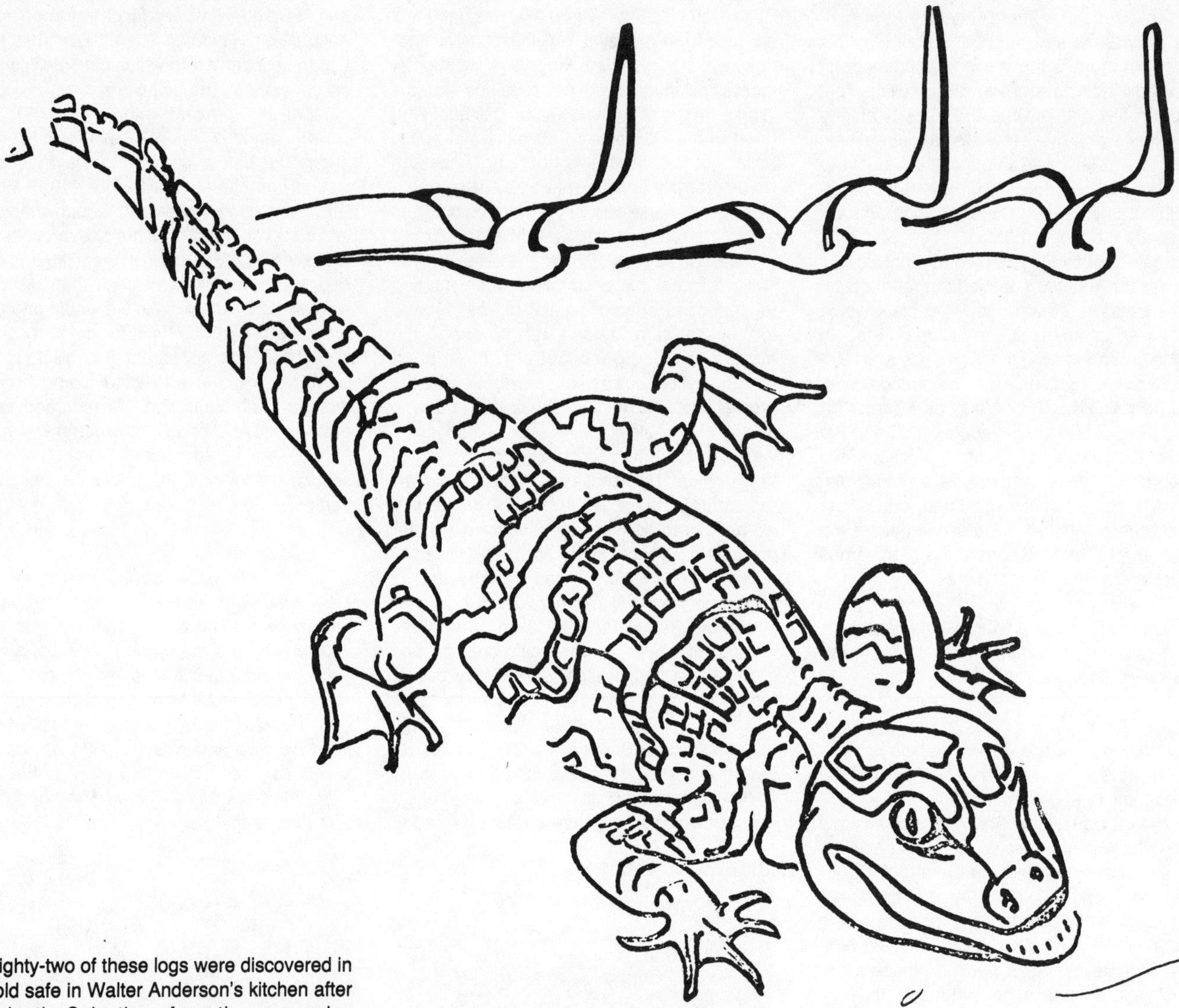

Eighty-two of these logs were discovered in an old safe in Walter Anderson's kitchen after his death. Selections from them comprise (along with many of his paintings and drawings) *The Horn Island Logs,* which are extremely interesting for the philosophy they illustrate; for what they tell us of the painter's eye at work; and for what they illuminate about Anderson's connection with nature that, along with his great talent, produced his "psalm." They detail his close and stark relationship with the flora and fauna of the Gulf Coast that live in his paintings. As one reads through these often minute descriptions of the activities and appearance of a tern, a duck, a frog, or a snake, one increasingly gains the impression that these wild things were Anderson's people. He related to them with the directness and wonder of a child. He joined their world probably as closely as a human could.

But he did not seem to see his activities—lying or standing in water up to his shoulders in order to make a sketch, or hiding in bushes eaten by mosquitoes in order to capture his subject on paper without disturbing it—as unnecessarily difficult or peculiar (though he would have admitted the lack of comfort). Being uncomfortable was apparently a small price to pay for being, as he said, the "court painter" to nature:

I saw a magnificent thistle bursting into bloom—every thorn tense with anticipation of the presentation of its first flower to the sun. I am to be court painter and celebrate the christening.

What he did find strange was the fact that this close relationship to nature (and, by extension, to their own nature) was not nearly as important to other men as it was to him. He wrote:

It is not enough to call a man a fool or a lunatic, yet it is hard to argue that he is dead. He can smell and touch and hear and taste and even see; but his relation to life, to being, to existence, is so incredibly vague that, to his intelligence, he can barely seem alive.

Whether he crawled on his belly through a swamp or lay on his back in a puddle, there can be no doubt that Anderson's own intelligence found him exceedingly alive. A watercolor he did of himself lying naked on his back in a "nullah" (puddle) displays such a lightness and joy of existence that he might have been a butterfly. In seeking an accommodation for himself within or without the world of men, he had apparently found for himself a kind of earthly paradise. The joy of it permeates all his paintings and creates their amazing luminosity. No wonder that, by contrast, the life of ordinary men seemed dead.

The accommodation that Anderson discovered for himself within (or on the fringe of) the natural world was literally that of medium. According to his theory, it was he who would help nature to, in a sense, discover itself. He would do this by studying, sketching, and

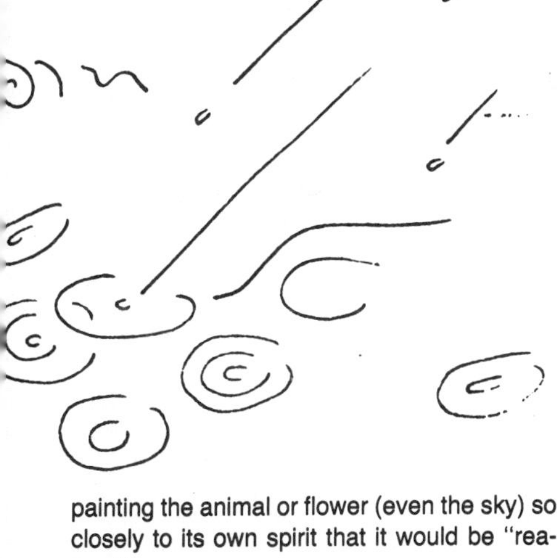

painting the animal or flower (even the sky) so closely to its own spirit that it would be "realized."

> *I saw a wonderful thick flock of them—a pattern of terns, almost a tone, changing from white to dark in flight so that the spiral form is brought out by the values of the bodies against the sky. A mosaic sky—of birds, of feathers: the celestial inverted cone of heaven, always there but needing to be realized.*

Almost—he was giving nature the gift of consciousness, a gift that Anderson did not seem to consider diminished by the fact that nature could in no way accept it. But as he accorded nature consciousness, he seemed to withdraw it from his own species. He might describe people (except for his relatives) from the point of view of an animal:

> *While I was painting, two ferocious hunters appeared with guns and a dog.*

Or from the point of view of an omnipotent painter:

> *.. fishing boat got in my way and out popped a pink man with yellow hair. . . . I saw a very black and active moccasin, and three fisherman—two white, one a deep and flowing pink, half a mile away—azalea pink.*

The Horn Island Logs give us a painter's-eye view of his world. We are allowed a peek at the process of creation. We can see how the forms arrange themselves for Anderson into a pattern, in a scene in which the rest of us would see only objects. Even his drawing of raindrops on water is perfectly organized by his creativity. And the birds, for him, would somehow always arrange themselves obligingly into a design:

> *The beauty was there. . . . There were tremendous cumulus clouds reaching to the zenith and with the wind behind them. Then the man o'war birds all floated facing this cloud three or four deep in strata with the concave fronts of their wings to the full convex forms of the clouds. They were innumerable, as the forms in a pattern repeat where if a small part is shown the effect is beyond counting. With this difference [that] there was a form created by perspective so that the effect was usually that of a cone elongated and horizontal to the earth or vertical and reaching to infinity.*

But color and light were his most joyous tools, as we might expect from one influenced by the Impressionists and Post-Impressionists. When we read that " . . . there were cows on the dunes which were pink . . ., " we accept that as the value accorded by the painter's eye because we trust Anderson, who has rendered nature for us so perfectly. We have understood that his pink and blue deer could have been no other color, certainly not a "realistic" brown; we have adored his short brush strokes of white, which (impossibly, yet inevitably) compose a possum; we have accepted his blue and green and pink cranes whose wings seem to melt out of the rushes. And so we believe it when he says:

> *It is approaching the magic hour before sunset, when all things are related, and are organized thru color. . . . But the variety of form will obviously be derived from the variety of color; instead of a round bird form being given a white coat the bird form will be round because it is white, like a marble or a white cloud. The grass will be elongated and thin because it is flat and green, so that one feels that the forms do change as the sun gets lower and the color more intense.*

It was not important to Walter Anderson that he be recognized or that his paintings be widely viewed. Indeed, quite the opposite was apparently his preference. However, seeing and being uplifted by his paintings is important to us Americans. Artists can do a great deal for their society. They can see visions for it. They can recognize its deepest dreams and express them for it. The expressions of its shared hopes can create a bond among the members of society and between them and the artist.

We Americans are often wary of the fine arts, perhaps supposing ourselves (such is the value placed on expertise in our society) not expert enough to relate to and understand them. But most of us are still inspired by the wonders of nature, its cycles and order, whether the inspiration comes from backpacking in the wilderness or merely seeing the Everglades on TV. We do not feel that we have to be "experts" in nature to relate to it and to feel that it has meaning for our lives. Perhaps nature may be the last common denominator of symbols and passion for such a widely heterogeneous people as Americans.

Through his transcendent portrayal of nature, Walter Anderson touches the shared hopes of more of his compatriots than he would ever have imagined. We need to know about him and see his work, feel the pride of understanding and the thrill of being transported by this great American artist.

—*M. J. H.*

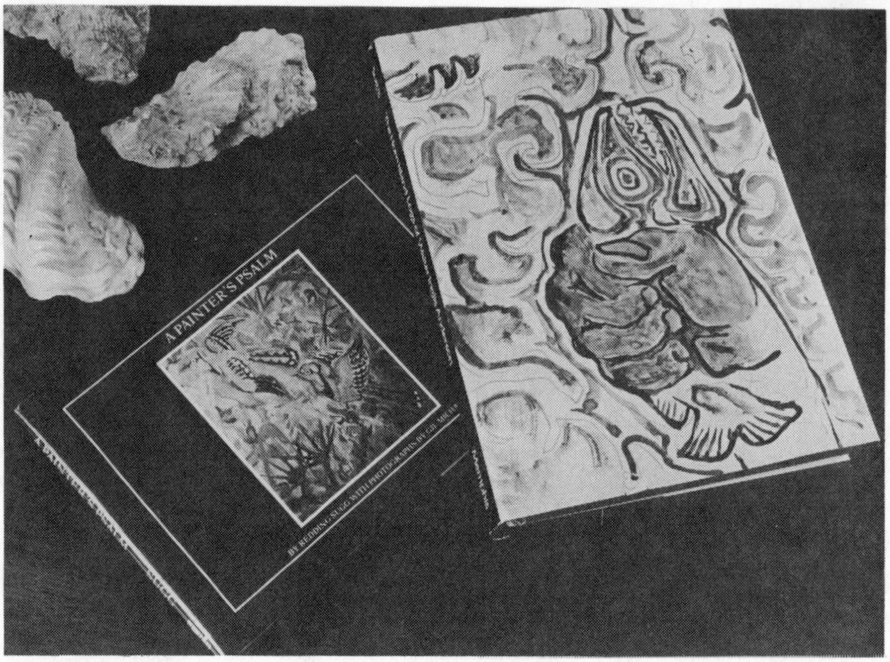

You can order either of these books (*A Painter's Psalm*—$17.50, and *The Horn Island Logs*—$19.95, Memphis State University Press) through Memphis State University Press or the Friends of Walter Anderson. Tours of the Anderson cottage can be made by appointment; call (601) 875-4678 or 875-7320 or write the address below. For $10.00 you can get a set of four reproductions of Walter Anderson's watercolors ("Water Lilies," "Palmettoes with Flowers," "Sweet Gum Tree," and "Cherokee Rose"), each approximately 12 by 15 inches. You can join the Friends of Walter Anderson ($10.00 membership) in their fight to keep the Gulf Coast weather from dealing its normal fateful blows to the treasure trove of Anderson drawings and paintings.

From the Friends of Walter Anderson you can also order a set of 10 postcards (of shepherds—pictured) for $2.00 plus postage or 10 folded cards with envelopes (of wise men) for $3.50 plus postage. There are two other postcard designs not pictured.

Friends of Walter Anderson, Inc.
P.O. Box 328
Ocean Springs, Mississippi 39564

Some excerpts and drawings from The Horn Island Logs of Walter Inglis Anderson *(copyright 1973 by Memphis State University Press) have been reprinted in the Earth section of this book with permission of the publisher.*

And now...sea and earth....

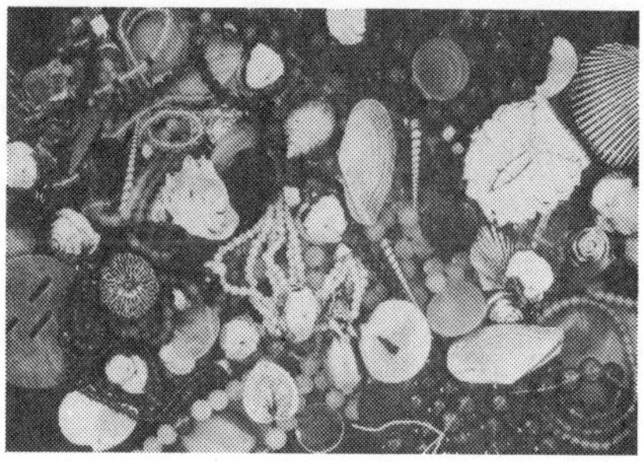

Many artists have been inspired by the sea—its depth and mystery and the fact that it is the cradle of life. Mignon Faget has focused her inspiration on jewelry. A jewelry designer whose training is in sculpture, Mignon Faget takes the beauties of nature and transforms them into silver, gold, and semi-precious stone designs.

"I like to play with the dynamics of a form out of context," she says, "the shell that is no longer a shell but a form in sterling or gold, juxtaposed with rich silks."

Mignon Faget made her first piece of jewelry in 1970. She melted some of her own sterling silver belongings in order to make a belt buckle, fashioned from a wax cast of a sand dollar she had found on the beach.

A look back over Mignon's ten years of designs shows that they have evolved naturally, one creation building upon another, almost like her favorite moon snail. She has been a collector of shells for years. She searches out ordinary as well as unusual shells. "A shell is one of the best primitive forms of architecture. When I reduce nature's forms to the least common denominator I discover endless possibilities," explains Mignon.

Her designs are timeless, always simple and therefore, versatile. She had a feeling for the "softening" of jewelry which led her into Slip Cords (her name for a series of tubular forms that can be moved up and down to create different effects). Then she decided to recreate the tactile qualities of silk and gauze in solid materials, as in her knot collection.

"I still do shells—they are classic now. And nature motifs like seeds and nuts and beans. I also love whimsical pieces from childhood recollections, like my animal cracker pieces," she said. Stones and beads have been added to the Mignon Faget collections. Important looks have been the two-strand bracelets of Austrian crystal with silver scarab clasps, or rose quartz beads with shell box clasp.

Commenting on her own recent concept and design development, Mignon says: "I find that my jewelry has evolved over the past few years from simpler, single-focus pieces toward more complex designs involving the structure of parts, the integration of contrasting textures, shapes, colors. An earlier almost exclusive involvement with gold and silver has gradually been joined by a fascination with gemstones, hence an investigation of carving as well as casting, color as well as the no-color of precious metals, and more abstract forms in addition to the reflection of nature's forms inherent in lost-wax casting. Rather than treating gemstones as an end in themselves, I want to use them as a medium for sculpture. I love their silky translucency, the glow of subtle colors, those accidents of nature that might ordinarily be considered flaws. Even their names invoke for me the air of mystery that surrounds them: moss agate, rose quartz, aventurine, smoky topaz. . . . "

Mignon Faget designs, produces, sells, and ships her creations from a century-old Victorian barge board cottage by the levee in New Orleans. The number of Mignon Faget enthusiasts is growing, as the line is carried in specialty and clothing shops throughout the United States. For information on the Collection and store locations, please contact:

Mignon Faget Limited
710 Dublin Street
New Orleans, Louisiana 70118
(504) 865-1107

GREENHOUSES FOR ALL SEASONS

Planning a greenhouse can be a most pleasant experience, but many gardeners need a little help in executing their plans. Problems such as the best type of structure to use, locations, correct heating, cooling, etc., confront the average buyer.

The construction of a greenhouse is probably the most important aspect; it is necessary that no corners be cut that would lower quality. Texas Greenhouse Company handles a complete line of greenhouses, and each piece of each house is given personal attention. They offer either aluminum or redwood as a framing material. The aluminum models have a steel substructure which allows you to hang heavy baskets without damaging the structure over the years. These models also feature vents which run the length of the greenhouse. The redwood models are made of clear heart redwood with aluminum gusset plates for extra strength, and they have individual roof vents. Double strength glass is also used to prevent breakage.

Ezyrected Greenhouses are available in several sizes as well as styles. Some may prefer the special glass-to-ground construction for added space, others to attach a greenhouse to an existing structure. Texas Greenhouse Company can adapt a greenhouse to practically any requirement. Greenhouses have been fitted to rooftops, on terraces, between buildings, against buildings, and as extensions to other buildings. *Ezyrected Greenhouses* can also be furnished in any number of sizes for commercial growers.

Send your request for a quotation and a free catalogue to:

Texas Greenhouse Company
Department ACS
2717 St. Louis Avenue
Fort Worth, Texas 76110

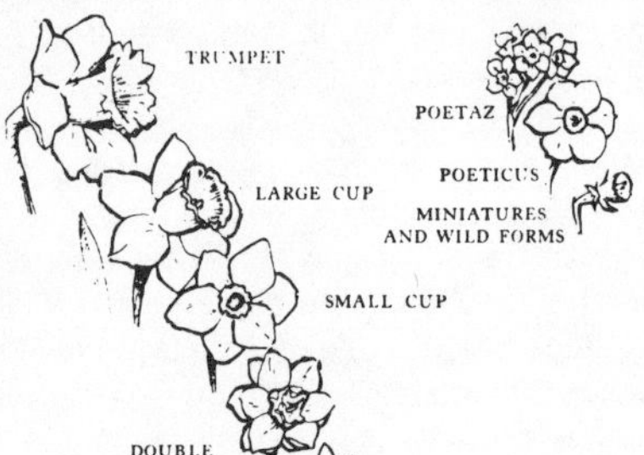

A CATALOGUE OF DAFFODILS

The Daffodil Mart in Gloucester, Virginia, sells daffodils, naturally. They grow 95% of the bulbs they sell. They are growing seedlings of their own in addition to over 2,000 established varieties.

Brent C. Heath is the owner of the Daffodil Mart, the third-generation Heath to manage it. His grandfather, Charles, founded the Mart when, as a gentleman farmer, he allowed the Dutch firm M Van Waverer & Sons to lease his land to grow their bulbs when Holland was plagued with a bulb-destroying worm around 1915.

In 1938, Charles's son George and his wife went into business for themselves and now Brent is continuing the tradition.

The Daffodil Mart prints a color catalogue of the many varieties of daffodils. The varieties are rated according to how well they grow. With each order, a set of detailed planting and growing instructions is sent. If you wish to receive a printed catalogue, send $1.00 to:

The Daffodil Mart
North, Virginia 23128

". . . there was quite a large alligator asleep with its tail in the water. He was about fifteen feet from me. I drew him then tried for a different point of view. Alligator rampant! in the air, then in the water." HORN ISLAND LOGS.

HEARTHSTONE LOG CABINS

Hearthstone Log Homes prides itself on building *real* log cabins. John Ricketson, who is a distributor, tells us that the 6" x 12" hand-hewn logs used in the cabins are the same kind of logs that our forefathers used. These homes will blend into any environment and can be used as permanent homes, second homes, guesthouses, and even commercial buildings, such as restaurants.

The uniqueness of these cabins and the thoroughness of their construction seem to depend on the use of the half-dovetail notch. This notch is cut so that the water always runs away from the cabin rather than back into the joints that are cut into the logs.

You may choose one of 16 pre-engineered homes or have your log home custom-built to your own specifications. On-site erection of your cabin can be furnished by Hearthstone, or you may choose to do the erection yourself or have your builder do it.

Write for additional details and a brochure.

Hearthstone Log Homes
P.O. Box 5092
Macon, Georgia 31208

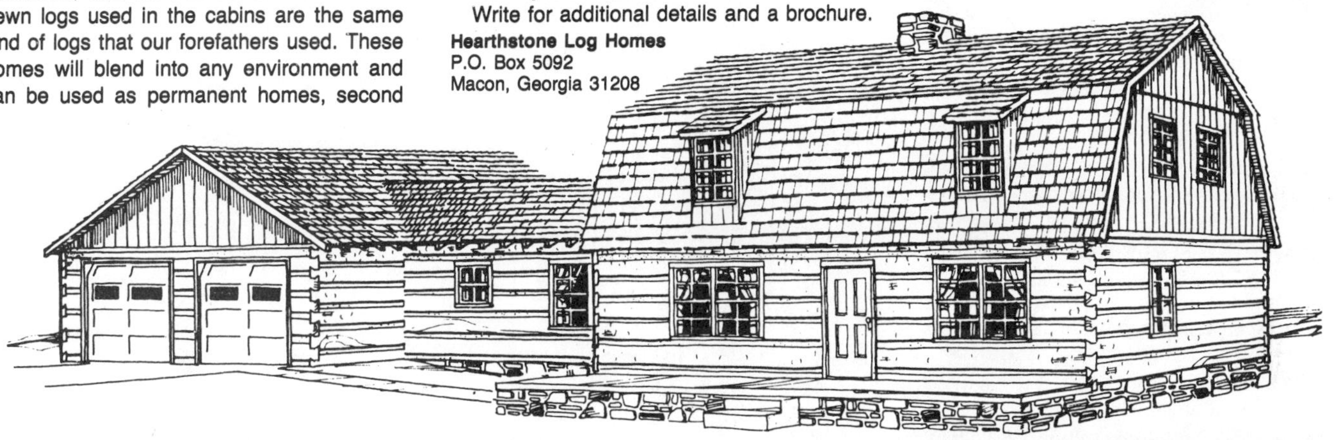

THE DO-IT-YOURSELF WEATHER BOOK
by Tim Campbell

Oxmoor House, Inc.
Birmingham, Alabama

The "blissfully ignorant attitude about weather is literally costing our economy hundreds of billions of dollars annually and yet, incredibly, no one really seems to care. For it is just naturally assumed, and casually accepted by all, that absolutely nothing can be done about it." This frightening observation makes Tim Campbell's *Do-It-Yourself Weather Book* invaluable reading in more ways than one.

Mr. Campbell is primarily concerned with the weather's effect on farming. As a qualified meteorologist, he tells farmers how they can "manage" the weather and obtain satisfactory crop results. Also, the general reader will be interested in some of the more amazing aspects of weather and climate, of which he is more than likely unaware.

Mr. Campbell attacks the unfortunate trend in television weather forecasting which has crept in in the last two decades. The direction has been increasingly away from quality and professional reporting, toward a melodious-voiced, beautiful body giving out gimmicky information on something she (or he) knows nothing about. This situation is all the more sad because eye appeal could be maintained if the television executives could be convinced that better information exists.

Also, the author points out, climate is just as variable as weather. Changes in the global climate affect every household in the world. For example, in 1815, the largest known volcanic eruption occurred when Tambora erupted in the Dutch East Indies. Two hundred and twenty million tons of ash were injected into the stratosphere. The result was a worldwide decrease in temperature. In 1816 there were frosts in the state of Pennsylvania every month of the year!

Mr. Campbell pictures and describes weather instruments measuring soil moisture, humidity-temperature indicators, wind-speed gauges, wind meters, and other instruments used in predicting the weather. All of these could be extremely helpful to the careful farmer who wants to insure a good crop yield. The author also includes an interesting section on cloud formations. At the end is a glossary of weather terms and expressions.

"It is not too far-fetched," says Mr. Campbell, "to assert that several hundred million dollars could be saved each year if every farmer in America knew what '50% chance of rain' meant." Sounds as if we could all be made a little weather-wiser, and this book could help.

—S.V.H.

PAPPY'S PINEY WOODS KINDLIN' KEG

Keep a supply of kindling on hand to start your cozy fires and have an attractive container as well: the reusable pine "Kindlin' Keg" from Piney Woods Products of Beaumont, Texas, comes with over 165 sticks of dry Southern pine kindling. The keg is an attractive addition to your fireplace accessories and can serve as a planter when empty.

Each keg is $7.50 plus $1.95 postage; or 2 for $18.50 prepaid. Order from:

Piney Woods Products
P.O. Box 7219
Beaumont, Texas 77706

> *"[I] did two water colors of Hermit Crabs. I'm beginning to feel like one of them without the protecting shell." HORN ISLAND LOGS.*

(The following article is reprinted by permission of *The Birmingham News*.)

PICK HERB GARDEN HINTS FROM CATALOGUE

By Pat McGuire

Just about every day, a new batch of catalogs arrives at our house. Some of them we read with delight, others fit the category of "junk mail."

But this past week, a most welcome little yellow catalog came in the morning mail. It's the 1979 offering from the Sandy Mush (N.C.) Herb Nursery and it's an absolute delight to read.

In 33 hand-lettered pages, the catalog presents the nursery's current listing of available herbs and tells you in a chatty, informative way about how to grow them, where to plant them, how much sun or shade they'll need and how they look in the landscape. There are even recipes for using dried herbs in potpourri and in wine and herb vinegars.

Charming line drawings of herbs with funny names like bee balm, rue and tansy are scattered through the pages. And in the back of the little booklet, there are five suggested herb garden plans which make you want to sit down and order everything necessary to start a Bee and Butterfly Garden, a Fragrant Garden or A Little Kitchen Border.

With spring just days away, the time to think about an herb garden is right now. The problem is in choosing just what kind of garden and how many plants you'll want to look after.

If you love to cook, there are dozens of herbs which, when picked fresh from your kitchen herb garden, add a special sparkle to almost any recipe.

French tarragon, with its anise-like flavor, is a "must" for gourmet cooking, according to the Sandy Mush Herb Nursery. You can grow your own horseradish, adding the leaves to salads in the summer and chopping the roots later for homemade horseradish sauce. A food processor makes quick work of the chopping.

Oregano is available in a creeping white-flowered variety and can be planted in a hanging basket near the kitchen door. A creeping rosemary is available, too. Just a few leaves do wonderful things for lamb, chicken or vegetables.

On your deck or terrace, you might try a sweet bay shrub in a clay pot or other container. The fragrant, glossy leaves are pretty to look at and are a special addition to stews, soups and sauces. When cold weather comes again, bring the sweet bay indoors and grow it as a house plant.

Thyme—a pleasant addition to poultry dishes, soups and salads—comes in many disguises. There are carraway, coconut, nutmeg, oregano and lemon scented varieties. Some of it grows upright and some creeps along the ground, making it ideal for rock gardens or to plant between stepping stones. Almost all varieties of thyme have pretty little blooms.

Some herbs have been used for centuries as medicinal aides. The juice from the crushed leaves of the aloe plant is often used to soothe burns. Feverfew once was used to treat fevers.

A garden planted with scented herbs is a special delight. Old fashioned lavender is a favorite and can be dried for use in sachets, soaps and potpourri mixes. There's lemon grass, which smells just like lemon drops, and lemon verbena, with its fresh lemon scent. And scented geraniums come in rose, lemon, spice, mint and pine scented varieties.

English pennyroyal is a welcome addition to rock gardens and its scent is said to repel insects.

You can dry herbs by hanging them upside down in bundles or placing them on a cookie sheet in the oven, with the door left open.

The best time for drying herbs is when they have just come into full flower, according to the Sandy Mush Herb catalog. Once the herbs are dried, it's important to store them in airtight bags or glass bottles, away from heat and light.

Since most herbs are perennials (they keep growing year after year), once you start your herb garden it will continue to produce for you—providing you give it tender loving care.

If you'd like to order an herb catalog for yourself, write to: Sandy Mush Herbs, Route 2, Surrett Cove Road, Leicester, N.C. 28748. There's a $1 charge for the catalog, but the Sandy Mush folks will subtract that amount if you place an order.

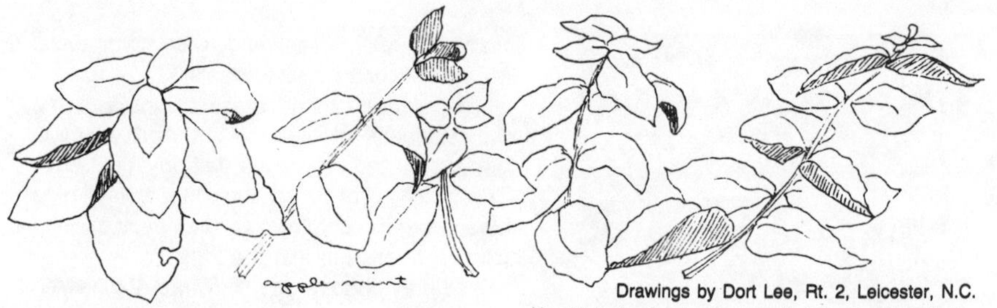

Drawings by Dort Lee, Rt. 2, Leicester, N.C.
Hand lettering by Jan Burkhead of Sandy Mush Herbs.

MINTS (MENTHA) - Especially easy to grow group of plants with a fascinating array of scents and tastes. All are good for teas - experiment! Also good with fruit dishes, jellies, lamb, peas. Root and stem cuttings, division.

APPLE MINT (Mentha suaveolens*) $.95 - 2 to 3 ft. tall, stiff stems have large, fuzzy, gray-green leaves with a slightly apple scent.

BLUE BALSAM TEA MINT (M. x piperita v.) 2 to 3 ft. plant has shiny, dark green leaves with a purplish tint. More pungent aroma and flavor than peppermint.

CORSICAN MINT (M. requienii) $2.00 - 1 inch, most unusual mint forms a dense, emerald green mat. Tiny round leaves have a strong creme-de-menthe scent. Use sharp knife to cut plugs for division.

CURLY MINT (M. aquatica v. Crispa*) $.95 - to 2 ft., has crinkly, light green leaves. Good mint flavor.

GINGER MINT (M. x piperita v.) $.95 - 1 to 2 ft. plant with tender, bright green leaves, strikingly variegated with gold. Combines taste of mint and ginger for a delicious change.

LEMON BERGAMOT MINT (M. x piperita v. citrata*) $.95 2 ft. plant with crinkly foliage. Refreshing lemon and mint flavor. Tolerates more sun than other mints.

ORANGE MINT (M. x piperita v.) $.95 - 1 to 2 ft. plant has broad, dark green leaves edged with purple. Has a definite citrus scent and taste.

PEPPERMINT (M. x piperita) $.95 - 2 ft. plant with narrow, dark green leaves, purple stems. Has true peppermint flavor. Makes a soothing tea for upset stomachs.

SPEARMINT (M. spicata) $.95 - 2 ft. plant with emerald green, shiny, heavily veined leaves. Traditional spearmint flavor.

SPEARMINT, NARROW-LEAVED (M. spicata cv.) $.95 - Same as Spearmint except narrow leaves.

DOOR STORE

Browsing through the Door Store catalogue makes you want to toss away all the furniture you now own in favor of some of the crisp, clean-lined, bright furniture pictured there. You need not worry that many others have had similar inclinations and that you'll end up with a living or dining room just like everyone else's. On the contrary, since the Door Store specializes in furniture-in-parts, you can choose from a large group of tabletops to match an even greater variety of pedestals and legs, and then you can finish to your own specification any of a large number of side chairs. And the end result will be a roomful of furniture like no one else's, with a distinct, yet classic, style.

The furniture available runs the gamut from Louis XV chairs, to Chinese Chippendale chairs, to classic bentwood rockers, to chairs designed by members of the German Bauhaus school of design, to steamer chairs like those used on Italian Line ships. The prices are reasonable; however, since many of the items are imported, prices are subject to more fluctuation than might be expected from other, domestic, lines of furniture.

Comfortable sofas are available, and several different styles of sofa-sleeping systems are shown. The shelf systems include a wide variety of elements from which to choose: walnut, mahogany, or rosewood shelves; steel, walnut, oak, or aluminum free-standing poles; brass, chrome, painted chrome, stained aluminum, or walnut wall-mounted standards; and brass, chrome, painted, walnut or wrought-iron brackets in a variety of styles. The possibilities end where your imagination stops.

A visit to the Door Store through its catalogue is the "next best thing to being there." Send $1.00 for 56 page catalogue. Express charges on orders are collect. No COD's.

The Door Store
3140 M Street, N.W.
Washington, D.C. 20007

Cartoon Chair
High gloss finish over aniline stain that lets wood grain show through. Gleaming in walnut, yellow, orange, red, or green. Sturdy natural rush seat. $69.

ORIGINAL PAWLEY'S ISLAND ROPE HAMMOCKS

Anyone who hasn't relaxed in a hammock has missed one of life's most pleasant moments. The Original Pawley's Island Rope Hammocks have been handicrafted for several generations in the coastal community of Pawley's Island, on the plantation coast of South Carolina.

The founder, A.H. "Doc" Lachicotte, Sr., began making rope hammocks some 60 years ago. He was taught the trade by his brother-in-law, Josiah Ward, an outdoorsman, who traveled to Charleston by boat to sell the rice from Waverly Mills. He had grown tired of sleeping on uncomfortable grass-filled mattresses that were excessively hot in the summertime.

Hammock weaving was introduced to the area 200 years ago by Portuguese sailors who made nearby Georgetown a port of call. The Pawley's Island Rope Hammock is handwoven from selected, high grade cotton twill twine. The staves are from giant oak trees in the area. They are sawed to size, boiled in a huge outdoor vat, and then shaped by forcing either end under a large beam across a curved surface. The supporting ropes at each end are secured to an ample sized metal ring. The coolness, softness and flexibility of the hammocks, plus their strength and long-lasting qualities, are outstanding features.

The most popular seller has a 54" x 82" body size with a 13' overall length. It is wide enough for you to lie crosswise as well as lengthwise. The price for the #13 medium model is $60.00 prepaid.

Order from:

The Hammock Shop
P.O. Box 308
Pawley's Island, South Carolina 29585

HATTERAS ROPE HAMMOCKS

For a memorable experience in leisurely living, stretch out and relax in a Hatteras Hammock. These hammocks are handcrafted by experienced weavers. Handsome oak stretchers keep the luxury size uniform. The soft, flexible cotton rope allows the breeze to cool you from all directions. Ideal for porches, patios, lawns, beach cottages and summer homes. The body size is 54" x 82" and 13 feet in length. The price is $58.00.

Order from:

Hatteras Hammocks, Inc.
P.O. Box 1602
Greenville, North Carolina 27834

"I went to Rabbit Springs for water and got both fire and water in the same place. All the ants of the island that was flooded have collected along the line of highest water and on the trash of rotten wood, tree bark, uprooted grass, etc. They have made temporary homes like people on the levee—and like people on the levee they don't like strangers and go for them blindheaded. So while I was filling jugs with water at one end of me, fire was consuming my lower half." HORN ISLAND LOGS.

The much admired mallard lands in a profusion of colors.

Winter Birding In the South

by STEVE PRICE

Each winter in the South, Mother Nature repeats one of her most spectacular, one of her most beloved, and one of her most baffling wonders: the mystery of waterfowl migration.

As early as August and September, ducks and geese begin leaving their nesting grounds in the far Canadian north on the long flight southward. Obeying some ageless instinct, untold millions of birds take wing, following the same four flyways their kind have taken since time began.

Three of those air corridors terminate in or pass through the South. The Atlantic Flyway follows the Eastern seaboard down to Florida; the Mississippi Flyway draws some 8 million ducks, geese, and swans down the Mississippi River drainage to the Gulf; and the Central Flyway, beginning in Alaska, swings over the Rockies and Great Plains through South Texas and Louisiana.

Located all along these flyways—on islands, coastal marshes, mountaintops, and lakes—are federally operated national wildlife refuges. These lands have been set aside and are managed as sanctuaries not only for birds and waterfowl, but for alligators, buffalo, elk, wolves, bighorn sheep, prairie dogs, and every other animal in between.

Southern refuges are managed primarily for waterfowl. America's two favorite ducks—mallards and pintails—funnel south in droves, with counts of well over 100,000 birds on a single refuge often reported.

Other birds come to the refuges, too. Bald eagles are frequently seen on some, while swans and pelicans are the main attractions on others. In the spring, shore birds and waders replace the waterfowl.

Virtually every national wildlife refuge is within a short distance of urban dwellers and is open daily, year-round, at no charge. Since the refuges are not part of the National Park System, visitors will find many of their favorite amenities lacking. Camping is usually prohibited, and there will be no restaurants, lodges, cabins, or other concessions so familiar in national parks. But picnicking is usually allowed, as is boating, fishing, and hiking.

Most wildlife refuges include a system of roads and trails leading throughout, overlooking vast marshes, ponds, and lakes or specially planted food plots. Many have high observation towers, strategically located photography blinds, and self-guided nature walks.

Many of the roads will be unpaved trails, and the only signs you are likely to see will read, "Animals have the right-of-way." In short, national wildlife refuges are managed for wildlife, not people.

Each refuge can provide free booklets and brochures describing its attractions and usually a bird list. Tours can be arranged for special groups, but most refuges are open for visitors to simply wander and observe at their own pace.

December is the best month for seeing the huge waterfowl concentrations, but peak populations may last into January. Don't go afield without a pair of binoculars and a bird identification book, and always check at refuge headquarters first; officials will normally be able to pinpoint the best viewing spots.

Of the more than 50 national wildlife refuges throughout the South, here is a close look at five that offer a variety of birding experiences and rank as alltime favorites.

St. Marks National Wildlife Refuge, Florida

Eighty thousand redheads can't all be wrong.

At least that's the feeling at St. Marks, where some 80,000 redhead ducks winter each year, along with 12,000 scaups, 6,500 widgeon, and 3,500 pintails. This is one of the largest redhead concentrations found anywhere in the South and is especially welcome, since this duck is usually off limits to hunters.

One of the older refuges in the system, St. Marks is about 20 miles south of Tallahassee along the Gulf Coast and includes approximately 65,000 acres of land and 31,700 acres in Apalachee Bay.

Wildlife habitat here is extremely varied, ranging from hardwood swamps to brackish bays, tidal flats, and pine uplands.

More than 300 species of birds have been recorded on the refuge, along with healthy populations of turkey, deer, and alligators. Bald eagles, ospreys, and red-cockaded woodpeckers—all endangered—nest here.

The refuge includes approximately 25 miles of dikes open to walking or bicycling and a short self-guiding nature trail leading to an observation tower overlooking a pond and marsh.

Another observation tower overlooks the tidal marsh of Apalachee Bay and is adjacent to the St. Marks lighthouse, constructed in 1831 and still in operation by the U.S. Coast Guard.

Additional information is available from the Refuge Manager, St. Marks National Wildlife Refuge, Box 68, St. Marks, Florida 32355; telephone (904) 925-6280.

Wheeler National Wildlife Refuge, Alabama

Wheeler annually contains the largest concentration of wintering Canada geese in the Southeast, with a peak population of about 27,000 birds. Along with 40,000 ducks, it's a crowded place.

This is one of the most unusual refuges in the system, since portions of the refuge actually lie within the city limits of Decatur, Huntsville, and the Army's Redstone Arsenal Reservation. It stretches 15 miles along both shores of the Tennessee River—the first national wildlife refuge to be established on a manmade waterpower impoundment, Wheeler Reservoir.

Over 250 species of birds have been identified here, including several endangered species. In late 1976, the birding world became quite excited by the unusual presence of a Hudsonian godwit in the refuge.

A number of dirt roads wind throughout the refuge, and a heated observation tower is open Friday, Saturday, and Sunday from 2:30 p.m. to dusk. The tower offers a panoramic view of much of Wheeler's 34,500 acres and is an excellent spot to begin refuge tours.

For additional information, contact the Refuge Manager, Wheeler National Wildlife Refuge, Box 1643, Decatur, Alabama 35602; telephone (205) 353-7243.

Anahuac National Wildlife Refuge, Texas

Certainly one of the premier winter birding spots on the upper Texas coast, Anahuac's 9,836 acres annually attract thousands of ducks and geese, herons, rails, and grebes. But the birds to look for are pelicans, which turn the ponds and marshes white with sheer numbers.

Careful observation may also yield a glimpse of bald and golden eagles, a masked duck or even a Ross's goose. Located in the coastal marshes beside East Galveston Bay, birders have identified more than 250 species here.

Anahuac includes not only a section of bay beach, but also bayous, canals, and vast wet grasslands. Because the refuge is so low lying, much of it becomes impassable in wet weather; however, a system of roads leads throughout the refuge and should be followed whenever possible. Shoveler Pond normally has some of the largest waterfowl concentrations and can be visited first after stopping at refuge headquarters for birding lists and maps.

For additional information, contact the Refuge Manager, Anahuac National Wildlife Refuge, Box 278, Anahuac, Texas 77514; telephone (713) 267-3337.

White River National Wildlife Refuge, Arkansas

This is one of the more unusual refuges in the national system in that approximately 75% of it normally gets flooded each year by the Mississippi and White Rivers. The flooding is extremely beneficial, however, for as the high waters recede, they leave behind 169 separate lakes and untold miles of water-filled channels and bayous.

These, in turn, attract as many as 500,000 ducks and 1,500 Canada geese during the winter months. Some of the lakes may have as many as 100,000 birds on them at once.

Mallards make up the majority of ducks at this time of year, but because the Mississippi Flyway bottlenecks here virtually all the flyway species, such as gadwall, teal, widgeon, scaup, and pintail, can be seen. White-tail deer are common, and there is a small black bear population.

Located along the lower White River near St. Charles, the refuge embraces some 113,000 acres of bottom land along the edge of the famous Arkansas Grand Prairie rice country. Most of the flooding occurs between March and

May and inundates most of the refuge roadway system.

For additional information, contact White River National Wildlife Refuge, Box 308, DeWitt, Arkansas 72042; telephone (501) 946-1468.

Pea Island, North Carolina

Located on the Outer Banks south of Nags Head, Pea Island is a primary wintering ground for snow geese. Twenty thousand of these birds may land here during the winter months, along with thousands more Canada geese, whistling swans, 25 species of ducks, gulls, terns, hawks, and even peregrine falcons. In all, 315 species have been identified. This is one of the finest places anywhere to observe wintering waterfowl and shorebirds.

Consisting of 5,915 acres of beach, dunes, salt flats, and tidal marsh, plus an additional 25,700 watery acres in Pamlico Sound, Pea Island National Wildlife Refuge is easily viewed by driving southward on State 12. Along the road, which passes between dunes and marshland, there are several parking pullouts and observation stands.

Walking trails lead beside ponds and planted fields, although the snow geese can often be seen without ever leaving your automobile.

Winter here can be bitter. Expect wind, and dress warmly. Most trails are dry, but waterproof boots are nice.

For additional information, contact the Refuge Manager, Pea Island National Wildlife Refuge, Box 1026, Manteo, North Carolina 27954; telephone (919) 987-2394.

The South's National Wildlife Refuges

In the South there are more than 50 national wildlife refuges. Chances are, one of these wildlife refuges is reasonably close to where you live. A complete listing follows.

Alabama

Choctaw, Box 325, Jackson 36545; (205) 246-3583.

Eufaula, Box 258, Eufaula 36027; (205) 687-4065.

Wheeler, Box 1643, Decatur 35601; (205) 353-7243.

Arkansas

Big Lake, Box 67, Manila 72442; (501) 564-2429.

Felsenthal, P.O. Building Room 314, Box 337, El Dorado 71730.

The South's wildlife refuges are harboring thousands of migratory waterfowl.

Holla Bend, Box 1043, Russellville 72801; (501) 968-2800.

Wapanocca, Box 279, Turrell 72384; (501) 343-2595.

White River, Box 308, DeWitt 72042; (501) 946-1468.

Florida

Chassahowitzka (Cedar Keys), Route 2, Box 44, Homosassa 32646; (904) 628-2201.

J. N. "Ding" Darling (Calloosahatchee, Egmont Key, Island Bay, Matlacha Pass, Passage Key, Pine Island, Pinellas), Drawer B, Sanibel 33957; (813) 472-1100.

Lake Woodruff, Box 488, DeLeon Springs 32028; (904) 985-4673.

Merritt Island (Pelican Island, St. Johns), Box 6504, Titusville 32780; (305) 867-4820.

National Key Deer (Great White Heron, Key West), Box 510, Big Pine Key 33043; (305) 872-2239.

St. Marks, Box 68, St. Marks 32355; (904) 925-6280.

St. Vincent, Box 447, Apalachicola 32320; (904) 653-8808.

South Florida Refuges (Loxahatchee, Hobe Sound), Route 1, Box 278, Boynton Beach 33437; (305) 732-3684.

Georgia

Blackbeard Island: See listing under South Carolina.

Harris Neck: See South Carolina.

Okefenokee, Box 117, Waycross 31501; (912) 283-2580.

Piedmont, Round Oak 31080; (912) 986-3651.

Savannah: See South Carolina.

Tybee: See South Carolina.

Wassaw: See South Carolina.

Wolf Island: See South Carolina.

Louisiana

Catahoula, Drawer LL, Jena 71342; (318) 992-5261.

D'Arbonne, P.O. Building Room 314, Box 337, El Dorado, Arkansas 71730.

Delta-Breton, Venice 70091.

Lacassine (Shell Keys), Route 1, Box 186, Lake Arthur 70549; (318) 774-2750.

Sabine, MRH 107, Hackberry 70645; (318) 762-5135.

Maryland

Blackwater (Martin, Susquehanna), Route 1, Box 121, Cambridge 21613; (301) 228-2677.

Eastern Neck, Route 2, Box 225, Rock Hall 21661; (301) 639-7415.

Mississippi

Noxubee, Route 1, Box 84, Brooksville 39739; (601) 323-5548.

Yazoo, Route 1, Box 286, Hollandale 38748; (601) 839-2638.

North Carolina

Mackay Island: See Virginia.

Mattamuskeet (Cedar Island, Swanquarter), Route 1, Box N-2, Swanquarter 27885; (919) 926-4021.

Pea Island, Box 1026, Manteo 27954; (919) 987-2394.

Pee Dee, Box 780, Wadesboro 28170; (704) 694-4424.

Pungo, Box 267, Plymouth 27962; (919) 793-2143.

Oklahoma

Optima, Box 628, Guymon 73942; telephone (405) 338-3479.

Salt Plains, Route 1, Box 76, Jet 73749; (405) 626-4794.

Sequoyah, Box 398, Sallisaw 74955; (918) 775-4931.

Tishomingo, Box 248, Tishomingo 73460; (405) 371-2402.

Washita, Route 2, Box 68, Butler 73625; (405) 473-2205.

Wichita Mountains Wildlife Refuge, Box 448, Cache 73527; (405) 429-3221.

South Carolina

Cape Romain, Route 1, Box 191, Awendaw 29429; (803) 928-3368.

Carolina Sandhills, Route 2, Box 130, McBee 29101; (803) 335-8401.

Santee, Box 158, Summerton 29148; (803) 478-2217.

Savannah (Blackbeard Island, Georgia; Harris Neck, Georgia; Tybee, Georgia; Wassaw, Georgia; Wolf Island, Georgia; Pinckney Island, South Carolina), c/o Savannah Complex, Box 9623, Savannah 31402; (912) 232-4321, extension 415.

Tennessee

Cross Creeks, Route 1, Box 229, Dover 37058; (615) 232-7477.

Hatchie, Box 187, Brownsville 38012; (901) 772-0501.

Reelfoot (Lake Isom), Box 295, Samburg 38254; (901) 538-2481.

Tennessee, Box 849, Paris 38242; (901) 642-2091.

Texas

Anahuac, Box 278, Anahuac 77514; (713) 267-3337.

Aransas, Box 100, Austwell 77950; (512) 286-3559.

Attwater Prairie Chicken, Box 518, Eagle Lake 77434; (713) 234-3021.

Brazoria (San Bernard), Box 1088, Angleton 77515; (713) 849-6062.

Buffalo Lake, Box 228, Umbarger 79091; (806) 499-3382.

Hagerman, Route 3, Box 123, Sherman 75090; (214) 786-2826.

Laguna Atascosa, Box 2683, Harlingen 78550; (512) 423-8328.

Muleshoe, Box 549, Muleshoe 79347; (806) 946-3341.

Santa Anna, Route 1, Box 202A, Alamo 78516; (512) 787-3079.

Virginia

Back Bay (Fishermans Island, Plum Tree Island, Mackay Island, North Carolina), Pembroke Office Park, Pembroke No. 2 Building, Suite 218, Virginia Beach 23462; (804) 490-0505.

Chincoteague (Wallops Island), Box 62, Chincoteague 23336; (804) 336-6122.

Great Dismal Swamp (Nansemond), Box 349, Suffolk 23434; (804) 539-7479.

Mason Neck (Marumsco), 9502 Richmond Highway, Suite A, Lorton 22079; (703) 339-5278.

Presquile, Box 620, Hopewell 23860; (804) 458-7541.

Drawing from HORN ISLAND LOGS.

History of Seafood Cooking in the Carolina Low Country

Long before the first Europeans journeyed to America's shores, the productive waters of the Carolina coast were famed among the Indians. Some of the finest seafoods in the world were available to anyone for the taking. River shrimp swam in profusion. Succulent oysters paved the beds of the salt water creeks. And the meaty, delicious Atlantic Blue Crab fought each other year around for the chance at any bait thrown their way.

As waves of explorers, then settlers, came to the Carolina coast the forms of preparing the seafood varied as much as the people themselves. French, Spanish, Scottish and English—all added their particular touches and tastes, many of which have survived to today to comprise the coastal, or low country, cookery.

From the beginning of time perishable seafood could not be transported but an hour or two from where caught. Therefore those inlanders hungering for the fruits of the sea in its many forms had to journey to the ocean. After the turn of the century, with the advent of refrigerated transport, seafood slowly moved inland. But not until a few decades ago, when the commercial processing of seafood was perfected, was it possible to universally enjoy marvelous low country recipes based on the sea's harvest.

This combination gift and cook-book offers some of these recipes, tailored to modern tastes in preparation and serving. The Blue Channel Company of Port Royal, South Carolina, hopes you will enjoy these dishes as have the generations of Americans of the Carolina low country since the forming and founding of our nation.

The Blue Channel Company is America's largest packer of Atlantic Blue crabmeat, and it is also known as a quality producer of seafood soups, stews, and spreads. Blue Channel offers eight gift boxes; the first four are samplers with a mixture of Blue Channel products. The last four, with the exception of Gift Package No. 7, have proportionately more of their famous blue crabmeat. (Gift Package No. 7 is the All Soup and Stew Sampler.) The prices of these gift boxes range from $10.50 to $39.50. They are delivered anywhere in the United States. In all of the gift boxes sent from Port Royal, a copy of *Carolina Low Country Cookery* is included.

Write to:

The Blue Channel Company
Port Royal, South Carolina 29935

APPALACHIAN TRAIL GUIDES

GREAT SMOKY MOUNTAINS NATIONAL PARK

If you are not a hiker, but merely appreciate a job clearly and thoroughly done, you will find pleasure in the guidebooks to the Appalachian Trail published by the Appalachian Trail Conference. Every inch of trail in Virginia, North Carolina, Tennessee, and Georgia is documented; you could be set down at any point on the Trail and find your place almost immediately by referring to the guidebook. Two sets of instructions for traveling the Trail are given: one for hikers going north on the Trail, another for hikers going south. As the section reproduced here will illustrate, the guidebooks were prepared by people who know their subject intimately, down to the least fern.

To order a guidebook or obtain information on other publications of the Conference, write:

Appalachian Trail Conference
P.O. Box 236
Harpers Ferry, West Virginia 25425

Memberships in the Conference support the Appalachian Trail and enable you to receive Appalachian Trailway News *(issued in February, May, August, and November). Dues are $12.50 a year. Write to the above address, giving name, address, and outdoor interests or experience, and enclose a check for the first year's dues.*

THE APPALACHIAN TRAIL

The Appalachian Trail is a continuous, marked footpath along the crest of the ranges generally referred to as Appalachian; hence its name. It extends through the eastern states from Katahdin, a massive granite monolith in the central Maine wilderness, more than 2,000 miles south to Springer Mountain in northern Georgia. This master trail has been completed, marked, and measured throughout its length.

The Appalachian Trail traverses 14 states. Virginia has the longest section with nearly 500 miles, approximately one-fourth of the total. West Virginia has the shortest section with some 20 miles along the Virginia-West Virginia boundary. The greatest elevation along the Trail route is on Clingmans Dome in the Great Smokies, 6,643 feet. The Trail is only slightly above sea level at its crossing of the Hudson River.

The proposal of the Appalachian Trail was originally advanced in 1921 by Benton MacKaye of Shirley Center, Mass. Forester, philosopher, dreamer, and frequenter of the New England forests, MacKaye had conceived the vision of a trail which for all practical purposes should be endless. He gave expression to his plan in an article "An Appalachian Trail, an Experiment in Regional Planning," in the October 1921 issue of the *Journal of American Institute of Architects.* Others had proposed extensive through trails but the conception of this supertrail, the Appalachian Trail, was solely MacKaye's. His proposal aroused interest among hiking clubs in the vicinity of New York City and in 1922 the first part of the Trail was constructed in the Bear Mountain section of the Palisades Interstate Park by clubs affiliated in the New York-New Jersey Trail Conference. Interest in the undertaking soon spread to New England and Pennsylvania.

This early enthusiasm died out before much work was done, however, and in 1926 Arthur Perkins, a retired lawyer of Hartford, Conn., undertook to translate the conception of an endless trail into an actual one. He interested various groups

2-1

in going to the mountains and locating and cutting through the wilderness the footpath which had been discussed for five years. Soon the Trail was no longer only a fireside philosophy. To the enthusiasm and momentum developed by Mr. Perkins' activities is due the practical completion of the Trail project. He interested Myron H. Avery, of Lubec, Maine, and Washington, D.C., who as Chairman of the Appalachian Trail Conference from 1931 to 1952 enlisted the aid and coordinated the work of hundreds of persons up and down the coast. With the activity and efforts thus aroused, the Trail was completed from Maine to Georgia.

When this project was first undertaken, all outdoor organizations in the East were confined to New England and New York. The Hudson River was the frontier to the south or west. The existing trail systems which could then be incorporated into the supertrail numbered four. First, there were the splendidly maintained Appalachian Mountain Club trails in New England. Until the completion of the Appalachian Mountain Club chain of huts, however, the system had been a series of north and south trails and its east and west axis did not appear. In Vermont the lower 100 miles of rapidly developing Long Trail could be utilized. Between the White and Green Mountains was the Dartmouth Outing Club trail system. In New York there were the comparatively narrow Bear Mountain and Harriman sections of the Palisades Interstate Park. In all, there were perhaps 350 miles of the more than 2,000. At that time the length of the Trail was thought to be only 1,200 miles; but when it was actually developed, it was almost twice that.

The completion of the Trail was also made easier by the existence in the South of the National Forests. Here connected skyline trails were developed to a degree not anticipated by those who early planned the route of the Appalachian Trail.

Beginning in 1927, clubs were formed in the Southern Appalachian states so that now all the Trail is under the supervision of organizations which maintain the route. They are federated in the Appalachian Trail Conference with headquarters at Harpers Ferry, W.Va. The Trail route is divided

2-2

into six districts, with three representatives from each, together with the elected officers, constituting the Board of Managers, the governing body of the Conference. The Chairman is the Conference's executive officer. Sessions of the Trail Conference are held at intervals of not more than every three years. The Conference membership consists of organizations which maintain the Trail or contribute to the project, individuals who maintain the Trail or are responsible for areas through which it passes, and individual dues-paying members.

At the Eighth Appalachian Trail Conference held in June 1937 in the Great Smoky Mountains National Park, Trail Conference member Edward B. Ballard proposed to the Conference a plan for an "Appalachian Trailway," which would set apart an area on each side of the Trail and dedicate it to the interests of those who travel on foot. This plan was adopted by the Conference and steps were taken to carry into effect this long-range program to ensure the perpetuation and protection of the Appalachian Trail. These efforts culminated in the execution on October 15, 1938, of an agreement between the National Park Service and the U.S. Forest Service for the promotion of the Appalachian Trailway. Thus, there was created a new type of recreational area to be known as the Appalachian Trailway, a zone extending through the National Parks and Forests for a distance of one mile on each side of the Appalachian Trail. Within this zone there were to be no new paralleling roads for motor transportation or any other development incompatible with the existence of this area. There was to be no cutting primarily for the production of timber within 200 feet of the Trail. A similar agreement, creating a zone one-quarter mile in width, was entered into with the states through which the Trail passes.

Protection of the Appalachian Trail was expanded under the National Trails System Act of 1968. Under it, a national system of trails was established, and as initial components the Appalachian Trail and the Pacific Crest Trail were designated National Scenic Trails. The Act provides that the Secretary of the Interior, in consultation with the Secretary of Agriculture,

2-3

will administer the Appalachian Trail, primarily as a footpath, and protects the Trail against incompatible activities and the use of motorized vehicles. Provision is also made for acquisitions of rights-of-way for the Trail, both inside and outside the boundaries of federally administered areas, by purchase, ex-

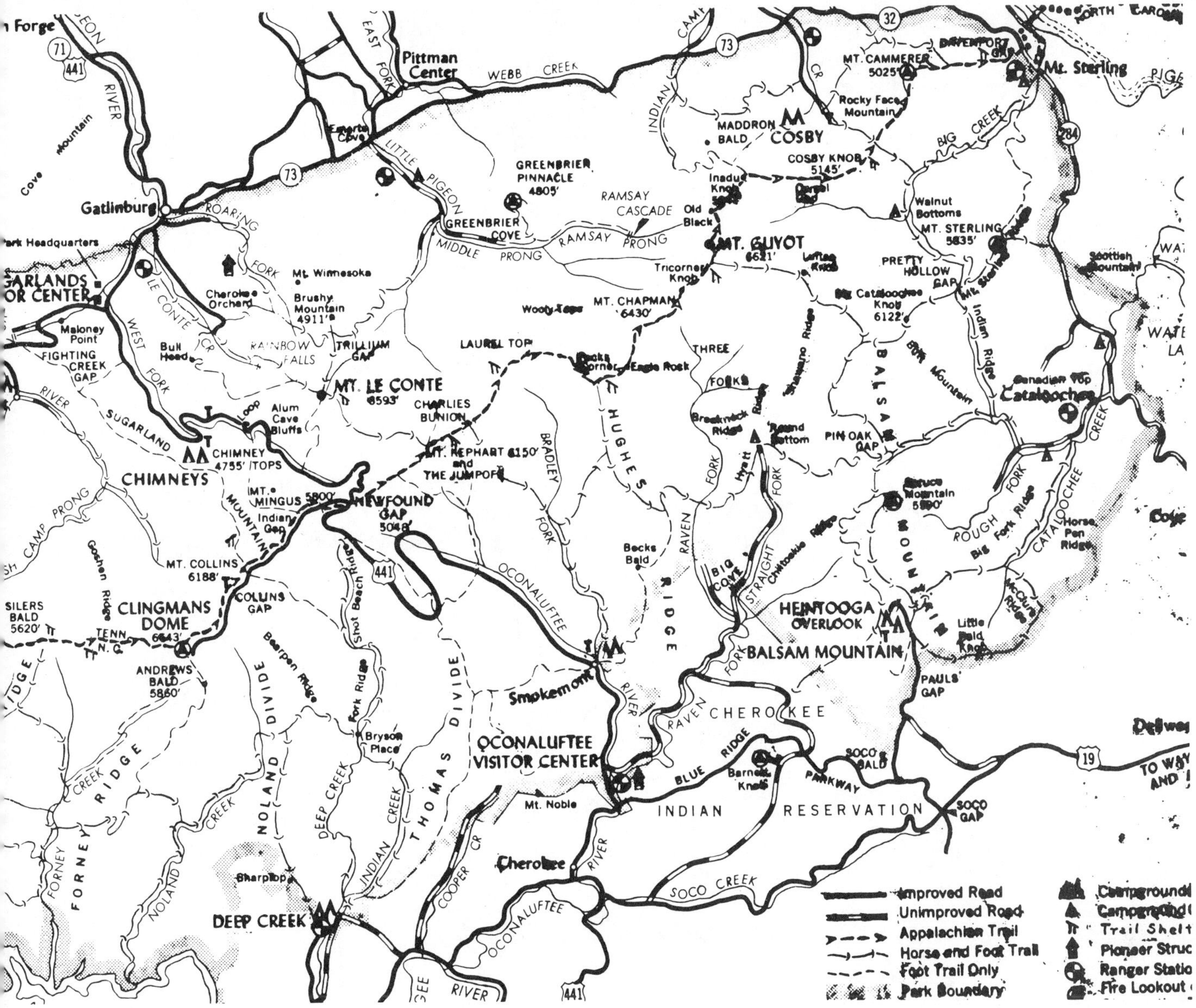

change, or, as a last resort, condemnation.

In 1970 the Act was implemented by supplemental agreements among the National Park Service, the U.S. Forest Service, and the Appalachian Trail Conference. These agreements established specific responsibilities of these three organizations for initial mapping, selection of right-of-way, relocations, maintenance, development, marking, acquisition of land, and protection of the Trail. The Conference and the Trail clubs in general retain their established responsibilities for Trail clearing and marking.

Agreements have also been drawn up between the National Park Service and the various states through which the Trail passes. These agreements encourage the states to acquire and maintain the right-of-way for the Trail outside of federally owned land.

A comprehensive statement of the Trail project, describing its history and route and containing the text of its constitution, the National Trails System Act, supplemental agreements, and a bibliography is in a booklet entitled *The Appalachian Trail* (ATC Publication No. 5), obtainable from the Appalachian Trail Conference, Harpers Ferry, W.Va. 25425, at a cost of $1.

Anyone who wishes to help support the Appalachian Trail or keep informed about it may join the Appalachian Trail Conference. Dues are $12.50 for the first year, $10 thereafter. Write to the Appalachian Trail Conference, Harpers Ferry, W.Va. 25425, giving name, address, outdoor interests or experience and enclosing a check for the first year's dues. Members receive several publications of the Conference, including *Appalachian Trailway News* (issued four times a year).

This volume is one of a series of guides to the Appalachian Trail. It comprises the Trail data from Damascus, Va., just north of the Virginia-Tennessee line, to the western end of the Great Smokies. For a guide to the Trail to the north, refer to

2-4

Guide to the Appalachian Trail in Central and Southwestern Virginia, and for a guide to the south, refer to *Guide to the Appalachian Trail in the Great Smokies, the Nantahalas, and Georgia*. Both guides, as well as guides to the rest of the Trail, may be obtained from the Appalachian Trail Conference.

For additional information on the Appalachian Trail see the following:

Campfires Along the Appalachian Trail, by Ramond Baker. New York, Carlton Press, 1971. 120 p. $3.

The Appalachian Trail, by Ronald M. Fisher. Washington. National Geographic Society, 1972. 199 p. $4.25 plus postage.

Appalachian Hiker; Adventure of a Lifetime, by Edward B. Garvey. Oakton, Va., Appalachian Books, 1971. 397 p. $5 postpaid.

The Appalachian Trail; Wilderness on the Doorstep, by Ann and Myron Sutton. Philadelphia, J. B. Lippincott, 1967. 180 p.

2-5

The Southern Appalachians

The Southern Appalachian Mountains, described in this *Guide* and in *Guide to the Appalachian Trail in the Great Smokies, the Nantahalas, and Georgia*, are the highest and considered by some the most rugged of the entire Appalachian chain. Except perhaps for Maine, they represent the superlative in the "wilderness" and the primitive made available by the Appalachian Trail. Much of the route is virtually ridge crest travel and for long distances is above the 5,000-foot elevation. The outlook is generally a vast bewildering sea of lofty mountain ranges in all directions.

Travelers from the other sections of the Appalachian Trail will find here much contrast. With increasing elevation, particularly in the Great Smokies, the trees and flora become similar to those in the north woods. Of much interest are the Southern Appalachian "balds," great clear summits, affording magnificent outlooks, comparable to the glaciated summits of New England.

Apart from the endless ridges, perhaps the most impressive feature of Trail travel in the Southern Appalachians is the profusion of flowering shrubs — rhododendron, azalea, and laurel. Their dense masses and "thickets" in full bloom make

1-2

the traveler's path one of almost indescribable beauty. The floral display is at its height in late June and early July. The blooming season is controlled by elevation, and on the summits the display occurs much later than in the valleys. The advantage of travel at this season to witness the floral display is offset, however, by the increased probability of the heavy rains characteristic of the region.

The varieties of trees encountered are of much interest. The Great Smoky Mountains National Park alone contains more species of trees than all Europe. An outstanding current book describing the Trail and its environment is *The Appalachians*, by Maurice Brooks (Houghton Mifflin Co., Boston, 1965).

The Trail route covered by this *Guide* also contrasts with sections farther north in that most of it is publicly owned. Much of it lies in the two National Forests, the Cherokee (in Tennessee) and the Pisgah (in North Carolina), and in the Great Smoky Mountains National Park. Such public ownership results in protection under the National Trails System Act and ensures the preservation of the primitive aspects of the Trail environment. Further purchases of land will increase the publicly owned areas. The completion of this purchase program will thus result in a continuous public domain for those who walk and camp.

1-3

Planting Bulbs for The Best Effect

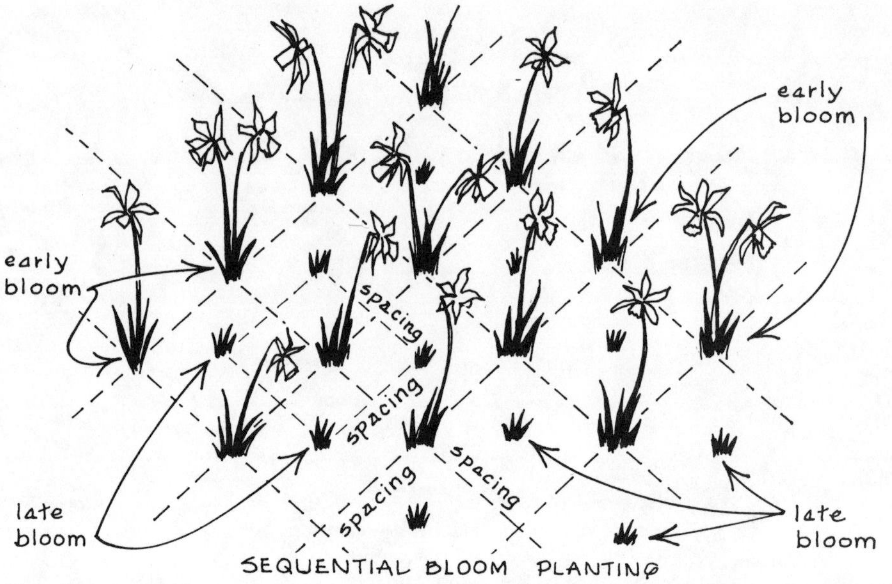

SEQUENTIAL BLOOM PLANTING

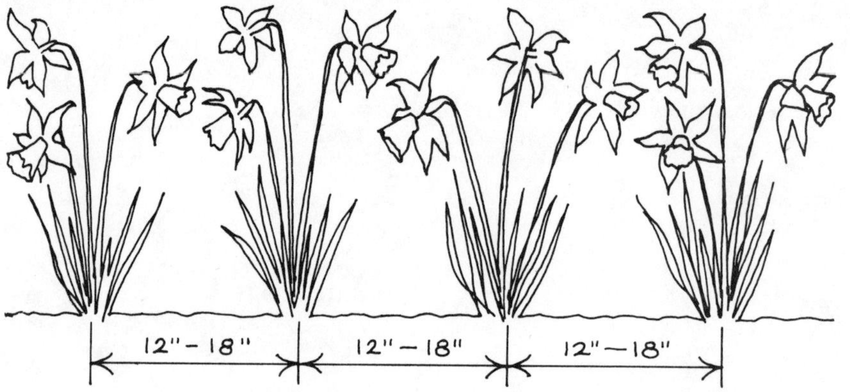

SPACING FOR MULTI-FLOWERING BULBS

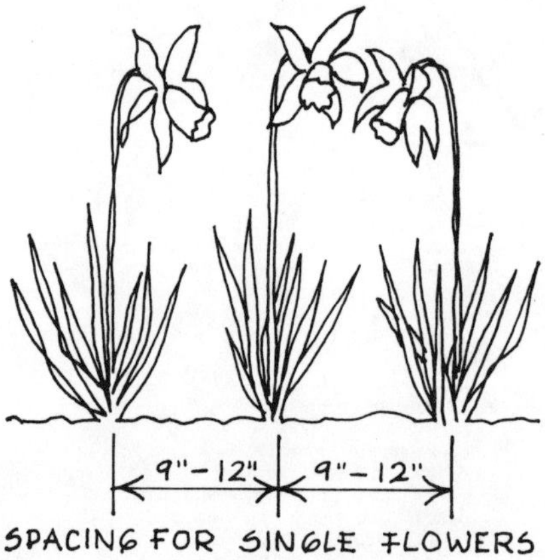

SPACING FOR SINGLE FLOWERS

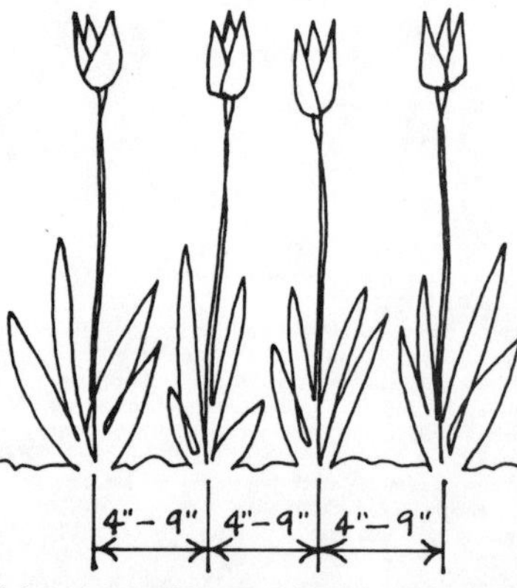

SPACING FOR TALL BULBS

November is the last month for planting bulbs in the Upper South and the beginning of the planting season in the Lower South.

Unless you are naturalizing bulbs, the spacing of bulbs in a mass planting should be influenced by the flowering habit of the bulb, the landscape effect desired, and the location of the planting on the lot. Considering these factors can give the landscape the maximum effect from a bulb display. Here are some design tips for bulb planting:

—Space bulbs according to flowering habit. Generally speaking, bulbs that produce multiple stems with several blooms to a stem (like paper-white narcissus or liberty bells) can be spaced farther apart than single-stem, solitary-bloom bulbs, like hybrid tulips. The profusely flowering bulb will appear as a dense, full planting when spaced as far as 12 to 18 inches apart, while willowy single-bloom plants sometimes need to be as close as 9 to 12 inches to read as a mass of bloom.

—Space bulbs according to color. Generally, scrambled bulbs will not read as strongly in the landscape as drifts of separate colors. Also remember that brilliantly colored bulbs will read more vividly than pastel shades and can be spaced farther apart for mass effect.

If combining drifts of brilliant and soft colors, plant the brilliantly colored flowers in the background and the softer color in the foreground. You may have to plant more of the softer colored flowers to balance visually with the brighter color, even though the brighter color may be spaced farther apart.

—Space bulbs according to height. Taller flowering bulbs should be planted closer together than shorter stem varieties. By concentrating the bulbs, attention is captured by the color instead of the expanse of bed beneath the flower.

If shorter stem flowering bulbs are planted adjacent to taller varieties with the same spacing between plants, the shorter variety will dominate the planting. For instance, in a mass planting of hyacinths and tulips, the taller tulips should be spaced closer together to balance the display of hyacinths.

—Space bulbs according to the terrain. On steeply sloping land, bulbs may be spaced a maximum distance apart since foreshortening causes the planting to appear more concentrated. On slopes viewed from an elevated position (the middle of the slope is at eye level of the viewer) bulbs should be planted closer together to read as a filled-in planting.

Other Tips

—Let distance work for you in planting. If a planting is to be viewed from a distance (from the street or across a large lot), a widely spaced bulb planting is best for mass effect. The bulbs may be planted 12 to 18 inches apart depending on the type. By contrast, plantings adjacent to a walkway or living area must be tightly spaced to create a mass effect.

—Plant bulbs in a sequential-bloom pattern to prolong the effect. Combine early- and late-flowering bulbs to extend the blooming season. For this purpose, plant bulbs in diamond patterns within the bed, based on the spacing considerations mentioned here. Plant the early bulbs at the corners of the diamonds and the late bloomers in the center of the pattern. This way, the plants that bloom at the same time are staggered in separate rows adequately spaced and the season of bloom is extended.

TREE-RIPENED TEXAS FRUIT

Through the efficient mail-order business of Pittman and Davis, Inc., of Harlingen, Texas, you can share in the delicious harvest of the famous Texas red grapefruit.

Pittman and Davis will be glad to send you their free catalogue which is filled with appetizing-looking pictures of tree-ripened citrus fruit, not only the red grapefruit—so called because of the rich red color of its meat, but also navel and Valencia oranges. The company offers the fruit in many different size containers, from the small six pack to half-bushel and bushel cartons and baskets. You can order a mixture of fruit, or all oranges, or all grapefruit. You also can join the Pack-a-Month Club in which you receive fruit during the 5 months from November through March. These represent the peak growing months around Harlingen.

Many of the fruit selections are attractively packaged for gift giving as are their other offerings: pecans, walnuts, almonds, Canadian bacon, smoked peppered boneless ham, smoked turkey, aged Cheddar cheese, fruitcake, and orange blossom honey. If any of these is to be a gift, you may send your card to Pittman and Davis and they will enclose it and ship directly to the recipient.

Pittman and Davis has been in business since 1926. They guarantee satisfaction, and you may either remit with your order or they will bill you. All the prices in their catalogue reflect shipping charges; the one price is all you pay. Write to:

Pittman and Davis, Inc.
P.O. Box 2227
Harlingen, Texas 78550

DIXIE GUN WORKS

Turner Kirkland, president of Dixie Gun Works, handlers of rare antique guns and gun supplies, bought his first gun in 1932, a Colt Model 1849 pocket revolver. He was 12 years old and the gun cost him $.75. After intervening years of college, Army duty, and work as a jewelry salesman, he finally decided that gun collecting and distributing were still his main interests and in 1954 cleaned out his father's coal house, sheetrocked the walls, and went to work. With the contacts he had made during his years as a jewelry salesman (when he would buy up rare guns and parts during his travels) Mr. Kirkland established himself as an able and reputable gun and gun parts dealer. His business now operates out of a 47,000 square foot building, with almost 40 employees.

The Dixie Gun Works' showroom houses antique automobiles, popcorn poppers, steam whistles, old headlights and sidelights, antique horns, hubcaps, radiator ornaments, a collection of Kentucky Rifles, Philadelphia Derringers, all military rifles from 1795 through 1873, horn tip powder measures, Confederate Reunion and Yankee Reunion Civil War badges, to name just a portion of the contents.

Anyone who happens by the Dixie Gun Works on a pretty day when one of the antique cars is out may get taken for a spin around the block.

Several catalogues are available from Dixie Gun Works. A 500-page catalogue of shooting equipment and modern reproduction guns, all for muzzleloaders, costs $2.00. Secondary antique arms catalogues, issued around three or four times a year, cost $1.00.

For additional information, write:

Dixie Gun Works, Inc.
Gun Powder Lane
Union City, Tennessee 38261

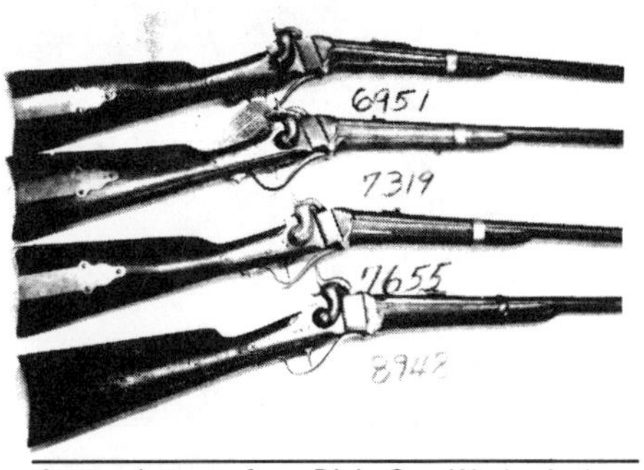

A sample page from Dixie Gun Works Antique Arms Catalogue

#6951 A MODEL 1852 SHARPS CARBINE. This particular carbine is scarce in that is in the original 45 caliber. Has 21 3/4" round tapered barrel. Bore is good with pitting. Rifling is still visible. Metal surfaces show pitting and dark brown patina. Front sight appears to be a new replacement. The original folding leaf sight had the leaf broken off. The base still remains. Breechblock action works fine. Lock has a good action. Markings are fair. The pellet priming feeding mechanism is missing. All markings are faint on this scarce carbine and are illegible. Has a new replacement saddle bar and ring. Has a brass barrel band, patchbox, and buttplate. These parts are in very good condition with minor nicks and scratches. The original walnut forearm is in very good condition with the original retaining barrel spring for the lever pin. The is the difference between the model 1853 and the model 1852, the type of lever catch. Buttstock is curly walnut. With minor nicks and scratches. Overall condition of this hard-to-get gun is good. $475.00

#7319 A SHARPS MODEL 1852 CARBINE. This is the scarce model with the barrel band on the forearm to hold the lever pin in place. Has a 21 1/2" round barrel. Bore is smooth with pitting. No original finish remains. A light brown patina with traces of surface age pitting. Has a replacement rear sight and the bar is missing. Brass buttplace, patchbox, and barrel band. Markings are good. Buttstock and forearm are in good condition with minor nicks and scratches. Gun is missing the saddle bar and ring. Markings are very good. Overall condition of this gun is very good. $625.00

#7655 A SHARPS MODEL 1852 CARBINE. This is a scarce model with a barrel band spring to hold the lever pin in place. Has a 21 1/2" round rifled barrel. Bore is very good with good rifling. Carbine is somplete with all original parts. Still retains 50% or better of the original blue and color casehardening. Serial number is 2761. Good markings. Lock action works fine. Original buttstock and forearm are in fine condition with some minor nicks and scratches. Brass buttplate, patchbox and barrel band. Has the saddle sling bar and swivel. Overall condition is very fine. $1425.00

#8948 A SHARPS MODEL 1863 PERCUSSION CARBINE. Serial number is C, 26146. Has new model 1863 markings on barrel. Barrel has a light brown patina. Some light surface age pitting. Lock action is very good. Good markings on lock. Has light brown patina. Bore is very good. Has nice original two piece walnut stock with minor nicks and scratches. Barrel has some light surface age pitting, underneath about 4" forward of the forearm. Has original barrel bands, that have a dark brown patina. Has good inspectors marks on the stock. Gun is missing lever catch. This is a part that we have, and you can purchase this from us to get the gun back in complete condition. A very nice Sharps percussion carbine that is in very good condition. $525.00

DUCK DECOY KITS

Bay Country Woodcrafts, located near the Chincoteague Wildlife Refuge on the Eastern Shore of Virginia and owned and operated by the Hornick family, is the largest decoy factory in the world. Duck decoy making is a revival of a folk art that America can truly call its own; decoy carving is an American folk art which originated with the American Indians in colonial times rather than from European cultures.

Decorative duck decoy kits that you may make yourself are available from Bay Country Woodcrafts—and these are for the beginner as well as the experienced. The kit parts are carefully carved from solid white pine, smoothly sanded, and ready for assembly; each kit contains a head, body, glass eyes, sandpaper, and instructions. The assembled duck (10 to 16 inches in length depending upon species) has many finishing possibilities: it can be stained, painted, or antiqued. Three of the most popular kits: the Mallard, Green Wing Teal, and Wood Duck include a detailed painting guide; it is a professional lesson in duck painting to finish the hen and drake of these three species.

Bay Country Woodcrafts offers a handsome, full-color catalogue for $1.00.

Bay Country Woodcrafts
U.S. Route 13
Oak Hall, Virginia 23416

BIRD CARVINGS

What Edward Boehm created in porcelain, Jim White of Cairo, Georgia, creates from a block of wood . . . exquisite carvings of birds, especially bob-white quail, owls, sandpipers, and ducks.

Starting with a block of sugar pine, Jim uses a bandsaw for the initial shaping process. Then, slowly and meticulously, he pares and whittles until the finished shape emerges. Careful handsanding of the figure's contours absorbs part of the long hours necessary to complete each figure. The specimen is painted in its natural color tones; Jim insists on the realistic appearance of his birds down to the toenails! Not content to just dab in varnish for eyes, he uses glass eyes from a taxidermy supply house. In the case of the owls, the eyes seem to actually follow a person around the room.

Special attention is given to the mounts. Most of the birds are mounted on carefully selected driftwood, gathered along the river banks and on the Gulf Coast. Some are mounted on cypress knees cut from the swamp on the Ochlocknee River in south Georgia.

A catalogue may be obtained for $.50—write to:

Jim White
Route 2, Thomasville Road
P.O. Box 329
Cairo, Georgia 31728

BAKER'S ROPE LADDER FOR HUNTING OR ESCAPING

In 1977, Baker Manufacturing Company realized that some trees were too large to accommodate their tree stand. But they knew that these same trees often had limbs that hunters would like to use. To solve the problem, they decided to manufacture a rope ladder.

Baker now has available for mail order a 15-foot rope ladder with 10 oak steps. The ladder has a 20-foot weighted throw rope at the top, enabling a man to get the rope over a limb. Then the ladder can be pulled up and the hunter will have enough rope to tie securely to the tree trunk. The ladder also has 6-foot sections of rope at the bottom that can be secured to minimize the swaying effect.

This rope ladder may also be used as a fire escape. The throw rope can be tied around a heavy object in the room, such as the bed frame. The ladder can be stored under the bed; in case of an emergency, it is light enough that a woman or child can throw the ladder out of the window.

Two models are available; #RL-2 (15 foot, second story) costs $19.95 and #RL-3 (25 foot, third story) costs $29.95.

Baker Manufacturing Company
P.O. Box 1003
428 N. St. Augustine Road
Valdosta, Georgia 31601

> *"Last night there was a beautiful sunset. One felt that it had been arranged with taste. So many sunsets seem to be simply wild explosions of color in order to stun people into a state of mute wonder. But this one had variety, vermilion red and purple together, and lilac and gold together against a heavenly clear green turquoise sky. You felt that there would never be bad weather again." HORN ISLAND LOGS.*

THE PURPLE MARTIN

The purple martin, largest of the swallow family, has been a favorite in North America for many generations. It's a very *American* bird; the migratory range is extensive, and in the spring and summer the martin inhabits all the United States and southern Canada, from coast to coast.

Mr. R.B. Layton of Jackson, Mississippi, has published several fascinating books on the purple martin which have been most successful. The first, *The Purple Martin,* is now in its fourth printing and is the only book about this species that is recommended by leading national and international ornithologists. This 192-page paperback with photographs and drawings covers such topics as arrival in spring, raising the young, diet, enemies, and migration. Mr. Layton has also put out a book entitled *Purple Martin House Plans*, enabling you to make a home for this cheerful, friendly bird—and have built-in pest control as well. One adult martin can eat 2,000 mosquitoes each day! The book includes 10 complete plans of various styles, each 8½" x 11", and his newest book on aluminum purple martin house plans appears to be as interesting as the others.

Mr. Layton has also written *30 Birds That Will Build in Bird Houses.* The book describes these birds and the types of houses they like. Robins, for example, prefer a shelf that is covered but open on two or three sides. The book contains forty birdhouse plans—and each plan has a note to indicate which birds will find the house acceptable.

These informative books are only available from Mr. Layton; all shipping and handling charges will be paid.

The Purple Martin $3.98
Purple Martin House Plans $1.50
Purple Martin New Aluminum House Plans $1.00
30 Birds That Will Build In Bird Houses $4.95

Write to order:

Mr. R.B. Layton
Nature Books Publishers
P.O. Box 12157
Jackson, Mississippi 39211

PLAN TWO–SURE-FIRE NINE-PLEX

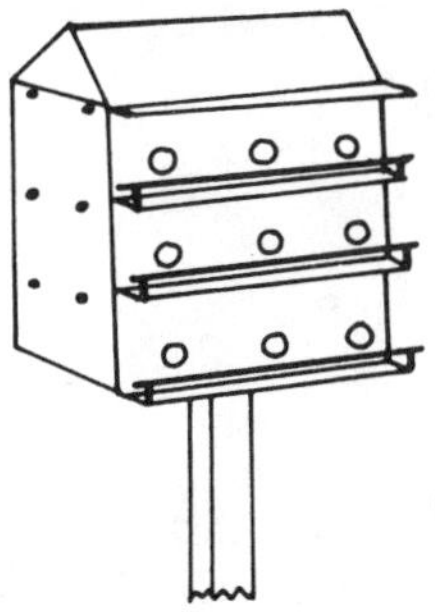

MATERIALS NEEDED

2 pieces, 8" x 24" (ends)
4 pieces, 10$\frac{1}{2}$" x 24" (floor and ceiling)
1 piece, 24" x 24$\frac{1}{2}$" (back)
2 pieces, 6" x 24$\frac{1}{2}$" (roof)
3 pieces, 7 2/3" x 24$\frac{1}{2}$" (fronts)

(Sheet of exterior plywood, $\frac{1}{4}$" thick)⟶

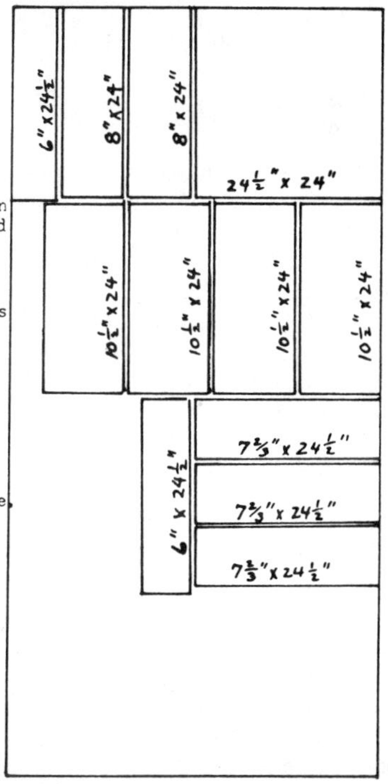

CONSTRUCTION TIPS - This sure-fire house always attracts martins. It is made to face in one direction only for close observation. Begin by nailing your end pieces to the bottom piece, evening the back edges and allowing the front flooring to extend for the porch. Next, eight inches higher, nail in the second floor in a similar manner. Use only a couple of nails in each end until you are sure the house is progressing properly, then add nails later when the house is completed. After the third floor has been added in a similar manner, add the fourth, which becomes the ceiling of the top floor. Now, you are ready to add the back to the house. The 24$\frac{1}{2}$" size is the length of the house. Now add the partitions eight inches apart. Nails through the back should be driven first, then the front as each is put into place. Be sure that you have cut the entrance holes properly before nailing the fronts into place. Sand the hole edges to remove the rough edges. The roof pieces should be nailed together and then spread out the width of the house as the attachment is made. Nail it into place. Then, cut a pattern the size of the two ends, gable pieces, and use it to cut the two end pieces from the plywood. Nail these into place. You have now constructed your house and ready to tack on a piece of roofing. Railings may now be installed across the front of the porches. Paint the house and when it dries, you will be ready to install it. Remember to drill drain and ventilation holes for each apartment.

OUTWARD BOUND

Question: What do these people have in common, besides obvious physical exertion and breathless expressions?
Answer: They are all attending the North Carolina Outward Bound School.

Outward Bound was developed in England during World War II as survival training for English merchant crewmen. (The idea was that rigorous outdoor adventure experiences could condition men better to survive shipwrecks and the other perils of wartime.) Outward Bound came to the United States in 1962 when the first Outward Bound School opened in Colorado.

But Outward Bound, as it is now, does not teach survival techniques or survival skills as a primary goal. What it does hope to do is to make its students more aware of their capacities. It tries to stretch them physically, mentally, and emotionally. It tries to teach them that they may have reserves of strength and cunning that they, living in a mechanized society, never thought they had because they never needed to use them.

An Outward Bound course (of which there are many, of different lengths and for different needs) consists of a variety of activities undertaken both in groups and alone in which physical and/or emotional stress is involved. Ages range from 16 to 60. Students at Outward Bound may find themselves (after a few days of training), rock climbing, rappelling, crossing a gorge on ropes, white water canoeing, etc. They learn to work in groups with an instructor advising when absolutely necessary. But the emphasis is on the groups working things out for themselves and depending upon each other. A final exercise may be planning and implementing an expedition (during which the group is totally responsible for its members) into the wilderness. There is also, toward the end of the course, a "solo," during which the student is left alone in a wild area with a sleeping bag and poncho, to meditate and get along totally on his own for several days. He can fast, forage, or subsist on a very tiny solo pack (two biscuits, two figs, two envelopes of hot chocolate, and a couple of tea bags).

After an Outward Bound experience, which must be similar to some that our forefathers had, one participant wrote: "We are better than we know. If we can be made to see it, perhaps for the rest of our lives we will be unwilling to settle for less."

For information write to:

North Carolina Outward Bound School
P.O. Box 817
Morganton, North Carolina 28655

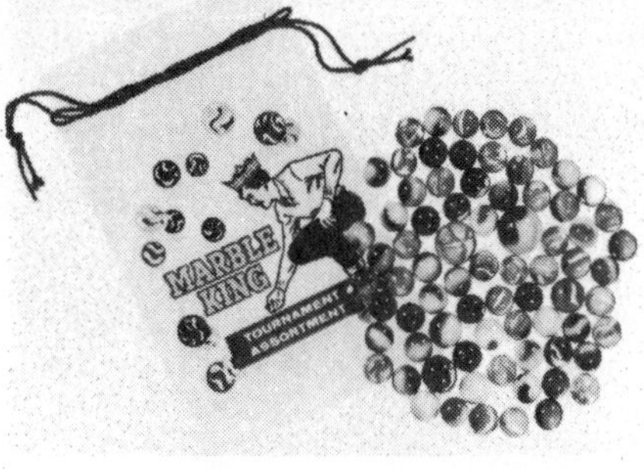

WHERE TO FIND YOUR MARBLES

West Virginia is a singular state in several ways, but one of the most interesting facts about this mountainous region is its preeminence in the field of marble-making. There are just about five plants in the whole United States which manufacture marbles, and four of them are in West Virginia.

Of course, the same qualities which make West Virginia an important glass-making state contribute to its prominence in the marble-making field, since marbles are glass products. But the manufacture of marbles has an interest-appeal all its own, and if you ever get a chance, you should try to visit one of the marble factories. C.E. Bogard & Sons, Box 162, Cairo, West Virginia 26337, allows visitors in its plant 7 days a week and at present is the only plant which encourages tours. The other three plants are Gladding Corporation, Box 247, Parkersburg, West Virginia 26101; Marx of West Virginia, 601 Railroad Street, Glen Dale, West Virginia 26038; and Marble King, Inc., Box 195, Paden City, West Virginia 26159.

Roger Howdyshell, the president of Marble King, is very high on a new book about marbles: their history, lore, and manufacture. The book was written by a man who grew up playing marbles on the playgrounds and sidewalks of New York City—but, of course, the "tools" of his games came from West Virginia. The book is called *The Great American Marble Book* by Fred Ferretti and is published by Workman Publishing Company, 251 East 51st Street, New York, New York 10022.

Marbles are readily available in your neighborhood stores, so there's not much need to mail-order them; however, just remember when you "shoot" them that they are an almost exclusively Southern item.

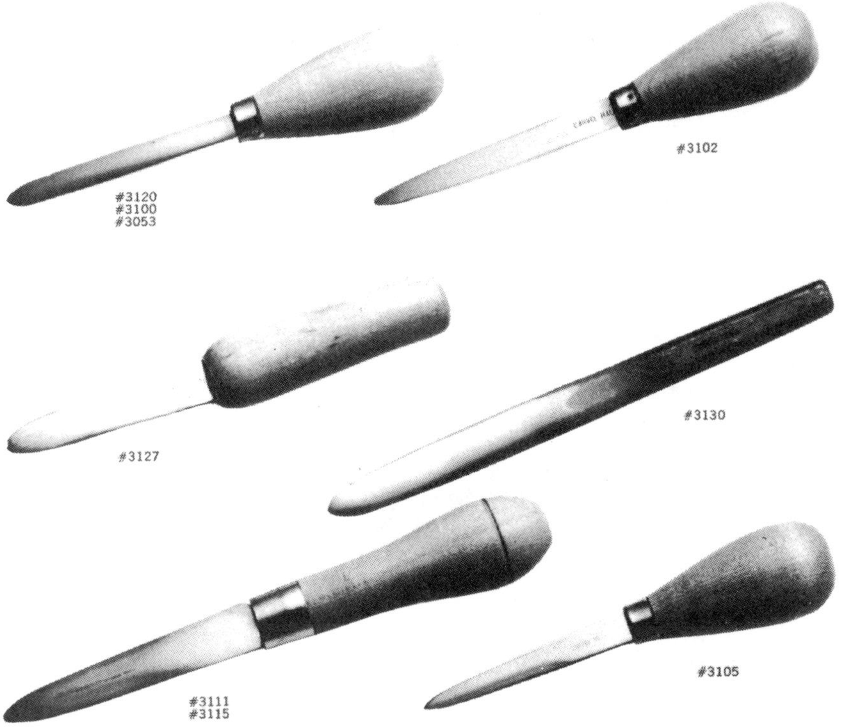

OYSTER OPENERS

Carvel Hall, a division of Towle Silversmiths, has its headquarters near the Chesapeake Bay shoreline in eastern Maryland. Consequently, when they mention that they make oyster knives, it's a safe bet that the knives are tried and true versions of the implement very necessary to the enjoyment of oysters on the half shell or oysters anything else.

There are six styles of oyster knives from which to choose: one, the "New Haven," is, as its name implies, more popular with New Englanders; another, the "Southern and Galveston," is used more in the Southern and Gulf Coast regions. All are designed by professional oyster openers and made by experienced knifesmiths.

Also available from Carvel Hall is a crab knife, designed to get the most meat from each crab—if you've ever picked a crab yourself, you know how valuable such a knife can be. And, for those of us who have to clean and prepare the catch of a freshwater, as well as saltwater, fisherman, Carvel Hall's fish fillet knife is a blessing.

Carvel Hall's entire line of cutlery (including steak, carving, paring, and utility knives) is available in department stores and hardware stores throughout the South. Or you may write the address below for information:

Carvel Hall
Crisfield, Maryland 21817

Prices of these knives are: #3120 (medium handle) $1.80 each; #3102 (special stabber) $1.90 each; #3130 (crack knife) $3.40 each; #3111 (Southern knife) $2.70 each; and #3105 (super stabber) $2.10 each.

SMOKED TURKEYS

Selwood Turkey Farm, located "on Hiway 76—between Winterboro and Childersburg—near DeSoto Caverns" (also near Talladega, Alabama), does a land office business during the holiday season around year's end, but can furnish you with a delicious smoked turkey at any time during the year. Each turkey is cured in a mixture of 15 different herbs and aromatic spices and smoked with hickory and other woods to just the right degree of doneness. The turkeys are available for $1.95 per pound (plus 4% sales tax if you live in Alabama). When ordering, just specify the particular weight turkey you desire—Selwood has just about any size you could hope for between 9 and 13 pounds. Postage is $2.00 a package except for West Coast deliveries which are higher.

To order, enclose a check or money order in the amount indicated by per pound cost and the weight of the turkey you wish and mail to:

Selwood Turkey Farm
Route 1, Box 230
Alpine, Alabama 35014

WHICH WAY IS THE WIND BLOWING?

If your actions are highly dependent upon which way the wind is blowing, you'll want to invest in one of these well-made but inexpensive heavy-duty aluminum weather vanes. The vanes are made by the Lassiter Lightning Protection Manufacturing Company, Mount Olive, North Carolina, and are currently priced at $19.95 postpaid.

You can select the ornament shown here (approximate size is 24" x 24") or choose a dog, horse, cow, hog, or rooster ornament. The weathervane comes complete, ready to install on your building.

Write to:

Lassiter Lightning Protection Mfg. Co.
Route 3, Box 32
Mount Olive, North Carolina 28365

ENVIROSOUTH MAGAZINE

If your interests include environmental conservation, you might be interested in a new magazine called *EnviroSouth*. The magazine is published quarterly in Montgomery, Alabama, and the publisher says that it is the South's only environmental quarterly.

Some of the articles in a recent issue include "A Lesser-Traveled Portion of the Appalachian Trail Promises Wilderness and a Measure of Solitude," "Sue Freeman Miller Guides You Through the Ambitious Plan to Re-Create Thomas Jefferson's Monticello Grove, Now Rising from the Devastation of Clearcutting," and "Southeast Overview: What's Happening to Environmental Issues Around the Region."

A subscription to *EnviroSouth* will cost you $6 a year if you live in the Southern states or the District of Columbia; it is $8 if you live outside the Southern states.

Write to:

EnviroSouth
P.O. Box 17111
Montgomery, Alabama 36117

OUR RESTLESS EARTH

by Edward T. Luther

The University of Tennessee Press
Knoxville, Tennessee

Because Tennessee has one of the strangest shapes in the Union, its terrain is one of the most diverse. With the sole exception of Missouri, Tennessee is bordered by more states (eight) than any other state. Bristol, Tennessee, in the northeastern corner is closer to the province of Ontario than it is to Memphis, in the southeastern corner of Tennessee.

Several major geologic provinces are represented in the Volunteer State. The geologic history of the area is a rich and varied one. *Our Restless Earth* succeeds in the difficult task of presenting the facts on each of the geologic regions in the state and making them interesting and comprehensible even to the geologically untrained.

In the winter of 1811-1812, the New Madrid earthquake shuddered through the area. This event created many lakes in the Mississippi floodplain section of Tennessee. The jewel in this province is Reelfoot Lake, a gorgeous souvenir of the quake. The floodplain itself is very flat, sloping southward toward Memphis.

Moving eastward from the Mississippi, one encounters the plateau slope. Seventy million years ago, it was covered by a shallow sea full of huge reptiles. This is one of the most famous fossil-collecting localities in the United States. Mr. Luther offers some interesting information and a history of the Tennessee River. The river actually flows north and was once made up of at least three rivers! Then there is the Central Basin which supports more bluegrass than there is in all of Kentucky. Further eastward looms the Cumberland Plateau which so inconvenienced our traveling ancestors with its height and massiveness. The main throughway, as every Daniel Boone fan can tell you, is the famous Cumberland Gap. The story of the formation of the Appalachian Mountains is included in this informative book. Mr. Luther also explains the lovely coves which nestle in the Smoky Mountains, and he reveals the reasons behind the mystery craters which are sprinkled throughout Tennessee.

When the reader completes *Our Restless Earth*, there will be very little he doesn't know about the geology of Tennessee. He will know the origins of the state's oil, coal, iron, marble, caves, coves, lakes, etc. This is an enjoyable way to bone up on geology and one of the South's most beautiful states. —S.V.H.

ISON'S NURSERY AND VINEYARD

Perhaps you are one of many who remembers eating scuppernong grapes under an old-fashioned arbor as a child. Scuppernong or muscadine-type grapes are native to most of the Southeastern states from Virginia along the Atlantic and Gulf Coast of Texas. The muscadine region of the South also extends well up into the Blue Ridge mountains and along the Mississippi River into the Central Plains to southern Missouri and along parts of the Tennessee River. Muscadines thrive best where the winter temperatures usually do not go below zero degrees F.

One of the largest producers of top quality scuppernong muscadine plants is Ison's Nursery and Vineyard in Brooks, Georgia. They have put together a booklet which should help anyone who is interested in planning a small home vineyard or a commercial planting. Ison's Nursery and Vineyard sells two kinds of muscadine plants: the Pistillate and the Self-Fertile. The booklet provides a description of each variety.

Also, the booklet has a section on the vertical trellis with diagrams and photographs. Other discussions include how to double yields by the third year and how to prevent possible cold injury to plants.

Write for the informative booklet and price list.

Ison's Nursery and Vineyard
Brooks, Georgia 30205

AUDUBON WITH A CAMERA

Perry D. Slocum has a busy life. He is, on one hand, the proprietor of Slocum Water Gardens, a Winter Haven, Florida, showplace and nursery for tropical water plants. He is also an excellent protographer of birds and has produced, in conjunction with the Florida Audubon Society, a fantastic book containing 145 full-color, full-page photographs of birds in their native surroundings. In addition, there is a complete commentary about each bird, when and how it was photographed, and a map showing its habitat in all seasons. Not surprisingly, Perry Slocum has been named one of the top five nature photographers in the world by *Who's Who in Photography*. The book, *Birds of North America and How to Photograph Them,* sells for $12.95 and may be ordered by writing Mr. Slocum.

To return to Mr. Slocum's role as president and founder of Slocum Water Gardens—he has been in the business for over 40 years and has established a 7-acre site in central Florida with 33 outdoor pools and 122 indoor pools for the production of water lilies, lotus, aquatics, and goldfish. Mr. Slocum will ship his plants and fish to every state. To order, write:

Slocum Water Gardens
1101 Cypress Gardens Road
Winter Haven, Florida 33880

OWEN'S VINEYARD AND NURSERY

A delight to both the eye and taste—that is a grape arbor. It will satisfy your aesthetic and gastronomic desires as well.

Owen's Vineyard and Nursery in Gay, Georgia, has become the largest producer of high quality muscadine grapes (*vitis rotundifloria*) since its beginning in 1934. They are in the business of supplying the best muscadine varieties available and to supply new and better varieties as they are developed. Owen's ships plants into all states where muscadines will grow and into many foreign countries.

Grape-growing can be profitable. The yield of the muscadine is only a few bunches of fruit per vine in the second year. However, well-tended vines may produce a ton or more of fruit per acre the third year. Production should increase until vines reach maturity, usually between 6 and 10 years. A production average of four and one-half tons of fruit per acre over a 20-year period is a realistic figure.

Owen's offers many varieties of the muscadine which may be bought individually or in collections (the latter, to obtain a longer fruiting season).

They will be glad to send you their booklet, "Muscadine Grapes," which includes information on muscadine varieties, their care, and harvesting, as well as complete price and ordering information.

Illustrated here are reprints from the booklet on trellis construction.

For further information, write:

Owen's Vineyard and Nursery
M. Aubrey Owen and Sons
Georgia Highway 85, 4 miles north of
Gay, Georgia 30218

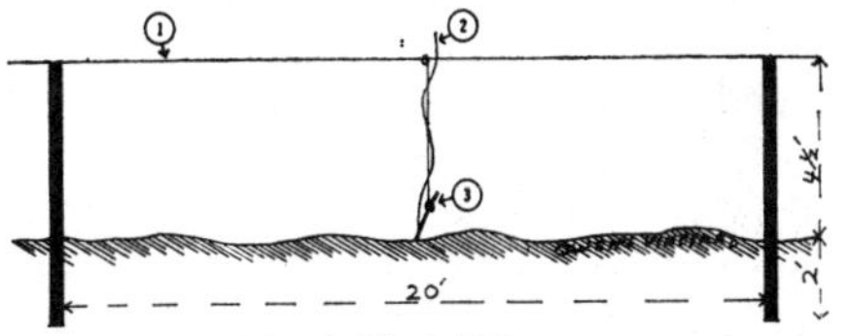

1. No. 9 Smooth Galvanized Wire
2. Vine
3. Sisal Twine

The end posts should be at least 7" in diameter, 8' long, set 3½' in the ground and securely braced. Line posts should be at least 4" in diameter, 6½' long and set 2' in the ground, and 20' apart in the row. One strand of No. 9 smooth galvanized wire is tied around one end post, run along the top of the line posts, stretched tight and stapled, then tied around the other end post. The trellis should be erected before the vines are set or at least before growth starts. Vines should be planted exactly half-way between posts and exactly under the trellis wire.

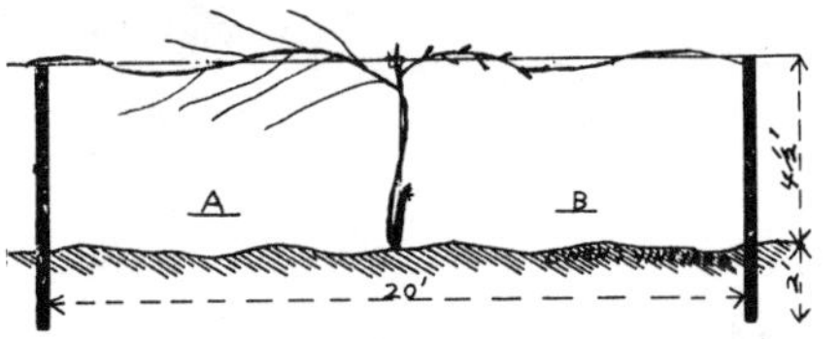

Diagram of the trellis showing a two year old vine.

A—Shows the beginning of lateral growth on the main arm.
B—Shows the beginning of fruit spur formation, which is the lateral growth pruned off to two or three buds.

The first year, do not remove the leaves from the trunk but cut off the lateral canes that arise just above each leaf. By the second year, the vine should have made enough growth so that all new growth is removed from the trunk. When the cane selected as the trunk has grown one foot above the trellis wire, tie the trunk tightly to the wire. This will provide support for the trunk until the arms are well-formed. Cut off top growth slightly above the wire so as to force lateral shoots to sprout all along the trunk. Select one cane from each side of the trunk, preferably 2 to 6 inches below the wire.

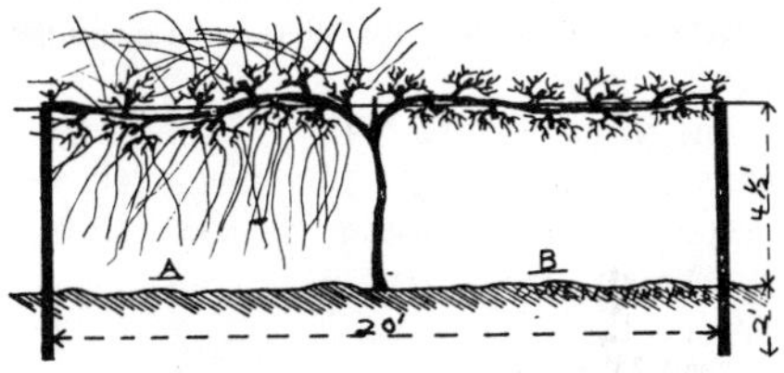

Diagram of a mature vine
A—Unpruned section
B—Pruned section

The fruit spurs are formed at the end of the second summer by cutting back the first lateral canes to two or three buds. Every year thereafter, dormant pruning consists of cutting back the current year's growth to two or three buds. Reasons for this pruning are to balance fruit and vegetable growth, increase berry and cluster size, increase yields, and to hold the size of the plants within convenient bounds.

Variety	Fruit Color	Additional Information
FEMALE FLOWERS (*need pollinating*)		
Fry	Bronze	Clusters very large, with very large fruit size of good quality. Ripens midseason. Vigorous and productive. Beautiful fruit. Susceptible to black rot. Excellent for the southern areas but too susceptible to cold injury for the northern muscadine areas.
Higgins	Bronze	Clusters large, with very large fruit of good quality. Skin thick but edible. Produces a heavy crop that ripens midseason to late. Plants vigorous.
Hunt	Purple	Clusters large, with medium to large fruits. Skin medium. Quality excellent. Ripens early. Vigorous.
Jumbo	Black	Clusters large, with fruit being the largest of any muscadine variety that has been introduced. Good quality and production. Good disease resistance. Ripens midseason to late, irregularly over several weeks, making it an excellent variety for home use.
Scuppernong	Bronze	Clusters medium, with medium-sized fruit. Skin medium thick with excellent quality. Ripens early. Moderately vigorous.
Summit	Bronze	Clusters medium, with large fruit of very good quality. Medium skin (thinnest of any large fruited variety). Ripens midseason. Vines vigorous and very productive. One of the best bronze varieties for home and commercial use.
PERFECT FLOWERS (*self-pollinating*)		
Cowart	Purple	Clusters good size, with large fruit that ripens uniformly. Fruit flavor very good. Vigorous and highly productive.
Dearing	Bronze	Clusters medium, with medium to small fruits of excellent quality. Thin skin. Heavy production that ripens midseason.
Magnolia	Bronze	Clusters are medium to large, with large fruit of excellent quality. Ripens late. Vigorous and productive.
Southland	Purple	Bears high-quality, non-glossy medium-sized fruit. Ripens midseason.

Blueberries

Owen's Vineyard and Nursery also ships blueberry plants and to quote Mr. M. Aubrey Owen—"We grow Southern Blueberries developed in the South for the South, (*Vaccinium ashei*) commonly called Rabbiteye blueberries."

You may send for their brochure (at the above address) which lists eight varieties of blueberries and provides helpful information on their cultivation.

If you're a gardener and have known the frustration of losing your crop to forces that you thought were beyond your control, then the Garden Monster is for you. Several garden predators like to feast on crops. But the Garden Monster's weird noises, movements, reflections, and vibrations scare off the birds, rabbits, squirrels, mice, and moles that may be devouring your garden, berry patch, grapes, or fruit trees.

Undoubtedly, at this point, you are curious to know—what is a Garden Monster? The Garden Monster has eight tentacles of super strong black plastic film which fan out around an aluminum grommet. The gardener tacks the Monster to a stick, pole, or stake. The Monster is activated by the slightest breeze and the tentacles set up a crackling, tinny chatter, which, along with the motions of the tentacles and light reflections, drive away the garden predators.

It is recommended that you use two Monsters to protect even the smallest garden. You may order two Monsters for $5.00 or four Monsters for $9.00 postpaid.

Garden Monster
Camden, South Carolina 29020

Start the Garden Early In a Cold Frame

A cold frame is a bottomless, enclosed soil bed covered with glass, plastic, or other transparent material. Although functional year-round, a cold frame is particularly useful at this time of year for starting flower and vegetable seeds early and for rooting hardwood cuttings of trees and shrubs.

The cold frame is also a good place to store potted plants, especially those that are recovering from insect or disease damage.

Here are some pointers on using a cold frame. For construction, use the sketch as a guide.

Plan a location for the cold frame where it will receive direct sunlight for a few hours each day. The frame will need to be partially shaded during warm winter days.

Dig a 4-inch hole in the ground to the dimensions of the frame; then set the frame in the hole. This will help provide insulation. If you prefer to place the cold frame on a flat surface, mound soil halfway up outside walls.

To create a good soil bed for the cold frame, spread a 3- to 4-inch layer of shredded leaves or other organic matter on the ground. Then add topsoil or garden loam mixed with equal parts perlite or builder's sand. Root cuttings or sow seeds directly in this medium.

If you prefer to use flats to hold the growing medium, spread a layer of shredded leaves, hay, or wood chips in the cold frame to provide sufficient insulation and ensure good drainage from the flats. Fill the flats with a mixture of equal parts potting soil and perlite, and insert cuttings or sow seeds in them.

A little pine straw scattered on the cover of the cold frame will provide the kind of filtered light required for rooting cuttings or germinating seeds.

Water and ventilation are important. Too much moisture and too little ventilation can cause cuttings and seeds to rot and fungi to thrive. Too much exposure, on the other hand, may result in cold damage or sunscald.

Keep the soil in the cold frame generally moist but not soaked. Water with a fine but gentle spray from the garden hose, taking care not to disturb the soil. Spray foliage as well as soil.

Adjust the ventilation by raising or lowering the lid of the cold frame.

On particularly cold nights, pile a small amount of actively fermenting compost in a corner of the cold frame to provide a little warmth for the plants.

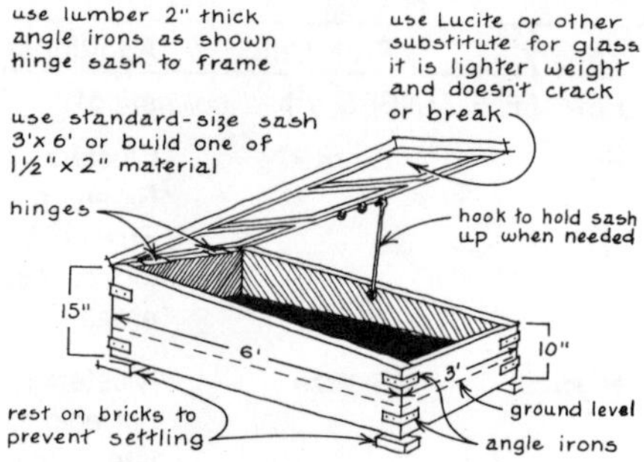

NATURE'S PANTRY

by David Wilson

Lorien House
P.O. Box 1112
Black Mountain, North Carolina 28711

Nature's Pantry was written to demonstrate just which plants, common to the woodlands of Eastern North America, are edible and could serve as emergency nourishment if necessary. As a side effect, the book is an extremely educational tool for "expanding one's range of experience, to serve in daily living as well. . . . " One hundred plants are itemized, and pen and ink drawings accompany the listings. Each entry includes a full description of the plant, preparation of the edible parts for eating, and any medicinal qualities of the plant. *Nature's Pantry,* which sells for $2.00, would be a perfect gift for anyone interested in the natural abundance of our land.

Lorien House also publishes books of poetry and philosophy and now has a series on solar energy.

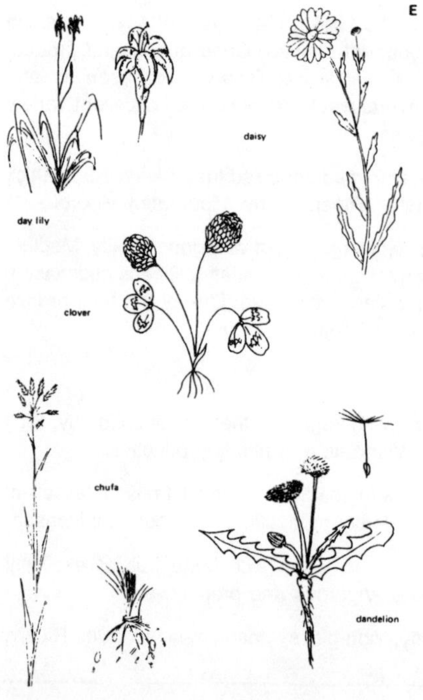

12

DANDELION (Leontodon taraxacum)

Description: It is a perenrial. The leaves are medium green, radiating at ground level; they are feather shape and jagged on the sides. The tips are usually curved (some pointed). The flower is yellow and multi-petaled on a single plain stalk (with milky juice). The seeds are a puffball on the stalk. The root is a single taper, fibrous and white.

Preparation: The leaves make an excellent raw salad, or may be cooked as a green. Late Spring finds them bitter, and slicing out the central vein will remove most of this taste. The roots may be dried and boiled for coffee or ground for flour.

Medicine: High in vitamins A, C, and protein; minerals calcium, magnesium, potassium. The dried root tea is used for a tonic and laxative.

*

DAY LILY (Hemerocallis fulva) - Tiger Lily -

Description: A perennial plant, it grows in dense patches, from bulbs and a root stock. The bulbs are white. Leaves are thin, 1 to 2 feet long, light green, one central vein. The stalk is 2 to 6 feet tall, with buds branching at the top. Flowers are orange (sometimes yellow), trumpet shape, flaring 6 petal with long stamen.

Preparation: The bulbs are good boiled. The flowers are dried and fried or put into soups or breads for flavoring.

*

BEN MEADOWS CATALOGUE

One of the most fascinating catalogues we have seen comes from the Ben Meadows Company, "the place to buy anything for the forester, tree farmer, engineer, draftsman, surveyor or utility." Indeed, in its 624 pages you're likely to find anything for anyone—it's a grown-up wish book for those who just like to imagine possessing the exact tool for the most precise job. For instance, you can buy through Ben Meadows Catalogue such things as templates for drawing all sorts of designs—from letters of the alphabet to electronic components; drafting equipment from paper to drafting lights and tables; map drawing materials; a huge selection of pens, pencils, nibs, inks, and erasers; all types of filing systems; notebooks; surveying equipment; stopwatches; barometers; public address systems; slide rules; measuring rods and types; first aid kits; snake bite kits; insect repellent; boots; axes; knives; backpacks; tents; sleeping bags; water pollution detectors; tool boxes; power tools—and an assortment of other items, ad infinitum.

The Ben Meadows Catalogue is obviously not cheap to produce; there is therefore a charge of $3.00 for each one ordered, but the charge is refundable on the first order of $25.00 or more. The catalogue itself would make a great gift for the person who *thinks* he has everything—after glancing through Ben Meadows Catalogue, he'll realize just how much he lacks!

Order from:

Ben Meadows Company
3589 Broad Street
Atlanta (Chamblee), Georgia 30366

THE ONLY TREE STAND THAT CLIMBS

If you're trying to get away from a charging wild boar, the Baker Tree Stand will not help you climb a tree in record time. What it will enable you to do, however, is establish a perch above your game so that the boar (or whatever else you may be hunting) will not be able to get you on the run anyway.

It's also generally better to be above your game: there is an advantage to being above the normal sight line; your scent will dissipate before being noticed by your prey; and firing your gun or arrow down toward the ground is a much safer practice than normal firing.

If you prefer to let others do the hunting, you might enjoy using the Baker Tree Stand for tree pruning or wild life photography and general observations. The stand can also double as a convenient shelf or seat when you're camping.

There are no nuts and bolts in the Baker Tree Stand; it is hinged to fold flat for light and quiet carrying. The stand weighs 10 pounds, but will hold up to 500 pounds. Cost is $68.95. (Georgia residents add sales tax).

Send $.25 for a brochure or order from:

Baker Tree Stand
P.O. Box 1003, Dept. CS
428 North St. Augustine Road
Valdosta, Georgia 31601

Safety belt, included with the Baker Tree Stand, lets you lean out from tree.

The Strap Assembly snaps into holes already in the frame of the Baker Tree Stand, lets you backpack the 10-lb. stand easily. Cost: $4.95.

"Then I went to Rabbit Springs and found a fable. In the pump house, I found a spotted frog, green and gold and black and copper—magnificently dressed. I caught him and started home. On the way I met a moccasin. When I thrust a stick at him, he opened his mouth wide—white and horrible inside. There I was with the stick in one hand and the frog in the other, and the moccasin had opened wide his mouth, almost at my invitation. I resisted and kept the frog, but I've been wondering ever since. Have I interfered with providence?" HORN ISLAND LOGS.

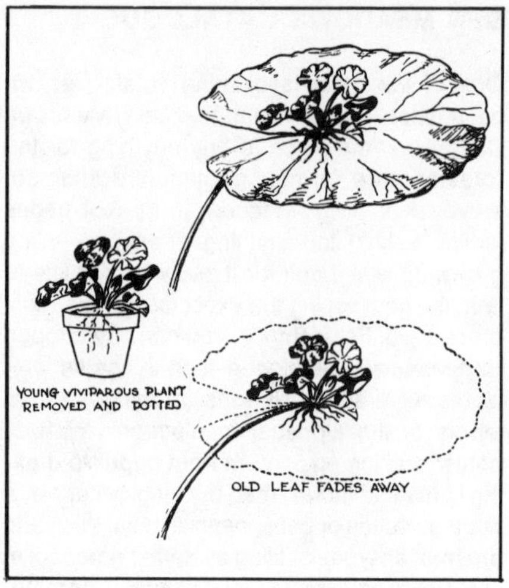

LILYPONS WATER GARDENS

Lilypons Water Gardens, which covers hundreds of acres of lower Frederick County in Maryland, is the world's largest producer and distributor of exotic aquatic plants, goldfish, and garden pool supplies.

To be more specific about the location, Lilypons Water Gardens is in Lilypons, Maryland. We'll let *them* explain the genesis of the name.

"Back in 1930 Three Springs Fisheries (as the firm was then named) was doing such a heavy business, shipping goldfish and waterlilies to all parts of the world, that postal phases of the business became a major problem. At the suggestion of fisheries executives, the Post Office Department agreed to establish a post office at the fisheries."

"What to do for a name? Something short, something descriptive. One postal official, an opera devotee, suggested the name of Lily Pons. Would the famous opera star permit the name? She was delighted! So, in 1932, the official name of our little community became Lilypons, Maryland."

"Later Lily Pons came to Lilypons to see the lily ponds. She sent many of her Christmas cards from the small post office and she wrote now and then to fisheries families."

The Gardens has everything you need to maintain a fish pond or aquarium including fish, which are shipped in polyethylene bags filled with oxygenated water and packed in conventional cardboard boxes, and scavengers—giant bullfrogs, clams, tadpoles, and snails. You can even purchase a small fiberglass pool kit for $39.95 and in one afternoon build your own.

Decorate your pond with plants and at the same time provide your bullfrog with his own lilypad. There is a stunning array from which to choose: hardy and tropical water-lilies, sacred lotus, shallow water plants, and oxygenating plants.

All of this may be seen in the color catalogue available for $1.00 from:

Lilypons Water Gardens
949 Southern Road
Lilypons, Maryland 21717
(also in Brookshire, Texas 77423)

ALL ABOUT BEES

Did you know that 95% of all bees in the United States are Italian? Not imports from the European boot, mind you, but a breed of bee noted—blessedly—for having an *average* temperament and for staying on his comb *well* when the hive is open!

Walter T. Kelley, who owns a beehive factory in Clarkson, Kentucky, must know just about everything there is to know about bees and beekeeping. He started learning when he received an encyclopedia on beekeeping for his 11th birthday. That was some 60 years ago.

For the initiated beekeeper, Mr. Kelley publishes an annual catalogue, at no charge, entitled *Bee Supply Super Market.*

For the aspiring beekeeper, he recommends you first buy his book, *How to Keep Bees and Sell Honey,* $1.25 postpaid. We might add, this book is fascinating reading to anyone who is curious about bees.

Mr. Kelley begins by telling you of the three kinds of bees in a hive—the queen, the mother of all the bees in her colony, who will lay between 1,000 and 2,000 eggs a day; the drones, the males whose only value is fertilizing the queen; and the workers, the undeveloped females who, as their name indicates, are the nectar and pollen gatherers, the wax builders, the honey processors, the housekeepers, and the hive guards. The workers have the stingers! (While the queen also has a stinger, she uses it only to sting another bee, usually another queen.)

Mr. Kelley continues with information both entertaining and practical, everything from A to W—"Advertising honey," to "Wiring frames." Many of the pictures he took himself during travels in the United States, Panama, Canada, and Western Europe.

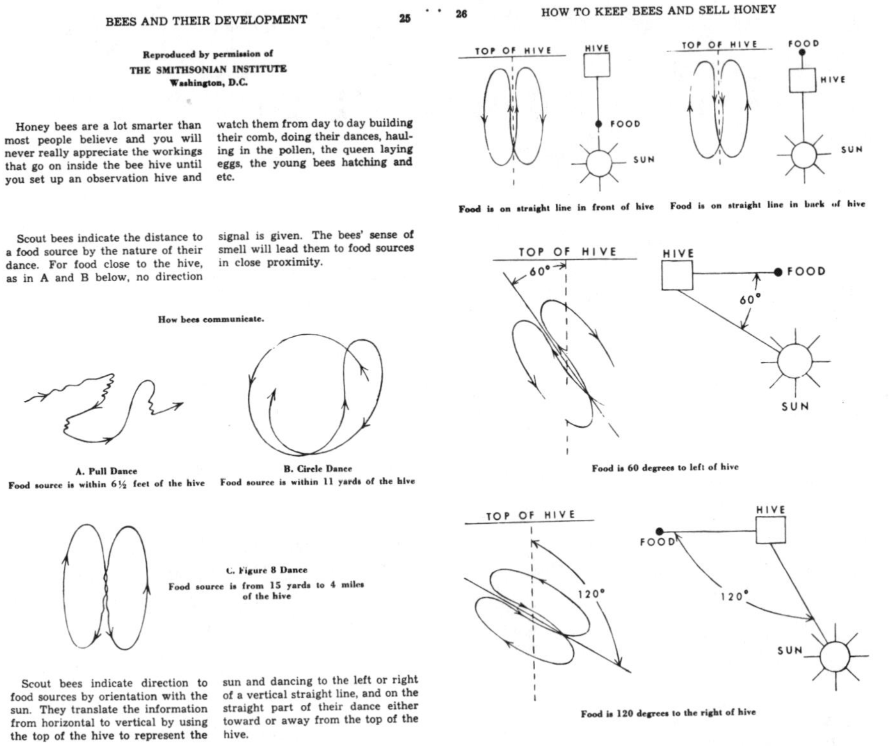

BEES AND THEIR DEVELOPMENT 25 · · 26 HOW TO KEEP BEES AND SELL HONEY

Reproduced by permission of
THE SMITHSONIAN INSTITUTE
Washington, D.C.

Honey bees are a lot smarter than most people believe and you will never really appreciate the workings that go on inside the bee hive until you set up an observation hive and watch them from day to day building their comb, doing their dances, hauling in the pollen, the queen laying eggs, the young bees hatching and etc.

Scout bees indicate the distance to a food source by the nature of their dance. For food close to the hive, as in A and B below, no direction signal is given. The bees' sense of smell will lead them to food sources in close proximity.

How bees communicate.

A. Pull Dance
Food source is within 6½ feet of the hive

B. Circle Dance
Food source is within 11 yards of the hive

C. Figure 8 Dance
Food source is from 15 yards to 4 miles of the hive

Scout bees indicate direction to food sources by orientation with the sun. They translate the information from horizontal to vertical by using the top of the hive to represent the sun and dancing to the left or right of a vertical straight line, and on the straight part of their dance either toward or away from the top of the hive.

Food is on straight line in front of hive

Food is on straight line in back of hive

Food is 60 degrees to left of hive

Food is 120 degrees to the right of hive

When you are ready to buy, check the *Bee Supply Super Market* for the Beginner's Outfit, which contains the necessary items you will need in starting one hive of bees including bee veil, bee gloves, etc., a book of instructions, and the hive which is shipped knocked down with complete directions and nails for assembling. The wood is so soft, the pictures and directions so complete, and the fit of the parts so perfect, that you will not have a bit of trouble in assembling the hive. Kelley's furnishes ready-wired comb foundation, so that all you have to do is to nail it in place.

You may order Kelley's Beginner's Outfit, without bees, F.O.B. Clarkson, for $48.00, or Kelley's Complete Beginner's Outfit, with bees, for $71.00. The Bees?—Italian, of course!

To order books or bees, write to:

The Walter T. Kelley Co., Inc.
Clarkson, Kentucky 42726

THE SPEEDY BEE

Troy Fore, Jr., and his wife Mary live in the village of Gardi just south of Jesup, Georgia. He is a beekeeper and a newspaper publisher. In fact, Troy publishes a newspaper about bees, *The Speedy Bee,* a monthly tabloid newspaper for professional and amateur beekeepers. It is, he believes, the only monthly beekeeping newspaper in the world.

What is there to say about beekeeping that will fill a 24-page newspaper every month? There are "Coming Events," dealing with meetings of interest to beekeepers; an editorial column by Mr. Fore and one by his wife appropriately entitled, "The Queencell;" many letters from readers; feature articles as well as reprints from other beekeeping publications; "Honey Market News," which is a monthly report issued by the U.S. Department of Agriculture; and many interesting advertisements, a certain sign of stability for the publication. Troy Fore, Jr., comes by his interest in beekeeping honestly. His father was a beekeeper specializing in raising and selling queen bees. This lifelong exposure to honey production is reflected in the 34-year-old Fore's wide-ranging knowledge of the subject. Coverage of the beekeeping industry in the U.S. and Canada requires travel to as many as a dozen beekeeping meetings and conventions a year.

Despite Troy Fore's considerable knowledge of his subject, articles in *The Speedy Bee* are aimed at the average beekeeper, staying away from the technical stuff without going altogether to the elemental. *The Bee,* as the Fores affectionately refer to their paper, has readers in every state and in two dozen foreign countries. Subscription rates are $6.00 per year in the U.S. and Canada and $10.00 in other countries. Sample copies are available for $.50 each. Order from:

The Speedy Bee
P.O. Box 998
Jesup, Georgia 31545

"I woke up to rain, and thought what a nice morning to sleep; then a mosquito bit me on the cheek. Some day I may write a book on man's debt to mosquitoes and gnats. Someone admitted that they increased the birth rate. . . .

"My perfect rapport with nature came when I found my first sea horse, the reconciling agent in time—motor magna—between the horrible monotony of the machine and the bomb of poetry—alive, and when I put it in water it hummed. Its motor or wings or fins worked—rainbow colored, blue-red-yellow, a tripart rainbow."
HORN ISLAND LOGS.

LIMB-I-NATOR

Meadows Manufacturing Company has come up with a new tool for the homeowner. It's called the Limb-I-Nator. The homeowner for whom this product is designed is the one who mows his own lawn, trims his shrubbery, cleans his gutters, and wishes that he had a way to safely and efficiently prune ugly, dying limbs.

The Limb-I-Nator allows you to prune high limbs while standing on the ground. Two forty-foot ropes are attached to a saw (one of them is weighted for placement) which can cut limbs up to six inches in diameter. The length of the rope will allow you to prune up to forty feet above the ground. The saw wraps almost around the limb. When it is pulled back and forth, the saw cuts the limb in such a way that no splintering occurs at the bottom of the limb. Due to the length of the rope, the user can stand out of range of a falling limb. It is safer to prune a limb than to have one fall unexpectedly.

You may order the Limb-I-Nator for $19.95, which includes UPS delivery. Also, this product carries a money-back guarantee.

Meadows Manufacturing Company
543 Whitehall, S.W.
Atlanta, Georgia 30303

Catalogs for Plant People

Gardeners always seem to be people in search of a special plant they've heard or read about. Here is a list of nurseries and seed producers that offer a catalogue or price list to the public. You may contact them directly to obtain the catalogue and perhaps answers to your questions.

Vernon Barnes & Son Nursery, Box 250-L, McMinnville, Tennessee 37110; (615) 668-8576. Landscape plants, fruit trees, berry plants, wildflowers. Catalogue is free. Will ship plants.

Bass Pecan Company, Lumberton, Mississippi 39455; (601) 796-2461. Pecan trees, fig trees, landscape plants, magnolias, all hollies. Catalogue is free. Will ship plants.

Beal's Nursery, Route 3, Box 142, Lincolnton, North Carolina 28092; (704) 735-5147. Landscape plants, bedding plants, some fruit and nut trees. Catalogue 50 cents. Will ship only bare-root plants, preferably in-state.

Bentley Nursery, Route 3, Box 215, Monticello, Florida 32344; (904) 997-2555. Landscape plants, general nursery stock. Wholesale only. Catalogue 39 cents. Will not ship plants but will refer inquiries to client nurseries all over the Southeast.

Bountiful Ridge Nurseries, Princess Anne, Maryland 21853; (301) 651-0400. Fruit trees, shade trees, nut trees, berry plants, grape vines. Catalogue is free. Will ship plants.

Finch's Blueberry Nursery, Route 1, Box 341, Bailey, North Carolina 27807; (919) 235-4664. Rabbit-eye blueberries. Catalogue is free. Will ship plants.

The Graham Center Seed Directory, Route 3, Box 95, Wadesboro, North Carolina 28170. Lists numerous sources of seeds and gives a brief description of what each source offers. Catalogue is $1.

Green Oak Nursery, Box 12219, Jackson, Mississippi 39211; (601) 956-5022. Zoysia and Bermuda seed, large trees. Brochure is free. Will ship both plants and seeds.

Hastings Seed Company, Box 4274, Atlanta, Georgia 30302; (404) 321-6981. Vegetable seeds, flower seeds, and bulbs. Catalogue is free. Will ship.

Iron Gate Garden, Route 3, Box 101, Kings Mountain, North Carolina 28086; (704) 435-9338. Lilies, hosta, and perennials. Catalogue is free. Will ship plants.

Kilgore Seed Company, 1400 West First Street, Sanford, Florida 32771; (305) 323-6630. Vegetable and flower seeds. Catalogue is free. Will ship.

Leafy's Greenhouse, Route 2, Box 41, Centre, Alabama 35960; (205) 927-5655. African violets, episcias, cyclamen, gloxinias. Price list available. Will ship plants.

McGill Greenhouses, 66 Oakland Avenue, Mobile, Alabama 36608; (205) 342-6822. Rare tropical foliage plants, orchids, bromeliads, horticultural supplies. Catalogue is free. Will ship plants.

Meadows Farms, Route 2, Box 102-A, Sterling, Virginia 22170; (703) 450-4240. Trees, shrubs, indoor plants, and landscape plants. Catalogue is free. Will ship anywhere.

George W. Park Seed Company, Box 31, Greenwood, South Carolina 29647; (803) 374-3341. Wide variety of seeds. Catalogue is free. Will ship anywhere.

Rayner Brothers, Department SL-1, Salisbury, Maryland 21801; (301) 742-1594. Strawberry, blueberry, asparagus plants, bramble fruit plants, and fruit and nut trees. Catalogue is free. Will ship plants.

Reasoner's Tropical Nurseries, 4610 14th Street West, Bradenton, Florida 33507; (813) 756-1881. Landscape plants (specialty hibiscus). Hibiscus variety list is free. Will ship only hibiscus plants. Will not ship to Texas, California, Arizona, or Canada.

Sandy Mush Herbs, Route 2, Surrett Cove Road, Leicester, North Carolina 28748; (704) 683-2014 or 683-2087. Herb plants and seeds. Catalogue is 50 cents (refundable with first order). Will ship plants and seeds.

Sunset Nursery, 4007 Elrod Avenue, Tampa, Florida 33616; (813) 835-6441. Landscape plants, unusual fruit trees, bonsai. Send stamped, self-addressed envelope for bonsai price list. Will ship.

George Tait & Sons Nursery, Box 5545, Norfolk, Virginia 23504; (804) 622-3385. Grass seeds, flower seeds and bulbs, vegetable seeds, berry plants, horticultural supplies. Catalogue is free. Will ship plants and seeds.

Texas Onion Plant Company, Department 506, Farmersville, Texas 75031; (214) 782-7171. Wide variety of onion plants. Catalogue is free. Will ship anywhere.

Thomasville Nurseries, Box 7, Thomasville, Georgia 31792; (912) 226-5568. Roses, daylilies, camellias, azaleas. Catalogue is free. Will ship plants.

Thrower Nursery, Route 1, Box 257, Baileyton, Alabama 35019; (205) 796-2245. Fruit, nut, and flowering trees. Catalogue is free. Will ship plants.

FOR THE BIRDS!

Feathered friends feel at home with houses and feeders made from rough materials. This nesting box/feeder combination, made from hollow logs and slabs, is ideal for any season. Patterns and instructions for making six other houses and feeders from inexpensive, rustic materials are available for $2.00 plus $1.50 postage and handling from:

Wood and the Works
Route 4, Box 1720
Alabaster, Alabama 35007

NATIONAL GEOGRAPHIC SOCIETY

The National Geographic Society publishes a plethora of interesting titles, records, maps, and globes.

The books of the society are as varied as they are beautiful; all are related to this Earth which man shares with plants and other animals. A sampling of titles—*Great Religions of the World, Marvels of Animal Behavior, The World of the American Indian, Our Continent, Ancient Egypt,* and, for young people, *A National Geographic World* magazine and a series called "Books for Young Explorers." Listed under special publications are 56 books, and among the subjects of these are *The Ocean Realm, Into the Wilderness, America's Sunset Coast,* and *Mysteries of the Ancient World.*

Records include "We Americans," "On Parade," "Songs of the Cumberland Gap," and "Dixieland Jazz."

There are political globes and physical globes. There are maps: atlas, special interest, enlarged ($6.00), and general reference (plastic $4.00, paper $3.00).

The National Geographic Society catalogue of publications is sent annually to members in the Society, and should you not be a member and wish to join or merely want the catalogue, write to:

The National Geographic Society
Washington, D.C. 20036

Covey of Quail

When it comes to fine dining, quail are hard to beat. Whether they're barbecued, braised, roasted, or southern fried, quail make a meal that is fit for a king.

Quail used to be a delicacy enjoyed only by a few. But now, thanks to modern pen-raising and processing techniques, everyone can serve these delicious game birds.

If you order Bobwhite quail from J. Garland Jones at Covey of Quail, you can be sure they're fresh. His birds are processed weekly; they are "flavor fed and packed (4) to a carton and quick frozen in water for delicious eating." He will ship a whole covey of quail (16 birds), packed in dry ice in a reusable styrofoam container, for $31.68. Add $8.00 for handling and prepaid shipping by United Parcel Service anywhere in the United States.

J. Garland Jones
2527 Poole Road
Raleigh, North Carolina 27610

WOODPLAY™

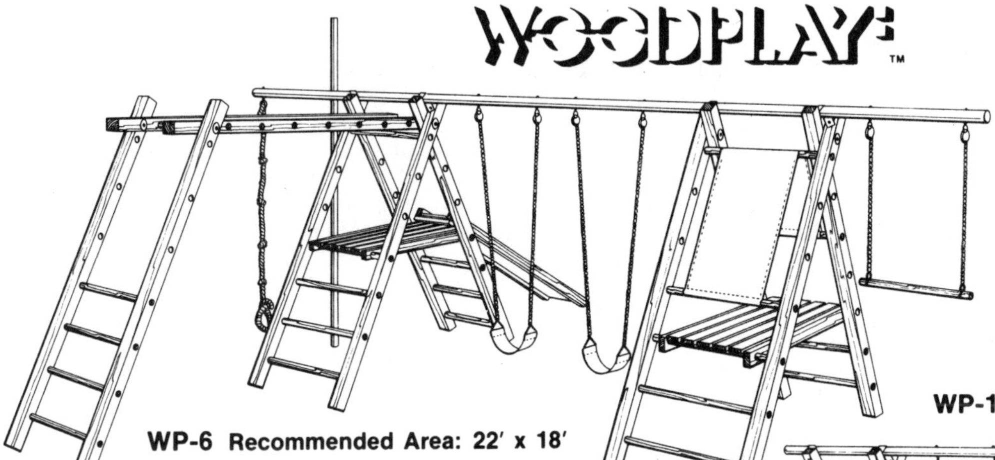

WP-6 Recommended Area: 22′ x 18′

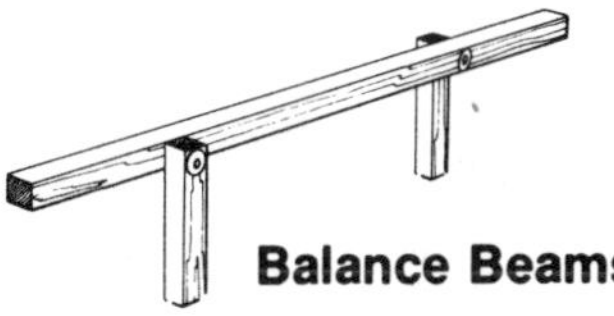

Balance Beams

See Saws

WP-1 Recommended Area: 12′ x 16′

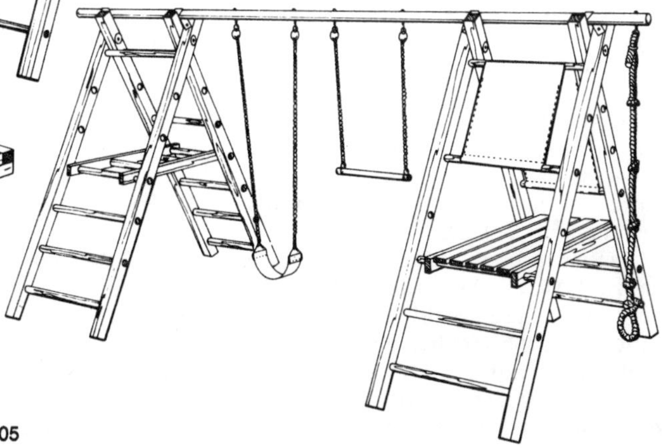

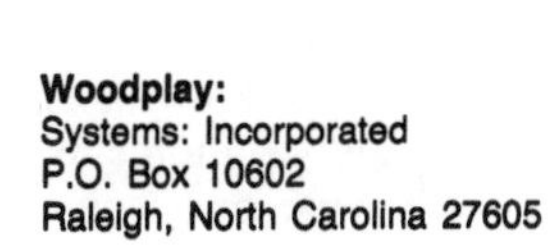

Sandboxes

WOODEN PLAY STRUCTURES

Woodplay backyard play units are built primarily of wood. Modular designs provide basic units or complete backyard activity centers. The units are easily assembled—or disassembled for moving. The units provide a variety of climbers, swings, and platforms to challenge the children in your yard. Prices on these units vary from $275.00 to $470.00. Also available are sandboxes, see saws, and balance beams.

For a free brochure describing the various units, write to:

Woodplay:
Systems: Incorporated
P.O. Box 10602
Raleigh, North Carolina 27605

Rock Climbing: It's a Vertical World

North Carolina's Stone Mountain offers a wall of heady resistance to a growing army of young mountain climbers. You can also just watch from below.

by GLENN MORRIS

Rock climbers deliberately seek progress the hard way. Given good weather, they flock to the hills in droves, becoming pairs of antlike figures that slowly inch their way up the mammoth rock faces of the Southern Highlands. Ever wonder who would try climbing? Men and women of all ages and backgrounds from every Southern state climb, and they are quite happy in their vertical world. Perhaps the only thing that sets them apart is that none of them can spell acrophobia.

In spite of the apparent hazards and the difficulty of getting started, the sport is rapidly growing. With more and more participants each year, the Southern states are responding by recognizing the legitimacy of climbing as a planned recreation. In North Carolina's Stone Mountain State Park, near Elkin (one of many fine climbing areas in that state alone), nonclimbers can lie back in a meadow beneath the 600-foot granite wall and watch the miniature figures stretch their way up the side.

To nonclimbers it may seem a crazy or suicidal sport. In fact, climbing has been called the hardest way in the world to accomplish absolutely nothing. But devotees of this adroit, almost arcane sport will tell you that understanding rock climbing begins with understanding the challenge.

Climber Chuck Mitchell states it simply, "All climbers, no matter how experienced, eventually come to that point where the smallest upward movement seems impossible, and they may hesitate or freeze. That moment becomes the most important in their life,

and solving that problem is the crux of the climbing challenge."

That point of crux has its particular expression in an affliction known as "sewing machine heel," when the knee and heel of a climber start hammering in an uncontrollable piston-like spasm. It is said that you haven't climbed until you have the "heel."

The sport, even on low boulder climbs, can become that serious, but it is usually immeasurably fun and satisfying. Part of the joy begins with recapturing the childlike fascination of scrambling over and around large rocks and boulders. The climber then refines his skills, slowly adapting them to larger and harder locations. Confidence in individual ability plays a tremendous part in climbing. Climbs that terrify beginners will, in as little as a year, become as easy as stairs.

The world of the individual on a climb is like a chess match. Slow, rhythmic movements, each carefully planned and evaluated, pace the climber from one resting place to the next. Movement through some stretches of rock requires a masterful artlike control of the body—like a vertical ballet.

To reach the top by any means possible (what would seem to be the ultimate goal) is not completely satisfying for experienced climbers. Fulfillment is inseparable from the active moments of climbing. There is a sense of accomplishment at "topping out," or finishing a climb, but this is a composite emotion constructed of the many small triumphs and successes that contribute to completing a route.

In spite of the intensely personal nature of climbing, climbers also develop strong ties with other individuals, for the simple reason that few climbers climb alone. Solo climbing is not safe. In fact, climbers develop strong loyalties with familiar partners and are hesitant to climb "blind"—with somebody of unknown ability.

Generally, climbing is done in pairs —two climbers to a length of rope usually 150 feet long. The purpose of the rope is to interrupt a severe fall. As the first climber, or leader, ascends, he places anchors, called protection, in the rock face.

The type of protection varies, but generally it is in the form of a chock— a wedge of metal with a steel or nylon loop that is placed in a crack in the rock so that a downward pull wedges it tightly. With a chock secured, a snaplink or carabiner (a steel oval with a spring loaded gate) is clipped into the metal or nylon loop of the chock, and the rope in turn is clipped into the snaplink. The leader then continues to climb while his partner, called the second, belays him by slowly releasing or feeding the leader rope.

Should the leader fall, the second would limit the fall by tightly grasping the rope, allowing the leader to fall only twice the distance he has climbed above the last point of protection.

When the leader climbs the length of the rope, the belay is reversed. The leader, from a secured anchor point, will bring the second climber up to the new position, and the sequence begins anew. Along the way up to the leader, the second will remove the protection placed by the first climber.

Technological developments of the last decade have radically altered the type of protection used. For years, pitons, small chisel-bladed, metal nails with a steel eye loop, were hammered into the rock. These were difficult to remove and damaged the rock by widening the cracks where pitons were repeatedly inserted.

Most climbers today use chocks, which are not only readily retrievable, but do not damage the rock when used. The incredible array of sizes and shapes of chocks looks like a hardware fantasy land—but each one is designed to reduce the severity of a fall.

Not all types of climbing are the same: There are different techniques and even different equipment according to the rock formation.

Vertical and overhanging wall is one

type of climbing. The rock formations are characteristically clifflike and may be pocketed with rough edges and secure natural grips affectionately called "Hail Mary" or "Acme" handholds. Larger chocks and heavy boots with a stiff edge are frequently employed in vertical wall climbing.

Chimney or crack climbs involve wedging part of the body, sometimes the entire body, between two opposing sides of a crack and forcing upward progress by leg strength.

Friction climbing is a technique developed for the smooth granite monadnocks (domes) of places like Stone Mountain, North Carolina. The climbs are over continuous slabs of granite almost void of cracks or spurs of rocks for protection. A special smooth-soled shoe is employed, and the technique is a delicate balancing act. On friction climbs the definition of a ledge is anything 2 inches wide.

All climbs are rated in degree of difficulty by a decimal system. In addition, many sport colorful, humorous names such as "No alternative," "Sufficiently breathless," and "Dum-de-dum-dum."

While climbing sounds simple, it should not be misconstrued as easy or hazard free. There is an inherent and obvious danger in rock climbing. Although it cannot be learned without practice, beginners should have some instruction in basic technique and safety, since trial and error learning can be painful and time consuming.

Chris Hall, of Atlanta's Georgia Outdoors North and vice president of the Southeastern Climbers Association, is a part-time teacher. He states, "Most good outdoor stores will know of a qualified climber who will give basic instruction and teach safe climbing. It is important to learn the elementary precautions early—they are the building blocks for climbing safely at any level of difficulty. One object of climbing is to be sure and come back to climb again."

Most Southern states allow climbs on a personal risk basis. While few states actively encourage climbing, they very rarely restrict the sport. Other popular locations outside of North Carolina include Seneca Rocks in West Virginia and Yonah Mountain in Georgia.

There are many other areas all over the South that are acclaimed by climbers. And many more are added to the list, as climbers continue their quest for new and varied climbs. But the sport of climbing remains ever remote, which doesn't bother climbers at all. They are used to being their own spectators and prefer to enjoy their time outdoors in their own very personal, very solitary way.

AUSTIN-HALL BOOT COMPANY

Austin-Hall Boot Company of El Paso, Texas, does not stock boots. Boots are *handmade* for a particular customer from a set of measurements. Styles for riding, hunting, hiking, or camping are available. So are decorated boots for performers. Everyday and dress boots in various styles are shown in the catalogue; in addition, you may order modifications on the regular styles.

We are showing here two examples of Austin-Hall Boots. The fancy boot is called "Powder River" and the less fancy boot is called "Oak Leaf." In the catalogue we saw, the base prices run from about $52.00 to about $144.00. The modifications you ask for your own pair will, of course, affect the price.

For your free copy of an Austin-Hall catalogue with its price list and full ordering instructions, write to:

Austin-Hall Boot Company
P.O. Box 12368 SL
El Paso, Texas 79912

SNAKE BOOTS

If you spend much time in the woods hunting, hiking, or camping, you'll need a pair of snake boots. The Russ Boot Company in Albany, Georgia, has developed a snake-proof boot that is lightweight, well-built, and affordable for the average sportsman.

Before the company developed these boots, they tested all kinds of leather. Boots were made with ordinary shoe leather two or three hides thick, and they discovered that a snake could strike through them easily. To make these boots snake proof, they now soak the leather for three months in a brine-type chemical solution that tightens and toughens the leather. Only the leather from the throat of a bull is used because this is the toughest hide. After the soaking process, the leather is hand-stitched into a boot.

Each boot is 17 inches high. (This is adequate since most snakes don't strike above 8 inches from the ground.) These boots are saturated with an oil-type substance and have rounded toes, which help them repel water.

Mr. Russ, owner of the company, gives us an added feeling of safety about his product when he says, "Periodically I select a pair of boots at random from our production line and send them to Ross Allen, the famed snake expert in Silver Springs. Allen tests the boots by letting rattlers, cottonmouth moccasins and

even cobras strike and chew on the boots repeatedly. No snake has ever penetrated the leather, and he considers my boots completely safe to wear into his rattlesnake pit."

For a free brochure and the dealer nearest you, write:

Russ Boot Company
P.O. Box 808
Albany, Georgia 31702

Carolina Log Buildings, Inc.

REAL LOG HOMES

The log cabin, once a familiar symbol of the American Frontier, is making a comeback, and Carolina Log Buildings, Inc., in Fletcher, North Carolina, expects to play a big role in its renaissance.

Development of the do-it-yourself, pre-packaged log cabin was undertaken in the early sixties by Jesse P. Ware, a one-time boat builder and founder of the parent company. The first pre-cut cabin was completed in January, 1964, and shortly thereafter the Vermont firm was incorporated as manufacturing unit. Now six plants, including the one in South Carolina, continually endeavor to keep up with the demand started by that one house in the Vermont countryside.

The building system is described in their brochure *Real Log Homes:*

"Whether the home is small or large, the same building system is standard. A ¼" wide and ⅝" deep groove is on the planed top and bottom surface of every log. Fitting tightly into this groove is a strip of hardboard material (spline) which is designed to be twice the depth of the spline groove. The logs are stacked on top of each other with the groove in the bottom surface of the upper log fitting down over the hardboard spline. Before this occurs, two strips of weatherproof foam gasket tape are applied to either side of the spline groove. To ensure a tight fit, the logs are joined together using ten-inch spiral spikes for superior holding power. This same system of spline and gasket tape is used around the doors and windows and the butt joints."

In addition to log homes, the Fletcher plant produces other log buildings such as motels, ski lodges, restaurants, and utility buildings.

The log homes are used as permanent and vacation residences from the cold mountains of Vermont to the warm coastal areas of the Carolinas. A brochure, an excerpt from which is reproduced here, is available for $5.00. Included are diagrams and prices for 26 structures. Blueprints for the homes are $25.00 per set. This amount is credited to the purchase price if and when a Real Log Home is purchased.

Carolina Log Buildings, Inc.
P.O. Box 368
Fletcher, North Carolina 28732

LOG HOMES COUNCIL
Quality Solid Wood Housing by a Member of the National Association of Home Manufacturers

Plymouth

Our most popular model, the **PLYMOUTH,** has achieved that status because of a unique combination of spaciousness, affordability and style. The 1552 to 1920 square feet of living space is more than ample room for the smaller families of today. All this space, however, does not leave a blank space in your bank book because the price of the **PLYMOUTH** is exceptionally economical. All this practicality is accomplished without compromising on style and beauty. The romantic charm of the distinctive gambrel roof is accented throughout the whole upstairs by the exposed ceiling beams and added headroom. Why sacrifice on size and style when you can afford a **PLYMOUTH**?

The beautiful Southern home above has an optional **CAVENDISH** dining room extension which is a very popular choice among our **PLYMOUTH A** and **B** owners. The dormers were an added touch provided by the homeowner.

OVERALL DIMENSIONS
PLYMOUTH A: 32′8″ × 24′4″
SQUARE FOOTAGE: 1552

OVERALL DIMENSIONS
PLYMOUTH B: 40′4″ × 24′4″
SQUARE FOOTAGE: 1920

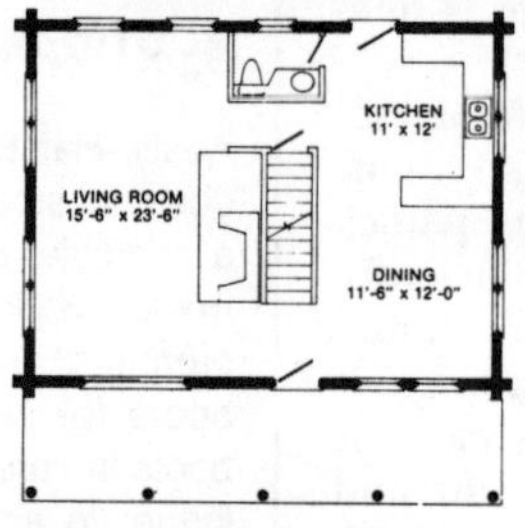

FIRST FLOOR PLYMOUTH A
Square Footage 776

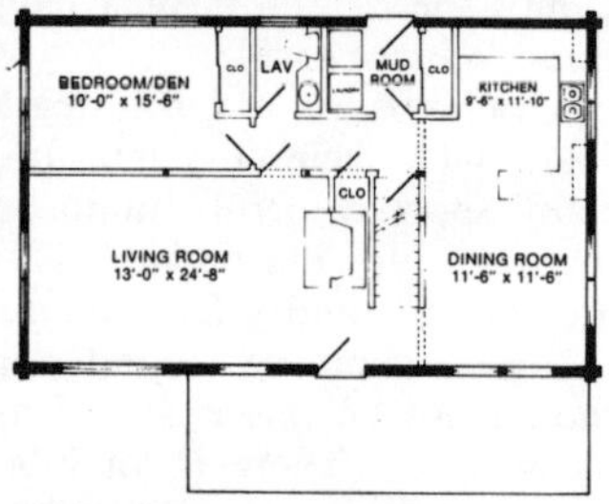

FIRST FLOOR PLYMOUTH B
Square Footage 960

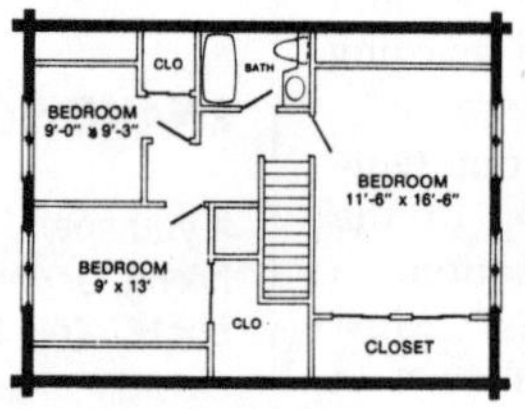

SECOND FLOOR PLYMOUTH A
Square Footage 776

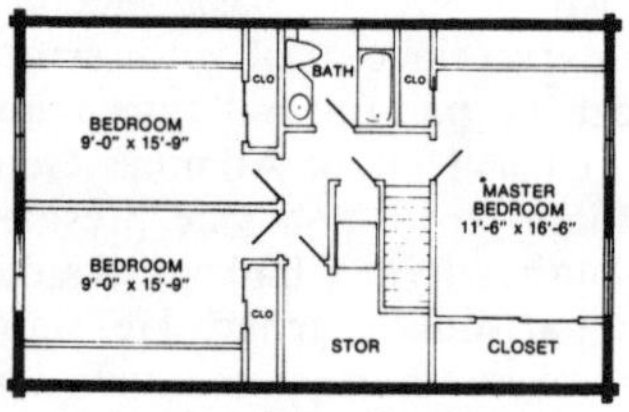

SECOND FLOOR PLYMOUTH B
Square Footage 960

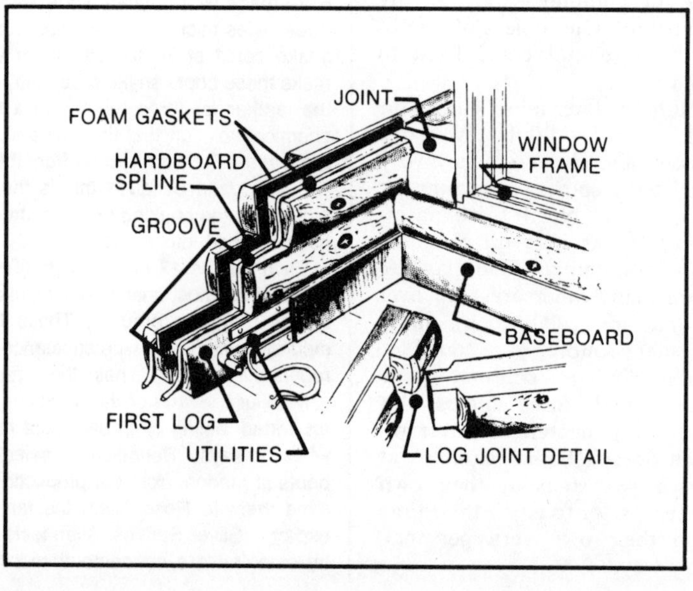

PACK FRAME KIT

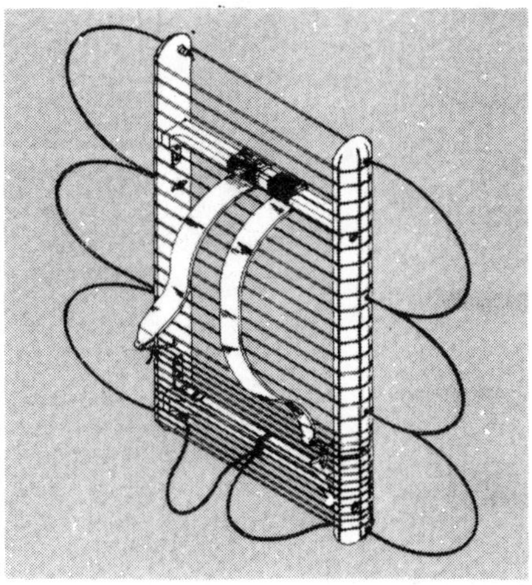

The components of this kit can be assembled into a most comfortable pack frame. The nylon cord allows full circulation of air under and around your pack keeping your back cool and sweat-free. The nylon cords also distribute the weight of the pack over the back and take quite a bit of lead off your shoulders.

The pack frame comes with complete instructions and is not difficult to assemble. The kit is $9.50 + postage unassembled or $12.50 + postage assembled.

Write to:

Klima Kraft
316 East Drive
Oak Ridge, Tennessee 37830

Energy Quest: *A game of strategy, chance, suspense, and surprise, played on a colorful 18¼" x 18½" gameboard with nine potential energy sources. Players generate as many kilowatt-hours of electricity as possible before an "oil embargo" strikes and ends the game. For 2-6 players, ages 9 to adult. Each, $9.95, plus $3.00 for postage and handling. Order from Carolina Biological Supply Company, 2700 York Road, Burlington, North Carolina 27215.*

> *"The breakers were very white and I found a field of yellow cosmos with white dunes and dark blue sea behind them. That was interesting. On the beach were a great many Portuguese Man o'War cast up by the waves—pink and green and indigo blue—and for a while I walked behind the dunes and saw the dark water thru two dunes with a flock of white Gulls flying past. And there were wonderful shells—bright blue in the shadow with the sky reflected on them. And I've never seen such pattern as the grass made on the sand." HORN ISLAND LOGS.*

JIMMY LILE—KNIFESMITH

Jimmy Lile's skill as a knifemaker is known throughout the United States; he produces the finest handmade knives to be found anywhere.

Lile makes all types of knives, including fishing, hunting, skinning, kitchen and camping knives, daggers and boot knives, hatchets, Bowie's and toothpicks. Many of those he does are special design knives with the shape and size of the blade and handle left to the customer's preference.

The methods Lile uses in making knives distinguish him further because he is one of the very few craftsmen in the United States capable of making knives by both forging or grinding them. He usually prefers the grinding or stock removal method because it results in a better edge due to the steel he uses.

Lile begins his knives with a bar of top quality, rust resistant steel and saws it to a rough shape or profile. The blade is then shaped on a grinder, the bevels are cut into it, and it is polished. Next, the blade is heat treated in an electric furnace to a durable hardness of RC60 and is then fitted with a handle, shaped again, and polished. Lile hand carves the finger grooves in the handles which are made out of everything from exotic woods and ivory to antlers and water buffalo horns.

Perhaps the most impressive of Lile's knives are his commemorative ones, usually large Bowie's or frontier knives with 10 to 12 inch blades. He has made several, including the James Black commemorative knife, in honor of the man who made the original Bowie. Lile's Arkansas River Navigational Knife commemorating the navigation of the river from its mouth to Tulsa, Oklahoma, has special meaning for Lile since his great-grandfather was the first licensed steamboat captain on the Arkansas River.

Travelers passing through the Russellville area can find a showcase of the knives at the Jimmy Lile Showroom, Highway 7 South (hours: 9:00 am.m to 5:00 p.m. Monday through Friday). Prices range from $80.00.

Write:

James B. Lile
Route 1
Russellville, Arkansas 72801

Start a Compost Pile

Spring is a good time to begin a compost pile since many gardeners are replenishing mulch, dethatching lawns, pruning shrubbery, and creating other garden waste. Don't make the mistake of throwing all this material away when it can be used in your garden. Any soil, good or poor, can be improved by working compost into it.

There are no mysteries to successful composting. To start your own compost pile, you need only a bin of some sort to contain the plant materials. Decomposition in the bin will occur by itself, but you can help speed it by sprinkling the pile with decay organisms (available at garden supply stores), dehydrated manure, or nitrogen fertilizer, such as ammonium nitrate. Keep the pile evenly moist, and turn it once a week to expose the material to the air and further hasten decomposition.

It's a good idea to separate materials into two compost piles according to the rate at which they will decompose.

Compost bins such as this one are available commercially, but you can also make your own from bricks or wood and turkey wire.

Herbaceous materials, such as weeds, lawn thatch, and green garbage from the kitchen, break down more rapidly than woody materials, such as pruning waste. The compost made from herbaceous material should be decomposed enough for garden use in 4 to 10 weeks. Compost from the woody material will take much longer.

A properly maintained compost pile is free from odors and flies. Should either become a problem, lightly sprinkle the pile with lime after turning the material.

The pile should heat up again after being turned. If much material remains undecomposed after three or four turnings and the pile no longer heats up, sprinkle more manure or ammonium nitrate on the pile.

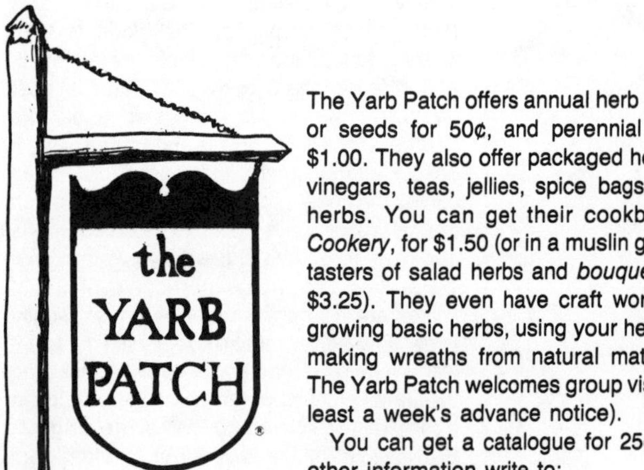

The Yarb Patch offers annual herb plants and/or seeds for 50¢, and perennial plants for $1.00. They also offer packaged herb blends, vinegars, teas, jellies, spice bags, and bath herbs. You can get their cookbook, *Yarb Cookery*, for $1.50 (or in a muslin gift bag with tasters of salad herbs and *bouquet garni* for $3.25). They even have craft workshops on growing basic herbs, using your herb harvest, making wreaths from natural materials, etc. The Yarb Patch welcomes group visits (with at least a week's advance notice).

You can get a catalogue for 25¢. For it or other information write to:

The Yarb Patch at Jubilee
3726 Thomasville Road
Tallahassee, Florida 32312
(904) 893-2647

HARVEST OFFERINGS

We use cork-topped antique reproduction bottles to package herb blends of our own creation. This year the bath herbs are finally a reality, and we are working on some additional herb items for introduction later this year, we'll keep you posted on our progress.

TASTER QUARTET - a trial packet containing tasters of our four blends (as described below) can be mailed to you for $1.75 including postage.

BOUQUET GARNI - our very popular blend of herbs in ready-to-use cloth bags to drop in your soup or pot roast. Glass spice jar, $1.75; mailing folder with recipes, $1.25; and taster for 35¢.

SALAD HERBS - a blend delightfully different with the many uses described on the label of the spice jar, $1.75; mailer with three individual packets and two recipes for $1.25; or a taster for 35¢.

HERBS FOR BISCUITS AND BREAD - tasty combination of herbs to add when making biscuits or breads, or for spreading with butter on prepared breads. In a glass spice jar, $1.75; or a taster for 35¢.

HERBS FOR BIRDS - not for feeding the birds, but for seasoning all fowl and game. Chicken salad should never be without it! Spice jar for $1.75; and a taster packet for 35¢.

REFILLS - if you already have a spice jar, and it is empty, we offer you a refill for any of the above blends for $1.00 in a carefully sealed small zip lock bag. Send us $4.50 (postage included) and we will see that all of your jars are filled!!!

A FIELDGUIDE TO SCREENPRINTING

©Coming Attractions, Ltd. 1976

COMING ATTRACTIONS, LTD.
SILKSCREENED SPORTSWEAR

Coming Attractions, Ltd., offers tee shirts with outdoor graphics. The tee shirts themselves can be chosen from the classic tee, a sport shirt style, a tee with striped shoulder inset, a tapered tee, a heavyweight tee, or a V-neck jersey. The designs available include those for the runner, the backpacker, the paddler, the wayfarer, the rock climber, and numerous others.

Coming Attractions also has a line of outdoor clothes in a variety of styles. Cotton jersey is featured in pull-over shirts. Men's and women's traditional Swiss Army shirts are available in 100% cotton hand-loomed plaids or plain chambray. Shirts of cotton chamois, cotton flannels, and dress wools are featured. Shorts and pants are available in twill or corduroy.

To select your favorite tee shirt and design or other outdoor clothing, write for a free catalogue from:

Coming Attractions, Ltd.
Outdoor Clothing
1524 Springhill Road
McLean, Virginia 22102

©Coming Attractions, Ltd. 1976

L RUNNER

©Coming Attractions, Ltd. 1976

G NATURE WALK

©Coming Attractions, Ltd. 1976

DD SOARING

©Coming Attractions, Ltd. 1976

X MOUNTAIN MAN

©Coming Attractions, Ltd. 1976

Q OLD GOAT

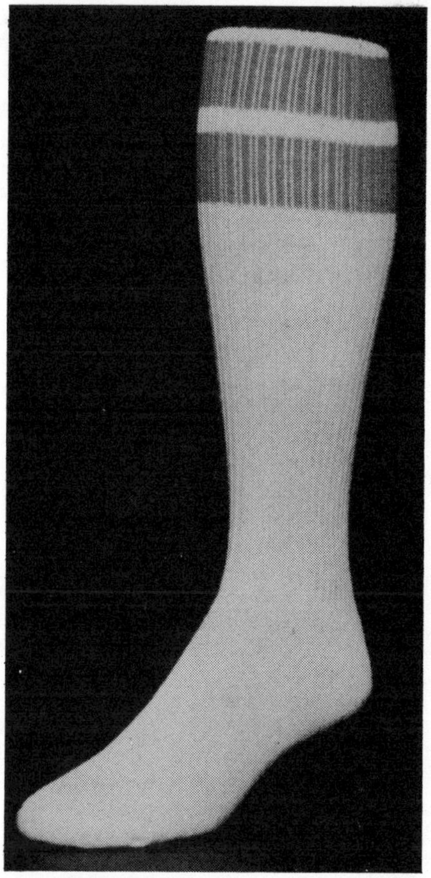

FOR SPORTSPEOPLE

Here is the sock for sportspeople, constructed so as to "wick" moisture away from the foot and absorb it in another layer of yarn. This patented process combines hydrophobic (moisture repelling) inner yarn and hydrophilic (moisture attracting) outer yarns. The result is Wick-Dry socks. Your feet stay dry and comfortable.

Write to:

Rockford Textile Mills, Inc.
McMinnville, Tennessee 37110
(615) 473-2195

"I went back to my boat and warmed a can of soup and went to bed with the mosquitoes. It is the first time that I have identified the mosquitoes with thought. I could feel and hear them thinking their way in to bite, to live to go on living. All of the mosquitoes on the island would identify themselves with one—that one would bore thru rock with their assistance to get at my blood and I would become identified with all men in order to keep it out—and I would win and I did—but not until several had bored their way in.

"Gravity is a wonderful thing—and if mosquitoes could use gravity to get in, I could use gravity to keep them out and I did—but I had to stay awake to do it." HORN ISLAND LOGS.

Nut Houses-Where To Buy Pecans

The pecan, (pronounced pe-kon') here in the South, is a delicacy we have long enjoyed. In the fall our trees are laden with brown nuts, and there are industries devoted to the processing, packaging, and marketing of this food that nourished the Indians and intrigued the early explorers to the Mississippi River Valley.

The following is excerpted from *Pecan Cookery, For the Gourmet*, a cookbook devoted entirely to recipes that use pecans, which was copyrighted in 1973 by Damco, Inc., Mobile, Alabama, and is sold for $2.00 by the H. M. Thames Pecan Company, P. O. Box 2206, Mobile, Alabama 36601:

History

"Of all of the foods contributed by the North American continent to international cuisine, none is of more importance nor destined to play a more prominent role in gastronomy than the pecan. Indigenous to a broad expanse of the southern portion of the United States, the golden-kernelled pecan has become a major crop in the agricultural economy of the nation.

"When and how the pecan tree originated is shrouded by the mists of history, but there is no doubt that the American Indian tribes inhabiting the Mississippi Valley and its tributaries from Missouri and Illinois to the southward, and also in western Texas and southern Oklahoma, knew and used the fruit of the 'pacan' tree as a major foodstuff long before the advent of the white man. The early Spanish explorers and soldiers of fortune who traversed the area found the pecan in use and have given us definite information on its use.

"Lópe de Oviedo, one of the adventurers who wandered through Louisiana and Texas wrote in his journal, 'There were on the banks of this river many nuts, which the Indians ate in their season, coming from 20 to 30 leagues round about. There, nuts were much smaller than those of Spain.'

"While de Oviedo and his companions were wandering in Texas or very soon thereafter, De Soto was on the Mississippi River. Notes of his expeditions record that in certain sections of what is now Louisiana, in 1541 the wild fruits of this region were abundant. The pecan nut, the mulberry, and two kinds of wild plums furnished the natives with food.

"The early French explorers ignored the agricultural aspects of the country in their journals and it was not until 1704 that we begin to find reference to pecans appearing in their records. Jean Penicant, a ship's carpenter with the first expedition of d'Iberville into lower Louisiana, visited Natchez, an Indian settlement on the Mississippi and described three kinds of nut trees, some with nuts as large as the fist which the Indians used in making bread for their soup; the others, and best ones, however, were scarcely larger than the thumb and were called 'pacane.' This is the first French description of the nut and the very first recorded use of the name applied by the Indians to the fruit, the spelling of which is, of course, French.

"In 1712, Father Gabriel Morest, a Jesuit missionary, wrote to a Father Germon of the same Order, telling him that there were different kinds of nut trees in southern Illinois, among them the pecans (Les pacanes) the name given to the fruit of one of the kinds by the Indians, were better flavored than the nuts of France.

"We get a good description of the fruit and tree from Xavier Charlevoix, a French missionary, who was in Cascashia in 1721 and the next year journeyed down the Mississippi to New Orleans. He wrote from Cascashia that, 'Among the fruits that are peculiar to this country, the most remarkable are the pecans. This is a nut having the length and form of a large acorn. There are those having a very thin shell, others have it harder and thicker which is to the detriment of the fruit; they are even somewhat smaller. All have a fine and delicate taste; the tree which bears them grows very high; its wood, its bark, the odor and the shape of the leaves appear to me similar to the walnuts of Europe.' It is certain that this refers to the pecan as we know it.

"It is evident that the early French settlers throughout the Mississippi Valley knew well and used the pecan. It is no foolish guess to say that many times individuals and communities found this product of the wild a valuable asset to their frontier existence.

"It remained for John Bartram, the well-known botanist of Philadelphia, to make the first recorded shipment of pecans from America. In August of 1761, he wrote his friend Peter Collinson of London, England, to this effect, 'I have not yet been to Ohio, but have many specimens from there. But in about two weeks, I hope to set out and search for myself, if the barbarous Indians don't hinder me.' Bartram evidently made his trip, in spite of the French and Indian War which was in progress, for upon his return from Fort Pitt, now Pittsburgh, he forwarded on December 12, 1761, a letter and package of seeds and plants to Collinson, who in answering him in April, 1762 says, 'I really believe my honest John is a great wag and has sent me some hard stony seeds, something shaped like an acorn, to puzzle us; for there is no name to them, I have a vast collection of seeds, but nothing like them. I do laugh at Gordon for he guesses them to be a species of hickory. Perhaps I may be laughed at in turn, for I think they may be, what I wish, seeds of the Bonduc Tree (Gymnocladus canadensis) which thou picked up in thy rambles on the Ohio.'

"Gordon made decidedly the best guess, as the stony seeds were undoubtedly pecans or Illinois hickory, for Bartram answers, 'The hard nuts I sent were given me at Pittsburgh by Col. Boquet. He called them hickory nuts and said that he had them from the country of the Illinois. Their kernel was very sweet. I am afraid they won't sprout as being a year old.'

"It is possible that Bartram had heard of the Illinois hickory or nut, as the pecan was called by the English along the Eastern coast, but it is evident none had come into his possession prior to the Ohio trip for he had not only sent seeds to England but also distributed them among his friends at home. A letter from John St. Clair during November, 1761, congratulates him on his safe return from Ohio and expresses thanks for the valuable hickory nuts that had been forwarded, it being apparent later that these were pecans.

"Brandel's sketch of American Botany from 1635 to 1840 says that the pecan was introduced into New York by fur traders in 1762 towards the close of the French and Indian War. All the early importations to the Atlantic Seaboard were from the northern range of the tree coming from the Ohio River and the territory of the Illinois Indians, hence the name of 'Illinois nuts' in common use at that time. The first recorded planting seems to have been in 1772 by William Prince, the outstanding nurseryman of the East. He set 30 nuts that season and raised 10 plants, eight of which he sold in England for 10 guineas each.

"Authentic reports of brother officers show that General Washington was fond of pecans and often had them in his pockets. His diary records that in 1774 he planted pecans about his home at Mount Vernon. During this period Thomas Jefferson was also interested in "paccans' as they were sometimes called.

"The East had no knowledge of pecans from the South, nevertheless the plant was receiving attention in that section. Antonia de Ulloa noted it in his travels along the lower Mississippi and in the published account of them, from Madrid, Spain, in 1772, states that, 'Two other kinds of trees are found there which appear to be peculiar to that country. One of these they call Pecands, which is a kind of walnut of greater body than ours, but in wood and leaf very similar. The fruit is in taste similar to the walnut, more delicate and finer with less proportion of oil. In form it is different and resembles dates, being in size almost the same or a little less. The shell is thin and smooth and without the roughness which the walnut has.'

"The first record of pecans being sent from Louisiana to the North appears in 1799 when, on the twelfth of November, Daniel Clark of New Orleans sent a box of nuts to Thomas Jefferson, then Vice President of the United States, and wrote him, 'I have presumed to send you a box of Peccan nuts. These last are not, I understand, common in the Atlantic ports of the United States, though they grow everywhere on the banks of the Mississippi, from the Illinois River to the Sea. The tree grows to the usual size of forest trees and affords a delightful shade in summer, it might be well to cultivate it in Virginia for use and ornament.'

"It is evident that Jefferson received the nuts and that there was correspondence with Clark for several years. The Jefferson letters are not obtainable, but Clark's answers give some idea of what they contained. From them we know that pecans had been planted at Monticello as early as 1780. Both Washington and Jefferson saw in the pecan a valuable addition to the gardens of the country but it remained for F. Andre Michaux to recognize it as a coming industry.

"He traveled west of the Allegheny Mountains in 1802 and then published in London an account of the trip in 1805. Michaux says, 'The Juglans pecane is not met with nearer than the mouths of the rivers Cumberland and Tennessee, from whence the fruit is sometimes brought to Lexington (Kentucky) to market. Neither does this tree grow east of the Allegheny Mountains.' It is interesting to note that land prices in the territory were governed by the species of trees growing thereon, and those on which 'Juglans hickory' were found commanded good prices.

"There seems to be no definite record of the first planting of pecans with nut production in view. Onderdank in 1911 reported trees set on irrigated land at Bustamente, Mexico, a hundred miles from Laredo, Texas, that are thought to be 200 years old; this is prior to any known plantings in the colonies. Prince's trees on Long Island that came from nuts planted in 1772 seem to be the first in the United States. Washington was planting pecans in 1774, calling them 'Mississippi nuts,' and Jefferson in 1781 described a two-year-old tree on his land, so we know he joined in the planting in 1779.

"It remained for Antoine, a slave gardener on Oak Plantation in Louisiana, to be the first to successfully graft pecan trees. In 1846-47 he successfully grafted 16 trees and later worked over more, so that by the end of the Civil War there were 126 trees of the variety, which was later named Centennial, on the plantation bearing nuts that found eager buyers. The slave Antoine had thus laid the foundation upon which was to be a great industry. For it may be safely said, therefore, that the pecan industry has developed during the past century and has moved forward to become one of America's great horticultural crops."

How The Pecan Got Its Name

"Having sketched the history of the pecan, it now remains to explain the philology of the common name and its pronunciation.

"At the time of the early Spanish explorations, the Indians along the Gulf Coast did not appear to have a definite name for this nut. Cabaca de Vaca writes of it in 1533 as walnut and likens it to those of Spain. About the same time Lópe de Oviedo speaks of 'the river of many nuts.'

"The old Spanish accounts of travel in the South continuously use the words 'neces' and 'nogules.' Not until 1704 do we find Penicant at Natchez using the term 'pacane.' Thus it is evident that the Indians along its northern range as well as those

continued

Here are 7 Southern companies from which you may order pecans and pecan products and a few words about each:

Sternberg Pecan Company—shelled pecan halves sent anywhere in U.S.A. prepaid; 2 lb. bag $9.75, 3 lb. bag $13.25, 5 lb. bag $20.50, 10 lb. bag $40.00. (Prices subject to change.)

Sternberg Pecan Company
P.O. Box 193
Jackson, Mississippi 39205

Sunnyland Farms—shelled pecan halves in different weight boxes; gourmet pecans (toasted, orange frosted, sugared and spiced); pecan fruitcakes, pralines, and other candies. Write for free color catalogue and pricelist.

Sunnyland Farms
Route 1—P.O. Box 549
Albany, Georgia 31705

Young Pecan Sales Corporation—sells butter-roasted and salted pecan halves for $8.85 per 2⅛ lb. tub; pecan halves for $8.30 per 2⅛ lb. tub; pecan pieces for $8.05 per 2⅛ lb. tub. Write for prices by the bag and shipping costs.

Young Pecan Sales Corporation
P.O. Drawer 5779
Florence, South Carolina 29502

H. M. Thames Pecan Company—sell strictly pecans (halves, mixed halves and pieces, midget pieces, meal); most orders less than 100 pounds shipped UPS or parcel post. Business gifts wrapped and mailed.

H. M. Thames Pecan Company
P.O. Box 2206
Mobile, Alabama 36601

Quality Pecan Company, Inc.—sell 4 lbs. pecan halves for $16.00; 5 lbs. in shell (Desirables); 5 lbs. in shell (Schleys) and gift packages. Shipped prepaid east of Rocky Mountains. Write for their "Old South Recipe" booklet.

Quality Pecan Company Inc.
5420 Newton Road
Albany, Georgia 31701

Priester's Pecans—pecan confections, fancy papershell pecans, roasted salted pecans, pecan fruitcake. Write for a free 32-page color catalog and pricelist.

Priester's Pecans
Fort Deposit, Alabama 36032

Fancy Mammoth Pecan Halves	**Delivered East of Mississippi**	**Delivered West of Mississippi**
2 lb. mammoth pecan halves	$ 9.50	$11.40
3 lb. mammoth pecan halves	14.25	17.10
(Packed in Christmas cellophanes)		
Carolina's Finest Papershell Pecans		
3 lb. papershell pecans—burlap bag	$ 6.25	$ 7.50
5 lb. papershell pecans—burlap bag	10.75	12.90

Golden Kernel Pecan Company
P.O. Box 613
Cameron, South Carolina 29030

toward the south had the same name for this plant and its fruit.

"Webster's new unabridged dictionary states that pecan comes from the Algonquin language and gives the spelling as 'pakan.' The French were very apt to write the Indian 'k' as a 'c,' thus 'pacane,' the 'e' being added so that the 'n' would be pronounced. The French seem to have completely adapted the 'pacane' as referring to a particular tree and its fruit for they called

the large native stand at the north of the Cumberland River 'la pacaniere,' and a village with the same name was found by Nuttall on the Arkansas River in 1818.

"The approved pronunciation has only recently been settled. The Century Dictionary gives: Pecan (pe-kan' or kon') indicating a preference for the first, hard 'a'; this was naturally the pronunciation of the Eastern colonies, but in the South and especially where there had been a French influence, the softer 'a' as in the second pronunciation became usage. The Webster's dictionary as well as the Oxford and others, follow the Century."

Pecans In The Daily Diet

"Pecans are rich in food value. Nutrition studies show they provide essential vitamins and minerals—are particularly good as energy food. It is interesting that the American Indians who first used them for food were aware of their nutritional benefits.

"Cabaca de Vaca, one of the early Spanish explorers, in the log of his adventures and travels, wrote 'The Indians came to the place of which we had been told, to eat walnuts (as pecans were then known). These are found with a kind of small grain, and this is the subsistence of the people for two months in the year, without any other thing.' The fact of the pecan's food value is well illustrated by this quotation.

"Pecans, in addition to being a welcome addition to the diet because of their superbly delicious flavor, are valuable for their contribution to good nutrition.

"Pecans are an excellent source of calcium, phosphorous, iron, protein, quality carbohydrates, Vitamin A and Vitamins B and G*. Calorically speaking, they are neither high or low in this list of fuel foods."

*Nutritional Data: Heinz Nutritional Research Division, Mellon Institute, Pittsburgh, Pennsylvania.

On The Storage Of Pecan Meats

"The life expectancy of freshly shelled pecan meats is three months *under refrigeration*. To store nuts over a longer period, freezing is recommended.

"No preparation is necessary. They may be packed in plastic freezer containers or screw top glass jars. The advantage of rigid containers over plastic bags is that no crushing or breakage occurs in the former.

"Pecans should *never* be left to deteriorate at room temperature."

PECAN PICKER-UP-ER

You'll be able to complete the "mechanization" of the pecan gathering-shelling process with the Pecan Picker-Up-Er devised by the H and K Company of San Antonio, Texas. No more stooping or scrambling around on your knees. However, you'd best plan a little exercise routine to otherwise use your muscles, else all those pecans you pick up with the Picker-Up-Er, shell with the Dynamic Nutcracker, and eat all by yourself will pick up a few pounds for you, too.

To order your Picker-Up-Er, send $5.95 to:

H and K Company
715 Camden Street
San Antonio, Texas 78215

SHELL PEAS THE EASY WAY

What kitchen could be complete without a pea sheller? "So simple a child can use it," says the Pea Sheller Manufacturing Company. You can save your fingers, fingernails and time by taking advantage of this handy utensil. It is made of durable plastic with a changeable, single-edge razor blade. Use it for fresh green blackeyes, cream peas, purple hulls, etc.

The pea sheller is $3.00, which includes postage, handling and tax. Send to:

Pea Sheller Manufacturing Company
P.O. Box 833
Baytown, Texas 77520

"I took a bath in the large bullrush pool and found the black and gold cloisonne sphinx. I've seen it before in the same setting, against a mosaic pattern of lilac and gold bullrushes, the concentrated pattern of the moth against the diffused pattern [of] almost identical elements in the background. Which sounds as tho it might have been almost invisible, but it was very conspicuous, all the source of other motives and values behind generated from a single center. The eye was irresistibly drawn to that center—protective coloration seems to have more to it than simply rendering the animal or bird invisible.

"I drew it standing in water up to my shoulders with each little riffle jiggling my elbow. I doubt if I've ever done anything in a more impossible position. It was as if some humorist stood just behind me watching what I was doing and whenever the drawing required care would wiggle my elbow and go into hysterical amusement each time." HORN ISLAND LOGS.

The Balloon Works

NATIONAL CLIMATIC CENTER

The largest facility of the five major operations in the Environmental Data Service is the National Climatic Center, located in Asheville, North Carolina. The NCC is the central source of historical weather information and the custodian of all current United States weather records. It obtains its data from the National Oceanic and Atmospheric Administration's Weather Service, the weather services of the Air Force, Navy, Federal Aviation Administration, the Coast Guard, and cooperative observers on land, at sea, and in the air. Also included are the cloud photography and other data obtained from environmental satellites.

Much of this information can be made available to individuals, and, as the chart reproduced here shows, many types of companies and individuals currently use the information generated at the NCC. Subscription publications include "Local Climatological Data," a monthly publication prepared separately for 290 cities and towns which records daily information on temperature, dew point, precipitation, pressure, wind, sunshine, and sky cover, and monthly averages of these elements. Also included in a subscription to the monthly publication is the annual "Local Climatological Data with Comparative Data," which summarizes by month and for the year the data recorded during the past calendar year and also contains a table of normals, means, and extremes based on long periods of record. Single copies of the annual publications are also available on request.

Other subscription publications include "Climatological Data," a statewide monthly summary; "Climatological Data, National Summary"; "Hourly Precipitation Data," by state; "Storm Data," nationwide; "Monthly Climatic Data for the World"; "Northern Hemisphere Sea Level Charts and 500-Millibar Charts"; "Daily River Stages," an annual; "Weekly Weather and Crop Bulletin," distributed from Washington about noontime each Tuesday; "Mariners Weather Log"; and "High Altitude Meteorological Data."

For a subscription to any of the above, write to the Superintendent of Documents, U.S. Government Printing Office, Washington, D.C. 20402.

Visitors are welcome at the National Climatic Center. Advance notice is desirable, especially if the visitor wishes to confer with specific specialists. Working space and assistance are provided as needed. For information, write:

The National Climatic Center
National Oceanic and Atmospheric Administration
Federal Building
Asheville, North Carolina 28801

REQUESTS FOR SERVICES

Requests should define data required, stations or geographical limits involved, desired carrier medium (magnetic tape, punched cards, microforms, hard copy), and such other pertinent information as a description of the problems for which the data are required. NCC personnel and the user consult on content and specifications, but non-government users who require assistance in specifying their needs are referred to a private meteorological consultant.

Work is performed on a reimbursable basis. Unit costs for some simple services have been established by the Department of Commerce; otherwise, the requester is provided a cost estimate before work begins.

BALLOONS! BALLOONS! BALLOONS!

Some people dream of ballooning; others actually do it. If you are a member of the latter group, you will be needing supplies. The Balloon Works of Statesville, North Carolina, is in the business of crafting sport balloons.

The people who make the balloons are themselves active and enthusiastic participants in the sport of aerostation. They speak fondly of the adventure of ballooning and plan to enhance the adventure and pleasure by improved design and construction of balloons.

Their balloons involve these components: an envelope with 121 possibilities for color combinations (and even an option for custom design or special logo balloons); a carriage of rattan trimmed in suede and including an instrument panel, a fuel pressure panel, and a blank panel with other optional equipment; a basic fuel system of burner, main tank, pilot light system, pressure gauge, fuel lines, and optional features; instruments including a mechanical rate of climb, altimeter, fuel pressure gauge, temperature gauge, etc.

For more information regarding the balloons, write to:

The Balloon Works
Rhyne Aerodrome/Rfd 2
Statesville, North Carolina 28677

GIFTS FROM CALLAWAY GARDENS

The Callaway Gardens Country Store puts a little Southern sophistication into the country with a variety of old South products ranging from the famous muscadine products to Georgia cured ham, bacon, and grits. All are a must on every breakfast table—and such an unusual gift!

The muscadine is a grape grown at Callaway Gardens. The co-founder of the Gardens, Cason J. Callaway, began raising muscadines back in the forties and later used an old family recipe to make the famous muscadine sauce. Jams and jellies are also made from the grape, all right on the premises. These are special products available only at the Callaway Gardens Country Store.

The Callaway Gardens Ham is Georgia cured and hickory smoked to the peak of perfection, and the Georgia cured bacon tastes just as if you own your own smokehouse. All this and the mellow corn flavor and old-timey goodness of Callaway Gardens Speckled Heart Grits makes breakfast, or any meal really, complete.

The Callaway Gardens Country Store also specializes in Southern crafts and the shelves are filled with items which afford a wide range of shopping. In addition, there is cane syrup, homemade bread, and galberry honey. It's like no other "country store" you've been to.

Pictured are a number of gifts you can order, but there are many more. Drop by when you are in the area. The Callaway Gardens Country Store is located on U.S. Highway 27 atop Pine Mountain, one mile south of Callaway Gardens. Call or write to order or to request a catalogue:

The Callaway Gardens Country Store
Pine Mountain, Georgia 31822
(404) 663-2281

CORNMEAL AND GRITS

Barry and Janell Ogletree operate Ogletree Grist Mill in Livingston, Texas. With their small grist mill, they turn out cornmeal and grits which use the whole kernel of corn. The meal is not meant to be sifted; the flakes of the husks of the corn contain most of the food value. When the flakes are moistened, they get soft. There are no preservatives added to the 100% human food corn, but the products can be stored indefinitely in the freezer or refrigerator.

A sample box containing one 2-lb. bag of cornmeal and one 2-lb. bag of grits sells for $2.00 plus UPS or U.S. postal charges.

Write to:

Ogletree Grist Mill
800 N. Drew
Livingston, Texas 77351

THE PEANUT KIDS

We thought we had found the best peanuts in the South when we recommended The Packing Shed and then The Peanut Shop of Williamsburg, but one other brand must definitely be added to the list—The Peanut Kids from Producers Peanut Company, Inc. They are especially good—and one must come to the conclusion that Virginia is the peanut capital of the South since all of these fine brands have hailed from that area.

Producers Peanut Company will send you a 3-pound can of salted peanuts for $6.45, providing they are delivered east of the Mississippi. If delivered west of the Mississippi, add $.40 per pound.

Write to order:

Producers Peanut Company, Inc.
Peanut Products
P.O. Box 250
Suffolk, Virginia 23434

This Table Is Rough And Ready

Designed for rugged use, yet attractive enough for entertaining, this table is an easy-to-build, practical piece of outdoor furniture. You can use it for outdoor dining or as an outdoor work surface. (The tabletop is an ample 3 x 6 feet.) The outdoor exposure will only add to the table's rugged good looks.

Our design was adapted from a table used by Ken Mahler at his Kiawah Island, South Carolina, beachhouse for serving and preparing fresh oysters. The "oyster" table is constructed entirely from rough-sawn cedar boards—a natural material for outdoor use. Although rough wood is not usually used for tables, it is the rough wood, with its rugged character, that keeps this table from being typical.

Materials needed to build the table are: three 6-foot pieces of 2 x 12, two 30-inch pieces of 2 x 4, two 62-inch pieces of 2 x 4, and four 28-inch pieces of 4 x 4—all in rough-sawn cedar. (These rough-sawn materials should be full dimensional in size; i.e., a 2 x 4 is actually 2 inches x 4 inches.) Fasteners needed include sixteen 3/8-inch lag screws, 4 inches long with flat washers, and 1 pound of 16-penny galvanized casing nails.

First, construct the 2 x 4 frame. Butt the two 62-inch pieces into the 30-inch 2 x 4's, fastening them with nails. Lay the three 2 x 12's side by side on the frame, evenly spacing the overhang approximately 3 inches on all four sides; then nail them to the frame.

Turn this assembly over and drill four staggered holes in each corner of the frame, two per side, to accommodate the lag screws. (Be sure the holes are properly staggered, so the screws will miss each other.) Then fasten a 4 x 4 leg in each corner with the screws (use washers to prevent crushing the wood). You can use a hammer or a drill to start the screws in the legs.

Should the legs of the table be uneven, causing the table to wobble, correct it by trimming each leg slightly. To even the legs, start with a thin, straight piece of material (such as a piece of 1/4-inch plywood) that is thicker than the space between the ground and the shortest leg. Steady the table on a level surface; place the plywood flat beside each of the three other legs and mark the legs along the top of the material. Then cut each leg to the mark to correct the movement.

Left natural, the table will weather outdoors to a rustic gray. The unweathered color may be preserved by treating the wood with a clear waterproof sealer. If you want to add color to the table, you can stain it with either a semi-transparent or solid-color exterior grade stain.

To build the table, construct the 2 x 4 frame first. Then place the three 2 x 12's on the frame, evenly spacing their overhang on all four sides, and nail them in place.

For outdoor dining, the rugged table takes on new character with the addition of a centerpiece, place mats, and settings.

Turn the tabletop over, and fasten the 4 x 4 legs to the frame using lag screws.

When drilling the pilot holes for the screws, carefully stagger alternate holes, so the screws will pass each other.

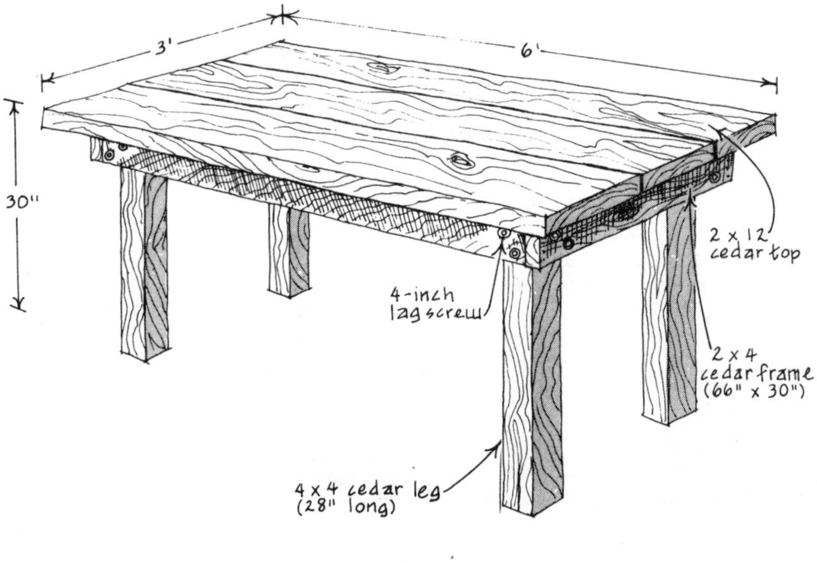

ANNAPOLIS SAILING SCHOOL®

You need not own a sailboat, live on the water, or be an accomplished sailor to participate in the courses offered by the Annapolis Sailing School. All you need is a desire to learn. This school is the oldest and largest sailing school in the country, headquartered in a lovely colonial house in Annapolis. The school operates a fleet of over 50 boats out of its own private marina; these new fiberglass boats are from 22 to 43 feet in length.

The curriculum includes over a dozen unique courses, from weekend and week-long instruction in basic sailing to a 10-day bluewater cruising course aboard a 43-foot custom sloop in the Grenadines. The courses combine comprehensive classroom work covering the fundamentals of sailing with closely supervised practice sessions aboard the sloops. Onboard classes are limited to no more than four students per boat.

The Annapolis Sailing School also offers vacation courses in three categories—Basic, Cruising, and Auxiliary—and within each category are courses of varying duration to accommodate individual vacation plans and schedules.

While the emphasis is on introducing would-be sailors to the fundamental skills and techniques of sailing, the Annapolis Sailing School also serves the instructional needs of more advanced sailors. The same concept has been incorporated into branches located in various vacation areas: St. Lucia in the Windward Islands; St. Petersburg, Florida; St. Thomas in the U.S. Virgin Islands; on Lake Geneva, Wisconsin; Puget Sound, Seattle, Washington; and in San Diego, California.

A 20-page color brochure is available by writing or calling the school. Maryland residents call (301) 267-7205. Outside Maryland call toll free 1-800-638-9192.

Annapolis Sailing School
P.O. Box 3334
Annapolis, Maryland 21403

Auto FIRE®

YOUR FIRE NEXT TIME

We didn't believe the claims the manufacturers of the Auto Fire Charcoal Lighter/Stove/Heater made—until we tried one. And we now wholeheartedly endorse the "world's fastest charcoal lighter and camp stove" which "lights charcoal in 90 seconds . . . searing hot in 6 minutes . . . guaranteed." It turned our regular grill into a close competitor to an automatic gas one—at a fraction of the cost: $7.95 each for an aluminized steel lighter (4-pack carton, $24.00 postpaid) or $16.95 for a stainless steel lighter (4-pack carton, $60.00 postpaid). A nickel chrome Bar-B-Que Grid, used to turn your lighter into a grill is $1.50 postpaid.

Order from:

Auto Fire Corporation
P.O. Box 487H
Corinth, Mississippi 38834

A WALK ON THE RIVER

Patuxent River Park in Prince George's County, Maryland, is a 5,000-acre park comprised of 21 parcels of land which range in size from ⅓ of an acre to nearly 2,000 acres. These parcels make up what is termed a "limited-use natural area" which means that only the activities which are compatible with nature and with each other are permitted. The park is managed by the Department of Parks and Recreation of the Maryland-National Capital Park and Planning Commission. All visitors are required to have an advance reservation or special-use permit. Nature programs and outdoor recreation activities such as camping are available by advance reservation.

The Jug Bay Natural Area, near Croom, is the headquarters for the park; this site is staffed and supervised year-round.

The Black Walnut Creek Nature Study Area, dedicated to nature study and environmental education, offers a boardwalk through the marsh and swamp combined with trails through the woods which permit close observation of the fragile wetlands. Naturalists lead hikes which cover plant and animal identification, natural history, folklore, and more. Photography blinds at the river's edge provide a place for observing and photographing waterfowl such as ducks, Canada Geese, or Whistling Swans.

Interpretive boat tours on Jug Bay aboard the "Possum" and "Muskrat" explaining marshland and ecology are available for groups. The "Possum" and the "Muskrat" are electrically powered making them perfect for silent observation of wildlife. River tours are conducted from April 15 to October 15, depending on the weather. All boat tours require advance reservation.

Both the boats and nature trails will accommodate special population groups, including senior citizens, visually handicapped, and physically handicapped.

A living history exhibit called Patuxent Village is open to visitors year-round. This program interprets the social history of the life along the river. Special programs are available for all types of groups. The "smoke house," "Jug Bay packing house," "hunting and trapping shed," and "Patuxent workshop" allow the visitor to see just how daily life might have been a hundred years ago. A person can learn how to "skin" and "hew" logs for building a cabin, how to "strip" tobacco and "prize" it for shipping on the sailing ships and steamboats, and how to smoke meat and fish.

Please remember that a permit or reservation is required for all activities. Groups or individuals may arrange tours by contacting the Patuxent River Park Office at 627-6074 or by writing to:

Patuxent River Park
RR Box 3380
Upper Marlboro, Maryland 20870

solar unlimited incorporated

According to Solar Unlimited, Inc., a company formed in Huntsville, Alabama, in 1976 by a former manager of NASA's Solar Heating and Cooling Program, the main obstacle to solar, nationwide, has been the cost of installation—often half the total system cost. Installation has run high because solar manufacturers failed to recognize the need to standardize and pre-build systems at the factory. Instead, many manufacturers simply sent system parts to the home-site, requiring a disproportionate amount of time for design and assembly. Solar Unlimited says it has surmounted the equipment-cost and installation obstacles with its six standard heating packages—all pre-assembled to the maximum degree possible. Homeowners and home buyers may select anything from domestic water heaters to full central heating packages. None requires more than three days to install.

The Federal Solar Tax Credit, again according to Solar Unlimited, represents a milestone in the nation's conversion to solar heating because it enables a family buying a home (new or existing) to add solar at no additional first-year cost. This is how: the Federal Solar Tax Credit (Public Law 95-618) gives taxpayers a dollar-for-dollar credit for the installed cost of solar equipment, amounting to 30 percent of the first $2,000, and 20 percent of the next $8,000. The maximum allowable credit is $2,200. If, for example, a family purchased a $50,000 home on a conventional mortgage, they would normally pay $10,000 down, or 20 percent. If the family added a $5,000 solar system into the mortgage, the home mortgage down payment would be increased by $1,000. However, the Federal Solar Tax Credit on a $5,000 solar system is $1,200, which is $200 more than the increase in the home down payment.

Solar Unlimited dealt with the question of comparative costs by comparing the heating costs of a super-insulated home using one of their "Suncatcher" systems with a home using "standard" insulation and electric baseboard heating. Based on Huntsville's 3 cents per kilowatt hour utility rates, the "standard" home was projected as using (in the first year) $950 worth of electricity for domestic water and home heating. The super-insulated, solar-equipped home was projected as using less than $150 worth. In many parts of the country, solar saves more in utility costs than it adds to the monthly home mortgage payment. As utility rates rise, the difference is expected to be more pronounced. The super insulation is also expected to cut air conditioning costs by more than 50 percent. Finally, if the home is in an area where property values are on the rise, the solar system should rise in value along with the home and bring proportionately more upon resale.

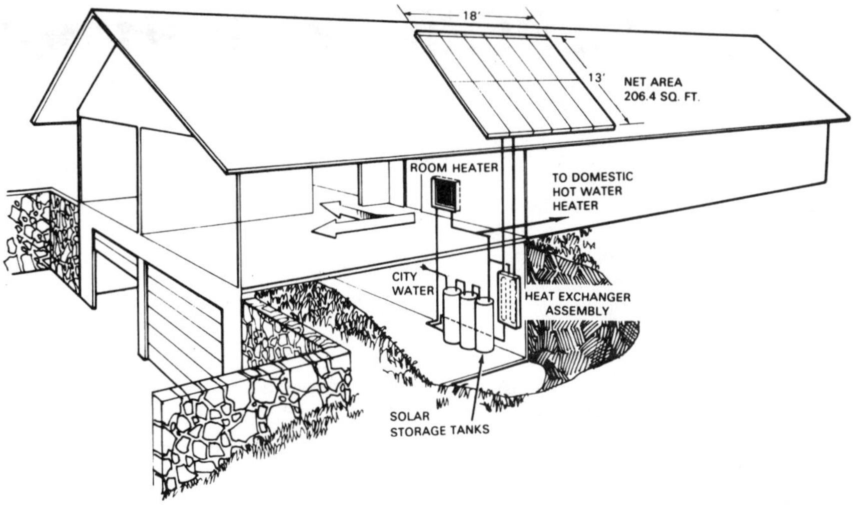

THESE COLLECTORS FEATURE SERPENTINE TUBE-AND-FIN ABSORBER PLATES

MODEL H1 SUNCATCHER

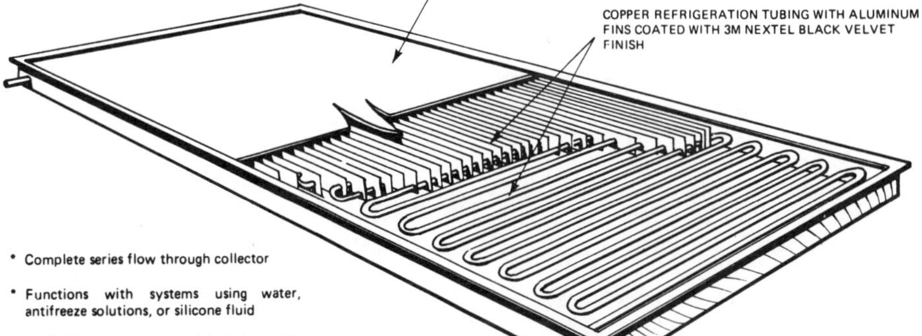

- Complete series flow through collector
- Functions with systems using water, antifreeze solutions, or silicone fluid
- Available in single- or double-glass models

THREE "H1" COLLECTORS WITH THREADED ROD MOUNT FOR PROPER SUN ANGLE.

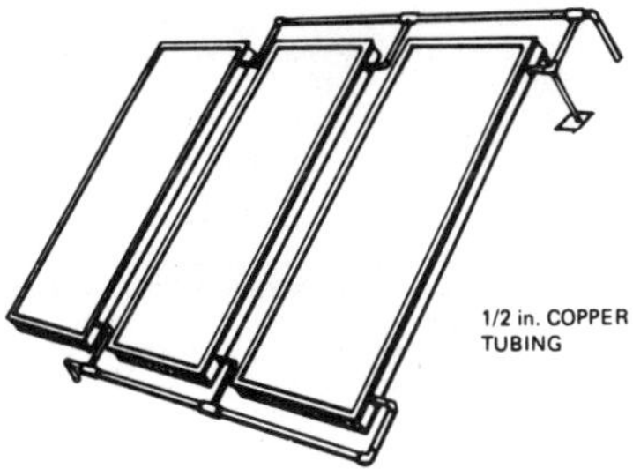

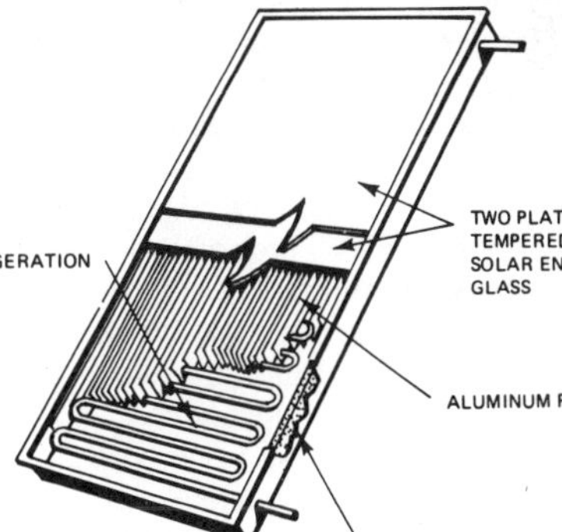

Dimensions: 35 3/8" x 77 3/8" x 4" deep

Net Glass Area: 17.2 sq. ft.

Model H1 Suncatcher – Stock No. 11101

Some people have been scared off by stories about systems freezing, boiling or generally not doing the job. Solar Unlimited has its own set of requirements which the company believes should be the bottom line for system acceptability. The company recommends that solar buyers look for systems which meet at least these criteria:

Eliminate freezing and boiling under any condition.

Eliminate corrosion for life of system.

Eliminate the need for fluid servicing and scheduled maintenance.

Use non-toxic fluids.

Operate fully automatically.

Be cost effective.

The Department of Energy expects solar to provide about 25 percent of the nation's energy needs by the turn of the century.

For further information, write to:

Solar Unlimited, Inc.
4310 Governors Drive West
Huntsville, Alabama 35805

WILDERNESS SOUTHEAST, INC.

Dick Murlless has two things going for him which are of particular interest to us: he is the author-editor of *Hiker's Guide to the Smokies*, a Sierra Club "Totebook," and he heads a group of experienced persons who conduct outfitted expeditions in wilderness areas of the Southeast—Wilderness Southeast, Inc.

To take *Hiker's Guide to the Smokies* first: this is the most complete and accurate guidebook that we know of, to all the trails of the Great Smoky Mountains National Park. (The Appalachian Trail in the park is covered completely and exhaustively in the book *Guide to the Appalachian Trail in Tennessee and North Carolina: Cherokee, Pisgah, and the Great Smokies*, published by the Appalachian Trail Conference. See the entry under "Appalachian Trail Guides" in this catalogue.) The book also covers the Joyce Kilmer Memorial Forest and Slickrock Creek. According to Mr. Murlless, "Within the park, the 67 miles of Appalachian Trail are being loved to death. The guidebook is a must for anyone wishing to hike along the park's other 580 miles of trails." We enjoyed browsing through the guidebook because it is not merely one dry trail description after another; on the contrary, some of the memorable exploits and incidents which have occurred in the Smokies have found their way into the trail write-ups. The book is available at the address given below and costs $8.50, including shipping and handling.

Wilderness Southeast, Inc., is best described by this excerpt from a brochure sent out to those people interested in exploring some of the wilder reaches of the Southeast:

"Wilderness Southeast, Inc. is a non-profit educational organization dedicated to running quality wilderness canoe, backpack, island camping, and skin diving trips. We will help you handle the everyday problems of wilderness camping so that you are free to discover, appreciate, and explore a new world. Our guides are trained and eager to interpret the ecology and conservation status of your trip area. Our trips are unhurried and small, with a maximum of 16 trippers. We teach, help, encourage, and let you share in camp responsibilities; but we never pamper. We give high priority to the protection of the areas we visit and guarantee minimal trip impact on these wild places. We cannot sanction the collecting of live specimens (except by those possessing a legal collecting permit). A sense of the importance of all life and the wholeness of nature is basic to our philosophy. We want you to get excited about wilderness and feel the sense of self-worth and inner peace it can bring. We want you to find the pleasure of being an integral part of a group fending for itself in the outdoors, and to share the joys of wilderness. Come with us to the southeastern wilds and let us show you that a wilderness experience can be meaningful and fun."

DEEP CREEK

(41) THOMAS DIVIDE 14.1 mi.

Gated road, horse and foot trail / Max.. elev. gain 3,310
Start: Deep Creek Road (0.9 mi.), 1,900 ft.
End: Newfound Gap Road, 3.5 mi. south of Newfound Gap, 4,650 ft.
USGS quads: Bryson City, Clingmans Dome, Smokemont, N.C.
Trail connections: Indian Creek, Deeplow Gap, Newton Bald, Sunkota Ridge, Collins Creek, Kanati Fork

Thomas Divide is a long ridge which arcs in a half-circle from the vicinity of Deep Creek Campground to the crest of the Smokies. The Thomas Divide Trail, although beginning in the valley where Indian Creek empties into Deep Creek, is mostly a ridge-top path, following Thomas Divide all the way to the Newfound Gap Road. It is well graded, open, well maintained and well marked. Five overlooks have been cleared to show broad vistas. Being a ridge route, it is generally dry, but there are a few sources of water along the way. Although there is no designated campsite on this trail, a suitable location may be found along the way near the end of the Newton Bald Trail. The proposed Indian Creek Motor Nature Trail would have caused the closing of a part of the lower section of the Thomas Divide Trail, but the Motor Nature Trail has been abandoned (as of 1977 update). You should check with the ranger at Deep Creek Campground for the latest information.

Thomas Divide takes its name from William Thomas, a white man and a native of Haywood County, N.C. He had been adopted by the great Cherokee chief Yonaguska and given the name *Wil-Usdi* or "Little Will." In 1839 Yonaguska died, and Thomas was elected chief of the Eastern Cherokees. During his early years as chief, he fought hard before Congress to gain the Indians their just rights, earning the reputation of their savior. He was, on the other hand, quite an operator, and was much criticized for his involvement in land speculation (at one time owning more than 100,000 acres in N.C.) and for promoting road and railroad construction in Indian territory. During the Civil War he was the leader of "Thomas's Legion of Indians and Highlanders," which was organized to guard the Smokies from attack by the North. Later his power waned and he lost control over his vast empire. He died in 1893, leaving his estate in terrible confusion.

Trailhead: The trail starts at a gate on the right, 0.9 mi. above the Deep Creek Campground, on the Deep Creek Road. This is also the head of Indian Creek Trail (see p. 169). There is limited parking.

Trail Details: Walk through the gate up Indian Creek Trail, which is a jeep road. At 0.1 mi. Indian Creek Falls is on the left. The trail crosses Indian Creek on a jeep bridge at 0.2 mi. and reaches a trail junction, with sign, at 0.5 mi. The Thomas Divide Trail goes to the right and immediately crosses Indian Creek on a foot log. Then it starts to climb at a moderate grade but with rough, washed out stretches, alongside a small branch, whose water is silted and unsuitable for drinking. At 0.8 mi. the trail turns sharply to the left, crosses a branch and ascends a small dry ridge. At 0.9 mi. it turns sharply to the right; note an old, unmaintained trail running to the left. The Thomas Divide Trail climbs on the right side of the ridge line. At 1.2 mi. it crosses a silted spring branch. Continuing its moderate climb, it leaves the zone of cove hardwoods behind and at 1.4 mi. reaches the crest of Thomas Divide at Stone Pile Gap.

At Stone Pile Gap the trail runs into construction for the Indian Creek Motor Nature Trail. For the next 2.0 mi. the trail has been affected by road work. Follow the road as it climbs gradually along the left side of the ridge line, which incidentally marks the park boundary. At 3.4 mi. (watch out; no sign) the trail leaves the road to bear right in a low gap. (The road bears left and leaves the ridge.) The trail continues to climb at a moderate grade along the crest of the Thomas Divide. At 3.5 mi. there is a small knoll and the park line veers to the right. The trail continues uphill on the crest through second-growth oak and dry-ridge hardwoods. At 4.4 mi. there is a view to the right into the valley of Cooper Creek. After passing over a wooded knob at 4.9 mi., the trail descends moderately down the crest, slabs to the right and reaches a good, small spring at 5.2 mi. At 5.8 mi. it arrives at an intersection at Deeplow Gap. To the left (W) the Deeplow Gap Trail leads 2.3 mi. to the Indian Creek Trail. To the right (E) the Deeplow Gap Trail leads first past a small spring (400 ft.), then past Little Creek Falls and on to Cooper Creek (see p. 162).

From the gap the Thomas Divide Trail continues straight on a moderate upgrade along the crest of Thomas Divide. At 8.9 mi. the Newton Bald Trail (see p. 146) terminates on the right (E) having come 4.8 mi. from the Newfound Gap Road. Along that trail a short distance is a campsite with a firepit and a spring.

At 9.4 mi., along a level area of the ridge, there is a sign and two trail intersections. To the left (W) the Sunkota Ridge Trail (see p. 168) leads 4.8 mi. to Martins Gap. To the right (E), about 150 ft. before reaching the trail sign, the unmaintained Collins Creek Trail leads east 4.2 mi. to the Collins Creek picnic area (see p. 147).

The Thomas Divide Trail continues along the ridge, crosses a wooded knob and descends into Tuskee Gap. It then climbs again to crest at Nettle Creek Bald, where there is a sign, at 11.8 mi. At 12.3 mi. the Kanati Fork Trail terminates from the right. A sign indicates that that trail leads east 3.0 mi. to the Newfound Gap Road. There is water 1.4 mi. down the Kanati Fork Trail (see p. 149).

Continuing along the crest of Thomas Divide, at 13.0 mi. the trail arrives at its highest point, 5,160 ft., in a clearing where there are extensive views to the east of Mt. Kephart and Charlies Bunion. This general area is known as Turkey Flyup: hunters used to flush wild turkeys there, causing them to "fly up." The trail then follows a knife edge to the crest of Beetree Ridge at 13.4 mi. It crosses the nose of the ridge through a birch forest and runs downhill, reaching a gap at 13.9 mi. Then it again climbs, moderately, to reach a large grassy area and the Newfound Gap Road at 14.1 mi. There is a trail sign at the upper edge of the grassy area, but it is hard to see from the highway because it is 250 ft. away. To the right 0.25 mi. down the highway, there is an overlook, with parking. Driving northbound, it is the first overlook on the left after crossing Beech Flats Prong. To the left Newfound Gap is 3.5 mi. away.

(42) COOPER CREEK 2.3 mi.

Gated jeep trail / Max. elev. gain 1,430
Start: Deeplow Gap Trail and Cooper Creek Road, 2,190 ft.
End: Mingus Creek Trail, 3,620 ft.
USGS quads: Smokemont, N.C.
Trail connections: Deeplow Gap, Mingus Creek

This short trail is an important segment in the lateral trail system leading from the Deep Creek Campground to the Oconaluftee Ranger Station. It connects the Deeplow Gap Trail, of which it amounts to a continuation, to the Mingus Creek Trail. Mostly, it follows the course of Cooper Creek,

Some of the trips planned by Wilderness Southeast include a six-day canoe trip through the Okefenokee Swamp in April, a week snorkeling in the Keys in August, a week-long family basecamp in the Smokies in July, a Sea Islands Photographic Workshop in June, a week of hiking and rafting on the wild Chattooga River in June, a week backpacking on Cumberland Island in February, and a week of exploring the Everglades after Christmas.

Participants need bring only their own clothing, sleeping bags, and personal articles; the rest is provided by Wilderness Southeast. Prices run from $185 to $300 per person.

In addition to the above trips, Mr. Murlless and his associate, John Crawford, are both professionally trained to teach environmental programs to elementary and high school students, as well as adults. Any group wishing an activity-centered approach to ecology lessons should contact them about arranging special trips.

For more information about Wilderness Southeast, Inc., or to order *Hiker's Guide to the Smokies,* write:

Wilderness Southeast, Inc.
Route 3, Box 619 CS
Savannah, Georgia 31406

Reprinted by permission of Florida Keys Keynoter-Sundial.

An Unusual Scientist

By GRETEL VONNOH

Stanley Becker, of Little Torch Key, is a zoologist and marine biologist, but if you think he goes around wearing a white coat doing experiments in laboratories, you would be mistaken.

This scientist wears plaid shirts open at the collar, blue jeans and his hair long.

A quiet man of 43, he has lived in the Florida Keys for 16 years, growing more interested in the peaceful surroundings each year.

He finds it very hard to ignore anything that is alive and so he has acquired a vast knowledge of native plants, shrubs, animals and birds. He says he has a working knowledge of about 700 species and a book knowledge of almost twice that number.

As a zoologist specializing in coral and related animals he collected specimens for U.S. Government experiments on radiation.

As a marine biologist he has collected and supplied many specimens to universities and government agencies. A very rare member of a microscopic group of marine organisms is named for Mr. Becker because of his participation in the discovery.

He discovered nature is at its best when not disturbed by noise or pollution so he bought a canoe and started gliding through the waterways getting to remote spots inaccessable by other means of transportation.

Enjoying himself so much, and wanting to share the beauty and quiet around the Keys, Mr. Becker has decided to give people the opportunity of seeing his quiet wilderness by canoe.

At present time he has four canoes which will accomodate up to 10 people. He says he can teach anyone enough about the art of canoeing in about five to 10 minutes and they will be able to glide through the water with ease.

If anyone gets tired of paddling, the canoes are equipped with anchors so everyone can take a breather. The canoes are also equipped with life preserver cushions.

Mr. Becker's canoe tours are from 9 a.m. to 4 p.m. and he provides lunch, either hot or cold, depending on the weather. Soft drinks are also provided.

Mr. Becker feels canoeing is the only way to see many of the interesting wildlife around the Keys, and it is not unusual to spot fish, birds and even the Key Deer—all in their native habitat.

For more information on the canoeing excursions, call him at 872-2620.

To combine fun with environmental education under the tutelage of Stan Becker, write to:

Stan Becker
P.O. Box 62
Big Pine Key, Florida 33043

"The first osprey has just caught a fish in my front yard. You miss things without realizing what it is that you are missing, then blame yourself for insensitivity—the truth is that things move fast, and life is interesting and there are many things to be enjoyed and digested. . . ."
HORN ISLAND LOGS.

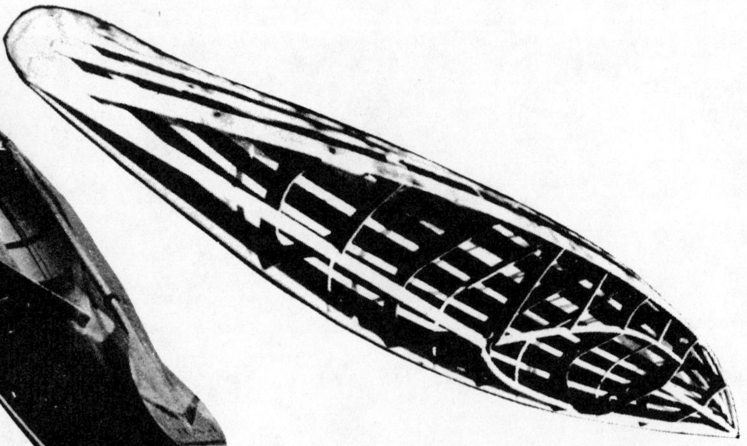

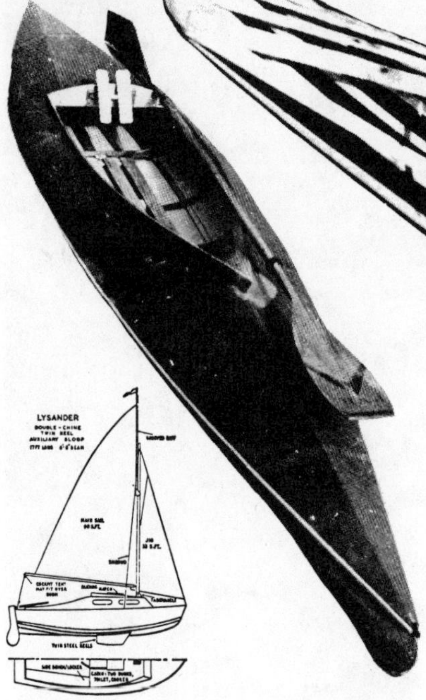

KAYAK, CANOE, AND SAILBOAT BUILDING PLANS

George Shelton started a business called Outdoor Sports out of his need to locate a quality building plan for a canoe he wanted to build.

Now he has a wide variety of plans available for kayaks, canoes, and sailboats. These plans are designed for the first-time builder, and dozens of boats have been built by youth groups, such as Scouts. To build one of these boats, it is only necessary that you be able to use basic hand tools.

As for the materials, simply take the materials list to a local cabinet shop or carpenter and let him cut the wood to the specifications of one boat. The cost of construction will vary, depending on what you want the craft to look like. But building a craft yourself will cost only a fraction of the retail cost of buying a similar craft.

The plans marked PBK are by Marine architect P. W. Blandford, with many clear drawings and full-size patterns of all shaped parts. Each set of plans includes detailed instructions and a complete materials list. All of the other plans are equally as clear and detailed as those by Mr. Blandford.

Write for a descriptive brochure.

Outdoor Sports
P.O. Box 1213
Tuscaloosa, Alabama 35401

Capt. John F. Vandegrift, Sr., Master Mariner - President

Captain Van INC.

Master Mariners

552 5TH STREET - P.O., BOX 53
PORT ARTHUR - TEXAS - 77640

CAPTAIN VAN, INC. - ACTIVITIES

INDEPENDENT MARINE SURVEYORS—CONSULTANTS
INTERNATIONAL CARGO GEAR BUREAU—INSPECTORS
ADMIRALTY INVESTIGATORS—COMPASS ADJUSTERS
MARINE ENGINEER & NAVIGATION SCHOOLS
NAUTICAL BOOK & INSTRUMENT SALES

BOAT GUIDE

What's the price of a 1975 Hatteras Long Range Cruiser? How much does a 1972 Morgan 27-footer cost? What's the current market value of a 1968 Chrysler Charger w/85 Johnson? One book will answer all of these questions. It's called *BUC's™ Used Boat Price Guide*.

If you're in the business of buying, selling, insuring, or financing pleasure boats, then you know that boat prices depend on many variables. The local economy, weather, accessibility to water areas, storm damage, model preferences, changes in supply and demand, and availability of boat loan money all play a part. Each of these conditions can vary from one area to another. However, all of these factors are taken into consideration when the current boat values are computed in the *BUC'S™ Used Boat Price Guide*.

The references are cross-indexed by trade name, manufacturer, and parent company. This makes the book an invaluable reference tool. Order a copy for $44 from:

BUC™ International Corporation
1881 Northeast 26th Street
Fort Lauderdale, Florida 33305

> *"I beached the boat in a bare stretch where there were no nests and took off my clothes and went along in the shallow water with only my head out, but the pelicans got up just the same and man o'war birds. I lay on my back in the water and looked up and the man o'war were in a long path pointing up wind, with their wings still except for an occasional flap. I went back to the boat and drew them. . . ."*
> *HORN ISLAND LOGS.*

A good fisherman knows his lake A typical lake will have both barren and productive areas. The productive areas are in the form of feeding or holding areas, and some can be both.

Like people, fish seek comfortable surroundings, and productivity of a particular area will vary with the seasonal water temperature. The general rule is fish shallow in Spring, deep in mid-Summer, shallow in Fall, and deep in Winter.

	1 4 5 7 9 10 11 12
	1 4 5 6 7 9 10 11 12
	1 3 4 5 6 9 10 11
	1 2 3 4 5 6 7 8 9 10 11 12
	1 3 4 5 6 9 10
	1 3 4 5 6 9 10 11
	1 2 5 6 7 8 10 11 12

1. **Brushy Bank:** Good feeding area.
2. **Submerged Rock Pile:** Holding and feeding area. Rocks usually harbor small forage fish and crayfish.
3. **Weedy Bay:** Good feeding area.
4. **Shallow Submerged Weedy Bar:** Good feeding area. Weeds harbor minnows and small forage fish.
5. **Drop-off:** Game fish forage in shallows, hold on edge of drop-off, dart into deeper water at sign of danger.
6. **Cliffs:** Holding and feeding area. Game fish school on shelves. Minnows, small fish, crayfish inhabit rocks and crevices.
7. **Submerged Island:** Holding area. Possible feeding area, depending on cover and depth.
8. **Creek Bed:** Edges with cover good holding areas during mid-summer and winter months.
9. **Creek Mouth:** Food washed into lake creates good feeding area.
10. **Sloping Point with Drop-off:** Shallow point good feeding area. Drop-off into deep water good holding area.
11. **Overhanging Bank:** Provides shade. Good holding area.
12. **Stump Patches and Brush Patches:** Provide cover for minnows and small fish. Good feeding and holding areas.

The *Whopper Stopper Fishing Guide and Catalog* combines descriptions of lures with descriptions of the most likely places and conditions for using the lures successfully. From that catalog/guide, we are reproducing a lake diagram which suggests a pairing of lures with lake areas. The lures—or series of lures—which match the fishing conditions of the lake are those explained and shown in beautiful color in the catalog from Whopper Stopper, Inc., P.O. Box 1111, Sherman, Texas 75090.

SOUTHERN FISH AND OYSTER COMPANY, INC.

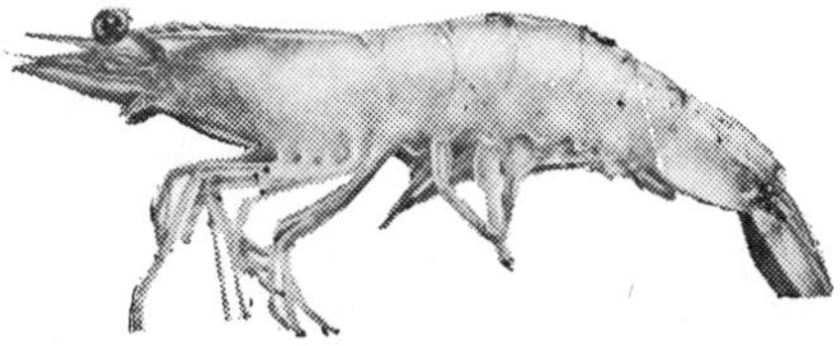

Most Southerners enjoy fresh seafood, and they like it to be really fresh. The Southern Fish and Oyster Company, Inc. is located in Mobile, Alabama, which is about as close to the Gulf of Mexico as a city can be. This company ships fresh seafood, packed in heavy-duty styrofoam boxes, to arrive at its destination no later than 12 to 24 hours from the time of shipment.

They offer a wide variety of seafood that is caught fresh daily from the bayous and the Gulf near Mobile. All sizes of shrimp, many varieties of fish, such as snapper, speckled trout, and flounder, as well as oysters and crabmeat, are available. Their seafood supply is seasonal, with the summer months yielding the best shrimp and crabmeat, the fall months yielding good fish, and the winter, oysters.

Call for further information about shipping and prices—(205)438-1271.

Southern Fish and Oyster Company, Inc.
P.O. Box 307
Mobile, Alabama 36601

A LURE FOR DEEPER DEEP-WATER FISHING

A new ⅞ oz., 5⅛" deep-running *Magnum* lure to catch big bass, stripers, muskie, and pike has been added to the Hellbender Series of Whopper Stopper, Sherman, Texas.

Designed for heavy casting and trolling, it reaches depths (35 feet trolling) not before attainable with a floating diving-type lure. The *Magnum* retains all the characteristics and fish-catching qualities of the regular Hellbender series.

For more information, write:

Whopper Stopper, Inc.
P.O. Box 1111
Sherman, Texas 75090

Courtesy of Tropical Shell Institute

A Close Look at the Beach

Your appreciation of the beach can be greatly enhanced if you understand more about the living things that inhabit the narrow arena of crashing waves and shifting sands.

by JAMES H. CARMICHAEL, JR.

Probably the most alluring geographical feature of the South is its salt-water coastline. Swimmers, fishermen, sunbathers, and rubberneckers, young and old—all seem to obey some instinctive urging toward the sea's edge, to that confluence of sand, surf, and sun which, in its mysterious way, enchants and revitalizes us all.

Your enjoyment and appreciation of a beach can be enhanced immeasurably, however, if you understand more about the multitude of living things enacting their ages-old drama of survival in that narrow arena of crashing waves and shifting sands.

An undisturbed beach reveals a beautiful balance of plants and animals adapted through millions of years of evolution to this specific environment. Unfortunately, too many sections of Southern coastline have been developed or polluted with reckless disregard for the beauty and function of the natural features—all too often with disastrous consequences.

Take the notable case of sea oats, the tall and graceful salt-tolerant grass that serves to hold sand dunes intact. Removal or destruction of sea oats leads to rapid dispersal of the dunes' sand by wind, subsequently exposing the upper beach to erosion during storm tides.

The biology of a beach can be an endless stimulation of your intellectual curiosity as well as an exercise of esthetic sensitivities. Consider just one of the many intriguing shore creatures, the **coquina**. Coquinas (*Donax variabilis*) are those strikingly colored little clams found by the thousands in the summertime on unpolluted beaches, squiggling in the sands washed by the very shallowest surf. They are sometimes called butterfly clams because the paired halves of the shells spread out flat on the sand to resemble butterfly wings.

A coquina's life is one of almost ceaseless activity. Burrowing in the sands between high and low tide lines, it feeds upon microorganisms filtered from the sea. Two pale, fleshy siphon tubes are extended upward out of the slightly parted shell. Water is drawn in through one of these (the intake siphon), passed over sticky internal gills, which collect diatoms and other plankton (minute animal and plant life), and is then pumped out through the other siphon.

When washed out of their burrow in the sand and tumbled about by a wave, coquinas hasten to dig in again, each one probing down with its muscular "foot" to gain a grip beneath the surface. Having done so, the smooth shell is tugged down into the sand, and once again the siphons pop up to circulate food-laden water through the feeding organs.

A less conspicuous but equally successful exploiter of the turbulent surf zone is the curious **mole crab** (*Emerita talpoida*), which is neither mole nor true crab, and which is sometimes called a sand flea or sand bug, though it's neither flea nor bug.

A rapid digger, protectively pale-colored, the mole crab emerges from the sand as waves swirl up the beach. Scurrying shoreward with the incoming rush of water, this hyperactive little crustacean usually starts to burrow just as the wave's surge diminishes. Disappearing backwards like magic into the sand, it digs in with a furious whirling motion of its tail appendages until only eyes, feathery antennae, and mouth parts are left protruding.

Mole crabs always face seaward when thus embedded, but they make no attempt to collect food from the incoming surf. Only into the stream of the wave's backwash does the creature extend its netlike antennae to "fish " for plankton, pulling the antennae through its mouth parts to scrape off a meal of minute sea life.

Mole crabs are eagerly sought by birds and fish. Surf fishermen dig them out of the sand where the surf is shallowest and use them as bait for pompano, whiting, and sheepshead.

Imagine snapping your fingers with such force that the concussion wave stuns a nearby enemy or prey animal. Such is the trick of a remarkable little creature of shallow coastal waters—the **pistol shrimp** (*Synalpheus*). Also called snapping shrimp, they live under stones or inside certain sponges and vacated shells, particularly along beaches where there are sheltering pilings or rocks.

One of the pistol shrimp's claws is greatly enlarged and has a moveable finger equipped with a peg that fits precisely into a socket on the opposing finger. When the claw is opened suddenly, and the peg is pulled out of the socket, the abrupt overcoming of suction causes an amazingly loud report.

Sometimes, as a small fish approaches, the shrimp eases toward it, aims its pistol at the victim, and pulls the trigger. The resulting shock wave stuns the fish momentarily, and the little gunman hastily retrieves its prey before the fish can recover.

Another of nature's ingeniously engineered animals, often exposed at low tide among sheltering rocks and in tide pools, is the **sea anemone**. Suggesting flowers, and giving little immediate indication of mobility, sea anemones usually attach themselves to stationary objects, although certain species actually hitchhike atop the shells of hermit crabs—apparently to partake of the crab's meals and in return to afford some measure of protection to the crab by presenting to predators their venomous tentacles.

Varying considerably in color, form, and size, all sea anemones have an array of fleshy, sticky tentacles surrounding an oral cavity into which captured prey is drawn. When an unwary fish brushes against an anemone's tentacles, out shoots a battery of microscopically small stinging darts, technically called nematocysts, which, though harmless to the touch, are sufficiently venomous to paralyze its natural prey. Once the darts have immobilized the fish, the sinuous tentacles enfold the helpless victim and pull it down into the mouth.

Another curious specimen is the short-spined **purplish sea urchin** (*Lytechinus variegatus*), found abundantly along some sections of the Southern coast. This fellow is unique insofar as it extends its sucker-tipped tube feet from between its stiff spines to pick up and pull little pieces of shell over its back. The bits of shell help conceal the sea urchin from would-be predators. Sea urchins might be difficult to detect, even when you are snorkeling, precisely because of this concealment, but once located you'll find they're usually abundant in that area.

Two other echinoderms (spiny skins)—the **sand dollar** and the **sea stars (starfish)**—are all too familiar in the coastal South as dried household ornaments. Alive in the sea, however, they are marvels of animal locomotion—particularly the sea star, which, as it walks up the glass wall of an aquarium, presents for observation the complex movements of its hundreds of tiny, sucking, tube feet. The combined suction of these strange feet allows the animal to adhere tenaciously to smooth surfaces and to pull open the shells of scallops and other bivalves to get at the meat inside.

A fascinating shore animal apparently caught in an evolutionary transition from sea to land life is the fleet-footed **ghost crab**, whose lightly speckled coloration camouflages it perfectly on the sand. Digging its burrows above the high-tide mark as if asserting its claim to a purely terrestrial habitat, this pale and nimble scavenger (*Ocypode albicans*) has really not yet severed its bond with the ocean. Unlike true land crabs, it is not an air breather. It takes its oxygen from a bit of the ocean carried in the branchial chamber surrounding its gills and must visit the surf periodically to replenish the water.

Down in the Florida Keys, creeping among the ancient coral rocks of which the islands are composed, is one of the South's most entertaining shore creatures. This is the colorful land hermit crab (*Coenobita clypeatus*), a true air breather. Stockier than the marine hermit crabs, the land hermit crab has one oversized claw with which it tears into edible carrion or fruit.

One of the curious habits of this little terrestrial decapod is its periodic "conferences" with a dozen or more of its kind to inspect and exchange each other's borrowed shells. The smaller crabs leave shells they have outgrown and move into those vacated by the next larger crab.

These whimsical creatures have also been discovered residing in small discarded bottles, hauling them around over coral stone with perfect aplomb.

GIFTS FROM THE SEA

For those who prefer the gifts from the sea *au naturel,* and are too far from the ocean or too lazy to collect their own, the Tropical Shell Institute can help you out. For your coffee table, curio cabinet, aquarium, or shell collection, you can get the collection pictured on the opposite page for $12.95 plus $3.00 postage and handling. Or you can get a 250 shell collection for $19.95 plus $4.00 postage and handling. For $1.00 you can get a portfolio on other shells.

Tropical Shell Institute
P.O. Box 21490
Fort Lauderdale, Florida 33335

SHELLS AND SHORES OF TEXAS
by Jean Andrews

The University of Texas Press
Austin, Texas

Shells tell the story of this earth as far back as the beginning of the Cambrian era 600 million years ago. Before the dawn of civilization, early man had many different uses for the sea shell. It could be an object of adornment, an implement, or even a medium of exchange. Grave sites all over the world give evidence of man's need for the mollusk. Remarkably, not much is known of the animals that created the shells and that have intrigued, and helped to feed, humans from time immemorial.

But today, the fossil-maker is beginning to be recognized as well as the fossil. The conchologist (one who studies shells) prefers to be referred to as the malacologist (one who studies the organism).

Unfortunately, fresh-water species of mollusks are quickly disappearing. Each new dam and inland waterway seals their fate tighter. Texas is not one of the states that has enacted laws designed to protect the mollusk (except in the case of the oyster). Thus, marine mollusks in the area are becoming extinct, beaten back into the past by the swelling oil-slick tides of the future. Coastal waters are virtually uninhabitable for these creatures. Also, Hurricanes Carla, Beulah, Celia, and Fern have eliminated most of the molluskan population from the shallow coastal waters of central and south Texas. But the diehard mollusks are slowly returning.

This book gives a great deal of Texas history and ecology. The casual beachcomber, the amateur shell fancier, and the scientist can all find something in Mrs. Andrews' book worth collecting. Drawings, maps, charts, and illustrations, following detailed descriptions of individual shells, are included. Also, 24 beautiful full-color plates grace *Shells and Shores of Texas*. —S.V.H.

When the wilderness calls

Sportsmen wanting to hunt and fish, and vacationers who love pack trips, photogenic scenery, and the outdoors now have a convenient source for recommendations concerning reliable guides, outfitters, and resorts in the great sports areas of this continent. Wayne Preston, Inc., can provide you with information for a hunting trip in the Rocky Mountain states, Texas, Canada, Alaska, or Mexico. And he also offers hunting and fishing for all species of game in the following areas: Africa, Asia, some parts of Russia, Central and South America. He started with 64 packages in 1969 and today these have been expanded to include as many as 500 different trips.

Wayne B. Preston is an avid sportsman himself who has enjoyed hunting and fishing throughout North America. He can give you information on personally selected facilities and personnel in the area of your choice as well as equipment. As part of his service, Preston can also give you assistance on many necessary details such as applications for permits and licenses, copies of season dates, and regulations for the particular area you wish to visit.

Mr. Preston's operation is based in Dallas, Texas, and he offers many interesting fishing and hunting safaris in the state of Texas. With approximately 4,500 square miles of inland waters and a coastline of 624 tidewater miles, Texas is one of the top three states in freshwater and saltwater fishing catches. Texas leads the nation in the annual harvest of whitetail deer, mourning dove, waterfowl, wild turkey, and exotic big game.

Some information on a few previous trips that have been offered are excerpted here for your scrutiny:

MULE DEER NEAR THE BIG BEND PARK—Season: Begins Saturday after Thanksgiving for 16 days

Nation-wide fame has been given the mule deer of the desert Southwest and we offer a fine 35,000-acre ranch in the heart of this country that has not been hunted for four years. A brand new hunting lodge, the WT Lodge, will accommodate up to 14 with all modern conveniences plus an enjoyable fireplace for recounting the day's adventure. You may prefer our real deluxe Oasis lodge for parties or families up to six. Either lodge offers fine Mexican-styled home cooking. You will be provided with a limited number of guides and vehicles. If you care to, you may bring your hunting vehicle or just land on our 2,300-foot sod airstrip adjoining the ranch headquarters.

Three 4-day hunts are planned over the three weekends. This allows ample time to find that trophy buck and you might like to try for a javelina plus a limit of blue quail without additional charge. Drop your deposit in the mail to confirm your individual or group reservations. We will be happy to provide additional details.

ANTELOPE IN THE TRANS-PECOS AREA—Season: Begins on Saturday nearest October 1st

No state drawing is needed for this prize trophy in the rolling country of Southwestern Texas. You will want to make your plans early as trophy permits are very scarce each year. Only 900 bucks were bagged state-wide last fall. This has made it necessary to take reservations on a first deposit basis only.

Our annually sponsored hunt has a real high success ratio over the years and we expect excellent results again next fall. You can choose between our regular hunt or our deluxe trophy hunt. In the regular hunt, we provide your trophy permit and a limited number of guides and vehicles. If you have your own "off-the-road" vehicle you may well want to bring it.

In the Deluxe Trophy hunt all you need to bring is your favorite rifle and personal gear. We provide guides, vehicles, food and lodging, meat processing, transfers from the airport, permits, spotting scope and special equipment needed. We can also arrange charter flights from Dallas if you wish.

WHITE TAIL DEER-90 Minutes from Dallas—Season: November 13th to January 3rd

You may enjoy a weekend of hunting for bucks or does under a guaranteed basis—no deer—no pay. Blinds are provided as well as a guide and vehicle on the ranch. No overcrowding is permitted and this is an ideal place to relax while being assured of success. Overnight accommodations are nearby plus a State Park where dinosaur tracks offer appeal. Pick out your weekend and let us hear your wishes.

Write:

Wayne B. Preston, Inc.
3444 Northaven Road
Dallas, Texas 75229
or call:
(214) 358-4477

BELLINGRATH GARDENS BOOK

Bellingrath Gardens and Home is known as "The Garden for All Seasons," a place where a huge variety of beautiful flowers and shrubs are cultivated in a carefully planned yet wonderfully natural setting throughout the entire year. The late Walter D. Bellingrath (who with his wife, Bessie M. Bellingrath, began the Gardens as a merely personal activity in 1927 to enhance the surroundings of their fishing lodge on the Isle-aux-Oies near Mobile) compared the Gardens to a lovely lady with 52 gowns, one for each week of the year. And Mr. Bellingrath was not exceedingly hyperbolic in this comment. Bellingrath Gardens makes spectacular use of the Southern climate and subtly changing seasons to display a dazzling array of azaleas in late winter; dogwood, roses, and hydrangeas in spring; roses, allamandas, daisies, and countless other flowering plants and shrubs in summer; over 900 varieties of camellias in autumn; and Confederate jasmine, sweet olive, magnificent oaks, and magnolias all year long.

A book, well-illustrated with color photographs of the Gardens in every season and several pictures of the Bellingrath Home's interior treasures (the fishing lodge long ago gave way to a lovely mansion), is available by mail for $3.75. Also, there is a 16-mm color and sound movie of the Gardens available for loan to garden clubs and other interested groups. The only cost is for the postage and insurance of the film both ways. For additional information, write:

Bellingrath Gardens and Home
Route 1, Box 60
Theodore, Alabama 36582

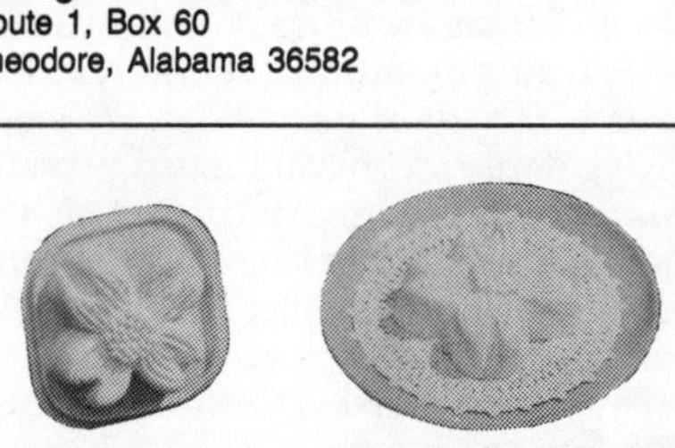

ICE CREAM FLOWER MOLDS: Now you can mold ice cream in exquisite flower shapes just the right size for individual servings. Just fill molds with ice cream; pop into freezer. When you are ready to serve them, the ice cream slips out easily, reproducing every detail of a zinnia, rose, daisy, dogwood, pansy, or blackeyed Susan. The molds are ideal, too, for gelatin desserts and salads. A set of six, all different, costs $3.95 plus $1.10 postage. Write to Artisan Galleries, 2100 North Haskell Avenue, Dallas, Texas 75204.

ON STAYING COOL

The Porta-Shade and the Tent Shade are products from Harold Cunningham and Company of Bowie, Texas.

The Porta-Shade, according to its manufacturer, can be set up in about 5 or 6 minutes by one person. The canopy has a reflective white top above a dark blue bottom. The Porta-Shade is seven feet tall to allow heat to escape, and it can be leaned to increase shade area. It comes complete with the waterproof canopy, strong 1" aluminum poles, corner clips that won't pull out, impact polystyrene stakes, and strong nylon guy-ropes. The most popular model is a 9 x 9 Dining Shade which sells for $29.75.

The Tent Shade is shaped like a tent and is also made of the blue/white heat-reflective, waterproof material. It comes complete and ready to set up. It consists of two 1" aluminum tubing poles, the tent material, 6 stakes, and pre-tied guy ropes. The 9 x 18 tent sells for $44.95.

Write to:

Harold Cunningham & Company
P.O. Box 552
Bowie, Texas 76230

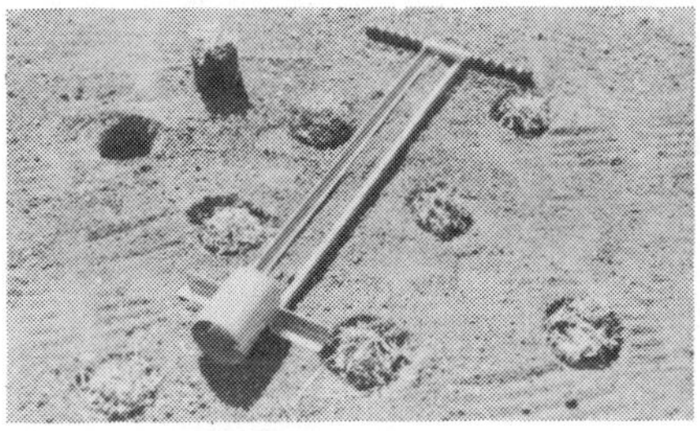

PLUG O GRASS ™

Now available is a tool for transplanting grasses that grow by runners (St. Augustine, Carpet, Bermuda, and Zoysia). The tool allows its user to perform several tasks: transplant grasses, remove weeds, transplant bulbs, and make planting holes for various small plants.

The transplanter with its 3½-inch-diameter cutting tube and two internal blades is pushed into saturated ground. A quarter turn breaks the connection between the plug and the surrounding ground. The plug is then lifted straight out of the ground. Using the same process, planting holes are dug.

The transplanter has no moving parts to break, a cutting area tempered to minimize sharpening, and heavy-gauge, all-steel welded component construction. The price is $15.95, including postage and taxes.

Contact:

Plug-O-Grass, Inc.
P.O. Box 17565
San Antonio, Texas 78217

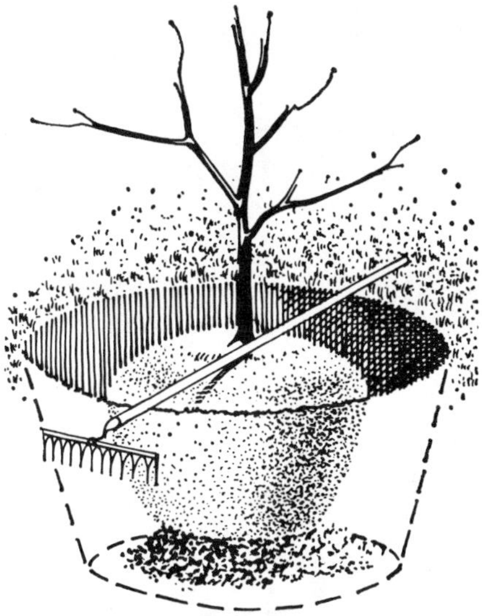

Plant Dogwoods With Care

There's more to planting a dogwood than just digging a hole in the ground. Although these popular trees are native to the South, they can be temperamental in the home garden. A little extra care at plantingtime can make the difference between a tree that thrives for many years and one that dies the first summer.

First, purchase a healthy tree from a reputable nursery rather than trying to transplant a tree from the wild. Once you've purchased a tree, don't delay planting it. Select a planting site that is partially shaded, especially from afternoon sun.

Dig a planting hole twice as wide and deep as the root ball. Dogwoods are more particular about drainage than they are about soil, but you can improve both soil structure and drainage if you dig the hole about 3 feet deep and mix leaf mold, pine bark, or peat moss into the backfill soil. On extremely heavy soils, break up existing hardpan before attempting to grow a dogwood.

On balled-and-burlapped plants, unfasten the burlap from around the trunk, but it is not necessary to remove the burlap from the root ball. On container-grown plants, loosen the roots if they have become matted around the soil ball.

Begin to refill the planting hole, firming the soil to adjust the plant to the correct height. The top of the root ball should be slightly above the soil surrounding the planting hole. Lay the handle of a shovel or a rake on the ground to check the level of the root ball; then firm backfill soil around the roots. Water thoroughly to settle the soil, and add more backfill if necessary.

The first year in the ground is crucial for a dogwood, so be sure to water during rainless weather.

Walking For Wildflowers

The blooming of the wildflowers is one of the season's most anticipated events. Here are some places you can visit to learn more about them.

When the first wildflowers peek through winter's mantle of fallen leaves, it's nature's official declaration of a special new season. Unless you happen to find skunk cabbage (*Symplocarpus foetidus*), you'll probably find bloodroot (*Sanguinaria canadensis*) to be the first wildflower in bloom, followed closely by trailing arbutus (*Epigea repens*) and liverleaf (*Hepatica americana*).

The interest in wildflowers has inspired many public gardens to create carefully cultivated plantings of hardy native wildflowers in natural habitats. Here is a listing of some of the gardens in the South that have wildflower areas. Most of the gardens have labeled plantings, and many have staff members to answer questions. Many gardens also offer guided wildflower walks or prearranged classes.

Alabama

The wildflower garden at the Birmingham Botanical Gardens is one of the finest landscape displays of wildflowers in the South. The plants, mostly shade-loving flowers, are representative of almost the entire state and are skillfully integrated into handsomely crafted rockwork. The species are labeled, and the garden is open during daylight hours year-round so an entire succession of bloom may be observed. The Birmingham Botanical Gardens is located at 2612 Lane Park Road, Birmingham 35223.

Arkansas

The Museum of Science and History in Little Rock offers wildflower walks each Saturday in April. These are guided tours into different habitats accompanied by a naturalist familiar with the flora in the area. One introductory lecture for all participants is scheduled at the museum to acquaint wildflower observers with what they should look for in the field. Some of the tours take all day, so visitors should bring a lunch. There is a charge for each trip, but it varies with the length of the excursion. For further information on the tours, write Wildflower Walks, Museum of Science and History, MacArthur Park, Little Rock 72202.

Florida

The Corkscrew Swamp Sanctuary near Naples is one of this state's finest preserves. A boardwalk more than 1 mile long leads through the sanctuary, and native plants are labeled along the walk. This 11,000-acre National Audubon Society sanctuary features one of the largest remaining stands of bald cypress *(Taxodium distichum)*. Admission is $3 for adults and $1 for students age 12 and over, and includes a 31-page self-guided tour booklet. The sanctuary is located in the Everglades on State 846 about 30 miles southwest of Fort Myers. For information, write National Audubon Society, Route 6, Box 1875A, Sanctuary Road, Naples 33999.

Georgia

Famous throughout the South, Callaway Gardens at Pine Mountain features wildflower walks that display plants from across the state. The garden features scheduled guided walks led by staff members. Plants are labeled for self-guided tours, but the weekend workshops and walks are a popular means to discover the wealth of plants featured at this recreation facility. Admission to the gardens is $2 for adults and $1 for children. Pine Mountain is on State 27, about 80 miles south of Atlanta. For further information, write Callaway Gardens, State Highway 27, Pine Mountain 31822.

Kentucky

Amid the 10,000 acres of forest preserve that comprise Bernheim Forest lie 300 of the most scenic landscape acres in the country. Modeled after the great park designs of England, and designed by the office of Fredrick Law Olmstead, the landscape arboretum offers a wealth of plant materials (some 1,500 species) that are labeled and displayed in the best horticultural fashion. Wildflowers (almost everything that blooms in Kentucky) abound on the property and can be observed near many of the shelters and along the trails that tour the preserve. Bernheim Forest is open daily 9 a.m. to sundown from the 15th of March to the 15th of November. There is no charge for admission. For further information, write Bernheim Forest, Clermont, 40110.

Louisiana

Visitors to the Caroline Dormon Nature Preserve at Briarwood in Natchitoches Parish will be treated to 120 acres of rare and unusual Louisiana plants. Briarwood is shown by tours and is open to the public every weekend in April, May, August, and November. Hours are 9 a.m. to 5 p.m. on Saturdays and noon to 5 p.m. on Sundays. The gardens feature a bay garden, where Caroline Dormon, owner of Briarwood, worked for years to hybridize the Louisiana iris. Briarwood is on State 9 between Saline and Campti. Further information is available from the Foundation for the Preservation of the Caroline Dormon Nature Preserve, Inc., Box 226, Natchitoches 71457.

Mississippi

The Gloster Arboretum in Gloster is a 350-acre tract that has extensive native flowers. The plants are labeled but are located throughout the grounds, so it is best to attend on weekends, when guides are available. The continually expanding collection boasts an extensive collection of native magnolias as well as the Dr. Clair Brown Wildflower Garden. For further information, write the John James Audubon Foundation, Box 1106, Baton Rouge, Louisiana 70821.

North Carolina

Preservation of the native woodlands is the underlying philosophy of the North Carolina Botanical Garden, and their outstanding habitat collection of plants is slowly growing. The species in the four

gardens (Mountain Habitat, Piedmont Forest, Sandhills Habitat, and Coastal Plain) are collected only from areas that are endangered by development. Other plants are propagated and grown on the grounds. The charm of the garden is that visitors can view the plants in habitats that are almost identical to their native sites. On the 11 acres of the grounds, one can walk from the mountains to the coast through a succession of bloom. There is no charge for admission. The North Carolina Botanical Garden is open weekdays from 8 a.m. until 5 p.m. and mid-March through mid-October from 10 a.m. to 4 p.m. on Saturday and from 2 p.m. to 5 p.m. on Sunday. Further information is available from Totten Garden Center, 457-A Botanical Garden, UNC-CH, Chapel Hill, 27514.

South Carolina

The Horticultural Gardens of Clemson University in Clemson give visitors the opportunity to see a fine collection of Piedmont plants. Trails are easy to follow, and most of the plants are labeled. The gardens are open year-round during daylight hours so visitors can see a succession of bloom. For information, contact Dr. David Bradshaw, Horticulture Department, Clemson University, Clemson 29631.

Tennessee

The Tennessee Botanical Gardens and Fine Arts Center at Cheekwood in Nashville features a self-guided wildflower walk through one portion of the Wildings garden. All specimens are labeled with both common and scientific names. A brochure is available with a description of the different areas and a map for a walk through Wildings. Cheekwood is open Tuesday through Saturday from 10 a.m. until 4:30 p.m. and Sunday from 1 until 4 p.m. For information, contact Tennessee Botanical Gardens, Cheek Road, Nashville 37205.

Texas

Wildflowers abound throughout the state because of vigorous efforts to encourage their growth, particularly along roadsides. Accordingly, it is a slightly different wildflower tour that highlights early spring—one that emphasizes the great expanse of ground that the flowers cover. The Official Wildflower Tour of Texas is a driving tour centered at the community of Hughes Springs. A tour map of featured flowers and their location is available at the beginning of the self-guided trip. For further information, contact the Chamber of Commerce, Box 218, Highes Springs 75656.

GREAT SMOKY MOUNTAIN WILDFLOWER OR PHOTOGRAPHY CAMPS

Globe Treks of Hendersonville, North Carolina, has two camps which focus specifically on (1) wildflower studies and (2) photography.

The wildflower camp involves primitive camping and hikes to different habitats with elevations between 2,000 and 5,800 feet. (This includes the valley floor and high ridge lines.) The hikes move at a leisurely pace under the guidance and instruction of a staff member from the North Carolina Botanical Garden. The participants come from different levels of camping experience and knowledge of botanical subjects. Globe Treks provides tents, sleeping bags, food, and utensils. You provide clothing, boots or shoes, camera equipment, etc. Lists of supplies are available with copies of the itinerary.

The Great Smoky Mountain Photography Camp involves photography instruction, geared to both the amateur and the knowledgeable photographer. At the base camp, family-style tents are used; two-man tents are set up in the Smokies. Lists of equipment needs would be furnished to you before the camp; clothing and photography equipment are basic.

Both camps are presently scheduled for 4-day sessions. For each session, the number of participants is limited (20 for wildflower camps and 15 for photography camps).

For more information, write to:

Globe Treks, Inc.
410 W. 5th Avenue—Suite 10
Hendersonville, North Carolina 28739

GARDENS OF THE BLUE RIDGE

If you have ever taken a hike in the mountains of the Southeastern United States, no doubt you have been tempted to bring back to "civilization" some of the beautiful ferns or other plants you have seen growing in the wild abundance along your path. *Please do not give in to your temptation!* There are several nurseries which specialize in the cultivation of these natural plants—go to them for your plants, and leave the woods and hiking trails untouched.

One of the nurseries which has a terrific stock of wild flowers, hardy trees, shrubs, plants and bulbs native to the mountains is Gardens of the Blue Ridge. The nursery is located at Pineola, 15 miles north of Ashford and 2 miles south of Linville, North Carolina, on U.S. 221. Here are grown and offered for sale such categories of plants as hardy native herbaceous perennials; hardy native plants for rock gardens and naturalizing; hardy native orchids; hardy native ferns; hardy aquatic and bog plants; hardy vines, climbers, and creepers; native lilies for naturalizing or specimens; mountain laurel; rhododendrons; hardy native deciduous trees and shrubs; and hardy native evergreen trees and shrubs.

A special Christmas season offering from the Gardens of the Blue Ridge is a good selection of evergreens for holiday decorations. Available are wreaths of double face balsam, double face white pine, or double face hemlock in sizes ranging from 13" to 36". Christmas roping in 25-yard coils can be obtained in either white pine, mountain laurel, a white pine and mountain laurel combination, hemlock, or Southern balsam. You may also buy American holly branches, balsam fir branches, galax leaves, ground pine for bouquets, and leucothoe sprays. Special assortments suitable for giving as Christmas gifts to friends are also available.

The fall planting season begins in August and they ship all winter according to weather and locality served. If you wish to visit the nursery yourself, the best time is between May and October.

For a complete catalogue of available plants, send $1.00 to:

Gardens of the Blue Ridge
P.O. Box 10
Pineola, North Carolina 28662

> *"Spring day—the ecstatic Grackles a little crazy—are being forced into nest building by their wives. They have I think established a small colony near a wild life refuge sign as if it were a token of safety—or good luck."*
> *HORN ISLAND LOGS.*

Books for Wildflower Lovers

It's almost impossible to see a field of Texas bluebonnets or a woodland creek bank of wild hepatica without wanting to know more about these beautiful plants that grow and thrive without the "helping" hand of humans.

To identify the plants that you find while hiking and camping, you will find one or more of these books useful in furthering your knowledge of the wildflowers in your area.

■ *Wildflowers of the Southeastern United States* ($12; University of Georgia Press). By Wilbur H. Duncan and Leonard E. Foote, this superb volume contains nearly 500 color photographs and descriptions of more than 1,000 species. The book is ambitious, depicting native and naturalized plant materials of 12 Southeastern states plus North Florida. Botanical terms used to describe plant and flower parts are illustrated with line drawings. The book may be ordered directly from the publisher in Athens, Georgia 30602. Indexed; 296 pages.

■ *Ozark Wild Flowers* ($2.95 paperback; Woods Brothers Agency). This slender volume, by Edith Lancaster Huey, is an impressionistic view of Ozark wildflowers. There is no descriptive text, but the photographs help identify plants. Order directly from the author at Box 97-H, Sylamore Route, Mountain View, Arkansas 72560. Indexed; 46 pages.

■ *A Guide to the Wildflowers & Ferns of Kentucky* ($9.50 hardcover; The University Press of Kentucky). Mary E. Wharton and Roger W. Barbour have produced a definitive volume on wildflowers and ferns in Kentucky. The book is also of interest to readers in northern Tennessee and western West Virginia, where plant materials are similar. Almost 500 color photographs accompany the text in which nearly 700 species are discussed. Line drawings illustrate botanical terminology. Order from the publisher in Lexington, Kentucky 40506. Indexed; 344 pages.

■ *Wildflowers of Louisiana and Adjoining States* ($12.50 hardcover; Louisiana State University Press). Author Clair A. Brown, a distinguished botanist of international reputation, has compiled this field guide to the native and naturalized plants of Louisiana and surrounding areas. Color photographs illustrate 430 plant species, which the author describes in non-academic language. There is a glossary of botanical terms, a bibliography of suggested reading, and an explanation of the botanical "regions" of Louisiana. Order the field guide directly from the publisher in Baton Rouge, Louisiana 70803. Indexed; 247 pages.

■ *Flora of West Virginia* ($13.25 paperback; West Virginia University Bulletin). This four-volume series is an update of a similar collection originally published in the early 1950's. Although rather academic, the books will interest the West Virginia wildflower enthusiast. The books describe over 2,000 species, with lengthy discussions of the natural history of the area. Order from the University of West Virginia Bookstore in Morgantown, West Virginia 26505. Indexed; 1,079 pages.

■ *Wildflowers of Alabama and Adjoining States* ($10 hardcover; University of Alabama Press). Authored by Blanche E. Dean, Amy Mason, and Joab L. Thomas, this book includes color photos and botanical descriptions of 400 species, plus a glossary of botanical terms. Order from the publisher, University, Alabama 35486. Indexed; 230 pages.

■ *Wild Flowers of Florida* ($4.95 paperback; Banyan Books). Authors Glenn Fleming, Pierre Genelle, and Robert Long have collaborated to produce this small but useful volume about the long-neglected wild flora of Florida. The plant descriptions are easy to read, and although the quality of the photographs varies, all are adequate. Two glossaries, one of which is illustrated by superb drawings, explain botanical terminology. Order from the publisher, Box 431160, Miami, Florida 33143. Indexed; 96 pages.

■ *Wild Flowers of North Carolina* ($10.95 hardcover; University of North Carolina Press). One of the best in the state-by-state series of wildflower books, this volume by William S. Justice and C. Ritchie Bell is a handy guide for the Upper South native-plant enthusiast. The 400 color photographs are generally high quality, and each accompanying text is both short and informative. Available in many North Carolina bookstores or from the publisher in Chapel Hill, North Carolina 27514. Indexed; 217 pages.

■ *Roadside Flowers of Texas* ($5.75 hardcover; University of Texas Press). In this superb book by Howard S. Irwin, a noted Texas botanist, the love of wildflowers is apparent. The 257 plants discussed are illustrated with watercolor paintings by Mary Motz Wills, the noted Texas artist. The one minor objection to the format is that the illustrations appear apart from the texts. Nonetheless, it is a must for Texas wildflower lovers. Available in bookstores throughout the state or from the publisher in Austin 78712. Indexed; 295 pages.

■ *Wildflowers in Color* ($8.95 hardcover; Harper & Row). This small book has chosen as its focus the great Southern wildflower refuges: the Great Smoky Mountains, the Blue Ridge Parkway, and the Shenandoah National Park. Authors Arthur Stupka and Donald H. Robinson have compiled valuable botanical information and superb color photographs of over 250 species of native and escaped plants, including trees, shrubs, vines, and herbaceous wild plants. The geographical range of the book is broad, discussing plants found over much of the Eastern United States. Available in bookstores across the South. Indexed; 144 pages.

■ *Roadside Flowers of Oklahoma* ($5 paperback; Doyle McCoy). In a private printing, Author Doyle McCoy of Cameron University has produced a layman's guide to the non-cultivated flora of his state. Nearly 300 species are illustrated and discussed in this small manual; a second volume, containing 150 additional photographs, is scheduled to be ready soon. A number of bookstores in the state stock the book. Copies are also available directly from Dr. McCoy at Cameron University, Lawton, Oklahoma 73501. Indexed; 116 pages.

■ *Great Smoky Mountains Wildflowers* ($3.75 paperback; University of Tennessee Press). Simple in format and direct in language, this pocket-size book is authored by Carlos C. Campbell, William F. Hutson, and Aaron J. Sharp. Although all three differ in background, their common interest in the flora of the Great Smokies has resulted in a usable field guide for the layman. Plant descriptions are short and informative; the photos, mostly by Dr. Hutson, range from adequate to exceptional. The book discusses about 170 of the most common species. Available from the publisher in Knoxville, Tennessee 37916. Indexed; 113 pages.

"Facts, facts, facts are amusing things—it seems that a bullrush is just wide enough for a little green frog to get on the other side of and have one eye on each edge so that he is completely hidden except for his eyes and fingers holding on."
HORN ISLAND LOGS.

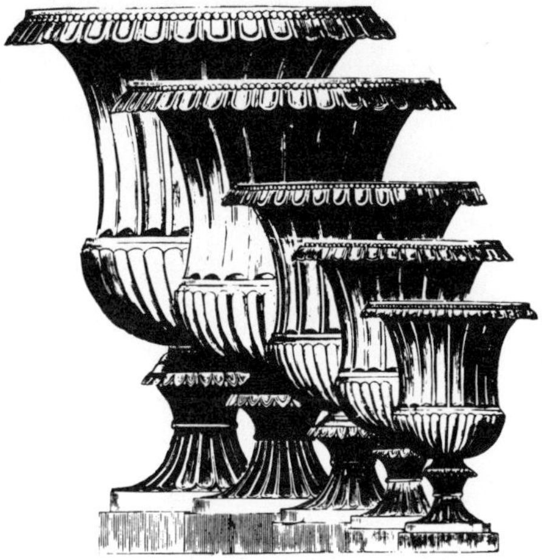

FOUNTAINS OF ANY AGE

A fountain of youth may be the most sought-after type of fountain, but until that discovery is imminent, we should be happy with the products of ornamental iron foundries such as Robinson Iron of Alexander City, Alabama. Here the "specialty of the plant" is the creation of one-of-a-kind fountains, although they will sell you one from their standard collection—and these are extremely beautiful creations, too.

The basis of their custom ironworking business is the Janney Collection of original patterns for fountains, birdbaths, urns, railings, gates, garden furniture, posts, and other ornamental iron. Long before the Civil War, the Janney Iron Works of Montgomery, Alabama, produced a great amount of the ironwork found on plantation homes, townhouses, and public buildings in the South. During the war, the foundry devoted itself to production of war materiel for the Confederacy. After the war, there was not much interest in ornamenting homes or buildings with decorative iron, so the patterns gathered dust. About 40 years ago, the patterns were moved from Montgomery to Alexander City, and once more the designs, which run the gamut from Greek to other revivals appearing in France, Spain, and Italy during the Renaissance, were put in production.

Robinson Iron does a great deal of restorative work. They have remade the gate posts at the entrance to West Point Military Academy and the figures on the Court Street Square Fountain in Montgomery and have recreated items for the Savannah historical district and the Selma, Alabama historic area. They love the challenge of a restoration but equally enjoy working up an entirely new pattern from an original design.

For $3.00 pre postpaid, they will send you a catalogue which shows you the types of things they have done. Dealer inquiries are also welcomed.

Write to them at:

Robinson Iron
Robinson Road
Alexander City, Alabama 35010

Gate posts at entrance to West Point Military Academy

Dance Urn

Magnus Roman Fluted Fountain

Georgia Post

Bill Haddox

HANDWORK

"The things men make are the best witness. They cannot lie. And what they say is of supreme importance. For they speak a man's soul and tell who are his gods."

Photograph and commentary from COMMON CLAY/INDIANA REVISIONS by Charles Counts, A. G. Halldin, publisher.

Handwork Index

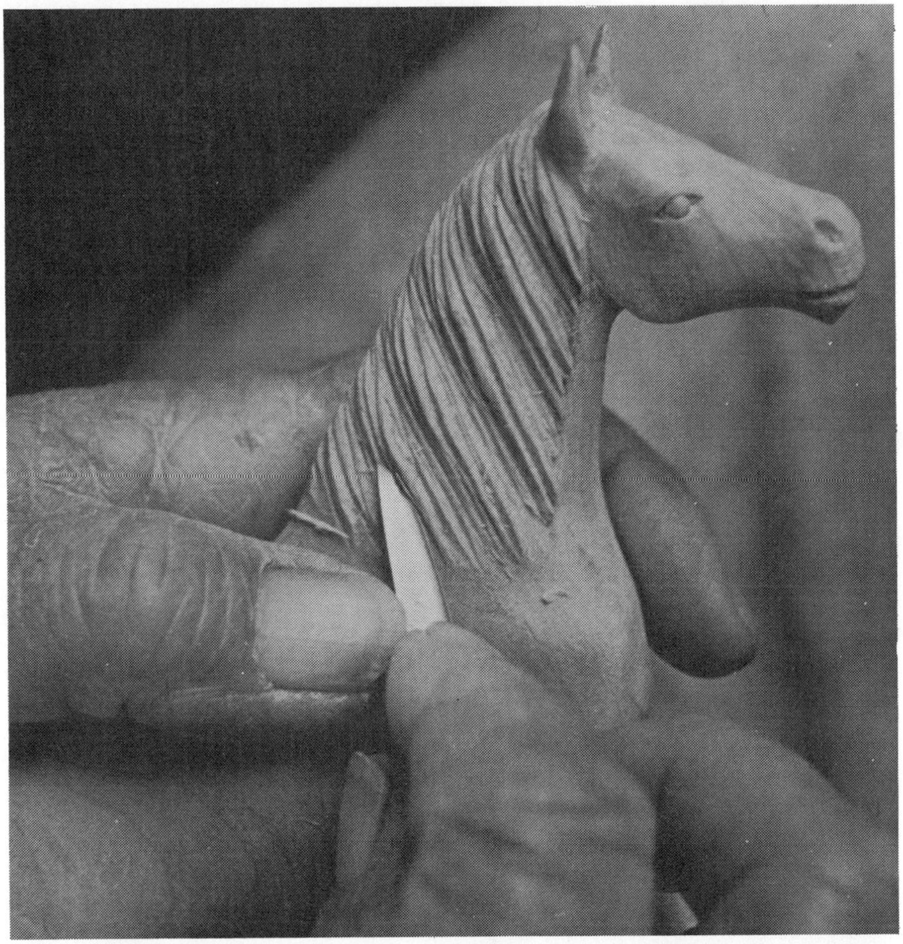

Schools That Teach the Art of Crafts

by Julia Hamilton and Karen Lingo

Craftsmen have long passed their skills and ideas from one generation to the next. Today, sculptors, weavers, potters, and blacksmiths continue the tradition by offering instruction to adults in schools across the South.

Today, students of all ages are rediscovering the skills as well as the satisfaction gained by creating something with their hands. It can be a project as involved as a stained-glass window or as simple as a shallow clay dish. And instruction is available in almost every city in the South.

Courses in arts and crafts are taught in community schools, colleges and universities, museums, and art centers. One of the best ways to receive concentrated instruction is to attend one of the region's art, craft, or folk schools. Here, students are immersed in the study of their chosen subject from daylight until dark, and sometimes into the night as well. Room and board are available, and the courses usually last from one to three weeks.

Three of the most popular schools in the South are Penland School of Crafts in Penland, North Carolina; John C. Campbell Folk School in Brasstown, North Carolina; and Arrowmont School of Arts and Crafts in Gatlinburg, Tennessee.

Penland has an academic atmosphere; college credit is offered and some work-study scholarships are available. But there is no sales gallery, and drop-in visitors are not encouraged. John C. Campbell and Arrowmont, on the other hand, both have sales galleries and welcome visitors on a limited basis.

To experience the arts and crafts schools firsthand, Karen Lingo enrolled in a pottery course at John C. Campbell and Julia Hamilton studied painting at Arrowmont. Here is what they found.

Head bent over her potter's wheel, the young lady from Atlanta was a study in concentration as her fingers guided the moist, spinning lump of clay into the shape of a teapot bowl. But it wasn't quite right, so she scraped it off and began another as less experienced students stopped to watch. This was her second course at John C. Campbell. In the first she had learned the techniques of throwing pottery. Now she was working on refinement.

A hundred yards away, in a rustic board building, a dozen students ranging in age from 25 to 60 were getting their first taste of wood carving. It was the first day, and by lunchtime bandaged fingers were in evidence. But by suppertime (it's called supper at John C. Campbell), everyone proudly exhibited a recognizable form emerging from beneath the flicks of the knife.

John C. Campbell is a rustic place, as comfortable as a favorite old jacket. The various crafts buildings, all within easy walking distance of the main house, are spread out over the rolling countryside outside Brasstown, North Carolina. The main building, which is called Keith House, contains student rooms, a kitchen, community room, school offices, and a crafts sales shop. In the living room students gather at a large fireplace at the end of the day to exchange classroom experiences, read the newspaper, tell ghost tales, or do a little more work on their carvings or quilts.

Mealtime at the school is akin to going home for a meal . . . like grandmother used to cook. It's simple fare, but filling. The vegetables are grown in the school garden and either eaten fresh during the season or canned for use during the fall and winter. The bread is homemade as well, and so are the desserts.

Back in the 1920s, John C. Campbell was started as a community education center, offering subjects ranging from forestry and history to public health. The community still uses some of the facilities. Choir practice is usually held at Keith House, and sometimes local residents will drop by for an evening of folk dancing with the students.

The majority of courses are taught in the spring and summer, with two held in the fall. In winter, special-interest weekend workshops are offered. The main crafts taught are wood carving, weaving, pottery, enameling, and blacksmithing. Once or twice during the year, classes are offered in woodworking, basketry, quilting, lapidary, and silversmithing.

Tuition at John C. Campbell is $65.00 a week. Rooms range from $31.50 to $77.00 a week, depending on whether they are single or dormitory space. Three meals a day for a week add up to $63.00. Craft materials used in class are extra, but are available at school at cost.

At the school, students can work as little or as much as they want. As both Pottery Instructor Lee Davis and Master Wood Carver Jack Hall say, "You can come in and work all day and night too, if you want."

Usually, it's the potters who head out the door of Keith House right after supper, going back to their wheels. Unlike the wood carvers and quilters, they can't bring their work back to the fireplace. And occasionally, there will be blacksmiths who just can't stay away from the forge. Far into the night the sparks fly from their anvils. And when all is quiet, they come tiptoeing back into Keith House for a few hours' sleep before the next day begins.

The Arrowmont School of Arts and Crafts sits in an airy woodland at the base of a mountain in Gatlinburg, Tennessee. It's a secluded place, far more private than you'd expect to find off one of Gatlinburg's busiest streets.

Each summer, Arrowmont conducts a concentrated series of workshops, although workshops are held at various times throughout the year. For the summer programs a faculty of over 40 instructors is assembled. Some are designers and craftsmen who operate independent studios for the production of stained glass, handmade furniture, or pottery. Several have produced books on subjects such as enameling, dyeing and textile design. They provide students with up-to-date instruction, including lectures, group demonstrations, slide presentations, and critiques of individual work. In the studios instructors emphasize aesthetic content as well as mastery of technique.

Among the students are working adults on vacation, artists, college students, and hobbyists who have always wanted to learn to paint, make pots, or sculpt in clay. Students can enroll at beginning, intermediate, or advanced levels. Many start the summer at a beginning level and finish a more advanced class several weeks later. College credit is available through the University of Tennessee.

Courses at Arrowmont include weaving, stained glass, watercolor, woodworking, jewelry making, creative writing, furniture design, and sculpture in fabric, clay, or metal. All classes meet with the instructors during the morning and afternoon. The pace is rigorous, and the students are ambitious. Most continue to work in the studios until late in the evening.

Students move freely from one class to another, observing others at work. In the stained-glass course, they might see a lesson in manipulating color and light to create designs. Or in a course in textile design, they may see duplicates of old family photographs being used in exploring a photo-silk screen technique. Most develop a real interest in the progress of others, watching step-by-step as a salad bowl hewn from a felled tree is polished to perfection.

Between classes, students often wander into the gallery in the main bulding to see exhibits of faculty crafts and artwork, which are displayed there. And in addition to regular class meetings, the school conducts a series of evening programs, which in the past has included concerts by musical performers and lectures on folk pottery in the South.

Arrowmont was founded in 1912 by Pi Beta Phi fraternity as the Gatlinburg Settlement School, an early source of public education in the area. Over the years the school developed into its present modern studio complex, and today students work in well-equipped studios and can move outdoors to work on sheltered terraces.

Some single rooms, as well as dormitory rooms, are available. Students can visit informally with instructors in the large dining room, where three meals are served each day. And there is a lounge where students can gather to share the experiences of the day. The school also maintains a library with an excellent collection on the subjects of arts and crafts.

Tuition at Arrowmont is $80 per week, plus an initial processing fee of $15. Room and board ranges from $105 a week for a single room to $85 a week for space in a dormitory for four people. Students supply most of their own materials for the classes, but a fee is charged for the use of materials supplied by the school.

FOR MORE INFORMATION

Below is a list of some of the South's most popular craft schools. Some offer live-in facilities and some do not. For information, write directly to each.

Grove House, 3496 Main Highway, Coconut Grove, Florida 33133.

Hambridge Center, Box 33, Rabun Gap, Georgia 30568.

John C. Campbell Folk School, Brasstown, North Carolina 28902

Penland School of Crafts, Penland, North Carolina 28765.

The Arrowmont School of Arts and Crafts, Box 567, Gatlinburg, Tennessee 37738.

Hill Country Arts Foundation, Box 176, Ingram, Texas 78025.

The Silver Shuttle, 1301 35th Street, N.W., Washington, D.C. 20007

Smithsonian Associates, Smithsonian Institution, Washington, D.C. 20560

SALUDA MOUNTAIN TOYS

SALUDA NC 28773

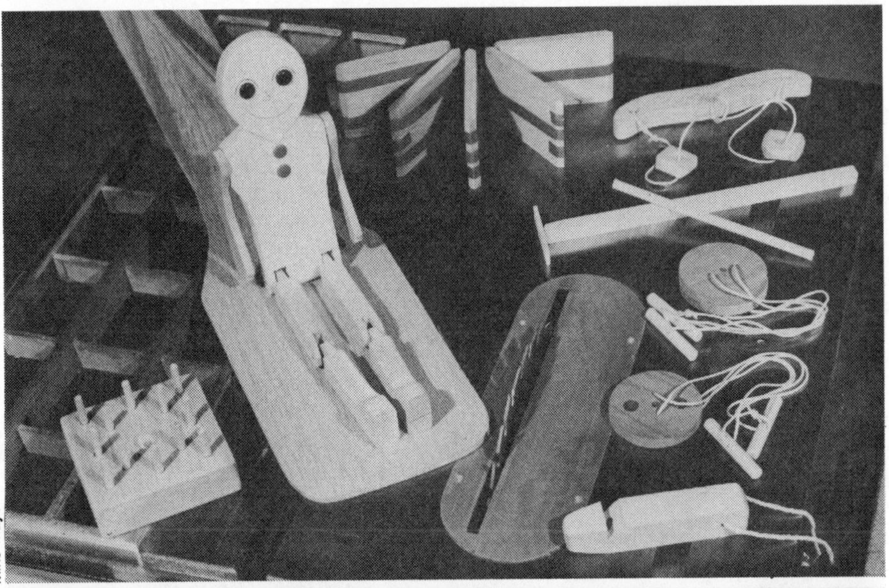

Mike Mayo

Mike Mayo

Saluda Mountain Toys is a family business that grew from a home workshop into its own home. The "Shop" is located in Saluda, North Carolina, where one can still see diesel engines pull the long, long trains up the Saluda grade, the steepest railway grade east of the Rocky Mountains.

This company produces both original and traditional hardwood toys. Some designs belong just to the family, but the Folk Toys belong to many generations of mountain fathers who handcrafted them for their children. All toys are made of assorted hardwoods: walnut, maple, cherry, and oak. Necessary instructions are included with the Folk Toys.

The prices of the Folk Toys are, clockwise, left to right:

Center Well Puzzle	$2.50
Lumberjack "Dancing Dan"	9.50
Jacob's Ladder	3.25
Ox Yoke Puzzle	2.50
Gee-Haw Whimmydiddle	1.75
Clapper	2.00
Moonwinder	1.75
Wood Whistle	1.75

The block train, shown at the back of the train photograph, is made of twenty-two blocks of walnut and maple for the young engineer to build and rebuild ($40.00). The mini-train, front of photograph, has an engine (2¼" x 5-½") with three cars ($15.00).

Shipping and handling charges are: up to $5.00—$1.00; $5.01 to $10.00—$1.50; $10.01 to $20.00—$2.00; $20.01 to $30.00—$2.50; $30.01 to $50.00—$3.00; over $50.00—$3.50. North Carolina residents add 4%.

Order from:

Saluda Mountain Toys
P.O. Box 26
Saluda, North Carolina 28773

A DOLL ARTIST

Ellen Turner, a doll artist from Horse Shoe, North Carolina, has made dolls or sculpted figures most of her life. She is a member of the Southern Highland Handicraft Guild, and her work has been exhibited at the Renwick Gallery of the Smithsonian.

The person who can best describe Ellen Turner's dolls is Ellen herself. She wrote us: "These sculptured dolls are characterizations of women, usually women of Southern Appalachia. I try to present a strong image, utilizing body posture, finger articulation, facial expression, and style of clothing. The figures are developed from my imagination, drawing from many memories I have of people who framed my life as a child and young adult. I am always working on some new character so I can only picture here these figures as an example of what I create. I do make new versions of some characters that I have already made. I enjoy doing special orders. All my work is of original design and involves quite a few different techniques.

"The construction is on a wire frame which is built up with excelsior and cotton padding, then covered with cotton knit. The faces have stitched features which are sized, then painted with acrylic paints. The wigs are usually of human hair but sometimes I use mohair or some more interesting material. The hands are very carefully constructed with wire and fabric. Their clothing is made from both new and old fabrics, which are cut and sewn for each one alone. No patterns. The accessories are fashioned from objects I find in the woods—dried flowers, baskets, walking sticks, etc.—or are made from fabric. The stands are mahogany or redwood, which are finished by me. I give them individual names and a verse as a way of introduction or explanation. They are 25 to 32 inches tall. $160 to $175 postpaid. Allow about 3 months for delivery. A deposit of one-third of the price is required with order.

"I also make a smaller doll, 15 to 18 inches tall. There are two designs as of now: Nellie, a young Asheville flower vender, who has a straw hat and flowers in hand; Maude, an old woman from the hills with sunbonnet and walking stick. Their bodies and faces are constructed as the larger dolls' are. I used patterns for the clothing, patterns which I have made. Their stands are of pine, $55.00 postpaid. Allow about 2 months for delivery. A deposit of one-third of the price is required with order. These dolls are all signed, dated and when appropriate, numbered."

Write to:

Ellen Turner
Route 1, Box 156
Horse Shoe, North Carolina 28742

Left to right: LILY MOSS, she follows the music of the falling leaves; DULLIA, little Dullia, where are you going? Leftwich Cave or home again; MYRTLE FAYE, the birds and me; ORA, solitary as the tree on the hill.

FRADY'S WIDOW, Never forget me.

MINNIE MOSES, Down in the hollow she wanders at dawn.

JENNY, Farmer Allen's daughter, from up Turkey Hill.

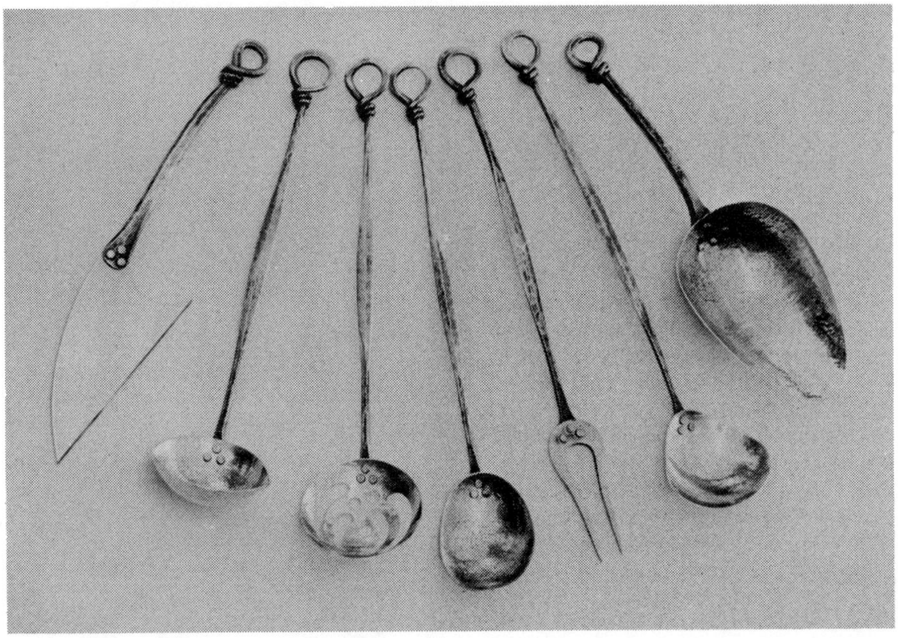

These kitchen utensils have solid copper handles and bronze bowls or blades, except the fork, which is all copper. Left to right, regular cake knife $36.00; double lip ladle $42.00; pierced ladle $56.00; oval spoon $31.00; fork $31.00; triangular spoon $31.00; scoop $56.00.

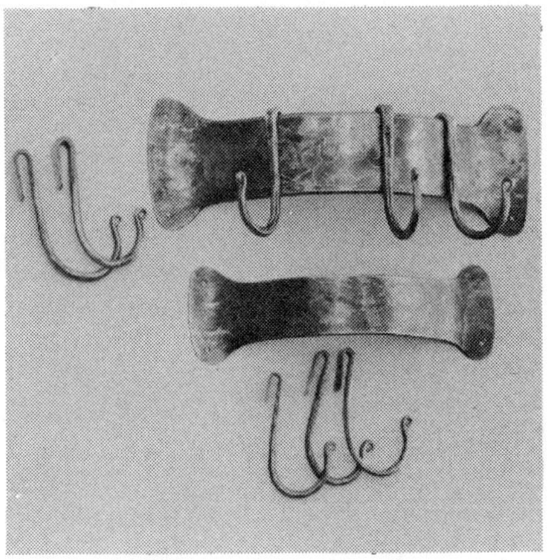

Utensil racks—8" rack $16.00; 12" rack $24.00; utensil rack hooks $4.00 each.

Small door knocker—$48.00.

HAND-FORGED COPPER

Dempsy R. Calhoun was born in 1947, in Rocky Mount, North Carolina. He grew up on the family farm, where the physical association with natural stimuli such as trees, rocks, bones, plants and animals had a definite impact on him as a young boy. While attending East Carolina University in Greenville, North Carolina, Calhoun took a B.F.A. in sculpture and an M.A. in design.

In 1971, as a graduate student, he began experimenting with forged metals—initially iron and steel. This immediately led into copper, brass, and bronze—the metals he predominately uses today. A broad line of gourmet kitchen utensils, accessories, hardware, and related items was to be developed over the coming years. At the same time, sculpture in wood and metal continued to balance out his creative endeavors.

Today his functional ware is handled by galleries throughout the country. Though he enjoys bringing together the utilitarian and aesthetic into what he terms "functional sculpture," he has never lost the need to produce the purely aesthetic sculptures that bring together many of the organic forms he finds in nature. "I'm actually reassembling forms the Lord has already put here—I didn't invent line, shape, color and texture, they have already been provided."

To order any of the items pictured, write:

Dempsy R. Calhoun
P.O. Box 417
Wingate, North Carolina 28174

THE 1921 FURNITURE CO. QUALITY HANDMADE WOODWORK

The 1921 Furniture Company, owned by Pat and Dan Jordan, has been in business for six years. All of the furniture is handmade by the owner and his two builders. Each piece is made of pine—hand-rubbed with an oil finish. Some of the items available for mail order include china cupboards, tables, trunks, beds, a full line for the kitchen, ladderback chairs, and couches.

Spice Rack—$13.35

Trunk—$38.05

Quilt Rack—$22.80

To order, you may write to the Jordans or call the store.

912 Arendell Street
Morehead City, North Carolina 28557
(919) 726-1800

In the summer of 1966, a group of traditional craftsmen living in two mountain counties in Eastern Kentucky, got together and organized a self-help cooperative for improved marketing of the crafts they produced. This organization was later to be called the Grass Roots Craftsmen of the Appalachian Mountains, and was incorporated in the spring of '68. They began selling many of the fine quilts that have traditionally been a heritage of Eastern Kentucky, to collectors and fine gift stores in other parts of the country. As word got around, other local craftsmen wanted to join and market their crafts. From a few quilters the Grass Roots Cooperative began to grow in membership and in the production of new craft items. Today the Craftsmen are affiliated with both the Federation of Southern Cooperatives and the Kentucky Guild of Artists and Craftsmen. Working as a self-help cooperative, the Grass Roots Craftsmen have become an important economic factor in the lives of many deserving people outside of America's vast labor force.

Wherever you go in Appalachia you see whittlers, many with nothing more to show for the whittling than a pile of shavings. The Craft Cooperative has attempted to seek them out and encourage them to whittle with a purpose. The pleasing result is an impressing array of walking canes, wooden dolls, animals and birds that highlight traditional Appalachian art forms. Hand carving, coupled with the inherent capability of mountain artisans to create useful and functional articles of furniture, have given the Grass Roots Craftsmen one of the most complete stocks of wood crafts to be found. The beautiful native Appalachian woods add to the desirability of these chairs, rockers, stools and many other works of art.

Making the art of quilting into a more economical business is how our patchwork pillows, place mats, ponchos and bonnets came into being. The traditional art of hand quilting was combined with today's modern colors and fabrics to create new ideas in quilted items. The high standard of hand quilting and traditional patterns are incorporated into all of these fine pieces. Patchwork, for the ladies of the cooperative, is not a hobby. It means money to keep their children fed and in school. It means human dignity, being proud of what they can make to sell. New ideas are always being experimented with which means new items will continually be introduced to the public.

The art of quilting has been handed down for centuries from mother to daughter in our counties. During these generations of hard close to the earth living, quilts became a necessary and colorful part of mountain family life. Many of our patterns were brought to Kentucky by the early settlers; others were developed by primitive artists, stitching by the flickering light of hearth fires. An old story tells of mountain women gathering around the camp fire of wagon trains to exchange patterns and quilt ideas with the pioneer women going west. Today, we still gather and exchange quilt patterns. Only now the setting is the common room of our community centers, but the modern mountain quilter, like her grandmother, takes great pains and pride in hand crafting each quilt she makes. For these reasons, the Grass Roots Craftsmen of the Appalachian Mountains has rightfully earned the reputation of selling the finest traditional quilts in the nation, even to having one of our quilts on display in the White House.

GRASS ROOTS CRAFTSMEN
Of The APPALACHIAN MTS., INC.

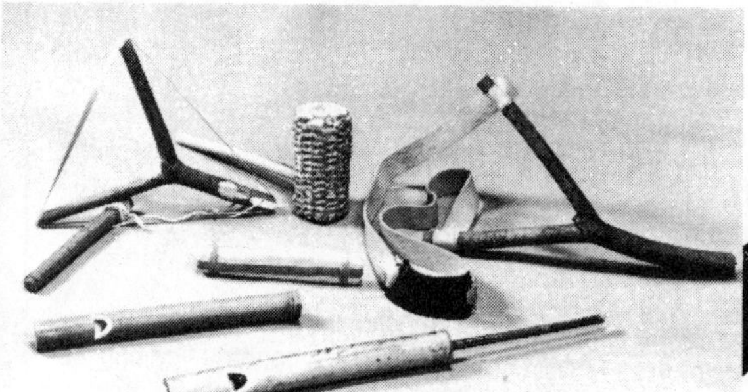

Grass Roots Craftsmen
of The Appalachian Mts., Inc.
Lost Creek, Kentucky 41348

Jerry Burns

JILL RUHLMAN, POTTER

Jill Ruhlman's work is all hand-built, colored porcelain. No two pieces are exactly the same. Most pieces are fired three times in an electric kiln. Lusters, decals, and handpainting are used for fine details.

Jill, who grew up in Nebraska, has been a teacher of emotionally disturbed children in Florida and a Peace Corps Volunteer in the Philippines. She studied at Penland School in North Carolina and was apprenticed to Jane Peiser. She now has her own studio in Atlanta. She is a member of Georgia Designer Craftsmen, Piedmont Craftsmen, Inc., Atlanta Art Workers Coalition, Atlanta Women's Art Collective, and the American Crafts Council.

Jill makes dramatic vases, mugs, goblets, toothbrush holders, and hand mirrors. Prices range from mugs at $12 to large vases and wall pieces at $600 and up.

Write to:

Jill Ruhlman
502 Page Avenue, N.E.
Atlanta, Georgia 30307

IRIS. 8 x 10 oval. Blossom is marbled blue-purple opaque glass and the foliage is three shades of green. Background blue-green to light blue. One of a series which includes calla lily, bird-of-paradise, nasturtium, and violet. The series can be color-cued for a set, or made of individual color choice. $30.00–$65.00.

THE OPEN WINDOW

The Open Window Stained Glass Studio designs and produces a variety of stained-glass articles, including traditional and non-traditional architectural windows. Hanging chandelier lampshades and shades mounted on bases as table lamps can be made according to the Tiffany art-nouveau style or in more contemporary designs and shapes. The studio especially likes to create a shade for a particular lamp base and can have custom bases handbuilt or thrown on a potter's wheel and glazed to suit a client's color scheme. The Open Window has been commissioned to create jewel boxes and other decorative boxes, as well as a bedside table incorporating beveled pieces.

Windows can be fabricated using the traditional lead came or copper foil—a method developed by Louis Tiffany. The design of the window and its eventual use (i.e., as an outside window or an interior room divider) will suggest which method is more appropriate.

The Open Window Stained Glass Studio is located in Midtown, a section of Atlanta which has long been associated with the arts and artists. It is part of an art collective called the "1-2-3 Shoe Repair Studios." Collaborative efforts with craftspeople there include firing painted glass in a potter's kiln, designs by architects and graphic artists, and silk screening on handblown glass roundels.

Linda Copley-Arnold, the owner of The Open Window, has an extensive background in fine arts and has studied ceramics and interior design. She worked in stained glass for three years, and, upon opening her shop, organized and became the first president of the Atlanta Glass Art Guild, an association of hobbyists and professionals working in stained glass.

The major portion of the work from The Open Window is commission work. Shown here are some items which have been made in the studio and can be repeated, but inquiries about custom work are equally welcome.

Write to:

The Open Window Stained Glass Studio
111 Tenth Street, NE
Atlanta, Georgia 30309

DOMED LAMPSHADE. 18" diameter. The body is tortoise-shell patterned glass, with the detail and butterfly in bright jewel tones of blue and green, red, purple and gold. $200–$600.

OZARK OPPORTUNITIES, INC.

The Rural Production and Marketing of Crafts Program is sponsored by Ozark Opportunities, Inc., which is a non-profit agency of the Community Service Administration. The program seeks to develop the economy of the impoverished mountain communities in northwest Arkansas while at the same time preserving the rich traditions of highland arts and crafts. In this traditional mountain-industry program, efforts are made to involve participants who might not be otherwise employed due to age, disability, or mountain isolation. The participants receive all of the proceeds from the sales. Most of the items have been produced for generations in the homes of the Ozark mountaineers.

You may order many items from Ozark Opportunities, Inc., by mail. Some of the items include an Acrobat Toy, a Bowl Basket, a Birdhouse, a Chicken Board, a Small Cedar Cradle, a Balancing Doll, a Corn Shuck Doll, a Dancing Doll, a Recipe Owl, a Hen Door Stop, a Hen Potholder, and a Wall Plaque.

Write to them for a catalogue and a price list.

Ozark Opportunities, Inc.
Crafts Program
CC#3
Harrison, Arkansas 72601

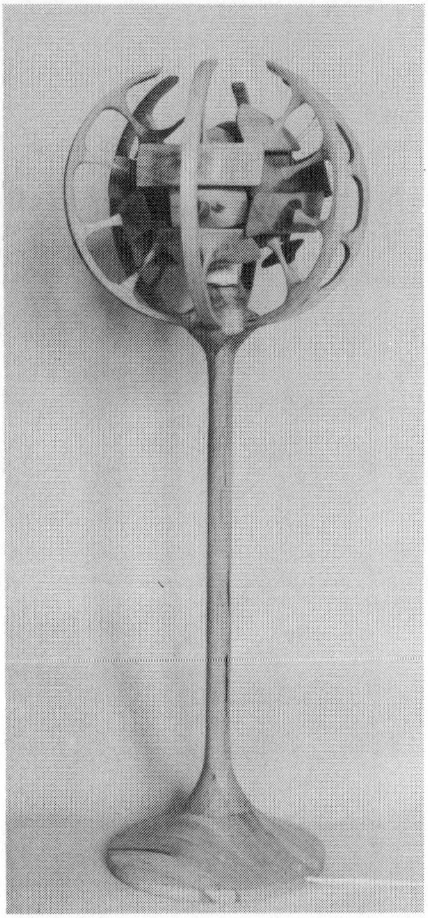

Fletcher's one-of-a-kind lamp, made of pecanwood grown in Louisiana, stands 36 inches high and is 14 inches in diameter at the top. It consists of a stem and base turned on the lathe, a ceramic socket, and arms which hold baffles which break up the light and make it indirect.

JAMES POWERS

Life-Sized Bald Eagle (6½ foot wingspread)—$3600.00

James Powers, a woodcarver, was born and grew up near Oakdale, Tennessee, which is a little mountain town in Morgan County in East Tennessee. He started carving when he was nine years old.

In the early sixties, James Powers quit his other job and started to carve full time. At first, it was hard to place his work in shops, but now he can hardly keep up with the orders he receives. James carves from basswood, painting the songbirds in their natural colors. He has several Limited Edition birds that are signed and numbered. You may write for a price list of these birds.

A member of the Southern Highland Handicraft Guild, the Foothills Guild, and the National Woodcarvers Association, James' work is in several museums: The Cherokee Indian Museum, The National Woodcarvers Museum, and The Smithsonian Institution.

For more information, write to:

James C. Powers
P.O. Box 63
Oakdale, Tennessee 37829

Pileated Woodpecker—$85.00

COX WOODWORK

Fletcher and Carol Cox, who live and work at Tougaloo just north of Jackson, Mississippi, design and make contemporary furniture and smaller wooden objects for sale by commission and through galleries. Working only with the finest hardwoods—some available locally and others imported from around the world—the Coxes sculpt many of their pieces in an effort to make functional items beautiful. They appreciate the natural colors and grain variations in woods and so use only oil finishes which will nourish the wood over a period of time.

Fletcher, who concentrates on making furniture, has worked both with architects and with individuals who commission pieces for private residences. He has made the sanctuary furniture for churches in Greenwood, Mississippi; McComb, Mississippi; and Mobile, Alabama. The Mississippi Museum of Art commissioned him to make the benches for the new building which opened in April, 1978. A chest which he made was chosen for a merit award in the Southeast Crafts '78 exhibit held in Berea, Kentucky, and the same chest was selected for a display in the Renwick Gallery in Washington, D.C. The lamp pictured here was selected as part of the "Fire and Light" exhibit at the Peters Valley Crafts School in Layton, New Jersey. Two of the Coxes' pieces appear in the *Fine Woodworking Biennial Design Book.*

Carol's work includes a variety of sculpted boxes, free-form weed pots, bowls, plates and platters. She has recently had a book of poems called *Woodworking and Places Near By* published by Hanging Loose Press in New York.

Write to the Coxes at:

Cox Woodwork
P.O. Box 188
Tougaloo, Mississippi 39174

Chair made by Fletcher for Immaculate Heart of Mary Church, Greenwood, Mississippi, of white oak with cherry highlight strip.

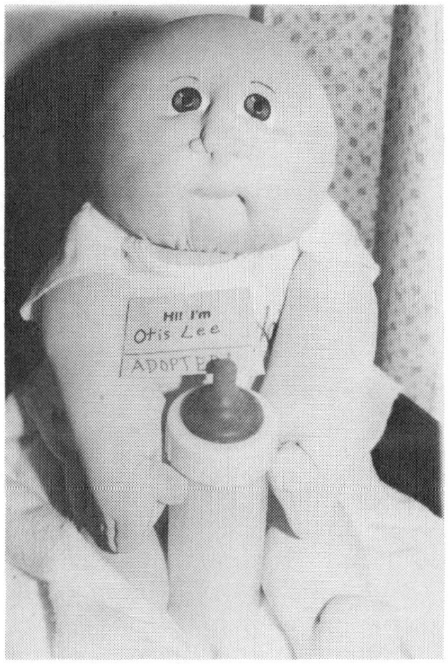

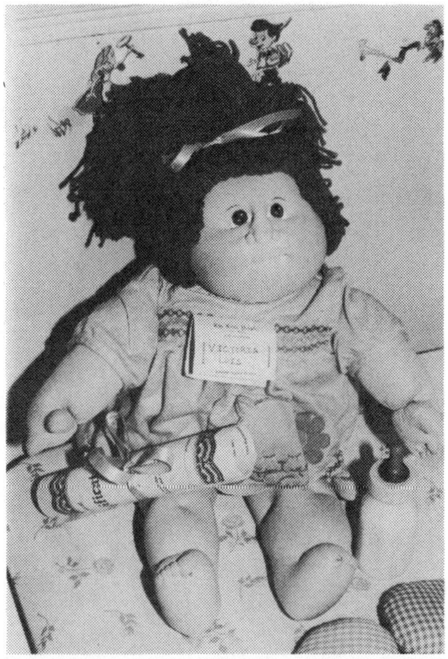

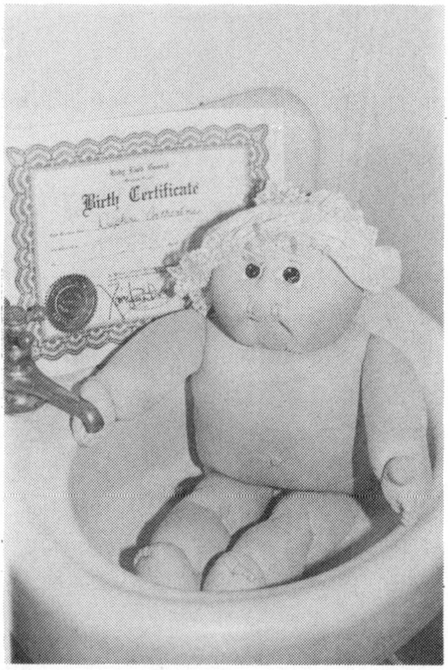

THE LITTLE PEOPLE

The Little People, copyright 1978, are "born" each day at BabyLand General in Cleveland, Georgia, where there is a maternity ward, nursery, and adoption office in an old, renovated doctor's clinic.

Actually, the Little People are soft sculptures, designed by a Northeast Georgia mountain craftsman, 23-year-old Xavier Roberts. Soft sculpture is an old German technique and a fast-growing art form. Each Little Person is a unique, signed original. They are "born" from creative hands, a special four-way stretch material, and polyester. The Little People wear real children's clothes, some of which may be slightly smudged or ripped. Roberts says, "That's because their wearers may burp a lot or like to climb trees, and there are even one or two who refuse to stay out of the dirt."

The adoptive parents receive an official, notarized birth certificate, complete with footprints. Some adults who are otherwise stodgy have been known to talk baby talk to the Little Person that they've decided to adopt. Not surprisingly, most of the Little People are adopted by adults.

Though some people slip and refer to the Little People as dolls, Roberts cautions them that this might hurt a Little Person's feelings. He says, "They are babies, artworks, Little People, collector's items, or soft sculptures, but definitely not dolls." A doll, after all, is something you might play with, whereas a Little Person is someone with whom you can live.

Little People are ordered by hairstyle. The babies' hairstyles include: Bald, Bald with Pacifier, Pigtails, Ponytails, Curls, and Afros. Adoption fees are $70 and up, according to hairstyle and age.

Although "Hospital Staff" only are allowed in the delivery end of the "Clinic," BabyLand General welcomes anyone to its nursery, maternity ward, and adoption center in Cleveland, which is 10 miles from the Alpine Village of Helen. Hours are 9-5 on weekdays, 10-6 on Saturdays, and 1-6 on Sundays. Don't be surprised to see the staff in white hospital jackets as well. If you decide to adopt, they may even give you an "It's a girl" or "It's a boy" cigar.

Babyland General
19 Underwood Street
P.O. Box 714
Cleveland, Georgia 30528
(404) 865-5249

THE TEXTILE MUSEUM

The Textile Museum was born of one man's love for rugs and fabrics, when in 1925 George Hewitt Myers opened the Museum primarily as a showcase for his growing collection of Oriental rugs. Over the years, it has grown into a comprehensive repository of mankind's skill in the decorative arts.

Today the Museum is one of only three institutions in the world concentrating on fabric arts—the other two are in France and India—and has developed an international reputation for its special collections.

Among these are textiles and classic rugs from Egypt, Turkey, India, China, Indonesia, East Asia, North and West Africa, and Spain. The Textile Museum is an unmatched reservoir of the world's finest carpets and fabrics. From the New World, the Museum owns one of the great collections of pre-Columbian textiles from Peru, as well as ethnographic textiles from 19th and 20th century American Southwest, Mexico, Panama, Bolivia, Peru and Guatemala.

In an effort to further knowledge of the textile field, the Museum has published 17 catalogues and books, produces an annual journal which presents information and analyses written by the staff and renowned scholars of textile arts, and a newsletter which keeps members of the Museum up-to-date about the activities at the Museum. The Textile Museum Shop, which was started in 1971, also maintains a large inventory of related publications which it makes available through mail order.

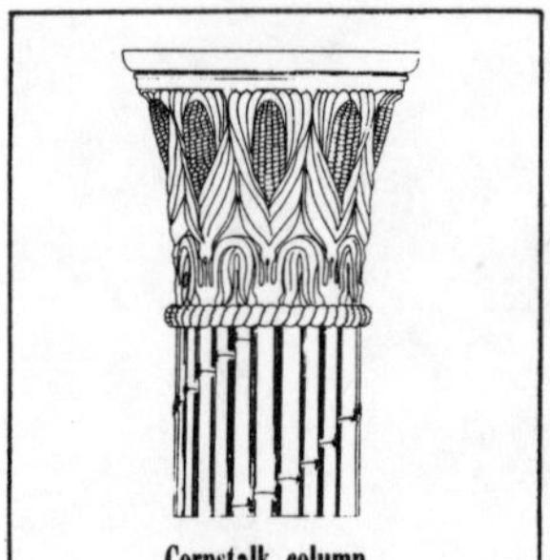
Cornstalk column

1976/1

Star and guilloche detail

1976/2

Rosette design

1976/3

Eagle, Senate Chamber ceiling

1976/4

Eagle, House Chamber ceiling

1976/5

George Washington Memorial Window

1976/6

A unique feature of the Shop is its effort to carry on the traditional role of designer and pattern maker for today's embroiderer by commissioning fine line drawings based on Museum fabrics. The contemporary craftsman's interpretation of each pattern serves as a link between past and present. There is a selection of more than 30 such transfers which come with instructions.

The Textile Museum's catalogue of "Museum Transfers" and its listing of publications will be sent upon request.

Inquiries should be directed to:

Museum Shop
The Textile Museum
2320 S Street, N.W. Washington, D.C. 20008

Sign Bracket. White Hardware Store, Savannah.

Griffin Railing. Indigo Plantation, South Carolina.

BAILEY'S FORGE

Ivan Bailey of Savannah, Georgia, produces his art from iron and other metals. He was educated at Portland University, the University of Georgia, and with Professor Fritz Ulrich at Northrhine/Westfalen Technical Institute.

Mr. Bailey is known best for his contemporary designs but he has occasionally made reproduction designs.

For a brochure giving more of his designs, send $.50 to:

Bailey's Forge
215 Whitaker Street
Savannah, Georgia 31401

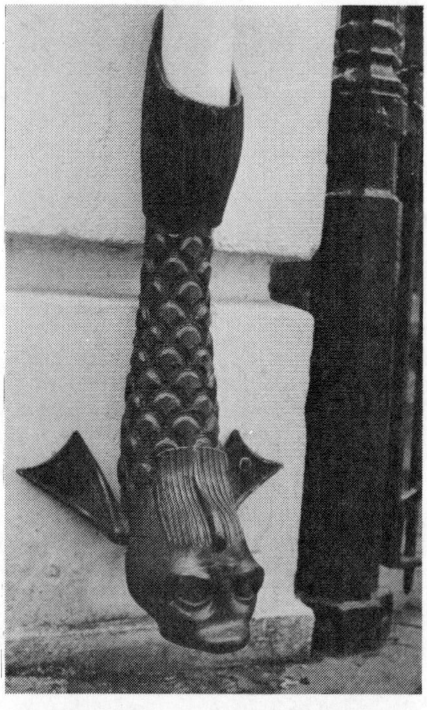
This dolphin downspout boot of cast aluminum is available exclusively from Bailey's Forge. 30" high, accepts 4" round or slightly altered square pipes. 28 lbs., can ship UPS. Price $120.00.

KEEP FINE CRAFTS ALIVE

That is the mission of Wood and the Works. Its young owners, Carol and Steve Tipton and Jo and Rick Kittinger, rebuilt an old grist mill on the road between Birmingham and Selma, Alabama, and word spread that this was a place where fine craftspeople could display and sell their work. "We try to maintain high quality crafts," said Steve Tipton. "We stay away from things that don't take talent."

Over fifty Alabama craftspeople, many of them members of the Southern Highland Craft Guild and the Alabama Designer Craftsmen Guild, show their work at Wood and the Works. The crafts range from stained-glass items to jewelry made from natural objects to pottery lanterns, bowls, and dishes to batik wall hangings to hanging baskets of pine straw to dried flower arrangements to tatted doilies and tablecloths to wooden and stuffed toys to walnut, cherry, or oak chests. Jo Kittinger, the potter, and Steve Tipton, the woodworker, are also the salespeople and are always ready to discuss fine crafts with visitors and give demonstrations of furniture-making and stoneware pottery-throwing. You might even get a cup of sassafras tea (not to mention a lesson in how to make it).

Handcrafted sewing chest—$295.

For a pleasant, leisurely, crafty experience, drop in at Wood and the Works. For information, write to:

Wood and the Works
Route 4, Box 1720
Alabaster, Alabama 35007
205/663-9575

Fern Stoddard is a glassblower from Kingston, Tennessee, who combines a love of sketching with a study of sculpture and training for scientific glassblowing. She started glassblowing in the early 1960s and trained for scientific glassblowing at Oak Ridge. She has exhibited in many states at craft shows, art shows, gift shops, and colleges. Mrs. Stoddard, who belongs to the Cumberland Mountain Crafts Association, also demonstrated her work at the Cooperative Crafts Exhibition at the Smithsonian Institution. Her handblown glass novelties and jewelry are available by mail order. Write to Fern Stoddard, Route 4, Box 365, Kingston, Tennessee 37763.

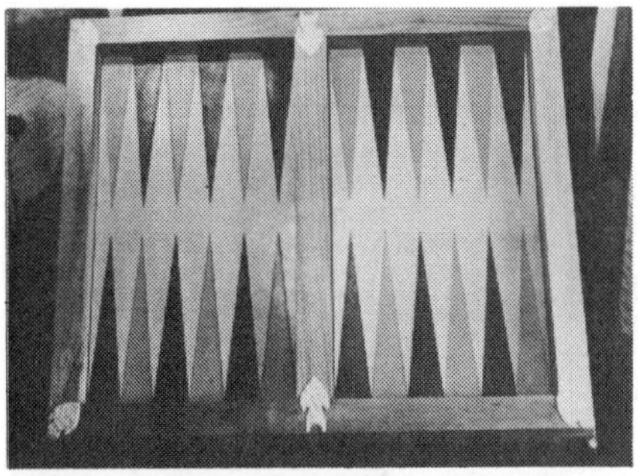

WOOD AND LEATHER

The January 1975 National Backgammon Championship Game was played in Las Vegas—on a Troll & Company board. Troll & Company is the business of John and Diane Corey of Knoxville, Tennessee.

John and Diane Corey have thirteen years combined experience. They have taught at the University of Tennessee, in the Free U Program, and for the Tandy Leather Corporation. In a span of three years under the name of Troll & Company, the Coreys instructed and graduated over thirty apprentices from their custom shop. Many of these graduates are still making leatherwork their living. Troll & Company is now working with mixed media.

Shown here is a backgammon table which combines the beauty of wood and leather. The backgammon board is regulation size. It is made of solid walnut with brass hand-hammered corner pieces. The playing surfaces are inlaid leather. Other mixed-media work from Troll & Company includes chess tables, wall hangings, and custom furniture.

Write to:

John and Diane Corey
P.O. Box 1212
Knoxville, Tennessee 37901

WOOD-WEAVES

Eleanor Quimby Wood, a handweaver, creates interesting hangings that would handsomely decorate the wall of a den or child's room. You may order the "O'Possum in the Persimmon Tree," a hand-knotted rya woven on linen with wool, cotton, and rayon, or the "Wise Old Owl," a colorful hand-knotted rya similarly woven. These two ryas sell for $39.00 each postpaid.

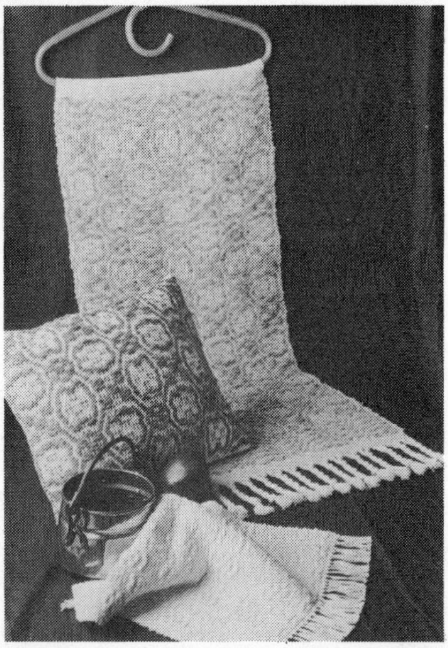

Dogwood Wall Hanging—Natural wool, tweed pattern on white nylon, 16" x 14" weaving, plus bamboo hanger (50" total height), $36.00. Dogwood Pillow—natural or brown wool tweed pattern on white nylon; 2 blooms about 13" x 16", $18.00; 3 blooms about 17" x 16", $27.00. Dogwood Place Mats—White pattern weft on natural cotton warp, 13½" x 20" plus fringe, $5.00 per mat. Inquire for prices of runners. Add $1.50 for shipping charges.

Wood-Weaves
Eleanor Quimby Wood
Route 1, Box 138
Gordon, Georgia 31031

OZARK WILDFLOWERS

Darien and Mark Russell of Mountain View, Arkansas, make these pressed flower pictures. The wildflowers and interesting foliage are picked and dried; through a trial-and-error process, the Russells have learned which flowers will dry well. The frames are made of barnwood. In order to make the pictures as permanent as possible, the Russells have discovered a method to press them permanently and seal them airtight.

Retail prices on the pictures are: 4 x 5 single frame $10.00; 5 x 7 single frame $15.00; 5 x 7 double frame $20.00; 8 x 10 single frame $25.00; 8 x 10 double frame $35.00.

Darien and Mark Russell
Rushing Route, Box 58
Mountain View, Arkansas 72560

The Gallagher Quality...

J. W. Gallagher has been involved in woodworking for years and years, but he decided to start making guitars in 1965. That turned out to be a blessing for the music world, because J. W. Gallagher takes great pride in making a top-quality guitar. He knew long ago that he would not mass-produce guitars but instead would make each one to the best of his ability with the best materials.

The backs and sides of the guitar are made of a select grade of either solid rosewood or mahogany. Spruce tops are used on all models, and the fingerboards and bridges are made of African ebony or rosewood. The necks are handcarved from solid mahogany, dovetailed, and glued into the body. Also, a heavy adjustable truss rod is used in the neck of all Gallagher guitars. Gallagher guitars are finished with several thin coats of lacquer that is handrubbed between coats, and the final coat is handrubbed and polished.

Gallagher guitars are special. The workmanship and finish on all of the guitars is the same regardless of the price or model. The difference in the cost of the various models is determined by the cost of the materials and the amount and type of trim used.

You may also purchase a hard-shell case made of heavy plywood and covered with grained black leatherette. Write to the Gallaghers for an attractive brochure, picturing many of the available models. They will enclose a price list for the various models.

J. W. Gallagher and Sons
Wartrace, Tennessee 37183

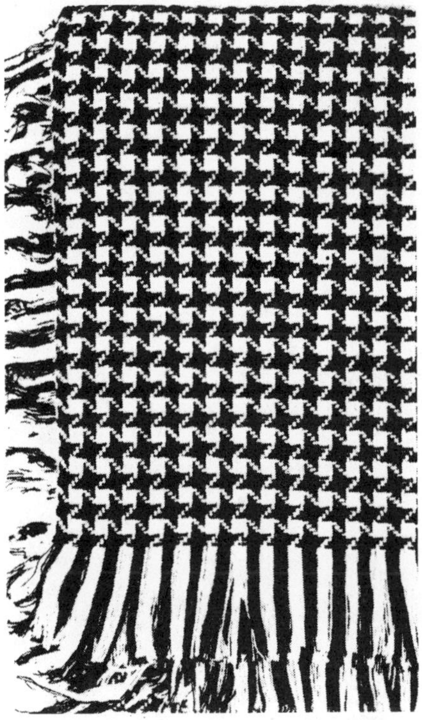

THE GOODWIN GUILD

In Blowing Rock, North Carolina, the Goodwin Guild Weavers are carrying on a family tradition that dates back to 1812. More than 167 years ago, John Goodwin had a weaving shed on his estate near Bolton, England. His son, James Goodwin, came to America in 1837, bringing with him "drafts," or patterns, and a knowledge of weaving beautiful spreads. He established a small wool-working plant in Virginia and passed on his weaving expertise to his son, Charles Goodwin.

More than half a century ago, Charles and his son John Owen Goodwin searched through the Appalachian Mountains for old handloom weaving patterns, which they began reproducing on power looms in Cedar Bluff, Virginia.

In 1951, John Owen Goodwin brought the Goodwin Guild Weavers to the small mountain town of Blowing Rock, North Carolina. Since his death in 1974, his two daughters and five grandchildren have carried on the family's craft. Using the same looms that were powered by waterwheel over a hundred years ago, the Goodwins have steadfastly held on to the old ways of weaving, making just one concession to advancing technology—the use of electrical power to run the antique looms.

Thousands of visitors each year visit their weave shed and watch as the weavers reproduce wool and cotton coverlets in patterns such as "Whig Rose," "Lover's Knot," and "Morning Star," as well as "Honeycomb" cotton coverlets, tablecloths, placemats and napkins. Other favorites include the all-wool afghans in the "Star Plaid" and "Scotch Plaid" patterns. Visitors are welcomed and given tours on an individual or group basis.

A trip to Western North Carolina is not complete without a visit to the Goodwin Guild to watch as skilled weavers keep a part of America's heritage alive.

The products of the Goodwin Guild may be purchased in their shop next to the weave shed or in selected gift shops around the United States. Their dedication to tradition and fine quality have made the Goodwin name synonymous with quality woven goods for six generations.

For a color brochure, write:

Blowing Rock Crafts, Inc.
Goodwin Guild Weavers
P.O. Box 314
Blowing Rock, North Carolina 28605
Telephone (704) 295-3577

MATTHEW RENNA—WOODCARVER

Matthew Renna of Philadelphia, Mississippi, carves many things from wood. He uses any variety of wood to carve. He carves in the round: animals such as dogs, goats, and mules; birds such as ducks and owls; caricatures of people; and fish. He says he will carve a plaque of anything he has a picture of. He carves and assembles arrangements; a bed of bream on cypress knees; a country store with caricatures of people around it; groupings of hillbilly caricatures. He carves different things by order as long as the customer sends photographs or pictures of the object to be carved.

The items pictured here are among the ones which are carved on a fairly regular basis. The bream (about 4½" long) sells for $16.00. The old shoe (about 1¾" high and 2½" long) sells for $10.00.

Write to:

Matthew Renna
531 Poplar Avenue
Philadelphia, Mississippi 39350

MAC-CRAFTER

The device shown here provides the other hand which always seems to be needed when doing macramé. This sturdy steel stand is assembled quite simply with bolts and wing nuts and adjusts to a comfortable working height with a twist of the hand. The U-shaped base is designed to prevent tipping, and a crossbar holds cords out of the way and a clip holds an instruction book. The hooks and swivels are designed to hold any project, even those in which round work must turn smoothly. With the crossbars removed, the Mac-Crafter becomes a plant hanger. How is that for a storage method?

To order your Mac-Crafter, send $29.95 plus $2.50 for shipping to:

Mac-Crafter
P.O. Box 190X
Duck Hill, Mississippi 38925

CLOWNS

If you like clowns, Sylvia Ellis makes the cutest clowns that we've ever seen—and she also makes adorable rag dolls, soft animals, and wall hangings for children's rooms. Her business started out as a hobby, as with many businesses where the creative arts are involved, but luckily a friend opened a new toy store in California and liked Sylvia's toys enough to feature them. From that point on, Sylvia's story is one of success.

Sylvia designed the patterns for 3 hanging clowns, which have subsequently become her best-selling items. Sylvia has sold thousands and thousands of them. The three hanging clowns are hung from the ceiling: one hangs from a ring, one sits on a swing, and the third hangs upside down. Also, she has two clown dolls: one is a baby clown in a bonnet called Peanut and the other is a larger clown named Popcorn. Three rag dolls you will cherish are a 36" Raggedy Ann, a 16" Laura (with long pigtails), and 12" Sunshine (blond with a happy face). Animals include a 30" mouse called Jelly (with quaint ears and a long braided tail), Henrietta the goose (with bonnet, apron, and purse over her wing), Casey the Engineer Duck and his sister, and a wallhanging called "Buckwheat" (a rocking horse).

Business has been so good that Sylvia cannot possibly make all of the animals herself anymore. She now has 12 ladies who sew for her in their homes, although Sylvia organizes the materials and coordinates the colors to make sure that each toy is made as she would make it herself. This frees Sylvia to spend some of her time designing new toys. She says, "I have so many toys in my head waiting to get out."

Prices for Sylvia's toys are listed below:

36" Raggedy Ann	$50.00
16" Laura	25.00
12" Sunshine	18.00
Ring Clown	17.50
Swing Clown	16.50
Upside Down Clown	16.50
Peanut	16.00

30" Jelly 25.00

Popcorn	22.00
Henrietta	26.50
Casey	13.50
Casey's Sister	14.50
Buckwheat	30.00

The toys may be ordered from:

Designer Arts
115 Valley View
Hot Springs, Arkansas 71901

CATAWBA POTTERY, A DYING ART

Mrs. Sara Ayers is a Catawba Indian. She was born and raised on the Catawba Indian Reservation near Rock Hill, South Carolina. Growing up as she did, Mrs. Ayers learned the art of making pottery the Catawba way. She uses no wheels, only her hands, and no modern finishes; the only colors come from the firing process.

The Educational Television station in Columbia made a documentary on Mrs. Ayer's pottery as it is a dying art.

The following is a partial list of the items she makes for mail-order:

Smoking Pipes	$2.50
Peace Pipes (4 stems)	$5.00
(6 stems)	$8.00
(8 stems)	$12.50
Bowls	$2.50 to $10.00
Book Ends	$15.00 a pair
Loving Cups	$5.00 to $15.00
Wedding Jugs	$5.00 to $15.00
Effigies (frog, owl, beaver, swan)	$3.00

You may have a special commission that you would like her to do or you may write to her for other pottery pieces she does:

Sara Ayers
1182 Brookwood Circle
State Highway 215
West Columbia, South Carolina 29169

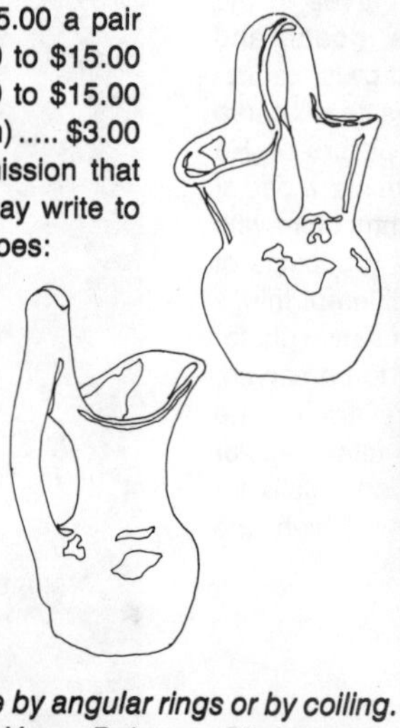

CATAWBA POTTERY can be made by angular rings or by coiling. Examples of finished Catawba pottery are left to right, Wedding Vase, Rebecca Pitcher.

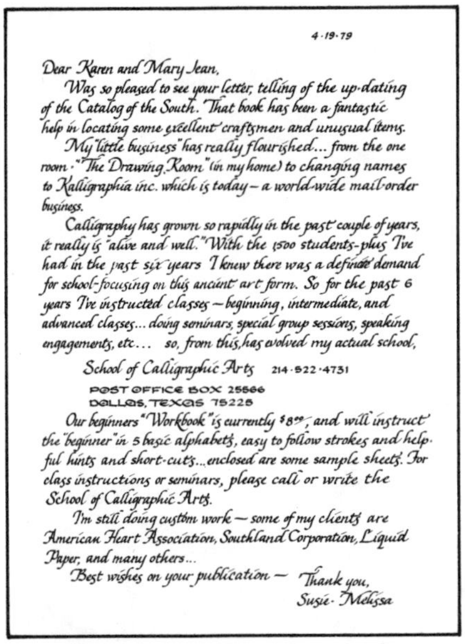

4·19·79

Dear Karen and Mary Jean,

Was so pleased to see your letter, telling of the up-dating of the Catalog of the South. That book has been a fantastic help in locating some excellent craftsmen and unusual items.

My "little business" has really flourished... from the one room · "The Drawing Room" (in my home) to changing names to Kalligraphia inc. which is today – a world-wide mail-order business.

Calligraphy has grown so rapidly in the past couple of years, it really is "alive and well." With the 1500 students-plus I've had in the past six years I knew there was a definite demand for school-focusing on this ancient art form. So for the past 6 years I've instructed classes – beginning, intermediate, and advanced classes... doing seminars, special group sessions, speaking engagements, etc... so, from this, has evolved my actual school,

School of Calligraphic Arts 214·522·4731
POST OFFICE BOX 25566
DALLAS, TEXAS 75225

Our beginners "Workbook" is currently $8.00, and will instruct the "beginner" in 5 basic alphabets, easy to follow strokes and helpful hints and short-cuts... enclosed are some sample sheets. For class instructions or seminars, please call or write the School of Calligraphic Arts.

I'm still doing custom work – some of my clients are American Heart Association, Southland Corporation, Liquid Paper, and many others...

Best wishes on your publication – Thank you,
Susie-Melissa

As can be seen from her signature, Susie-Melissa Cherry is a calligrapher, one of a rare breed of persons who are devoted to the fine art of free-hand lettering and elegant penmanship. Susie-Melissa is bent on spreading the particular beauty of this craft throughout the South by reproducing her original lettering and marketing the results by mail-order and through specialty shops.

We have reproduced her letter to us. As you can tell, she is spending much of her time teaching others how to do this beautiful work. But she also does custom works and you can write to her at the address below for information about commissioning a special calligraphic artwork.

Kalligraphia, Inc.
4227 Herschel
Suite 302
Dallas, Texas 75219

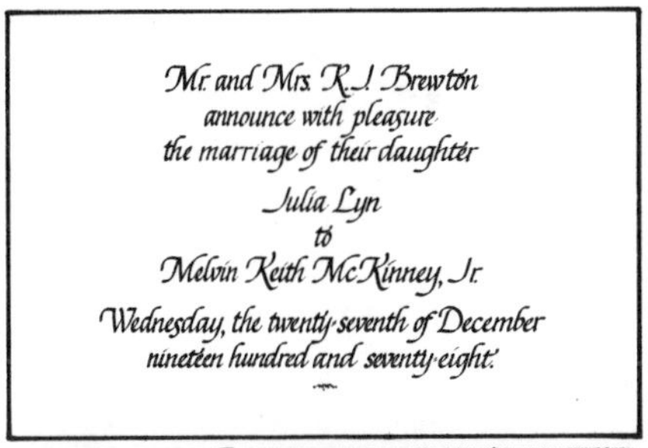

Mr. and Mrs. R. J. Brewton
announce with pleasure
the marriage of their daughter
Julia Lyn
to
Melvin Keith McKinney, Jr.
Wednesday, the twenty-seventh of December
nineteen hundred and seventy-eight.

AN ANCIENT COCK from a 6th-century Sassarid silk in the Vatican museum. In rusty reds, moss, ivory, black, and brown on old gold. Handpainted. Kit $40.00.

ADAPTATIONS FROM THE PAST—IN KITS

Jane Whitmire has adapted designs from cultures that are far away in time and place. These adaptations are now available to you in kit form. The needlepoint designs may be either by chart, often partially drawn on the canvas, or by handpainted pictorial designs; sometimes a combination of chart and painting is used. The method chosen reflects the easiest and best method for the particular design being used. Paternayan Persian wool is used. The imported canvas is usually #12 mono.

For reproduction pieces of small furniture worthy of the needlework used in or on them, check with Jane Whitmire for stools, luggage racks, or glass-lined trays in Chinese Chippendale; a Sheraton stool in 3 sizes; a Queen Anne stool; a firescreen; and a candle screen. The pieces are of solid Honduras mahogany and are available for immediate delivery. In addition, you can expect the needlepoint pieces and the furniture reproductions to match each other in size; a number of the patterns have been adapted to the different sizes of stools.

To order these kits, add $2.00 each for postage and handling. Virginia residents add 4% sales tax. For a catalogue of the many kits offered (including some of contemporary design), send $1.00 to:

Jane Whitmire
Masterpiece Needlepoint
2353 South Meade Street
Arlington, Virginia 22202

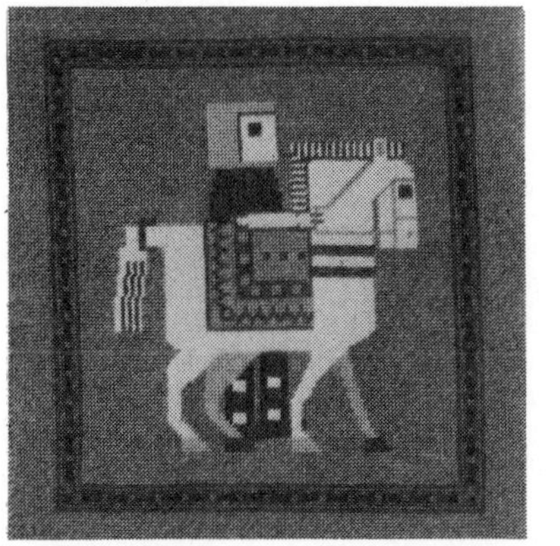

SCYTHIAN HORSE from the famed Pazyryk Carpet in the Hermitage Museum, Leningrad—the oldest existing knotted carpet, from around 300 B.C. Rosy copper, blue, browns, golds, and beiges. Kit $35.00.

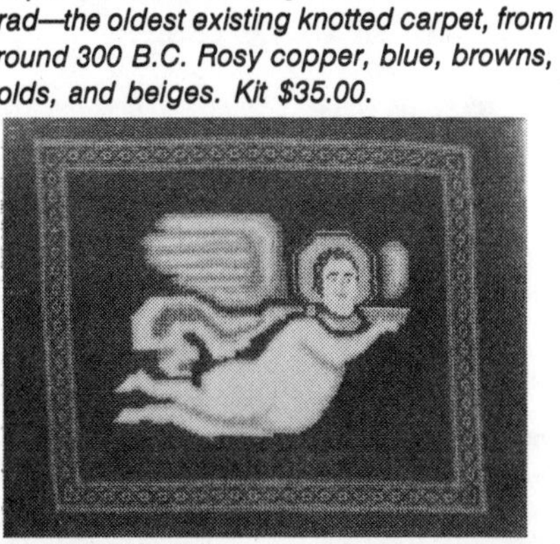

COPTIC CUPID from a 7th-century tapestry. Or maybe he is an angel; the Copts (early Egyptian Christians) mixed pagan and Christian symbols. Rich browns, golds, greens, blues, and persimmon. Kit $35.00.

Nancy Patterson, shown with one of Iron Mountain's newest creations: ceramic drinkware. The stemware and barware include a 14-ounce, all-purpose goblet; 10-ounce red wine goblet; 6-ounce white wine goblet; 12-ounce double old-fashioned; 8-ounce single old-fashioned; and 2½-ounce shot cup.

IRON MOUNTAIN ODYSSEY

The story of Nancy Patterson and her trek from Southern California to Laurel Bloomery, Tennessee, from her study of ceramics to the founding of Iron Mountain Stoneware, is nothing less than an odyssey. As proof, consider this rundown of Nancy's life since 1948:

After undergraduate study at UCLA and USC, Nancy entered Los Angeles' Art Center College of Design. She intended to study illustration and design of textiles and wallpaper, but instead found herself fascinated by the ceramics and porcelain work done by Albert King, one of the world's leading ceramists who was teaching a course in the use of color at the College of Design. So caught up was she in Mr. King's work that she asked him to accept her as an apprentice, which he promptly did. In 1954, Christian Christiansen, managing director of Denmark's Royal Copenhagen Porcelain Manufactory, visited King's studio and was very impressed with Nancy's work. He invited Nancy to come to Copenhagen as a guest artist for a month, telling her that although he couldn't pay her, she would be able to keep every product she created.

As soon as she could, Nancy took off for Copenhagen, to work in the factory she considers to be the producer of the world's finest porcelain—at that time she was the only American to ever work at Royal Copenhagen. She finished up her month, then was asked to stay on for another, then another—finally, Royal Copenhagen offered her a paying job. During the next 2 years, Nancy worked with top artists—from factory processing to hand-decorating to kiln-firing—designing and producing a variety of ceramics. In the process, she found herself more and more drawn to stoneware, a hard dense ceramic first developed by the ancient Chinese. Stoneware is similar to porcelain except that it retains minerals that porcelain does not. This difference makes stoneware warmer and more natural. High-fired porcelain and stoneware emerged about 250 A.D. in China. Marco Polo brought stoneware to Europe and it has been made there continuously since.

On the quality scale, stoneware is rated right under porcelain and above fine and commercial china and above earthenware. (Ceramic ratings go up with quality of clay and heat of firing.)

In the stoneware context, Nancy kept hearing about Arabia in neighboring Finland, a company which employed artists in pure design. She applied for a job there and soon relocated in Helsinki. It was a job that was more like a dream come true—each morning she could start work on whatever interested her, because Arabia felt that freedom of experimentation sooner or later resulted in striking new stoneware designs. But after 12 months there, Nancy, who at this time had stretched her 1-month European visit to a 3-year stay, decided it was time to come home.

She had always wanted to tour the ceramic museums of Europe, the Middle East, and Asia, so her homeward journey involved a 7-month tour of these. She landed in Taiwan just as her money ran out. Friends told her that if she stayed in Taiwan for 3 months she could buy a ticket home for one-third the regular tourist fare—using Taiwan currency. But when

Shown here are examples of three of Iron Mountain's stoneware patterns: A) White Top; B) Blacksburg; C) Roan Mountain. Iron Mountain makes twelve other dinner patterns, plus items such as ashtrays, salts and peppers, teapots, pie plates, casseroles, pitchers, creamers and sugars.

The Iron Mountain pitcher.

her 3 months was up, the law changed, requiring a 6-months' residency for reduced fare. With 3 more months to wait, Nancy found a job as a consultant to the Peitou Ceramic Plant near Taipei. At the time, the plant made ceramic insulators, tiles, plumbing ware, and serving dishes, but they were very interested in making porcelain products for export to the United States and asked Nancy to help. Her investigation of the clays available revealed that Taiwan did not have the right kind of clay for porcelain, but that they did have the kind needed for stoneware. Soon Peitou was sending baskets of stoneware to the United States, much to the pleasure of the Chinese government and Madame Chiang, who congratulated Nancy personally over lunch. After 4 years the factory was doing exceedingly well in sales, but their expansion was hampered by lack of capital. Nancy was asked to go back to the United States to find investors for Peitou. Nancy agreed, and after more than 7 years, returned to California.

During her visit home, she crushed a vertebra in a horseback-riding accident. Deciding during her recuperation that she would like to remain in the United States, she began to formulate a plan: to design and produce her own stoneware. Her only obstacles were that she had no idea of where she could work or how she could go about starting her business. A friend, Albert Mock, suggested *where:* in his native Appalachia, where people share a long handwork tradition. Although they probably hadn't worked much in ceramics, he was certain they could adapt.

Nancy went to Damascus, Virginia, to see the region for herself, and she was captivated by it. She immediately began looking for the *how* of her plan: financing. She was eventually successful in finding a loan from the Area Redevelopment Administration, a Federal agency established to aid economically depressed areas. She also got two local banks to provide a loan and she sold stock to family, friends, and local people.

In 1965, the plant opened on a site on Iron Mountain, midway between Mountain City, Tennessee, and Damascus. Back in 1870, an iron-mongering plant had turned out *blooms* of metal against a background of mountain *laurel.* Hence, Laurel Bloomery. Iron Mountain's inaugural crew was trained on-the-job by a Department of Labor grant. The handcraft tradition ran strong; soon the plant was humming *continued*

and by 1967, Iron Mountain Stoneware was showing a slight profit.

With the growth of the plant came new responsibilities, and Nancy found herself spending almost all her time on production supervision, employee training, finance, sales, and general administration. Design was left out—Nancy was a designer who had no time to design. But in 1966 she called upon Joe Lamb, a ceramics machinery engineer, to join Iron Mountain to handle those more mundane, but essential, aspects of the company so that she could return to designing. Today Nancy is Mrs. Lamb and she and Joe share the responsibilities of the company as well as the responsibilities of three children.

Not many people could claim the variety of experiences that Nancy Patterson can—and an even smaller number could claim the success she has had in her chosen field. In addition, Nancy's devotion to her craft has meant the improved chances for a meaningful life for the people around Laurel Bloomery. Nancy's "wanderings" are probably over, but the products of her art continue to find their way to all parts of the globe. From Laurel Bloomery come thousands of pieces of stoneware each year, to be sold in over 600 retail stores in this country, including Rich's, Neiman-Marcus, Tiffany's, Gump's, and Bloomingdale's.

For literature and current prices of the stoneware, write:

Iron Mountain Stoneware
Laurel Bloomery, Tennessee 37680

BATIK

Batik is a process of dyeing a print into a fabric by covering up parts of the cloth (silks, linens, and cottons) with wax that can be removed. Louise Janin of New Orleans, Louisiana, excels at designing and printing batik. She has worked with architects, designers, and individuals to create custom pieces (shades, wall hangings, room dividers, and skylight/ceiling backlit panels) for commercial and residential uses. Also, some of her items can be seen and/or purchased at the New Orleans Museum of Art and Alternatives Gallery.

Several of her items are available for mail order. Each piece is handmade—one of a kind. Some of the items are: kimonos (long from $88, short from $48); caftans (from $48); wraparound and drawstring skirts (from $42); pillows (from $23); silk scarves (12" x 72", $18; 36" square, $20); and wall hangings (any size).

Since each piece is an original, the fabric content, intricacy of the design, color scheme, and number of colors all affect the cost of the finished piece.

When inquiring, be specific about what you would like to purchase, and send a stamped, self-addressed envelope with your letter.

Sonny Carter

Louise Janin
Sans Souci
5535 West End Blvd.
New Orleans, Louisiana 70124

BATIK WALL HANGINGS

Kenlyn Stewart is the artist who created these wall hangings. The hangings use wax as a resist and fiber reactive dyes in a series of dye baths on 100% cotton. Kenlyn, with a BA from the University of California at Santa Barbara, now lives in Knoxville, Tennessee. The landscape shown here is 23" round and sells for $75.00. Kenlyn does pieces in price ranges from $15.00 and up. She also does commissions. You may contact her:

Kenlyn Stewart
c/o Sue Draper
17 Hawthorne Drive
Knoxville, Tennessee 37919

WEST VIRGINIA SCENES

West Virginia Scenes by Marcia Sontheimer Kincaid

West Virginia Scenes by Marcia Sontheimer Kincaid

Marcia Sontheimer Kincaid, a graduate of West Virginia University, has exhibited her work in a number of one-artist shows. If you have not been fortunate enough to catch these shows, you can still enjoy her pictures. *West Virginia Scenes* is organized to market them. Marcia's pen and ink drawings and lithographs depict scenes from all areas of West Virginia. Limited edition reproductions of various scenes are available. There are more than thirty scenes to select from.

Note cards in unlimited editions are printed in black on white stock and available in units of 8 single or 8 assorted reproductions. A set of 8 notecards and envelopes is available for $1.80 plus $.50 postage.

To inquire about the limited edition reproductions or to order the note cards, contact Marcia at:

West Virginia Scenes
Route 1, Box 101
Morgantown, West Virginia 26505

SCULPTURAL KNOTTING

Lyn Sterling is a fiber artist specializing in knotting. She teaches macramé and sculptural knotting at Callanwolde Fine Arts Center in Atlanta, Georgia. She is a member of Chattahoochee Handweavers Guild, Georgia Designer Craftsmen, and Piedmont Craftsmen. Her work is currently sold through the Signature Shop in Atlanta, The Craft Shop in Winston-Salem, and Storehouse throughout the South. Ms. Sterling has also done commissioned work for Reynolds World Headquarters in Winston-Salem, Family Federal Savings and Loan in Macon, and Southern Bell in Atlanta. Her work has also been purchased by The Mint Museum in Charlotte and the Georgia Art Bus.

For more information about her work, write:

Lyn Sterling
1322 McLendon Avenue, NE
Atlanta, Georgia 30307

From pure white china silk, June Manville crafts roses and irises which are colored with a permanent art marker. The petal edges are hand rolled. One flower can be used in a bud vase, perhaps with baby's breath or a few straw flowers. Each large-size rose or iris is $6.50. Buds are $4.00. Mailing charges are extra. Write to June Manville, 403 Trailwood Drive, Clinton, Mississippi 39056.

BASKETS are being rediscovered as functional household items and decorative pieces. Linda Parker adapts ancient techniques for the contemporary home, using a mixture of materials which includes Mississippi plant life. For information regarding orders, write to Linda Parker, 5433 Hartsdale Drive, Jackson, Mississippi 39211.

TENNESSEE STRINGS

by Charles K. Wolfe

The University of Tennessee Press
Knoxville, Tennessee

Country music cannot be thoroughly understood without a knowledge of the culture from which it came. For a variety of reasons, Tennessee has been able to maintain a suitable climate for both the pop and the traditional culture. The incredible diversity of the sound in this particular state is the basis of a unique music.

It all began with fiddling and banjo picking in the mountains. "Uncle" Dave Macon took the 19th century folk music and transformed it into the 20th century country sound. He is considered the "grandfather of country music." By the early 1920s, the string band was formed. This was done by adding the guitar to the already well-known combination of the banjo and the fiddle. In this informative book, Mr. Wolfe charts the careers of the early pioneers in country music with a precision that musicians as well as non-musician readers can appreciate. One of the most outstanding of these early founders was Jimmie Rodgers—the first country music superstar—and it is fitting that Mr. Rodgers is honored with the title "father of country music."

Mr. Wolfe includes a fascinating history of The Grand Old Opry in *Tennessee Strings*. The Opry began in 1925, its foundation cemented largely through the efforts of one who is not generally associated with the country sound: Henry Ford. It was through his efforts that a number of fiddling contests were sponsored throughout the South. His motives were to infuse fiddle music into the mainstream of American life as an antidote for jazz and the "loose morals" that jazz implied (according to Mr. Ford).

This book also discusses the origins and founders of honky-tonk music (Hank Williams); tuxedo music (Eddy Arnold); and of course, bluegrass (Flatt and Scruggs). The development of the Nashville sound is traced. The recording industries there (including the famous Sun label which first promoted the efforts of Elvis Presley, Johnny Cash, and Jerry Lee Lewis) so fostered the growth and acceptance of country music that after 1968, Bob Dylan, Paul McCartney, and Ringo Starr were recording there. Why Nashville? Mr. Wolfe has some interesting explanations.

The synthesis of the polished "Nashville Sound" with the lonesome sounds of the fiddle produces responsive chords in almost every listener. And the blend of the personal with the geographical perspective makes this book an alluring luxury. —S.V.H.

Harpsichord model 168

Spinet harpsichord model "Silbermann"

DEALER IN GERMAN-MADE HARPSICHORDS

The material we received from Robert Taylor is self-explanatory. Should you desire further information, write him at the address given below. Remember that since the harpsichords are imported items, the current prices may vary quite a bit from those printed here.

HARPSICHORDS ••••• SPINETS ••••• CLAVICHORDS

made by SPERRHAKE of Passau / Germany

CLAVICHORD	MODEL HUBERT	5 octaves	Legs or trestle	$2050

SPINETS

KLEINSPINET	8' register	Lute stop	4½ octaves	$ 2200
MODEL SILBERMANN	8' register	Divided lute stop	4½ octaves	$ 2400

ONE-MANUAL HARPSICHORDS

MODEL 145	MODEL 168	MODEL 206-2	MODEL 206-3
8' and 4' registers Divided lute on 8' Hand stops, knee lever 4½ octaves 4'9" long $ 3500	8' and 4' registers Divided lute on 8' Hand stops, knee lever 4½ octaves 5'7" long $ 3700	8' and 4' or 8' and 8' Lute on one 8' Hand stops, knee lever 5 octaves and 2 notes 6'9" long $4700	8', 8' and 4' registers, or 8', 4' and 16' registers Lute on one 8' Handstops, knee lever 5 octaves and 2 notes 6'9" long $ 5200

TWO-MANUAL HARPSICHORDS

MODEL 170 H	MODEL 216 H	MODEL 230 H	MODEL 220
8', 8', 4' registers Lute on upper 8' Manual coupler Hand stops 4' by knee lever Shifting coupler for 4' 4½ octaves 5' 7¾" long $ 5450	8', 8', 4' registers Lute on both 8's Manual coupler Hand stops 4' by knee lever Shifting coupler for 4' 4¾ octaves 7' 2½" long $ 6550	8', 8', 4' registers Lute on both 8's Manual coupler Hand stops 4' by knee lever Shifting coupler for 4' 5 octaves and 2 notes 7' 8½" long $ 7700	16', 8', 8', 4' registers Lute on 16', 8', 8' Manual coupler Pedal operated Lutes by hand stops Shifting coupler for 4' 5 octaves 7' 4" long $ 9000
MODEL 198 H	**MODEL 216 P**	**MODEL 230 P**	**MODEL 270**
Same as above, but 4¾ octaves (A to F) 6'6" long $ 6000	Same as above, but Pedal operated Lutes by hand stops $ 7200	Same as above, but Pedal operated Lutes by hand stops $ 8300	Same as above, but 8' 10" long 5 octaves and 2 notes $ 10100

PEDAL HARPSICHORDS	16' 8' 4' registers	30 notes	$ 6200

These prices include all costs delivered in the Washington, D.C. area. Elsewhere shipping charges from Washington, D.C. paid by the customer.

These prices are for walnut, oak, ash, elm, teak, pear, cherry or mahogany finish. Rosewood is more. These prices subject to change in case of any substantial change in the value of the German Mark.

For further details or illustrated brochure:

Robert S. Taylor 8710 Garfield Street Bethesda, Maryland 20034

QUILTS AND PATTERNS

Marilyn Califf has poked around attics, gone to flea markets and auctions, and generally made every sale in the mid-South to gather a fine assortment of antique and contemporary quilts. Her small white cottage on a hill houses her quilt collection. Her shop is both a museum and a retail store, because she has quilter's supplies, cotton fabrics, toys, baskets, thimbles, frames, and books on quilts. There are usually 40-50 quilts for sale, plus many samples from which to order (double size, $150.00–$300.00). She will quilt your tops, too. Marilyn is one of the few quilt designers in the country and publishes 150 quilt patterns.

Marilyn sent us a copy of her catalogue, which is called *Marilyn Califf's Wonderful World of Contemporary Quilts*. This catalogue (which you may purchase for $2.50) is a guide to Marilyn's patterns for quilts: pieced quilts, appliquéd quilts, crib quilts. Some of the quilts in this catalogue are Lovebirds, the Amish Friendship Plume, Dutch Doll, Morning Glory, Joan of Arc, English Rose, Cartwheels, Chicken Gizzards and more. There are 80 designs to choose from.

Each quilt pattern has yardage estimates figured for several bed sizes. Instructions are given for making each quilt by the traditional method and, except for quilts with blocks set together on the diagonal, for the new quilt-as-you-go method. The pattern pieces are exact size.

Supplies for quilters include a lap frame, a leather thimble, a pencil with which you trace a design and transfer to fabric by ironing on, marking pencils, needles, thread, 90"-wide white cotton quilt lining, quilting designs to transfer to fabric with dressmaker's carbon, and a tracing wheel.

Marilyn's *Pillow Book* introduces the reader to quilting through making a miniature—used as a pillow but including the skills and techniques required for large quilts. Ten patterns are included: Crazy Quilt, Double Wedding Ring, Dresden Plate, Drunkard's Path, Dutch Doll, Eight-Pointed Star, Grandma's Flower Garden, Quilting Design, 9 Patch, and Overall Sam.

Write to:

Marilyn Califf's Contemporary Quilts
3466 Summer Avenue
Memphis, Tennessee 38122

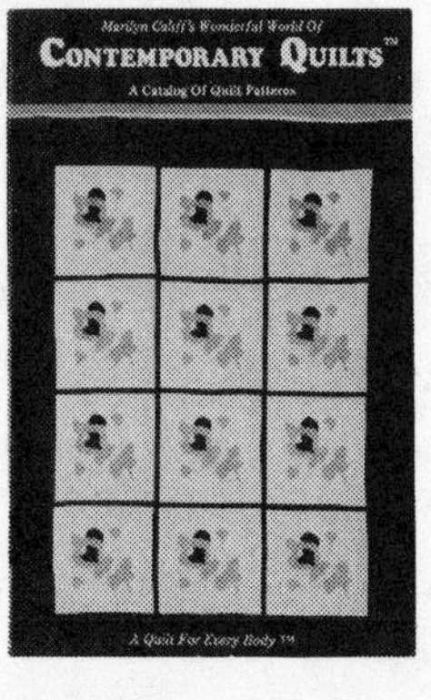

THE ELEGANT ELEPHANT

We first saw John Mee's elephant on a knick-knack shelf—an elegant sculpture of smooth wood with the grain rubbed to glowing. Then we realized that it came apart. It was an elegant elephant puzzle.

The elephant stands eight inches high, of walnut, laminated to a two-inch thickness and hand rubbed with tung oil. The baby elephant can nestle into the mother or stand separately. What is especially interesting is that the separation marks of the puzzle create the design. The butterfly shown in the picture comes apart along the lines of a butterfly's markings. And the rabbit comes apart along the lines that make its eye and legs. Also available are a snail, squirrel, owl, turtle, bear, cat, snake, mouse, train, and car. Most of these can be ordered in a one-inch thickness, which has no tung oil finish and is ideal for young children. They can also be made of mahogany.

"I am an engineer by profession," says Mr. Mee, "and have had a woodworking hobby for over 20 years. Several years ago, I was short on funds and decided to make all of my Christmas gifts. I designed several animal puzzles and other items which became gifts for my family and friends. Since that time interest in my designs has increased to the point where I have over 100 designs and handcraft thousands of items each year. The price range is $4.00 to $50.00 with most items selling in the $6.00 to $10.00 range."

Send 25¢, to cover handling, for a brochure or price list to:

Hardwood Creations by John and Susan Mee
3556 Bermuda Drive
Birmingham, Alabama 35210
(205) 956-4756

14" Cowboy Tumbleweed $35.00. 14" Railroad Mac $30.00.

FRECKLES . . . LEVEL LAND DOLLS

These charming freckled characters are created by Winifred Holloway of Chattanooga. Winifred's interest in dolls surfaced when she made George and Martha Washington dolls for her daughter to use in a school project. Her husband noticed the pleasure that creating those dolls gave Winifred, and he presented her with a book on making dolls. The gift and the pleasure led to a business.

Freckles . . . Level Land Dolls are all based on book characters or people Winifred knows. Huckleberry Finn, Tom Sawyer, and Becky are, of course, based on the Twain characters. Becky looks just as saucy as she should. Huck, on his way to a fishing hole, is smiling broadly. Poor Tom reveals by his expression how he feels about *school*.

The "Oz" characters are easily recognizable. Like all of Winifred's dolls, they carry small items which add to their charm: the oil can, the hatchet, the basket.

Contact:

Winifred Holloway
221 Shawnee Trail
Chattanooga, Tennessee 37411

11" Dorothy and Toto $25.00. 14" Scarecrow $25.00. 14" Lion $30.00. 17" Tin Man $30.00.

11" Huckleberry Finn $25.00. 10" Tom Sawyer $25.00. 9" Becky $25.00.

Most popular girl doll: 16" Laura $35.00.

Most popular doll of all: 19" Frankie $40.00.

Springles

Springles are formed of fine wire, then covered with a thin clear film on which hand painting is done with three kinds of paint—four coats for flowers, three for leaves, and 11 or 12 for butterflies. The special painting keeps Springles flexible and strong. We received a sample of Model V, a brilliant bouquet with butterfly in variegated colors 10½" high on a walnut base, and of three tiny angels delicately painted: one white, one blue, one pale pink—each with gossamer wings.

Springles are permanent, washable, and flexible. The Springles line includes a wide selection in size and color of permanent flowers sold singly; butterflies in several colors sold as pins, hairclips, and on stems for use in flower arrangements; boxed flower arrangements in walnut bases; a series of flying angel figures in three colors designed to hang in flight or as Christmas tree decorations.

The makers of Springles, Gay and Joe Fox, are former members of the U.S. Foreign Service who are now settled in North Carolina and are members of the Southern Highland Handicraft Guild.

The nonsense name, Springles, was chosen by the Foxes when they decided that their flowers should bring the same happiness as do those first flowers of spring.

Springles may be bought in fine gift shops. For the name of a shop near you, write:

Springles
c/o Gay and Joe Fox
P.O. Box 308
Black Mountain, North Carolina 28711

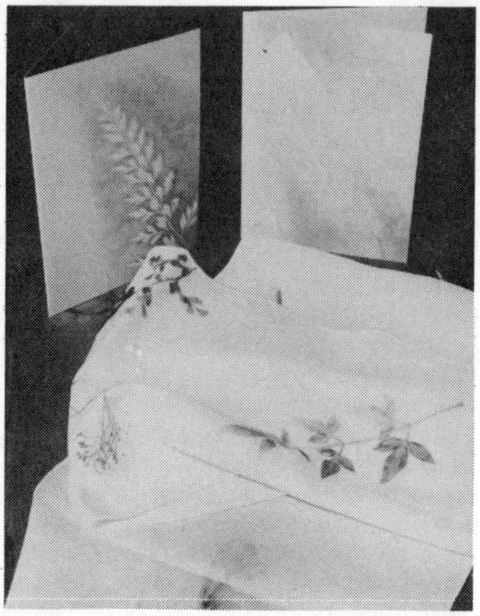

These scarves and the notepaper are made by using a dry-dye colored paper and natural leaves and flowers. Each print is an original. Eight notes with envelopes are priced at $1.50 plus $.50 postage; 8" x 36" polyester scarves are $5.00 plus $.25 postage and the square chiffon scarves are $10.00 plus $.25 postage. For more information, write to: Mini Rhea Calder, Box 645, Magee, Mississippi 39111.

Mahogany Stearman, 17", $55.00. Mahogany 18-wheel Tanker, 25", $125.00.

TOWERY "TOYS FOR COLLECTORS"

Bob Towery of Yazoo City, Mississippi, specializes in realistic wood sculptures of twentieth-century transportation. His 18-wheelers and World War I era airplanes seem to appeal equally to tiny tots and "boys" of considerably more advanced years. These (are they "toys" or "collectors' items"?) are made of fine Honduras mahogany. The numerous airplanes in the collection are part of what Bob calls his "new heritage": "With a four-year stint in the Air Force, a wife that cut her teeth on the seat of an airplane, a sixty-seven year old father-in-law who is still flying professionally, and a son in college studying aerospace engineering, what else can you expect? We like airplanes!"

Bob Towery also likes wood. When he was thirteen, he painstakingly constructed a what-not shelf for his mother. Thirty years later—after careers as teacher, contractor, and cabinetmaker—he has turned to toymaking and children's furniture, areas in which he is able to apply his belief in the dignity of work with modern skills and equipment. His children's furniture of Ponderosa pine is proportioned for specific age groups. His maple and mahogany toys include sixty original designs from tiny cars to large trucks and airplanes.

He is a member of the Craftsman's Guild of Mississippi and the Mississippi Woodworkers Association. His work is currently on display in sales galleries of the Mississippi Museum of Art in Jackson and the Old Capitol Museum, also in Jackson.

Write to:

Bob Towery
P.O. Box 1
Yazoo City, Mississippi 39194

SPIRITS OF THE FOREST

R. Morgan is the son and grandson of carvers. Naturally he became interested in woodcarving when he was quite young. Morgan, while stationed with the army in Germany, studied the art of carving from roots. Morgan's *Who's* (What else would you name objects about which people kept asking, "Who?") are his own interpretation of root carving. The spirits of Morgan's forest bear a strong resemblance to the lumberjacks and loggers that were a part of his childhood in Maine.

Write to:

R. Morgan Woodcrafts
1427 Lottie Street
Spring Lake, North Carolina 28390

CHURCHILL WEAVERS

It is said that Churchill Weavers grew from a dream of David Carroll Churchill, a man who had graduated with honors from M.I.T. in 1899. Carroll Churchill became interested in handweaving while in India, where millions of native artisans still worked at this ancient art, an art being slowly destroyed by the mass production of the growing machine age in England. The solution was to speed up native weaving production with new types of faster handlooms—and Churchill's genius developed them. Finishing his work in India, Churchill returned to America in 1917, and a few years later came to visit in Berea, where he found that handweaving still lingered in the Southern mountains.

Churchill decided to stay in Berea and make use of his world-wide knowledge and experience by starting an industry. The first loom was pieced together from scraps, but with Mr. Churchill's mechanical ability and Mrs. Churchill's flair for color and design, their first product was recognized for its superior quality. Successfully expanded over the years, it is now the largest handweaving company in America.

Now Lila and Richard Bellando pioneer a new era in the Churchill tradition. Personally selected by Eleanor Churchill upon her retirement to continue the handweaving industry of Churchill Weavers, the Bellandos work together to maintain the tradition of quality and craftsmanship that has long been the hallmark of Churchill products.

When you are in Berea, you are invited to visit both the loomhouse and gift shop. To shop by mail, send $1.00 for a catalogue to:

Churchill Weavers
P.O. Box 30
Berea, Kentucky 40403

MARY'S MACRAMÉ

Mary McCrocklin of Brandon, Mississippi, began to make macramé purses while she was recuperating from surgery and needed something to do. She sent her husband out to buy materials for macramé—and an instruction book. She studied the book and sat down to make a purse. She liked the purse and so did other people who saw it. That year, Mary made purses as Christmas presents for family members. People who saw Mary's purse or the ones she had made as presents began to order purses for themselves. Mary was in business.

The purses are made of strong cords which are washable and come in many colors. The lining is a silk material which matches the bag. There is an inner pocket sewn onto the lining for holding keys or whatever.

Besides the purses, Mary also makes bathroom towel holders, kitchen towel holders, napkin holders, key rings, sunglasses or cigarette holders, and wine racks which hold eight bottles.

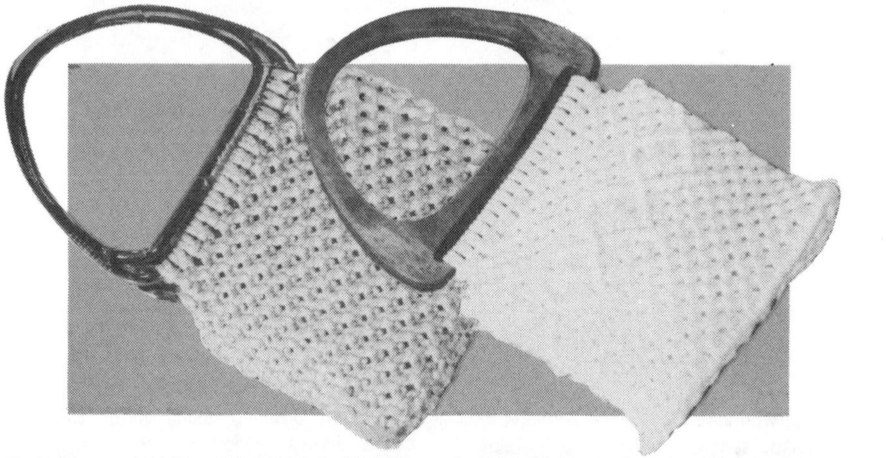

Prices for some items include purses with macramé handles $22.50, purses with plastic or wooden handles $24.50, child's purse $6.50, towel holders $6.00, napkin holders $6.50, key rings $.75, sunglasses or cigarette holders $4.00, and a wine rack for eight bottles $25.00.

Write to:

Mary E. McCrocklin
110 Firecrest Drive
Brandon, Mississippi 39042

TULLY TOYS INC.

Meet Tully Hall and his menagerie of lovable wooden toys. Made of red oak and ash (fine Southern hardwoods) these toys can be shipped anywhere by UPS. The dinosaur, hippopotamus, ostrich, rhinoceros, cow, alligator, elephant, lion, razorback, chicken, armadillo, ram, and shrimp cost $35.00 (shipping charges extra). The giraffe costs $45.00 (shipping charges extra).

Write to:

Tully Toys Inc.
4606 Warrenton Road
Vicksburg, Mississippi 39180

ICARD CABINET WORKS

A footstool will often accent your favorite room and will be useful for various purposes. A company in West Virginia makes rush or split footstools, and cane or rush chairstools. They are of hardwood and can be stained to the desired color.

Elwanda Icard is a native West Virginian who started craft work in conjunction with Icard Cabinet Works, her husband's business of custom cabinets and fine woodwork. Her work is of excellent quality, and she is helping to preserve and promote a craft that is very much in danger of being lost.

Write to:

Icard Cabinet Works
Route 2, Box 299
Point Pleasant, West Virginia 25550

BUCKBRUSH BASKETS

The Arts and Crafts Store of the Cherokee Nation of Oklahoma is an outlet for the handcrafted items which are produced by the Cherokees of the area. The store is owned and operated by the Cherokee Nation. Among the many items sold in the store are double-woven buckbrush baskets, beadwork, turtle shell shakers, ball sticks, buffalo grass dolls, rag dolls, woodcarvings, stone carvings, pottery, quilts, saddle blankets, the traditional Cherokee tear dresses, and ribbon shirts.

The buckbrush baskets featured here utilize a plant that is plentiful in the Cherokee country of northeast Oklahoma. Jennie Sapp, a traditional Cherokee basket weaver, says that buckbrush can be gathered from late September to early April and coiled in bundles for storage. The outer skin must be removed by two hours of boiling in water; then the skin will slide off easily when it is rubbed with an old cloth. At this point, the buckbrush is white or cream colored. The traditional colors are brown, black, red, and orange. Natural dyes used are walnut hulls for brown and bloodroot for orange. Some commercial dyes are also used.

To the buckbrush runners and traditional colors, the creative ability of the Cherokee basket weaver is added to produce baskets such as these.

Contact:

Cherokee Nation of Oklahoma Arts and Crafts Store
P.O. Box 948
Tahlequah, Oklahoma 74464

NEEDLEPOINT AND NEEDLEART

Rosene Hill works with Edna Looney at Hill-Looney Products in Wewoka, Oklahoma. Rosene designs needlepoint kits, and Edna designs kits of decorative items to be made of felt. Rosene's Creative Needlepoint Kits include painted canvases (with or without yarn) for such items as wall hangings, tennis covers, luggage rack straps, bell pulls, plus pillows or pictures. Edna's Creative Needleart Kits include all the material necessary to make such felt and sequined items as Christmas stockings and tablecloths, holiday centerpiece decorations, Christmas tree skirts and ornaments, a United States map picture and individual state map pictures, calendars, birthday banners, alphabet banner, and yardstick wall hanging. All items are available at specialty shops and department stores across the country or a brochure and pricelist may be obtained from:

The Corner Shoppe
Box 1532
Wewoka, Oklahoma 74884

STAINED GLASS OF BETHANIA

This independent stained-glass studio is operated by Randy Sewell in Bethania, North Carolina, which is a Moravian community founded in 1759 on the outskirts of Winston-Salem. Randy does custom designs for the specific needs and places of his customers. His designs range from traditional to contemporary and realistic to abstract. His work is for businesses, restaurants, churches, homes, etc. He is an exhibiting member of Piedmont Craftsmen, Inc., and his work has been shown and/or purchased by the Corning Museum of Glass, Renwick Gallery of the Smithsonian Institution, Mint Museum of Charlotte, Southeastern Center for Contemporary Art (SECCA), and other galleries and museums. Most of his designs require personal consultation with customers, their architects, or interior designers. The studio is open for visitors, but a telephone call for an appointment is recommended.

Stained Glass of Bethania
5650 Main Street
Box 130
Bethania, North Carolina 27010

CABIN CREEK QUILTS

Not all great American artists live in big cities. Some of them live in Ohley, Lookout and Jordan's Creek. Their medium is patchwork and their creations are quilts, comforts, clothing, tablecloths, mats and toys. They offer 10 quilt patterns in single, double, queen, and king sizes.

Quilt catalogs are $1.50 each from:

Cabin Creek Quilts
P.O. Box 383
Cabin Creek, West Virginia 25305

QUILTING TIPS

From a company that specializes in mass production of bedding items, a book for those who wish to make theirs an individual effort. For *Barbara Taylor's Book on Quilting,* send $1.00 to:

Taylor Bedding Manufacturing Company
Department CA
P.O. Box 979
Taylor, Texas 76574

LILLIE EXPRESSIONS IN GLASS

Don Lillie and his associates show their creations in the Lillie Studio at Omni International in Atlanta. Don Lillie started glassblowing at the Mayo Clinic, holds a degree in Physics from Georgia Tech and is the Master Glassblower there.

The glassblower working at his bench uses glass tubes and rods of various diameters and, by free blowing, shapes the glass without the use of molds or forms.

Among the many items available from Lillie are animals (alligator, bear, cat and mouse, large caterpillar, deer, dragon, elephant, Canadian goose, hummingbird, Piglet, unicorn, woodpecker); flora (dogwood in clear or white, dogwood as a plaque or a pen set, iris, jonquil, morning glory, mushroom, spruce tree, sweet pea); Christmas ornaments (see our Christmas section); miscellaneous items (angel, Atlanta skyline, candleholders, gavel, napkin rings, Pythagorean theorem, treble clef, vases); jewelry (dove or teardrop earrings, acorn or strawberry necklaces). These are only a few items taken at random from a listing sent to us. Selected antique reproductions and restorations can also be ordered.

All mail orders are carefully packed and are insured for a safe arrival. A minimum shipping charge of $3.00 applies to the majority of orders.

The white dogwood bloom shown here sells for $15.00. To order or to send for a free brochure, write to the main office:

Lillie Expressions in Glass
3431 Lake Drive, S.E.
Smyrna, Georgia 30080

THE SOUTHERN HIGHLAND HANDICRAFT GUILD

The Guild, probably the best known of the many craft guilds throughout the South, operates four retail shops through its merchandising subsidiary, Crafts of Nine States, Inc.: Allanstand, 16 College Street, Asheville, North Carolina 28801; Guild Crafts, 930 Tunnel Road, Asheville, North Carolina 28805; Guild Gallery, 501 State Street, Bristol, Virginia 24201; and the Parkway Craft Center, Blowing Rock, North Carolina 28605. Although the individuality of craft work makes a catalogue impossible, the shops do accept mail-orders and offer a mailing service to customers.

For additional information about the Guild, write:

Southern Highland Handicraft Guild
15 Reddick Road
P.O. Box 9545
Asheville, North Carolina 28805

PORTRAITS: Harvie Brown, a native of Florida who now lives in Decatur, Georgia, is a portrait painter and illustrator. His degree is from Georgia State University, and he has won numerous awards for his drawings. He paints from private sittings or from a photograph. His portraits are done in pastels or oils. Write to him at Contemporary Creations, Harvie Brown, 2265 Ponte Vedra Court, Decatur, Georgia 30032.

The Copper Shop

COMMISSION HOUSE COPPER SHOP

Allen H. Green II and Allen H. Green III handcraft lamps, weathervanes, family crests, and commissioned items. Each piece is an original, since no molds are used. Instead the pieces are beaten out by hand on a sand bag.

The patented hurricane lamp, which has been established as the Fredericksburg Lamp, is designed and handcrafted in five distinctive versions: spring bracket, table lamp, chandelier, patio lamp, and table lamp with reflector.

Weathervanes are designed to order. Prices start at $200 and are dependent upon the intricacy of the design.

To request additional information about Mr. Green's copper products, or to order, write:

The Copper Shop
Commission House
Frederick and Sophia Streets
Fredericksburg, Virginia 22401

Fredericksburg Table Lamp, $34.00 plus $3.00 shipping

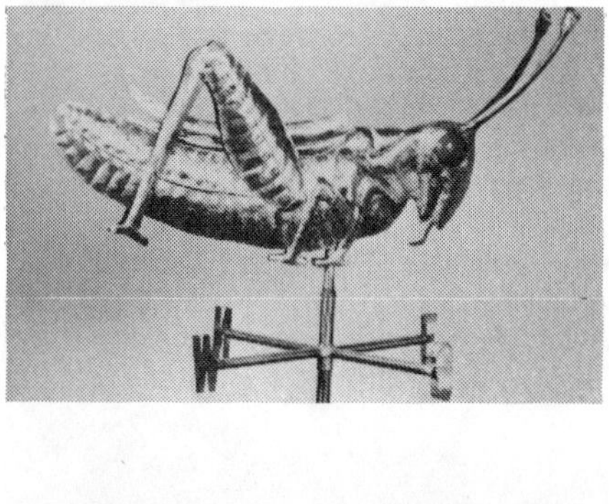

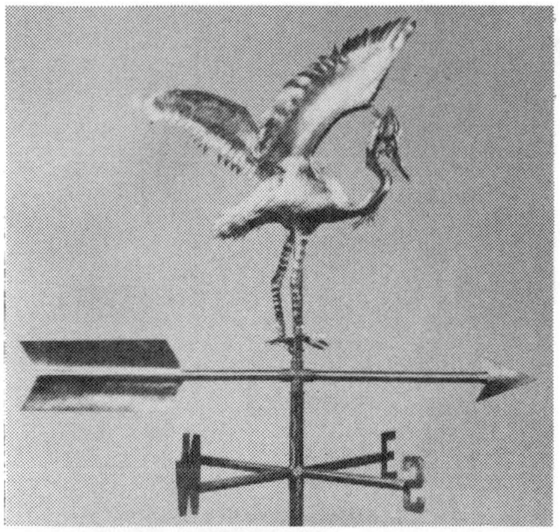

The Copper Shop's Weathervanes

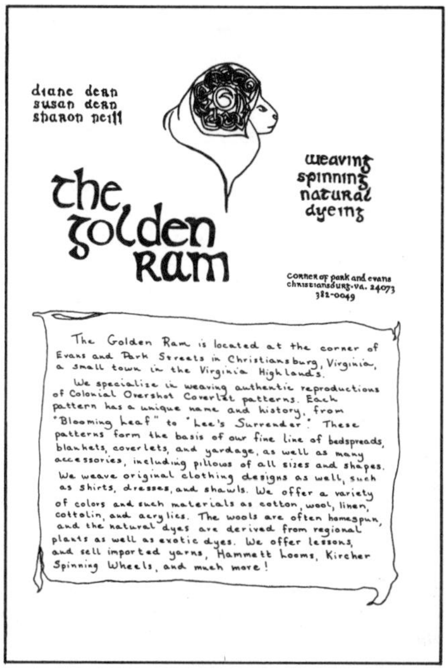

Reproduced here is the cover of the catalogue of The Golden Ram. Besides the handwoven reproductions of Colonial overshot patterns in a line of bedspreads, blankets, coverlets, and yardage, The Golden Ram also sells looms and spinning equipment, yarns and fleeces, and handmade items. Among the handmade items are shirts, jackets, skirts, caftan dresses, ponchos, shawls, scarves; pillows, sheepskin rugs, handmade sheep, sheep ornaments (see our Christmas section of this book), sheep breed pillows; coiled jewelry: barrettes, chokers, necklaces, headbands, and bracelets.

For your copy of their 16-page catalogue, send $1.00 to:

The Golden Ram
P.O. Box 246
Christiansburg, Virginia 24073

Write to Country Living for one of their catalogs—they have unusual, stylish items at prices that are affordable. The address is 320 King Street, Alexandria, Virginia 22314.

THE DULCIMER—INSTRUMENT OF THE SOUTHERN HIGHLANDS

A. W. Jeffreys, Jr., maker of new and collector of old dulcimers, sent us a rather complete description and history of this mountain folk instrument which we pass along to you.

Mr. Jeffreys, his wife, and children are all involved in the process of dulcimer making—for them it is a family craft. The Jeffreys' dulcimer is made of cherry and walnut hardwoods. The three-string model is slightly less than the four-string one, and both sell for under $100.00. You may write the Jeffreys at their business:

Appalachian Dulcimers
232 West Frederick Street
Staunton, Virginia 24401

"The Appalachian dulcimer is a 3-string folk musical instrument peculiar to the Southern Highlands. It was used by the early settlers to accompany their English and Scottish ballads and folk songs. How it got to be called a dulcimer is a mystery since it is a plucked instrument, not hammered, and thus belongs to the psaltery or zither class of stringed instruments. But a dulcimer it was called by the mountain folk, or in some hollows and hilltops, a "dulcymore," until it was chased to the attic and outbuildings about the turn of the century by the manufactured guitar and banjo.

"Recent interest in folk music has stirred a rediscovery of the Appalachian dulcimer's unique sounds and simplicity. It is the easiest of all stringed instruments to learn to play in the traditional manner with most people learning to play a familiar tune within 5 to 20 minutes after

This handsome dulcimer with the heart designs is made from cherry and walnut by the Jeffreys family.

becoming acquainted with tuning and holding the instrument. Musicians find it challenging to accomplish the complexities of playing when all the methods and tunings are utilized. Sounds vary according to the tuning and method of playing—now like a German zither then like an early spinet and even like a Scottish bagpipe. It may be tuned to the major and minor scales (modes) as well as the other four modal scales all popular before the 16th century.

History

"The history of the Appalachian dulcimer can now be traced with almost certainty to folk instruments of Norway and Sweden. Some early instruments found in Virginia and now contained in the Jeffreys collection of mountain dulcimers are like the folk instruments found in the museums of Norway and Sweden. These folk instruments were used in the Scandinavian countries during the 15th, 16th, and 17th centuries and a bare thread of lineage enabled them to find their way to America to be utilized by isolated pockets of Southern mountain folk to accompany their ballads and love songs. In preparation (by the Jeffreys) is a limited edition of an album of dulcimer playing that will include contemporary artists, traditional Southern mountain playing and a unique recording made in Europe on an Edison cylinder of a progenitor of the Appalachian dulcimer—the Swedish hummel.

3-String and 4-String

"The traditional Appalachian dulcimer has been mostly a simple and flexible 3-string instrument. Some early folk instruments had four strings which were really 3-string instruments with double melody strings to make four strings in all. This was done because early makers did not always have quality acoustical woods available to them, and the melody string was often overriden in volume by the two drone strings. More recently some players have preferred a 4-string dulcimer with one melody string and three drones tuned differently from each other to produce a richer chord group."

The Dulcimer Shoppe (McSpadden Musical Instruments) in Mountain View, Arkansas, performs what you might term "a labor of love." It is obvious from the way they describe their business:

"Ordering through the mail can be a very impersonal transaction. Because we believe that a dulcimer is a personal instrument, we want you to know the people whose hands, minds, and hearts shape our instruments. In the workshop are George Looney, Richard Stoltze, Mike McGhee, Larry McSpadden, and Lynn McSpadden. Lynn founded the Dulcimer Shoppe in 1962, and the dulcimer designs are his, but all five craftsmen are responsible for the final quality of each instrument. Their combined experience in fashioning more than 5,000 dulcimers totals nearly a half century. We believe the product of their experience is an instrument that is superior in musical tone, visual beauty, and quality of construction. We back this belief with a written life-time warranty. Each dulcimer is numbered and signed by one of the makers. The numbers enable us to keep a record of the original owner of each instrument."

Besides making dulcimers, which are described in their catalogue, the McSpaddens make kits for dulcimers (one hourglass and one teardrop shaped). Complete details and photographs of the instruments (kits and finished), with prices and ordering instructions, are included in *Mountains Dulcimers in the Ozarks*, their catalogue, which may be ordered by sending $1.00 to The Dulcimer Shoppe. Also included in the catalogue are other folk instruments not made by the McSpaddens, such as the Ozark Clog Doll, Melody Flute, Jew's Harp, and Fretless 5-String Banjo kit; numerous books and records in the area of folk music, especially dulcimer, are listed.

Among the books available are three by the McSpaddens: *Four & Twenty: Songs for the Mountain Dulcimer,* a basic instruction book by Lynn, which is included in the price of each dulcimer and kit from The Dulcimer Shoppe; *Brethren, We Have Met,* a book of shape-note hymns and Christmas carols, by Lynn McSpadden and Dorothy French; and *Merrily Strum: Mountain Dulcimer for Children,* a simplified instruction book featuring familiar children's songs, by Mary Catherine McSpadden, Lynn's wife.

Two records of particular interest are *Stone County Dulcimer* and *Ozark Mountain Dulcimer.* Both albums have instrumental dulcimer music only (no singing), played by Jean Simmons and her daughter Pam on McSpadden dulcimers. Jean works at The Dulcimer Shoppe year-around and Pam has worked there in the summers. The Simmons Family (including husband and father Tommy Simmons) are well known throughout the Ozarks for their enjoyable presentations of regional folk music.

When you write or call The Dulcimer Shoppe, you will probably talk to or hear from Jean Simmons or Mary Catherine McSpadden, who handle all orders and correspondence. They work year-around on mail and phone orders. If you are in the area between March 15 and October 31, stop by McSpadden Musical Instruments between 9 and 5, any day but Sunday, to see dulcimers being made and to learn to play one. All Dulcimer Shoppe employees are also dulcimer players. Write to:

McSpadden Musical Instruments—The Dulcimer Shoppe
P.O. Drawer E, Highway 9 North
Mountain View, Arkansas 72560

DAVIS DULCIMER SHOP

The Davis Dulcimer Shop, located in the mountains of Gatlinburg, Tennessee, has just about everything for the dulcimer enthusiast and is open year-round. All items available for mail orders from the shop are shown here. They can be ordered from:

Davis Dulcimer Shop
P.O. Box 515
Gatlinburg, Tennessee 37738

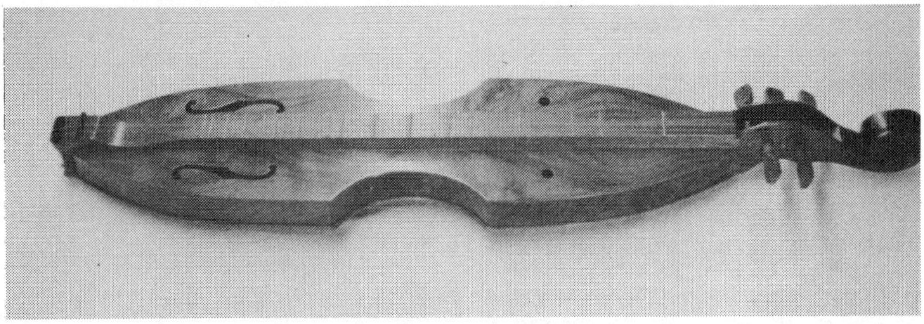

The completed 5-string dulcimer sells for $250.00. The wood is solid walnut. If you prefer to try your hand at dulcimer making, the Davis Dulcimer Shop sells this kit of precision-cut, pre-sanded parts for $100.00. The kit is the same model as the dulcimer, 5 strings and solid walnut. The instruction record "How to Tune and Play" is free with the order of a kit or dulcimer. Add $6.00 to cover postage and insurance for each item.

The shop's owner, Bill Davis, has recorded LP albums as follows: "Sounds of the Smokies," BWD-71; "Smoky Mountain Melodies," BWD-72; "Echoes from the Valley," BWD-75. All LP albums sell for $4.95 each. All albums are also available in 8 track tapes and cassettes and sell for $6.50 each. Instruction record "How to Tune and Play" sells for $6.00. To order, add $.75 for each item to cover postage. For more information, write for free brochure.

Homer C. Ledford is a member of the Southern Highlands Handicraft Guild and the Kentucky Guild of Artists and Craftsmen. He makes handmade musical instruments in his shop in Winchester, Kentucky, and sells not only these, but some dulcimer accessories, books, and records: black walnut dulcimer model No. 0046 with butternut top and rosewood pegs, 3 strings, $85.00 plus $4.00 postage and insurance; 4-string model No. 0446, $90.00 plus $4.00 postage and insurance; model No. YP-1900, same as the previously mentioned models but with special antique yellow poplar top over 100 years old, 4 strings, limited production, $95.00 plus $4.00.

The Ledford dulcimer accessories include a wooden carrying case for any one of the three models, $45.00; machine-quilted, heavy cotton, print carrying bag lined with acrylic, with drawstring and shoulder strap, same carrying bag except made of heavy cotton corduroy or denim, $9.25 each.

Instruction Books and Records

The Dulcimer Book by Jean Ritchie. 45 pages. Illustrated..........................$2.95

The Plucked Dulcimer & How to Play It by John Putnam................................$1.50

The Appalachian Dulcimer by A. W. Jeffreys, Jr...$3.00

How to Play the 5 String Banjo by Pete Seeger.................................$2.00

How to Play the Appalachian Dulcimer—music and instruction, 45 rpm with Edna Ritchie Baker singing "Four Marys," etc. 10 min. playing....................................... $1.50
(Free with purchase of dulcimer.)

Ledford Family "Songs We Love to Play and Sing," LP album of dulcimer music, guitar, fretless banjo, musical saw, etc. Traditional folk songs. 16 selections. (Free with purchase of dulcimer.)............................$4.95

Allow $1.00 shipping on all small items, and please send check or money order when ordering. Allow 3 to 4 weeks for delivery.

You may address orders to:

Homer C. Ledford Crafts
125 Sunset Heights
Winchester, Kentucky 40391

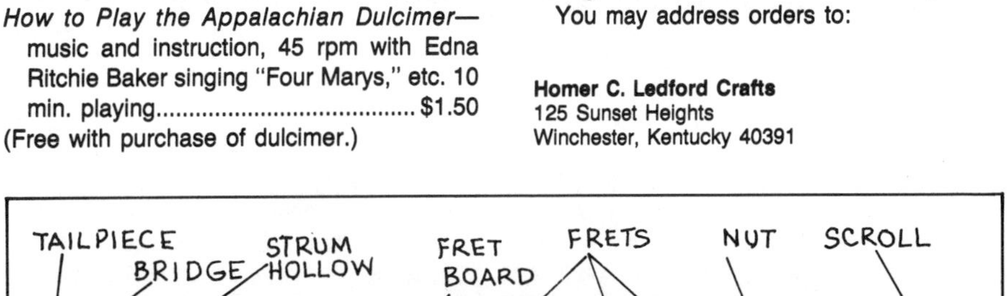

SALTER PATH

Fania Tuomey makes two types of baskets: wall baskets and the full-shaped melon baskets. The handles are made of grape or wisteria vines. The rest of the weaving is done with reeds, with some of the reeds dyed, to add color to the baskets. The baskets range in price from $8.00 to $50.00, according to size. Write to Fania Tuomey, Route 1, Box 237, Higden, Arkansas 72067.

Salter Path Audubon Quilted Pillow Kits are hand-screened in England on fine cotton and are from authentic Audubon paintings. There are four different prints in each series, and the kits are $9.95 each, plus 90¢ postage. These four prints have matching borders in brown, soft blue, and mossy green, foliage in mossy greens and twiggy browns, and come with a backing of handsome brown velveteen. The four are (1) the Zenaida Dove, browns with soft blue and russet, one bird in flight; (2) the White-crowned Pigeon, a stunning design in deep blues with a touch of white, a bit of russet in the flowers; (3) the White-winged Crossbill, two males in a pretty red with black and a touch of white on the wings, the two females in olive tones, and (4) the Band-tailed Pigeon, graceful birds in medium blues with a touch of bittersweet, on a flowering branch. The finished pillow is about 11 x 15 inches.

Salter Path also has other kits with such names as "Smithsonian" Birds, "Birdwatcher" series, "Bewick's Ducks," and "Four Wise Owls." For a flyer about these, send a self-addressed, stamped envelope to:

Salter Path
Shandy Lane
RFD 3, Box 346-B
Wilmington, North Carolina 28403

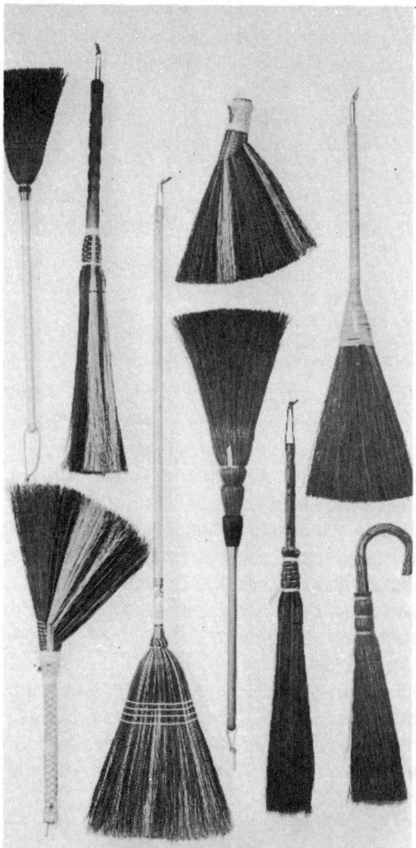

STUDENT CRAFT INDUSTRIES

Berea College, located in Berea, Kentucky, was founded in 1855. They have an enrollment of 1,400 students of high ability but limited economic resources. Approximately 80% of them are selected from 230 Appalachian counties of eight Southern states. Berea has no tuition. Board, room, health, and incidental fees for each student are only about $1,284 for the school year.

Yet, with all of this, Berea has a student program which enables the student to earn his way through college. The Berea College Student Craft Industries produce quality crafts, such things as: ceramics, of traditional as well as unique designs; furniture of solid wood in Early American design, carefully selected and expertly finished; handmade brooms, made with handles of sassafras and leather thongs for hanging; needlecraft; toys with character out of lively prints; fireside weaving, with a wide selection of everything from ponchos to panels for the wall; woodcraft, games, and cutting boards.

Berea College Student Craft Industries are center members of the Kentucky Guild of Artists and Craftsmen, the Southern Highland Handicraft Guild, and the Blue Ridge Hearthside Crafts Association.

For their attractive catalogue, send $.50 to:

Student Craft Industries
Berea College
Berea, Kentucky 40404

STUART NYE SILVER SHOP

The dogwood is the state flower of both North Carolina and Virginia; and most Southerners are also aware of the breathtaking beauty the dogwood provides in the spring.

The Stuart Nye Silver Shop has been making silver jewelry patterned after the dogwood for over 40 years. Simple tools are still used to fashion the silver. Each piece is cut by hand with metal shears and the design work is done with sharp chisels on the anvil, reminding one of the blacksmith's shop. The craftsmen form the jewelry with blunt tools or hammers on a soft background (lead). Any necessary assembly is done with an acetylene torch and silver solder. After the piece is cleaned and oxidized it is polished and anti-tarnish treated; the finished jewelry is then inspected and attached to its individual display card. The result: jewelry that is delicate in design and beautiful to look at, appealing to all ages, and reasonable in price.

A catalogue is available for $1.00.

Stuart Nye Silver Shop
940 Tunnel Road
Asheville, North Carolina 28805

A STOOL YOU CAN MAKE

This footstool kit makes a woven rush footstool for any room of your home. The frame (14" x 11" x 11¾"), completely assembled and sanded, is made from selected hardwood, mostly maple. Fiber rush and weaving instructions for several designs are included. The manufacturer suggests two hours as the weaving time. The stool may then be stained, varnished, or painted. The price is $14.99, postpaid.

Write to:

Lucel Products
210-C Marray Drive
Chamblee, Georgia 30341

CANOPIES

"Rosemont" has been the homestead of a single family for generations and today serves as the headquarters for Laura Copenhaver Industries. Laura Copenhaver Industries was born out of an effort by Laura Scherer Copenhaver to help mountain families during the Depression. Until that time, this energetic and talented woman had been teaching college English and writing. When she became aware of the economic plight of Virginia sheep farmers and mountain folk, she devised a scheme to combine the raw products of wool with the handicraft of the mountain people into beautiful rugs, curtains, quilts, and canopies. These items are now found in homes throughout the world. The proceeds of this industry provided the sorely needed funds to these impoverished country families; many of the people helped by Mrs. Copenhaver's energies are still selling their handicraft through Laura Copenhaver Industries.

Some of the most beautiful items that are made at "Rosemont" are the hand-tied fishnet canopies. Exquisite designs hand-tied by ladies who have passed the art from generation to generation are produced in the mountains of North Carolina and Virginia. The canopies are tied by hand with natural cream-colored or white thread. Four designs are available for straight or curved tester frames: the designs are "Tasseled Top Canopy," "Double Diamond Point Canopy," "Single Diamond Point Canopy," and "The Margaret Winston Canopy."

When ordering a canopy, please give the following information:

Length and width of tester frame?
Straight or curved? (If curved, give length along curve.)
Natural cream or white?
Design?
Length of hang-over (usually 18 inches)?

Laura Copenhaver Industries also makes quilts, coverlets, and petticoat valances. Send $.50 for their booklet. A "Margaret Winston Canopy" (shown) sells for $140.00, twin and double; $160.00, queen; and $190.00, king.

Laura Copenhaver Industries
"Rosemont"
Marion, Virginia 24354

SHEARWATER POTTERY: A FAMILY TRUST

By Mary Jean Haddin

The lawns come right up to the narrow streets of Ocean Springs, Mississippi—streets that are lined with ancient, spreading oaks. You feel as if you were driving into your past. Memories of a small, close world press in. Here is a community (a fast-disappearing species) where families have stayed and known each other for generations.

One of the old streets crosses a small bridge over a piece of the harbor and goes by a wooden sign saying simply, "Shearwater Pottery." You turn here onto the rutted dirt driveway into the woods along the harbor. The first building you see, nestled in the woods to the right of the bumpy driveway, is the pottery. (Since this is a weekend, the pottery itself is not open, though during the week visitors may tour the pottery. But the showroom is open 10:00–5:30, Monday through Saturday, 1:00–5:30 Sundays.) Your car jolts on, past a small white house, to another building almost hidden behind trees. You park among tree roots to enter the doorway, guarded by large bushes, of the showroom of the Shearwater Pottery. The still, greenish light of the forest glade is carried inside the showroom by the large windows and reflected by the walls and shelves of "pickled" cypress (wood painted white and then wiped off). It is quiet inside—with almost the air of a shrine—a little dusty, and friendly. On the shelves are pots of all shapes and sizes. They have the exquisitely smooth lines of clay objects that have been coaxed to rise from a wheel by hands that have no doubts. The simple flares and closings and mellow glazes decline further enhancement. They are perfect as they are. A silver-sheened green bowl, flecked with brown, flares out as gently as a flower. (Gazing into it is hypnotic.) A vase is of rich, smooth blue with a soft chocolate brown at the top. (You recall the fame of Shearwater Pottery's glazes.) Both of these bear only the mark: "Shearwater Pottery." Another vase is interestingly carved and painted in white and rusts and browns. This vase is marked "Adele Lawton" on the bottom. On another shelf a small figurine, a fox with blue-green fur, smiles at you.

Down some steps you find a beautiful white bowl, shaped like a magnolia. Near it is a tiny watercolor of a boatman silhouetted against a pale yellow sky. In the same corner is an unbleached muslin apron, hand-printed in earth red with a curving flower and heart-shaped leaves. These seem to be the work of yet another person: James McConnell Anderson. Standing in the opposite corner of this room is a large mushroom carved out of wood—big enough to sit on.

You wander on. In another room still another name appears: Walter Anderson. Here are plates—one carved and painted with a bird flying between two deep green trees into a golden sun. On these works, marked "not for sale," a bold, sure hand has drawn birds and animals: a whisk here makes a beak; a swirl there, a tail.

Shearwater Pottery, you have heard, is a family enterprise. But can all these different styles of pottery (thrown and molded, glazed and carved) not to mention the paintings, carvings and printed fabric—can these all be the work of one family? Do family members come like elves across the wood from the other houses along that bumpy driveway? You pounce upon a notebook lying on the shelf among the pottery—an old family album.

Within is the story of the business—Shearwater Pottery—that, you discover, has expanded to include four generations of a remarkable family. First appear the browning Victorian photographs of the patriarch, George Walter Anderson (a New Orleans grain merchant, born in Scotland) and the matriarch (Annette McConnell Anderson). It was Annette Anderson, you discover, who bought this property (at that time twenty-five acres of wilderness) sight unseen in the early 1920s. Annette Anderson was herself an accomplished artist, having graduated from the Newcomb School of Art and the Pennsylvania Academy of Fine Arts. In fact, she bought the land originally as a summer retreat where she could paint and sculpt, but later moved there permanently with her husband and three sons.

Yellowing newspaper accounts in the family album explain that what is now the Shearwater Pottery began when Annette Anderson bought a potters' wheel at an auction and "decided it was time to teach her three sons to use their hands in the name of art." Apparently they took to it. All had been educated at various art schools. In 1928, the eldest son Peter built the kilns and began making pottery. Annette and her two younger sons, Walter and James McConnell Anderson (ah, here came some of the names) designed the molds and decorated the pieces. When talented sisters, Patricia and Agnes Grinstead, married the two elder brothers (Peter and Walter), these young wives took over the business end of the family affair. (You begin to long, as when reading a Russian novel, for a family tree.)

Today, seventy-seven-year-old Peter Anderson is the master potter. Having designed and built the kilns still used today and developed the glazes for which Shearwater Pottery is famous, he contributes a large number of the exquisite pottery pieces. (The pottery has always been made from a mixture of Mississippi clay and a special clay from Tennessee—whose location is a family secret.) However, since 1968, Peter's son James has also been responsible for much of this beautiful pottery. James's wife Margaret is business manager of the pottery. Another of Peter's sons, Michael, returned to Shearwater in 1978 to produce its cast pieces. Peter's daughter Marjorie Ashley works in the showroom and workshop. Another daughter, Patricia Findeisen, is a designer and painter. Steven Ashley (son of Marjorie and grandson of Peter), a high school senior, assists his uncle Jim in the pottery. He is a talented apprentice potter and colorist.

James McConnell Anderson, Peter's youngest brother, still designs figurines and is known for his decorative work—reticulated bowls, carved vases and slip-glazed wares. He also does murals, watercolors, oils, carves wood, and makes furniture. His wife Sarah assists in the pottery showroom and workshop. His daughter Adele Lawton has made a specialty of carved vases. She is the major colorist of the third generation. She also watercolors the block prints that were designed by her uncle Walter.

Walter Anderson, the eccentric and extravagantly talented second son of the matriarch and patriarch, died in 1965. His drawings and paintings, block prints and decorated pottery are only lately beginning to receive some of the national acclaim they deserve, due largely to the energy of two people: his daughter, Mary Stebly, who as curator for the Walter Anderson Estate Collection, lectures and arranges exhibits of her father's work. His wife Agnes has catalogued his work and helped to publish two books about it. She and her granddaughter, Amy Stebly, also assist in the Shearwater showroom. Carolyn Anderson, wife of Walter's son Billy, serves as chief conservator at the pottery, repairing and reconstructing sherds.

Still another talented family member, though from a different branch of the family, shows his work in the Shearwater showroom. Robert Sidney (whose great-grandfather was the brother of Annette McConnell Anderson) is an accomplished wood carver, and, inspired like his relatives by the Gulf Coast fauna, carves birds and fish.

You close the family album reluctantly—loathe to leave this compelling story that does read almost like a novel—or a fairy tale. ("There was once a woman who had three sons and they lived in a wood by the sea.") Whence comes this fairy tale quality? Is it the sense of a guiding presence or set of standards that makes the characters involved seem somehow larger than life?

This family has, through four generations, maintained a trust in several senses of the word. They have accepted the family heritage—both a duty and a business entrusted to them from earlier generations. The family heritage has something to do with standards for life and something to do with standards for art and something to do with standards for the self in relation to the former two and to the family. The trust was a part of the life of innocent confidence of the 1920s. Fifty years later (unlike so many earlier acts of trust) it remains not only viable but vibrant and flexible. Did the custody of this heritage give family members a trust (or confidence) in themselves and their own talents?

Your car jolts back out the bumpy driveway toward the little town—back toward the interstate highway, to gas shortages and big cities. You wish you could stay in this corner of the woods where the sun glints from the pine needles and the waves, where family members go to work by walking through woods to their family enterprise. Where they work with their hands and brains, producing beauty. Where they participate each day in a family heritage and trust and seem somehow anchored by an act of their own will and belief.

You feel lucky to have been allowed to buy and carry away a talisman—a gently flared, silver-sheened bowl.

Drawing from HORN ISLAND LOGS.

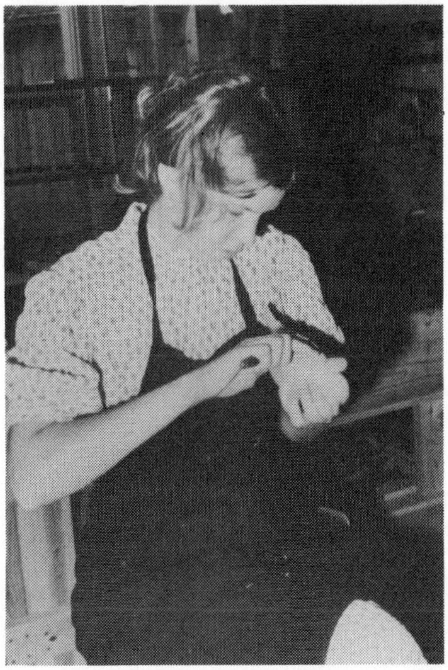

WOODCARVERS

For Gerry and Sharon Phillips-Chisholm, limited-edition wood sculpture has been their livelihood since 1972. They live and carve in Mountain View, Arkansas.

Wild and domestic animals, songbirds, hawks, owls, and ducks are among their subjects. The animals are carved in natural woods with a Danish oil finish, and the birds and ducks are handpainted.

The wood for their carvings comes from small "groundhog" mills whose primary product is crossties. The mill owner saves carving trees for Gerry and Sharon; then they must let the trees dry for three or more summers. By that time, the wood is seasoned and will not crack when it is carved. Gerry and Sharon write, "Wood is an honest medium with a warmth and life all its own. It can't be pushed around like clay can. Carve through it counter to the grain and the wood works with you, lending its strength to fine detail."

Songbirds are available in life size or as 3/5-size scaled miniatures. Life-size birds feature a featherlike texture over the body, glass eyes, sculptured metal feet and legs, and painting by individual strokes of color. All birds are mounted on driftwood.

The availability is limited because of the nature of the craft. Please write for a current price list.

Gerry and Sharon Phillips-Chisholm
Rushing Route, Box 92-B
Mountain View, Arkansas 72560

Mary Darby in her studio, working on a stained glass panel (8 square feet) to be installed in a new home in an outside wall at a stair landing.

GLASS WEB STUDIO

Mary Darby's studio is located in the Old Cotton Warehouse on the historic Savannah waterfront. Mary accepts commissions for custom-made ecclesiastical or domestic stained glass windows. She also will repair and restore items in need of that attention.

To consult Mary about commissioning a new window or repairing a present treasure, write:

Glass Web Studio
221 West River Street
Savannah, Georgia 31401

NEEDLEWORK DESIGNS

Doris Drake of Thomasville, Georgia, has compiled five books of needlework designs, done with the cross-stitch advocate in mind, but also suitable for use by the needlepoint fan. Book I has several beautiful alphabets. Book II has additional alphabets plus some small designs, mostly of animals. Book III is an oversize book with designs of a more intricate nature. Book IV, also oversize, has designs for mottos and sayings. Book V is an oversize book of whimsical designs. Books I and II sell for $6.50 each. Books III, IV, and V sell for $12.00 each. Add $.50 for tax and mailing for each book.

Order from:

Doris Drake Needlework Designs
P.O. Box 442
Thomasville, Georgia 31792

PRODUCTS OF A CENTURIES-OLD CRAFT—ENAMELING

Betty Jones Whitfield is an artist *par excellence* when it comes to enameling. She is a member of the Southern Highlands Handicraft Guild and exhibits at the Guild's fairs.

A selection of her most popular enamels are shown here and may be ordered directly from her. The apple tree, flowers, and tree of life reflect the endearing charm of folk art.

Stickpins and Scatter Tacs	$4.50
Earrings	$7.00
Bird Pendant	$4.50
Cloisonne Trees 1" oval	$11.00
1½" oval	$16.00
1½" round	$16.00
2" round	$26.00
Apple Tree	$21.00
Cloisonne and Silver Foil Daisy	$26.00

(Rose, Bluebell and other available)

All are gift-boxed and postpaid. Order from:

Mrs. Betty Jones Whitfield
116 Lakeview Drive
Birmingham, Alabama 35209
(205) 942-5208

ANDREA BODET—POTTER

Andrea Bodet became interested in pottery-making several years after learning techniques of working with clay during a post-graduate sculpture course. Initially, she used hand-building techniques and worked with low-fire clay. Although she was primarily self-taught, time spent working with several independent potters helped change her sense of direction and emphasis to the area of wheel-thrown production work. Greater refinement of these skills was achieved through study at Penland School of Crafts.

Andrea now operates a production studio on a full-time basis with emphasis on wheel-thrown functional items. One-of-a-kind studio pieces are still an important and necessary statement and are exhibited periodically. Andrea Bodet's work is sold at gift stores, specialty shops, and galleries; is exhibited regularly at juried shows and exhibitions; and is in private collections throughout the United States. Andrea is also an exhibiting member of the Craftsmen's Guild of Mississippi. Andrea is available by appointment and can be reached at the address given below. Currently a line of thirty-five items is being produced. All pieces are signed. Variations in size and color are to be expected in handmade pottery.

Andrea Bodet—Potter
Route 1, Box 30
Oakland, Mississippi 38948

BATTER BOWL. This stoneware batter bowl is wheel-thrown with a pulled handle, trimmed foot, and a pouring spout that makes it the perfect mixing bowl for almost anything. Capacity, 6 cups. Colors available: earth tones (burnt orange, beige and iron red combination with hand-painted slip design, or white with hand-painted blue slip design—not necessarily that shown). Price: $15.00 postpaid. Wooden spoon not included.

CANDLESTICK. This old-fashioned candlestick with matching snuffer is approximately 6" tall; it is wheel-thrown stoneware with a pulled handle for carrying. The matching snuffer hangs on the side ready for use. Colors available: earth tones (burnt orange, iron red, and beige in varying combinations), white with a hand-painted blue slip design, or celadon green and white (upper portion) combination with hand-painted slip design. Price: $12.50 postpaid. Candle not included.

PAPIER JEWELRY

Mrs. Lena Anderson of Dallas works with papier maché. Mrs. Anderson's education includes a degree from East Texas University and the study of oils, sculpture, design and color with various artists. For the past fifteen years she has designed many different things: flowers, containers, Christmas angels, wig stands—and now jewelry. The necklace shown here is painted on both sides with either gray or ivory elephants. The elephants sell for $22.50 postpaid. Texas residents add 5% sales tax. Mrs. Anderson is not able to send out brochures or catalogues but please contact her for orders at:

Anderson Papier Maché
5810 Waggoner Drive
Dallas, Texas 75230

COLORS FROM NATURE

Helen Bryant, a weaver of considerable talent, uses only natural dyes to color the wool she uses. She discovered that the yarns she had been buying were not as pretty as the yarns she had seen that were naturally dyed. Mrs. Bryant loves to gather the ingredients that she uses for her dyes. She goes to the yard or the forest and gathers elderberries, walnuts, pecan blossoms, lichens, bayberries, eucalyptus, and black-eyed Susans.

Starting from scratch, Mrs. Bryant taught herself the basics of weaving about seven years ago. She uses an old-fashioned spinning wheel to spin some of her own yarn but cannot do enough spinning for all the weaving she does. Helen Bryant has become nationally recognized for her art and has exhibited her work in many shows. She also has held workshops in colleges and schools and a mini-workshop for the American Craft Council.

Some of the items she makes that you may order include afghans, pillows, wall hangings, and bedspreads. Mrs. Bryant uses lots of raw silk in her full-sized bedspreads. Prices range

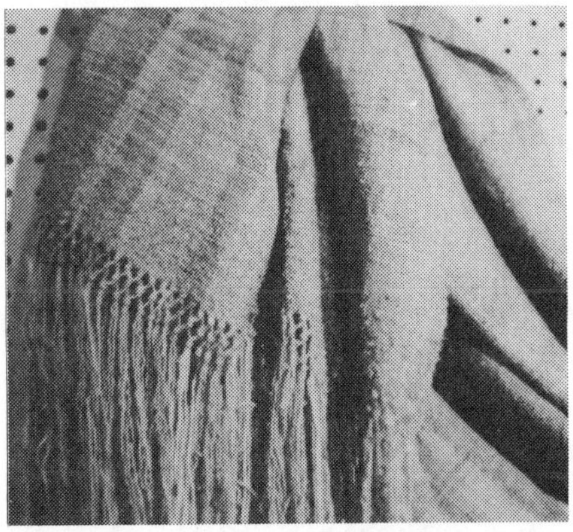

from $35.00 for pillows to $100.00 for afghans that measure 46" x 72" (not including the fringe). Her wall hangings are priced from $50.00 to $250.00 and her bedspreads are priced at $350.00. Every piece is original; no two items are alike.

To inquire about her exquisite work, write to:

Helen Bryant
4250 Athens Drive
Jackson, Mississippi 39211

The Freedom Quilting Bee

In her letter to us, Mrs. Estelle Witherspoon, manager of the Freedom Quilting Bee, explains the genesis of this south Alabama cottage industry.

The Freedom Quilting Bee is housed in this many-angled building in the tiny south Alabama town of Alberta.

Dear Friend,

We members of the Freedom Quilting Bee are very proud of our little organization, a cooperative of 30 skilled artisans. "The Bee," as we call it, is one of this country's only all-Black women's cooperatives.

We have been in operation for fourteen years, and in that short time we have achieved national recognition for our quilts. We have participated in many exhibitions and demonstrations—including those at the Smithsonian Institution. We members of the Freedom Quilting Bee have had the tremendous satisfaction of being told that the quilts we produce are "the most charming, the boldest, the most different quilts produced in America today."

Then too, the Bee's quilts have been featured in magazine and newspaper articles such as Vogue, House and Garden, *the* New Yorker *and the* New York Times.

But our organization was not formed for the purpose of becoming famous. Our cooperative is situated in a rural area of Wilcox County, Alabama, a poverty region where employment is difficult to find, and where as late as 1970, family incomes averaged $800 a year.

In 1966 we women banded together to organize a small business in order to provide supplementary income for our families. We were adept at quilt-making and were familiar with traditional Southern patterns learned from our mothers and grandmothers. These are the designs we began to use in our sewing of quilts, and today these designs are still used, almost exclusively, in our quilting work at the Bee.

You would like our quilts. They are bright, colorful patterns suitable for use on your bed, your wall, as a tablecloth, picnic blanket—or other imaginative use.

Laundering the quilts is no problem. Except with the velvet patterns, an automatic washer (warm water) and dryer can be used.

We think so much of our products that we cheerfully return the money if our customers are not satisfied and return the item within ten days.

Our brochure is free. Send for it and choose something you would like for yourself or for a gift to a friend.

Sincerely,
Mrs. Estelle Witherspoon, Manager

Mrs. Estelle Witherspoon is the busy manager of The Freedom Quilting Bee.

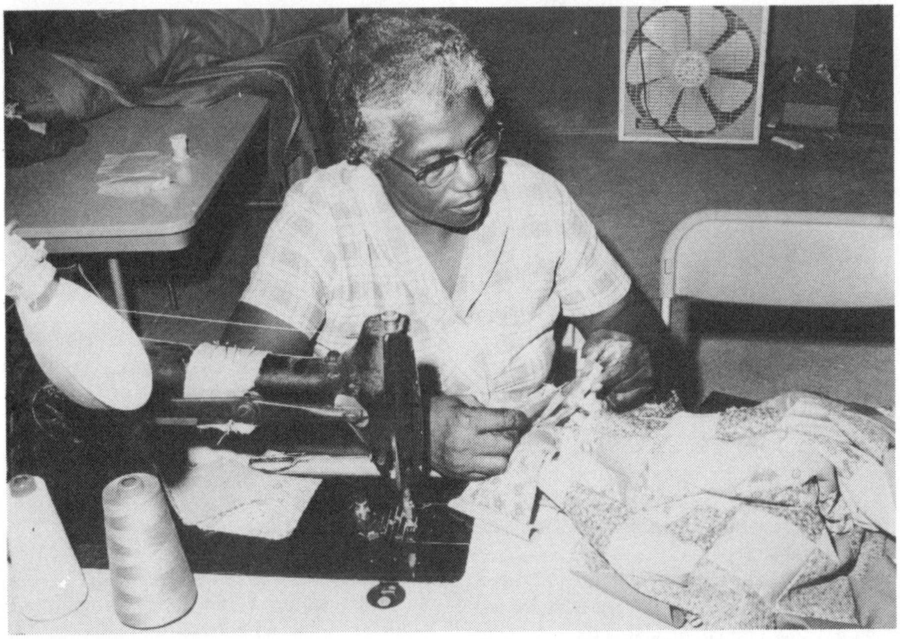

Quilt tops are carefully assembled.

Potholders: perfect for gifts, these generously-sized potholders brighten kitchens with their colorful patchwork. Available in all colors. Made of fine cotton calico prints with coordinating solids or ginghams. Dacron-fill, approximately 8" x 8". Priced at $3.00. Minimum order of 3.

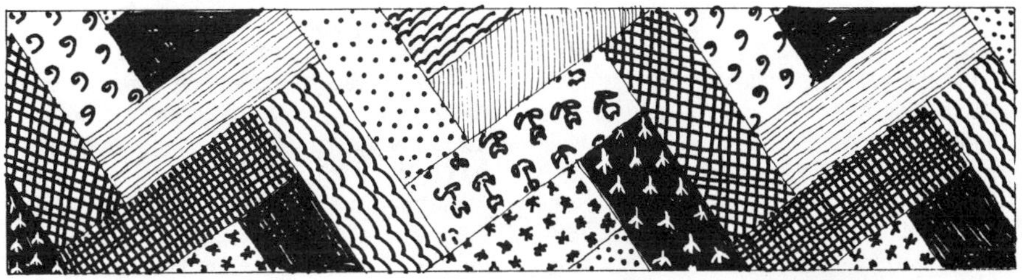

The Freedom Quilting Bee has a colorful brochure and order form which they will be glad to send you free. Here is a sampling of their handmade articles for sale at reasonable prices.

The Bee makes five different quilt patterns in five sizes—single, double, queen, king, and crib. Prices for quilts range from $235 to $360; crib quilt, $60.00.

The Bee also makes boutique items: patchwork pot holders, $3.00; patchwork pillows, $9.00; children's patchwork blocks.

On all their mail-order items you are given a choice of color. Prices are exclusive of handling charges which are clearly explained on the brochure.

Write to:

The Freedom Quilting Bee
Route 1, Box 72
Alberta, Alabama 36720

A CRAFT SHOP ON THE SOQUE RIVER

One of the places that we would most like to visit but feel that we already know a great deal about, through the communication we've had with its owner, John LaRowe, is a contemporary craft shop called the Mark of the Potter. We can't say enough for John LaRowe—his kindness in helping us to gather names of other craftsmen in the general area as well as imparting such enthusiasm for his own operation left us with a good feeling.

Grandpa Watts' Mill on the Soque River near Clarkesville, Georgia, was the victim of a flood in 1966 causing it to cease its corn grinding operation. Powered by the swift-flowing waters of that river, the spillway was swept away and costs were too great to replace all that was necessary. But Glen and John LaRowe reopened Grandpa Watts' Mill (after many repairs and much hard work) in 1968 and called their home and studio Mark of the Potter.

Mark of the Potter, a longtime dream come true, is now celebrating its tenth anniversary offering contemporary crafts in clay, fabric, wood, and metal. Visitors can see Glen and John throw pots in the shop area and they may watch other craftsmen work from the throwing of the pottery through the glazing and firing operations.

The LaRowes throw pots from their own stoneware clay body containing Georgia red clay, ball clay and fire clay, and their pots are wheel-thrown on kick wheels that they designed and built themselves. They use glazes that they have compounded for beauty, permanence and, of course, food safety. The pottery is fired to stoneware temperature at 2400° F. in a 36 cubic foot gas kiln that the LaRowes built for reduction firing. Each pot is an original work: handmade, virtually as pots have been made for centuries. The Mark of the Potter also carries crafts and pottery by several other Southeastern craftsmen.

Mark of the Potter
On the Soque River at Grandpa Watt's Mill
Georgia 197; Route #3
Clarkesville, Georgia 30523

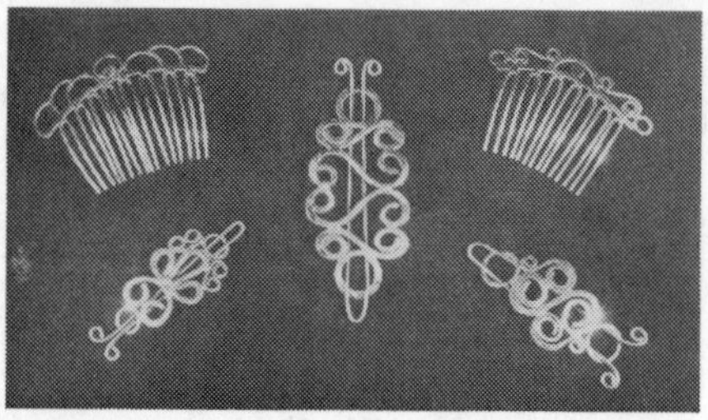

BRASS ROOTS

Courtney Miller designs these hand-crafted barrettes and combs. Solid brass wire is cut, shaped, forged, and buffed. Each piece is unique since the component parts (circles, scrolls, etc.) are made first and then laid out into an arrangement of barrettes or hair combs. The pieces are soldered together and put into a pickling solution to remove fire scale. They are forged with a chasing hammer on a miniature anvil and polished to a smooth and shiny surface. (The jewelry is not given any plastic coating because the coatings will chip and be worse than without coating; steel wool is to be used if there is ever any tarnish.)

The designs are not only pretty; they are functional. Please state if your hair is thick or thin, fine or coarse; this will help in making your barrette or comb particularly yours.

Hair combs are priced at $16.00 a pair. Small barrettes are $6.00. Medium barrettes are $10.00 each; large barrettes, $12.00 each. Shipments can be sent C.O.D. through the U.S. Post Office.

Write to:

Courtney Miller
Route A, Box 222A
Yellville, Arkansas 72687

STAINED GLASS

Stephen Ware's stained glass appears throughout the South. His clients vary from private individuals to commercial businesses. Stephen's work with stained glass began in 1970, through an interest in light transmission of color and functional art work. His first venture was a stained-glass shop with two fellow craftsmen.They concentrated on lamps, windows, and candleholders. After four years, Stephen left to open a shop of his own. Most of his early works were for residential use with themes that grew out of the wishes of clients and commissions. The popular themes were traditional designs. Later works deal with floral, oriental, and fantasy themes.

Stephen's glass has been seen in art shows in Atlanta, Nashville, Huntsville, Birmingham, and New Orleans. He has given demonstrations to high school and university art students. Stephen attended classes in technical illustration and engineering drawing at Calhoun Trade School and the University of Alabama in Huntsville. He has worked for the Army, Lockheed, and IBM in their graphics and drafting departments. In 1975, he as-

sisted in the construction of the second largest mosaic in the United States: the mosaic front of a Baptist Church in Huntsville.

Some of Stephen's works are the result of collaboration with fellow artists. The painted faces which appear on several works are the work of painter Al Byers. Multi-panel pieces also represent the designer efforts of Bette Young; such a piece is the 3-panel Dragon (19 feet long) exhibited in the Kaffeeklatsch in Huntsville.

Contact:

Stephen Ware
4418 Shelby Avenue
Huntsville, Alabama 35801

THE LONESOME PINE

When Helen Standifer moved to Knoxville a few years ago, she became interested in crafts in general and then in making wire trees. As she explains, "Putting two of my favorite things together—metal and trees—I started making wire trees, and 'The Lonesome Pine' was started." Each year, Helen adds several new trees to her group. She now makes about twenty-five basic trees, though each individual tree has its own character.

Helen tells us about her trees: "Several sizes of wire are used depending on if the tree has to support something (leaves, stones, etc.) or has a great deal of branch detail. Color is determined by type of wire—brass, copper, or steel—since I don't paint any of the trees. For those who find the dead or winter tree cold, I have spring dogwood trees with delicate shell blossoms, trees adorned with semiprecious or precious stones and summer trees which have as many as two thousand handcut leaves. The tree's elaborate root system clings to either a stone or mineral base. . . . I buy many beautiful and unusual stones to create unique combinations. The one pictured on the wooden base is a brass tree with fresh water Tennessee pearls on honey onyx."

Helen's trees are priced over quite a range: $15.00 to $1,000.00. She will do custom work using ideas or pictures or stones which customers have collected. Make inquiries by sending a self-addressed, stamped envelope to:

The Lonesome Pine
406 Monitor Lane
Knoxville, Tennessee 37922

NOISY CROW PAPERS

K. Franklin Spoor's beautiful marbled papers (the kind you love to see as the end papers in old books) can be ordered made up into such things as note cards and gift boxes. Or you can order them by the gorgeous sheet for your own creations. The method of production is described by Spoor:

"Noisy Crow Papers are imprinted by free-flowing and controlled colors to produce the endlessly varied decorative paper for covering such objects as fiber gift boxes, basswood hinged boxes, stitched-bound Strathmore sketch books, wood tiles, folding letter boxes, and matted and framed monoprints.

"Using contemporary materials, mainly kraft or rag paper and pigments in acrylic polymer emulsion, but employing techniques known and guarded since the middle of the sixteenth century in Europe and Asia, each sheet produced becomes a record of the selection of color, the movement of the pigments on the surface of the carragheen size, and the lifting of the pattern from the surface with the sheet of paper. Variously known as Turkish, clouded, marbled, or vat dyed paper, such papers are still produced by individuals and commercially in India, Turkey, France, Sweden, England, and the United States where it has been the subject of renewed interest and its production the subject of books and magazine articles.

"Noisy Crow Papers are the product of my growing study for over ten years and experimentation for the last five years in the attempt to decorate objects that please the eye and compliment the person who receives them as a gift."

To order from Noisy Crow Papers, you may write for a price list and samples, or you might order note cards with envelopes for $1.00 each or $10.00 a dozen; these come in assorted papers. Other items available are fiberboard gift boxes and hinged basswood boxes in various sizes. Sketch books with hard covers and stitched bindings are available with or without initials. The Marmorate Monoprints are appropriately framed. Finally, there are sheets of marbled paper; their use is left entirely to your imagination and ingenuity.

Write to:

Noisy Crow Papers
K. Franklin Spoor
Beechwood Hills
Newport News, Virginia 23602

BENCHMARK GALLERY

Rude Osolnik, owner of the Benchmark Gallery, works with wood, and he is a master craftsman. Each piece is chiseled from one solid block of wood. The various hardwoods, with which he works, come from all over the world, and they are aged for at least two years. Needless to say, no two Osolnik pieces are alike. And, as Rude puts it, he "bows to Mother Nature in following grain patterns to achieve the most beauty." All of these pieces are exquisitely finished. Hours of meticulous handwork are involved—applying fillers, oil, and sealers before the final finish.

The Benchmark Gallery was created as a place to display and sell Osolnik originals, but they have added many fine crafts from leading craftsmen and artists from many states.

Write to Rude for more information about his work or visit his gallery when you're near Berea, Kentucky.

Rude Osolnik
Box 422
Berea, Kentucky 40403

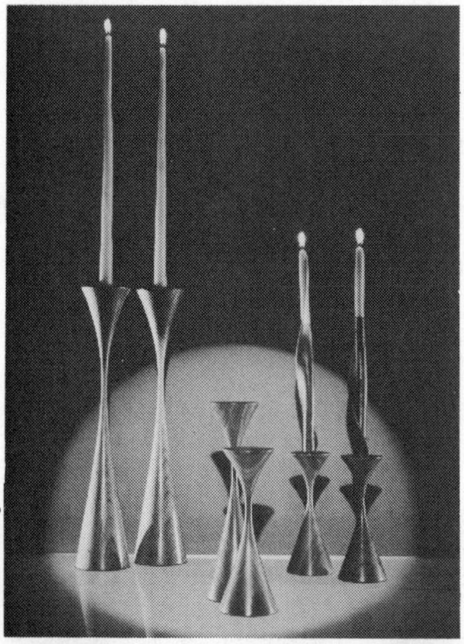

Hedrick-Blessing

John Scarlata

David Gaynes

BLOWN GLASS

Robert Levin is presently the Resident Glassblower at Penland School of Crafts, Penland, North Carolina. He says, "I am trying to capture some of the fluidity of glass in its molten state, while at the same time imposing a strong sense of form and balance. My pieces are essentially decorative works of art with a functional connotation."

Robert Levin is affiliated with the American Crafts Council, the Glass Art Society, and Piedmont Craftsmen, Inc. His work can be found in the collections of the Mint Museum, the Corning Museum of Glass, the Kunsthaus an Museum of Cologne, Germany, and other museums and foundations.

Write to:

Robert Levin
Penland School
Penland, North Carolina 28765

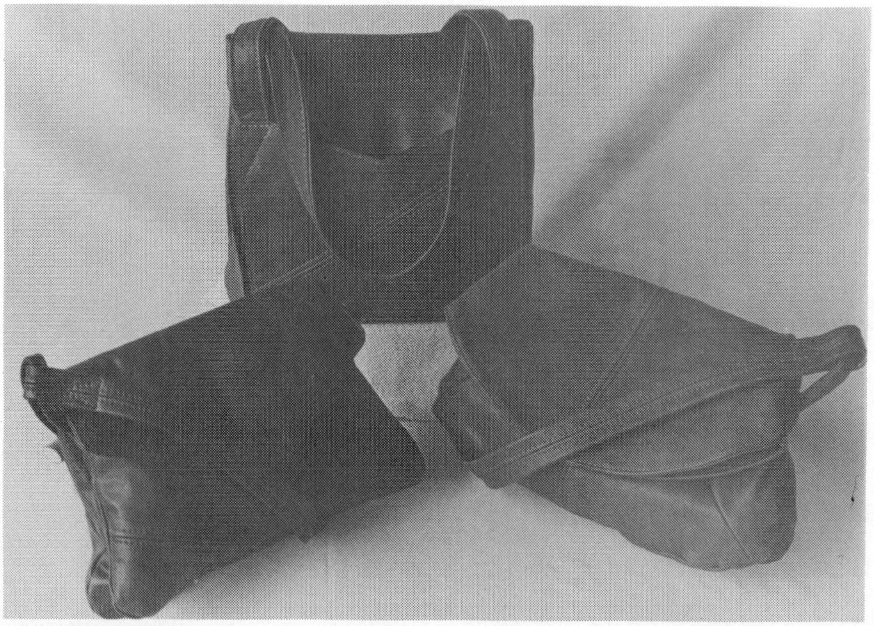

LEATHER PURSES

The Rudy Tell Design Group of Cosby, Tennessee, have been making hand-finished leather handbags for the past six years. The group holds membership in the Piedmont Craftsmen Association and the Southern Highland Handicrafts Guild. They sell primarily through a limited number of leather shops and craft stores throughout the South, but you may order directly. Payment should be by check, money order, or C.O.D. Prices include all shipping and handling charges. The handbags are available in tan, brown, cordovan, black, and navy.

Prices on these Rudy Tell Design Group purses are: left, style 895, $51.50; center, style 800, $55.00; right, style 837, $48.00.

Order from:

Rudy Tell Design Group
Route 2
Cosby, Tennessee 37722

BROOKS LEATHER DESIGN

Steve Brooks has been working with leather for eleven years and plans to continue for a long time: "I find great pleasure in playing with shape, color, form, volume. As long as I am still discovering new ways to use leather, I will be a leather craftsman." His intention is to begin with the best materials available and to create something with a clean, bold design.

Steve has a studio/shop near Chapel Hill, North Carolina, where he specializes in briefcases, luggage, and handbags. He also welcomes custom orders. His work is produced, from Steve's original designs, by himself and an apprentice.

A free brochure is available to you. Besides purses and briefcases, the brochure lists a Gladstone (an overnighter), a doctor's bag (also usable by photographers and plain travelers), the Portmanteau (weekend size), a variety case, and a handstitched Western hat with braided band and rakish lines. The brochure is updated each year to reflect the current popular designs.

Write to:

Brooks Leather Design
Route 1, Box 343
Pittsboro, North Carolina 27312

EGGS—SCRATCHWORK AND HANDPAINTED

These eggs feature original designs with much fine detail by Barbara Middleton. Mrs. Middleton of North Little Rock, Arkansas, is a member of the Ozark Foothills Handicraft Guild. She practices the nearly forgotten art of scratchwork eggs, which was once a Pennsylvania Dutch tradition. The scratchwork eggs are prepared by dyeing the eggs with a natural dye made from suitable plant materials such as onion skins (ruddy brown), sedge grass (ocher), or blueberries (dark blue). She then uses a sharp tool to scratch a design through the dye, revealing the white shell where the design has been scratched. The egg is then given a protective coat of varnish.

The painted eggs display detailed miniature scenes of wildlife, flowers, and butterflies on either the natural brown eggshell or black enameled eggs.

Mrs. Middleton also fashions jewelry boxes from eggshells; the eggshell is cut into two pieces with either scratchwork or handpainting decorating the hinged lid. The jewelry boxes are lined with delicate fabric complementing the color of the eggs.

	Price List
Scratchwork:	$15.00 (Hen size) and up
Painted:	$12.00 and up
Jewelry Boxes:	Individually Priced

Send inquiries to:

Mrs. Barbara Middleton
9107 Peach Tree
North Little Rock, Arkansas 72116

The Owl's Nest

Have you ever seen one of those stained wood plaques with apples and grapes—so real you want to take one off and pop it in your mouth? This is an example of tole painting.

Carole Hancock, who is a self-taught tole painter, has been teaching the art of tole for over four years. Her studio, The Owl's Nest, in Hot Springs, Arkansas, is a home studio that is open to the public by appointment.

In her home studio, Carole enjoys making special, made-to-order items. She has tole painted unusual wood pieces, as well as tinware, crock canisters, rub-outs, personalized family trees, and she welcomes requests for her paintings.

Whether you would like to have instruction in beginning, intermediate, or advanced tole painting; would like to place a special order; or just to visit, write:

Carole Hancock
Akers Road
Route 6, Box 654A
Hot Springs, Arkansas 71901

Country Homestead, Low Country Series

She-Crab Soup

Ringbearer's Pillow

THE COUNTING HOUSE

The Counting House at the Hammock Shop is on Pawley's Island—the South Carolina Low-Country coast's oldest summer resort—where a locally produced hammock is almost invariably found on the porch of the summer cottages.

The Counting House carries a complete line of counted-thread cross-stitch supplies. The designs we are showing here are from a group by Ginnie Thompson; she is also the author of the leaflet "The Case for Cross Stitch."

Write to:

The Counting House
at the Hammock Shop
Box 155
Pawley's Island, South Carolina 29585

Piney Woods, Low Country Series

People In A Boat, Low Country Series

LITTLE RIVER POTTERY

A small house in Townsend, Tennessee, which faces Highway 73 and has the Little River flowing past the back door, is the studio/shop of Alice and Jim Nichols. Jim is a potter, and Alice is needlecrafter and business manager. The shop is open weekends from the middle of April until the end of October, and mail orders are accepted year round. If you are in the neighborhood (it is only a few miles down the road from the northwest entrance to the Great Smoky Mountains National Park), stop by to see all the handcrafted items they have. Or order by mail some of the items shown here. The pottery is dishwasher- and oven-proof, but it will not survive if used directly on a range cooking element.

Prices for pottery items:

Candlesticks	$ 4.00 ea.
Planter, with rim (5" x 5")	6.00 ea.
Planter, with rim (includes jute hanger) (7" x 7")	9.00 ea.
Pitcher (16 oz.) (includes jute hanger)	5.00 ea.
Pitcher (32 oz.)	7.00 ea.
Honey Pot with Twirl (12 to 16 oz.)	9.00 ea.
Pig-Pen Holder	12.00 ea.
Pig Bank with Cork in Belly	12.00 ea.
Wren House	6.00 ea.
Candle Lantern (2½"-3" wide; 3"-4" tall)	4.00 ea.
Candle Lantern (3½"-4" wide; 5"-6" tall)	5.00 ea.

Ruth Carey

Prices for needlework items:

Eyelet pillows in 3 shapes (lace and ribbon trim, 10½" plus width of lace)	$ 8.00
Calico cat pillow (hand-embroidered features, 19" high)	$10.00

Measurements may vary slightly, since the items are individually made. When ordering, Tennessee residents should add 6% sales tax. For orders under $10.00, add $1.00 handling fee. Write to:

Little River Pottery
P.O. Box 143
Townsend, Tennessee 37882

QUALLA ARTS & CRAFTS MUTUAL, INC.

These Indian products come with a guarantee of authenticity. The name of the artist, the description of the object, and the materials used are all listed on a tag from the Indian Arts and Crafts Board of the U.S. Department of the Interior.

Qualla Arts & Crafts Mutual, Inc., is an Indian-owned and -operated cooperative of the Qualla Indian Boundary, Cherokee, North Carolina. This cooperative was founded in 1946 to encourage high standards for the products it sells and to find markets for handmade products. The sales shop was begun in 1960 and expanded in 1976.

To keep alive the arts and crafts of the Eastern Band of Cherokee Indians, workshops and exhibits are arranged. Three or four times a year, a gallery exhibition of outstanding craft work is arranged; so far, over twenty-five artists have had this exhibition. For each exhibition, a four-page brochure about the person and the craft is made available; samples of the front pages of these brochures are reproduced here.

Items sold in the shop usually are the work of women who produce crafts in their spare time. The person is paid at the time of purchase and, as a member, benefits from dividends and equity in the organization. Qualla has around 275 members; in the past five years, the organization has paid close to a million dollars for purchases.

For a brochure listing items which may be purchased, write to:
Qualla Arts & Crafts Mutual, Inc.
P.O. Box 277
Cherokee Indian Reservation
Cherokee, North Carolina 28719

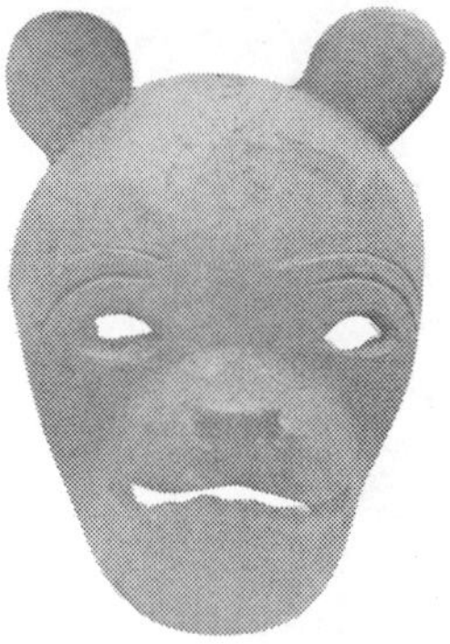

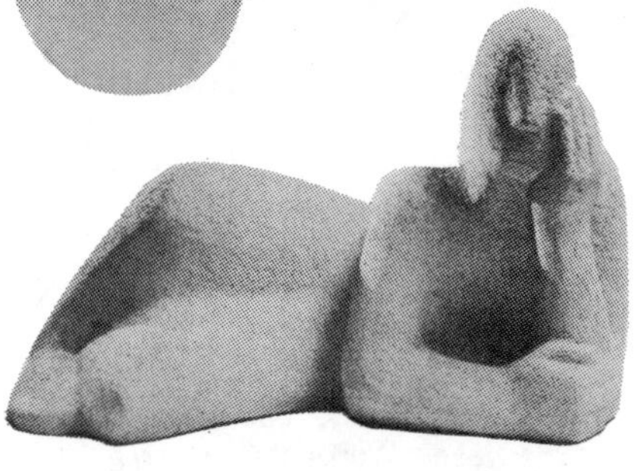

Brochures reproduced by permission of Indian Arts and Crafts Board, U.S. Department of the Interior

THE CHEROKEE INDIAN NATION

edited by Duane H. King

The University of Tennessee Press
Knoxville, Tennessee

"Indian Nations before the Whites are like balls of snow before the sun," declared a Cherokee chief in 1775 who correctly feared that the whites' desire for land would become insatiable. The ultimate effect of this action would leave a great many Cherokees homeless. This book gives the lie to the assertion that Cherokees spurned the white man and his ways and stoically refused to yield in the face of the enemy. The truth of the matter is that the Cherokees tried desperately for over 200 years to accommodate their ways and traditions to the whites, who steadily encroached upon their land.

There is an incredible chapter detailing the Cherokees' attempt to "civilize" themselves in white Southern eyes by becoming slaveholders. The traditional economics of the Cherokees decreed that they should shun both the accumulation of property and the acquisition of wealth beyond basic needs. Thus, Cherokee culture, which possessed no sense of racial identity before the advent of the whites, modified the system of human bondage that they had adopted from the whites. The result was expressed by the slave of a Cherokee removed to Oklahoma, "If I must be a slave, I had by far rather be a slave to an Indian than to a white man."

It would be a mistake to place all Cherokees in the "noble savage" category or to classify all whites as "devils." Some white men devoted long and tireless hours to the frustrating and unpopular Indian cause. Among the most notable were William A. Bowles and Will Thomas. Bowles, the son of a Maryland Tory, lived with the Creeks and later masqueraded as a Cherokee in England, gaining a position briefly in some of the highest places there. Constantly conniving and writing flamboyant letters, Bowles endeavored to establish trade relations between the Creek and Cherokee Indians and British free ports. Although his motives were suspect to many, Bowles led a dashing, adventurous life which is compelling enough to warrant serious study.

Will Thomas, less colorful than the flashy Bowles, nonetheless probably did more than any other white man to secure the Indians' claims to the land. In this thankless capacity, Thomas achieved true greatness. As a self-appointed attorney in Washington for the Cherokees, he devoted his life to an unpopular—even radical—cause. This 19th century humanitarian has long been neglected by most professional historians. The rights and financial claims of the Cherokees in North Carolina were the primary concern of this selfless man.

In this absorbing book, twelve contributors examine every aspect of Cherokee life: the hostilities of the 18th century, the turmoil caused by the forced removal from their lands in the 19th century, and the condition of the

Indian today. In shaking the truth out of the legends, many feet of clay are exposed. The voluntary martyrdom of Tsali is questioned and the greatness of Andrew Jackson is undermined by his callous handling of the Indian "situation." But the future holds the promise and must forgive the past as best it can. The Cherokees in North Carolina and Oklahoma are taking some remarkable steps to secure a better life. They are even beginning to revive their ancient tribal government.

Archaeologists, historians, anthropologists, and sociologists will find in this book new insights into the lives of these native Americans. Also, anyone at all interested in the American Indian cannot afford to pass up this fascinating study. —S.V.H.

HANDCRAFTED COAL FIGURINES

West Virginia is one of the leading coal producing states in the country and most often associated with the hardworking coal miner. Lillybrook House, Inc. in Coal City, West Virginia, specializes in handcrafted figurines made from coal.

"Big John," the coal miner, is one of the most interesting of them all, especially typifying the area. He stands 8" tall on a ¾" base made from coal—his dinner pail at his feet, also made from coal, holds his lunch and water supply for the day. The "at rest" stance emphasizes the weight he carries around his waist, the heavy mine belt with his tools and battery for safety light. In his mouth is the tobacco "chew" all miners use as protection against the fogging dust they constantly breathe. Heavy safety-toed shoes protect his feet as he crawls on his knees during his entire time inside the mines.

Other figurines available are: a rough textured bear, panther, cat, rabbit, elephant and a large or small owl.

Lillybrook House, Inc. will send you a catalogue upon request with a pricelist included—"Big John" retails for $10.00, including shipping. Check or money order must accompany all orders.

Lillybrook House, Inc.
Dept. 405, Jenkins Building
4 Parker Street
Coal City, West Virginia 25823

GAIL BOLVIG'S NEEDLE WORKS

The headline to this article can be interpreted in a couple of ways: one way is to translate it "The Needle Works of Gail Bolvig," the other is to read it as "Gail Bolvig's needle does work." Either is correct but even then the full significance of "Gail Bolvig's Needle Works" is not revealed, for while Gail Bolvig does excel in needlepoint and is an excellent teacher of the art, what she does the very best—better than almost anyone else we know about—is to design canvases for others to work.

There is no way that a catalogue such as this can show exactly how good Gail is at designing canvases, for part of her excellence is revealed in the subtle shadings she manages, first with her canvas design and then with her selection of yarns with which to work the design. Gail does only custom designs—she has no standard kits—but she will attempt to execute a custom design for almost any type of item which lends itself to needlepoint. She has created designs for such items as pictures, posters, picture frames, handbags, chair seats, church kneelers, pillows, belts, cummerbunds, ties, wastebaskets, rugs, phonebook covers, golf club covers, tennis racquet holders. . .the list is endless. And almost as endless are the types of designs she has created in the few years since her hobby became her business: coats of arms, home "portraits," portraits, hobby emblems, "potpourri" of family interests, flower prints, bird prints, a child's original drawing, abstract art, matching fabric designs, ad infinitum.

If you are interested in having Gail do a design for an item of yours, plan to spend at least $45.00 for the design, canvas, and yarn. This is a minimum price, but since each piece done by Gail is a custom one, the price for your design will depend upon the type of design, its size, and intricacy. Gail uses only Paternayan Persian wool yarns and mono-mesh canvas. Her living room is a sea of rainbow-colored yarns, kept in a floor-to-ceiling stack of ice cream containers.

Gail will be happy to correspond with you about doing a design. She has just finished filling the orders that resulted from the fact that she designed a needlepoint crest for her college sorority and when the other "sisters" got wind of it, they all wrote to Gail for one of their own.

You may write to her at this address:

Gail Bolvig's Needle Works
3404 Montevallo Road
Birmingham, Alabama 35213

FINE QUILTS

Martha Mitchell has received many blue ribbons for her work as an artist and for her exquisitely quilted covers and spreads. Her quilts are of traditional patterns in bright colors on sateen, satin, or fine cotton materials and are finished in intricate designs of quilting in small and symmetrical stitches. Her special trademark on each finished quilt is a dainty Briar stitch all around the edge. Mrs. Mitchell works on a commission basis: you can request color, size, and pattern and she will make your quilt.

Quilting is not Mrs. Mitchell's only talent; she paints in oils and will accept commissions to suit your decor. Her specialty is renderings of ancestral homes.

You may write to her and negotiate your quilt or painting.

Mrs. Martha Mitchell
Route 2, Box 34
Huntsville, Texas 77340

The Bird Nest

Glenna Grimmer, who is the "Bird Lady" of The Bird Nest, began her now flourishing profession just as a hobby. Today she devotes full time to carving birds out of balsa wood, painting them, and mounting them on pieces of driftwood or other natural pieces of wood she gathers during family vacations. In addition, she also makes bronzes of various birds, first sculpting them in wax, then reproducing them through the lost wax method of casting. All of her bronzes are signed and numbered as part of limited editions. Among the birds now available as bronzes are a roadrunner (both life-size and "mini-size"), wren, hummingbird, and owl. If you should desire a bird other than these, Ms. Grimmer will be happy to consider your request and execute the bronze on a special commission basis.

A particularly charming wood carving which Ms. Grimmer does is the "owl in a knothole." Each one is different, using a real knothole and the wood of that particular knothole for the owl carving. Ms. Grimmer considers the knothole "nature's frame," and indeed, no more perfect frame could be chosen for these owls. Of course, the sizes of the owls will vary, depending upon the sizes of the knotholes available. Ms. Grimmer has made some as small as 4" high, others as large as 15". When you order a "knothole owl," you take potluck, although Ms. Grimmer will make every effort to find a knothole of the size most suitable to you.

Ms. Grimmer also designs nature jewelry, primarily stick pins and tie tacks. She has a number of designs—the two shown are the owl and the roadrunner. The jewelry is made in sterling silver or antique gold over sterling; 14k gold is also available. Write to her for prices.

The Bird Nest
1106½ West Third
Carrollton, Texas 75006

"Wren on a Stump" in bronze—about $100.00.

WOODSTOCK TOYMAKER

Harry Griffith of Columbia, Mississippi, has a smile on his face—and another in the names of his toys. The animals are Tobias the Turtle, Denny the Dino, Oink the Pig, and the Corn-Fed Mouse. For those who fancy the fanciful, there is a Boone's Farm Dragon or a Unicorn Turning Somersault. Among the toys here are pull toys that do funny things and a number of trucks, trains, and planes. Puzzles are available in the shape of a lion, an elephant, a giraffe, a rabbit, a raccoon, or a deer. A telephone and an iron are also available. Rocking horses sell for $35.00. The giraffe is $45.00. The doll bed is $25.00 and the wheelbarrow, $30.00. Add 10% to all orders to cover shipping and handling.

Each toy is designed to be functional, safe, and fun to play with. Each is handmade of maple or black walnut hardwoods with dowel construction. There are no metal fasteners. The materials are non-toxic.

For orders or a free brochure, write to:

Woodstock Toymaker Harry Griffith
114 Marion Avenue
Columbia, Mississippi 39429

BULLRUSH BABY BASKET™: Start a family tradition with a charming classic portable bassinette. 30"L x 19"W x 18"H. $35.00 (ppd.) with free lining instructions or optional 2 piece quilted gingham liner and coverlet $13.00. (Specify yellow or light blue.) Write for catalogue of infant gifts and practical necessities. New Orleans Baby Company-Dept. OH; 5007 River Road; Box 4190; New Orleans, Louisiana 70178.

SCULPTURE—ONE DROP AT A TIME

In Eureka Springs, Arkansas, Mel and Marj Soderquist maintain a shop in which they sell handcrafted items. Marj takes care of the shop which sells their work and that of other people in the area. Among the items in their brochure are coat racks, candle lanterns, candle rachets, candle holders, and lamp stands of wood. These are made by Mel.

Mel also makes sculptures from flame-molten steel. Mel's father, who came from Sweden to Minnesota, was a blacksmith who started a garage. Mel grew up with a torch in his hand; his father taught him welding and blacksmithing. After a career in office equipment supply, Mel "retired . . . to be creative," says Marj in her letter. She also says, "He always loved wood and we bought old houses and office buildings and remodeled them. He has his woodworking shop and makes special order items, replaces broken parts of antiques, etc."

The sculptures which Mel makes take quite some time. He recently completed a group of miners for Ozark Lead Company; they took about twenty hours each. The sculpture shown in the close-up is called "Priming the Pump." Other items he has done are called "Going Fishing," and "Fisher in Boat."

To contact the Soderquists, write:

Mel Mar Shops
Route 1, Box 225
Eureka Springs, Arkansas 72632

NOTE CARDS. Katy Fidler of Morgantown, West Virginia, silk-screens traditional patchwork and appliqué designs to note cards. Silk-screening, though not considered a traditional craft, lends itself well to this use. The designs are applied to a creamy paper which provides a pleasant background for the colors used in the patterns. All of the printing and most of the other work involved in producing the cards is done by Katy, by hand. Katy currently produces 18 designs which are sold individually for $.65 or in packages of six assorted cards for $4.00. Write to Katy Fidler, 51 Richwood Avenue, Morgantown, West Virginia 26505.

Steve Payne

FOR WOOD PEOPLE

Are you a "wood" person? Do you love to run your hand over smoothly shaped wood and savor the grain and texture and almost feel the growing of the tree? The collector's box shown here will make you want to do just that. It is red oak, 13 inches by 9 inches by 6 inches deep, to hold your most precious collection. This exquisite box is the artistry of Bert Lustig, who made it at his workshop in his home. He also makes lamp bases out of a variety of woods: red oak, walnut, and cherry. Since he welcomes custom work, try him for imaginative treatment of wood pieces whose grain and texture you want enhanced.

Bert Lustig
Route 3, Box 194
Berkeley Springs, West Virginia 25411

APPALACHIAN STOOLS

Appalachia, along with areas of the Southwest and New England, is known to be one of the nation's centers for traditional handcrafted work. Items produced in this area are usually simple, yet elegant in design, sturdy, and able to fit in with almost any decor.

Appalachian Industries, Inc., has designed a line of stools, handcrafted, peg-legged, split-top, and wedged with contrasting Appalachian hardwoods. They are pictured along with a child's table and chair set. The stools shown are oil-finished and sanded. You may also order an Appalachian baby cradle, a rocker, a deacon's bench, a parson's table, and other pieces.

Write to them for prices.

Appalachian Industries, Inc.
Route 1, Box 6A
Vanceburg, Kentucky 41179

AMERICAN WICKER, INC.

The craftsmen around Boone, North Carolina, have gotten themselves somewhat together and their wares are being marketed throughout the country in specialty shops and department stores. Some of these items are shown here, but for the name of the store nearest you where you may buy these and a hundred other mountain crafts from the Blue Ridge area, write:

American Wicker, Inc.
Route 3, Church Road
Box 541-C
Boone, North Carolina 28607

MOLAS: BEAUTIFUL "BLOUSES"

On the Caribbean coast of northeastern Panama lies the Comarca de San Blas, a territory occupied by the Cuna Indians. Here, on a string of lovely islands called the Archipelago de las Mulatas, the Cuna Indian women still create the bright and beautiful panels of cloth which, sewn together, make their blouses. Called "molas," these blouses are actually several rectangular pieces of cloth which are layered and then cut and sewn into designs of great beauty and interest. The process could be called "reverse applique" and this is the term used by *Woman's Day* to describe the technique in an article published on "molas" several years ago: "Conventional applique is usually done by cutting shapes from fabric, turning under the raw edges to the shapes and then sewing them to another, larger piece of fabric to form a complete design. But the Cuna women work in reverse. They take several pieces of cotton fabric of different colors and baste them together along the outer edges; then working from the top layer down they cut through the various layers to create fanciful designs. As the shapes are cut out, the edges of the openings created are turned under and sewn to the fabric layers underneath. The color that shows through the openings depends upon the number of layers which are cut through in a particular place."

Nowadays the molas are prized by collectors and make marvelous wall hangings or framed prints. Alexander diFronzo is both a collector and importer of molas and is eager to spread the word about this truly ancient and relatively little-known craft. Mr. diFronzo became interested in molas when he conducted an army band and chorus which gave "people to people" concerts in the remote interior of Latin America. While conducting Christmas programs for the Cuna Indians of the Comarca de San Blas in 1964, he first saw and began acquiring molas. Since then he has built up quite a collection of them which has been exhibited throughout the South, and he also takes orders for molas and sells them through Pan-Am Exhibits, his shop in San Antonio.

Each mola is an original, so if you wish to order one, just state the size you desire and list the colors you wish to predominate in your design. You may also designate the motif you prefer, anything from birds, animals, fish, flowers, trees, geometrics to religious or op-art designs. Mr. diFronzo will take your request and match it as closely as possible to an existing mola or will commission one expressly for you.

For more information and current prices of the molas, write:

Alexander diFronzo
Pan-Am Exhibits
3743 Highcliff
San Antonio, Texas 78218

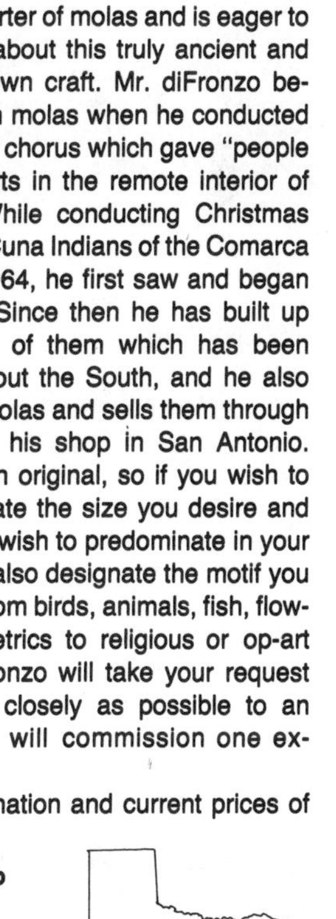

Sign of the Peacock

An interesting—and free—catalogue is available from the Sign of the Peacock. Below are shown several of the items that may be ordered.

Sign of the Peacock
Cashiers, North Carolina 28717

Gnomes from J.L.T. Needlepoint on front and back. The large kits (10" tall) sell for $16.50 prepaid; small ones (shown) (6" tall) are $11.50 prepaid. Male and female versions of gnomes are available in both sizes.

American primitive artist Clementine Hunter is the genius of Melrose Plantation in Louisiana. Reproductions of her work, hand painted on #12 needlepoint canvas, are now available for you to stitch.

In the Baptizin', red robed clergy do the honors. The complete kit is $43.50 prepaid; the canvas only, $33.50 prepaid.

Pecan Harvest is a bright and happy scene of a bountiful crop. The complete kit is $43.50 prepaid; the canvas only is $33.50 prepaid.

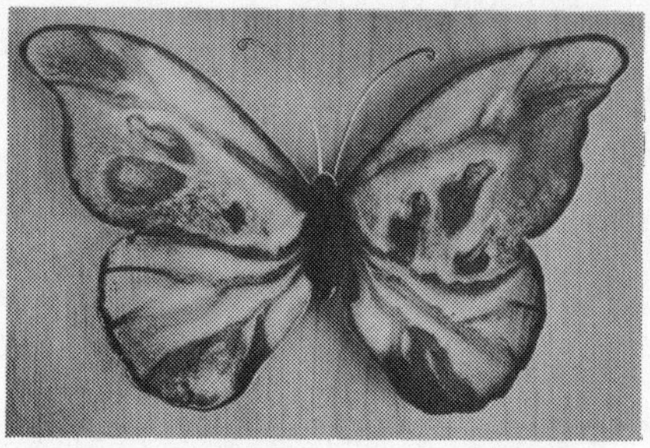

COPPER ENAMELING

Copper enameling, particularly that done in miniature, is a time-consuming and exacting work.

Peggy Palmitier of Pampa, Texas, is a copper enamelist who creates miniatures from 2" square to 5" x 7". These come either mounted on blocks of walnut or framed. She designs still life and floral sprays. She also does boxes with colorfully enameled tops. These Peggy does by using stencils of real leaves pressed flat or by using an aluminum screen. Sometimes she cuts her own stencils using a contemporary design. Prices for her work range from $10.00 up depending on the intricacy of design and whether framed or mounted.

Peggy also makes beads which are enameled on ⅛" and 3/16" copper tubing. She cuts butterflies from copper and then enamels them. Some are mounted on wood and some are framed. A picture of one of her butterflies is reproduced here for you. You may write to her to request a miniature copper enameling in your choice of color and style.

Peggy Palmitier
Box 1820
Pampa, Texas 79065

WILDFLOWERS IN THREE DIMENSION

A bit of nature preserved for your enjoyment—whether you select a picture designed with preserved flowers, one of preserved butterflies, or a combination of the two, or a dome with preserved butterflies "in flight," the work of Janice Logan and her family will truly be a joy for all seasons. All of the flowers are mounted on velveteen and trimmed around the outside of the picture using the same material. Please indicate your first and second color choice from antique gold, black, avocado green, French blue, royal blue, or chocolate brown. Your own color swatches are welcome.

Also available are butterflies arranged as if "in flight" on driftwood collected by the Logans on their own farm. The arrangements are completed with real lichens, brackets, fungi, and preserved leaves, which the Logans also collect and preserve. Mr. Logan completes the effect by making all of the wooden bases himself of solid hand-rubbed walnut or cherry, which he personally logged. The entire arrangement is then sealed under glass or plexiglas for your enjoyment.

Three of Ms. Logan's arrangements are shown here. To order or to inquire about other designs, write:

Wildflowers in Three Dimension
Janice Logan
Route One
Fayetteville, Tennessee 37334

WEAVERS WORKSHOP LTD.

Weavers Workshop, Ltd., is a very unique store. Located in the Riverbend area of New Orleans, it is a block from the trolley line and another block from the Mississippi River levee. The old cottage that houses the Workshop has a tin roof and barge board walls in the front room gallery.

Four professional weavers—Annette Adler, Phyllis Mayronne, June Steinbaugh, and Barbara Threefoot—have been running the shop for seven years now. They have an eclectic selection of yarns—mostly natural fibers—lush mohairs, Donegal tweeds, Mexican yarns, silks, cottons, and linens. They have a collection of over four hundred fiber books and are dealers for Leclerc, Schacht, and Ulltex looms. Their stock also includes Ashford and Haldane spinning wheels and a good selection of spinning fibers. Everything for the handweaver and spinner is under the old tin roof.

In the front room gallery is a beautiful assortment of handwoven things. Draped over the old skeinwinder and drying rack are handsome, handwoven woolen afghans, mohair and wool shawls, and scarves. Sitting on top of the old wooden bobbins is a wonderful collection of wool and mohair hats. Every piece is individually crafted, and there are no two alike.

Afghans, shawls, scarves, and hats are available from the shop in the following sizes and price range: wool or wool and mohair afghans approximately 45" x 72", $100 and up; shawls of mohair or mohair and other fibers approximately 24" x 82", $50 and up; scarves of mohair, mohair and wool, or wool approximately 10" x 60", $25 and up; hats, mostly mohair and brushed wool, $20 and up.

Weavers Workshop Ltd.
716 Dublin Street
New Orleans, Louisiana 70118

WILDFLOWER DESIGNS FOR NEEDLEWORK

by Adalee Winter

Oxmoor House, Inc.
Birmingham, Alabama

Even the most hardened cynic usually has a touch of the romantic in him when it comes to wildflowers. Whether they bring back childhood memories, fantasies, or simple hopes for spring, flowers are always a welcome sight to adults and a perpetual delight to inquisitive children.

Mrs. Winter makes the interesting observation that a study of wildflowers also provides a study of geography, botany, and history. An example of the latter is found in the story of the fleur-de-lis. The king of the Franks was trapped with his army on a riverbank by the Goths. He noticed that throughout the riverbed in certain places there were irises growing. Deducing from this discovery that the river must be shallow in those spots, the king and his army waded across the river and escaped annihilation by the Goths. Later, when this king became Charles V of France, he deliberately chose the iris or fleur-de-lis as the royal emblem of France.

In *Wildflower Designs for Needlework*, there is, first of all, a section devoted to a description of the flower, the derivation of its name, the places where it can be found, and a bit of history concerning it. Beautiful watercolor illustrations of the flower accompany this information. The second part of the book gives the needlework chart and lists the colors you should use when working. Then follow instructions on how to make a rug, working from a charted design, working cross-stitch and needlepoint, blocking needlepoint, and how to choose colors and materials.

This colorful multi-faceted book is just as much for the flower fancier as for those who do needlepoint. The book should enjoy a potpourri of fans and readers. —S.V.H.

HANDMADE VIOLAS

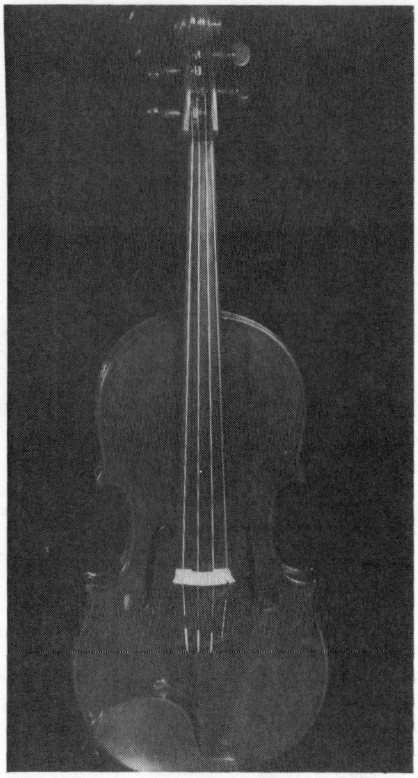

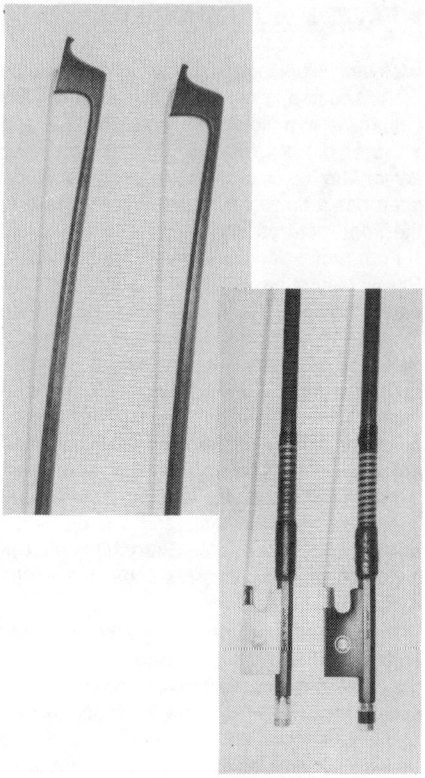

John Sipe makes violas—he inherits his craft from relatives who migrated to America in the 1760s from Germany.

One of the most beautiful of his violas is designed to suit the needs of the player in a large orchestra. It is 17 inches in body length with a string length of 15¼ inches. Although this viola is of large dimensions, it is very comfortable to handle; the upper bouts are sloping to make shifting into the higher positions easier. Acoustically, the viola plays well in all positions from the high notes to the low C string. A specially designed tailpiece allows more tension on the C string, therefore giving it greater ability.

The varnish is made entirely by Mr. Sipe from natural ingredients created in the beginning of time, and could have been used by the Italian makers of Cremona. Varnishing the viola is a most delicate operation, requiring a lot of time and skill to bring it to a state of perfection—and Mr. Sipe has achieved exquisite perfection.

A testimonial to Mr. Sipe's work from James McCauly, Violist—Fayetteville Orchestra—Fayetteville, North Carolina:

> "The 17-inch symphony model viola you made for me is the most exciting instrument I have ever played. The increased dynamic range and tone quality is much greater than one might expect after playing smaller instruments. This new instrument is easier to play and offers superior tone quality to many of the older instruments I have tried, at much less cost."

The price of this symphony viola is $3,000.00; purchasers will be given approximate delivery time when ordering and trade-ins will be accepted as part payment.

Mr. Sipe is also a Bow Maker. He has studied bow making in England with W. E. Hill and Son, renowned experts in violin and bow making. Mr. Sipe describes his bows: "Bows are made from *Pernambuco*, a wood that grows in Brazil, South America, and is imported here. The frog or nut is made from ebony, ivory, horn, and T'shell. The fittings are silver and gold on these frogs. In some ways it is even more of an art to make a fine bow. The bow prices range from $500.00 to $1200.00, depending on the fittings and general outcome of the bow."

Write to:

John Sipe Violin Company
708 Central Avenue
Charlotte, North Carolina 28204

"Pillow Talk" will brighten your home with soft sculpture. You will find them so cheerful and easy to make that you will want several. Choose flower, butterfly, tulip, mushroom or ladybug in yellow, blue, pink, green or red. Pattern, $2.00 each postpaid; Kit, $7.95 each postpaid. (Stuffing not included.) Brochure $.50 or free with order. Order from Stitch 'n Stuff, Dept. OH, 4900 Winthrop West, Fort Worth, Texas 76116.

PRESSED FLOWER STATIONERY. Stationery fashioned from pressed flowers and plants is designed and made by Edna N. Staley. The stationery includes 10 notes to a box and sells for $5.00 retail; gift enclosure cards come 12 to a box and are $2.50 retail.

Mrs. Staley also makes ceramic original plates. Her 10¾" wedding plate is $25.00; 8" child's birth plate, $10.00. The plates are hand-painted with sgraffito decoration. These are designed according to the customer's desired color and pattern. Order from: Mrs. Edna N. Staley, 66 Orchard Drive, New Martinsville, West Virginia 26155.

CREATIONS

Rt. 1 - Box 405
Millstone
West Virginia 25261

Alice Stough sounds like a very nice lady (from her letters), and she is *obviously* a very talented one. Alice spins, knits, and crochets, and, in the summer of 1978, she was one of only five craftspersons to win an Award of Excellence at the Mountain State Art and Craft Fair, held in West Virginia.

Alice lives with her husband and their three children on a 111-acre farm. They raise their own flock of colored-sheep—different shades of browns, blacks, and grays. Alice tells us that her husband grows all of the food for the flock and cares for them, and she cards and spins their wool to use in her knitting and crocheting. She uses only hand-spun yarns and only natural undyed colors. Also, she leaves all the oils in the wool, making the finished products naturally waterproofed, mothproofed, and dirt resistant.

The pullover sweaters (pictured) are available in small, medium, and large. A woman's sweater costs $65.00; man's sweater costs $70.00; and a child's sweater costs $35.00. Alice also makes cardigan sweaters, which are $8.00 higher than the cost of the pullovers.

Yarn color (natural undyed shades only) samples will be sent upon request for $1.00, which is refundable on the first order.

Alice makes several other items that you might be interested in writing to her about—rugs made from jute welt cord and poncho and hat sets.

SAND CREEK LEATHER

Sand Creek Leather, located at 7045 Old Canton Road, may be reached by taking the Natchez Trace Parkway north of Jackson and exiting at the Ross Barnett Reservior exit, 3 miles from Interstate 55. The gallery is located one mile to the south (to the right) on Old Canton Road.

Marion and Chuck Cuendet opened Sand Creek Leather in 1972. This custom leather shop specializes in everything from apparel such as suits, capes, and sandals; accessories such as attachés, legal journals, and doctor's cases; to home furnishings such as wall pieces and screens. The Cuendets write, "Though providing a continual variety of pieces for sale in our gallery off the Natchez Trace north of Jackson, Mississippi, we also create many custom and commissioned pieces for leather lovers all over America. We combine a unique blend of exotic hardwoods and bark-tanned leather, giving our work a contemporary quality with traditional styling."

Their prices range from $20 to $500 and up.

DOCTOR'S BAG. 14" x 10" x 10". Hand-dyed, vegetable-tanned cowhide with sculpted walnut handle and latches. Molded end pockets. $200.00.

Three items that may be ordered through the mail include a camera case, a doctor's bag, and a grip. Write to:

Sand Creek Leather
7045 Old Canton Road
Jackson, Mississippi 39211

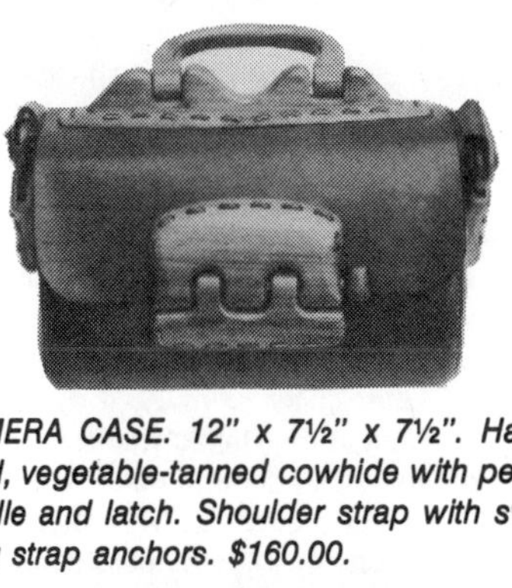

CAMERA CASE. 12" x 7½" x 7½". Hand-dyed, vegetable-tanned cowhide with pecan handle and latch. Shoulder strap with swiveling strap anchors. $160.00.

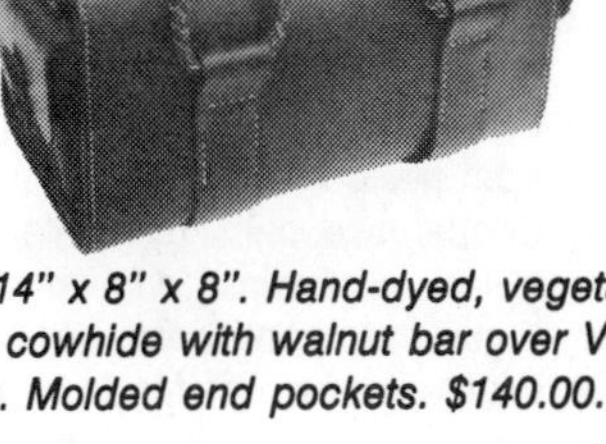

GRIP. 14" x 8" x 8". Hand-dyed, vegetable-tanned cowhide with walnut bar over Velcro closure. Molded end pockets. $140.00.

PEACHTREE NEEDLECRAFTS

Here is a kit which includes everything necessary to complete a woven afghan which is 48" x 63": 100% cotton basketweave material, 7 oz. of wool yarn, needle, directions, and diagram. The kit is available in a choice of three colors: spring, autumn, and blue. The yarn is variegated and insures the random pattern of the flame stitch.

The afghan kit is $18.00 plus $1.00 postage.

Peachtree Needlecrafts also sells a flame stitch skirt kit for $16.00 plus $1.00 postage and a pillow kit for $6.00 plus $1.00. The skirt is available in a combination of orange, gold, and green; pink, green, and brown; or shades of blue. The pillow comes in shades of blue, shades of gold, or shades of olive green. Order from:

Peachtree Needlecrafts
435 Heritage Way, N.E.
Atlanta, Georgia 30328

Owners of Peachtree Needlecrafts are, left to right, Barbara Hyde and Nancy Crowther. Nancy is wearing a flame stitch skirt.

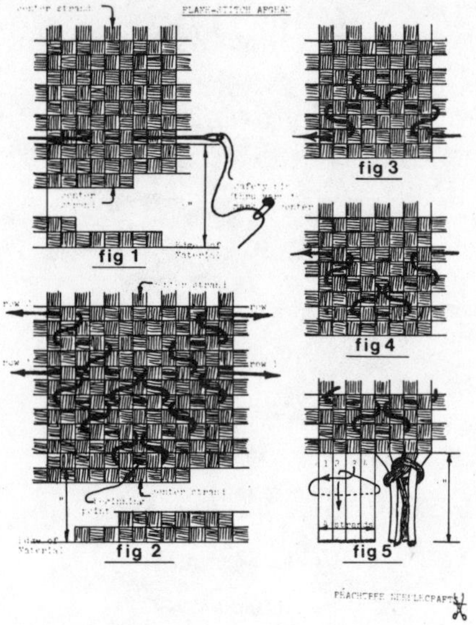

OKLAHOMA INDIAN ARTS AND CRAFTS COOPERATIVE

The Oklahoma Indian Arts and Crafts Cooperative, through its shop located in the Southern Plains Indian Museum and Crafts Center in Anadarko, offers for sale a diverse line of authentic Indian arts and crafts.

Founded in 1955, the Cooperative is comprised of more than 50 members representing 12 Indian tribes of Oklahoma. Each member of the Cooperative owns a share of the enterprise and receives an annual dividend based on a percentage of his total annual production for the Cooperative. Included among the Cooperative's membership are some of the most talented Indian artists and craftsmen in Oklahoma.

Jewelry pieces are among the distinctive items produced by the Cooperative. We are featuring here jewelry made by the Indians from German silver.

German silver, also known as nickel silver, is a non-ferrous alloy of copper, nickel, and zinc which was invented in Hildburghausen, Germany, in the second decade of the 19th century. Later in the century, it came to be manufactured in the United States. The silver is tough yet malleable and takes a good polish. It was first brought to the Indians of the Southern Plains by traders. More durable and less costly than true silver, German silver appealed greatly to the practical nature of the Southern Plains Indian craftsmen, who were essentially nomadic people. With no elaborate workshop needed to fashion German silver into ornaments of beauty, the craftsmen could easily transport their equipment as they moved from place to place.

The Cooperative sells many items other than jewelry: moccasins, original paintings, suede bags, and Indian costumes. You can own a double warbonnet for $200.00 or an adult warbonnet for $100.00. They also have on hand a large selection of pow-wow drums priced from $35.00 to $100.00.

You may write the Cooperative and obtain a complete list of what is available and the prices.

Oklahoma Indian Arts and Crafts Cooperative
P.O. Box 966
Anadarko, Oklahoma 73005

WHITE WEDDING DRESS. Bride or party beautiful. Pure white stitched Mexican cotton, square yoke, lavish with lace, yards and yards of pure loveliness. Sizes 6-14. $130.00.

OAXACA WEDDING DRESS. A classic. Lavish hand embroidery in joyful multi-colors, hand-crocheted edging. A stunning at-home or party dress, and it's machine washable, dryer perfect. White background. Sizes 3-12 only. $62.00. Also comes with short embroidered cap sleeve.

BOUTIQUE BEAUTIES

Angelita Boutique of San Antonio, Texas, capitalizes upon the cultural relationship between Texas and Mexico. Angelita carries Mexican designer clothes, wedding dresses, and an international collection of beautiful things. The emphasis is upon natural fibres, hand-weaving, embroidery, color, and design.

Besides the things shown here, a catalog which is available upon request also shows long gauze dresses, a Mexican fisherman's sweater, a pure Alpaca cap or poncho from Bolivia, a Mexican village blouse with exquisite hand embroidery, and for men, a Mexican wedding shirt. Imports other than Mexican include a caftan and a clutch which is a melange of peacock, guinea, and pheasant feathers and comes from China.

Prices given in captions include shipping costs, but Texas residents should add 5½% sales tax. For orders or a catalogue, write:

Angelita Boutique
416 Paseo De La Villita
San Antonio, Texas 78205

ARROWCRAFT SHOP AND CONTEMPORARY GALLERY

In 1912, as a memorial to its founders, the Pi Beta Phi fraternity established a Settlement School in Gatlinburg, Tennessee, in the foothills of the Great Smoky Mountains. In 1925, Pi Phi opened the Arrowcraft Shop in Gatlinburg in order to furnish an outlet for the crafts produced in the area. Another milestone came in 1945 with the beginning of the Summer Craft Workshops in conjunction with the University of Tennessee, which provided college accreditation and paved the way for the present Arrowmont School of Arts and Crafts.

"Arrowcraft" is the registered name applied to all articles produced and marketed through the Arrowcraft Shop. Contemporary, as well as traditional, designs are created by a weaving specialist and translated into table linens, handbags, stoles, towels, and other articles by men and women working on their looms at home. Arrowcraft Shop is also a treasure house of fine native wood carvings, basketry, broom making, modern ceramics, and metal work.

You may visit the Arrowcraft Shop and Gallery on the Parkway between 8:00 a.m. and 5:00 p.m. Monday through Saturday, or send for their catalogue "Arrowcraft" which gives pictures, prices, and mail-ordering information on all their products.

Arrowcraft Shop and Gallery
P.O. Box 567
Gatlinburg, Tennessee 37738

SELECTIVE CREATIONS in Tamarac, Florida, is a new company which offers hand-sculptured mirrors with hand-beveled edges. The mirrors include a 14" x 16" butterfly, a 22" x 10½" seagull, a 12½" x 13" angelfish, and a 15" x 8½" dolphin. The price of each is $19.95 plus $3.00 postage. Write to Irene at 8 Pleasant Hill Lane, Tamarac, Florida 33319.

KENTUCKY HILLS INDUSTRIES

Kentucky Hills Industries of Pine Knot is an association of craftspeople making and marketing choice homecrafts that adorned the homes of our early pioneers. The "Bootjack Shelf," "Butterfly Table," and the "Old Milk Stool" are replicas of those used in the days of Daniel Boone and John Finley when Cumberland Gap was a part of the "Old Warriors Trail."

Kentucky's genuine mountain crafts are widely known as a part of the true culture of the land of horse racing, mint juleps, Cumberland Falls, majestic lakes, and beautiful hills.

Once Kentucky Hills Industries was a part of the household of Elma and Smith Ross of Pine Knot. Through the cooperation of the Farmers Home Administration, Kentucky Hills Industries has been broadened and developed into a nonprofit marketing association. Crafted items reproduced by families of the Appalachian Region of Kentucky are being marketed over a wide area by direct mail and from a sales room in Pine Knot, Kentucky.

The purpose of the nonprofit corporation is twofold:

1) To perpetuate the superior homecrafts of pioneer days, for which Kentucky has long been noted, and bring them to the outside world at reasonable prices.
2) To help the mountain folks find a market for the products of their skills so they too may have a better life—better homes, better clothes, better food, better medical care, and the extended opportunity for educating their children.

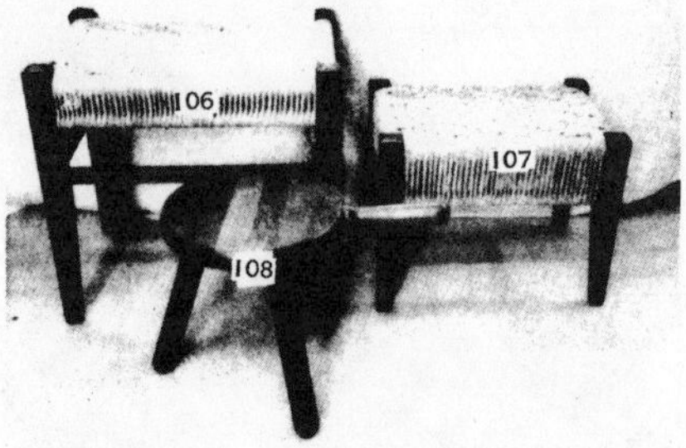

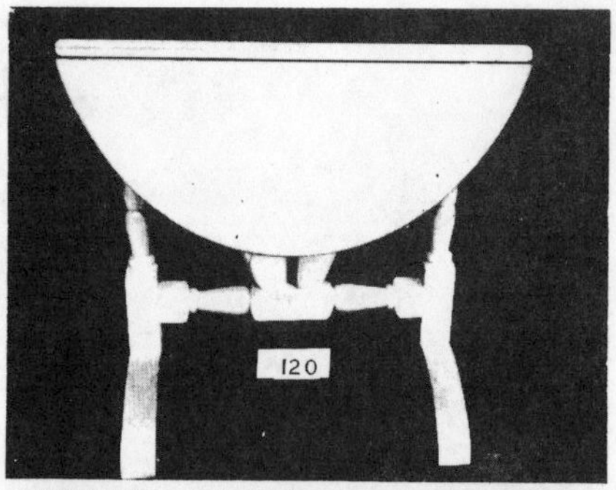

Kentucky Hills Industries has a catalogue picturing 146 handcrafted items which they will send you along with a pricelist free. This catalogue has a number of furniture items handmade from walnut or cherry including a four-poster bed, several varieties of tables, a gun cabinet, corner cupboard, serving tray and stand, and hutch.

Write for the complete listing of these crafts of the Kentucky hills:

Kentucky Hills Industries, Inc.
Box 186
Pine Knot, Kentucky 42635

DOROTHY LINSLEY, POTTER

In 1971, Dorothy Linsley fired her first load of pots in a home-built kiln and embarked on a career in stoneware pottery, to which she now devotes full time. Dorothy uses two clay bodies which she designed. They are a toasty brown stoneware and a burnt-brick red flameproof ware. Most of her work is done on a potter's wheel, but a good many pieces have hand-built parts added. The clays and glazes are mixed from dry milled clays and other chemicals, biscuit-fired to about 1900 degrees, then glazed and fired a second time to 2300 degrees in a reduction atmosphere. About three times every two months, she fires 28 cubic feet of pots in a downdraft kiln with four natural-draft gas burners. Dorothy and her husband, Clyde, built the kiln and are nearing completion on a new studio and gallery which they call "Turtle Creek Pottery". Located five miles from Little Rock in the woods off Arkansas Highway 10, it is a unique post-and-beam, rough-sawn cypress, board-and-batten structure, oriented solar south.

Dorothy's 25 years' experience as a painter prior to becoming a potter has made her sensitive to visual, as well as tactile, aesthetics, and she tries to create functionally proper ware that is visually exciting. She has had no formal training in pottery and has learned through books, discussions with potter friends, and, more importantly, from reams of notes made from results of endless experiments.

Dorothy is a member of Ozark Foothills Handicraft Guild and wholesales to their shops in Hardy, Heber Springs, Mountain View, and the Arkansas Folk Center. The bulk of her work is retailed at various crafts fairs, including War Eagle, and from Turtle Creek Pottery in Little Rock.

Shown here, as one example of Dorothy's work, is a large salad bar or chip-and-dip ("Shard Plant" series) with a hinged lid, ladle, four wine goblets, and a one-quart decanter with corked stopper. Sets similar to this are $180.00 plus shipping costs and a $2.00 packing fee. Two or three months should be allowed for delivery.

Write to:

Dorothy Linsley
Turtle Creek Pottery
Hwy. 10, Rt. 5, Box 473-A4
Little Rock, Arkansas 72212

A FEATHER IN YOUR HAT

Once during a slack time at a craft fair, Victoria Huey started playing with some pheasant feathers she had brought along. "I made a few pieces of feather jewelry and put them out on the card table and sold them all. That encouraged me to start working with feathers on a serious basis. Since my husband and I both wear western hats all the time, I started making feather hatbands." Soon she was getting orders for these as well as pins, brooches, and necklaces made from feathers.

For information on an elegant hatband or other feather jewelry, write to:

Victoria Huey
Leatherwood Crafts
Southwest Mall
Little Rock, Arkansas 72209

OLD FASHIONED WOODEN TOYS BY ED THE TOYMAKER

Edward Law makes old fashioned wooden toys. Ed has attempted to copy, as nearly as possible, the construction methods of old, and where possible, the joints are wood, with wooden pins locking them in position. The painting of the toys is done by Ed and his wife Eleanor.

"Ed the Toymaker," as Mr. Law is known, is a member of the Ozarks Craft Guild and exhibits each year at the Guild's craft fairs in Mountain View and Heber Springs, Arkansas.

The following wooden toys are made in Ed's workshop:

ACROBAT (Man on a trapeze)
AX MEN (Two men chopping a log)
BALANCING DOLL
CAPERING TOYS (Clown, Hillbilly, Raggedy Ann and Andy)
CHICKEN BOARD (Chickens and rooster pecking at seed)
DANCING BOY ON A BOARD
DANCING HILLBILLY DOLL AND PADDLE
DONKEY CARTS
MALLARD DUCK BOARD
MARIONETTES
MYSTERY SPINNERS
PAINTED WALKING DOLLS WITH STICK (Boys, Girls, Indians, George Washington, Grenadier Soldier)
PULL TOYS (Dog, Horse, Rabbit)
RECIPE OWL
RING TOSS (Boys, Duck, Elephant)
SAW MEN (Two men sawing a log)
SNOW GOOSE BOARD
TUMBLING CLOWN ON PARALLEL BARS
TIC TAC TOE BOARD
UNPAINTED WALKING DOLL WITH STICK

A brochure and prices (please specify retail or wholesale) will be mailed upon request.

Mr. Edward Law
Route 6, Box 51
Mountain Home, Arkansas 72653
Telephone: 501-492-5938

MYTIK

"Mytik" is what Molly Voight calls her own personal style of batik. The piece we saw was startling—a rainbow of what appeared to be streams of stuffed plush, surrounding a rectangular mirror. The rainbow was in the brightest primary and secondary colors. The entire piece was 25" x 25".

Molly described her process. She uses "batik (wax resist), block print, screen print, direct application, and combinations of these techniques. These are all applied to various types of fabrics, using procion fiber-reactive dyes, which are of industrial strength and totally colorfast." The dyed fabrics are then stitched and stuffed using a trapunto technique.

Molly also does more traditional batik. She says she uses a particular innovation until other people start copying it. Then she simply invents another process.

Her work currently is either in full rainbow colors or progressions of brown. She can match color samples, and if you will send her a picture of the area of your house where you need a piece of her work, she can suggest what she might have to suit it and will send slides. Her price range is $15 to $500.

Here are some examples of her work. The plush rainbow with mirror is approximately 25" x 25". For information write to:

Molly Voight
9616 Red Lane Drive
Birmingham, Alabama 35215
(205) 833-1903

"There is a lesson in tradition, a sense of right FORM, a correctness in ordinary utilitarian utensils, that express a whole culture." From COMMON CLAY/INDIANA REVISIONS by Charles Counts, A.G. Halldin, Publisher.

SOME OLD-FASHIONED DOLLS

"Jed Clampett" (15 inches high) and "Granny" (11 inches high) sell for $25.00 each (postage $1.00 each).

"Will Rogers" and "Carrie Nation" each sell for $25.00 a kit (plus $1.00 each doll for postage).

Pink bisque dollhouse dolls include a grandfather, grandmother, little girl, mother, father, little brother, nurse, chauffeur, and baby. Each kit costs $7.50 (postage $1.00).

Ann Decker of Eureka Springs, Arkansas, has the right approach to retirement: "Find a hobby and enjoy it if you want to be happy, healthy, and interesting—at least to yourself—in your retirement. Get started before it is time to retire and hold on to your enthusiasm whether it is for pleasure or profit."

The hobby Ann found, actually many years before her retirement time came about, was the creation of bisque doll kits. It all started when Ann's daughter and her five nieces were collecting storybook dolls, and Ann decided to use a little of what she had learned in a ceramics course she had taken in a college in her hometown of Chickasha, Oklahoma, to add to their collections. She got so interested in making dolls that she set up a studio in her home which she continued until the death of her husband forced her to devote all her time to running a bookkeeping service office. The hundreds of molds she had made over the years she gave to a senior citizens center.

The hobby was put aside, but not forgotten, and while watching the television program "The Beverly Hillbillies," Mrs. Decker decided to try her hand again at modeling "Granny" and "Jed Clampett." She was soon back in the swing of things about dollmaking: modeling the doll, making the mold, pouring, painting, glazing, and firing the doll to completion.

Ann's newest doll is Carrie Nation. The doll is made of clay from the local Onyx Cave. As Ann describes her character, "Carrie traveled everywhere—giving lectures, breaking up saloons with her hatchet, getting herself in and out of jails. She had a home here which is now a museum—Hatchet Hall." Eureka Springs is celebrating its centennial this year, and Ann's Carrie Nation is the official centennial doll.

In the picture with Carrie Nation, who lacked a sense of humor, is Will Rogers, who certainly did not. Of this doll, Ann says, "I modeled my Will Rogers doll about 30 years ago. Since 1979 is 100 years from his date of birth, I took the head off and made a mold and now have put the dolls on the market. I modeled mine from a statue in the Will Rogers Museum in Claremore, Oklahoma. On my doll I put two left feet as he always said he was so awkward because he had two left feet. The dolls I sell do have a matched pair."

Ann Decker's wonderful bisque doll kits are available to you. The kits include head, arms, legs, body pattern, and easy to follow instructions. The variety of dolls available is large, from dollhouse dolls made to a scale of 1 inch equals 1 foot, to regal 18-inch dolls. The kits cost from $7.50 to $35.00 each. Ann makes sixty-five different dollhouse dolls. For a fully illustrated catalogue, send $1.00 to:

Dolls by Ann Decker
Department SL
79½ Spring Street
Eureka Springs, Arkansas 72632

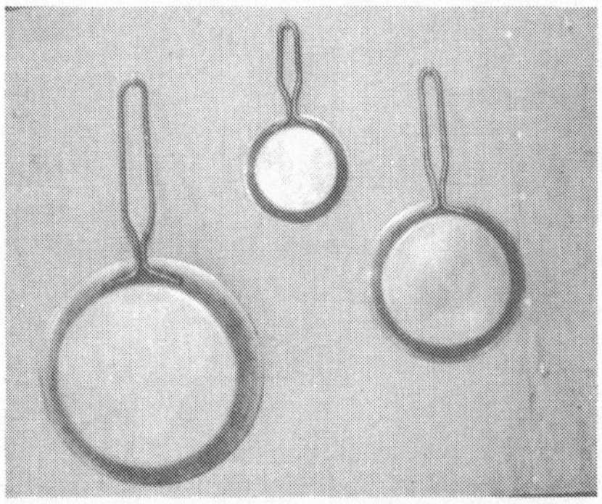

SPUN METAL CRAFTS

Metalspinning, one of the oldest crafts in the world, is another of the crafts that is in danger of becoming a lost art in this age of push button mass production. But one of those craftsmen who still spin metal to absolute perfection is Helmut Koechert and he has been doing so for over 25 years.

Koechert spins pewter, copper, and brass in his shop; all are elegantly plain in design. Each item is signed and will become an heirloom of tomorrow.

To learn to spin metal, a person must serve an apprenticeship lasting about five years. During this time he learns to make his own tools and forms, to maintain and repair his spinning lathe, and to know the characteristics of each kind of metal. It takes strength as well as skill to spin the various metals over the forms, and he must develop an eye for spinning as well as a feel for it. Helmut Koechert has done all these things.

Write to:

HeDKo Spun Metal Crafts
Route 1, Glades Road
Gatlinburg, Tennessee 37738

MILDRED ATKINS, POTTER

Mildred Atkins is a potter who makes both wheel-thrown and hand-built pottery. A number of her works are shown here for your information. To order, you may write:

Mildred Atkins
1208 Des Moines Avenue
Morgantown, West Virginia 26505

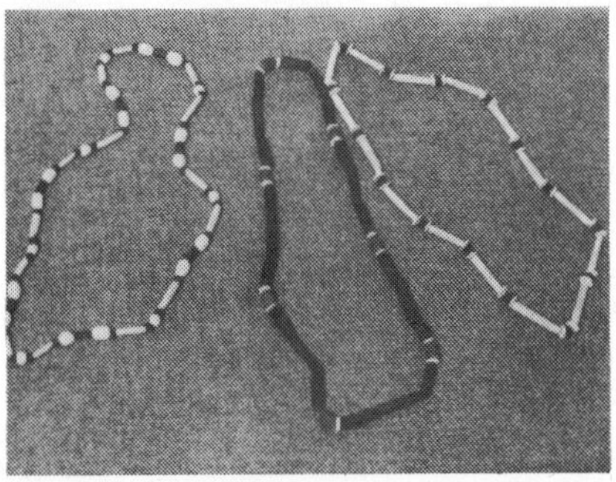

NECKLACES of unglazed hand-formed clay beads. 26" long. Earth tones or pastel blues or greens. $16.00. Matching earrings, ¾" to 1½" dangles, for pierced ears, $3.00. Postage $1.00 for necklace or set, $.50 for earrings only.

WIND CHIMES—"You Gotta Kiss A Lot of Frogs Before You Find a Prince." Pale, muted greens in unglazed porcelain. Dozens of frogs surround the princess, producing a singing, tinkling waterfall of sound in the faintest breeze. Small (pictured) $25.00; large, $45.00. Postage, $2.00.

CAMPUS CRAFTS

Weaving has long been an important part of the cultural heritage in the Southern Appalachian region. For many years the Campus Crafts at Annville Institute have contributed extensively to this valuable tradition. Their handsomely woven articles have been admired by people from all over the United States.

We feel that you will be more than pleased with the crafts you receive from Campus Crafts.

Dorothy and Enos Brockman, who worked in this project at Annville Institute for 30 years, bought the equipment and are teaching people to weave on their own since the closing of the school in the spring of 1978.

You may write for their free brochure and pricelist showing all the items made at Annville and are welcome at any time to visit their shop:

Campus Crafts
Dorothy Brockman
Annville, Kentucky 40402

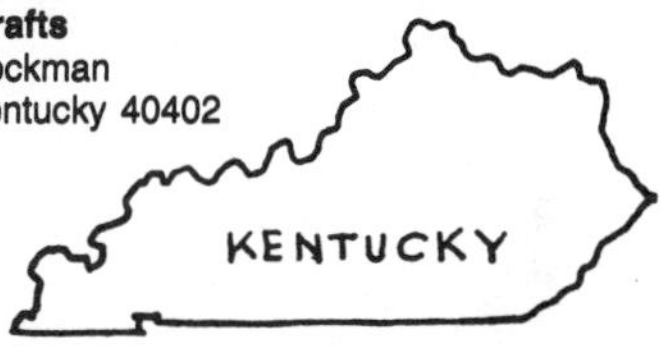

THE FRONT PORCH

The Front Porch, in Greenville, South Carolina, is a miniature shop owned and operated by Tom Henry and his family. In the beginning, this was a retail "full size" furniture store specializing in renovations of homes and businesses. About three years ago, Tom Henry was asked by one of his friends to build a dollhouse for her small daughter. Mr. Henry, the father of four boys, had no conception of what "scale" a dollhouse should be, so he simply built what looked all right to him. The mother and daughter were delighted. However, at that time, there were no miniature shops in Greenville, and the mother complained that she could not find furniture for her dollhouse. Mr. Henry then decided there might be a market for miniatures. The search began to find furniture suppliers. Since that time, miniatures have taken over the greater portion of the shop.

Among some of the lines carried at The Front Porch are Chestnut Hills Studios, Ltd., Houseworks, Ltd., X-Acto, Concord, Sonia Messer, Fantastic Mdse., and handmade pieces by The Miners, Verl Kraeger, and many others. Porcelain handmade dollhouse dolls by Penny are carried at The Front Porch. This shop offers all the necessary materials to finish a dollhouse: wall paper, moldings, siding, windows, doors, lighting kits and fixtures, plus just about anything else you may need.

Besides the miniatures and dollhouses, period rooms are a specialty. These individual rooms are especially nice if a person doesn't have a place for a whole dollhouse. Mr. Henry has built and installed rooms that were recessed into walls.

Copy of the Sotille House, located on the campus of the College of Charleston, S.C., built for Dr. Keller Freeman of Greenville, S.C.

Trains and accessories are also a big business at The Front Porch; the upstairs portion of the building is devoted to the different scales of trains, buildings, track, etc.

The Henrys are still doing renovations of big homes, doing custom and specialized work in historic homes as well as in the newer ones and in office buildings.

A register kept at the door for people to sign when they visit The Front Porch relates a story within itself. Just about every state is represented. A flip through the pages will verify the fact that miniatures are one of the most sought-after items of hobbyists and collectors. People from Canada, France, England and Puerto Rico have come to the shop.

The Norwood house is an exclusive design, but other dollhouses can be purchased. The miniatures may also be ordered. For a 90-page catalog of miniatures and dollhouses, send $3.50 to:

The Front Porch
804 Augusta Street
Greenville, South Carolina 29605

Copy of another house located on the campus of the College of Charleston, S.C. The outside is a copy, inside designed and built by Tom Henry.

Copy of the Norwood home in Greenville, S.C.This is one of the most outstanding Victorian-style homes in Greenville and is listed in the National Historical Register. This house was built for one of the heirs, Susannah Norwood Ross.

Grandma Pattern: utilizes head made from darning egg with painted face, 15" body, instructions for clothes and broom. $2.50 postpaid.

Grandpa Pattern: construction similar to Grandma, flannel shirt and bib overalls. $2.50 postpaid.

DILLON'S DOLLS: PATTERNS

Jane Dillon's craft books and patterns emphasize calico. Jane, a native of New York who received a Bachelor of Fine Arts Degree from the University of Buffalo and did graduate work at Syracuse University, has taught art in Tennessee and Alabama and tole and quilting in Virginia. She now lives in Newport News, Virginia, where she makes her patterns for items with a country accent. The particular patterns shown here illustrate some of her dolls. Individually, these patterns sell for $2.50, but any two of the $2.50 patterns may be purchased for $4.00.

A brochure of individual patterns illustrates her designs for dolls other than those shown here, as well as a hen string holder; a gingham dog or calico cat broom holder; hen, cat, or pig pin-ups that are used as pin cushions; a calico Christmas angel; a Mrs. Bunny Rabbit with calico dress; a Granny towel holder; a calico weathervane; and several other items.

A book, *Jane's Calico Country Crafts,* includes actual-size patterns and complete instructions for making twenty items: hen on nest, calico cow, rocking horse, cardinal, ice cream cone, country rabbit, etc. Some small dolls are included. A spoon doll is built around a wooden spoon. A scarecrow has a 1⅛" styrofoam ball for a head. A clothespin chicken uses an old idea with a new twist. The price of the book is $4.00, postpaid.

Another book, *Jane's Calico Christmas Crafts*, also gives actual-size patterns and full instructions—again for twenty items. These are mostly items which would pleasantly decorate a Christmas tree or a mantel of evergreens: a calico Christmas cat, Poor Robin with a scarf to keep him warm, a mini-mouse, a Colonial mouse, a partridge in a pear tree, and Sunbonnet Sue. A Granny tea bell uses a bell with a face painted on the handle and dressed in calico. The price of this book is also $4.00, postpaid.

To order the two books, the specific patterns of dolls, or a brochure of other patterns available, write to:

Dillon's Dolls
P.O. Box 2478
Newport News, Virginia 23602

Dinnerware in shell with mother-of-pearl. Dinner plate, 11" in diameter, $20.00. Salad plate, 8" in diameter, $18.00. Soup bowl, 5" in diameter, $9.00. Napkin ring, $4.00. Wine goblet, 8" x 3½", $15.00. Prices do not include shipping.

CHESTER OLD—POTTER

Chester Old studied pottery at Penland School of Crafts, Penland, North Carolina. He is now a fulltime studio potter in Atlanta, Georgia, with gallery affiliations at such places as the Storehouse (Atlanta, Houston, Dallas, Raleigh); New Morning Gallery in Asheville, North Carolina; The Craft Shop, Piedmont Craftsmen, Inc., Winston-Salem, North Carolina; Makers Gallery, New York City; The Artisan Shop, Wilmette, Illinois; Whichcraft Studio, South Orange, New Jersey; and Gallery 2, Roanoke, Virginia.

His work is hand-built from thin slabs of clay with a high-gloss clear glaze and hand-painted with lusters (gold, silver, mother-of-pearl, brown, blue, gray and green).

To contact Chester at his studio, write to:

Chester Old
562 Greenwood Avenue N.E.
Atlanta, Georgia 30308

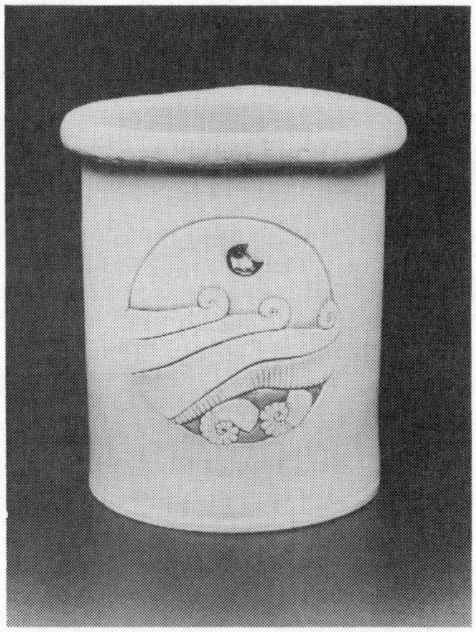

This container can be used as a planter, vase, or wine cooler. Shell or landscape design. 9" tall and 7" in diameter. $45.00 plus shipping.

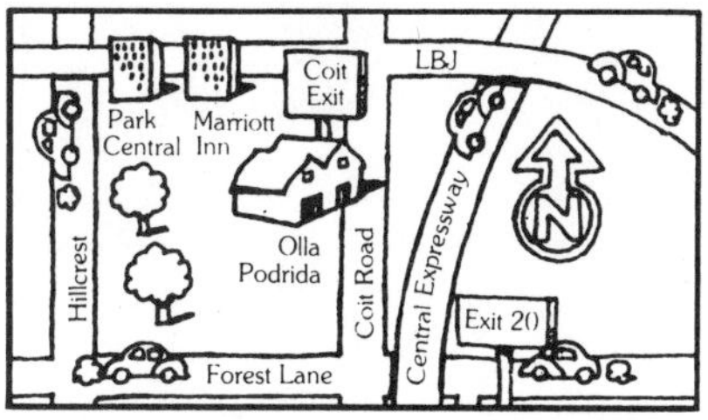

THE OLLA PODRIDA

Olla Podrida means "all in the pot," and The Olla Podrida is definitely a place that lives up to its name. Located in an old barn in North Dallas, it's an artist's paradise of paintings and photographs, weaving, pottery, brass, greenery, leather, jewelry, and whatever-you-will.

A step inside is a step into a different world. Open spaces, skylights, and healthy green plants blend with huge weathered timbers from Waco, iron grillwork, bars and cell doors from the old Abilene jail.

You'll open doors with brass pulls and handles, stand under revolving ceiling fans, take a rest on English railroad station benches, pass through old saloon doors, and admire Dutch lampshades and spot old railroad ties. Colorful stained glass windows are everywhere you look, including windows from the Dreyfuss estate and the old Dallas County Courthouse.

The Olla Podrida contains over 75 individual shops—only slightly less unique than the individuals who keep them. They're artists and craftsmen who specialize—who take pride in what they create and sell.

The Olla Podrida
A marketplace for artists, craftsmen and collectors
12215 Coit Road, in the same barn as Granny's Dinner Playhouse.
Open weekdays and Saturday 10 a.m.
to 5:30 p.m., Thursday until 9 p.m.

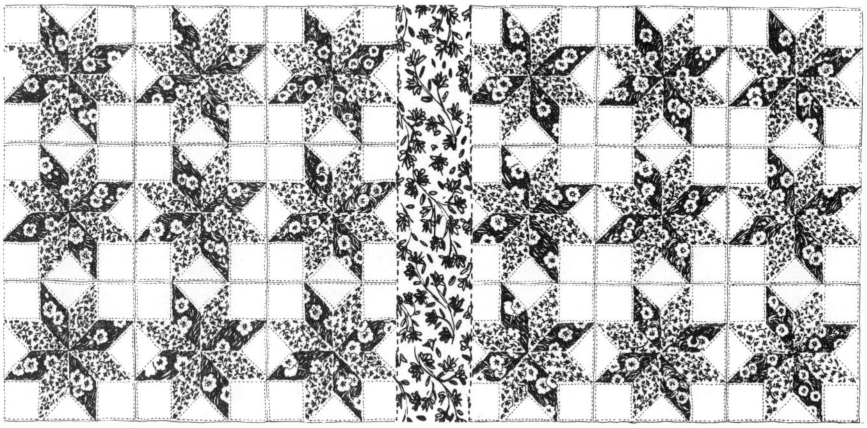

Appalachian Craftsmen

Appalachian Craftsmen is an organization of over 120 ladies in four rural counties of West Virginia. It was originally begun as an effort of the Junior League of Huntington to assist a local group in selling handcrafted ladies fashions using traditional patchwork and quilted designs. The product line has now been expanded to include childrens' clothing, toys, quilts, and other items. The independent, self-help organization changes quilting from a hobby to supplemental family income while maintaining the heritage and life style of the mountains.

The quilts that are made to order are available in these sizes (with a possible variance of a few inches for differences in quilt patterns) and prices (plus postage):

Crib	38 x 56	$ 80.00
Twin Coverlet	66 x 98	280.00
Twin Spread	80 x 112	340.00
Double Coverlet	76 x 98	300.00
Double Spread	96 x 112	365.00
Queen Coverlet	84 x 102	325.00
Queen Spread	102 x 118	400.00
King Coverlet	102 x 110	385.00
King Spread	120 x 120	435.00

Mail inquiries to:

Appalachian Craftsmen, Inc.
1209 Third Avenue
Huntington, West Virginia 25701

THE OLD MILL

Mountain Industries, a center of native crafts and skills, is located in a building called the *Old Mill* which has been in existence since 1877. The water-powered stone grinding of cornmeal and whole wheat flour still practiced there is almost a lost art, with only a few such mills now in operation in Appalachia. Guests may see the actual grinding of corn or wheat on early millstones and the cornmeal may be purchased. One may take a tour of the mill—the guide will show you the early equipment; you will see many of the original belt-and-pulley arrangements made when the mill was first established and still in use.

On the second floor of the mill, ceramics and other native crafts are on display. During the summer months skills of bygone days are demonstrated in the grist-mill. These skills include rugmaking, wool carding and spinning, handweaving of cloth, and basketmaking. There is a demonstration of grinding each Saturday at 2:00 p.m.

The program and crafts at Mountain Industries are carried out in affiliation with Penn Alps and the Council of the Alleghenies. The *Old Mill* is located about one mile north of Harman, West Virginia, on Route 32 in the heart of the Appalachian mountain range.

Mountain Industries
Harman, West Virginia 26270

Jack Jeffers

PLEASURES & PLACES

Birds know things
that people don't
from going places
that people can't—
never into a pressurized cabin
but to wind on each feather,
to soaring and swooping,
to claiming the mystery of going,
not just the getting there.
JV

Pleasures and Places Index

A DASH OF TABASCO

By John McNulty

Reprinted from *The New Yorker*, copyright June 13, 1953, and *The World of John McNulty* Doubleday and Company, 1957.

One evening, eating dinner alone in a restaurant on East Seventy-second Street, I was tossing a drop or two of tabasco on my clams when I fell prey to a habit I picked up a long time ago. I read the label on the bottle, right down to the small print. I have always been a steadfast reader of labels on bottles, even from as far back as when it used to say on ketchup bottles, "Contains one-tenth of one per cent of benzoate of soda as a preservative." The contents of any bottle, as set down by the manufacturer, have always made good reading to me. So I read the label on the tabasco bottle. It said, "Tabasco is the pepper sauce manufactured since 1868 by McIlhenny, New Iberia, La. Tabasco is made of vinegar, red pepper, and salt. A few drops mixed with soup or gravy, with breakfast eggs or glass of milk give a piquant and delicious flavor. No sea food should be eaten without tabasco. There is only one tabasco, McIlhenny's. THIS IS THE GENUINE ARTICLE. Made in U.S.A."

Well, I was in step, all right. I wasn't eating sea food without tabasco. I was putting it on the clams. A man eating dinner alone is apt to think thoughts that are quite idle—trivial, perhaps. I thought to myself how often I'd read that label, and how often the name "New Iberia" had struck me as a resonant sort of name. By the time the soup came, I was saying to myself, "Why don't I go down there and have a look at the Deep South, where I've never been?" Many a time I've heard people say, "One thing leads to another," and now I'm beginning to believe this is one of the great, irrefutable declarations in any language. I went to New Iberia and the Deep South and had a look at it, or them.

The day after reading the label, I telephoned to New Iberia. Tell the truth, I didn't really know if there were still any McIlhennys around. It's a long while since 1868, and it seemed quite possible that only the name had been retained by the makers of the sauce. (As one thing led to another, I was destined to learn that there are indeed McIlhennys around, and Averys and Clarks and Simmonses, and many more—all, in a manner of speaking, centered about the small bottle whose label also says, "Net Measure 2 ozs.")

When I got the tabasco factory on the phone, I asked for Mr. McIlhenny, regardless. A magnolia-tinted voice told me that he was not there at the moment but that I could speak to his assistant, Mrs. Fisher Simmons. I explained to Mrs. Simmons that I was thinking of coming down to see the place. Mrs. Simmons said they have numerous visitors and I would be welcome. She told me that New Iberia, a town of about sixteen thousand population, had a comfortable hotel, the Frederic, where I could stay. "It's about ten miles or so from Avery Island, where we are," Mrs. Simmons said. "But you'll have no trouble getting back and forth to visit."

I took the train, the Crescent, at Pennsylvania Station at 1:45 P.M., railroad time, the next day, which was a Sunday.

I am a city man, proficient to some degree in combat with the perils of Second Avenue and Seventy-second Street but ill-equipped to fend off whatever dangers there may be around the bayous and marshes of Louisiana, especially snakes. I am afraid of snakes anywhere. As marshes began to show up occasionally outside the train window after we were in Louisiana, I mentioned this fear to the porter. He was a slow but thoughtful speaker.

"Them snakes don't want to mess with you any more than you want to mess with them," he said. "They trying mighty hard day and night keep away from you, maybe more than you trying keep away from them."

"I guess that's so," I said.

"Course," he went on, "if a snake do just zackly the wrong thing, and a man do just zackly the wrong thing, and they both do just zackly the wrong thing just zackly the same wrong time, something bound to happen and it do."

From New Orleans, out across the Mississippi, New Iberia is, by rail, a hundred and twenty-six miles west and slightly north; the place was named by homesick Spanish, back in the days when Louisiana belonged to Spain. On my first morning there, in the Hotel Frederic, I phoned for coffee to be brought to my room.

"Light or dark?" the girl said.

"Oh, I thought you'd send the cream on the side and I could mix it myself," I told her.

"I don't mean that," she said. "I mean do you want Northern or Southern coffee?"

Perplexed a little, I asked for whichever was stronger.

"You want the Southern," the girl said.

In remarkably fast time, much faster than is usual up North, there was a knock on the door. I opened it, and there, holding the coffee tray, was a tall, lean, deeply tanned man of middle age, in a white coat and khaki trousers, and shod in moccasins. He had a brief, sharply pointed mustache, and he looked precisely as D'Artagnan would have looked had he been a room waiter in a white coat, khaki trousers, and moccasins. "*Bonjour!*" he said. "Good morning!"

He was the first of many Cajuns I was to meet during my visit. They are, as is well known, descendants of the French Acadians, who, around 1755, were exiled by the British from Nova Scotia and painfully made their way to Louisiana, because Louisiana was at that time a colony of France.

The waiter's accent baffled me at first. I know a few words of Fraser and Squair or Chardenal French, but Cajun is something else again. When he talked in English, he splashed in a word or two of French here and there.

"*Est* nice weather fo' travellin'," he said, putting down his tray.

I agreed, and he asked politely where I was from. When I said New York, he said, "*Est* nice place, New York? *Est* New York nice place up there?"

It was the first time anybody had ever asked me, simply, whether New York was a nice place, as if never having heard whether it was or not, and I was stuck for an answer. I said I thought it was a nice place.

"*Est bon*, good, you have nice place up there at that New York," he said. "*Merci*, thanks." He left silently on his moccasined feet.

Early that afternoon, after telephoning Mrs. Simmons at Avery Island, I went out there by a cab. The driver was Robert Broussard, another Cajun. Everywhere, as we drove along, were French names, on stores, filling stations, and such—names like Delahoussaye, Breaux (there pronounced "Brurr"), Louviere, and, as frequent as any, Teche, which is the name of a big bayou nearby. For years, "bayou" has struck my ears as a gentle, musical, and beckoning word. In New Iberia, I was told it is not a French word, as I had surmised, but Choctaw Indian.

Leaving the outskirts of the community and heading south, we followed a long, straight road with flat fields on the left, interrupted at infrequent intervals by small houses, some of them not much more than shacks; on the right was a narrow stretch of water. Beyond the bayou was a vast stretch of marshy land. "In there, plenty muskrat, plenty mink, plenty nutria," Broussard said. "They trappin' all winter plenty furs around here. Louisiana got pret' near most furs anywhere."

As we neared Avery Island, there were marshlands on our left, too. Our road, indeed, ran right across the marshes. Broussard explained to me that the Bayou Petite Anse, or Little Cove, meanders on three sides of Avery Island—north, west, and south—and the fourth side is cypress swamp. So watery, indeed, that the place has always been called an island, even if technically it may not be one.

Unwittingly, Broussard reminded me that one thing leads to another when he said, "My wife is boss of the bag room at the salt mine on the island." It was the first I had heard of a salt mine there, although I learned later it is one of the famous salt mines of the world; it is run by the International Salt Company. There's another famous salt mine under part of Detroit, I also learned later.

"Is nice place, salt mine," Broussard said. "Good place to see."

"I'll try to," I told him.

The long, straight road crossed a bridge over the Bayou Petite Anse and ended at a tollgate—the entrance to Avery Island. Tourists are charged a quarter admission. After I stated my business, the gateman waved us past. Immediately, we were in a world of lush and amazingly varied growths—palms, bamboos, palmettos, magnolias, and, most striking of all, majestically large live oaks, their seemingly eternal sturdiness accented by the delicate, mysterious grace of Spanish moss hanging from their strong, twisty limbs.

Overhead, at times, great-winged white birds that I recognized as egrets flapped their way. It was hard to believe that an industry lay ahead. Soon we reached a crossroads with the sign

LOUISIANA LAW
STOP

We halted, then turned a bend, crossed a railroad track I was astonished to find there, and came to the tabasco factory.

It isn't a big place at all, as factories go—three stories high in one part, four in another, made of brick painted gray, and covering the area of perhaps an eighth of a city block. To the left, as we approached, was a great cage, about twenty-five or thirty feet high. In it, I could see several score pheasants, the brilliantly colored males strutting happily about, and a lean, tanned man (nearly all Cajuns seem to be lean and tanned), wearing spectacles, who was scattering grain around for the birds. A gentle breeze suddenly brought the scent of tabasco in the making. It was delightful—pungent and spicy, with overtones of vinegar, but of vinegar sort of under control. As I stepped inside, I saw eighty or ninety covered oak casks standing in rows. Two women, each with a wooden paddle, were going from cask to cask, lifting the covers, then stirring the aromatic sauce within. I peered into a cask and saw the rich, bright red of the mixture. The woman stirring it told me that this was one of the last steps in the long process of making the tabasco I'd been shaking on the clams up in New York a couple of nights before.

The factory is unlike most factories, for it has an unhurried, almost sauntering air. Walking toward a stairway that leads to the offices above, I stopped for a moment at a room from which there came the siren fragrance of strong coffee. Two workmen, in khaki, and three girls, one in khaki and the others in fluffy summer dresses, were sitting around a table, each with a demitasse in hand, chatting. The accents of some of them were Cajun. The coffee was in an urn, in a corner close by. Whenever anyone in the factory feels like having coffee, it's there, waiting. There are no specific "coffee breaks," as there are in more bustling operations. I tried a demitasse and it came near lifting the top of my head off. "That's pure coffee, Louisiana roast," one of the men told me. "They roast it right near here in Lafayette. No chicory. Those New Orl'ns people use chicory. Not here."

The office, on the second floor, appeared to be a parlay of McIlhenny and Charles Dickens—quiet, air-conditioned, lacking in the frenzy of efficiency that plagues some Northern offices, and with a high, four-legged, slant-topped desk, bookkeeper-style, against one wall. Mrs. Simmons—gracious, busy, blond, and the grandmother of four children—came forward to greet me. She is a widow. Her grandchildren are the offspring of Fisher Simmons, Jr., the oldest of her three sons. The two others are Edward McIlhenny Simmons and William Matthews Simmons. Later, she candidly told me that she will be fifty-one in July. Mrs. Simmons is the daughter of the late Edward Avery McIlhenny, known always as "Mister Ned," who, after many memorable years as the lord of the island and head of the tabasco company, died in 1949, at the age of seventy-seven. Soon after his death, Walter Stauffer McIlhenny, who is the son of the late John Avery McIlhenny, a brother of Mister Ned, was made president of the company, and Mrs. Simmons became his assistant. Mister Ned had three daughters and no sons.

With easy courtesy, which to my ears was enriched by her accent, Mrs. Simmons asked me if the hotel in town was all right. I said something about its being perfectly comfortable—not the Ritz-Carlton, but perfectly comfortable. "With the right frame of mind, you can make any place you are into a Ritz-Carlton, can't you?" she remarked cheerily. "Besides, isn't the Ritz-Carlton torn down? I don't get up to New York much. Cousin Walter does, though, now and then." She turned and introduced me to her cousin Walter Stauffer McIlhenny, who had been busy at the telephone when I came in. He is a dark-eyed, handsome man of forty-one, over six feet tall and muscular, with a certain dignity about him and a direct gaze. Behind his desk, on the wall, was a banner with the inscription "U.S.M.C. Reserve." Gossiping around the hotel lobby that morning, I had been told that he holds the rank of lieutenant colonel in the Marines, following a distinguished record of service in the Pacific, including two awards of the Navy Cross. He became a major in combat, I'd been told, and was released from active duty as a lieutenant colonel. One of the great marksmen of this country, he is a life member of the National Rifle Association of America and was formerly captain of the Marine Reserve Rifle Team.

Mr. McIlhenny seemed a trifle incredulous when I told him I had come down to visit merely on an impulse inspired by reading the label on a tabasco bottle. "I didn't know that anyone read the label so fully," he said, smiling. "Personally, though, I've always thought it's rather quaint on the Lea & Perrins Worcestershire Sauce label where it says, 'From the Recipe of a Nobleman in the County.' " He went on to tell me that he and various other members of his family, and of the Simmons and Avery families, all related, live on the island, and are all generally referred to as "The Family." Each family has its own place, he said; his is in the old slave quarters, and he'd like me to lunch with him there one day. It was hot outside that afternoon, around ninety, with the humidity running a Louisiana eighty-six or so, and Mr. McIlhenny, no doubt thinking of that, added, "The slave quarters are air-conditioned these days."

Mrs. Simmons then turned me over to a man in his early twenties, Matthew Louviere by name, a medium-sized, good-looking chap who was wearing a linen jacket and dark trousers. Mrs. Simmons said that Matthew knew a great deal about Avery Island, since he had been born and raised there, and that he would be glad to act as my guide.

Matthew and I started out for a look around an island that I did not even then suspect could be so wondrous.

Matthew's manner of speech was that of an exceptionally well-educated young man from somewhere up North, almost professional in its precision and choice of words. In view of what Mrs. Simmons had said about his having been born and raised on Avery Island, I was surprised that he had not the slightest trace of a Southern accent. "My mother came from up North," he explained when I commented on this. "My father was a Cajun." I was even more surprised to discover later that afternoon that he had never so much as finished high school. Gradually it came out that he had for the most part educated himself, by diligent study at home and at libraries in the region. Moreover, several years in the Army, which included additional schooling and a period in Japan, had given his obviously avid mind an opportunity to pick up matters far beyond the ken of most of the people on the island, which, with equal obviousness, he loved profoundly.

Right from the start, however, it was clear that Matthew was reluctant to talk about himself, and preferred to talk of the island. Riding away from the factory in a company car, we passed the great cage of pheasants. "They are for use on The Family's table when the occasion demands," he said. "Mister Ned greatly admired pheasants, as he did almost every form of animal and bird life. Miz Polly does, too." "Miz Polly" is the name by which Mrs. Simmons is known and by which she is addressed by nearly everybody on the island.

Quite suddenly, the road turned and ahead of us lay a wide opening surrounded by thick woods. I caught my breath. Out in a large pond, on a bamboo platform perhaps three hundred feet long and twenty feet wide, and rising about ten feet above the water, were thousands and thousands of great white egrets—of startling beauty every one—nesting. Thousands and thousands, and the trees that closely bordered the pond, like a jungle, were crammed with more of them. They were snowy egrets, Matthew said, among the loveliest of birds, and this pond was the heart of a sanctuary for them that Mister Ned had created way back in 1895, when he captured eight young egrets on the island. So lovely, indeed, are these birds that man once killed them by the thousands for their plumage; a law protecting them was passed in 1913 largely as a result of the efforts of Mister Ned and the Audubon Society. "In the eighteen-nineties and early nineteen-hundreds, the slaughter of snowy egrets was utterly abominable," said Matthew. "Women at that time coveted the dainty, exquisitely delicate plumes of the egret, and these plumes were called aigrettes when used for millinery purposes. On the bird, these plumes are beautiful, but there were many people, including Mister Ned, who thought they were brutally ugly on a woman's hat. To be sure," he continued, as we left the car and walked to the pond's edge, watching the ceaseless activity around the nests, "Mister Ned was a hunter famous all over the world, and a marvellous man with a rifle. But he shot only creatures used for food—not pure beauties, like egrets."

I told Matthew I was happily flabbergasted at the sight before us. Up in Rhode Island a couple of years ago, I saw twenty-four egrets that had been staying for some time in the marshlands near the sea, and bird people there thought that was a great many. They were of the type called American egrets. I remember looking up the pronunciation in the dictionary, and it says the accent is on the first syllable, "EE-grets." Matthew said "e-GRETS," and I asked him about that.

"Possibly we here accent the last syllable because of the French influence in our speech," he replied. "However, *revenons à nos moutons*—back to our sheep. To get aigrettes, hunters used to shoot the egrets on their nests, because those special plumes grow on the birds—both male and female—only during the nesting season. So, with their parents killed, the young birds in those days starved to death in their nests. It was despicable. The law had not yet been passed when Mister Ned captured these eight birds, and here at the pond he built a cage for them. When they grew old enough to leave, he tore down the cage and bade goodbye to them, fearfully, and sure that he would never again see them. But when the next March arrived—the last days of March—back came these beauties to this very spot, and bringing friends with them. A cage was no longer necessary, and year after year they came and multiplied. Now look!"

I asked if anyone had any idea how many birds made their homes on the pond and around it.

"Understandably, the number can't be computed precisely," said Matthew, "but it is perhaps safe to say that there are between seventeen thousand and possibly twenty thousand on that platform. We have reached that estimate by taking one small square of the platform, counting the birds in the square, then multiplying that number by the number of squares. The result is approximate, of course. The total in the whole sanctuary may easily be over a hundred thousand."

Matthew said there were undoubtedly some American egrets on the platform, such as I had seen in Rhode Island, but that most of the birds were snowies. The American is taller, being more than three feet high, while the snowy is about two feet high. The American has a yellow bill and all-black legs. "The snowy has a black bill, black legs, and yellow feet," Matthew said. "That's why he is often called the bird with the Golden Slippers."

We walked up the road a piece, and came to several large piles of twigs. "Bamboo twigs," Matthew said. "Miz Polly has a couple of men assigned to gather those twigs every day, cutting them off the bamboos and putting them in piles at different points around the pond. The egrets know all about that. When they're making their new nests, after they come here from Central and South America in March, and when they need new material to repair their nests after a storm, they know just where to go–where Miz Polly has had the twigs put."

At that moment it occurred to me that Avery Island, where men spend hours piling up bamboo twigs for visiting egrets, is far, far away, both in miles and mores, from the restaurant on East Seventy-second Street where, ninety-six hours earlier, I'd been shaking some tabasco on some clams.

We got back in the car, and Matthew drove me to a clearing in a small forest of bamboo. "This is called timber bamboo," he said. "It is sold to people all over the country for landscape purposes, such as the building of decorative stockades, and also for other uses. Perhaps you do not know that bamboo is one of the fastest-growing plants in the world?" I didn't know it, of course, and when he showed me a young bamboo, green and erect, about thirty feet tall, and said it was only four weeks since it had come out of the ground as a sprout, I expressed skepticism. "Very well," Matthew said. "Let's choose a shorter and younger bamboo, and check its growth."

It was at that moment 2 P.M. on a Tuesday. We found a younger bamboo (the young bamboos are a tender, subdued green, in contrast to the darker tan of the older ones) and we recorded its height–it came about up to our waists–by making a mark on a full-grown tree a few inches away. (Two days later, at 10 A.M. on Thursday, Matthew and I returned to the bamboo glade and found our young bamboo. It had grown exactly thirty-six inches, or, as we ascertained by doing a little paper work then and there, at the rate of about four-fifths of an inch an hour in the forty-four hours that had elapsed. That's something like nineteen inches a day. Bamboos in Louisiana eventually get up to around forty or fifty, sometimes even sixty, feet.)

As Matthew and I were riding away from the bamboo glade, we encountered a two-wheeled cart, filled with brush and drawn by a placid mule. Its driver was sitting in comfort beneath a large and dusty unbrella. "That's brush for the New Year's bonfire," Matthew said. "We'll come to the bonfire pile in a minute." The driver, a colored man, tipped his hat as we went by and said, "Good evenin'." It was only midafternoon, but down there they say "Good evening" when the noon hour has passed.

Soon we were on a road skirting the foot of an unwooded hill on our right. To our left was a meadow, and in the middle of it was a vast pile of brush, perhaps twenty-five feet high, perhaps forty feet across. "Every New Year's Eve," Matthew told me, "all the people on the island, white and colored, come and stand on that hill and watch the New Year's bonfire, and the children have a wiener roast. During the rest of the year, the brush that's cleared off the land is brought over here and put on that pile. It is a custom that has gone on since plantation days. I used to come as a child, and, like the others, I used to believe that all the bad demons of the old year were burning up in the bonfire. and that in the new year to come there would be no malevolent demons around. Sheer voodooism, of course, but it was pleasant to believe as a child. On Christmas morning, too, I remember, Mister Ned used to sit on the porch of his house, and all the men on the island came visiting. Punch was passed around. Old-timers used to shake hands with Mister Ned, and some made speeches, I remember."

I said such scenes seemed to me to belong to the distant past, maybe more than a hundred years ago.

Matthew, with the almost apologetic reluctance that beset him whenever he spoke of matters unrelated to the island, said, "Do you recall what Henri Bergson said about the past?"

I said I didn't recall it, because I never knew it.

"Henri Bergson said, 'The present contains nothing more than the past.' "

A few turns in the road through the green shadows of some coolish woods and we paused again, for two reasons. One was that, soundlessly and unafraid, two young deer came out of the woods on legs whose grace would shame the finest ballerina, and stood, big-eyed, not twenty-five feet away, watching us. One was male, one was female, and both were of the most tender shades of brown. The other reason was that on our left, by a smallish pond, were some birds that no one could pass unheeding. Among them was a crane, his plumage shading through four or five tones of gray into black, with what seemed a touch of deep blue along his slender neck. Hanging from the back of his head was a pure-white manelike feathering.

"That white part looks like Einstein's hair, doesn't it?" I said.

"It does," said Matthew. "That white on the back of the head is, I believe, called a *mèche* in French, and I believe Napoleon had a *mèche*. That bird is an African demoiselle. Mister Ned imported a family of them."

Sharing the banks of the pond with the demoiselle were two white swans, at least eight pairs of Canada geese, their young waddling around behind them, and a bird that looked fantastically like a gaudily painted hen and had a walk that was chickeny, too. Its neck was purple, its back was green, its legs were yellow, and its bill was red with a yellow tip.

"That is a purple gallinule," Matthew told me. "I often think of him as a swimming chicken. He swims adeptly, even though he hasn't webbed feet, like most swimming birds."

We turned to look at the deer and found them still gazing curiously at our car. A moment later, the female decided to go back into the woods. The male, on the top of whose head were small velvet-covered antlers, or the beginnings of antlers, was bolder, and he was still watching as we drove away.

Just about then a demitasse seemed to be indicated, so we started back toward the tabasco factory, perhaps a mile off. Driving along, Matthew told me that the island is roughly oval in shape, about three miles long and two miles wide, and that it has thirty-eight hundred and forty acres of "high land." There are also hundreds of acres of marshy land that are regarded as part of the island. "The marshland is quite an asset, too, because of all the furs it produces," he said. "I don't know how many pelts each winter, but it's a great many. Muskrat, mostly, but also mink and nutria. Mister Ned was one of the original breeders of nutria. The Fish and Wildlife people here in Louisiana imported some from South America and gave them to him, so that he could experiment with raising them. The nutria is something like an otter. In fact, I believe I am correct in saying that 'nutria' is the Spanish word for 'otter.' The fur is in considerable demand. I think it was around 1930 when Mister Ned first brought them here. He kept them in an enclosed portion of the marsh. Mister Ned was very upset when he discovered one day that the nutria had broken out of the enclosure and scattered all over the marsh. It worked out well, though, because they survived and multiplied in the marsh, and there they remained, to be trapped in great numbers every year."

A person can get used to anything, even hanging, they say, and this time the "Louisiana roast" coffee tasted better than pretty good and had no shock to it. While we were having a second demitasse, Boss Jim Markey, a white-haired man of seventy, came in for coffee and said that he'd like to show me around a little in the factory. Boss has been working there for forty-eight years, and he's now the man responsible for the making of the tabasco.

Boss told me that the factory is not big and employs only sixty-two persons. Even so, it turns out five million bottles of tabasco a year. He said the oak casks containing the beautifully red and memorable pungent mixture represented the last three weeks in the process of making tabasco. "The peppers in those casks were harvested almost three years ago," he went on. "I guess you know we grow all the peppers here on the island. After they're harvested, they're crushed, and a small amount of salt is added to them. Next, we put them in oak barrels with covers that have tiny air holes in them, and spread a thick layer of salt on top of the covers. Then we move the barrels into the aging rooms, where fermentation starts and continues for three years, while the juices and gases from the peppers escape through the air holes and the salt above them. At the end of that time, fermentation ends, and the salt hardens and automatically seals the barrels until we're ready for them. Then we remove the covers, add the vinegar, and for three weeks, in this room here, we stir the mixture. After that, we filter it, and it's ready for bottling, upstairs. That's all there is to it–peppers, vinegar, and salt."

"Just as it tells you on the label," I said.

"Just like on the label," said Boss. "But it takes three years and a little bit more."

As I was leaving the factory a short time later, preparing to go back to the hotel in New Iberia, I came across Mr. McIlhenny, talking to one of the foremen. They were both speaking Cajun French, and when the foreman had left, I asked Mr. McIlhenny if he had any difficulty with the Cajun patois. He smiled and said, "Not in the least." He told me that as a child he had spoken nothing but French at home. Not Cajun, but pure French. His mother, Mrs. Anita Stauffer McIlhenny, a granddaughter of General Zachary Taylor, is of French and German blood. Her family has lived a long time in Louisiana and French is her natural and beloved language. She now lives in Baton Rouge.

"There's a little family story about speaking French that might amuse you," Mr. McIlhenny said. "When I was in the Marines, I got to Melbourne, Australia, and I telephoned to my mother in Baton Rouge. It was wartime, of course, and it was quite a task putting the call through. However, after a day or two the connection was made, and I spoke to my mother, with a military monitor listening in, as was required. To my astonishment, my mother hung up on me. After another long wait, the operator got her on the wire again and told her that her son wished to speak to her from Australia. 'That's not my son,' my mother said. 'My son knows better than to address me in English!' I got on the phone again, and spoke to her in French. Immediately, the military monitor cut us off. He couldn't understand French and therefore couldn't let the conversation go on. After looking around some, I found an officer who knew French well. He monitored the call, and I finally talked with my mother."

The next morning, Matthew and I went back to the pond where the egrets nest. The bamboo platform was still crowded with them. There were also some wading at the edge of the pond, on their long black legs with the golden-slippered feet, fishing for frogs. Matthew pointed to an almost indiscernible wake in the water beneath the platform. I spied an alligator's head. Matthew handed me a pair of binoculars, and through them I could more plainly see the ugly, prehistoric-looking old fellow. "He'd love to have some of those birds," Matthew said. "But only when one dies and falls off the nest, or is pushed off by the other birds, does he get one."

Egrets kept taking off from the nests and flapping away in the sky in the direction of the big bayous, miles from the island. "They go fishing in the bayous," Matthew said. "The males and females take turns sitting on the nests; one stays while the other goes fishing and brings home food. Then the other goes fishing."

At that moment, twenty or thirty egrets soared toward the sky in a group. As we watched them, clouds of smoke rolled over the treetops, momentarily obscuring the birds, and we heard, coming strangely out of the deep woods, the sound of a locomotive. "They're hauling empty cars out to the salt mine to bring back the salt this afternoon," Matthew said. "How'd you like to go see the salt mine?"

I thought it a splendid idea, and so we started for the other end of the island, where the mine is. On the way, I told Matthew that to me the phrase "the salt mines" had always had a sinister sound, because of the many things I'd heard and read about people being exiled to the salt mines of Siberia.

"In reality, it doesn't seem an unpleasant place to work at all," Matthew said. "All year round, the temperature is a steady seventy-two down there, and the ceilings are certainly high enough to permit proper ventilation, with the help of mechanical fans."

At the mine, Lester Jay, a young engineer, took us in hand. He led us to an elevator, on which four-ton carloads of salt are brought up to the surface, and we stepped aboard. There were no lights as the elevator went slowly down the shaft. Mr. Jay's voice came through the pitch-dark. "We're working at around the five-hundred-and-thirty to five-hundred-and-fifty-foot level," he said. "It's been at that level for about fifty years."

We reached the bottom of the shaft, stepped out, and saw in the light of numerous powerful bulbs, strung on poles as tall as telephone poles, the far-reaching streets of a cavernous underground city. Over our heads, in that particular spot, the roof, of solid salt, was about sixty feet high. The tracks of a narrow-gauge railway fanned out into the distance. Small electric locomotives were hauling trains of dump cars, filled with salt that looked like crushed rock. Mr. Jay picked up a handful from a passing car. Most of it was gray, but there were fragments as clear as crystal. "It's very easy to prepare for commercial use, it's so pure," he told me. "It'll run ninety-nine and a half pure sodium chloride." He said that about thirty persons work in the mine, and that most of them live on the island. The remainder are from New Iberia and neighboring communities.

We climbed into a jeep to tour the mine. I noticed now that, as Matthew had said, the temperature was cool, in comfortable contrast to the ninety-two it was five hundred and fifty feet or so above us. In most mines, you aren't allowed to smoke, but in a salt mine you can, because there are no inflammable gases. The walls, the roof, and the huge pillars that support it are all of almost pure salt—no rocks, no dirt, no other element except that possible one-half of one per cent. "This whole deposit is called a salt plug," Mr. Jay said as we set out through the eerie light. "The theory generally held about it is that millions and millions of years ago, perhaps billions, part of the ocean got trapped in here by some geological upheaval. Then, in the Ice Age, fresh water was added by the melting of glaciers. After millions of years more, all the water evaporated and left the salt. That's simplifying it pretty much, but that's a rough idea of the theory most scientists hold to."

At one point in our jeep ride, which took us more than a mile, we turned a bend and came to a vast, lighted cavern, where the ceiling, Mr. Jay said, was more than a hundred feet above us. A large, complicated drilling machine stood against one of the walls of salt, but the crew was working elsewhere. Mr. Jay called my attention to a number of holes that had been drilled in the wall at regular intervals. "They'll blast here this afternoon," he said. "That machine drills four holes at a time, until there are over a hundred of them. Then charges of dynamite are put in the holes and all set off at once. Each blast brings down from a thousand to twelve hundred tons of salt."

When our tour of the enjoyably macabre world beneath the earth's surface had ended and we were again "up top," Mr. Jay explained that the salt from the mine needs only to be crushed and graded to make it ready for industrial use. As for the daintier end product of the mine—the kind of table salt, say, that I had sprinkled on the clams before I shook the tabasco on them—Mr. Jay told me that it is made by an evaporating process, in great tanks that stand not far from the mine shaft. "It's made from the dust that accumulates while crushing salt," he said. "That word 'dust' isn't a good one, because everyone thinks of dust as impure. Really, it is pure, or ninety-nine-and-a-half-per-cent pure, salt dust. Water is added to it and heat applied, and the evaporation carries off that one-half of one per cent impurity."

Now, here is the story of the salt mine as I have pieced it together from what various people on the island told me—Mr. McIlhenny, Mr. Simmons, Matthew, and some others.

One day in 1790, a young man named John Hayes was out deer-hunting on the island, which was then called Petite Anse Island. He stopped at a spring for a drink and found the water briny. He got curious, and he and his family began going to the spring, taking home water, and boiling it off to get the salt. That became a regular thing with them, and with other people of the region, and they went on that way, evaporating water for salt, right up to the War Between the States.

In those days, salt was even more important than it is now, because it was one of the most efficient ways then known to preserve food. When the war broke out, the Confederate States were hard put to it for salt, because they were blockaded by the forces of the North. Providentially for the Confederates, a great discovery was made at the spring around 1862, shortly after the start of the war. In that year, Daniel Dudley Avery, a Yale graduate and a district judge in Baton Rouge, moved to the island with his wife, the former Sarah Craig Marsh. She was the daughter of John Craig Marsh, who settled on the island about a hundred and fifty years ago and was the first ancestor of "The Family" to live there. The Judge and his wife had a son named John Marsh Avery, who, being too young to go to war, was given the job of getting salt from the spring. He put some men to making the spring deeper and widening it. In doing so, they ran into rock salt about thirteen feet below the surface. This was wonderful news for the South. Shafts were speedily dug to get at the salt, and each Confederate state was assigned one. With prodigious labor, a "plank road" of cypress logs was built from New Iberia through the marshlands to the island. Along the plank road, oxcarts lumbered day and night, carrying the salt away.

"Then, in the War Between the States, the Federals came and defeated us," Mr. McIlhenny told me. "The Federals came in and seized the salt mines. Then, as they had every right to do under the rules of war, they burned and destroyed everything in the region. They flooded the salt mine to make it unworkable. It was a punitive expedition, and that's what you do in a punitive expedition." At that moment, Mr. McIlhenny appeared to me, admirably, in two roles: He was both the proud descendant of Confederate fighters and the former major of Marines serving the whole United States, North and South.

After the war, the salt mine was restored to working condition, but it was not until 1869 that it was operated commercially. It wasn't very successful, largely because of transportation difficulties, and in the eighteen-seventies the mine closed down. In 1880, expanding railway facilities made it feasible to resume operations. Nineteen years later, in 1899, the International Salt Company, then called the Avery Rock Salt Mining Company, leased the mine, and it has been digging there ever since. The island was given its present name at around the beginning of this century.

As we were leaving the salt mine, Matthew said, matter-of-factly, "Perhaps you'd like to see the oil wells, too. There are fifty-three of them." I hadn't known there *were* any oil wells on the island, but I replied that I supposed I might as well, so we drove out to the far rim of the island and there they were. I didn't count them, but there were a large number of oil wells, all right. Somehow, though, by that time they seemed to me to be a mere incidental, and later it occurred to me that any island on which fifty-three oil wells seem incidental is an uncommon island. The oil fields, owned by "The Family" and leased to the Humble Oil & Refining Co., have been in operation for about ten years, Matthew said.

The next morning, Thursday, I again met Matthew on the island. It was a hot yet lovely day, and after we had made our check on the growth of our bamboo, he said he had something altogether unexciting in mind for us—a visit to the old burying ground of "The Family." We ascended a gentle hill, serene and deeply wooded, and came upon a partially cleared grassy circle, about fifty yards in diameter. Neatly bordered with a privet hedge and scented with magnolias, it was indeed a place of peace. There were four magnolia trees growing in the burial ground and five great live-oak trees, all with their pennons of Spanish moss.

Matthew pointed to one granite headstone and said, "There is the man from whom all the possessions you have seen really came." On the headstone was the barely decipherable inscription "John Craig Marsh. Pioneer. Born at Cherry Bank Farm, N.J. July 28, 1789. Died at Baton Rouge, April 26, 1857."

Below this, near the ground, skillfully set into the granite, was a reddish stone, roughly oblong, into which the date 1703 was chiselled, and over it was a bronze plaque that read:

This is the cornerstone from Cherry Bank, at Rahway, N.J., home of John Marsh and his wife, Elizabeth Craig, birthplace of his son, David, his grandson, Moses, his great-grandson, Jonathan Alston, and his son, John Avery Marsh, who lies buried here.

I walked a few steps over the silky grass, and examined another headstone. The inscription on it moved me with its grace and gentility, its old-fashioned reverence for the dead. It read:

Sarah Craig Marsh, wife of Daniel D. Avery. Born New York City, March 30, 1813. Died New Iberia, La., March 29, 1879. Possessed of a vivacity of temperament that no burdens could chill, with a sympathy so tender and steadfast that no appeal seemed able to exhaust it. She was one to whom others turned in trouble with a confidence that was never disappointed. In her life illustrating that love is the fulfillment of the law.

We stayed at the burial ground only a little while and didn't talk very much. The headstone for Mister Ned was the simplest of all I saw. It said only:

Edward Avery McIlhenny. Born March 29, 1872. Died August 8, 1949.

As we were leaving the clearing, we came to an opening in the hedge. Matthew led me through it. Beyond were a number of untended, hardly noticeable mounds. "Here is where the colored folks were buried, from away back in plantation days," Matthew said. Only one had a headstone. It bore no inscription.

Matthew walked over to the grave with the headstone. "This is where Doc Russell is buried," he said. "He was a childhood playmate of Mister Ned's, and worked in the factory for years and years and years. We always called him Doc. I loved him. He taught me how to tell time. He had a great big watch on a great big gold chain and he was very proud of it. I learned how to tell time on that watch."

On my last day on the island, I had lunch with Mr. McIlhenny, Mrs. Simmons, and some others at Mr. McIlhenny's air-conditioned home in the slave quarters, where he has a superb staff to care for him and his frequent guests, who most often are former comrades in the Marines. Crawfish Newburg–the crawfish gathered right over in the swamp nearby–was the main dish. In plantation days, rows and rows of buildings constituted the slave quarters. Two of the buildings, constructed of brick handmade on the island, have survived in fine condition. They are low buildings, and in the century or more they have stood there, sun and rain have given the brick a texture and tint to be acquired by no hastier means. These two houses, overlooking a large pond, Mr. McIlhenny has made into the bedrooms of his home. The two are connected at one end by a newer building, constructed of bricks as like the old bricks as skill can make them, which contains a high-ceilinged, open-beam living room, a kitchen, and quarters for the staff. The three sections of the house face on a patio.

Before lunch, a number of us–Mr. McIlhenny; Mrs. Simmons; her daughter-in-law Lanier Simmons, the wife of Edward McIlhenny Simmons; Matthew; and I–sat around chatting, while a colored boy, Willie, moved quietly about, preparing a buffet table near a picture window. I asked the host to tell what the other guests would doubtless consider the oft-told story of tabasco.

"It *is* an oft-told story," Mr. McIlhenny said, "and oft-told with some inaccuracies. There really isn't any secret formula. It's just peppers, vinegar, and salt. Of course, the proportions are our own and the patience it takes also seems to be our own. So's the name." The McIlhennys are of Scotch origin, he went on. The family went from Scotland to Donegal, in Ireland, whence Ezekiel McIlhenny, the first of the clan to come to America, emigrated in 1745 to Nova Scotia. He moved later to Hagerstown, Maryland, and then to Philadelphia. A grandson, Edmund, was probably the first McIlhenny to venture into the South. That was around 1830.

"Edmund was a banker, and he married the daughter of Judge Daniel Dudley Avery," Mr. McIlhenny said. "Now, there's a lot of stuff frequently mentioned about the island originally being a land grant from the Spanish king, which is romantic and high-sounding, but we prefer to believe it was obtained by purchase by the Marshes and the Averys, a matter of simple buying and selling. In the early days, sugar cane, corn, and cotton were its principal products. Anyway, Edmund had a friend who went to the Mexican War in 1846, and when it was over, he hung around Mexico for a while. From the state of Tabasco, way down near Guatemala, he brought Edmund back some peppers the people there grind up with spoons on their plates and mix with their food.

"Matter of fact, the McIlhennys started growing these peppers merely because they were so beautiful. Had them in their gardens. Then, more or less for fun, they experimented with making a hot sauce from the peppers for their own use. They gave a few jars to friends, and gradually it came to be known as McIlhenny's Sauce.

"To make a long story short, the family had to get out when the Federals came in during the War Between the States. The Federals–and I repeat that they had every right to do so–destroyed and burned everything around here. When the family came back after the war, they were impoverished. It happened that the peppers were unharmed. And so it came about that the manufacture and the sale of the sauce, which was started in 1868, was really what held the family fortunes, such as they were, together for those bad years. That's about all."

In the reminiscences that followed, it became apparent that Mister Ned was the one who spread the fame and use of tabasco. He was a man of singular energy and interests. He served as a naturalist with an Arctic expedition with Dr. Frederick Cook in 1892, and headed his own Arctic expedition in 1897. He was a friend of Teddy Roosevelt and Jim Corbett, to name a couple of the celebrities he knew. "He was a splendid man with a rifle," Mrs. Simmons said. "Even after he had had a stroke, and was confined to his room, he proved that. He could not leave the room, but one day, when he was seventy-seven and with only a few months to live, he looked out the window and saw a big buck deer eating the buds on one of his favorite camellias. He sent for his rifle, the boy brought it, and ill though he was, Father dropped that buck with a bullet between the eyes at two hundred yards." One of Mister Ned's hobbies, they said, was the breeding of new varieties of camellias, many of which are today sold commercially. His particular pet was a delicately tinted one, which he named Virgin's Blush.

While we talked, the buffet had been made ready. In many homes, there's an awkward moment when lunch is ready and whoever is to serve it tries, furtively, to catch the eye of host or hostess to make known that fact. Not here. Everybody was talking easily, and Willie waited for no gap in the conversation. Instead, he just took his place with his back to the fireplace, set his feet precisely so, put his arms to his sides, and, bowing from the waist, said, "Lunch is served."

Everyone strolled over to help himself at the table. The crawfish looked–and presently proved–delicious. I tossed a dash of tabasco on mine and tried to make a small joke. "No sea food should be eaten without tabasco," I said.

"Quite right!" said Mrs. Simmons. Then Mr. McIlhenny added, "And thank you so much for saying so!"

GLASSES . . . IN WHICH TO PUT YOUR "DASH OF TABASCO"

The McIlhenny Company, about which the article "A Dash of *Tabasco*" was written, sells a set of four Double Diamond Label Glasses: 11 ounce, stemmed glasses with the *Tabasco* label on two sides. Now we don't know what *you're* planning to serve in those glasses, but we know exactly what *we* plan to mix in them. They are a perfect size, shape, and color for that most potent of "top of the morning" drinks, the Bloody Mary. And a Bloody Mary worth its salt is liberally seasoned with *Tabasco*—as if you didn't know. And if you want to serve your *Tabasco* in style, the McIlhenny Company has an elegant silver holder for the little bottle.

For your set of *Tabasco* glasses, send a check for $4.75; for your silver holder send $3.75 and your complete address to:

Department Double Diamond
McIlhenny Company
Avery Island, Louisiana 70513

TRYON PALACE RESTORATION COMPLEX

Although Williamsburg, Virginia, comes more quickly to mind when one mentions colonial restorations, the Tryon Palace Restoration Complex, in New Bern, North Carolina, rivals the more familiar one in beauty and accuracy, if it does not rival it in size. Indeed, there are those who say that the Palace is *the* most beautiful building which was built in colonial America. Suffice it to say, however, that one should by all means visit both Williamsburg and Tryon Palace to get the best possible picture of life and art in colonial America.

The construction of Tryon Palace was begun in 1767 under the supervision of John Hawks, the English architect who was "the first professional English architect to remain in America." The Palace was to serve as the colonial Capitol, and in that, the Palace was unique, as it also was in the fact that it was designed as a London vicinity house, "in the pure English taste." William Tryon was the Royal Governor who received appropriations for the construction of the Palace-Capitol, and he was the first Royal Governor to occupy it upon its completion in 1770. A year later, Governor Tryon was made Royal Governor of New York and he was succeeded by Josiah Martin, who served as Royal Governor until May 1775, when he took refuge aboard a vessel of the Royal Navy when the Patriots took control of the Palace. Prior to the actual possession of the Palace by the Patriots, the first Provincial Convention of North Carolina—the first anywhere in America to be called and held in defiance of British orders—had met in New Bern in 1774. Three years later, on January 16, 1777, the first Governor of North Carolina, Richard Caswell, and other State officials elected under the first Constitution of the independent State of North Carolina, were inaugurated in the Palace. From then until 1794, when the capital was moved to Raleigh, the North Carolina General Assembly held its meetings in the Palace. After 1794, the Palace fell into disrepair, and on the night of February 27, 1798, the main building burned. The East and West wing buildings were saved from the fire, but at some unrecorded date the East wing disappeared and the West wing was so altered that when it came into the possession of the State of North Carolina again, it was unrecognizable as an 18th-century structure.

Restoration of the complex was begun in 1952, with the completed Palace being opened to the public in 1959. Since then the gardens and other outbuildings have been restored also. Currently, the complex is open to the public, with guided tours by costumed hostesses, weekdays (except Mondays), Sunday afternoons, and National Holiday Mondays.

On the grounds of the complex are two other restored homes. The John Wright Stanly House was moved to the Tryon Palace Complex and restored in 1966-1972. It depicts the house of a prosperous merchant of the late eighteenth century and is furnished primarily with American pieces of 1750-1780. The Stevenson House (ca. 1805) is furnished with antiques of the Federal and Empire periods; it was opened to the public in 1966.

One of the strong points in the Tryon Palace restoration program is its emphasis on education. Consequently, there are many items available by mail which would be of interest to the casual student of colonial history. A *Tryon Palace Slide Set* (36 slides of the Palace's interiors and gardens with script), is available on loan for $1.00 plus guaranteed insured postage. There is also a *Tryon Palace Gardens Slide Set,* available under the same arrangement, which has a mimeographed script specifically designed for garden club use.

Several books, booklets, and leaflets have been printed about the Palace, its history, and restoration. Two cookbooks are available: *Tryon Palace Trifle—18th Century Cookbook* (hardcover—$2.50; paperback—$1.50) and *18th Century Tryon Palace Hostesses Are 20th Century Cooks* ($1.00).

Among other items available from the Palace Shop are a *Monte Original* Tryon Palace model, made of heavy paper, to be cut out and assembled ($1.75); colonial dolls—ladies, gentlemen, soldiers—($3.65 each); *Monte* dolls—First Ladies series, a complete set of seven 3-dimensional paper dolls ($3.85 per set). Engraved maps, in color, of Carolina in 1640, 1672, 1775, 1795, and 1825, executed by Lewis and Clark of Kitty Hawk, North Carolina, may be obtained from the Palace Shop—please write about current prices and selections available. You'll also need to write about the availability and current prices of the following: colonial reproductions in porcelain, tin, pewter, and pottery. The newest publications are 1978 ones: *Three Decades of Devotion, A History of the Tryon Palace Commission and Tryon Palace Restoration* (hardcover, 357 pages, $5.84), and *A Tryon Treasury* (guidebook, 64 pages, color and black and white photos, $4.50) by Taylor Lewis and Joanne Young. Both prices include tax and postage.

Tryon Palace Shop
Box 1007
New Bern, North Carolina 28560

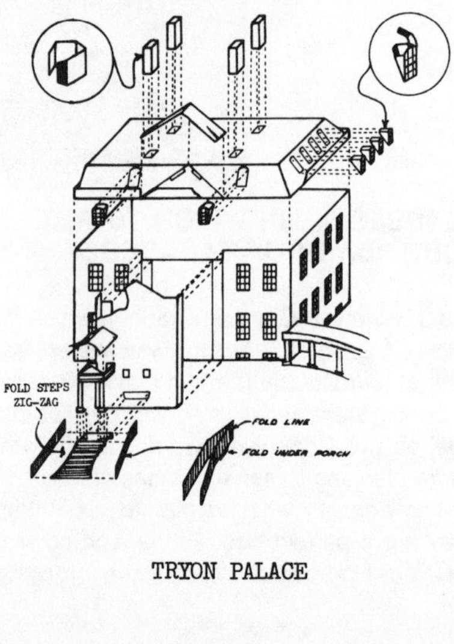

TRYON PALACE

ABOUT THE CAPITOL

The United States Capitol Historical Society was founded in 1962 as a non-profit educational organization with the purpose of encouraging knowledge about the Capitol.

Memberships in the Society now number more than five thousand. Various types of memberships are available; membership entitles one to a quarterly newsletter, an invitation to an annual meeting in Washington, and the right to purchase most of the Society's publications and products at special prices. One-time entry fees (ranging from five to one thousand dollars) are used to finance new ventures of the Society.

Anyone can order the two books shown here. *We, The People: The Story of the United States Capitol* ($2.25 postpaid) is a guidebook with over 175 pictures, most of which are in full color. This book is also available in foreign languages. Wouldn't it make a nice gift for any friend who does not speak English?

Our Nation's Capital Coloring Book ($1.70 postpaid) provides young people with illustrations to be used with crayons or water color. Each scene has a one-page description.

Also of possible interest to children—or school teachers—are accurate pasteboard models of the Capitol building. Among the other things available from the Society are an annual calendar, a book on the Magna Carta, a journal of Congressional studies, prints and Christmas cards, medals, a phonograph record of dramatic incidents in the history of the Capitol, transfer designs from architectural details and decorative seals for needlework (some in kits).

To inquire about a complete listing of items available, order the books, or inquire about membership, write to:

U.S. Capitol Historical Society
200 Maryland Avenue, N.E.
Washington, DC 20002

THE SPORT OF THE TWENTY-FIRST CENTURY

Photograph by Bettina Gray

Men have never been content to stay on the ground. The vast blue sky has challenged them since the days of the mythical Daedalus, who built feathered wings for himself and his son to escape imprisonment. Now that travel in airplanes has become as common and easy as bus travel, certain adventurers are eager to try their own, more personal "wings." Attached to their bodies with harnesses, hang gliders (whick look like great big kites) may be as close to wings of their own as humans will ever come.

Two pioneers of hang-gliding in Tennessee are Dick Stern and Don Guess. They read an article about it in the early 1970s. When Dick suggested to Don that they try it, Don's response was, "Shoot, you think I'm crazy? You think I'm gonna jump off a mountain?" But they did. They ordered a hang glider which arrived without instructions. They managed to put it together by trial and error—the same way they taught themselves to fly. When they outgrew their training hills, they sought another site and finally came upon a narrow strip of cleared land on Lookout Mountain. They received permission from the landowner to use it. The site proved to be ideal and soon hang-glider pilots were coming from neighboring states to try its "super soarability." The angle of the mountain, the slopes and air currents make it one of the best hang-gliding locations in the United States.

Tracy Knauss, an energetic young man with a BS in business, a BA in philosophy and a MA in business management, saw them fly and from that point became, as he put it, an "air space junkie." After taking a course, he became the first person to fly the complete 25-mile flight from Trenton, Georgia, to Chattanooga. His love for the sport led to his moving to Chattanooga solely for the purpose of hang-gliding.

Knauss decided that hang-gliding needed a central information bureau on techniques, hang gliders, pilots, kites, equipment, competition, coverage, etc., and, in 1976, went into business publishing *Glider Rider*, which today is the largest hang-gliding publication in the world. About the same time, he joined the Tennessee Tree Toppers, a club which promotes hang-gliding activities in the Chattanooga area, and was elected president. Under his leadership, the flying site on Lookout Mountain, discovered by Guess and Stern, was preserved via the Regulatory Program which Knauss designed and implemented. Later, when the property went up for sale, Knauss and two other investors formed a company, Air Space, Inc., and purchased the launch site specifically for the purpose of promoting the sport through daily flying and organized competition. It is called Lookout Mountain Flight Park.

After producing, with Dave Murchison of North Carolina, the Masters Championships at Grandfather Mountain, Knauss, with Murchison, decided to venture into a new area of hang-gliding services—namely, meet management. Sport Aeronautics was born—to provide regulated sites, uniform rules and informed officials for meets. In October of 1978 Sport Aeronautics organized the American Cup meet with hang-gliding teams from Britain, Canada, and Japan besides the United States team.

For beginners: it is advisable not to put together your own hang glider and go and "jump off a mountain." There are a number of professional hang-gliding schools that offer lessons. Instruction would include discussion of the glider, harness, helmet, ground team, and flights, and how to handle the glider. Practicing takeoff and a number of supervised flights at increasing altitudes would be important.

If you are interested in what Tracy Knauss calls "the purest form of flight," write to:

Tracy Knauss, Publisher/Editor
Glider Rider
P.O. Box 6009
Chattanooga, Tennessee 37401
(615) 867-4970

Pictured here is the Official American Cup Hang Gliding Game. For information, write T&M Enterprises, P.O. Box 2755, Chattanooga, Tennessee 37407, (615) 886-5677.

Flea markets may not be historically southern, or even unique to the South, but they have become an institution in the South as shown by the following article, reprinted with permission from Brown's Guide to Georgia, *copyright December, 1978.*

Cheap Thrills

A Guide to the Best Flea Markets in and near Georgia

by Beth Bassett

Need a bit of adventure in your life? A change from the daily dolor of pencils, the misery of Manila folders? Why not put on your jeans and an old T-shirt and spend a weekend treasure-hunting among the goods at the many flea markets accessible to Georgians? I guarantee you will find no duplication of objects among the merchandise and very few standard faces among the free-spirited owners and dealers.

To free your outing of hassles, we have listed in descending order the nine markets with the largest number of dealers, giving a thumbnail sketch of the flavor and wares of each. All of the businesses we list are open on a permanent, regular basis, and, with the exception of the Atlanta Swap Meet, all of them are held indoors. In addition to the ranking by size, I have indicated my personal bias by use of a rating system of one to five stars, with five designating the markets I like best.

Since 1973, flea markets have become increasingly popular. At the nine major markets we list, goods displayed over a total of 500,000 square feet of floor space and 10 acres of asphalt may attract up to 70,000 shoppers per day on a given weekend. So come on! Join the crowd!

☆☆THE JOCKEY LOT, Anderson, S.C. Cross into South Carolina on I-85, and exit on U.S. 76 East. Just after you reach Anderson, take U.S. 29 North. Jockey Lot is 10 miles out of town. 700 dealers. Fri 8 until all customers have gone, Sat 6–until, Sun 1–6. (803) 224-2027. Owners D.C. Bryson, W.R. McClellion. Established 1974. *Not my cup of tea. I'd like to see more collectables.*

Wear your walking shoes to this one. Strung end to end, the 100,000 square feet of floor space in these long, narrow sheds would total one mile in length. Big crowds under the tin roof make this a rather noisy shopping place, especially when it rains. Parking space for 10,000 cars.

Merchandise here is 95% new and slightly discounted. Jewelry, leather goods, cosmetics, clothing, tombstones, kitchen items, furniture, light fixtures, bathtubs, lumber, tools, bedding plants, farm products, hubcaps, and more. Five eating places. Best bargain: the dentist, who extracts teeth for as little as $6 and makes partial plates at reasonable prices. Customers line up and take numbers in his mobile office on Saturday from 9 till 1. Owners plan to bring in an M.D., a general practitioner, as well.

☆☆☆☆☆GEORGIA ANTIQUE FAIR AND FLEA MARKET, 2000 Lakewood Ave, Southeast Atlanta. Exit I-85 at Lakewood Freeway eastbound. Lakewood Ave leads to the Lakewood Park Fairgrounds. 500 dealers. Held 9–6 second Sat and Sun of every month. Owners Ellen Peabody, Cookie Levetan. Established 1973. *Because of its variety and bargain-priced finds, I give it top marks.*

Always something different here because dealers on the nationwide circuit bring goods from all over the U.S. (including Alaska and Hawaii) to show in four large buildings at the fairgrounds. Plenty of well lighted parking spaces.

Antiques and collectables that form the bulk of the merchandise have been known to include a $13,000 vase, a $20,000 diamond necklace, and a 1930 truck. Less exotic goods are secondhand items and new, discounted merchandise: Corning Ware, braided rugs, oriental rugs, furniture. A good buy: round unfinished oak tables for $80. Compare them at $200 (finished), retail. A large number of the buyers here are dealers who come from their own markets.

☆☆☆☆**ATLANTA FLEA MARKET, 2424 Piedmont Rd NE at Lindbergh, Atlanta. 391 dealers. Fri & Sat 12–9:30, Sun 12–7. (404) 266-2495. Owners Jack Hodgkins, Bill Malone, Don McQuinn. Established 1974.** *A great place to shop. I knock a point off for some overpricing.*

Expect to encounter crowds at this market, housed in 145,000 square feet of floor space in a building that used to contain an Arlan's discount store. The merchandise is now all but devoid of the clean-out-the-basement wares formerly to be found here. Most dealers are permanent and sell substantial goods about which they are knowledgeable. Find your way around by means of street signs and booth numbers.

Antiques and collectables form the backbone of the merchandise, but also represented are original oil paintings, new and used furniture, new and used clothing, household necessities, sports and electronics equipment, farm produce, gift items, and more. Services include a deli, which claims to be the only one in Atlanta serving New York-style fare, and a hair stylist. Goods are not uniformly good bargains, so be cautious. Among one collection of Early American hand tools, I found items priced at up to three times what they are elsewhere. Some copper and some brass objects in gift shop discounted, others at retail level. Tennis rackets actually overpriced.

"Happy coats," sold by Mrs. Rose Chen, are delightful bargains. Made in the People's Republic of China, the satin wraparounds are embroidered with colorful oriental designs and priced at $22. Bea and Harry Levitt sell open-stock McCoy ironstone at two-thirds retail price. Jerry's feathers in booth 128 are good buys. Books sold by Mrs. Emily Cooper are steals, many new ones less than half price, and attract many schoolteachers who buy children's volumes for their classrooms.

The booth I most enjoyed contained Toni's collection of "previously owned" furs. Monkey jackets are $550, full-length mink coats $600 and up. Red-squirrel coats complete with Joan Crawford shoulder pads and Art-Deco buttons, stone-marten fur pieces, and fur muffs are $20 to $40. These old furs have so much personality. And at those prices, almost anyone can afford at least a muff.

☆☆☆☆**ATLANTA SWAP MEET, located at the Storey Twin Drive-In Theater on the access road at Shallowford Rd and I-85 in Northeast Atlanta. 200 dealers. Open every Sun 8–5. Owners Ken Campbell, Jack Peay. Established 1974.** *This is a flea market in the truest sense of the term. I rate it high on the adventure scale.*

Ten acres of asphalt are spread with the results of hundreds of house cleanings. Dealers come before sunup to get choice spots near the concession stand. No firearms, liquor, pornographic literature, nor fireworks are allowed, since many families come to spend the day buying and selling.

Lots of bargains here: suitcases for $1, saddles for $10, shoes 25¢ a pair and up, cereal bowls 6 for $1, vases five cents, twin-bed set complete with frame, box springs, and mattress $22. Collectables available also: coins, bottles, primitives, Depression glass, and more. Many prices are lowered near the end of the afternoon.

☆**FLEA MARKET AT FOREST SQUARE, 4855 Jonesboro Rd, Forest Park. Exit off I-285 on Jonesboro Road going south, and travel 1½ miles to Forest Square. 110 dealers. Fri & Sat 10–9, Sun noon–6. All holidays except Christmas Day 10-9. (404) 361-1221. Manager Joan Brown. Established 1977.** *In any rating, one of the stores has to come in last. This is it.*

Open for only one year, this market hasn't quite gotten off the ground yet. Lots of empty space remains in the 75,000 square feet of this old Grant City building.

New and used clothing, jewelry, some farm produce, used household items, records, tapes, plants, tools, handmade articles, books, old comics. Tools (wrenches, sockets, etc.) and wooden ax and hammer handles are good buys. Macramé gift items made by 14-year-old Sandy Green are lovely and include a baby swing decorated at the corners with ABC blocks for $40. Mrs. Maxine Sandman presides over articles made by shut-ins. These include made-to-order doll dresses and furniture, mother-daughter dresses, and costumes.

☆☆☆**SOUTH AUGUSTA FLEA MARKET, 1558 New Savannah Rd. Exit I-20 on Bobby Jones Expressway (I-520), go east on Lumpkin Rd, then north on New Savannah Rd (Ga Hwy 56 Loop). Market is just north of Rocky Creek. 80 dealers. Sat 10–7, Sun 12–7, antique auction Sat 7 pm–1 am. (404) 798-8996. Manager Gerald Wight. Owners Sylvia and Harold Rhodes. Established 1976.** *Something in the air here arouses my curiosity. I give it a middling grade for being a latent source of treasure.*

Anything but fancy, this market convenes in an old corrugated-tin cattle-auction barn.

Some jewels among the mostly garage-sale items. Example: a 1916 Mascot stove, half wood-, half gas-burning. Has a warming oven, a gas oven, and a wood-heated oven. The stove is five feet tall and sells for $300. Example: half-price pet supplies, hair-care products, sewing notions, school supplies, and model kits for children. Example: a cut-glass crystal decanter among the items of an estate sale: $6.

☆☆**THE JUNCTION, 211 Roosevelt Ave, Albany. Take Washington St east off U.S. 19**

continued

A GOOD GUIDE

Brown's Guide to Georgia was first published seven years ago. In the years since then it has become obvious that *Brown's Guide* was just what a lot of Georgians had been looking for (and a lot of non-Georgians, too): a well-written, well-illustrated, genuinely informative guide to the state. From a quarterly selling 4,000 copies, *Brown's Guide* has become a monthly, with subscriptions doubling from 30,000 to 60,000 in the last twelve months.

Focusing on the people, places, history, culture, and recreational opportunities throughout the state of Georgia, the magazine typically contains articles on where to go, do-it-yourself ideas, hiking, biking, cooking, shopping, tours, historic homes, canoeing, fishing, eating out, and consumer service, as well as an extensive listing of Georgia restaurants, fairs, festivals, sports, and outings. Additionally, *Brown's Guide* carries in-depth profiles of active people throughout the state whose work might otherwise go unhighlighted, as well as features on the complex social and political dynamics of cities and towns across Georgia.

The magazine was the brainchild of publisher Fred Brown. "The reader I had in mind was really someone a lot like me," Brown recalls. "I had always enjoyed hiking, biking and canoeing, but I didn't know enough about it. I liked to get away and see other parts of the state up close and my aim was to put together a guide for people to make it possible for them to enjoy doing that kind of thing more easily."

His first issue, produced with the help and support of his family, appeared in 1972. He printed 8,000 copies and "got rid of about

4,000." "We weren't very sophisticated about our distribution at that point," Brown explains. "Manuel's Tavern in Atlanta was our first outlet. Other than that, we just threw the magazines in the back of a VW and delivered them to people who said they would help us get them out. We had no investors, no subscribers, no advertising, and no real idea about circulation."

This success story may be partly due to good timing. (According to a recent story in *Advertising Age*, an industry bible, local publications are the wave of the future.) But even more, we think, it is due to a real need being filled, and well filled. We wish someone would or could do the same for the other states as Fred Brown has done for Georgia.

The subscription rate is $10.00 per year. Back issues are $3.00 per copy.

Write to:

Brown's Guide to Georgia
Box 87306
College Park, Georgia 30337

(Oglethorpe Blvd). Roosevelt runs parallel to Oglethorpe. 25 dealers. Fri, Sat, & Sun 9–5:30. (912) 439-0138. Owners Mr. Snelling, Ed Mason Jones. Manager Mr. Shiver. Established 1976. *Not enough antiques and collectables for my taste, so I can't give it a higher rating.*

Trains still rumble down the railroad track smack in the middle of Roosevelt Avenue, and in former days the three-story red-brick flea-market building was a shipping warehouse. Now the interior is sectioned into chicken-wire booths.

Lots of bric-à-brac here. A few collectables—Depression glass, dishes from Occupied Japan, silverware, bottles—and a few antiques. Tools in Mr. Shiver's booth on lowest level are good buys. Example: impact wrench, used, for $40, which would cost up to $115 new. Mr. Shiver sells skill saws, sockets, and parts for hydraulic jacks and lawn mowers, and repairs those items. Market houses a furniture-refinishing shop.

******ATHENS FLEA MARKET, 364 N Thomas St, a block north of intersection of Thomas and Broad (U.S. 78), east of University of Georgia campus. 10 dealers. Mon–Th, 11:30–10, Fri & Sat 12–11, Sun 12–9. (404) 549-3534. Owners Al Templeton, John Stevens. Established 1974.** *My grade is based on the enthusiasm of the owners and dealers and on bargain prices.*

Sparky's Seafood Café and the Oyster Bar that looks like a set from a Humphrey Bogart movie open right onto the market and give the old grocery warehouse an intimate feeling. Booths are large. Lots of goods are just sitting around in the back room, as yet unclassified.

Furniture reproductions, primitives, out-of-print books, bric-à-brac, baskets and plants, waterbeds and accessories, gourmet coffee by the cup or pound, sandwiches and deli items, and used furniture sold here. Two companies who build solar-heated homes have offices and displays in the market.

Dr. and Mrs. Jim Cantrell (he is head of the Math Department at the University) have a large collection of primitives here, selling at prices well below those you'll find elsewhere. Example: hand planers for $12 and a cherry-wood level for $5. Baskets, plants, and waterbeds are bargain-priced.

*******SAVANNAH FLEA MARKET, 230 West Bay, on Savannah's riverfront. 8 dealers. Mon, Tu & Th–Sat 12–5. (912) 232-9251. Manager Mrs. Myra Chapman. Established 1969.** *For so much Savannah charm, what else but top marks?*

For goodness' sake, when you go to this one, leave your urge to organize, your inclination to rush around asking questions, at the door. If you just go with the flow, you won't miss the best features of the establishment: the unhurried charm of the dealers, and the stacked-up merchandise located on four labyrinthine levels that are stairstepped up the riverbank and look much as they did when the building was a cotton warehouse.

Antiques, collectables, and very good used furniture here. Mrs. Caroline Kimble on the street level has a large collection of glassware lining four window shelves and coloring Bay Street blue, green, and amber. A short flight of steps up, in The Attic, Sally and Mark Davys sell antiques: an English pub table bargain-priced at $225; a folding, traveling preacher's desk; a Pennsylvania Dutch dower chest. Mr. and Mrs. Flowers refinish furniture one level below the street. On the lowest and most picturesque level, three dealers offer collectables in a shop called the Upstairs, Downstairs. It opens on one end to the river, on the other to a cobblestone lane below the level of Bay Street. A first edition of *Robert's Rules* was selling there for $3, and old postcards (thousands of them) for from 10¢ to $5. A bronze-and-ivory figure of Isadora Duncan was marked $2,000, a clear cut-glass pitcher was $450.

The L. C. Gosney Company in Louisville, Kentucky, offers a product to help you remember the last six Triple Crown winners. A set of six tumblers with a Triple Crown winner on each glass in full color is available for $17.50 per set. In addition, they offer 12" x 16" prints of the Kentucky Derby winners in color for $6.00 per print and $17.50 with a frame; 12" x 16" prints of 11 winners of the Triple Crown are available for $9.00 per print and $19.50 with a frame. Other items that you may order include notes, playing cards, ice buckets, and waste baskets. Write to: L. C. Gosney, P.O. Box 6051, Louisville, Kentucky 40206.

THE PEANUT SHOP OF WILLIAMSBURG

The first peanuts grown in the United States were planted in Surry County, Virginia, not far from the present-day site of The Peanut Shop and its kitchen. The nuts were transported from Africa via the slave ships which stocked them as food for their human cargo. The peanut is among the oldest seed crops known to man and certainly has contributed to the economy of the South so abundantly that King Cotton is the only crop out-ranking it.

The Peanut Shop of Williamsburg's order form states that their peanuts are: "crunchier, meatier, more delicious than you have ever tasted." Having indulged in ample sampling from their 2½ lb. tin, we can only say their description is an understatement!

These are Virginia peanuts, and while we don't know what the generic differences are among peanuts, we can only tell you these look bumpier and are indeed the crunchiest peanuts we have ever eaten. They are blanched, cooked in pure peanut oil in small batches, and lightly salted. Nothing artificial has been added; consequently the information on the side of the tin states "to refrigerate."

The 2½ lb. tin sells for $7.25 postpaid (add $2.00 west of the Mississippi). Virginia residents add 4% state sales tax.

Order from:

The Peanut Shop of Williamsburg
Merchants Square
P.O. Box GN
Williamsburg, Virginia 23185

KEY WEST HAND PRINT FABRICS, INC.

Be one with the sun! Go in a shower of flowers, a paisley fair, or a bird in flight. Let them take you through a day or a night. Pick a design to sew into a free spirit wardrobe or to wrap a gift in sunshine.

Key West Hand Print Fabrics, Inc., creates material that pulsates with color. The famous Lilly and styles by Liza, Vanda, and Erio Bocci are made from this material.

Uses of the fabric are limited only by your imagination—of course, try dresses, slacks, pants, ties, jackets, bathing suits, hats, or any article of clothing. But how about using your scraps for patchwork placemats or quilts, or to cover boxes of stationery, diaries, or pencil boxes—anything you can cover, you can make it come vibrantly alive with the hand printed fabric.

The fabrics are a generous 44"—45" wide. Some are 60". All are washable, guarantee minimum shrinkage, and have designs that are not only original, but are individually copyrighted. They print on a variety of fabrics and prices range from $7.00 to $9.00 per yard.

Now you can also buy material for lining and finishing garments:

a) Plain white batiste lining, 65% polyester—35% cotton, at $1.60 per yard.

b) Plain background fabric (base fabric on which designs are printed), same fiber content, in colors to match materials, at $2.00 per yard.

Once you have had the delightful pleasure of owning a piece of Key West Hand Print Fabric, you will want to keep up with their ever evolving color combinations and patterns.

Visit one of their shops located, in Florida, at Key West, Marathon, Islamorada, Coconut Grove (Miami), Ft. Lauderdale, Clearwater Beach, Daytona Beach, Jacksonville, St. Petersburg Beach, Silver Springs, Vero Beach, and Winter Park. There are also stores in Virginia Beach, Virginia; Southern Pines, North Carolina; St. Simons Island, Georgia; Nantucket, Maine; Myrtle Beach, South Carolina; Kiawah Island, South Carolina; Hilton Head, South Carolina; Baltimore, Maryland; and Annapolis, Maryland.

Key West Hand Print Fabrics, Inc.
529 Front Street
Key West, Florida 33040

Artist "ZUZEK" creates original design.

Paint is poured into screen and transferred to fabric by means of the "squegee," the long, wooden board. The printing tables are 60 yards long.

Fabrics are then cured in ovens at high temperatures.

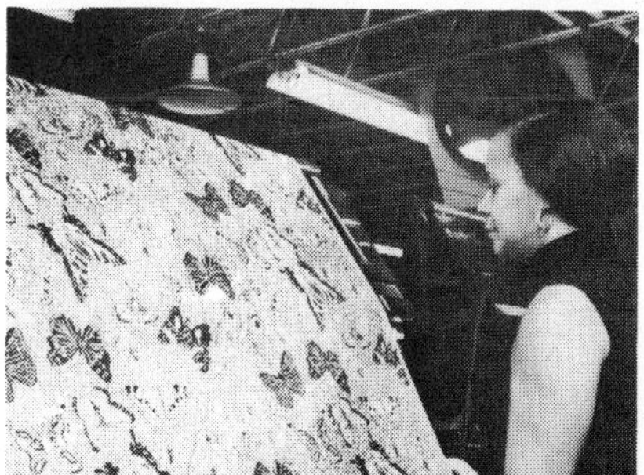

Finally each yard of fabric is carefully inspected for imperfections.

	ALABAMA	ARKANSAS	FLORIDA
JANUARY	Birmingham—Birmingham International Indoor Tennis Tournament Birmingham—Birmingham Symphony Presents "The Pops" Mobile—Senior Bowl Game Scottsboro—First Monday Trade Day, first Monday of each month	Fort Smith—Boat Show Hot Springs—Coin Show	Key West—Old Island Days Miami—Orange Bowl Game Sarasota—International Kite Flyoff Tampa—Can/Am Bowl Game Tarpon Springs—Epiphany "Greek Cross Day" White Springs—Stephen Foster Memorial Week
FEBRUARY	Birmingham—Dixie Jamboree Square Dance Festival Mobile—Azalea Trail Festival Mobile—Mardi Gras Day Union Springs—National Shooting Dog Championship, Sedgefield Plantation	Dardanelle—Bird Dog Field Trials Hot Springs—Oaklawn Racing, Oaklawn Park	Dade City—Heart of Florida Folk Festival Fort Myers—Edison Pageant of Light Tampa—Gasparilla Pirate Invasion
MARCH	Birmingham—Old-Time Fiddlers' Contest Eufaula; Lowndesboro; Mobile; Selma—Tours of Historic Homes Montgomery—Livestock Week and World Championship Rodeo	Hot Springs—Outdoor Art Show Rison—Pioneer Craft Festival	Bradenton—DeSoto Celebration Dunedin—Highland Games and Festival Palatka—Azalea Festival St. Petersburg—Festival of States Sanibel—Sanibel Island Shell Fair
APRIL	Birmingham—Alabama Jubilee Square and Round Dance Birmingham—Festival of Arts Birmingham; Decatur; Dothan; Montgomery; Selma; Tuscaloosa—Home and Garden Tours	Batesville and El Dorado—Historic Homes Tours Mountain View—Arkansas Folk Festival	St. Augustine—Blessing of the Fleet
MAY	Birmingham—Southern Appalachian Dulcimer Festival Clayton and Fort Payne—Historic Homes Tours Eufaula—Alabama Fresh Water Fishing Rodeo Mobile—America's Junior Miss Pageant Steele—Folk Music Festival, Horse Pens 40 Talladega—Winston "500" NASCAR Grand National Stock Car Race	Fort Smith—Arkansas-Oklahoma Rodeo Melbourne—Pioneer Day Stuttgart—Grand Prairie Grand Prix	Fernandina Beach—Eight Flags Shrimp Boat Races Ft. Lauderdale—Hall of Fame International Diving Meet Miami—International Folk Festival Sarasota—International Sandcastle Contest Tallahassee—FSU Flying High Circus
JUNE	Clanton—Peach Festival	Hot Springs—Arkansas Fun Festival Marshall—Buffalo River Canoe Race	Cypress Gardens—All-American Water Ski Championship Cypress Gardens—Classic Car Meet Fort Walton Beach—Billy Bowlegs Festival Pensacola—Fiesta of Five Flags

	ALABAMA	ARKANSAS	FLORIDA
JULY	Anniston—Alabama Shakespeare Festival Bayou La Batre—Blessing of the Shrimp Fleet Decatur—Spirit of America Pageant, Point Mallard	Fairfield Bay—USTA Mixed Doubles Tennis Tournament Springdale—Rodeo of the Ozarks	Daytona Beach—Firecracker "400" and Paul Revere "250" Race Miami—Bowling Tournament of the Americas Miami Beach—Shakespeare-By-The-Sea
AUGUST	Eufaula—Lake Eufaula Festival Talladega—Talladega "500" Grand National Stock Car Race	Batesville—National Explorer Scout Canoe Race Batesville—White River Water Carnival Prairie Grove—Clothesline Fair	Cypress Gardens—World Delta Glider Championships St. Augustine—Days in Spain Festival
SEPTEMBER	Gadsden—Mid-South Marching Band Festival and Parade Selma—Alabama River Raft Races	Mountain View—State Old-Time Fiddlers' Championship Russellville—Bluegrass Festival Stuttgart—Grand Prairie Festival of Arts	Cypress Gardens—National Ski Jumping Championship White Springs—Florida Folk Festival
OCTOBER	Athens—Tennessee Valley Old-Time Fiddlers' Contest Dothan—National Peanut Festival Gulf Shores—Shrimp Festival Steele—Horse Pens 40 Fall Folk Festival	Eureka Springs—Ozark Folk Festival Yellville—National Wild Turkey Calling Contest	Naples—Swamp Buggy Days Perry—Florida Forest Festival
NOVEMBER	Birmingham—Festival of Sacred Music Gulf Shores—Speckled Trout Rodeo	Stuttgart—World's Championship Duck Calling Contest	Key West—Offshore Powerboat Race Ormond Beach—Antique Car Meet
DECEMBER	Birmingham, Arlington; Mobile, Oakleigh; Montgomery, Ordeman-Shaw House; Selma, Sturdivant Hall—Christmas Celebrations at Antebellum Homes Montgomery—Blue-Gray Football Game	Arkansas Second Deer Season, Statewide Hot Springs—Christmas Pageant Siloam Springs—"Pool of Siloam" Pageant	Coral Gables—Junior Orange Bowl Sports Events: football, bowling, tennis, soccer Orlando—Tangerine Bowl Sports Week Pompano Beach—Christmas Boat Parade White Springs—Open House of Antiques and Christmas Concert

	GEORGIA	KENTUCKY	LOUISIANA
JANUARY	Atlanta—Children's Theatre	Prestonsburg—Annual "Old Christmas" Shakertown—Tours of Shakertown, year-round	Cameron—Louisiana Fur and Wildlife Festival New Orleans—Sugar Bowl Football Game
FEBRUARY	Atlanta—International Sport and Travel Show Savannah—Celebration of the Founding of Georgia	Hodgenville—Lincoln Day Celebration	Baton Rouge—LSU Livestock Show and Championship Rodeo New Orleans—Mardi Gras Celebration Shreveport—Louisiana Square Dance Festival
MARCH	Atlanta; Savannah—St. Patrick's Day Parades Dublin—St. Patrick's Festival St. Simons Island; Savannah; Washington; Waycross—Tours of Homes	London—Folk Festival	Baton Rouge—LSU National Quarter Horse Show Baton Rouge; St. Francisville—Tour of Homes Bogalusa—Dogwood Festival and Tour of Homes Lafayette; New Orleans—Opening of Horseracing
APRIL	Americus; Athens; Atlanta; Columbus; Thomasville—Homes Tours Atlanta—Atlanta Dogwood Festival Savannah—Night in Old Savannah Thomasville—Rose Festival	Benton—Tater Day Berea—Mountain Folk Festival Lexington—Blue Grass Tours	Baton Rouge—Louisiana Heritage Tour New Orleans—New Orleans Jazz and Heritage Festival New Orleans—Spring Fiesta Shreveport—Holiday in Dixie
MAY	Atlanta—Atlanta River Raft Race Dalton—Prater's Mill Country Fair Hiawassee—Spring Country Music and Bluegrass Festival Pineville—National Freestyle Water Ski Championship, Callaway Gardens	Berea—Artists and Craftsmen Spring Fair Louisville—Kentucky Derby Pineville—Mountain Laurel Festival	Lafitte—World Championship Pirogue Races Lake Charles—Contraband Days
JUNE	Cordele—Bluegrass Festival and Craftsmen Fair Pine Mountain—Florida State University Flying High Circus, Callaway Gardens	Grayson—Kentucky Folksong Festival Louisville—Bluegrass Music Festival Slade—National Mountain-Style Square Dance Contest	Galliano—Cajun Festival Gonzales—Jambalaya Festival

	GEORGIA	KENTUCKY	LOUISIANA
JULY	Atlanta—Stay and See Georgia Week, Lenox Square Pine Mountain—Masters Water Ski Tournament, Callaway Gardens	Slade—Mountain Music Festival South Union—Shaker Festival	Baton Rouge—LSU Paint Horse Show Galliano—Louisiana Oyster Festival Golden Meadow—Golden Meadow International Tarpon Rodeo Grand Isle—Grand Isle Tarpon Rodeo
AUGUST	Hiawassee—Mountain Fair Jekyll Island—Square Dance Jamboree, Aquarama Pine Mountain—Gardens Water Ski Show, Callaway Gardens	Cloverport—Sacajawea Festival Fulton—International Banana Festival Louisville—World's Championship Horse Show	Morgan City—Shrimp Festival New Orleans—Food Festival
SEPTEMBER	Helen—Bavarian Oktoberfest Newman—Powers' Crossroads Country Fair and Art Festival Stone Mountain—Yellow Daisy Festival	Prestonsburg—Kentucky Highlands Folk Festival Slade—Western-Style Square Dance Festival	Morgan City—Louisiana Shrimp and Petroleum Festival New Iberia—Louisiana Sugar Cane Festival
OCTOBER	Dalton—Prater's Mill Country Fair Hiawassee—Fiddlers' and Bluegrass Festival Stone Mountain—Scottish Festival and Highland Games	Louisville—Oktoberfest Paintsville—Apple Festival	Crowley—International Rice Festival Opelousas—Yambilee Festival Raceland—Sauce Piquante Festival and Pirogue Races Ville Platte—Cotton Festival
NOVEMBER	Lumpkin—Westville's Fair of 1850 Macon—Star of Bethlehem Show	Louisville—World Championship Quarter Horse Show	Baton Rouge—LSU Dixie Jubilee Horse Show Colfax—Pecan Festival
DECEMBER	Stone Mountain—Living Christmas Nativity Pageant	Bethlehem—Living Nativity	Many—Hodges Gardens Festival of Lights Natchitoches—Christmas Lighting Festival, Cane River New Orleans—Midwinter Sports Carnival: yachting, tennis, basketball; climaxed by Sugar Bowl Football Classic

	MARYLAND	MISSISSIPPI	NORTH CAROLINA
JANUARY	Baltimore—International Indoor Tennis Championships	Meridian—Meridian Symphony Orchestra Concert Natchez—Natchez Little Theatre	Hoffman—Southeastern Brittany Field Trials Pinehurst—Pinehurst Field Trials Southern Pines—Mid-South Horse Shows Winston-Salem—Piedmont Sportsman Show
FEBRUARY	Salisbury—National Indoor Open Tennis Championship	Biloxi and Waveland—Mardi Gras Celebration Jackson—Dixie National Rodeo	Charlotte—Mid-Atlantic Boat Show Charlotte—Southern Living Show
MARCH	Baltimore—Historic-Harbour House Tour McHenry—Winterfest St. Mary's City—Maryland Day	Biloxi; Carrollton; Columbus; Gulfport; Natchez; Ocean Springs; Pass Christian; Vicksburg—Spring Pilgrimages McComb—Lighted Azalea Trail Festivities	Rockingham—Carolina "500" Race Winston-Salem—Longhorn World Championship Rodeo Pinehurst—Sandhills Open Skeet Shoot
APRIL	Butler—Grand National Point-to-Point Steeplechase Races Glyndon—Maryland Hunt Cup Race Meet Monkton—My Lady's Manor Hunt Race Meet Statewide—House and Garden Pilgrimage	Jackson—Mississippi Film Festival	New Bern—Spring Tryon Garden Tour Southern Pines—Stoneybrook Steeplechase Race Statesville—Carolina Dogwood Festival Union Grove—World Champion Old-Time Fiddlers' Contest Wilmington—North Carolina Azalea Festival
MAY	Baltimore—Annual Preakness Baltimore—Kite Festival Baltimore Inner Harbor—Sailboat Regatta Rockville—Scottish Festival and Highland Games	Jackson and Tupelo—Arts Festival Monticello—Tours of Homes and Churches Vicksburg—Riverboat Festival	Charlotte—Southern Crafts Show Fontana—Square and Round Dance Festivals Winston-Salem—Winston "200" Auto Race
JUNE	Cumberland—Heritage Days Salisbury—Delmarva Chicken Festival	Biloxi—Blessing of the Fleet Biloxi; Ocean Springs—Fishing Rodeos	Brevard—Music Festival Linville—Annual "Singing on the Mountain," Grandfather Mountain Pinehurst—State Trapshooting Championships

	MARYLAND	MISSISSIPPI	NORTH CAROLINA
JULY	Frederick—Motorcycle Races Hagerstown—Frontier Crafts Days Ocean City—Seafood Festival	Gulfport—Mississippi Deep Sea Fishing Rodeo Philadelphia—Choctaw Indian Fair	Asheville—Craftsman's Fair of the Southern Highlands High Point—World Championship Boat Drag Races Linville—Grandfather Mountain Highland Games and Gathering of Scottish Clans Waynesville—Smoky Mountain Folk Festival
AUGUST	Brunswick—Potomac River Festival Cordova and Port Republic—Jousting Tournaments	Columbus—Folklife Festival Pass Christian—Round Cat Island Race	Asheville—Mountain Dance and Folk Festival Hendersonville—North Carolina Apple Festival
SEPTEMBER	Chestertown—Candlelight Historic Walking Tour Crisfield—28th Annual National Hard Crab Derby Towson—State Skeet Championship Westminster—Steam Show Days	Natchez—Old Natchez Territorial Fair	Elizabeth City—Albemarle Craftsman's Fair Linville—Masters of Hang Gliding Championship, Grandfather Mountain
OCTOBER	Annapolis—Chesapeake Appreciation Day Princess Anne—Olde Princess Anne Days Westminster—Fall Harvest Day	Natchez—Fall Pilgrimage	Mount Airy—Autumn Leaves Festival Rockingham—"American 500" Stock Car Race
NOVEMBER	Easton—Waterfowl Festival		Charlotte—Southern Christmas Show Winston-Salem—Piedmont Craftsmen's Fair
DECEMBER	Annapolis—Christmas Greens Show, Hammond-Harwood House Baltimore—Christmas at Mount Clare Baltimore—Holly Tour	Greenwood—Delta Band Festival and Winter Carnival Leland—Christmas Festival on Deer Creek Meridian—"Trees of Christmas" Tours, Merrehope Antebellum Home	Charlotte—"Singing Christmas Tree" Kill Devil Hills—First Flight Celebration Winston-Salem—"Salem Christmas of 1800"

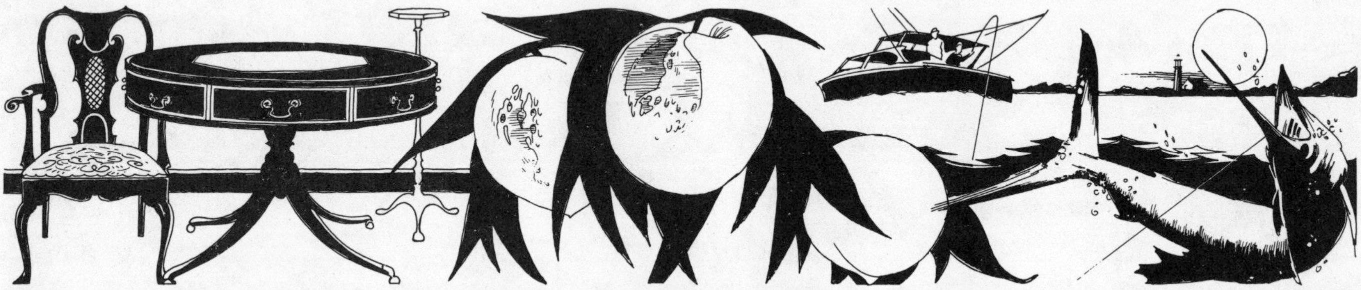

	OKLAHOMA	SOUTH CAROLINA	TENNESSEE
JANUARY	Tulsa—International Finals Rodeo	Charleston—Antique Fair and Sale Charleston—New Year's Celebration at Charles Towne Landing	Nashville—Boat Show
FEBRUARY	Carnegie—World Championship Domino Tournament	Columbia—Carolina Capers Square Dance Festival Greenville—Boat, R/V and Sports Show	Grand Junction—Grand National Field Trials, Ames Plantation Memphis—National Indoor Tennis Championships Memphis—Mid-South Sport, Boat and Travel Show
MARCH		Aiken—Triple Crown Racing (Harness Racing, Thoroughbred Trials, and Steeplechase) Beaufort; Charleston; Summerville—Tours of Historic Homes Camden—Carolina Cup Races	Erin—Wearing o' the Green Festival
APRIL	Guthrie—89'ers Day Celebration Muskogee—Azalea Festival	Camden; Charleston; Columbia; Edgefield; Florence; Greenwood; Hilton Head Island; Spartanburg—Home and Garden Pilgrimages Charleston and Georgetown—Plantation Tours	Gatlinburg and Elizabethton—Wildflower Pilgrimage Knoxville—Dogwood Arts Festival Paris—World's Biggest Fish Fry
MAY	Canton—Walleys Rodeo Enid—Tri-State Music Festival Prague—Kolache Festival	Charleston—Greek Spring Festival, Middleton Place Charleston—Spoleto Festival Myrtle Beach and the Grand Strand—Grand Strand Fishing Rodeo Orangeburg—South Carolina Festival of Roses	Memphis—Cotton Carnival Nashville—Iroquois Steeplechase
JUNE	Ardmore—Indian Fair Madill—National Sand Bass Festival Marietta—Frontier Days	Myrtle Beach—Sun Fun Festival North Myrtle Beach—Tennis Cup Nationals Tournament	Bristol—Spring National Drag Races Elizabethton; Roan Mountain—Rhododendron Festival Nashville—Sinking Creek Film Celebration

	OKLAHOMA	SOUTH CAROLINA	TENNESSEE
JULY	Oklahoma City; Pawnee—Homecomings and Powwows Stroud—International Brick and Rolling Pin Throwing Contest	Beaufort—Water Festival Greenwood—South Carolina Festival of Flowers Mountain Rest—Hillbilly Day	Smithville—Old-Time Fiddlers' Jamboree
AUGUST	Anadarko—American Indian Exposition Hugo—Bluegrass Music Festival	Myrtle Beach—Art in the Parks Sidewalk Show	Chattanooga—Hang Gliding Exhibition Lawrenceburg—Davy Crockett Day Shelbyville—Walking Horse Celebration South Fulton—International Banana Festival
SEPTEMBER	Perry—Cherokee Strip Celebration Tahlequah—Cherokee National Holiday	Charleston—Scottish Games and Highland Gathering Darlington—Southern "500" Festival	Cosby—Folk Festival of the Smokies Nashville—Longhorn World Championship Rodeo
OCTOBER	Stilwell—Indian Summer Festival Yukon—Czech Festival	Charleston—Lancing Tournament Spartanburg to Erwin, Tenn.—Autumn Leaves Cannonball Steam Train Trip	Bristol—Southeastern Band Festival Chattanooga to Crossville—Autumn Leaf Special Train Trip Knoxville—Craftsman's Fair of the Southern Highlands
NOVEMBER	Claremore—Will Rogers Day Celebration Enid—Grand National Quail Hunt	Camden—Colonial Cup Camden—The Camden Hunt Salley—Chitlin' Strut	Nashville—Annual Christmas Village Show and Sale, Fairgrounds
DECEMBER	Oklahoma City—National Finals Rodeo Waynoka—Christmas Pageant at Little Sahara	Beaufort; Charleston; Union—Christmas Tours of Antebellum Homes	Knoxville—Nativity Pageant Nashville—Trees of Christmas, Cheekwood

	TEXAS	VIRGINIA	WEST VIRGINIA
JANUARY	Dallas—Cotton Bowl Game El Paso—Sun Bowl Football Game and Carnival Hallettsville—Championship Domino Tourney Mission—Texas Citrus Fiesta	Stratford—Open House at Stratford Hall Williamsburg—Colonial Weekends in Williamsburg	Parkesburg—Winter Carnival
FEBRUARY	Brownsville—Charro Days Houston—National Indoor Championship Motorcycle Races Houston—Salt Grass Trail Ride	Alexandria—George Washington Birthday Celebration	Davis—State Snowmobile Championship Slatyfork—West Virginia Ski Pro Classic, Snowshoe Resort
MARCH	Houston—Azalea Trails McAllen—International Spring Fiesta Shamrock—St. Patrick's Celebration Tyler—Azalea and Spring Flower Trail Woodville—Tyler County Dogwood Festival	Lorton—Kite Festival Monterey—Highland County Maple Sugar Festival	Davis—Tucker County Alpine Festival
APRIL	Beaumont—Neches River Festival Corpus Christi—Buccaneer Days Dallas—World Championship Tennis Finals Fredericksburg—Easter Fires Pageant San Antonio—Fiesta de San Antonio Waco—Brazos River Festival and Pilgrimage	Cape Henry—Cape Henry Day Charlottesville and Vinton—Dogwood Festivals Norfolk—International Azalea Festival	Parkersburg—Heritage Days
MAY	Athens—Old Fiddlers' Reunion Waco—Texas Highland Games	Chincoteague Island—Seafood Festival, Tom's Cove Park, Eastern Shore of Virginia Jamestown—Jamestown Day Winchester—Shenandoah Apple Blossom Festival	Beckley—American Heritage Antique Show Lewisburg—Greenbrier Valley Bluegrass Festival Richwood—Cranberry Mountain Spring Nature Tour
JUNE	Denison—National Sand Bass Festival, Lake Texoma Odessa—Shakespeare Festival San Antonio—Fiesta Noche del Rio San Marcos—Texas Water Safari	Hampton—Jazz Festival Virginia Beach—Virginia Beach Music Festival	Glenville—West Virginia Folk Festival Webster Springs—Mountain State Bluegrass Festival

	TEXAS	VIRGINIA	WEST VIRGINIA
JULY	Corpus Christi—All Texas Jazz Festival Fredericksburg—"A Night in Old Fredericksburg" Odessa—Shakespeare Festival Stamford—Cowboy Reunion	Alexandria—Virginia Scottish Games and Gathering of the Clans Chincoteague—Wild Pony Roundup Millboro Springs—Big Bend Jousting Tournament	Huntington—Square and Round Dance Festival
AUGUST	Burnet—Old-Time Fiddlers' Contest Dalhart—XIT Rodeo and Reunion De Leon—Peach and Melon Festival	Abingdon—Virginia Highlands Arts and Crafts Festival Galax—Old-Time Fiddlers' Contest Mount Solon—Natural Chimneys Jousting Tournament Warrenton—National Championship Country Music Contest	Charleston—Folk Festival Salem—Western Square and Round Dance Festival
SEPTEMBER	El Paso—Fiesta de las Flores Magnolia—Texas Renaissance Festival Port Arthur—Mexican Independence Day Celebration San Marcos—Republic of Texas Chilympiad	Richmond—International Festival	Moorefield—Heritage Weekend
OCTOBER	Fort Worth—Oktoberfest Huntsville—Annual Texas Prison Rodeo Port Arthur—CavOilCade Tyler—Festival of Roses Winnsboro—Autumn Trails Festival	Richmond—National Tobacco Festival	
NOVEMBER	El Paso—Southwestern Sun Carnival McAllen—International Art Festival New Braunfels—Wurstfest Salado—Scottish Clans Gathering	Charlottesville—Thanksgiving Hunt Weekend	
DECEMBER	Dallas—Cotton Bowl Week: climaxed by Cotton Bowl Football Classic Mission—Poinsettia Show	Alexandria—Christmas Walk in Historic Alexandria Big Stone Gap; Lorton; Mt. Vernon; Norfolk—Tours of Antebellum Homes Richmond—"The Nativity" Williamsburg—Christmas in Williamsburg	Charleston—Trees of the Nation Exhibit

THE PHOENIX BIRD. 39" wingspan. Order 20 lb. string. Paper: 619486 $6.50 (Members $5.85) s/h $1.00. Silk: 612663 $20.00 (Members $18.00) s/h $1.00.

THE WRIGHT FLYER. Balsa wood and paper kite to make. 4½ foot wingspan. Order 20 lb. string. 618082 $12.00 (Members $10.80) s/h $1.00.

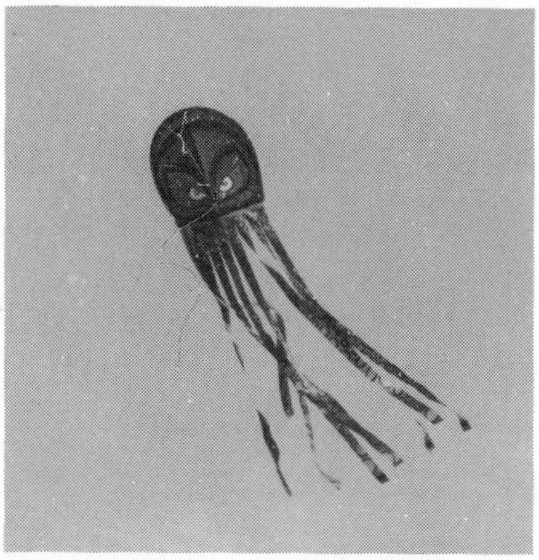

OCTAR THE OCTOPUS. Made of mylar. 5 feet long. Order 20 lb. string. 636951 $4.00 (Members $3.60) s/h $.50.

ICARUS. Made of sturdy ripstop nylon. 56" wingspan. Order 75 lb. string. 629279 $60.00 (Members $54.00) s/h $1.00.

FLY KITES FROM THE SMITHSONIAN

The Smithsonian Institution surely has the most unique, colorful, elegant kites in existence—at least we think so! Some of them are awesome in size and will capture everyone's fantasy in flight. These magnificent kites, which actually come in brilliant shades of blue, red, yellow, green, and other colors, can be ordered through the mail. We have pictured several of them, with prices and shipping costs for each.

And when you are in Washington, D.C., you must visit the glorious, new National Air and Space Museum. While you are there, wander into the Museum Shop where you can see the Smithsonian Institution's complete selection of kites.

Smithsonian Institution
P.O. Box 2456
Washington, D.C. 20013

For a good kite, use good string. You may order the string with which to fly the kites in various quantities:
500 feet of 20 lb. twisted nylon string on a plastic spool. 636894 $5.00 (Members $4.50) s/h $.65.
500 feet of 20 lb. string on wooden spool. 612549 $2.25 (Members $2.00) s/h $.25.
500 feet of 30 lb. string. 604561 $1.50 (Members $1.35) s/h $.25.
500 feet of 75 lb. braided string. 634774 $3.50 (Members $3.15) s/h $.50.

COFFIN HOLLOW AND OTHER GHOST TALES

by Ruth Ann Musick

The University Press of Kentucky
Lexington, Kentucky 40506

What do you think of when you think of West Virginia? Green lush mountains patched with strip-mined bald spots? A song by John Denver? Crazy feuds conducted by people with Dogpatch determination? Well, how about a dead Rebel soldier chasing his murderer and riding on his coffin? Or a ball of fire rolling over the grave of a strangled child? Or a headless dog that steals rides behind a man on horseback? These bizarre events maybe or maybe not really happened in West Virginia.

Indeed, the ghosts and folk legends of West Virginia are the focus of Ruth Ann Musick in her delightfully chilling collection of stories called *Coffin Hollow and Other Ghost Tales.* Particularly interesting is the colorful variety of ghosts provided by this unusual region. During the Civil War, a portion of Virginia refused to separate from the Union and this gamey section was referred to as West Virginia (among other things). Still, supporters of the Confederacy abounded in this region, and internal conflicting loyalties characterized the state. So (in the legends handed down in the state) there are many stories of the apparitions of soldiers—both Yanks and Rebs. Also, like the rest of the country, West Virginia contributed its young men to the tragic Viet Nam conflict and there is a tale involving a fairly contemporary ghost from that period. And, because much of the state was traversed by peddlers and salesmen, many of them ended up as murderers or victims or, at the very least, guests at non-existent stately mansions greeted by hosts who were "legally" dead years before.

So, for the lonely scholar of West Virginia folklore, this book constitutes a rare find. And for the many horror lovers in every state, there is plenty here to satiate their appetites. Poe might have been writing of the content of *Coffin Hollow* when he wrote, over 100 years ago,

"much of Madness, and more of
Sin
And Horror the soul of the plot . . . . "

—*S.V.H.*

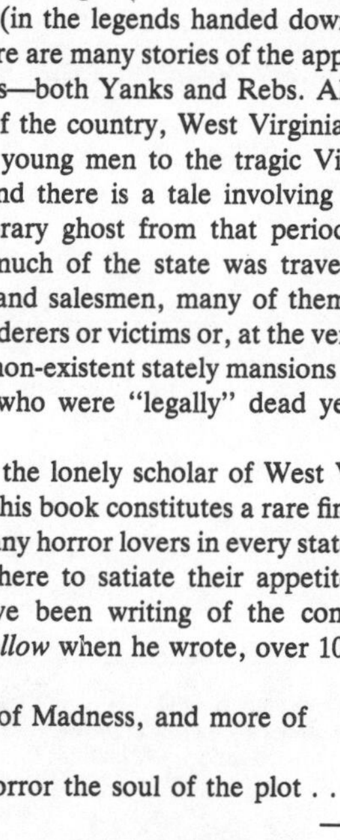

Folbot 17½-foot "Super" twoseater

FOLDING BOATS—FOLBOT

Folding boats first appeared during the Civil War in 1863 on Southern rivers. Many designs followed but the forerunner of today's Folbot was invented around 1900.

Today the Folbot Corporation of Charleston, South Carolina, manufactures finished Folbots and also sells kits for the industrious do-it-yourselfer.

In selecting a Folbot you should consider type and construction, model and size, and preferred color.

There are two types of Folbots: the folding kind, and the rigid portable. The folding one is best suited to limited storage space and is intended to be taken along in a car trunk. Like setting up a tent, it takes 15 to 30 minutes to assemble and after use, when wet, must be opened up for drying before storing permanently.

The rigid portable Folbot can ride atop any car and can be stored suspended from a garage ceiling or along a wall. There is hardly any difference in the nautical performance of the two types.

The folding types of Folbots are factory finished, but portables are available in a prefab kit form at substantial savings. Hard shell plastic Folbots are available only as factory-finished portables which are about 8% heavier than other models.

Folbot's hull consists of strong woven fabrics, impregnated and surfaced with vinyl. It is equally suited to arctic or tropic environment. Tearing strength of several hundred pounds per square inch prevents ripping.

Folbots come in different models, from single seaters to the five-passenger model. They can be adapted for sailing and are great for fishing or paddling along clear quiet streams and rivers. They come in basic colors of blue, red, yellow, green, or aqua.

The 17½-foot "Super" is a popular 2 seater model with a safe capacity of 720 pounds and space for 2 to 4. The cockpit size is 96 inches long and 23 inches wide. The folding type Super TSF packs in two bags: short, 38" x 19" x 8"; and long, 55" x 9" x 9". The "Super" is available direct in these models at these factory direct prices (not including shipping):

Super Prefab TSK	$246.00
Super Portable TSP	$432.00
Super Folding TSF	$464.00
Super hard-shell Portable TSPhs	$482.00

All accessories are purchased separately and as they are needed or desired.

From Folbot you may also order *The Grandiose Rio Grande* by Walter F. Burmeister, a 6" x 9" soft-cover book of beautiful photographs and text about the Rio Grande from north of Big Bend National Park through Colorado Canyon.

To view the complete line of Folbots and boating accessories and compare prices, write for the free colorful catalogue.

Folbot Corporation
Stark Industrial Park
P.O. Box 7097
Charleston, South Carolina 29405

FINE PRINTS

Although constantly changing, the inventory of the Baton Rouge, Louisiana firm of Taylor Clark—Fine Prints, Paintings, and Framing is always marked by an extensive collection of Audubon bird prints, from the original Havell edition, the Bien edition, the 1971 Amsterdam edition, and the small-sized Octavo edition, as well as by the prints done on textile, circa 1830. Clark's also seeks to keep on hand a good selection of Audubon and Bachman quadruped prints and Gould bird prints, plus a wide assortment of additional animal and fish prints. Rare maps; American and European view prints; botanical drawings; English, European, and American paintings; bronzes; fine and rare books; costume and Oriental prints are also well represented in the Clark catalogue. The current catalogue may be obtained by writing:

Taylor Clark
2623 Government Street
Baton Rouge, Louisiana 70806

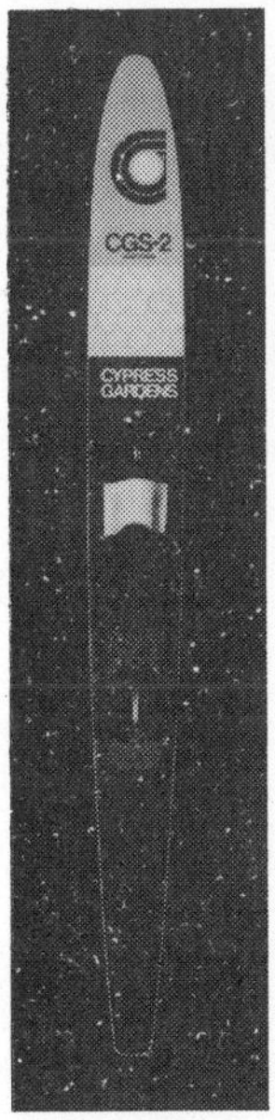

CYPRESS GARDENS SKIS, ACCESSORIES, AND FLOTATION

Cypress Gardens, the swamp that was transformed into a major tourist attraction by Dick Pope, Sr. and his wife Julie, is famous for its skiers and water shows.

Skis, accessories, and flotation equipment—representatives of which are shown here—can be purchased through Cypress Gardens Skis, a division of Florida Cypress Gardens, Inc.

A catalog of Cypress Gardens water skis and accessories is available. Write:

Cypress Gardens Skis
P.O. Box 8
Cypress Gardens, Florida 33880

BASIC RIBBONPOINT™ TECHNIQUE

by Patricia Mabry

Oxmoor House, Inc.
Birmingham, Alabama

In a great many villas and palaces in Europe, tiny silken ribbons adorn the furnishings as well as the dress of the people. Ribbons add a colorful gaity and festiveness to old world settings. Now Patricia Mabry has woven ribbons into the southern lifestyle. In *Basic Ribbonpoint™ Technique* she gives the reader some needlepoint with a twist. And the results are best described in terms of rugs, pillows, wall hangings, Christmas ornaments, belts, vests, yokes, pockets, and anything that can be made with a canvas base.

In this colorful, imaginative book, illustrated with sumptuous photographs, she guides the reader to an understanding of the application of Ribbonpoint™ technique. Directions are given for such articles as an evening jacket, plaques, mirror frames, and beautiful evening bags. A unique and lovely addition to your wardrobe may be your motive for doing Ribbonpoint™ work. Or maybe you just want to surprise a friend with something rare. Whatever the reason, Ribbonpoint™ technique is an exquisite way to achieve a new and exciting look whether it be on or around you. It is also the perfect solution for those people who are allergic to wool-fiber. And it is much cooler than wool.

Although the invention of Ribbonpoint™ technique was an accident, according to Mrs. Mabry, the result of her "accidental" discovery is a great expansion of the needlecraft concept. So, re-thread your needles with something else for a change and spend some quiet creative hours making some surprises with the basic ribbon. —S.V.H.

IN SEARCH OF BUDDY BOLDEN FIRST MAN OF JAZZ

by Donald M. Marquis

Louisiana State University Press
Baton Rouge, Louisiana

I first heard of Buddy Bolden while researching a story of New Orleans jazz (*Southern Living*, May 1968). He was a cornet player. The first "King" of jazz. An early interpreter of that musical form. But it was all very hazy. He was "the man with the golden horn" at the turn of the century, but he lost his sanity before he was 30. And that was it, the public record of Buddy Bolden.

But that was before Donald M. Marquis, a resident of New Orleans, went *In Search of Buddy Bolden* ($9.95; Louisiana State University Press).

Charles Joseph "Buddy" Bolden was born at 319 Howard Street on September 6, 1877. The Baptist Church was an early musical influence on Bolden. And seeing and marching behind the brass bands to the elaborate funerals. "Because death was a release from earthly burdens the inclination was to 'cry at birth, rejoice at death.' " In about 1894 Buddy chose to play the cornet perhaps "because he saw it as a lead instrument." And his first teacher was a neighbor, Manuel Hall, a cook at Nelson Quirk's Cafe on Royal Street.

"Between the late 1880's and 1894 or 1895, Buddy was sorting out what appealed to him, what he could handle, and what he wanted to experiment with." He was working out his own style. "His efforts took the form of playing 'wide-open' on the cornet and of playing in up-tempo or ragging the hymns, street songs, and dance tunes to create a musical sound that people were unfamiliar with."

It took five years of trial and error. Then in 1900 came the "King," Buddy Bolden and his band, with Willie Cornish, trombone; Jefferson Mumford, guitar; Jimmy Johnson, bass; and Henry Zeno and Cornelius Tillman alternating on drums.

Jazz became a reality in the years 1900-1910. And until 1905 or 1906, Bolden's "was the only jazz band in town." He could play it loud and he could play it easy.

It lasted five flaming years. "As 1906 dawned Buddy Bolden was the king of New Orleans black music. It was a perilous position, however, constantly threatened by those who were picking up on his ideas and doing other things with them."

By March 1906, he began having severe headaches. And spells of depression when he seemed to be afraid of his own cornet. His last job was at a Labor Day parade in 1906. His behavior became so erratic that for his and their own protection his family was forced to call the police. Always a heavy drinker, by spring he was a drunk. "On March 13, 1907, almost exactly one year after his first attack, Mrs. Bolden again called the Twelfth Precinct and for the third time Charles Bolden was booked for insanity." This time he was committed to the Insane Asylum at Jackson, Louisiana, where he lived until his death, November 4, 1931, at age 54. He was buried in a pine box in city-owned Holt Cemetery, unwaked and unremembered.

No recording survives of Buddy Bolden's music, if any was ever made. One advertising leaflet exists of his many jobs, an invitation to a Mardi Gras ball, February 18, 1903, the music to be provided by 'Prof. Bolden's Orchestra.' Only one photograph of him survives. And yet, American music was forever different after he lived and played his cornet. Lucky for us, Donald Marquis not only searched for Buddy Bolden. He found him.

—John Logue

Nostalgia Station

The B & O Railroad Museum includes Mount Clare Station, the nation's first railroad depot, and extends through the enormous Roundhouse, the old Print Shop, and the Gift Shop. Through a catalogue of railroad memorabilia, many of the nostalgic items related to the railroads are available to you.

China from the railroad dining cars is a popular item. B & O's "Blue China" depicts famous scenes along the railroad with special and newly produced items available; a Sesquicentennial Plate, for example, is available. Dining-car china is available in these pieces and patterns: a cocoa pot in the exclusive pattern of the Sante Fe, "California Poppy"; an 8" platter with the "Violets and Daisies" pattern of the CB & Q; a bouillon cup in "Traveler" from CMSTP & P; a tea plate in Pullman Company's "Indian Tree."

Numerous other mementos and collectors' items are available: B & O tablecloths, Missouri Pacific milk bottles, New York Central souvenir glasses, engineer hats, bandanas, belt buckles, T-shirts, Chessie towel sets or blankets, conductors' lapel emblems or buttons, badges, railroad lamps or lanterns, and a number of books, records, and calendars featuring railroad lore.

For your catalogue, send $1.00 to:

Nostalgia Station
B&O Railroad Museum
Pratt and Poppleton Streets
Baltimore, Maryland 21223

Dunn's

Home of the National Field Trials

Dunn's Supply, Inc., is located in Grand Junction, Tennessee, home of the National Field Trials. Dunn's naturally sells Field Trial equipment. As a matter of fact, Dunn's sells quite a few things—enough to fill an 80-plus page catalogue. In it, you will find a stainless steel belt buckle with your favorite dog emblem or a weathervane on which the emblem is a pointer dog. There is a coon call, a duck call, a squirrel call, a deer call, a turkey call—and others. There are hunting clothes, hunting knives, traps, dog cages, pigeon traps, and numerous other items. A number of books on dogs are available, including *Field Trials History, Management and Judging Standards*, and *National Field Trial Champions 1956-1966*, both by William F. Brown, official Field Trial Reporter.

For your free copy of the Dunn catalogue, write to:

Dunn's Supply, Inc.
Grand Junction, Tennessee 38039

THE GOLDEN EAGLE AND THE GOLDEN AGE PASSPORTS

In 1978, the National Park Service made available two passes—the Golden Eagle Passport and the Golden Age Passport—that will help you enjoy the parks and recreation areas managed by the Federal Government.

The Golden Eagle Passport is an annual entrance permit to national parks, monuments, and recreation areas which charge entrance fees. It admits the permit holder and a carload of accompanying people. Where entry is not by private car, the Golden Eagle Passport admits the permit holder and family group—parents, children, and spouse. The Golden Eagle Passport does not cover use fees, such as fees for camping. It costs $10.00 and is good for one calendar year. The passport may be purchased in person or by mail from the National Park Service, Washington, DC 20240.

The Golden Age Passport is a free lifetime entrance permit to those national parks, monuments, and recreation areas which charge entrance fees. To qualify, you must be a citizen or permanent resident of the United States who is 62 years of age or older. It also provides a 50 percent discount on Federal "use" fees charged for facilities and services such as camping, boat launching, and parking. The Golden Age Passport admits the permit holder and a carload of accompanying people. Where entry is not by private car, the Passport admits the permit holder and his or her spouse and children. You may only obtain a Golden Age Passport in person—it is available at most Federally-operated recreation areas where it may be used.

If you would like to obtain some basic information about the facilities and recreational opportunities available to users of National Park System camping areas, write to the Superintendent of Documents, U.S. Government Printing Office, Washington, DC 20402—Stock Number 024-005-00753-9.

MARDI GRAS MASQUERADE COMPANY

Anyone would enjoy going to a costume party if he could obtain a costume from The Mardi Gras Masquerade Company. They have thousands of original, authentic costumes available for rental. Many of these were acquired at a Metro-Goldwyn Mayer Studio auction; they were worn by stars and featured players in almost all of M.G.M.'s greatest movies. This company, while serving the New Orleans area as well as the entire South, also supplies community theatres in the Southern states with costumes on a regular basis.

Contact:

M.G.M. Costumes
1433 Melpomene Avenue
New Orleans, Louisiana 70130

ART FROM ST. SIMONS

Bill Hendrix does several things very well, among them flying his airplane from art class to art class, teaching those art classes, and capturing the special beauty of Georgia's "Golden Isles" in pen and ink drawings.

The flying came about when, with classes of students in widely scattered places constantly waiting while he negotiated traffic jams and congested highways, Hendrix decided to solve that problem by taking to the air. Now, where it once took him 45 minutes to travel between St. Simons and Jekyll Island, it now takes him only 2 minutes airborne. And the times from St. Simons to such places as Savannah, Douglas, Albany, and Fitzgerald have similarly improved.

The pen and ink drawings in which Hendrix excels are now available both as 11" x 14" frameable prints and as a notepaper collection. Ten notes and 10 envelopes are included in each box of notepaper which features 10 different island scenes for $3.00; prints are available in black and white at $4.00 each or individually hand-tinted at $15.00. Smaller black and white scenes are available, 6" x 8" matted, at $3.00 each. To order, add $.50 per box of notes and smaller scenes and $1.00 for 11" x 14". Information may be obtained by writing:

Island Art Center
St. Simons Island, Georgia 31522

Robert Preston and Barbara Cook in The Music Man.

EXITS AND ENTRANCES

You and your friends—or models of your choice—can be the stars of this unique program featuring original costumes worn by the stars of stage and screen. You can hear fascinating and amusing stories of famed performers and their work set in an atmosphere of backstage fun from the world of film, theatre, dance, opera, and television.

Mr. Bob Cahlman produces and narrates this distinctive program, which has received national attention. Mr. Cahlman was Director of Special Projects at the American National Theatre and Academy; he also was one of the founders of Houston's famed Alley Theatre and The Gallery Circle Theatre in New Orleans.

For further information:

Exits and Entrances
1433 Melpomene Avenue
New Orleans, Louisiana 70130

TRAIN THE UMPIRE

Some of the umpires on your television screen this year will be "Harry's Boys." Every spring, some 80 to 100 physically sound and reasonably sane young men migrate to Daytona Beach, Florida, in search of a dream. Their destination is the internationally known "Harry Wendelstedt Umpire School," which has trained 80% of the umpires in pro baseball.

Harry Wendelstedt, a 14-year National League veteran, leads a staff that has trained 40 of the current Major League umpires. Harry served as Chief Instructor of the Al Somers Umpire School for 18 years. Al Somers, who trained more Major League umpires than anyone in history, still serves on the Wendelstedt staff.

Of the students, Harry states, "We look for young men who are intelligent, physically sound, and able to operate efficiently under stress situations. We assume they know nothing of baseball and we teach a complete knowledge of umpiring skills."

Why would anyone want to be an umpire? Most say because they like being where the action is, and all have a great love for baseball. Those who make it to the Big Leagues will tell you it is worth every hour of the struggle to the top. They receive from $19,000 to $42,000, with $53.00 per day on the road, plus a first class travel expense on airlines all over the United States. They also pick up big Playoff and World Series checks.

Fewer than 40% of any class actually get a job in professional baseball. Many return to jobs as teachers, lawyers, coaches, plumbers, or electricians. They also use their training to become the nation's top collegiate, high school, and semi-pro umpires. They always look back at their "Day in the Sun" at Daytona Beach and feel their six weeks' training was one of the great experiences of their life.

In 1978, 15 of Harry's former students worked the Major League All Star Game, Playoffs and World Series.

The course convenes the first week of January and lasts for six weeks. Tuition is $350.00. Room rent is approximately $200.00 for six weeks. If you are interested in applying for umpire training, write to:

Harry Wendelstedt
School for Umpires
88 South St. Andrews Drive
Ormond Beach, Florida 32074

MR. MEAT SMOKER

Mr. Meat Smoker is a homestyle smokehouse; it smokes meat the ancient oriental way by cooking with humidity and indirect heat. The smoker gives you this secret by placing a pan of water between the fire and the meat. The steaming pan of water catches the drippings from the meat, and the vapor bastes the meat in its own juices. It takes approximately 15 minutes from the time you light the fire until the meat is in place. The type of food and its weight determine the length of smoking time, but you can count on at least an hour for seafood, while poultry, beef, and pork will take anywhere from three hours (as for cooked ham) to 12 hours (as for a large turkey). The manufacturers recommend, therefore, that you go play golf or tennis, watch football or take a nap.

The meat smoker is sold in well-known stores nationwide and comes in two sizes: a single grill smoker, which sells for $54.95 and will cook up to 20 lbs. of meat at one time; a double grill smoker, $69.95, which cooks up to 50 lbs. of meat. It comes in decorative colors of orange, yellow, and brown. Mr. Meat Smoker also has an electric model for $99.95 which comes only in the double grill size and the orange color. A complete gourmet recipe book is furnished with each unit.

The smoker is constructed of cold-rolled steel, the charcoal and water pans are porcelain enamel, and the grills are heavy chrome plated with support brackets in the middle. Replacement parts are available for order.

In smoked meat, to achieve maximum perfection, the secret is trapping the humidity. Mr. Meat Smoker's top fits on the outside to seal the heat, vapor, and smoke in the unit.

Accessories are available for Mr. Meat Smoker and include: a rib rack for $9.95; a drip pan, $5.95; hickory, $1.99 per bag; and Mr. Meat Smoker Preferred Seasoning, $3.50.

For the name of your local dealer or further information write:

Mr. Meat Smoker
Drawer S
Mabauk, Texas 75147

FOR THOSE WITH THE RIDING HABIT

Deluxe Saddlery, Importers, of Baltimore, Maryland, puts out a yearly catalogue entitled "Boots and Saddles." A great portion of the catalogue, however, is devoted to things other than boots and saddles—such things as riding coats, jodhpurs, stocks, gloves, riding goggles, hunting appointments (including a sandwich box and silverplated flask), bits, bridles, horse blankets and vacuum groomers, and many gifts with an equestrian flavor.

At Christmastime, Deluxe publishes a catalogue with an emphasis on gifts that might appeal to just about everyone, not only the horsey set. Its specialty remains, however, quality riding apparel and saddlery.

Write to:

Deluxe Saddlery, Importers
1817 Whitehead Road
Baltimore, Maryland 21207

THE DOLL DOCTOR

For 12 years Hazel Edwards has been taking fragile, old dolls with broken legs, missing arms, or over-stretched elastic bands and has been reviving them, making them like—or sometimes better than—new. Actually, Hazel has been practicing doll medicine since her childhood, when all her friends would ask her to try to fix up their broken treasures. But since she hung out her shingle professionally, she has probably repaired over 2,000 dolls.

Hazel also sells a kit containing all the parts necessary to make a doll—she makes the parts herself using her part molds and kiln. But her real love is bringing once beautiful, always cherished, but time-ravaged dolls back to life.

Hazel's Doll Hospital
1805 Winfield Road
Winfield, West Virginia 25213

STEAMBOATS ARE A-COMING!

"Ol' Man River" just keeps rolling along—and, happily, so do the steamboats that ply her—though the steamboat is something of an endangered species, at least insofar as the overnight passenger is concerned. But two steamboats, the oldest and the newest, are still owned and operated by the Delta Queen Steamboat Company.

The *Delta Queen,* last of the old-time steamboats, daily steams the rivers carrying contemporary passengers who can experience her nostalgic grandeur by participating first hand in what she was always meant to be: an overnight, passenger steamboat. The *Delta Queen* is almost as long as a football field and has a passenger capacity of 192 and a crew of 75. She calls at hundreds of little river towns along the 3,000 miles of river system she travels. Teakwood handrails line the outside decks. Stained glass windows set with copper rather than lead decorate the Forward Cabin Lounge and the Texas Lounge. The Orleans Room features a Siamese ironbark floor. Cut glass crystal fills the door of the Gift Shop. And throughout the boat, the fittings are brass, and the posts and paneling are either oak or mahogany. The *Delta Queen* is an American institution, but she is also a working cruise vessel. She operates eleven months out of the year and never ties up for more than twelve hours.

The *Delta Queen's* history is intriguing. She was built (1926) in Scotland in prefabricated pieces (many of the old steamboats were built or designed in Europe). Her pieces were shipped across the oceans to the Sacramento Bay where she was completed at Stockton, California. There she made regular cruises on California waters. During World War II, the U.S. Navy pressed the *Delta Queen* into service as a yard ferry boat to transport troops and wounded within San Francisco Bay. She was decommissioned in 1946 and auctioned off to Tom Greene who ran Greene Line Steamers of Cincinnati, Ohio. After painstakingly crating the superstructure, Greene had the shallow-draft riverboat towed across 5,000 miles of open sea down the Pacific Coast, through the Panama Canal, and up the Gulf of Mexico to New Orleans. It was a feat many said couldn't be done. From New Orleans, the *Delta Queen* traveled upriver under her own power to the Dravo Shipyards at Pittsburgh, where she was remodeled and re-outfitted. On June 30, 1948, the *Delta Queen* made her maiden voyage on the Mississippi River system. She continued the steamboat tradition almost singlehandedly. Greene Lines operated her strictly as a tourist boat—something of a novelty in the declining age of packet steamboats. She was successful.

In 1966, the operation of the *Delta Queen* ran into a legal snag. That year the United States Congress passed the Safety and Sea Law which required any vessel carrying more than 50 overnight passengers to be constructed entirely of steel. The law was actually intended to apply to ocean-going vessels. But the broad terminology of the bill embraced river-bound vessels as well. It looked as if the *Delta Queen* might have to be retired, but the famous boat gained the support of the people of the United States. And since 1966, they have persuaded Congress to give her six exemptions from the law. In return, the Delta Queen Steamboat Company has undertaken a major program of safety and restoration. She is regularly inspected by the U.S. Coast Guard. The boat's current exemption from the law expires November 1, 1983.

America's newest steamboat was commissioned in 1976. The *Mississippi Queen* is the biggest steamboat ever and was the first overnight passenger steamboat built in fifty years. She has the capability of sailing the entire 3,000 miles of the Mississippi River system. Her cruise speed is about 7 MPH and she

cruises fifty weeks out of the year. As her predecessors did, the *Mississippi Queen* operates on steam, is propelled by a red paddlewheel, and is considered a boat rather than a ship. (She has only an 8 foot draft and she never cruises on waters which rock her back and forth). Still, she is elegant and sophisticated; she has elevators, a beauty shop, a movie theater, a complete on-board telephone and public address system, air-conditioning, a swimming pool, and a sauna. Her big steam calliope is the largest in the world. She sails under the American Flag and her crew is American. Her major ports of call presently include Cincinnati, New Orleans, St. Louis, and St. Paul/Minneapolis.

Both ships feature good food, lively entertainment, and a view which cannot be found except from a boat on the river.

The sailing schedules of the two boats include 3-night or 4-night cruises. The names of the cruises are "Deep South," "Bayou," "Plantation," "Dixieland," "Ohio Valley," "Frontier," "10-State," "Midwest," "Northwest Territory." Special adventure cruises are "Mason-Dixon Cruise," "Bluegrass/Dixieland Cruise," "Crescent City/Queen City Cruise," "Great Discovery Cruise," "Kentucky Derby Cruise," "Rollin'-On-The-River Cruise," "Ohio Valley Expedition Cruise," "Autumn Foliage Cruise," and "Autumn Adventure Cruise."

The 4-night "Plantation Cruise" from New Orleans to Natchez round trip is planned like this: Monday, depart from New Orleans at 6:00 p.m. and cruise upriver; Tuesday, try your hand at the calliope or flying a kite topside as the day is spent cruising the Mississippi; Wednesday, in early afternoon, arrive in Natchez and tour several of the antebellum homes; Thursday, arrive in St. Francisville, tour the mansion and gardens of Rosedown Plantation, depart in the early evening; Friday, cruise into busy New Orleans harbor at 9:00 a.m.

Prices vary according to accomodations and to the length of the cruise.

For further information on the schedules and fares of the *Delta Queen* and the *Mississippi Queen,* write:

Delta Queen Steamboat Company
511 Main Street
Cincinnati, Ohio 45202

THE DELTA QUEEN: LAST OF THE PADDLEWHEEL PALACES

By August Perez and Associates
Edited by Myron Tassin

Pelican Publishing House
630 Burmaster Street
Gretna, Louisiana 70053

The Delta Queen: Last of the Paddlewheel Palaces is a 96-page pictorial volume compiled in the interest of preserving the *Queen* and the heritage she represents. The photographs include such items of interest as a close-up of the ship's bell or a sumptuous light fixture, the performers who have made the music for the cruises, and the view of the boat just off Cave-In-Rock, Illinois, where pirates were known to rob steamboats. Photographs of the *Delta Queen* show her as she served Californians, as she was boarded up to come through the Panama Canal, as she moves through the river at New Orleans, at Memphis, at St. Louis, or at Cincinnati. The book also contains numerous photographs of 19th century sternwheelers and traces the history of steamboating on the Mississippi River and its tributaries.

The *Delta Queen,* which travels between Cincinnati and New Orleans, is a 20th century boat in the tradition of the sternwheelers of a century ago.

Also featured in the book is the description of one person's trip from Memphis to New Orleans—complete with notes on the music, the sleeping accomodations, the food, the bands, the crew. —*J.V.*

DELICACIES FROM NEW ORLEANS

The Creole Delicacies Company, Inc. is located at 533 St. Ann Street in New Orleans—in the heart of LeVieux Carre, facing Jackson Square. You may order delicious pralines or try some of the other delicacies they picture in their brochure. French Market Style Doughnuts, Hot Pepper Jelly, New Orleans Soups, and Praline Topping look especially inviting. Send $.25 for their illustrated brochure.

Creole Delicacies Company, Inc.
P.O. Box 51042
533 Saint Ann Street
New Orleans, Louisiana 70116

Where To Hear Bluegrass Music

In a season that runs mainly from spring to fall, there are some 400 bluegrass festivals around the South each year. Most are held outdoors, blending weekend camping with music.

Locations of the festivals range from farm fields to permanent bluegrass music parks. A handy item to bring is a folding chair, since most festivals do not have seating in the stage area. Admission ranges from $5 to $15 per day.

Following is a sampling of some of the bluegrass festivals held in the South. A comprehensive calendar of bluegrass and folk festivals in the United States is available for $3.25 from the National Council for the Traditional Arts, Inc., 1346 Connecticut Avenue NW., No. 1118, Washington, D.C. 20036.

Alabama

Tennessee Valley Old Time Fiddlers' Convention, Athens State College, Athens. Free camping, no hookups; admission, $2, $3. For more information, write Bill Harrison, 305 Stella Drive, Madison 35758.

Arkansas

Bluegrass Music Festival, fairgrounds, Harrison. Camping, hookups. For more information, write Bluegrass Festival, Box 939, Harrison 72601; or call (501) 741-2659.

Florida

Country Western Bluegrass Festival, Stephen Foster Center, White Springs. For more information, write Box 265, White Springs 32096; or call (904) 397-2192

Georgia

Jekyll Island New Year's Bluegrass Festival, convention center, Jekyll Island. Camping nearby; admission, $5, $6. For more information, write Box 731, Dahlonega 30533; or call (404) 864-2600.

Louisiana

Luke Thompson's Bluegrass Festival, Bluegrass Park, Folsom. For more information, write Luke Thompson, Box 2063, Baton Rouge 70821; or call (504) 775-9576.

Maryland

Bluegrass Unlimited Annual Fall Bluegrass Festival, Indian Springs, KOA campground, near Hagerstown. For more information, write to *Bluegrass Unlimited,* Box 111, Broad Run, Virginia 22014; or call (703) 361-8992.

Oklahoma

Grant's Oklahoma Bluegrass Festival, Salt Creek Park, Hugo. Camping. For more information, write Bill Grant, Route 2, Box 11-K, Hugo 74743; or call (405) 326-5598.

Texas

Kerrville Bluegrass Festival, Quiet Valley Ranch, 9 miles south of Kerrville. Camping; admission; $15 for three-day ticket. For more information, write Rod Kennedy. Box 1466, Kerrville 78028; or call (512) 896-3800.

Virginia

Mid-Summer Bluegrass Festival, Orange Blossom Park, Waynesboro. Camping; admission, $14 for a three-day ticket. For more information, write Jim Orange, 2487 Calf Mountain Road, Waynesboro 22980; or call (703) 942-2165 or 942-1068.

West Virginia

West Virginia Bluegrass Festival, Cox's Field, Walker. Free camping; admission, $15 for the weekend. For more information, write John Cox, Route 1, Walker 26180; or call (304) 428-3171.

AUTO TAPE TOUR

Seeing is believing, but listening is educational and entertaining. So think the creators of Auto Tape Tours which are now in use in the Great Smoky Mountains National Park. At any of four points (in Cherokee, North Carolina: Boundary Tree Lodge, U.S. 441; Museum of Cherokee Indians, Route 441; Tipton Terrace, U.S. 441; and American Historical Wax Museum, U.S. 441) you can pick up and return a tape player with a tape which thoroughly describes the history and geology of the Great Smokies. You'll hear such tidbits as a fantastic legend about two hill families who feuded for two generations over a pig; the story of the Appalachian Revolution, a violent disturbance that took place 200 million years ago; the history of "bear jams" and "boomer" squirrels. There's no doubt that Auto Tapes can expand your enjoyment of travel through the park; probably the best thing about them is that you control, by the push of a button, the pace of your tour, enabling the grandeur of your surroundings to exert whatever length hold on you it wishes.

Auto Tape Tours—$6.95 for your entire group (whether bus or car).

Request information from:

Auto Tape Tours
Division of Comprehensive Communications, Inc.
% Larry Johnson
P.O. Box 385
Scarsdale, New York 10583

GEORGIA PEANUTS

Some of you may want to find out if Georgia peanuts are all they're cracked up to be—Rhea's of Atlanta offers 5 lbs. of fresh roasted peanuts in the shell (and salted) in an old-fashioned burlap bag. They also have an attractive brochure, picturing delicious-looking candies, pralines, peanut brittle, pecans, dates, fudge, and other goodies. Write for it. To order the peanuts, send $6.60 plus $1.90 shipping charge (Georgia residents add 3% tax) to:

Rhea's of Atlanta
6214 Roswell Road, N.E.
Atlanta, Georgia 30328

THE BEST FROM BRENNAN'S

BRENNAN'S COOKBOOK

Who has not heard of "Breakfast at Brennan's"? Milk Punch, Eggs Sardou, Bananas Foster or Crepes Fitzgerald . . . once experienced, never forgotten. You may not be able to reproduce the ambience of Brennan's at 11 a.m. of a mid-Fall or mid-Spring day, but the information for recreating the menu of that hour is at hand in *Brennan's, A Souvenir Cookbook.*

These recipes are specialties of the house at Brennan's; you may be able to duplicate the taste, but it would be hard to duplicate the unique atmosphere of New Orleans.

Brennan's combines the Creole sense of the dramatic of its founder Owen Brennan with the home cooking of his wife Maude and the efforts of Dutch chef Paul Blangé—blended through what Maude referred to as "the holler and scream method." The result achieved by Owen Brennan is nothing less than unique; Brennan's is New Orleans at its best—gifted cooks preparing excellent ingredients in an atmosphere of happy tolerance of ethnic mixtures and serving in the grand manner. Brennan's breakfasts are not for everyday; they are for leisurely enjoyed special occasions. Don't plan too many other things for the same day; the afterglow of such gastronomic pleasures should be indulged, not wiped away by hurry and scurry.

To order *Brennan's, A Souvenir Cookbook,* send $5.00 plus $1.00 for handling to:

Brennan's
417 Royal Street
New Orleans, Louisiana 70130

BANANAS FOSTER

(for four)

4 tablespoons butter
3½ tablespoons brown sugar
½ teaspoon cinnamon
2 tablespoons banana liqueur
4 bananas, cut in half lengthwise, then halved
about ¼ cup rum
4 scoops vanilla ice cream

Melt the butter over an alcohol burner in a flambé pan or attractive skillet. Add the sugar, cinnamon, and banana liqueur and stir to mix. Heat for a few minutes, then place the halved bananas in the sauce and sauté until soft and slightly browned. Add the rum and allow it to heat well, then tip the pan so that the flame from the burner causes the sauce to light. Allow the sauce to flame until it dies out, tipping the pan with a circular motion to prolong the flaming. Serve over vanilla ice cream. First lift the bananas carefully out of the pan and place four pieces over each portion of ice cream, then spoon the hot sauce from the pan over the top.

This is one of Brennan's most famous and most popular desserts. It's really quite simple to prepare. Wait until the rum gets hot, so that you get a good flame when it's ignited. This can alse be prepared over a stove burner, then brought to the dinner table and flamed.

SAUTERNE or CHAMPAGNE EXTRA DRY

CRÊPES FITZGERALD

(for eight)

16 dessert crêpes, preferably warmed slightly (to prepare, see following recipe)
2 cups Creole cream cheese (or 4 parts Philadelphia cream cheese to 1 part heavy sour cream; see directions, p. 8)
3 cups fresh strawberries
3 to 4 tablespoons sugar
⅔ cup Maraschino liqueur

Have the crêpes and Creole cream cheese ready. Place a flambé pan or attractive skillet over an alcohol burner and mash the strawberries in the pan with a fork. Add the sugar and cook for about 3 to 4 minutes, until the strawberries are beginning to get soft. On each of eight preheated plates place two crêpes. Fill each crêpe with ¼ cup Creole cream cheese and roll up. Add the Maraschino liqueur to the sautéed strawberries and heat until quite hot. Tip the pan to ignite and flame until the flame dies out. Tip the pan with a rolling motion to prolong the flaming, if desired. Ladle the syrup from the pan evenly over the portions of filled crêpes and serve immediately.

CHAMPAGNE EXTRA DRY or BARSAC

MILK PUNCH

(for four)

6 ounces bourbon
1½ cups half and half
1 ounce simple syrup
6 drops vanilla extract
ice cubes
nutmeg

Combine all the ingredients except the nutmeg in a cocktail shaker. Shake vigorously, then strain into old fashioned glasses. Sprinkle each drink with nutmeg before serving.

EGGS SARDOU

(for eight)

creamed spinach:
1 cup butter
¾ cup white onion, chopped
1½ cups flour
4 cups milk
about 1 teaspoon salt
about ½ teaspoon black pepper
1½ cups cooked spinach, chopped

8 large cooked artichoke bottoms, heated
16 poached eggs
hollandaise sauce

To prepare the creamed spinach, melt the butter over low heat in a heavy saucepan. Add the chopped onion and cook until just soft. Add the flour gradually, stirring constantly. Stir in the milk, still stirring, and cook until evenly blended and warmed through. Add the salt, pepper, and spinach and cook a few minutes more, just until the spinach is warmed through and the mixture evenly blended. Put equal amounts of creamed spinach on 8 heated plates, then place an artichoke bottom on top of the spinach. Poach the eggs as directed for Eggs Hussarde, then place two poached eggs side by side on each artichoke bottom. Prepare the hollandaise sauce as directed for Eggs Hussarde, then ladle an even coating of hollandaise over each portion.

MUSCADET or CALIFORNIA CHABLIS

IRISH COFFEE

(per drink)

1 cube sugar
1½ ounces Irish whiskey
hot chicory coffee
fresh whipped cream

Place the cube of sugar in an 8-ounce wine glass. Add the Irish whiskey, then fill to one inch below the rim of the glass with hot chicory coffee. Top with a generous tablespoon of whipped cream.

Spring Winds Bring Kite-Flying Contests

Spring is the favorite time for kite-flying contests and festivals. Here is a list of kite-flying events in the South. (Circumstances occasionally force changes in dates of events. We recommend you check with local sponsors before driving long distances.)

District of Columbia

March—Washington; Kite Carnival; Washington Monument, west side. Sponsors: Smithsonian Institution, National Capital Parks, and D.C. Department of Recreation. Information: Resident Associate Office, Smithsonian Institution, Room 1271, A & I Building, 900 Jefferson Dr. S.W., Washington, D.C. 20560.

Louisiana

March—New Orleans; annual kite-flying contest; Harrell Stadium. Sponsor: New Orleans Recreation Department. Information: Morris Jeff, 303 Gallier Hall, New Orleans 70130.

March—New Orleans; annual kite-flying contest; City Park. Sponsor: Kite Shop. Information: Sally Fontana, Kite Shop, Jackson Square, 542 St. Peter, New Orleans 70116.

April—Shreveport; Holiday in Dixie Festival's kite-flying contest; LSU, Shreveport campus. Sponsor: KEEL radio. Information: Joe Callicoatte, Suite 1003, Fountain Tower, Shreveport 71101.

Maryland

March—Takoma Park; Annual Ben Franklin Kite Contest; Takoma Park Recreation Center. Sponsor: Takoma Park Recreation Department. Information: Takoma Park Recreation Department, 7500 Maple Avenue, Takoma Park 20012.

May—Baltimore; Preakness Cultural Festival, Kite Fly; Location varies. Information: Ralph Elsmo, Preakness Cultural Festival, Maryland Jockey Club, Baltimore, Maryland 21215.

North Carolina

April—Charlotte; annual "Great Outta Sight Kite Flight"; South Park. Sponsor: Charlotte Park and Recreation Department. Information: Charlotte Park and Recreation Department, 310 No. Kings Drive, Charlotte 28204.

Oklahoma

March—Tulsa; kite fly; Johnson Park. Sponsors: River Parks Authority, KMOD radio, and City of Tulsa Parks and Recreation. Information: Vivian Steele, River Parks Authority, 411 South Denver, Tulsa 74103.

Tennessee

April—Nashville; Annual Kite-Flying Contest; Percy Warner Park, steeplechase area. Sponsors: Horizons, Ltd. and Metropolitan Board of Parks and Recreation. Information: Horizons, Ltd., 2224 Bandywood Road, Nashville 37215.

Texas

March—San Antonio; Annual kite-flying contest; Brackenridge Park, polo field. Sponsor: Parks and Recreation Department. Information: San Antonio Department of Parks and Recreation, 950 East Hildebrand, San Antonio 78212.

March—Austin; Annual kite-flying contest; Zilker Park. Sponsors: Parks and Recreation Department, Downtown Exchange Club, and KNOW radio. Information: Parks and Recreation Department, Box 1088, Austin 78767.

Virginia

March—Alexandria; Alexandria Kite Festival; Chinquapin Center. Sponsor: Department of Recreation. Information: Alexandria Department of Recreation, 115 North Patrick, Alexandria 22314.

DAISY COUNTRY

"In 1860, spring-action air guns became popular with marksmen. These 'spring air guns' used a strong coiled spring behind a plunger encased in a closefitted cylinder. When the trigger was released, the spring rammed the plunger forward, compressing air into the barrel which shot out the bullet.

"Most of these guns were owned by commercial shooting galleries. Consequently they became known as 'gallery guns.'

"The popularity of gallery guns naturally led to the search for less expensive models that individuals could enjoy.

"In 1886, W.F. Markham introduced an inexpensive spring air rifle called 'The Challenger.' It looked more like a club than a rifle, but it shot common B-B's with enough force and accuracy to be used for target practice or to keep the sparrows out of the corn crib.

"A year later, C.J. Hamilton patented an improved B-B gun made entirely of metal. When he showed his first model to Lewis Cass Hough, the enthusiastic Hough exclaimed, 'Clarence, it's a daisy!'

"The name has stuck ever since."

Such is the background of the "Daisy" as related by the renowned air gun company. In the years since, Daisy has built a strong reputation as a manufacturer of quality products for young shooters. Now, with the increasing costs of shooting firearms and a growing urbanism that is limiting available space for powder shooting, adults in growing numbers are turning to air gun shooting as an alternative. To meet this new demand, Daisy has developed a Power Line series of adult air guns designed and engineered for shooters 16 years of age and older. With 3 to 5 times the power of traditional air guns, the Power Line rifles and pistols have the sophisticated look, feel and performance of conventional firearms demanded by advanced shooters. Yet, they can be used any place, indoors or out, anytime, and at a fraction of the cost of firearms.

Daisy Manufacturing Company
Rogers, Arkansas 72756

The air guns shown here are just a few of those made by Daisy Manufacturing Company. Approximate prices on the air guns shown are: Daisy Model 840 single pump pneumatic B.B/pellet rifle, $25.50; Power Line Model 917 pneumatic pump-up clip-fed pellet repeater, $53.50; and Power Line CO_2 1200 B.B. pistol, $36.50.

CHALET SUZANNE: A RARE TREAT

Chalet Suzanne, in Lake Wales, Florida, is several things to many people: a restaurant, a country inn, a soup cannery, an airfield. Remarkably, it is all these things with excellence: the restaurant and inn are models of old-world charm and service; the soup produced in the cannery is the only soup to have received the Gourmet Society Culinary Merit Award and to have gone to the moon on Apollo flights 15 and 16; the airfield is adjacent to the thirty charming rooms of this inn.

Who got this all together, and who keeps it together? Bertha Hinshaw, who started Chalet Suzanne as a restaurant when she was widowed in 1931 and needed something to stave off the threat of the Depression, gathered things she liked whenever she went around the world—and she went 18 times before her death, at age 90—brought them back to Chalet Suzanne and found, or built, a place for them, spawning the Inn. Architecturally, the result is a bit daft, but fun; as one architect said, "Bertha Hinshaw broke every rule in the book and got away with it." Such things as slanting floors, sloping walls, and variously-pitched roofs, along with a room with three washbasins (Bertha loved decorative china washbasins, which she insisted on being made into hot and cold running water

sinks) and guest rooms designated "Banana," "Soup Pot," and "Doctor," contribute to an overall feeling of *joie de vivre* while you're at Chalet Suzanne.

Today Carl, Bertha's son, and his wife, Vita, keep things going. Carl took a recipe for Romaine soup that Bertha had made up for serving in the Inn's dining room and, with a four-quart pressure cooker and a hand canner, made up a batch for guests who wanted to take some home. Today, over a half million cans of Romaine and 18 other soups and sauces are processed annually in the "soup kitchen" which adjoins the hangar at one end of the airfield. Such growth undeniably acknowledges the excellence of the product.

For more information on the inn and restaurant, write:

Chalet Suzanne, Inc.
c/o Carl Hinshaw
P.O. Drawer AC
Lake Wales, Florida 33853

A cookbook of recipes favored by Bertha Hinshaw and served at the Chalet Suzanne is available for $4.50. Also, the bowls in which the soups are served at the Chalet are reproduced for sale. These bowls were originally Norwegian ceramic ashtrays, but leave it to Bertha to discover an altogether different, but clever, use for them! The bowls are $13.50 each.

THIS HAUNTED LAND
by Nancy and Bruce Roberts

McNally and Loftin Publishers
Charlotte, North Carolina

The Robertses are back again with more things that go bump in the night. This time not only do the skeletons come out of North Carolina's closet, but five other states give up their ghosts as well. With unique photographs and graphic stories, *This Haunted Land* will keep the reader on a delightful edge.

In the wild and unexplored mountains in Western Carolina, several people over the years have observed an unusual sight. Floating around Hickory Nut Gorge with its steep cliffs, narrow ledges, dizzying falls, and grotesque rock formations, are huge crowds of dazzling white phantom-like beings. The Cherokee Indians who inhabited the region first saw the wispy, ethereal "little people." They are still seen on rare occasions. Some say these guardians to the gateway to the mountains are angels; some say spirits; skeptics say the figures are simply cloud formations.

A couple in West Virginia reluctantly allow a traveler into their home to pass the night. The stranger dies later on, pleading to no avail with his hosts to send for a priest. Since that time, the couple is plagued with spectral scissors which clip crescent-shaped slits in their linens and tablecloths and even the clothes of their visitors. In desperation, they finally send for a priest to see if the "Wizard Clip" can be exorcised.

Occult occurrences of this kind abound in *This Haunted Land*. Near Marshall, North Carolina, a tavern was located which saw guests in and checked them out *literally*. The owners of the place were a gruesome couple who robbed their victims after killing them. Needless to say, strange cries and apparitions haunt the vicinity. Turning further south, a plantation in Georgia belonging to the Surrency family exudes a tense supernatural aura. Indeed, from 1872-1877 (when the frightened Surrencys could stand no more and moved) a railroad ran a special train for people to watch the amazingly regular visitations of the Surrency spirits.

Of course, all wars breed their own ghosts. So, if you're down South, expect to see the dead sweetheart of a Confederate lieutenant killed in Tennessee gallop by on her lover's horse, his thick cavalry coat wrapped around her. Or, if you're in North Carolina, you might be asked directions by two horsemen trying to

get to Charlottesburg. They have been looking for Charlottesburg for 200 years and are lost forever somewhere between King's Mountain and Salisbury. These are Tory messengers trying to get some information to Cornwallis.

Haunted cars, phantom ships, the gray lady of South Carolina, a bewitched gold mine: these are just a few of the tales the Robertses have to tell. And since a picture is worth a thousand words, let's just say a few about the photographs of the restless apparitions. In relentless black and white, the stark silhouettes of trees, grim priests, and delicate Spanish moss send delicious shivers down the spine. And Bruce Roberts' photographs blur suggestively in all the right places, capturing the sensation of something seen but not seen. So for all the computer-age rationalists, the Robertses offer a few things that defy explanation.
—S.V.H.

Deck the Halls With Boughs of Holly

Tradition and Christmas are a part of the South's heritage for it was here that Christmas was first observed in the new colonies. The Southern states of Louisiana, Arkansas, and Alabama were the first to recognize Christmas as a legal holiday.

While Puritans banned the celebrations, Southerners reveled in them. Christmas has long been a holiday as well as a holy day, and the Southerner has always combined the temporal with the holy.

To help you locate those ornaments, cards, wreaths, and green garlands which will add dimension to your holiday decorating and celebrating, we have compiled this handy shopping guide.

CALICO CHRISTMAS ORNAMENTS

Frankie Eason has great patience and manual dexterity. This is evident from her delightful handmade ornaments.

Prices on the small ornaments range from $3.00 to $4.50 each. The stockings cost $7.50, and the wreath and pillow are $20.00 each. For postage add $1.00 for ornaments and stockings; add $2.00 for wreath and pillow.

Interested persons may obtain a brochure and current price list by sending a large self-addressed, stamped envelope to:

Frankie Eason
Route 2
Box 269-A
Creston, North Carolina 28615

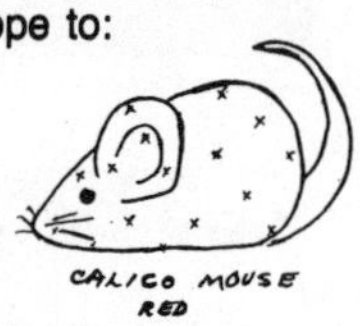

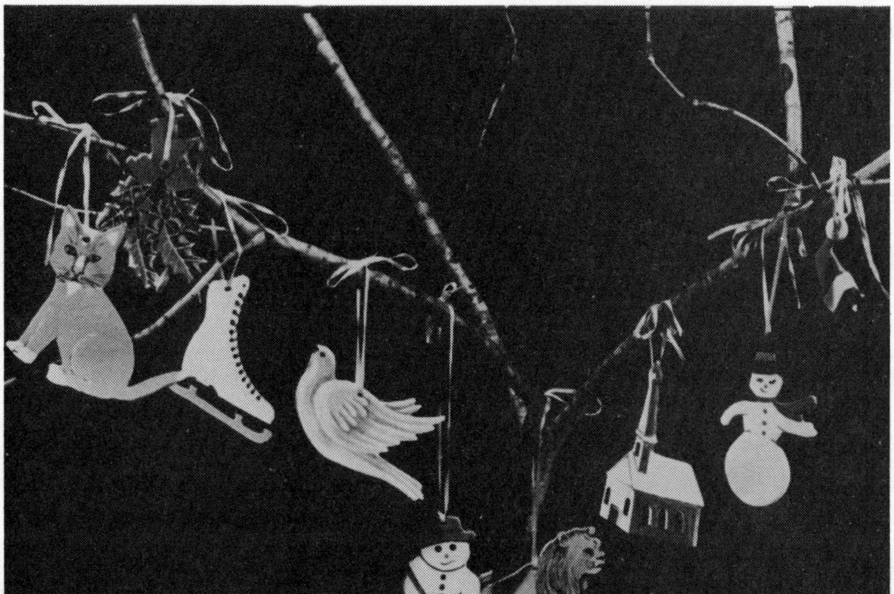

CERAMIC TREE TRIMS—Mrs. Edna N. Staley, 66 Orchard Drive, New Martinsville, West Virginia 26155, makes ceramic Christmas tree ornaments which include a variety of designs as shown here. Her ornaments are priced from $.50 to $3.00. You may write to her to order.

THE COUNTRY ACCENT

Judy Williams has put the sewing machine in its place. When Judy uses the machine in making her appliquéd wall hangings, there is no doubt about who controls what. The machine is a tool in the same way that a needle or crochet hook is a tool. Judy uses this tool to create her "Twas the night before Christmas" and "Christmas Cupboard" wall hangings and the personalized stockings shown here. Between September and December each year, Judy makes over 100 appliquéd Christmas stockings from a file of designs which keeps growing as people request new designs. The stockings sell for $13.50 each.

Since Judy's method is unlike others we have seen, it is a little difficult to describe exactly. The stockings and wall hangings have a layer of stuffing so that the effect is one of both quilting and appliqué. The detailing of small items is quite precise; the keyhole on the cupboard hanging and the mouse beside the fireplace in "Twas the night before Christmas" are examples of the delicacy and expertise of the designs of the hangings.

"Twas the night before Christmas" (21" x 30") sells for $65.00, and "Christmas Cupboard" (35" x 46") sells for $125.00.

Write to:

Judy Williams
A Country Accent
Route 17, Box 216
Hot Springs, Arkansas 71901

EVERGREEN GARLANDS

These evergreens carry, as nothing else can, the spirit of Christmas. They breathe the beauty and fragrance of the Southern mountains, and they find a ready place in every room of most of the notable homes in America during the Christmas holiday season. Orders must be prepaid.

Gardens of the Blue Ridge
P.O. Box 10
Pineola, North Carolina 28662

ROPING BALSAM

FRESH WREATHS

ROPING WHITE PINE

WREATHS	13"	16"	20"	26"
Double Face Balsam	$5.50	$6.50	$8.50	$14.00
Double Face White Pine	5.50	6.50	8.50	14.00
Double Face Hemlock	5.50	6.50	8.50	14.00

Decorative Items

CHRISTMAS ROPING—25 Yard Coils

	Each
White Pine	$15.00
Mountain Laurel	15.00
Southern Balsam	25.00

AMERICAN HOLLY (Branches). Deep green leaves with bright red berries. Excellent quality. 1 to 2 feet— per doz. $7.00

BALSAM FIR. Choice branches 1 to 2 feet long with a woodsy fragrance— per doz. 7.00

GALAX LEAVES. Medium and small sizes, green— per 1000 8.00

GROUND PINE (Bouquet Green). Very effective— 5 lbs. 8.00

LEUCOTHOE SPRAYS. Beautiful foliage, naturally in the shape of a partial garland or wreath. Deep green, 2 feet— per 100 7.00

GANELL'S CORNSHUCK CREATIVITY

Ganell Marshall, her husband, and two sons live on Sandy Ridge in Southwest Virginia. With the help of her family, Ganell uses shucks, cotton, flax, and other materials to create figures which may be used for Christmas decorations or keepsakes. Her work has been shown widely, particularly through the Southern Highland Handicraft Guild. The mountain people dolls were featured on the White House Christmas tree. Her work features storybook characters, country people, historical characters, and Christmas figures and decorations. Ganell is pleased that her cornshuck creativity continues the crafts heritage of the region.

Angel .... $1.50 each

Large Nativity (17 figures and shelter) $37.50

Nativity Set (Baby in manger, Mary, Joseph, shepherd, Wise Men, angel, camel, sheep, and cornstalk shelter) .... $25.00 set

Additional figures (camel, sheep, cow, donkey, angels, shepherd, Wise Men) ...... $2.00 each

Flight to Egypt (Mary and Baby on donkey, and Joseph) .... $8.00 set

Holy Family (Mary, Baby in manger, Joseph) .... $6.00 set

Angels or cherubs, 8" high .... $2.00 each

"Madonna" cornhusk doll, $12.00 each, ppd.

Santa Claus, sleigh, and 9 deer .. $25.00 set

Santa, sleigh, Rudolph .... $7.50 set

Christmas carolers .... $2.00 each

Mr. Snowman .... $2.00 each

Reindeer .... $2.50 each

Mrs. Claus .... $2.50 each

Santa Claus .... $2.50 each

Santa's Helpers .... $2.50 each

"Grandma" knitting and "Grandpa" in cornstalk chairs, $12.00 each, ppd.

"Prospector with pack mule" cornhusk doll, $15.00 for the set.

Mrs. Marshall also makes apple-head dolls with cornhusk bodies, and her two Christmas models are Mr. and Mrs. Claus, at $6.50 each.

She requests that you place your doll orders at least a month ahead of the time you will be needing them.

For a more complete listing than our space allows, send a stamped, self-addressed envelope to:

Mrs. Ganell Marshall
Route 1, Box 228
St. Paul, Virginia 24283

Macrame Christmas Tree—attractive wall or door hanging tied in green and decorated with pleasant sounding jingle bells. $11.00 plus $1.25 for postage. Write:

Koinonia Partners
Route 2
Americus, Georgia 31709

CAJUN CHRISTMAS CARDS: James Rice, whose winsome character, Gaston the green-nosed alligator, has become an authentic folk hero in many parts of the South, is the author-illustrator of seven books and is widely recognized as one of the nation's leading illustrators of children's literature.

Two sets of Christmas greeting cards feature full-color reproductions of scenes from his two biggest sellers, Cajun Night Before Christmas *and* Gaston The Green-Nosed Alligator.

The scenes depicting the Christmas season on the bayou feature a Cajun Santa Claus dressed in muskrat skins riding a gift-laden pirogue pulled through the sky by eight alligators.

A package of eight sells for $3.25 plus $.75 a set for postage and handling. From Pelican Publishing Company, 630 Burmaster Street, Gretna, Louisiana 70053.

*The **Springles** line includes a series of flying angel figures designed to hang as tree decorations. Each of three kinds comes in pink, blue, yellow, and white. The praying angel sells for $4.00, choir angels for $4.50, and trumpeter for $5.00. Each is washable and flexible. Write **Springles,** c/o Gay and Joe Fox, P.O. Box 308, Black Mountain, North Carolina 28711.*

***Springles** Wreath with the Bow (red) and red **Springles** (flowers) with gold centers and one hundred green leaves is $88.00.*

sheep ornaments

These darling little rams made of light wood and covered with real sheep wool are ideal ornaments to hang on your tree, in your car, in baby's room, or anywhere else you want a friendly sheep companion. Also availabe is a mobile which has a family of ram, ewe, and three little lambs. Colors in stock include white, gray, cream, black, brown, tan, gold, pink and blue. Also red and green for Christmas.

To order your sheep ornament ($2.50 plus $.50 postage) or the mobile of ram, ewe, and three little lambs ($7.00 plus $1.50 postage), write to:

The Golden Ram
P.O. Box 246
Christiansburg, Virginia 24073

HANDBLOWN TREE ORNAMENTS

The exquisite delicacy of these handblown ornaments from Lillie Glassblowers in Atlanta will make them special as gifts to friends—or to yourself.

Rocking Horse	10.00
Angel	6.00
Mushroom	6.00
Icicle	3.00
Clear crystal ball with indentations Round or oval	8.00
Star	6.00
Bell engraved with date of present year (it really rings)	7.50
Plain Christmas Bell	6.50
Teardrop	5.00
Lantern	6.00

UPS postage plus insurance $3.00 per each address U.S.A.
Order from:

Lillie Expressions in Glass
306 Omni International
Atlanta, Georgia 30303

THE SANTAS

Mr. and Mrs. Santa are designed and crafted by Alice Warriner. They are made of starch-impregnated fabric and are handpainted. They are made in two sizes: the 12" size which sells for $30.00 a pair (plus $1.50 postage); the 22" size which is $40.00 a pair (plus $1.75 postage). To order these or to inquire about a Mr. and Mrs. Pilgrim or angels by the same person, write:

Alice Warriner
Route 5, Box 204
Poplarville, Mississippi 39470

CHRISTMAS

THE OLD FASHIONED WAY

Return to the nostalgic past with hand crafted ornaments and decorations for Christmas. Each is a unique work of art in bright red and green calicos. All ornaments are filled with lightweight poly-fil and have grosgrain ribbon hangers. Ornaments vary in size from 2½" to 6".

ORNAMENTS

14A—PATCHED CALICO STAR ORNAMENT . . . trimmed with rick rack

14B—PUFFED BALL WREATH ORNAMENT . . . topped with plaid ribbon

14C—PATCHED HEEL AND TOE STOCKING ORNAMENT . . . sports white top

14D—PATCHED CANDY CANE ORNAMENT . . . tied with plaid ribbon

14E—PATCHED CALICO BELL ORNAMENT . . . trimmed with rick rack and ribbon

14F—YULE BIRD ORNAMENT . . . hand embroidered with calico wings

14G—BRAIDED CALICO WREATH ORNAMENT . . . tied with a bow

14H—ANGEL ORNAMENT . . . dressed in calico and lace, embroidered face. A real sweetheart.

14I —CALICO BIRD ORNAMENT . . . Bright calicos, solid wings

14J—MINI STRING QUILTED STOCKING ORNAMENT . . . mixed calicos with red or green top.

14K—GINGERBREAD MAN ORNAMENT . . . Brown polka dot, rick rack trim

Appalachian Craftsmen sell several Christmas ornaments. Reproduced here is a page from their catalog. The prices of ornament 14F is $3.25. The price of 14H is $3.75. The other ornaments (14A–14E, 14G, 14I–14K) are $2.75. The NOEL patchwork stringer with letters 7" tall sells for $15.00. Shipping charges for purchases under $10 are $1.50; $11–$25, $3.00; $26–$50, $4.00; $51–$100, $5.00; $101–$300, $6.00. West Virginia residents should add 3% tax. Order from:

Appalachian Craftsmen, Inc.
1209 Third Avenue
Huntington, West Virginia 25701

FRUITCAKES

Traditionally, fruitcake is eaten at Christmastime, and here are four sources for ordering this taste-tempting treat:

Koinonia Products—2 lb. 4 oz. tin, $7.65; 2 lb. 10 oz. box, $6.95; 1 lb. 5 oz. box, $3.75.

Koinonia Products
Route 2
Americus, Georgia 31709

Claxton Bakery, Inc.—3-pound light or dark (packed either solid or in three 1-pound cakes), $6.50; 5-pound light or dark (packed either solid or in five 1-pound cakes), $9.50. A light fruitcake is one made without jam. Add $.75 to a 3-pound or $1.00 to a 5-pound shipped west of the Mississippi.

Claxton Bakery, Inc.
P.O. Box 367
Claxton, Georgia 30417

Collin Street Bakery—Cakes sold in "keepsake" tins at no additional cost. 2-pound cake, $7.65; 3-pound cake, $10.90; 5-pound cake, $17.70. Prices include postage.

Collin Street Bakery
Corsicana, Texas 75110

Gordon Smith Bakery—3-pound cake, $11.50; 5-pound cake, $16.75. These are white fruitcakes and are shipped in metal tins.

Gordon Smith Bakery
1100 Dauphin Street
Box 109
Mobile, Alabama 36601

Christmas Events In The South

ALABAMA

A CHRISTMAS PAST AT THE ORDEMAN-SHAW HISTORIC HOME—Montgomery, Alabama. Each year beginning two Sundays before December 25, this beautiful home is decorated in the style of the Victorian Yuletide. Events include candlelight evening tours and musical events. Open 7 days a week, closed Christmas Day. Contact: Mrs. John F. Vaughan, Landmarks Foundation of Montgomery, 220 North Hull Street, Montgomery, Alabama 36104.

OLD FASHION CHRISTMAS AT ARLINGTON—Birmingham, Alabama, held the second weekend in December. This historic home is decorated in the authentic atmosphere of the years before 1860, with hostesses dressed in antebellum costumes. Christmas carols are sung by local school choirs, and refreshments are served. Open Saturday, 10 a.m. until 5 p.m.; Sunday, 12 to 6 p.m. Contact: Mrs. Catheriene M. Lackmond, Arlington, 331 Cotton Avenue, S.W., Birmingham, Alabama 35211. Phone: 780-5656.

CANDLELIGHT CHRISTMAS AT OAKLEIGH—Mobile, Alabama, held at this historic home generally the first weekend in December. The home is beautifully decorated, and candlelight tours are conducted. Contact: Mrs. Havadna Ford, Historic Mobile Preservation Society, 350 Oakleigh Place, Mobile, Alabama 36604. Phone: 432-1281.

HOLIDAY FLOWER SHOW AT BELLINGRATH GARDENS—Theodore, Alabama, near Mobile. For the entire month of December, the show features thousands of poinsettias in mass display throughout the gardens, along with other complementary flowers. One of the most unusual and unexpected colorful seasonal displays. Contact: Paul Cook, Bellingrath Gardens and Home, Theodore, Alabama 36582.

FESTIVAL OF SACRED MUSIC—Birmingham, Alabama. Each year, for three days beginning the day before Thanksgiving, a special festival of Christmas music is held at the Municipal Auditorium. Music is provided by the Birmingham Symphony Orchestra and Birmingham Civic Chorus, and personalities from the Lawrence Welk Show are an added attraction. Contact: Public Affairs Department, *The Birmingham News,* 2200 Fourth Avenue North, Birmingham, Alabama 35203.

ARKANSAS

CHRISTMAS CONCERT—Hot Springs National Park. Held at the Convention Auditorium the second Sunday in December, the concert features the Arkansas Symphony Chamber Orchestra, Garland County Community College Chorus, and featured soloists. The program includes selections from Handel's "Messiah" and Tchaikowsky's "Nutcracker Suite." Contact: Chamber of Commerce, Convention Auditorium, Box 1500, Hot Springs National Park, Arkansas 71901.

FLORIDA

CHRISTMAS BOAT PARADE—Pompano Beach, Florida, held each year on the Sunday preceding Christmas. Over 100 boats, decorated with gaily colored lights and bearing carolers, cruise the Intracoastal Waterway. Spectators line decorated seawalls to view the beautiful aquatic caravan. Contact: Greater Pompano Beach Chamber of Commerce, 2200 East Atlantic Boulevard, Pompano Beach, Florida 33062.

CHRISTMAS CONCERTS AND CHRISTMAS CRAFTS SHOW-SALE at the Stephen Foster Memorial—on the Suwannee River, White Springs, Florida. The first two days in December at 2:00 p.m. musical groups perform special music and concerts are played on the 97-bell Foster carillon. December 1–22 guests can view and purchase Christmas ornaments and gifts, all hand-made by the Suwannee River Crafts Guild. Contact: Stephen Foster Memorial, White Springs, Florida 32096.

GEORGIA

CALLAWAY GARDENS' CHRISTMAS—Pine Mountain, Georgia. Callaway Gardens celebrates Christmas with 12 days of holiday festivities which include "getting-to-know-you" hospitalities, nature walks, craftsmen demonstrating and teaching their talent, tree trimming, special horticultural workshops, and candy-making classes. The Christmas at Callaway Gardens begins on December 20, kicked off with a Madrigal Dinner in the tradition of Old England. The merrymaking continues through December 31, when the New Year's Eve Dinner Dance brings the celebration to a pleasurable end. For information and reservations write: Christmas at Callaway Gardens, Pine Mountain, Georgia 31822.

CHRISTMAS AT THE CLOISTER—Sea Island, Georgia, offers a week of holiday activities. All the cottages are lighted and many parties are held up and down Sea Island Drive each night. Special feature is the Yule Log Ceremony on Christmas Eve. The entire hotel is decorated and after the Yule log is lighted, guests join in caroling to the accompaniment of a harp. Santa Claus visits the children at their special party on Christmas Eve. Contact: Ted Wright, Managing Director, The Cloister, Sea Island, Georgia 31561.

TREE OF LIGHTS IN DAFFIN PARK—Savannah, Georgia. A crew picks a 60- to 70-foot pine each year. It is stripped of its branches; holes are drilled in the trunk; limbs are replaced until symmetrical proportions are assured; then the limbs are strung with multicolored lights. On the last Sunday before Christmas, a lighting ceremony is held, as viewers join in Yuletide caroling. Contact: Al Ray, AMBUCS, P.O. Box 22001, Savannah, Georgia 31403.

HOLIDAY YULE LOG CEREMONY OF WESTVILLE—Lumpkin, Georgia. The ceremony, held in this restored 1850s village, is a Yule log lighting, traditional in Southern communities in the 18th and early 19th centuries. Caroling and the ritual "hanging of the greens" are included in the ceremony. It is held on the Saturday nearest December 12. Contact: Norma Holloway, Westville Historic Handicrafts, Inc., P.O. Box 1850, Lumpkin, Georgia 31815.

ANNUAL LIVING NATIVITY PAGEANT—Stone Mountain, Georgia, 16 miles east of Atlanta on Highway 78. December 17 through 21 at 7:30 p.m. A narrated drama of the birth of Christ is portrayed on Memorial Plaza lawn with a cast of Atlanta area young people, live animals, lights and music heard over a giant outdoor stereo system. To watch the free pageant, visitors may relax on the sloping five-acre lawn that provides a natural amphitheater in front of Stone Mountain carving. Vehicle parking cost is waived from 5 p.m. to midnight from mid-December to December 25. Contact: Betty Franklin, Public Relations Dept., Stone Mountain Park, P.O. Box 778, Stone Mountain, Georgia 30086.

CHRISTMAS AROUND THE WORLD—Macon, Georgia. The Museum of Arts and Sciences offers its popular annual Christmas exhibit to the public, opening on the first Sunday before Thanksgiving each year. The exhibit features the themes of the Music of Christmas, Colonial Christmas at Williamsburg and Christmas Trees of the World. The Museum's Mark Smith Planetarium presents its traditional planetarium production, "The Star of Bethlehem," which seeks to offer scientific explanations of what that mysterious object in the sky might have been that guided the Wise Men to Bethlehem. The Museum is open weekdays from 9:00 a.m. to 5:00 p.m., reopening on Fridays at 7 p.m. for a public planetarium show at 7:30 p.m., followed by the laser light show at 9 p.m. Museum hours on Saturday are from 9:00 a.m. to 5:00 p.m., with a public planetarium show at 2:00 and laser light show at 3:30 and on Sundays from 2:00 p.m. to 5:00 p.m. with a public planetarium show at 2:00. Contact: Mr. D.R. Noble, Director, The Museum of Arts and Sciences, 4182 Forsyth Road, Macon, Georgia 31210.

KENTUCKY

LIVING NATIVITY—Bethlehem, Kentucky, held December 22 through December 25, 6:30 p.m. to 9:00 p.m. The Nativity scene is a tableau with characters wearing authentic dress and live animals adding to the realism. Recorded carols and scripture are played over a loud speaker. Contact: Alvin L. Roberts, Bethlehem Living Nativity, Bethlehem, Kentucky 40007.

LOUISIANA

HODGES GARDENS CHRISTMAS LIGHTS—Many, Louisiana, usually held for three weeks during the holiday season. Multicolored lights around the shore of the 225-acre gardens' lake illuminate the scene for the festival. Larger-than-life papier-mâché figures, arrayed in colorful robes, realistically depict the Holy Land of long ago. Admission charges to the Gardens, located midway between Shreveport and Lake Charles, are waived for the festival and the gates are open from 6 to 9 p.m. Contact: Carol Vinson, Publicity Director, Hodges Gardens, P.O. Box 921, Many, Louisiana 71449.

PATIO PLANTERS' CHRISTMAS CAROL CELEBRATION—New Orleans, Louisiana, held the Sunday before Christmas at Jackson Square. Guests assemble at 6:30 p.m. and form at each of the four gates into Jackson Square. As the St. Louis Cathedral bells toll 7 p.m., candles are lit and the procession into the square begins with thousands of voices singing Christmas carols. Contact: John Bogie, 7216 Zimple, New Orleans, Louisiana 70118.

CHRISTMAS EVE BONFIRE CELEBRATION IN THE LUTCHER-GRAMERCY AREA ALONG RIVER ROAD—between New Orleans and Baton Rouge, Louisiana. For two months before Christmas Eve, citizens begin to build more than one hundred 30-foot tall, pyramid-shaped bonfires along the river. At 7:30 p.m. on Christmas Eve, the bonfires are lit and burn into the night. Rockets, sparklers, and other fireworks add to the gaiety of the spectacular affair, and to enjoy it all, you need only to drive up the levee on the River Road. Contact: Louisiana Tourist Commission, P.O. Box 44291, Baton Rouge, Louisiana 70804.

MARYLAND

COLONIAL CHRISTMAS AT HAMMOND-HARWOOD HOUSE—Annapolis, Maryland. Each Christmas this beautiful Georgian mansion is decorated as it was in the 18th century. A greens sale is conducted in addition to a candlelight tour of the house. Hostesses in authentic costume welcome visitors. Contact: Administration, The Hammond-Harwood House, 19 Maryland Avenue, Annapolis, Maryland 21401.

CHRISTMAS OPEN HOUSE AND BAZAAR AT CARROLL COUNTY FARM MUSEUM—Westminster, Maryland. Usually during the first part of December, the Gift Shoppe is open and filled with numerous Christmas gift ideas. Later the Main House is decorated as it was in the 19th century. Special music is provided each evening. On the last night of the tour, a Friendship Candle Lighting Service is held, along with a community carol sing. Contact: Cindy Hofferberth, Director, Carroll County Farm Museum, Westminster, Maryland 21157.

VICTORIAN CHRISTMAS AT MILLER HOUSE—Hagerstown, Maryland. For about 10 days during the Christmas season, the historic Miller House is decorated as it was in days gone by. Special exhibits in the various rooms of the house include a cedar tree decorated with rare old Christmas ornaments. Hostesses dressed in original gowns of the late 19th century greet visitors. Contact: Mrs. Kenneth Peters, 135 W. Washington, Hagerstown, Maryland 21740.

CHRISTMAS AT MOUNT CLARE—Baltimore, Maryland, is held each year about 10 days before Christmas. Mount Clare is a museum house of 18th-century furnishings and at Christmastime each room is bedecked with Christmas arrangements in the Colonial manner. Costumed hostesses serve visitors refreshments and various musical programs are held. Contact: Mount Clare, Carroll Park, Baltimore, Maryland 21230.

MISSISSIPPI

CHRISTMAS PAGEANT—Leland, Mississippi. Each year about the second week in December, Deer Creek, which runs through the Delta town of Leland, becomes alive with floats depicting the spirit of Christmas. There are floats representing the life of Christ and floats representing the worldly aspects of Christmas. These floats can be seen until New Year's day. One night during the week, children await the arrival of Santa Claus on a gaily decorated float. Contact: Leland Chamber of Commerce, P.O. Box 67, Leland, Mississippi 38756.

TREES OF CHRISTMAS TOUR AT MERREHOPE—Meridian, Mississippi. Within the first two weeks in December, the historic Mississippi home, Merrehope, features live 12-foot trees, each decorated with hundreds of handmade ornaments representing other countries and different sections of the United States. A craft show features many handmade ornaments and gifts for sale. Contact: Merrehope, 905 31st Avenue, Meridian, Mississippi 39301.

CHRISTMAS HOMES TOUR—McComb, Mississippi. Each year, two homes in the McComb area are chosen and tastefully and artistically decorated. They are open for visitors beginning the second Sunday in December. Contact: Mrs. John Wardlaw, Wardlaw Road, McComb, Mississippi 39648.

NORTH CAROLINA

WORLD'S LARGEST LIVING CHRISTMAS TREE—Wilmington, North Carolina. A large water oak, 75 feet tall with a limb spread of 210 feet, is decorated each year and is considered to be the world's largest living Christmas tree. It is draped with 5 tons of Spanish moss and lighted by over 4,500 multicolored lights. Christmas carols are played and sung. The official ceremonial lighting is generally scheduled about the 10th of December, and the lights are turned on nightly during the holiday season. Contact: Greater Wilmington Chamber of Commerce, P.O. Box 330, Wilmington, North Carolina 28402.

OLD WILMINGTON BY CANDLELIGHT—Wilmington, North Carolina. The warmth and charm of historic Wilmington is experienced during this tour by the opening of the gracious homes and churches. Refreshments are served, carolers stroll through the streets, music is presented in the churches, and candles light your way. Truly an experience in Christmas Past. Contact: James R. Warren, Chairman, P.O. Box 813, Wilmington, North Carolina 28402.

SALEM CHRISTMAS—Winston-Salem, North Carolina. This is a one-day event held around the middle of December. The sights, sounds, and smells of Christmastime long ago are recreated in the restored old Moravian town of Old Salem. The streets are blocked to traffic and visitors may walk through the historic area and enjoy the unhurried, warm-hearted atmosphere of the town as it was nearly 200 years ago. Traditional Christmas music is provided by roving bands. All participants are appropriately costumed in early Moravian dress. Contact: Department of Information, Old Salem, Inc., Drawer F., Salem Station, Winston-Salem, North Carolina 27108.

SINGING CHRISTMAS TREE—Charlotte, North Carolina. This magnificent musical program has grown in popularity since its first performance 25 years ago. When the curtain opens, the audience is held breathless at the sight of a giant green tree with hundreds of shining lights that gradually glow from soft light to a brilliant splendor. The music that fills the air is rendered by approximately 100 male and female voices who compose the Charlotte Choral Society. Each year the theme of the show is different and depicted in new and beautiful sets, costumed dancers and musical selections. Often the show will include one or more well-known guest artists, as well as an appearance by Santa and falling snow on stage. A beautiful show for young and old alike. For tickets and information, contact: The Charlotte Choral Society, Spirit Square, 110 E. 7th Street, Charlotte, North Carolina 28202.

OKLAHOMA

SINGING CHRISTMAS TREE—Antlers, Oklahoma. A frame is built with stair steps in the shape of a Christmas tree. Some 125 choir members, robed in white, stand on the steps, forming the "singing Christmas tree." The tree is decorated with greenery and lights with a large star at the top. It usually opens a week before Christmas with singing each night between 8 and 9 p.m.. It is located off the Indian Nation Turnpike where parking is available for some 2,500 cars. Contact: Rev. H. L. Morrison, Box 517, Antlers, Oklahoma 74523.

OLD-FASHIONED CHRISTMAS AT THE OLD TOWN MUSEUM—Elk City, Oklahoma. This celebration is held at the historic museum, which is an authentic western Oklahoma home built at the turn of the century and furnished with Victorian furniture. On a Sunday afternoon, generally a couple of weeks before Christmas, a tree is placed in the gazebo on the grounds of the museum. It is decorated with green garlands and red bows and ornaments. Carols are sung and refreshments served, followed by Santa Claus's timely visit. The tree is spotlighted each night during the holiday season. Contact: Curator, Old Town Museum, P.O. Box 542, Elk City, Oklahoma 73644.

SOUTH CAROLINA

HOLIDAY FIESTA—Myrtle Beach and the Grand Strand, South Carolina. November 18–December 31. The special holiday activities include turkey shoots, community worship services, golf tournaments, Christmas observances, community caroling, Christmas concerts, home tours, art exhibits, and package plans at motels and hotels. Contact: Greater Myrtle Beach Chamber of Commerce, P.O. Box 2115, Myrtle Beach, South Carolina 29577.

WINYAH ACADEMY CHRISTMAS HOMES TOUR—Georgetown, South Carolina. Included in this tour are a number of homes, chosen each year—some older, historically important homes, and some new—decorated in a variety of ways. Contact: Claudia Walker, Winyah Academy, P.O. Drawer C, Georgetown, South Carolina 29440.

CHRISTMAS IN CHARLESTON—Charleston, South Carolina. The whole month of December will see the business district and historic districts filled with singing groups, story tellers, beautifully decorated museum mansion houses, and historic churches decorated for the holidays. Christmas concerts, ballets, and plays will be presented. Most important of all is the mild December weather with temperatures in the sixties and seventies. For a schedule of events, write: Christmas in Charleston, P.O. Box 975, Charleston, South Carolina 29402.

TENNESSEE

NATIVITY PAGEANT—Knoxville, Tennessee. A cast of 84 local actors, live animals, and a 200-voice choir all make this production of the Nativity most impressive and realistic. It is usually held for three days during the middle of December. Contact: Mrs. John Ray, 9713 Panama Drive, Knoxville, Tennessee 37919.

THE TREES OF CHRISTMAS AT CHEEKWOOD—Nashville, Tennessee, held at Cheekwood, the Tennessee Botanical Gardens and Fine Arts Center. The display of trees includes those decorated in the tradition of some seven or eight countries as well as other novelty trees, such as the "Sugarplum Fairy Tree" (suggested by the well-known character from Tchaikovsky's "Nutcracker Suite"). Also on hand is a display of locally made handcrafts. All of this usually starts the 1st of December. Contact: The Tennessee Botanical Gardens and Fine Arts Center, Inc., Cheekwood, Nashville, Tennessee 37205.

TEXAS

POINSETTIA SHOW—Mission, Texas. In the second week in December each year, Mission, Texas, reminds the Rio Grande Valley of the advent of the Christmas season with a display of the beautiful traditional Christmas flower in the only all-poinsettia show in the nation. Contact: Mrs. T. L. Duncan, Box 706, Mission, Texas 78572.

DICKENS'S EVENING ON THE STRAND—Galveston, Texas. First Saturday in December, 2 p.m. until 10 p.m. Named Texas' most outstanding winter event, this unique yuletide celebration authentically rekindles the spirit of Christmas Past by recreating a "living" Victorian street scene in the Historic Strand District. This event includes Dickens's characters—Scrooge, Tiny Tim, Oliver Twist, and a host of others—come to life. Along the streets you see strolling carolers, musicians, dancers, and vendors selling dancing dolls and roasted chestnuts. More than 60 Victorian "shoppes" are housed in the 19th-century buildings. Victorian specialty houses, dining salons, and pubs cater authentic Victorian wares and fares to genteel customers. Contact: Galveston Historical Foundation, P.O. Box 302, Galveston, Texas 77553.

THE GLOW OF CHRISTMAS—Galveston, Texas. Ashton Villa, an 1859 restored Galveston mansion, is decked throughout in holiday splendor and open free to the public for a few days in early December. Visitors are given a special tour of Ashton Villa by docents dressed in period costume. The house is elaborately decorated inside and out with traditional Victorian decorations. To highlight the spirit of "The Glow," a dozen or more choirs perform Christmas carols throughout the house, and volunteers dressed as Victorian family members go about their duties of preparing a home for Christmas before the turn-of-the-century. Refreshments are served. Contact: Judy Schiebel, Ashton Villa, 2328 Broadway, Galveston, Texas 77550.

MIDWESTERN-BURNS FANTASY OF LIGHTS—Wichita Falls, Texas. Four of the campus buildings of Midwestern University each year are decorated with some 12,000 red, white, and yellow bulbs. These and over 30 Christmas exhibits, many of which are animated, form the "Fantasy Of Lights." They are turned on the first Friday in December and continue to shine throughout the holiday season. Contact: Mr. Steve Holland, Midwestern University, 3400 Taft Street, Wichita Falls, Texas 76308.

LOS PASTORES—San Antonio, Texas. Held at the San Jose Mission, this is an old, primitive pageant depicting the birth of Christ. Contact: San Antonio Conservation Society, 107 King William Street, San Antonio, Texas 78204.

CHRISTMAS CELEBRATIONS—San Antonio, Texas. Three celebrations are held in conjunction with each other, usually the week before Christmas. "Las Posadas" is held in the streets of downtown San Antonio and along the River Walk. It is the traditional Mexican depiction of Mary and Joseph seeking shelter. "Fiesta de Las Luminarias" is a festival of lights, with local high schools and churches presenting musical entertainment. "Fiesta Navideña" is held at the Mexican Market and is a festival of Christmas music, along with an arts and crafts show and sale. Contact: Greater San Antonio Chamber of Commerce, Box 1628, San Antonio, Texas 78296.

VIRGINIA

CHRISTMAS AT BOAR'S HEAD INN—Charlottesville, Virginia. Each year Boar's Head Inn treats its guests at Christmas with a most unique and interesting program of activities. The inn is colorfully decorated, and entertainment is provided during the entire Christmas week. Each evening there is caroling before a Christmas fire. Festivities include: a Christmas puppeteers show for the children, search for the Yule Log and a lighting ceremony, folk-plays, and much more, all in the tradition of merry old England. Contact: The Boar's Head Inn, Ednam Forest, Charlottesville, Virginia 22901.

CHRISTMAS WALK—Alexandria, Virginia. Now in its ninth year, the theme of this Christmas celebration is "A Scottish Christmas in Alexandria," emphasizing the Scottish origin of this historic city. The schedule of activities includes Scottish bagpipe bands providing stirring music, a special Scottish Advent Service, tours of decorated historic homes, a special "Wonderful World" for children, a display of early American, Scottish, and English fire-fighting equipment, plus sales of Christmas greens, antiques, and taste-tempting goodies. Contact: Christmas Walk, 602 Cameron Street, Alexandria, Virginia 22314.

THE NATIVITY—Richmond, Virginia, a continuous pageant for over 50 years. It is held each Christmas Eve at 6 p.m. at the Carillon in Byrd Park. The pageant is the story of the Nativity done in pantomime with narration and music. Contact: Department of Recreation and Parks, City of Richmond, 900 East Broad Street, Richmond, Virginia 23219.

CHRISTMAS IN WILLIAMSBURG—Williamsburg, Virginia. This Christmas program is a fortnight of traditional and Colonial activities featuring dramatic lighting, games, feasting, and special events. Usually beginning the third weekend in December. Contact: Colonial Williamsburg Foundation, Williamsburg, Virginia 23185.

WEST VIRGINIA

OLD-FASHIONED CHRISTMAS—Harpers Ferry, West Virginia. This celebration is held the first full weekend in December. Visitors can take a candlelight walk through the streets of Harpers Ferry. Shops are lighted by candles, and the streets, by old-fashioned lamps. Carolers and roving musicians provide the Christmas music. Contact: D. D. Kilham, Hilltop House Hotel, Harpers Ferry, West Virginia 25425.

GASTON, THE GREEN-NOSED ALLIGATOR

Written and Illustrated by James Rice

Pelican Publishing Company, Inc.
630 Burmaster Street
Gretna, Louisiana 70053

What happens to Christmas if all the reindeer call in sick? If Prancer sprains his ankle, Donder catches cold, and Vixen and Dasher are recovering from crash landings? But, worst of all, what if the light goes out on Rudolph's nose???

In this delightful tale, author-illustrator James Rice comes up with an unusual solution. He is aided by a lovable alligator with the festive name of Gaston! Gaston is the epitome of Southern charm and he usually can be found soaring gracefully above the Louisiana bayous. And, most important, he has his own light—on his nose!!

With the help of Gaston, Santa assembles a new team. Tiboy, Alceé, Ninette, Suzette, Celeste, and Reneé are going to follow Gaston's glowing green nose and deliver all the presents and candy to the children. But, as all kids know, not every alligator can fly like Gaston can. So, Gaston holds practice sessions in the swamps to make sure that all the gators will be aloft on Christmas Eve. All you children, young and old, can relax. Christmas will come on schedule and everything will be the same with just a little bit of extra greenery!

—S.V.H.

JUBILEE!

Occasionally, on the eastern shore of Alabama's Mobile Bay, there occurs a unique phenomenon: shrimp, crabs, and fish race to the water's edge, as if suddenly compelled to become land-bound. When the phenomenon is observed, you'll hear the cry *"JUBILEE!"* ring up and down the beach—and every available bucket, net, and gig is brought down to the shore, to aid in gathering up this unexpected and largely unexplained harvest of the sea.

When the Junior League of Mobile was casting about for a title to their cookbook in 1964, *Recipe Jubilee!* naturally came to mind, since they intended to publish a cookbook of tried and true recipes which they hoped would cause a stir of excitement not only along the Gulf Coast, but across the country as well. Since their initial printing of 7,000 copies in 1964, an additional 90,000 copies have been printed and sold—a bonanza for the Junior League of Mobile and their educational, cultural, and welfare projects in the community.

As could be expected, the "Seafood Jubilee" chapter is a particularly outstanding feature of the book, and the book could be recommended on the strength of that chapter alone. The chapter also includes some helpful advice on seafood preparation, no doubt the result of countless hours of experience of the best seafood cooks in Mobile.

Recipe Jubilee! sells for $6.25 plus a $1.00 handling charge. (Mobile residents add 6% sales tax; Alabama residents add 4% sales tax.)

Order from:

Recipe Jubilee!
350 Church Street
Mobile, Alabama 36602

WAKEFIELD-SCEARCE GALLERIES

The Wakefield-Scearce Galleries are located in one of the oldest buildings in Kentucky; the building had its beginning in 1790. From 1825 until 1939 it served as one of the most outstanding girls' schools west of the Alleghenies. Today historic Science Hill houses one of the largest collections of fine English antique furniture, rare and unusual silver, and porcelain in the country.

An item handmade at Wakefield-Scearce Galleries is a sterling silver Mint Julep cup—copied from an original which was made in Kentucky about the year 1795. It is traditional in every detail.

The prices of the julep cups:
Regular Julep Cup, $98.50;
Nip Cup, $39.50;
Baby Julep, $72.00;
Double Jigger, $54.50.

Order from:

Wakefield-Scearce Galleries
Historic Science Hill
Box 469
Shelbyville, Kentucky 40065

THE MINT JULEP

"Wherever there is a mint julep there is a bit of the Old South. For the julep is part ceremony, tradition, and regional nostalgia; part flavor, taste, and aroma; and only by definition liquor, simple syrup, mint, and ice."

Richard Barksdale Harwell has collected for us the history and the traditions surrounding the julep. Anecdotes connect the drink with the colorful people who have made it a part of the history of the South in the grandiose antebellum days, the Civil War, the Victorian years, Prohibition and even overseas during World War II. Recipes from letters and cookbooks from the nineteenth century to the present give the subtle variations of the julep.

The Mint Julep by Richard Barksdale Harwell is available from the University Press of Virginia, Charlottesville, Virginia.

FRENCH FRAGRANCES FROM NEW ORLEANS

Hové, Parfumeur, was started in 1932 by Mrs. Alvin Hovey-King, whose hobby had always been the collection of perfumes from all over the world, first as an "Army daughter," then as a "Navy" and "Diplomatic" wife. Today the business is carried on by her daughter, son-in-law, and grand-daughter and is noted for its wide variety of outstanding fragrances at a relatively low cost.

All the formulas for the perfumes and colognes are composed and developed, and the resulting perfumes are mixed, bottled and packaged at Casa Hové, the Museum-shop home of the business on Toulouse Street, in the French Quarter of New Orleans. The perfumes are sold in the shop by mail order—the firm claims over 10,000 customers in the United States, Canada, Europe, and South America.

Among the fragrances listed in Hové catalog (available free of charge) are *Exciting New Orleans Bouquets:* Carnaval, Corduroy, Creole Days, Eau de Cologne Napoleon, El Capitan, Grandee, Kiss in the Dark, Rue Royale, and Spring Fiesta; and *Fascinating Fragrances:* Azalea, Carnation, Clochettes des Bois, Easter Lily, Elan d'Orange, Gardenia, Ginger Blanc, Heliotrope, Honeysuckle, Jasmin, Lavande, Lilas d'Avril, Magnolia, Pois de Senteur, Purple Violet, Rose Coleste, Rose Geranium, Tea Olive (Hové's most popular fragrance), Verveine, Vetivert, and Vetivert Root Fans.

For a free catalogue, write:

Hové, Parfumeur
723 Toulouse Street
New Orleans, Louisiana 70130

The Joys of Southern Skiing

The bitter cold of the last few winters brought the South its best ski seasons ever. Jumping from eiderdown to longjohns, more than a million enthusiasts a year turned out on the slopes for a real taste of a Southern winter. Following is a list of some of the ski areas in Alabama, Georgia, Maryland, North Carolina, Tennessee, and West Virginia.

Alabama

Cloudmont Resort, Mentone 35984; telephone (205) 634-3841. Cloudmont has a 1,000-foot beginner-intermediate slope serviced by a pony tow. Night skiing every night in season, late November through March 1; 100% snowmaking. Ski school and rental service. Lodging available at five A-frame chalets and four log cabins.

Georgia

Sky Valley Ski Area, Dillard 30537; telephone (404) 746-5301. Caters exclusively to beginners and intermediates on three slopes; the longest is 2,200 feet with a vertical drop of 250 feet. There is a double-chair lift and a rope tow. Ski school and rental service; 100% snowmaking but no night skiing. Condominiums and chalets for rent.

Maryland

Wisp Ski Area, Route 219, Oakland 21550; telephone (301) 387-5581. Offers 12 miles of slopes and trails (4 slopes and 16 trails), serviced by a double-chair lift, Poma lift, and rope tow. Highest vertical drop is 610 feet. Snowmaking capability on three-quarters of the slopes; night skiing on several slopes weeknights January 4 through February 24. Ski school, rental service. Lodging at the slope and other accommodations in the area.

North Carolina

Appalachian Ski Mountain, Inc., Box 106, Blowing Rock 28605; telephone (704) 295-7828. Five slopes and a wooded, 2,700-foot forest trail. Slopes serviced by two double-chair lifts and three rope tows. Night skiing every night except Monday and Thursday, 6 to 10 p.m., on all slopes; 100% snowmaking. A ski school, ski rental service, ski shop, and a large restaurant with fireplace that occasionally hosts dinner dances on Saturday evenings. Lodging is not available at the ski area, but Appalachian Ski Mountain has working arrangements with motels and can make reservations.

Beech Mountain, Box 277, Banner Elk 28604; telephone (704) 387-4231. Twenty-three trails covering 35 acres of slopes make Beech Mountain one of the largest ski areas in the South. Two new advanced slopes run from the top of the mountain, averaging a vertical drop of 805 feet. Eight lifts, including one J-bar and a new, very fast double-chair lift. Lifts and tows combined transport a record 10,000 skiers per hour up the slopes. Illuminated for night skiing; 90% snowmaking.

The Beech Mountain Ski Complex has three inns, a cafeteria, a ski school and rental service, and a "Bavarian Village" of shops.

Cataloochee Ski Slopes, Inc., Route 1, Box 500, Maggie Valley 28786; telephone (704) 926-0285. Cataloochee advertises as a "skier's ski area," long on skiing, short on nightclub-like entertainment. Six slopes (one advanced, three intermediate, and two novice areas) have 100% snowmaking capability; night skiing Monday through Friday. Longest run is 5,000 feet with a 740-foot vertical drop. Double-chair lift with midpoint loading and unloading, T-bar, and two rope tows service the slopes.

Cataloochee has a base lodge with restaurant, ski school, and ski rental and sales shop. Lodging is available in Maggie Valley.

Hound Ears Lodge and Club, Box 188, Blowing Rock 28605; telephone (704) 963-4321. Skiing at Hound Ears is open only to members and guests at the lodge. The 27-chair lift services a 1,250-foot intermediate slope with a vertical drop of 107 feet and a beginners area. One hundred percent snowmaking. The resort has a large clubhouse with a dining room and a ski rental shop.

Seven Devils Resort, Route 1, Highway 105, Banner Elk 28604; telephone (704) 963-4061. The four slopes are fairly steep, catering to serious skiers. They range from a 3,800-foot advanced run with a vertical drop of 607 feet to a beginners area. Two double-chair lifts and two rope tows; 70% snowmaking. The resort has 15 rooms at the inn, 30 chalets and condominiums.

Sugar Mountain, Box 369, Banner Elk 28604; telephone (704) 898-4521. Eleven trails on 70 acres of slopes; the largest vertical drop in North Carolina. Four lifts; one, a mile-long chair lift, services the 1.3-mile advanced run, one of the longest in the South with a vertical drop of 1,200 feet. Other slopes include a 4,100-foot expert, five intermediate, and five novice. Night skiing Monday through Saturday on six slopes; 100% snowmaking capability. Ski center with cafeteria, nursery, ski school, and equipment rental and sales shop; 32 units of overnight lodging.

Wolf Laurel, Mars Hill 28754; telephone (704) 689-4111. Wolf Laurel, called the "friendly ski slope," stresses family skiing on eight slopes (three expert, four advanced, one intermediate, and a novice area). Longest run is 3,500 feet with a vertical drop of 700 feet. Double-chair lift, Poma lift, and Mighty Mite tow bar service the slopes. Snowmaking covers five areas; night skiing Wednesday, Friday, and Saturday, including a Christmas special the entire week of December 26-30. Restaurant, ski school, and rental shop. Overnight accommodations available.

Tennessee

Ober-Gatlinburg Ski Resort, Gatlinburg 37738; telephone (615) 436-5423. Expert slope is 4,800 feet with vertical drop of 800 feet. The expert and the three other slopes (advanced, intermediate, and beginners) are serviced by two chair lifts and two rope tows. Night skiing Monday through Saturday on beginner, intermediate, and advanced slopes; 100% snowmaking. The first resort in the South to offer an Alpine Slide (a bobsled-type ride), which careens through a half-mile of wooded trails. Ski school, rental shop, accommodations in the area.

West Virginia

Alpine Lake, Terra Alta 26764; telephone (304) 789-2481. Three slopes: an advanced, 2,200-foot run with vertical drop of 400 feet, a 700-foot intermediate slope, and a beginners area, serviced by two Pomas and a pony lift. Nighttime skiing on all slopes, Friday and Saturday; 100% snowmaking. Ski school, rental shop, and a rustic lodge with dining room.

Canaan Valley Resort, Box 39, Route 1, Davis 26260; telephone (304) 866-4121. A complete concession-operated winter resort. Summit elevation of 4,280 feet with a vertical drop of 850 feet ensures exciting skiing on 7 slopes and 14 trails, ranging from expert to novice. Accommodations available in the new 250-room lodge, with restaurant, and in 15 deluxe cabins. Rental service, ski school, and nursery.

Chestnut Ridge, Box 590, Morgantown 26505; telephone (304) 292-4773. The two slopes at Chestnut Ridge (1,200 feet with a 170-foot vertical drop and 900 feet with a 130-foot drop) are lighted for night skiing; no artificial snowmaking equipment. The shorter slope is serviced by an electric rope tow. Rental service available.

Oglebay Park, Wheeling 26003; telephone (304) 242-3000. Oglebay's 40-acre ski area includes intermediate and beginner slopes ranging in length from 900 feet to a quarter of a mile and averaging a 20-degree slope. Two Poma lifts and a rope tow; 100% snowmaking. Ski school, rental shop. Night skiing on all slopes. Dining and overnight lodging at Wilson Lodge and at a series of cabins and chalets.

Snowshoe, located just outside Slatyfork 26291; telephone (304) 799-6600. At Snowshoe you can ski outside the horseshoe mountain basin or inside its bowl. There are 13 slopes in the north-facing, elliptical bowl; three triple-chair lifts service the inner bowl. Another triple-chair lift takes skiers to the outside of the basin for a 9,000-foot run with a vertical drop of 1,500 feet. There are 10 miles of groomed trails for cross-country skiers. Ski school, rental service; 90% snowmaking. Slopeside lodging at the 100-room budget hotel, at the deluxe Timberline Lodge, or in 86 one- and three-bedroom townhouse condominiums.

THE ROUND HOUSE

The people at Rondesics Homes, Corp., in Asheville, North Carolina, figured that if locomotives could turn around comfortably in a round house, surely the average family could rattle around with ease in a home built on the same order as a roundhouse. What was even more fundamental to the designers and engineers at Rondesics was the creation of a low-cost, but spacious, sight- *and* site-pleasing home, a home that could be built in the mountains, at the seashore, or beside a lake with equal ease and success.

To achieve this goal, Rondesics spent over 13 years working out the best designs and discovering the best materials with which to execute them. The final designs incorporated the idea of the geodesic dome, with the addition of an important factor: the Rondesics are beautiful to look at on a site—the geodesic dome is most often not. The dome does have some excellent attributes, however: it contains increased floor space; it is inexpensive, quick and easy to erect; it offers maximum window area, an essential ingredient in a home. These qualities were retained in the Rondesics design by the division of the homes into sections, enabling interchange among units, stacking of units, and the connecting of units in a variety of ways.

The cost of a Rondesics Home starts as low as $20,000.00 and goes on up. A roomy, two-bedroom model runs about $40,000.00, but since you can get as elaborate as you wish in combining and rearranging the basic home units, only your own pocketbook need limit your imagination.

There are Rondesics dealer/builders in most areas east of the Mississippi. Tom Fawcett, president of Rondesics, requests that you get in touch with him if you'd like to pursue the idea of a Rondesics Home as your vacation (or permanent) home. A complete brochure, with sample plans and a cost calculator, is available by writing:

Mr. Tom Fawcett
President
Rondesics Homes Corporation
527 McDowell Street
Asheville, North Carolina 28803

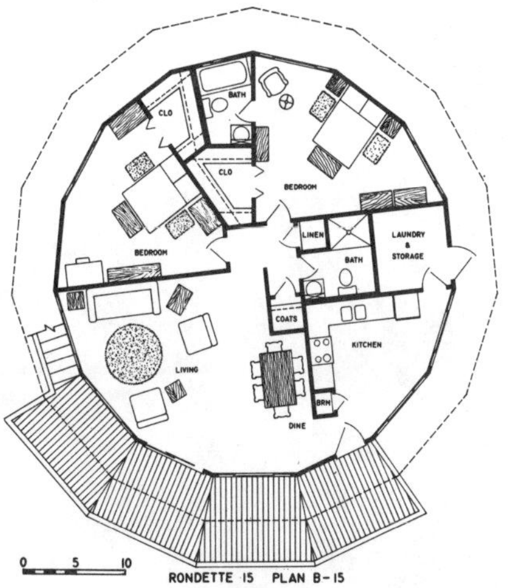

RONDETTE 15 PLAN B-15
TWO BEDROOM PLAN

Southern Zoo Guide

Visit A Zoo Near You

The encroachment of civilization upon the plain and forest homes of animals has provided man with additional territory but summarily undermined the balance of nature.

Animals that are particularly valuable for their hides have been hunted to near extinction.

Fortunately, there is growing worldwide concern for these victims of man's excesses. One refuge for animals is the zoo, and the concept of the zoo is changing from a compound where man and beast peer at each other through bars, to an environment duplicating as nearly as possible the animal's natural one.

In our own South there are zoos in almost every area; those that don't have zoos are building them. Columbia, South Carolina, and Wheeling, West Virginia, have new zoos.

A visit to a zoo is educational, tranquilizing to the spirit, and relatively inexpensive.

While this is a guide to municipal zoos, those funded wholly or in part by cities, there are others, including private animal preserves, where you are permitted to drive through and view animals from your car. We hope this Guide to Zoos in the South will inspire you to visit one near you.

ALABAMA

Birmingham Zoo
2630 Cahaba Road
Birmingham 35223
Open: daily 9:30 a.m.—5 p.m. Charge: adults $1.00, children 2-17 $.50.

Montgomery Zoo
329 Vandiver Boulevard
Montgomery 36109
Open: summer 9:30 a.m.—6 p.m.; winter 9:30 a.m.—4:30 p.m. Charge: adults $.50, children under 14 $.25.

ARKANSAS

Little Rock Zoological Gardens
#1 Jonesboro Drive
Little Rock 72205
Open: daily 9:30 a.m.—5:30 p.m. except New Year's, Thanksgiving, and Christmas. No charge.

DISTRICT OF COLUMBIA

National Zoological Park
Washington 20008
Open: summer 9 a.m.—6:30 p.m.; winter 9 a.m.—4:30 p.m. except Christmas. No charge.

FLORIDA

Jacksonville Zoological Park
8605 Zoo Road
Jacksonville 32218
Open: 9 a.m.—4:45 p.m. except Christmas and New Year's. Charge: adults $1.75, children 6 to 12 $.75, no charge 9 a.m.—10 a.m. weekdays to local residents.

Crandon Park Zoo
4000 Crandon Boulevard
Key Biscayne 33149
Open: summer 9:30 a.m.—5:30 p.m.; winter 9:30 a.m.—4:30 p.m. Charge: adults $.50, under 12 free with adult.

Dreher Park Zoological Gardens
1301 Summit Boulevard
West Palm Beach 33405
Open: 9 a.m.—5 p.m. except Thanksgiving, Christmas, and New Year's. Charge: adults $1.00, ages 3-12 $.50.

GEORGIA

Atlanta Zoological Park
800 Cherokee Avenue S.E.
Atlanta 30315
Open: 10 a.m.—5 p.m. except Christmas and New Year's. Charge: adults $1.50, ages 3-16 $.50.

KENTUCKY

Louisville Zoological Garden
1100 Trevilian Way
Louisville 40213
Open daily except Mondays September—May, Christmas, and New Year's; summer 10 a.m.—6 p.m.; winter 10 a.m.—5 p.m. Charge: adults $1.50, children 4-14 $.50

LOUISIANA

Alexandria Zoological Park
Box 71
Alexandria 71301
Open: summer 9 a.m.—dusk; winter 9 a.m.—5:30 p.m. except Christmas and New Year's. No charge.

Greater Baton Rouge Zoo
Box 60
Baker 70714
Open: 10 a.m.—5 p.m., weekends 9 a.m.—5 p.m. except Christmas and New Year's. Charge: adults $.50, ages 7-17 $.25.

Louisiana Purchase Gardens and Zoo
Box 123
Monroe 71201
Open: summer 10 a.m.—6 p.m.; winter 10 a.m.—5 p.m. except Thanksgiving, Christmas, and New Year's. Charge: adults $1.00, children 5-12 $.50.

Audubon Park and Zoological Garden
Box 4327
New Orleans 70118
Open: 9:30 a.m.—5 p.m. except Thanksgiving, Christmas, and New Year's. Charge: adults $1.25, children 2-14 $.25.

MARYLAND

Baltimore Zoo
Druid Hill Park
Baltimore 21217
Open: 10 a.m.—4:30 p.m. (buildings)—10 a.m.—dark (grounds). Charge: adults $.75, under 15 $.25.

Salisbury Zoo
750 South Park Drive
Salisbury 21801
Open: summer 8 a.m.—8 p.m.; winter 8 a.m.—5 p.m. except Thanksgiving and Christmas. No charge.

MISSISSIPPI

Jackson Zoological Park
2918 West Capitol Street
Jackson 39209
Open: summer 9 a.m.—6 p.m.; winter 9 a.m.—5 p.m. except Christmas and New Year's. Charge: adults $.50, children 6-12 $.25.

NORTH CAROLINA

North Carolina Zoological Park
Route 4, Box 73
Asheboro 27203
Open: summer 9 a.m.—5 p.m. (buildings)—9 a.m.—6 p.m. (grounds); winter 9 a.m.—5 p.m. Charge: adults $1.00, ages 2-15 $.25.

OKLAHOMA

Oklahoma City Zoo
2101 North East 50th
Oklahoma City 73111
Open: summer weekdays 9 a.m.—6 p.m. weekends and holidays 9 a.m.—7 p.m.; winter 9 a.m.—5 p.m. Charge: adults $1.00, ages 3-11 $.50.

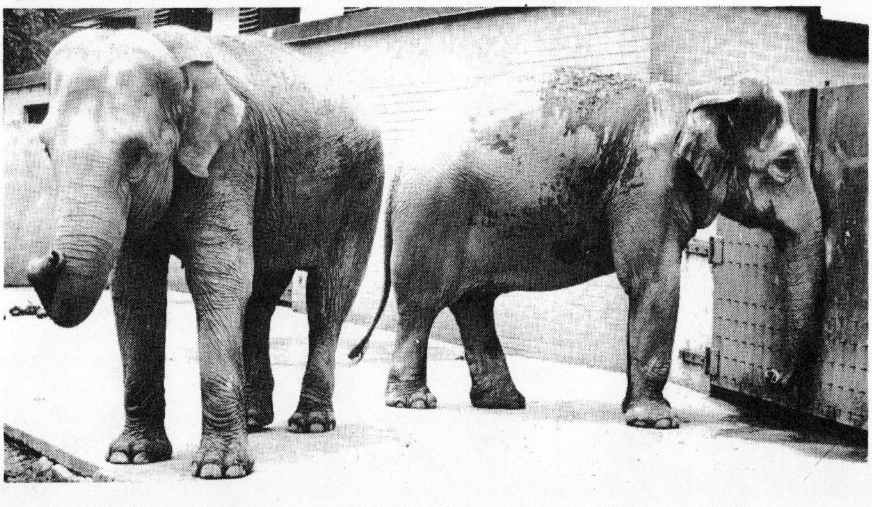

Tulsa Zoological Park
5701 East 36th Street North
Tulsa 74115
Open: 10 a.m. to one hour before dusk. Charge: adults $2.00, ages 6-11 $1.00.

SOUTH CAROLINA

Riverbanks Zoological Park
500 Wildlife Parkway
Columbia 29210
Open: summer 9 a.m.—6 p.m.; winter 9 a.m.—5 p.m. except Christmas. Charge: adults $2.25, children 2-12 $.75.

Greenville Zoological Park
Cleveland Park
Greenville 29601
Open: 9:30 a.m.—5 p.m. except Thanksgiving, Christmas, and New Year's. Charge: adults $.50, children under 16 $.25.

TENNESSEE

Knoxville Zoological Park
Box 6040
Knoxville 37914
Open: summer 10 a.m.—7:30 p.m.; winter 10 a.m.—4:30 p.m. except Christmas and New Year's. Charge: adults $2.00, ages 6-18 $1.00.

Memphis Zoological Gardens and Aquarium
2000 Galloway Avenue
Memphis 38112
Open: summer 9 a.m.—6 p.m.; winter 9 a.m.—5 p.m. except Thanksgiving and Christmas. Charge: adults $1.00, under 12 $.35; Aquarium: adults $.25, under 12 $.10.

TEXAS

Abilene Zoological Gardens
Box 60
Abilene 79604
Open: 10 a.m.—5 p.m., weekends and holidays 10 a.m.—7 p.m. except Thanksgiving, Christmas, and New Year's. Charge: adults $1.00, ages 2-12 $.50.

Gladys Porter Zoo
500 Ringgold Street
Brownsville 78520
Open: summer 10 a.m.—6:30 p.m.; winter 10 a.m.—5:30 p.m. Charge: adults $2.00, students $1.50, children under 12 $1.00.

Dallas Aquarium
3203 Junius Street
Dallas 75218
Open: 8 a.m.—5 p.m. Monday—Saturday, 1 p.m.—5 p.m. Sundays and holidays except Christmas. No charge.

Dallas Zoo
621 East Clarendon Drive
Dallas 75203
Open: summer 9 a.m.—6 p.m. (buildings), 9 a.m.—sundown (grounds); winter 9 a.m.—5 p.m. (buildings), 9 a.m.—sundown (grounds) except Christmas. Charge: adults $.75, 12 and under free with adult.

El Paso Zoological Park
Evergreen and Paisano
El Paso 79905
Open: summer 10 a.m.—6:30 p.m.; winter 9:30 a.m.—5 p.m. except Thanksgiving, Christmas, and New Year's. Charge: adults $.50, children 7-17 $.25.

Fort Worth Zoological Park and James R. Record Aquarium
2727 Zoological Park Drive
Fort Worth 76110
Open: Summer 9 a.m.—5:30 p.m. (buildings), 9 a.m.—6 p.m. (grounds); winter 9 a.m.—5 p.m. (buildings), 9 a.m.—5:30 p.m. (grounds). Charge: adults $1.00, children under 12 free.

The Houston Zoological Gardens
Box 1562
Houston 77001
Open: 10 a.m.—6 p.m. (buildings), 9:30 a.m.—8 p.m. (grounds) summer; 10 a.m.—4 p.m. (buildings), 9:30 a.m.—6 p.m. (grounds), winter. No charge.

Ellen Trout Zoo
P.O. Drawer 190
Lufkin 75901
Open: summer 10 a.m.—5:30 p.m. (buildings), 9 a.m.—6 p.m. (grounds); winter 10 a.m.—4:30 p.m. (buildings), 9 a.m.—5 p.m. (grounds). No charge.

San Antonio Zoological Gardens and Aquarium
3903 North St. Mary's Street
San Antonio 78212
Open: summer 9:30 a.m.—6:30 p.m.; winter 9:30 a.m.—5:00 p.m. Charge: adults $1.00, children 1-16 $.25.

Central Texas Zoo
Route 10, Box 173E
Waco 76708
Open: summer 9:30 a.m.—6 p.m.; winter 9 a.m.—5 p.m. Charge: adults $1.00, ages 4-12 $.50.

VIRGINIA

Lafayette Zoological Park
3500 Granby Street
Norfolk 23504
Open: summer 10 a.m.—6 p.m.; winter 10 a.m.—5 p.m. except Christmas and New Year's. Charge: adults $.50, children 12 and under $.25.

WEST VIRGINIA

Oglebay's Good Zoo
Oglebay Park
Wheeling 26003
Open: summer 11 a.m.—dark; winter 11 a.m.—5 p.m. except Thanksgiving, Christmas, and New Year's. Charge: adults $1.50, children 13-17 $1.00, 2-12 $.75.

Outdoor Dramas in the South

For specific dates and times contact local Chambers of Commerce.

Alabama

Tuscumbia, *The Miracle Worker,* late June to mid-August, Friday and Saturday nights.

Arkansas

Eureka Springs, *The Great Passion Play,* early May to late October, nightly except Mondays and Thursdays.

Hot Springs, *Hernando De Soto, Conquistador,* mid-June to mid-August, nightly except Sundays.

Hardy, *The Arkansaw Traveller,* late May to early September, nightly except Sundays, Mondays, and Wednesdays.

Florida

St. Augustine, *Cross and Sword,* mid-June to early September, nightly except Sundays.

Georgia

Jekyll Island, Jekyll Island Music Theatre, *Oklahoma, Guys and Dolls,* and *Fiddler on the Roof* in rotating repertory, mid-June to early September.

Kentucky

Bardstown, *The Stephen Foster Story,* early June to early September, nightly except Mondays.

Berea, *Wilderness Road,* late June to early September, nightly except Sundays.

Harrodsburg, *The Legend of Daniel Boone,* mid-June to late August, nightly except Sundays.

Van, *The Little Shepherd of Kingdom Come,* late June to late August, Thursday-Saturday nights.

Louisiana

Monroe, *Louisiana Legend,* early July to late August, Friday and Saturday nights.

Natchitoches, *Louisiana Cavalier,* late June to mid-August, Thursday-Saturday nights.

North Carolina

Boone, *Horn in the West,* late June to mid-August, nightly except Mondays.

Cherokee, *Unto These Hills,* mid-June to late August, nightly except Sundays.

Halifax, *First for Freedom,* late June to late July, Wednesday-Sunday nights.

Kenansville, *The Liberty Cart,* late June to early August, Thursday-Sunday nights.

Manteo, *The Lost Colony,* mid-June to late August, nightly except Sundays.

Pembroke, *Strike at the Wind,* early July to late August, Thursday-Saturday nights.

Snow Camp, *Sword of Peace* and *Cane Creek Calamities Continued* in repertory, early June to early September, Wednesday-Saturday.

Valdese, *From This Day Forward,* mid-July to mid-August, Thursday-Sunday nights.

Waxhaw, *Listen and Remember,* mid- to late June, nightly.

Wilmington, *The Immortal Showboat,* early June to early September, nightly.

Oklahoma

Tahlequah, *Trail of Tears,* mid-June to mid-August, Tuesday-Saturday nights.

Tulsa, *Oklahoma* and *Dust on Her Petticoats,* mid-June to late August, alternating nights, except Sundays.

Tennessee

Townsend (near Gatlinburg), *Smoky Mountain Passion Play* and *Damascus Road,* mid-June to late August, alternating nights, except Sundays.

Lawrenceburg, *The Gentleman from the Cane,* July-August, Friday and Saturday nights.

Texas

Canyon, *Texas,* late June to late August, nightly except Sundays.

Livingston, *Beyond the Sundown,* late June to late August, nightly except Sundays.

Galveston, *The Lone Star,* early May to early September, nightly except Mondays.

Virginia

Radford, *The Long Way Home,* late June to early September, Thursday-Sunday nights.

Strasburg, *Passion Play,* late June to early September, nightly except Mondays and Thursdays.

West Virginia

Beckley, *Hatfields and McCoys,* late June to early September, Tuesday, Wednesday, Thursday, and Saturday nights.

Beckley, *Honey in the Rock,* late June to early September, Friday and Sunday nights.

AN ILLUSTRATED GUIDE TO GHOSTS AND MYSTERIOUS OCCURRENCES IN THE OLD NORTH STATE

by Nancy Roberts
Photographs by Bruce Roberts

McNally and Loftin, Publishers
Charlotte, North Carolina

"Twilight is the hour to see a town if you would sense its true spirit." So says Nancy Roberts in her opening to the story of the "Ghost of the Old Mine." The same might be said of all of her collection: twilight is the hour to read these gripping tales. A deft writer, Mrs. Roberts' stories continue to haunt the memory even after the book is closed.

The beginning, fittingly enough if one considers rank, introduces the reader to the ghost of a Confederate general, mounting the parapet at Fort Fisher. Then a series of ghosts drift through these pages from all walks of life, in all kinds of circumstances. Also, there are eerie lights like the flickering light waved across the dark railroad tracks near Maco Station. This is the ghost lantern of a conductor trapped in a runaway railroad car, frantically signalling a following train to slow down. The appeal fails and in the ensuing collision, the conductor is decapitated. His light, however, can still be seen. Its signal is so convincing that the signalmen at the station now use two lanterns to avoid confusion with the unearthly one. And visual apparitions are not the only ones in these stories. Some ghosts shroud themselves in music. The organ at Kadesh Methodist Church occasionally can be heard although the church is empty and there is no organist. The weird music emanating from the building is not made by human hands.

Entertaining, enlightening, and eerie, this book is a marvelous collaboration between the Robertses. Bruce Roberts has illustrated the book with excellent photographs, especially when one considers that his subjects are unreal. The pictures are blurred in all the right places and Nancy Roberts' prose is delightfully horrifying in all the right places. Through their combined and chilling efforts, a good read is provided for those inevitable dark and stormy nights. —S.V.H.

NOSTALGIA UNLIMITED

If you like Coca-Cola and are the least bit nostalgic, you owe it to yourself to own a tray, old bottle, purse mirror or at least a pencil emblazoned with the famous trademark.

Palmetto Antiques of Ulmer, South Carolina, are purveyors of Coca-Cola mementoes. Some are originals, others, reissues, and still others are left in question—many illustrations are used to accompany the ample descriptions in their catalogue.

The price readily reflects what is authentic and what is reproduced; an original Coca-Cola Siphon Bottle with pewter screw pump and "Panama City, Fla., Bottling Company" stamped on it is $49.50; pencils, which anyone around 25 may have used to take a spelling test, are red imprinted with the Coke trademark in white, were issued in 1959, and sell for $.69 each.

Palmetto is the exclusive distributor for a series of re-issue pocket or purse mirrors depicting Coca-Cola advertisements. These mirrors sell for $1.85 each (with special prices for larger orders).

The Palmetto catalogue also offers political campaign buttons, some with candidates' pictures; reproductions of Confederate belt buckles in solid brass; German World War II military memorabilia, or pocket knives and railroad memorabilia.

One antique ladies' high top shoe from the early 1900s (no pairs—salesmen's samples) sells for $8.50.

For your copy of the 96-page Palmetto Warehouse catalogue, send $2.66, of which $2.00 will be deducted from your first order. For orders less than $25.00, shipping charges are 20% of total order.

Palmetto Warehouses & Collectables Unlimited
Highway 321
Norway, South Carolina 29113

DE SOTO NUT HOUSE

The DeSoto Nut House of DeSoto, Georgia, sells Georgia peanuts raw, shelled, and ready to use or roasted and salted in one-pound to 4½-pound packages. Their raw peanuts in the shell are sold in 3-pound to 10-pound boxes; roasted peanuts in the shell are sold in amounts from six one-pound packages to a ten-pound box.

Their "handmade in small batches" candies include peanut brittle (prepared by a secret process!), sugar nuts (peanuts with a crunchy sugar frosting), peanut chocolate fudge, peanut butter fudge, peanut clusters, and pecan brittle.

To sample the various offerings of the Nut House in a single package, the Deluxe Gift Box appears to be the perfect solution. It contains one-half pound portions of roasted and salted peanuts, raw shelled peanuts, peanut chocolate clusters, sugar nuts, peanut brittle, and roasted and salted pecan halves, and it sells for $12.95. (No extra for delivery in eastern U.S., but add $1.00 per order for Rocky Mountain and west coast states.)

Also available from DeSoto Nut House is a delightful book, *Peanut Receipts from Georgia* ($2.00). Published by Peanut Promotions of Americus, Georgia, the 64-page book (see introductory paragraph reproduced here) contains recipes for main dishes, soups, candies, breads—all the things that people have found to make with peanuts.

For a free brochure listing products and prices, write to:

The DeSoto Nut House
P.O. Box 44
DeSoto, Georgia 31743

A Word about Peanuts

The peanut, or "goober" as it is called in some parts, has been around a long time. It came to us from South America, where it was known and appreciated at least 40 centuries ago. The ancient Peruvians had regarded the peanuts flavor and restorative powers so highly that they included jars of them among the treasures placed in the tombs so they would accompany the departed to the next world.

Throughout the South, there are many former homes of famous people which are open to the public.

One may visit the home of "the father of our country" or "the father of jazz." The birthplace of Abraham Lincoln is open to the public; so is the birthplace of Robert E. Lee. Sequoyah's log cabin contrasts with the elegant home of industrialist James Deering.

For those who enjoy visiting the homes of the famous, we have compiled a list of some of the ones which are open to the public. We remind you, though, to check ahead regarding times to visit; each house has its own schedule.

Visit the Homes of the Famous

Thomas Wolfe's home in Asheville, North Carolina, provided the setting for Look Homeward, Angel.

ALABAMA

Gorgas House
University of Alabama Campus
Tuscaloosa

Home of the Gorgas family, 1878–1953: GENERAL JOSIAH GORGAS, famous Confederate soldier and President of the University; GENERAL WILLIAM CRAWFORD GORGAS, well known for his work in Panama and as Surgeon General of the United States Army during World War I; AMELIA GAYLE GORGAS, wife of Josiah, mother of William Crawford, librarian at the University. A "low-country raised cottage" beneath ancient oaks and magnolias.

W. C. Handy Home and Museum
620 West College Street
Florence

The restored cabin in which WILLIAM CHRISTOPHER HANDY was born in 1873. See the piano on which the "Father of the Blues" composed *St. Louis Blues,* Handy's famous trumpet, his library, and personal memorabilia.

Ivy Green
Tuscumbia

Home of HELEN KELLER. Here is the fountain where Helen learned the word "water" and the cottage where she lived with her teacher, Anne Sullivan. The home contains much of the original furniture of the Keller family, but hundreds of mementos of Miss Keller's life have been added. "The Miracle Worker," based on William Gibson's play, is staged on the grounds each summer on Friday and Saturday evenings during July and August.

First White House of the Confederacy
Corner of Washington and Union
Montgomery

The residence of JEFFERSON DAVIS and his family for only a brief time during the period when Montgomery was capital of the Confederacy. The two-story house contains period furnishings and personal possessions of the Davis family. There are many Civil War mementos.

ARKANSAS

Hatchet Hall
35 Steele Street
Eureka Springs

The three-story home and boarding house of CARRY NATION, the temperance leader who smashed saloons while preaching to the startled customers about the evils of alcohol and tobacco. Across the street is Carry's Cave, which she dynamited out of a rock cliff to find the underground spring she was told of in a "vision." (There was water there.)

Royston House
Old Washington Historic State Park
Washington

The Greek Revival home (1845) of GRANDISON D. ROYSTON, delegate to Arkansas' first constitutional convention (1836) and its sole survivor to attend the 1874 constitutional convention, where he served as president. The furnishings of the house reflect the life of the state leader in the mid-1800s.

Headquarters House
118 West Dickson Street
Fayetteville

JONAS TEBBETTS was an esteemed lawyer and state senator until he remained a "Union Man" during the Civil War. He was jailed, threatened with hanging, had his property confiscated, and escaped into Union country. His Greek Revival home was used as headquarters for both armies.

In 1931, FDR's "Little White House" cost $8,738 to build.

Museum of Science and History
MacArthur Park
Little Rock

The birthplace (1880) of GENERAL DOUGLAS MACARTHUR will be different from other homes in this list; the building is now a Museum of Science and History. It was once a part of Little Rock Arsenal. The Arsenal was commanded by General MacArthur's father who was given quarters in the building. After the Arsenal was closed, and the land turned over to the city of Little Rock, the building became a museum.

DISTRICT OF COLUMBIA

Frederick Douglass Home
1411 W Street SE
Washington

The preserved home of FREDERICK DOUGLASS, outstanding 19th century American Negro leader. Douglass escaped slavery to become an abolitionist, anti-slavery editor, the first Negro U.S. Marshal in the District of Columbia, and finally U.S. Minister to Haiti.

Woodrow Wilson House
2340 S Street NW
Washington

The Georgian Revival town house where WOODROW WILSON lived from the end of his Presidency in 1921 until his death in 1924. The house contains mementos of Wilson's public career—and his golf clubs and Victrola with record collection.

Hillwood
4155 Linnean Avenue NW
Washington

The opulent red brick Georgian home of MARJORIE MERRIWEATHER POST contains extraordinary items: dinner services used by Catherine the Great; jeweled Easter eggs by Carl Fabergé; Wedgwood; an exceptional collection of 18th century French furniture; rare tapestries; and the C. W. Post exhibit which consists of paintings, sculpture, and furnishings assembled by Mrs. Post's father (founder of Postum Cereal Company).

FLORIDA

Edison Winter Home
2350 McGregor Blvd.
Ft. Myers

The winter home of THOMAS A. EDISON for forty years includes his chemical laboratory, botanical garden, and museum. On display are the more than 200 Edison phonographs, both cylinder and disc type, and Edison's unique Model T Ford, a prototype presented to Edison by his friend Henry Ford.

Vizcaya
3251 South Miami Avenue
Miami

This Italian villa on Biscayne Bay was the home of JAMES DEERING of the International Harvester Company. The seventy rooms comprise what has been called the finest private house ever built in America.

Ernest Hemingway Home and Museum
907 Whitehead Street
Key West

Home of ERNEST HEMINGWAY from 1931 to 1961. Here he wrote *A Farewell To Arms, To Have and Have Not, The Snows of Kilimanjaro,* and *For Whom The Bell Tolls.* Among the mementos expect a living memorial: many cats and kittens, descendents of the nearly 50 cats Hemingway kept when he lived there.

Henry Morrison Flagler Museum
Whitehall Way
Palm Beach

The home of HENRY MORRISON FLAGLER, founder (with John D. Rockefeller) of Standard Oil. In addition to period rooms, there are special collections of porcelains, paintings, silver, glass, dolls, lace, costumes, and family memorabilia. Mr. Flagler's private railroad car, "Rambler," is also open to visitors.

GEORGIA

Wren's Nest
1050 Gordon Street SW
Atlanta

Home of JOEL CHANDLER HARRIS, creator of the *Uncle Remus* stories. The mid-19th century house was named by Harris when a family of wrens nested in the mailbox.

Little White House
Georgia 85-W and US 27-A
Warm Springs

President FRANKLIN DELANO ROOSEVELT'S Georgia home, which he built in 1932 for therapy at nearby Warm Springs. The house is exactly as it was the day he died there in 1945.

Sidney Lanier Cottage
935 High Street
Macon

Birthplace of Georgia poet SIDNEY LANIER. The Victorian cottage houses period furniture and historic exhibits.

Liberty Hall, Alexander H. Stephens Museum
Georgia 22 within city limits
Crawfordville

Home of ALEXANDER H. STEPHENS, Vice-President of the Confederacy. The antebellum home (circa 1830) is of the Federal style with later additions.

Juliette Gordon Low Birthplace
142 Bull Street and Oglethorpe Avenue
Savannah

Home of JULIETTE GORDON LOW, founder of the Girl Scouts of America. The 1820 Regency house, perhaps designed by William Jay, contains furnishings and memorabilia from Juliette Low's life (1860-1927).

KENTUCKY

Ashland
Richmond Road
Lexington

The country estate of HENRY CLAY, "The Great Compromiser." This estate is set in a woodland which provided a retreat for the man who was a Congressman, U.S. Senator, and Secretary of State—and who wanted the Presidency, a prize which eluded him.

Hopemont (Hunt-Morgan House)
In Gratz Park across from Public Library
Lexington

Built in 1814 by JOHN WESLEY HUNT, the house was later the home of his grandson Confederate General JOHN HUNT MORGAN, leader of Morgan's Raiders and "Thunderbolt of the Confederacy." THOMAS HUNT MORGAN, Kentucky's first Nobel Prize winner, was also born here.

Locust Grove
561 Blankenbaker Lane
Louisville

Last home of General GEORGE ROGERS CLARK. The Georgian frontier plantation house contains Kentucky and Southern period furniture and the surveyor's office. Among visitors here were Aaron Burr, John James Audubon, Cassius Marcellus Clay, and three Presidents: James Monroe, Andrew Jackson, and Zachary Taylor. William, General Clark's youngest brother, and Meriwether Lewis told of their adventures when they returned to Locust Grove from the Pacific.

Sinking Spring Farm
3 miles south of Hodgenville
Hodgenville

The one-room log cabin in which ABRAHAM LINCOLN was born and lived until he was 2½ years old. Robert Collier, the publisher of *Collier's Weekly* magazine, purchased the farm in 1905 and helped to organize the Lincoln Farm Association which acquired the farm and built the Lincoln Memorial Building to contain and preserve the traditional Birthplace Cabin.

Knob Creek (Lincoln's Boyhood Home)
Hodgenville

The home of ABRAHAM LINCOLN from the time he was two until he was almost eight. In the creek Lincoln would have drowned if his friend Austin Gallaher hadn't held a branch for him to grab and then pulled him to safety. A reproduction of the Lincolns' cabin is open to visitors.

LOUISIANA

Beauregard-Keyes House
1113 Chartres Street
New Orleans

Home of General PIERRE GUSTAVE TOUTANT BEAUREGARD, who, on instructions from the Confederate Government, on April 12, 1861, ordered the bombardment of Fort Sumter, South Carolina. This is the home to which Beauregard returned after his participation at Manassas (Bull Run), Shiloh, Bermuda Hundred, in the defense of Charleston, and the siege of Petersburg. After many owners (one of whom seriously threatened to turn it into a macaroni factory), the house was purchased by FRANCES PARKINSON KEYES in 1944. Mrs. Keyes restored the house and made it her winter residence. Here she wrote *Dinner at Antoine's, Steamboat Gothic,* and *Victorine*. One of her books, *Madame Castel's Lodger,* is about General Beauregard.

Viala Plantation House
West Bank of Mississippi River between Baton Rouge and New Orleans (at the foot of Sunshine Bridge)

Home of Dumay St. Martin and headquarters for the pirate JEAN LAFITTE. St. Martin was the local agent for the contraband slave trade, and the house served as Lafitte's residence for many months each year. The home is now downriver from its original site. It has been thoroughly restored and houses Lafitte's Landing Restaurant.

Bayou Folk Museum
Cloutierville

The restored home of KATE CHOPIN, author of the short stories "Desiree's Baby" and "Madame Celestin's Divorce." One collection of her stories about the simple people of the Cane River area, *Bayou Folk,* serves as the focal point of the museum, a typical Louisiana-type structure of about 1813.

Edward Douglass White Home
Five miles north of Thibodaux in Lafourche Parish on State Hwy 1.

Home of EDWARD DOUGLASS WHITE, lawyer, legislator, U.S. Supreme Court Chief Justice. The story-and-a-half raised cottage was built in 1790 by slaves and is furnished in the style of the 1830-1890 period.

MARYLAND

Babe Ruth Birthplace Museum
216 Emory Street
Baltimore

The restored 1895 birthplace of the "Sultan of Swat." Rare photographs, mementos, a slide presentation, and a life-size wax figure of BABE RUTH celebrate the man who hit in two different years more home runs than any other entire team in the American League (54 in 1920; 60 in 1927).

Edgar Allan Poe House
203 North Amity Street
Baltimore

Tiny house in which EDGAR ALLAN POE occupied the Garrett Chamber from 1832 to 1835. Poe lived and wrote here at the time he was courting the cousin he was to marry.

St. Elizabeth Seton House
600 North Paca Street
Baltimore

The home of MOTHER SETON, the first American-born Roman Catholic Saint, founder of the Daughters of Charity in 1808, and originator of the parochial school system in the United States.

Clara Barton House
5801 Oxford Road
Glen Echo

Home of CLARA BARTON, founder of the

American Red Cross. Until 1904, this was her headquarters.

Roger Brooke Taney House
123 Bentz Street
Frederick

Residence of ROGER BROOKE TANEY, the U.S. Chief Justice who wrote the majority opinion in the Dred Scott Decision, which held that slavery was legal under the Constitution.

The Star-Spangled Banner Flag House
844 East Pratt Street
Baltimore

The home of MARY PICKERSGILL who made the star-spangled banner—15 stars, 15 stripes—which flew over Fort McHenry and was watched by Francis Scott Key in the dawn of September 14, 1814.

MISSISSIPPI

Beauvoir
U.S. 90 overlooking Gulf of Mexico
Biloxi

Last home of JEFFERSON DAVIS, where he wrote *The Rise and Fall of the Confederate Government.* An important item is the rain cloak Davis wore when he was arrested May 10, 1865. The cloak was locked away by the Department of the Army in Washington for 100 years; it is evidence that Davis did not try to escape in women's dress.

Rowan Oak
Old Taylor Road
Oxford

The antebellum home of WILLIAM FAULKNER, now owned by the University of Mississippi. The furnishings and memorabilia are just as they were left at the time of Faulkner's death in 1962.

At Beauvoir, Jefferson Davis spent the last twelve years of his life.

NORTH CAROLINA

James K. Polk Birthplace
Hwy. 521
Pineville

A log house and outbuildings thought to be similar to the home in which JAMES KNOX POLK was born were reconstructed on the site in 1967. The story and a half, two-pen log house has two rooms on each floor and a fireplace on one end; the house contains furnishings dating prior to 1806 when the Polk family moved to Tennessee.

Biltmore House and Gardens
U.S. 25 South of Asheville, 2 blocks off I-40

This "country-home" castle built by GEORGE W. VANDERBILT was completed in 1895 and contains 255 rooms, some of which are open. Things to see include prints by Landseer and Albrecht Dürer; Napoleon's chess set; two Renoir paintings; portraits by Sargent, Whistler and Boldini; and five rare, middle 16th century, Flemish tapestries.

Thomas Wolfe Memorial
48 Spruce Street
Asheville

The rambling Victorian boarding house in which THOMAS WOLFE grew up became the "Dixieland" of his autobiographical stories. The interior of the house has been arranged to look as it did during the period described in *Look Homeward, Angel.* One room contains furnishings from Wolfe's last New York apartment, including his writing table and typewriter.

Duke Homestead
2828 Duke Homestead Road
Durham

The home of WASHINGTON DUKE, who began the first mechanical mass production of cigarettes in the 1880s and eventually controlled the largest tobacco company in the world. The simple four-room dwelling and first factory are from the period just after the Civil War.

Carl Sandburg Home: Connemara
Little River Road
Flat Rock

Home of CARL SANDBURG, poet, author, lecturer, minstrel, onetime political activist, social thinker—and for the last 22 years of his life, a resident of this farm. (He wrote; his wife managed the 240-acre farm.) Besides touring the main house, the visitor is free to stroll about the farm.

Reynolda
Winston-Salem

The home of RICHARD JOSHUA REYNOLDS, founder of the R. J. Reynolds Tobacco Company, was the heart of a self-sustaining farm and village. Enjoy many American paintings.

Wright Brothers National Memorial
On the Outer Banks of North Carolina about midway between Kitty Hawk and Nags Head on Alt U.S. 158

A reconstruction of the 1903 camp of WILBUR AND ORVILLE WRIGHT, built by the Park Service in 1963. One building duplicates the hangar; the other is similar to the one used as a workshop and living quarters. A large granite boulder at the first flight area marks the spot where the plane left the ground. Markers show distances for the flights.

OKLAHOMA

Sequoyah's Home
11 miles northeast of Sallisaw on State Highway 101

The 1829 log cabin in which SEQUOYAH lived has been preserved by the construction of a store building as a protective covering. Sequoyah's eighty-four character alphabet became a widely used method of communication among Cherokees.

Pawnee Bill Museum
1 mile west of Pawnee on Hwy. 64

GORDON WILLIAM LILLIE was a friend of the Pawnees (who made him their white chief), a teacher in the Pawnee agency, a cattle driver on the Chisholm Trail, traveller with Buffalo Bill's Wild West Show, and world famous with his touring Pawnee Bill Wild West Show. In the winters, he lived in his hand-built log cabin on a 2,000-acre ranch and accumulated the world's largest privately owned buffalo herd. Bill's wife was Mae Manning, a refined Philadelphian—and marksman and bronco rider in the show.

Frank Phillips Home
1107 Cherokee
Bartlesville

Twenty-six room mansion of FRANK PHILLIPS, founder of Phillips Petroleum Company. Built in 1909, the house has been elaborately restored.

Will Rogers Birthplace
About 4 miles northeast of Oologah

The ranch house where American humorist WILL ROGERS was born November 4, 1879. The house was relocated because construction of Oologah Dam caused flooding of the original home site.

SOUTH CAROLINA

Woodrow Wilson's Boyhood Home
1705 Hampton St.
Columbia

The home of WOODROW WILSON from 1871-74 when his father was a professor at the Columbia Theological Seminary. The house contains the bed in which Wilson was born and the desk he used as Governor of New Jersey.

Fort Hill
Clemson University Campus
Clemson

Home of JOHN C. CALHOUN, Vice-President of the U.S. and Secretary of War, and of THOMAS G. CLEMSON, founder of the University.

Heyward-Washington House
87 Church Street
Charleston

Built in 1770, this was the home of THOMAS HEYWARD, JR., a signer of the Declaration of Independence. When GEORGE WASHINGTON was on his Southern tour in 1791, he resided here.

Robert Mills Historic House
1616 Blanding Street
Columbia

This house, intended for Columbia merchant AINSLEY HALL, was designed by ROBERT MILLS, who served as a Federal architect under seven U.S. Presidents.

TENNESSEE

The Hermitage
12 miles east of Nashville on Hwy. 70-N

The Pre-Civil War Southern Colonial architecture of ANDREW JACKSON'S home features white pillars, wide verandas, and a graceful spiral staircase. The furnishings belonged to the Jackson family. A museum houses countless personal items belonging to President and Mrs. Jackson. A favorite attraction is Jackson's carriage.

Casey Jones' Home
211 West Chester Street
Jackson

On April 30, 1900, JOHN LUTHER (CASEY) JONES was at the throttle of "Old 382" as he approached a stalled train on the same track. Jones made a valiant effort to slow the train and was killed, the only casualty in the wreck. The home of the folk hero is maintained as a railroad museum.

The Crockett Cabin
Off U.S. 45W on the grounds of the high school in Rutherford

In 1823, DAVID CROCKETT moved to the wilds of West Tennessee. This reproduction of Crockett's cabin was built in 1956, using many of the logs from the original cabin. A rocking chair made by Crockett is on display, along with tools and household utensils dating back to the early nineteenth century.

Ancestral Home of James Knox Polk
301 West Seventh Street
Columbia

In 1816, Samuel Polk moved his family to Columbia; his son JAMES KNOX POLK was attending the University of North Carolina that year. Here James began his law career. The furnishings are those used by the President and Mrs. Polk in the White House and in his law office, along with some from the Samuel Polk family. Mrs. Polk's ballgown and the Inaugural Bible are on display.

Alvin York's Farm and Grist Mill
On Hwy 28, South of Jamestown

SGT. YORK, World War I winner of the Congressional Medal of Honor, was described by General Pershing as "the greatest soldier of the war." The York historic area encompasses the small town of Pall Mall where Alvin York grew up and spent his life.

Cordell Hull Birthplace
On State Hwy. 42, 1.2 miles south of Byrdstown

The log cabin birthplace of CORDELL HULL, Secretary of State for President Franklin D. Roosevelt and winner of the Nobel Peace Prize in 1945 for his work toward the establishment of the United Nations.

Andrew Johnson National Historic Site
Depot and College Streets
Greeneville

ANDREW JOHNSON, tailor, also became Alderman, Mayor, Governor, Congressman, Senator, Vice-President, and President. This home is where Johnson lived from 1851 to 1875 when he was not in Washington. The home has been restored to the period 1869-1875 and contains many pieces used by his family.

TEXAS

O. Henry Home
Austin

Residence of WILLIAM SYDNEY PORTER, the short story writer who is better known as "O. Henry." Among the furnishings of the period when he lived in Austin (1885-95) are his desk and writing materials.

LBJ Boyhood Home
Johnson City

LYNDON JOHNSON'S boyhood home has been restored to its appearance in the 1920s. In the area, one may also see the Johnson Settlement Area with its log cabin, which was the home of LBJ's grandparents. The LBJ Ranch is a private home and not open to the public, but it is possible to take a bus ride around the ranch.

Sam Rayburn House
Bonham

The home of SAM RAYBURN, who served as speaker of the U.S. House of Representatives longer than any other person. The house has been restored to 1961 condition with its original furniture, china, and personal items.

Eisenhower Birthplace
208 East Day Street
Denison

The two-story white frame house where DWIGHT D. EISENHOWER was born on October 14, 1890. The home has been restored to its 1890 appearance.

VIRGINIA

Mount Vernon
Mount Vernon

Designed and enlarged by President GEORGE WASHINGTON, the farmhouse became a mansion which is a unique and beautiful example of mid-Georgian architecture. In the fourteen rooms which are open can be found numerous original furnishings which have been returned as gifts, loans, or purchases. George's drafting instruments and Martha's kitchen compete for attention with the elegance of the formal rooms.

Monticello
Charlottesville

This classic example of American architecture and ingenuity was the place of which THOMAS JEFFERSON said, "All my wishes end where I hope my days will end . . . at Monticello." The house and gardens are much as they were when Jefferson retired to his home and family.

Ash Lawn (Highlands)
Charlottesville

The farm home of President JAMES MONROE belongs now to his alma mater, William and Mary. The home is 2.5 miles from Monticello, the home of Monroe's close friend, Thomas Jefferson.

Sherwood Forest
Virginia Route 5
Charles City County

Built in 1730 and altered by President JOHN TYLER in 1844, Sherwood Forest has been continuously occupied by members of the Tyler family and has been a working plantation for 240 years. There are superb period furnishings and original furniture, portraits, and books.

Woodrow Wilson Birthplace
24 North Coalter Street
Staunton

The Greek Revival-style Manse of the Presbyterian Church in which President WOODROW THOMAS WILSON was born December 28, 1856. In the carriage house may be seen a 1919 Pierce-Arrow, the Presidential limousine which was purchased by the President when he left office.

Lyndon Johnson's Boyhood Home.

Scotchtown
Hanover County

Built about 1719, Scotchtown was purchased by PATRICK HENRY in 1770. The Manor House has been restored and furnished with 18th century antiques.

Stratford Hall Plantation
Westmoreland County

Home of THOMAS LEE, acting governor of Virginia and founder of the Ohio Company; RICHARD HENRY LEE, who introduced the motion for independence in the Continental Congress; and birthplace of ROBERT E. LEE, General of the Armies of the Confederacy.

Arlington House
Arlington

Built by GEORGE WASHINGTON PARKE CUSTIS, the adopted son of George Washington and the father-in-law of ROBERT E. LEE, this home was the scene of Lee's wedding to Mary Randolph Custis and their home until Virginia seceded from the Union.

John Marshall House
Ninth and Marshall Streets
Richmond

The home of JOHN MARSHALL, a soldier in the Revolutionary War, a diplomat, U.S. Secretary of State during the French Revolution, and Chief Justice of the United States from 1801 until his death.

WEST VIRGINIA

Stulting House
On U.S. 219
Hillsboro

The birthplace of PEARL COMFORT SYDENSTRICKER BUCK, author of *The Good Earth,* winner of the Pulitzer Prize for Literature in 1932 and the Nobel Prize for Literature in 1938. A historic house museum of 1892 (the year of Pearl Buck's birth), Stulting House contains some of the original furniture and the memorabilia of Pearl Buck.

Jackson's Mill
Near Weston, about 2 miles off U.S. 19

The Jackson of this mill is STONEWALL JACKSON; he worked in the mill as a boy. The mill now houses a museum. The boyhood home was destroyed by fire, but its site is marked by a granite monument. The mill is a part of the West Virginia State 4-H Camp.

Geographic Index

General Index